Wastewater and Waste Treatment: Overview, Challenges and Current Trends (Volume II)

Wastewater and Waste Treatment: Overview, Challenges and Current Trends (Volume II)

Guest Editors

Dimitris Zagklis
Georgios Bampos

Basel • Beijing • Wuhan • Barcelona • Belgrade • Novi Sad • Cluj • Manchester

Guest Editors

Dimitris Zagklis
Department of Industrial
Engineering and
Management
International Hellenic
University (IHU)
Thessaloniki
Greece

Georgios Bampos
Department of Chemical
Engineering
University of Patras
Patras
Greece

Editorial Office
MDPI AG
Grosspeteranlage 5
4052 Basel, Switzerland

This is a reprint of the Special Issue, published open access by the journal *Processes* (ISSN 2227-9717), freely accessible at: https://www.mdpi.com/journal/processes/special_issues/G630734U50.

For citation purposes, cite each article independently as indicated on the article page online and as indicated below:

Lastname, A.A.; Lastname, B.B. Article Title. *Journal Name* **Year**, *Volume Number*, Page Range.

ISBN 978-3-7258-3918-6 (Hbk)
ISBN 978-3-7258-3917-9 (PDF)
https://doi.org/10.3390/books978-3-7258-3917-9

© 2025 by the authors. Articles in this book are Open Access and distributed under the Creative Commons Attribution (CC BY) license. The book as a whole is distributed by MDPI under the terms and conditions of the Creative Commons Attribution-NonCommercial-NoDerivs (CC BY-NC-ND) license (https://creativecommons.org/licenses/by-nc-nd/4.0/).

Contents

Dimitris P. Zagklis and Georgios Bampos
Editorial for the Special Issue "Wastewater and Waste Treatment: Overview, Challenges and Current Trends (Volume II)"
Reprinted from: *Processes* **2025**, *13*, 1097, https://doi.org/10.3390/pr13041097 1

Georgios Manthos, Dimitris Zagklis, Christos Georgopoulos, Constantina Zafiri and Michael Kornaros
Life Cycle Assessment of Waste Glass Geopolymerization for the Production of Sustainable Construction Materials
Reprinted from: *Processes* **2025**, *13*, 331, https://doi.org/10.3390/pr13020331 7

Laura Pozo-Morales, Antonio Rosales Martínez, Enrique Baquerizo and Germán del Valle Agulla
Simulation Tool for the Techno-Economic Assessment of the Integrated Production of Polyhydroxyalkanoates as Value-Added Byproducts of a Wastewater Treatment Plant
Reprinted from: *Processes* **2025**, *13*, 295, https://doi.org/10.3390/pr13020295 20

Jakub Jurík, Barbora Jankovičová, Ronald Zakhar, Nikola Šoltýsová and Ján Derco
Quaternary Treatment of Urban Wastewater for Its Reuse
Reprinted from: *Processes* **2024**, *12*, 1905, https://doi.org/10.3390/pr12091905 41

Lei Hu, Lin Shi, Edwin Hena Dawolo, Ning Ding and Hong Liu
Cobalt-Modified Biochar from Rape Straw as Persulfate Activator for Degradation of Antibiotic Metronidazole
Reprinted from: *Processes* **2024**, *12*, 1596, https://doi.org/10.3390/pr12081596 80

Linjing Jia, Ankita Juneja, Erica L.-W. Majumder, Bandaru V. Ramarao and Deepak Kumar
Efficient Enzymatic Hydrolysis and Polyhydroxybutyrate Production from Non-Recyclable Fiber Rejects from Paper Mills by Recombinant *Escherichia coli*
Reprinted from: *Processes* **2024**, *12*, 1576, https://doi.org/10.3390/pr12081576 98

Salah Jellali, Wissem Hamdi, Majida Al-Harrasi, Malik Al-Wardy, Jamal Al-Sabahi, Hamed Al-Nadabi, et al.
Investigations on Amoxicillin Removal from Aqueous Solutions by Novel Calcium-Rich Biochars: Adsorption Properties and Mechanisms Exploration
Reprinted from: *Processes* **2024**, *12*, 1552, https://doi.org/10.3390/pr12081552 118

Emilia A. Jiménez-García, Salvador Pérez-Huertas, Antonio Pérez, Mónica Calero and Gabriel Blázquez
Recycling PVC Waste into CO_2 Adsorbents: Optimizing Pyrolysis Valorization with Neuro-Fuzzy Models
Reprinted from: *Processes* **2024**, *12*, 431, https://doi.org/10.3390/pr12030431 136

Senouci Boulerial, Carlo Salerno, Fabiano Castrogiovanni, Marina Tumolo, Giovanni Berardi, Abdelkader Debab, et al.
Optimal Mesh Pore Size Combined with Periodic Air Mass Load (AML) for Effective Operation of a Self-Forming Dynamic Membrane BioReactor (SFD MBR) for Sustainable Treatment of Municipal Wastewater
Reprinted from: *Processes* **2024**, *12*, 323, https://doi.org/10.3390/pr12020323 150

Luis A. Franco, T. Dwyer Stuart, Md Shahadat Hossain, Bandaru V. Ramarao,
Charlene C. VanLeuven, Mario Wriedt, et al.
Apple Pomace-Derived Cationic Cellulose Nanocrystals for PFAS Removal from Contaminated
Water
Reprinted from: *Processes* **2024**, *12*, 297, https://doi.org/10.3390/pr12020297 . . . . **161**

Hee-Jun Kim, Sangjun Jeong, YeonA Lee, Jae-Cheol Lee and Hyun-Woo Kim
The Crucial Impact of Microbial Growth and Bioenergy Conversion on Treating Livestock
Manure and Antibiotics Using *Chlorella sorokiniana*
Reprinted from: *Processes* **2024**, *12*, 252, https://doi.org/10.3390/pr12020252 . . . . **182**

Maja Čolnik, Mihael Irgolič, Amra Perva and Mojca Škerget
The Conversion of Pistachio and Walnut Shell Waste into Valuable Components with Subcritical
Water
Reprinted from: *Processes* **2024**, *12*, 195, https://doi.org/10.3390/pr12010195 . . . . **196**

Gabriel Sperandio, Iterlandes Machado Junior, Esteefany Bernardo and Renata Moreira
Graphene Oxide from Graphite of Spent Batteries as Support of Nanocatalysts for Fuel
Hydrogen Production
Reprinted from: *Processes* **2023**, *11*, 3250, https://doi.org/10.3390/pr11113250 . . . . **214**

Mario Alejandro Parra Ramirez, Stefan Fogel, Sebastian Felix Reinecke and Uwe Hampel
Techno-Economic Assessment of PEM Electrolysis for O_2 Supply in Activated Sludge
Systems—A Simulation Study Based on the BSM2 Wastewater Treatment Plant
Reprinted from: *Processes* **2023**, *11*, 1639, https://doi.org/10.3390/pr11061639 . . . . **230**

Georgios Manthos, Dimitris Zagklis, Sameh S. Ali, Constantina Zafiri and Michael Kornaros
Techno-Economic Evaluation of the Thermochemical Energy Valorization of Construction
Waste and Algae Biomass: A Case Study for a Biomass Treatment Plant in Northern Greece
Reprinted from: *Processes* **2023**, *11*, 1549, https://doi.org/10.3390/pr11051549 . . . . **252**

Federico Micolucci, Jonathan A. C. Roques, Geoffrey S. Ziccardi, Naoki Fujii,
Kristina Sundell and Tomonori Kindaichi
Candidatus Scalindua, a Biological Solution to Treat Saline Recirculating Aquaculture System
Wastewater
Reprinted from: *Processes* **2023**, *11*, 690, https://doi.org/10.3390/pr11030690 . . . . **267**

Rosa Paola Radice, Vincenzo De Fabrizio, Antonietta Donadoni, Antonio Scopa
and Giuseppe Martelli
Crude Oil Bioremediation: From Bacteria to Microalgae
Reprinted from: *Processes* **2023**, *11*, 442, https://doi.org/10.3390/pr11020442 . . . . **281**

Siti Safirah Rashid, Siti Norliyana Harun, Marlia M. Hanafiah, Khalisah K. Razman,
Yong-Qiang Liu and Duratul Ain Tholibon
Life Cycle Assessment and Its Application in Wastewater Treatment: A Brief Overview
Reprinted from: *Processes* **2023**, *11*, 208, https://doi.org/10.3390/pr11010208 . . . . **292**

Editorial

Editorial for the Special Issue "Wastewater and Waste Treatment: Overview, Challenges and Current Trends (Volume II)"

Dimitris P. Zagklis [1,*] and Georgios Bampos [2,*]

1 Department of Industrial Engineering and Management, International Hellenic University (IHU), GR-57400 Thessaloniki, Greece
2 Department of Chemical Engineering, University of Patras, GR-26504 Patras, Greece
* Correspondence: zagklis@ihu.gr (D.P.Z.); geoba@chemeng.upatras.gr (G.B.)

1. Introduction

Liquid and solid waste management is one of the most important challenges of the 21st century, as continued population growth, intensive agriculture, urbanization and industrialization have led to increased pollutant loads on natural ecosystems [1–4]. Innovative, efficient and environmentally sustainable treatment technologies are imperative [5], as conventional systems often fail to meet new requirements [6], both in terms of the removal of persistent pollutants and the reuse of treated effluents [7–9]. In the context of the circular economy, the conversion of waste into resources takes on a central role, offering solutions that combine environmental protection with the production of useful products such as biopolymers [10], fuels [11], adsorption materials [12] and clean water [13–16].

This Special Issue, entitled "Wastewater and Waste Treatment: Overview, Challenges and Current Trends (Volume II)", brings together recent scientific papers covering a wide range of thematic areas [17]: from life cycle assessments (LCAs) and technoeconomic analyses of sustainable processes to the applications of biological, nanotechnological and thermochemical solutions for waste decontamination and utilization. These approaches address the environmental impacts of pollution while demonstrating new possibilities for the recovery of energy and raw materials. Examining multidisciplinary approaches and applications in realistic conditions, the published articles capture contemporary trends and prospects for a more sustainable and circularly organized society.

2. Overview of Contributions

The papers published in the second edition (Volume II) of the Special Issue (S.I.) entitled "Wastewater and Waste Treatment: Overview, Challenges and Current Trends" can be separated into four (4) distinct categories: life cycle assessment (LCA) in the service of sustainable technologies for waste management (two papers), biological waste treatment (three papers), circular economies based on waste-to-energy utilization (four papers), innovative technologies for water and air purification (six papers) and industrial processes based on resource recovery from waste (two papers). The distribution of publications (%) is depicted in Figure 1.

The role of LCA is vital for ensuring waste management technologies are sustainable [18], as demonstrated by the two relevant papers published in this S.I. The application of LCA to wastewater treatment (WWT) methods showed that energy consumption produced the greatest environmental burden (ca. 80% of the total footprint), whereas the greenhouse gas emissions corresponded to 14–36% CO_2 and 23–43% N_2O of the total emissions of WWT methods, as demonstrated by Rashid et al. [19]. The use of biogas in resource recovery processes may reduce CO_2 emissions by up to 102 kt annually. Similarly, an LCA conducted for waste glass geopolymerization showed a decrease in CO_2 emissions of up to 26 kg_{CO2}/ton, while the use of NaOH contributed significantly to the environmental burden of the process in terms of impact to human health (9×10^{-5} DALY/ton$_{\text{waste-glass}}$) as presented by Manthos et al. [20]. Overall, the proposed method had an environmental benefit equal to ca. 20 mPt/ton, introducing an alternative to traditional recycling.

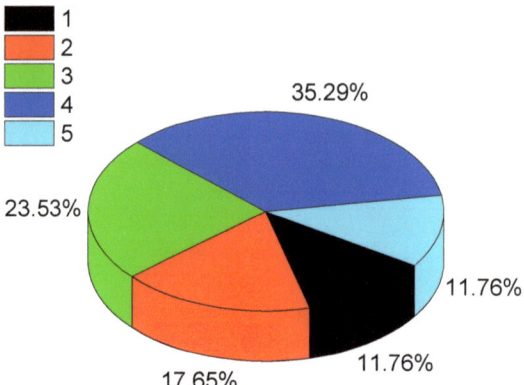

Figure 1. Publication distribution (%) based on subject: life cycle assessment (LCA) in the service of sustainable technologies for waste management (1, black), biological waste treatment (2, red), circular economies based on waste-to-energy utilization (3, green), innovative technologies for water and air purification (4, blue) and industrial processes based on resource recovery from waste (5, cyan).

Biological treatment methods have a special role in waste management technologies [21,22]. Radice et al. [23] highlighted the role of bioremediation in environmental decontamination. The use of microorganisms (bacteria and microalgae) could be a key strategy for removing oil pollutants. Specifically, the application of the microalga *Chlorella vulgaris* resulted in an 80% removal of emulsified oil after 5 days, whereas the combination of the abovementioned microalga with bacteria increased this percentage by up to 92%. The bacteria *Candidatus Scalindua* achieved a 98.9% removal of NH_4^+ and a 99.6% removal of NO_2^- from aquaculture wastewater, as presented by Micolucci et al. [24]. The presence of antibiotics in wastewater has been found to reduce the growth rate of *Chlorella sorokiniana* by up to 61%, thus negatively affecting biofuel production, as reported by Kim et al. [25].

The utilization of waste for energy production is based on the circular economy [26,27]. Four papers within the present S.I. are related to this intriguing subject, thus underscoring its significance. Gasification was shown to be the most economically sustainable solution for the utilization of construction waste and algae biomass, resulting in an income equal to 0.13 EUR/kg and a treatment cost of 0.09 EUR/kg, as demonstrated by Manthos et al. [28]. The internal rate of return of the gasification process was found to be equal to 9%, thus making it competitive compared to other thermochemical methods. The synthesis of graphene oxide (GO) using recycled Zn-C batteries was investigated by Sperandio et al. [29] with a view to application as a support in Ni/Co nanocatalysts for $NaBH_4$ hydrolysis in H_2 production. The estimated performance for energy production was 90%, while the as-prepared catalytic system was active after seven consecutive operation cycles. According to Jiménez-García et al. [30], the recycling of PVC using an optimized pyrolysis process allowed the synthesis of CO_2 adsorbents capable of capturing up to 45.6 mg CO_2/g. Activation with the use of KOH at 760 °C, maintaining an activation agent/carbon ratio equal to 2/1, resulted in an enhanced adsorption capacity, whereas the use of NaOH at 840 °C increased the adsorption capacity by 25%. Pozo-Morales and co-workers [31] performed a technoeconomic assessment of the production of polyhydroxyalkanoates (PHAs) by a WWT plant in Spain. The aerobic dynamic feeding (ADF) strategy exhibited the highest yield, producing 0.226 kg of CODPHA/kg COD with a cost equal to 0.11 EUR/kg CODPHA, while reducing sledge production by 6%.

Water and air purification technologies take the lion's share of published works in this S.I. (six contributions). The potential introduction of proton exchange membrane (PEM) electrolysis process for O_2 supply in activated sludge systems was investigated with a technoeconomic analysis [32]. It was revealed that electrolysis employing a PEM could replace effectively a conventional ventilation system covering 99% of the O_2 needs of a unit serving 80,000 citizens. The estimated cost was 128 EUR/ton. The use of cellulose nanocrystals for per- and poly-fluoroalkyl substance (PFAS) removal from contaminated water was studied by Franco et al. [33]. Cellulose nanocrystals, modified with the *Moringa oleifera* cationic protein, improved PFAS adsorption, thus increasing the removal capacity of perfluorooctanoic acid (PFOA) from 47.1 to 61.1 mg/g. Equilibrium was achieved within 15 min, thus highlighting the effectiveness of the proposed approach. The removal of amoxicillin (AMX) from aqueous solutions utilizing biochar materials rich in calcium was studied by Jellali et al. [34]. Ca-rich biochar materials derived from the co-pyrolysis of poultry manure, palm oil waste and marble dust were used, and achieved an AMX removal rate equal to 56.2 mg_{AMX}/g. The highest AMX adsorption was found for the biochar derived after a heat treatment at 900 °C.

Operational parameters such as mesh pore size and air mass load were investigated for the effective operation of a dynamic bioreactor used for municipal WWT by Boulerial et al. [35]. The use of a 20 μm mesh combined with a 5 min aeration after 4 h resulted in a steady flow and low turbidity. Co-modified biochar was employed for metronidazole (MNZ) degradation by Hu and co-workers [36], demonstrating a removal higher than 90% within 60 min. Lastly, as it concerns novel water and air treatment processes, the review of Jurík et al. [37] related to the quaternary treatment of urban WWT discussed various intriguing aspects. In general, quaternary WWT is performed with coagulation, membrane filtration (UF/NF) and UV disinfection, ensuring the effective removal of micropollutants. The European Union (regulation 2020/741) promotes the reuse of treated wastewater due to increasing water demand. By implementing this technology, agriculture can benefit from the safe use of recycled water while addressing scarcity problems.

Finally, industrial processes based on resource recovery from waste are of great significance, since they provide practical solutions to processes that are already utilized [38,39]. Jia et al. [40] studied the production of polyhydroxybutyrate (PHB) from paper mill waste. The fermentation of non-recyclable paper mill fiber with recombinant *Escherichia coli* produced 6.27 g/L PHB. Waste pretreatment was optimized by increasing the cellulose yield to 83%, allowing high sugar concentrations for fermentation. Subcritical extraction was used to recover phenolics, flavonoids and antioxidants from waste nut shells [41]. Walnut shells treated at 300 °C for 15 min yielded the highest amount of total phenolics (127.08 mg_{GA}/g), while peanut shells treated at 200 °C for 60 min contained the highest number of flavonoids (10.18 mg_{QU}/g).

3. Challenges and Perspectives

In conclusion, our analysis of the 17 contributions to this Special Issue highlights the urgent need to develop sustainable technologies for waste management, recycling and environmental remediation. LCA underscores the significance of reducing the environmental impact of industrial processes, emphasizing reducing energy consumption and utilizing environmentally friendly chemicals. Biological and nanotechnological solutions exhibited high efficiency in pollutant degradation, but require further thorough investigation in order to be implemented in real environmental systems. Circular economies and the production of high-value products from waste introduce significant opportunities, but the economic viability and the potential scaling up of the proposed processes remain challenging.

The development and implementation of innovative technologies for wastewater and waste treatment is accompanied by significant challenges. First, despite the environmental benefits of technologies such as geopolymerization and PHA production, their dependence on high-impact reagents such as NaOH increases their environmental and economic costs. Furthermore, the stability and efficiency of biological technologies (e.g., bacteria and microalgae) are affected by the presence of toxic pollutants, such as antibiotics, requiring an enhanced biotechnological approach. Beyond the technical issues, the industrial scaling of many of these solutions is still in its early stages, with a need for cost reduction and better integration into production structures. Finally, their adoption also depends on product safety and on their compliance with environmental requirements.

Future prospects are focused on optimizing innovative technologies to make them more efficient and sustainable. The development of energy-efficient and environmentally friendly catalytic materials can improve the performance of adsorbent and geopolymer materials. The use of synthetic biology offers the potential to enhance the resilience of microorganisms in toxic environments, thus improving the biodegradation of pollutants. Also, combined treatment techniques—mixing physical, chemical and biological methods—are a powerful approach for removing difficult pollutants, such as PFASs. The utilization of waste for biomaterial production may further promote the circular economy, while the integration of digital tools and artificial intelligence promises better prediction, monitoring and optimization of the proposed waste treatments. The successful implementation of these directions requires close cooperation between the scientific community, industry and institutional bodies.

Funding: This research received no external funding.

Acknowledgments: We are thankful to all the authors who submitted their impressive work to this Special Issue and to the reviewers for their time and effort in reviewing the manuscripts.

Conflicts of Interest: The authors declare no conflicts of interest.

References

1. Rashid, S.; Sultan, H.; Rashid, W.; Talpur, B.D.; Supe Tulcan, R.X.; Khan, M.T.; Bohnett, E.; Korai, M.S.; Zhang, L. A critical review of opportunities and challenges of solid waste management in an emerging economy- evidence from Pakistan. *Environ. Dev.* **2025**, *55*, 101182. [CrossRef]
2. Bano, S.; Singh, K.; Chaudhary, A.; Chandra, R. Innovative methods for the valorisation of solid wastes from sugar mill and refineries for sustainable development: A review. *Clean. Waste Syst.* **2025**, *10*, 100230. [CrossRef]
3. Dhenkula, S.P.; Shende, A.D.; Deshpande, L.; Pophali, G.R. An overview of heavy metals treatment & management for laboratory waste liquid (LWL). *J. Environ. Chem. Eng.* **2024**, *12*, 113165. [CrossRef]
4. Kumareswaran, K.; Ranasinghe, S.; Jayasinghe, G.Y.; Dassanayake, K.B. Systematic review on liquid organic waste (LOW) characteristics, processing technologies, and their potential applications: Towards circular economy and resource efficiency. *J. Clean. Prod.* **2024**, *447*, 141286. [CrossRef]
5. Ahmad, A.L.; Chin, J.Y.; Mohd Harun, M.H.Z.; Low, S.C. Environmental impacts and imperative technologies towards sustainable treatment of aquaculture wastewater: A review. *J. Water Process. Eng.* **2022**, *46*, 102553. [CrossRef]
6. Salem, K.S.; Clayson, K.; Salas, M.; Haque, N.; Rao, R.; Agate, S.; Singh, A.; Levis, J.W.; Mittal, A.; Yarbrough, J.M.; et al. A critical review of existing and emerging technologies and systems to optimize solid waste management for feedstocks and energy conversion. *Matter* **2023**, *6*, 3348–3377. [CrossRef]
7. Shamshad, J.; Ur Rehman, R. Innovative approaches to sustainable wastewater treatment: A comprehensive exploration of conventional and emerging technologies. *Environ. Sci. Adv.* **2024**, *4*, 189–222. [CrossRef]
8. Mishra, V.; Mukherjee, P.; Bhattacharya, S.; Sharma, R.S. Innovative sustainable solutions for detoxifying textile industry effluents using advanced oxidation and biological methods. *J. Environ. Manag.* **2025**, *380*, 124804. [CrossRef]

9. Tahmasbi, F.; Khdair, A.I.; Aburumman, G.A.; Tahmasebi, M.; Thi, N.H.; Afrand, M. Energy-efficient building façades: A comprehensive review of innovative technologies and sustainable strategies. *J. Build. Eng.* **2025**, *99*, 111643. [CrossRef]
10. Getahun, M.J.; Kassie, B.B.; Alemu, T.S. Recent advances in biopolymer synthesis, properties, & commercial applications: A review. *Process. Biochem.* **2024**, *145*, 261–287. [CrossRef]
11. Stančin, H.; Mikulčić, H.; Wang, X.; Duić, N. A review on alternative fuels in future energy system. *Renew. Sustain. Energy Rev.* **2020**, *128*, 109927. [CrossRef]
12. Yu, J.; Zhu, J.; Chen, L.; Chao, Y.; Zhu, W.; Liu, Z. A review of adsorption materials and their application of 3D printing technology in the separation process. *Chem. Eng. J.* **2023**, *475*, 146247. [CrossRef]
13. Begum, Y.A.; Kumari, S.; Jain, S.K.; Garg, M.C. A review on waste biomass-to-energy: Integrated thermochemical and biochemical conversion for resource recovery. *Environ. Sci. Adv.* **2024**, *3*, 1197–1216. [CrossRef]
14. Shahzad, H.M.A.; Almomani, F.; Shahzad, A.; Mahmoud, K.A.; Rasool, K. Challenges and opportunities in biogas conversion to microbial protein: A pathway for sustainable resource recovery from organic waste. *Process. Saf. Environ. Prot.* **2024**, *185*, 644–659. [CrossRef]
15. Feng, L.; Tian, B.; Zhu, M.; Yang, M. Current progresses in the analysis, treatment and resource utilization of industrial waste salt in China: A comprehensive review. *Resour. Conserv. Recycl.* **2025**, *217*, 108224. [CrossRef]
16. Zhang, T.; Liu, X.; Qu, G.; Lu, P.; Wang, J.; Wu, F.; Ren, Y. Secondary resource utilization of metallurgical solid waste: Current status and future prospects of wet extraction of valuable metals. *Sep. Purif. Technol.* **2025**, *361*, 131278. [CrossRef]
17. Zagklis, D.P.; Bampos, G. Editorial for the Special Issue "Wastewater and Waste Treatment: Overview, Challenges and Current Trends.". *Processes* **2024**, *12*, 853. [CrossRef]
18. Bisinella, V.; Schmidt, S.; Varling, A.S.; Laner, D.; Christensen, T.H. Waste LCA and the future. *Waste Manag.* **2024**, *174*, 53–75. [CrossRef]
19. Rashid, S.S.; Harun, S.N.; Hanafiah, M.M.; Razman, K.K.; Liu, Y.-Q.; Tholibon, D.A. Life Cycle Assessment and Its Application in Wastewater Treatment: A Brief Overview. *Processes* **2023**, *11*, 208. [CrossRef]
20. Manthos, G.; Zagklis, D.; Georgopoulos, C.; Zafiri, C.; Kornaros, M. Life Cycle Assessment of Waste Glass Geopolymerization for the Production of Sustainable Construction Materials. *Processes* **2025**, *13*, 331. [CrossRef]
21. Takata, M.; Fukushima, K.; Kawai, M.; Nagao, N.; Niwa, C.; Yoshida, T.; Toda, T. The choice of biological waste treatment method for urban areas in Japan—An environmental perspective. *Renew. Sustain. Energy Rev.* **2013**, *23*, 557–567. [CrossRef]
22. Sravan, J.S.; Matsakas, L.; Sarkar, O. Advances in Biological Wastewater Treatment Processes: Focus on Low-Carbon Energy and Resource Recovery in Biorefinery Context. *Bioengineering* **2024**, *11*, 281. [CrossRef] [PubMed]
23. Radice, R.P.; De Fabrizio, V.; Donadoni, A.; Scopa, A.; Martelli, G. Crude Oil Bioremediation: From Bacteria to Microalgae. *Processes* **2023**, *11*, 442. [CrossRef]
24. Micolucci, F.; Roques, J.A.C.; Ziccardi, G.S.; Fujii, N.; Sundell, K.; Kindaichi, T. Candidatus Scalindua, a Biological Solution to Treat Saline Recirculating Aquaculture System Wastewater. *Processes* **2023**, *11*, 690. [CrossRef]
25. Kim, H.-J.; Jeong, S.; Lee, Y.; Lee, J.-C.; Kim, H.-W. The Crucial Impact of Microbial Growth and Bioenergy Conversion on Treating Livestock Manure and Antibiotics Using Chlorella sorokiniana. *Processes* **2024**, *12*, 252. [CrossRef]
26. Islam, N.F.; Gogoi, B.; Saikia, R.; Yousaf, B.; Narayan, M.; Sarma, H. Encouraging circular economy and sustainable environmental practices by addressing waste management and biomass energy production. *Reg. Sustain.* **2024**, *5*, 100174. [CrossRef]
27. Atstaja, D.; Cudecka-Purina, N.; Koval, V.; Kuzmina, J.; Butkevics, J.; Hrinchenko, H. Waste-to-Energy in the Circular Economy Transition and Development of Resource-Efficient Business Models. *Energies* **2024**, *17*, 4188. [CrossRef]
28. Manthos, G.; Zagklis, D.; Ali, S.S.; Zafiri, C.; Kornaros, M. Techno-Economic Evaluation of the Thermochemical Energy Valorization of Construction Waste and Algae Biomass: A Case Study for a Biomass Treatment Plant in Northern Greece. *Processes* **2023**, *11*, 1549. [CrossRef]
29. Sperandio, G.; Junior, I.M.; Bernardo, E.; Moreira, R. Graphene Oxide from Graphite of Spent Batteries as Support of Nanocatalysts for Fuel Hydrogen Production. *Processes* **2023**, *11*, 3250. [CrossRef]
30. Jiménez-García, E.A.; Pérez-Huertas, S.; Pérez, A.; Calero, M.; Blázquez, G. Recycling PVC Waste into CO_2 Adsorbents: Optimizing Pyrolysis Valorization with Neuro-Fuzzy Models. *Processes* **2024**, *12*, 431. [CrossRef]
31. Pozo-Morales, L.; Rosales Martínez, A.; Baquerizo, E.; del Valle Agulla, G. Simulation Tool for the Techno-Economic Assessment of the Integrated Production of Polyhydroxyalkanoates as Value-Added Byproducts of a Wastewater Treatment Plant. *Processes* **2025**, *13*, 295. [CrossRef]
32. Parra Ramirez, M.A.; Fogel, S.; Reinecke, S.F.; Hampel, U. Techno-Economic Assessment of PEM Electrolysis for O_2 Supply in Activated Sludge Systems—A Simulation Study Based on the BSM2 Wastewater Treatment Plant. *Processes* **2023**, *11*, 1639. [CrossRef]
33. Franco, L.A.; Stuart, T.D.; Hossain, M.S.; Ramarao, B.V.; VanLeuven, C.C.; Wriedt, M.; Satchwell, M.; Kumar, D. Apple Pomace-Derived Cationic Cellulose Nanocrystals for PFAS Removal from Contaminated Water. *Processes* **2024**, *12*, 297. [CrossRef]

34. Jellali, S.; Hamdi, W.; Al-Harrasi, M.; Al-Wardy, M.; Al-Sabahi, J.; Al-Nadabi, H.; Al-Raeesi, A.; Jeguirim, M. Investigations on Amoxicillin Removal from Aqueous Solutions by Novel Calcium-Rich Biochars: Adsorption Properties and Mechanisms Exploration. *Processes* **2024**, *12*, 1552. [CrossRef]
35. Boulerial, S.; Salerno, C.; Castrogiovanni, F.; Tumolo, M.; Berardi, G.; Debab, A.; Haddou, B.; Benhamou, A.; Pollice, A. Optimal Mesh Pore Size Combined with Periodic Air Mass Load (AML) for Effective Operation of a Self-Forming Dynamic Membrane BioReactor (SFD MBR) for Sustainable Treatment of Municipal Wastewater. *Processes* **2024**, *12*, 323. [CrossRef]
36. Hu, L.; Shi, L.; Dawolo, E.H.; Ding, N.; Liu, H. Cobalt-Modified Biochar from Rape Straw as Persulfate Activator for Degradation of Antibiotic Metronidazole. *Processes* **2024**, *12*, 1596. [CrossRef]
37. Jurík, J.; Jankovičová, B.; Zakhar, R.; Šoltýsová, N.; Derco, J. Quaternary Treatment of Urban Wastewater for Its Reuse. *Processes* **2024**, *12*, 1905. [CrossRef]
38. Mansouri, S.S.; Udugama, I.A.; Cignitti, S.; Mitic, A.; Flores-Alsina, X.; Gernaey, K. V Resource recovery from bio-based production processes: A future necessity? *Curr. Opin. Chem. Eng.* **2017**, *18*, 1–9. [CrossRef]
39. Velenturf, A.P.M.; Purnell, P. Resource Recovery from Waste: Restoring the Balance between Resource Scarcity and Waste Overload. *Sustainability* **2017**, *9*, 1603. [CrossRef]
40. Jia, L.; Juneja, A.; Majumder, E.L.-W.; Ramarao, B.V.; Kumar, D. Efficient Enzymatic Hydrolysis and Polyhydroxybutyrate Production from Non-Recyclable Fiber Rejects from Paper Mills by Recombinant Escherichia coli. *Processes* **2024**, *12*, 1576. [CrossRef]
41. Čolnik, M.; Irgolič, M.; Perva, A.; Škerget, M. The Conversion of Pistachio and Walnut Shell Waste into Valuable Components with Subcritical Water. *Processes* **2024**, *12*, 195. [CrossRef]

Disclaimer/Publisher's Note: The statements, opinions and data contained in all publications are solely those of the individual author(s) and contributor(s) and not of MDPI and/or the editor(s). MDPI and/or the editor(s) disclaim responsibility for any injury to people or property resulting from any ideas, methods, instructions or products referred to in the content.

Article

Life Cycle Assessment of Waste Glass Geopolymerization for the Production of Sustainable Construction Materials

Georgios Manthos [1], Dimitris Zagklis [2], Christos Georgopoulos [3], Constantina Zafiri [4] and Michael Kornaros [5,*]

[1] Department of Environmental and Resource Engineering, Quantitative Sustainability Assessment Section, Technical University of Denmark, Bygningstorvet, Building 115, DK-2800 Kongens Lyngby, Denmark; gema@dtu.dk

[2] Department of Industrial Engineering and Management, School of Engineering, International Hellenic University (IHU), 57400 Thessaloniki, Greece; zagklis@ihu.gr

[3] Department of R & D, Enalos Research and Development PC, 51 Metamorfoseos Str., 15234 Chalandri, Greece; georgopoulos@enalos.com

[4] Green Technologies Ltd., 5 Ellinos Stratiotou Str., 26223 Patras, Greece; nzafeiri@tee.gr

[5] Laboratory of Biochemical Engineering & Environmental Technology (LBEET), Department of Chemical Engineering, University of Patras, 1 Karatheodori Str., University Campus, 26504 Patras, Greece

* Correspondence: kornaros@chemeng.upatras.gr

Academic Editor: Andrea Petrella

Received: 1 December 2024
Revised: 8 January 2025
Accepted: 14 January 2025
Published: 24 January 2025

Citation: Manthos, G.; Zagklis, D.; Georgopoulos, C.; Zafiri, C.; Kornaros, M. Life Cycle Assessment of Waste Glass Geopolymerization for the Production of Sustainable Construction Materials. *Processes* **2025**, *13*, 331. https://doi.org/10.3390/pr13020331

Copyright: © 2025 by the authors. Licensee MDPI, Basel, Switzerland. This article is an open access article distributed under the terms and conditions of the Creative Commons Attribution (CC BY) license (https://creativecommons.org/licenses/by/4.0/).

Abstract: Replacing conventional materials with new recycled materials is one of the goals of sustainable development, as it promotes the creation of environmentally friendly products while reducing the amount of waste to be treated. A common recyclable waste stream associated with urban living is waste glass, which typically comes from packaging or product containers. Although most of this stream can be reused and/or recycled, it is worth exploring alternative uses, especially for areas with high fluctuations in waste glass production. An example would be the sudden increase in waste glass in tourist areas during the high season. To this end, the present work presents the results from the life cycle assessment of waste glass geopolymerization for the production of cement tiles. The methodology includes the estimation of mass and energy balances by dividing the whole process into several sub-processes (NaOH addition, energy consumption, etc.). The NaOH addition was found to be the most burden-intensive process, with a total damage of 9×10^{-5} DALY per ton of waste glass in the human health category, while a minor contribution in all damage categories was attributed to process electricity demands (7.7 to 19.4%). By comparing the geopolymerization process with conventional recycling, an environmental benefit of 20 mPt and 26 kg CO_2 per ton of waste glass was demonstrated, indicating the process's expediency. The present study is a valuable tool for the up-scaling of processes towards a circular economy.

Keywords: geopolymerization; waste glass; life cycle assessment; recycling; construction materials

1. Introduction

In the last decades, there has been a growing need for a transition to more sustainable systems regarding the three different aspects of sustainability: economic feasibility, environmental sustainability, and societal expectations [1,2]. The first goal is related to the economic challenges between a proposed process/product and its environment (market instabilities, investor decisions, etc.). The environmental sustainability goal can be achieved by minimizing the environmental footprint of a process/product compared to the existing regime. Social sustainability is the most overlooked part of a sustainability assessment, due to the lack of a clear methodology [3]. However, as the methodology matures and expands, it is necessary to include it when possible.

Waste glass constitutes a substantial portion of urban solid waste due to its large production volumes. Although this type of waste is easily recyclable, it tends to accumulate in landfills and recycling facilities [4]. The most common form of glass in the municipal waste stream is food and beverage containers. Specifically, in the European Union, about 19 million tons were generated in 2015, and the recyclable fraction of this amount reached a percentage of 86% [5]. Several factors can be crucial for glass reuse, such as glass dimensions and its concentration of heavy metals [6]. Also, the color of broken and mixed waste glass can affect the performance of the recycling process and the properties of the new material [7]. In most municipalities in Greece, recyclable packaging is collected as a separate stream and transported to sorting and recycling centers. Seasonal variations, especially in tourist areas during high tourist seasons, can result in quantities of glass exceeding the capacity of such recycling facilities.

Geopolymerization is a promising technology that facilitates the recycling of hazardous wastes (such as slag, dust, etc.), with the goal of creating new products [8]. The process mechanism involves the dissolution of any pozzolanic compound in an alkaline solution to initiate the formation of an aluminum, oxygen, and silica structure [9]. The underlined process is characterized by low energy requirements, low carbon footprint values, and low installed equipment costs. One of the main factors influencing geopolymerization is the nature of raw material. Calcined materials (such as waste glass) have shown faster dissolution and improved mechanical properties for this type of treatment [10]. Regarding the economic feasibility of geopolymerization, the addition of NaOH has been reported as the main factor affecting the sustainability of the process [11]. At the same time, the energy cost of geopolymer brick production is found to be much lower than that of conventional brick production, as the conventional process requires temperatures in the range of 1100 °C to 1400 °C [12].

Life cycle assessment (LCA) is a method that measures the resources consumed and emissions produced throughout the life cycle of a material or process and evaluates its environmental impact. This type of analysis is a tool increasingly considered necessary for research and policy-making purposes by institutions and companies. The core concept of this assessment is to connect the environmental impact of a process to the materials and energy required for product creation [13]. In addition, this analysis can be used to identify the stages of the process with the highest environmental impact in order to achieve further targeted optimization at these specified process stages [14].

The objective of this study was to evaluate the environmental impact of the geopolymerization of waste glass for the production of sustainable building materials, namely pavement tiles, and to compare this process with the recycling of waste glass. The general methodology followed was the estimation of mass and energy balances according to experimental data and the literature, and the implementation of these results in the LCA software (SimaPro 8). Several assumptions were made regarding the system boundaries and the yields of the sub-processes. The geopolymer production process has been studied in the literature with respect to its environmental impact [15,16]. In the work of Petrillo et al. [17], the production of tiles using geopolymerization showed the environmental benefits of the process. Additionally, the work of Salas et al. [18] addressed the up-scaling of geopolymer concrete production from the laboratory to industrial scale. The analysis showed that the NaOH addition was the step with the highest environmental impact. Although geopolymerization has been studied in the existing literature, data on a direct comparison between waste glass recycling and this technique are lacking. Moreover, this assessment offers insights into the geopolymerization technique, identifying the process's hotspots and providing direction to material engineers and researchers toward a sustainable society's transition. The present study aims to highlight the use of environmentally friendly techniques for new product formation using solid waste streams in synergy with established municipal recycling processes.

2. Materials and Methods

2.1. Goal and Scope

The mandatory steps to be followed for a life cycle assessment of a process are as follows: (1) goal and scope definition, (2) life cycle inventory analysis, (3) life cycle impact assessment (LCIA), and (4) life cycle interpretation [19]. The goal of the analysis was not to completely replace conventional recycling technology, but to propose an alternative sustainable solution for the residual waste that can be processed in recycling facilities. Thus, a functional unit (FU) of 1000 kg of waste glass was used as the basis for the analysis; so, all results presented here refer to the treatment of this amount of waste. This functional unit was selected considering that approximately 2.7 tons of waste per capita are generated annually and a percentage of 60% of this waste is recycled (1.7 ton per capita) [20].

The life cycle inventory (LCI) data were derived using SimaPro 8 software [21] and the Ecoinvent 3.5 database [22]. Background processes covering the whole region of Europe was selected in order to assure a wide applicability of the assessment. The environmental impact of the processes was calculated using the IMPACT 2002+ v2.15 method, which groups the LCI data into 15 midpoint categories, which are then aggregated into 4 damage categories, as shown in Figure 1. The graph shows that elementary flow results with comparable impact pathways are combined into midpoint impact categories. The differentiation between midpoint and endpoint categories reflects the distribution of impacts at an intermediate stage between inventory results and environmental quality changes [23]. All midpoint categories use units as reference compounds that can be converted to the units of the damage categories.

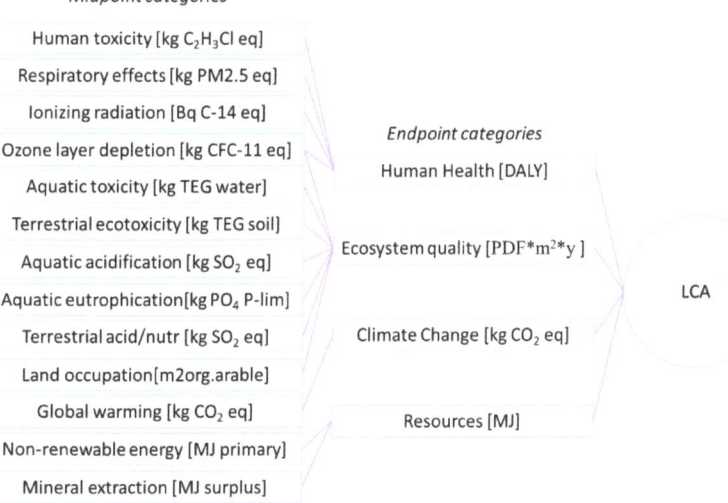

Figure 1. Scheme of the IMPACT 2002+ based on the work of Humbert et al. [24].

An LCA can stop at the LCI generation step. However, grouping the LCI results into impact categories is usually necessary to facilitate the understanding of the results, their interpretation, and comparison with the literature data. The midpoint damage categories aggregate the LCI results into categories that are not easily understood, such as land occupation or water extraction, but with fewer assumptions. On the other hand, endpoint damage categories are easier to understand, with damage categories such as climate change and resources used, but with more assumptions in aggregating the results. Several studies present results only in midpoint or endpoint damage categories. In this study, the midpoint damage categorization was first performed using the results from the LCI, and then a second grouping into endpoint categories was performed, allowing results to be presented at both levels.

For the final normalization of the endpoint categories, the exposure of an average European citizen (Pt) during one year was used. The normalization values from the IM-PACT 2002+ method were 0.0071 DALY/Pt, 13,700 PDF*m^2*y/Pt, 152,000 MJ/Pt, and 9950 kg CO_2/Pt.

2.2. Mass Balances and Assumptions

The process stages included in the analysis were divided into those directly affected by the process design (foreground) and those indirectly affected through mass and energy balances (background). The processes included in the analysis for both the geopolymerization method and conventional recycling up to the crushed glass production stage are shown in Figure 2. More specifically, the geopolymerization process includes the collection of waste glass, its crushing, the addition of reagents and mixing, a curing stage, and finally, the production of tiles. The modeling of the recycling process was based on data from the work of Blengini et al. [25] and includes the transport of waste glass, the washing stage using oxygen to avoid anaerobic conditions, the drying and grinding stage, and the production of crushed glass. In the case of geopolymerization, the final product displaces the production of concrete tiles, while conventional recycling displaces the production of silica sand [25]. The construction materials of the process equipment are not included in the analysis, which is quite common in such analyses, because the environmental impact of constructing the equipment is considered minimal compared to the impact of its operation, due to the equipment's long lifespan [14].

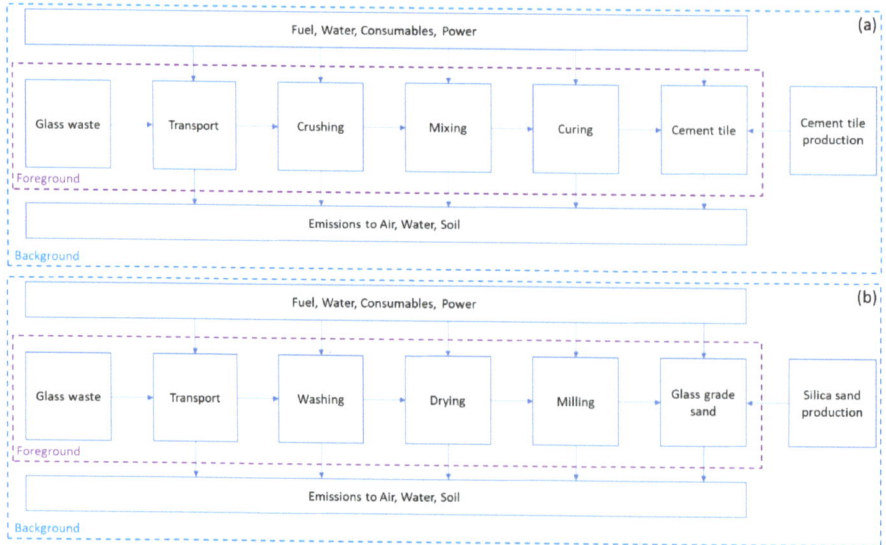

Figure 2. Process stages for the different treatment methods of waste glass ((**a**) geopolymerization, (**b**) recycling).

2.3. Geopolymerization Process Modeling

The geopolymerization process was modeled according to the data presented in Table 1. The processed product displaces the production of cement tiles, while the raw materials used in the process are sodium hydroxide and water. Since the scope of the present assessment is the environmental study of a small plant capable of processing seasonal waste glass that cannot be recycled, it was assumed that the plant would be located within the geographic boundaries of a city; therefore, a small transport distance of 5 km was assumed. This was the only transport burden considered in this analysis, as the handling of material during the processing and transport of NaOH to the pilot geopolymerization unit are expected to have a minimal impact on the overall process. It was also assumed that the cement tiles produced would be used to pave the local sidewalks. Typically, the impact of transporting raw materials and products is a small part of the total impact (shown in the following analysis). In this analysis, a total transportation impact of 5 tkm (ton-kilometers) was assumed.

Table 1. Input data for LCA of the geopolymerization process of waste glass.

	Avoided products		
Cement tile		1068	kg
	Materials/fuels		
Sodium hydroxide		56	kg
Tap water		200	kg
Transport, freight, lorry		5	tkm
	Electricity/heat		
Electricity, medium voltage		87.5	MJ

The Municipality of Megara, Greece has a separate glass collection system utilizing bell-shaped containers. Part of this stream was supplied for pilot operation and obtaining the data used in this study. No separate glass types were investigated as the provided waste glass stream was a mixture of all the available glass containers.

The input data for the geopolymerization process were based on experimental data obtained during the operation of a pilot geopolymerization unit (0.5 t/h capacity) in the Municipality of Megara, Greece, for the treatment of excess waste glass during the high tourist season.

The product of the geopolymerization process was modeled by displacing cement tiles. This was based on the literature data that highlight the physical properties of this product, comparable to conventional construction materials [26,27].

Background processes were modeled using the Ecoinvent 3.5 database. More specifically, data representing Europe, excluding Switzerland, were utilized. If European data were unavailable, global data were used instead.

2.4. Recycling Process Modeling

Although the geopolymerization process will not be used in competition with the recycling process, as it is recommended for periods when the quantities of waste glass exceed the capacity of the recycling plant, the process is presented here for comparison purposes. The analysis of this process is based on the literature [25]. The input data for SimaPro are shown in Table 2. The process was studied up to the stage of crushed glass production, which displaces silica sand production. Several raw materials were included in the analysis in order to perform the necessary washing (water and oxygen to avoid the growth of anaerobic microorganisms), drying of the material (thermal energy), and finally, its crushing (electric energy).

Table 2. Input data for LCA of the recycling process of waste glass.

Avoided products		
Silica sand	850	kg
Materials/fuels		
Oxygen, liquid	0.49	kg
Tap water	830	kg
Transport, freight, lorry	20	tkm
Diesel	0.425	kg
Electricity/heat		
Heat, district or industrial, natural gas	103.59	MJ
Electricity, medium voltage	25	kWh

3. Results and Discussion

3.1. Characterization

The mass and energy balances of the processes were aligned with raw materials extracted from the environment and emissions of pollutants/compounds released into the environment, using SimaPro 8.0 and the Ecoinvent 3.5 database to compile the life cycle inventory. The IMPACT 2002+ v2.15 methodology was used to aggregate the LCI into 15 midpoint impact categories. To identify the hot spot in the process, the analysis was performed by dividing it into five different sub-processes. The NaOH sub-process included the amount of NaOH required for the production of cement tiles, while the avoided product (displacement of cement tiles) was included in the product sub-process. To assess the results of various impact categories, a percentage-based analysis was conducted by dividing the value of each impact category by the damage in the scenario with the highest absolute value for that category. The normalization values are provided in Table 3, while the comparative results are presented in Figure 3.

Table 3. Normalization values for midpoint damage categories.

Damage Category	Unit	Maximum Absolute Value
Mineral extraction	MJ surplus	0.20
Non-renewable energy	MJ primary	14×10^2
Global warming	kg CO_2 eq	27
Aquatic eutrophication	kg PO_4 P-lim	13×10^{-3}
Aquatic acidification	kg SO_2 eq	0.7
Land occupation	m^2 org.arable	1.4
Terrestrial acid/nutr	kg SO_2 eq	3.3
Terrestrial ecotoxicity	kg TEG soil	36×10^2
Aquatic ecotoxicity	kg TEG water	11×10^2
Respiratory organics	kg C_2H_4 eq	3.2×10^{-2}
Ozone layer depletion	kg CFC-11 eq	4.5×10^{-5}
Ionizing radiation	Bq C-14 eq	10×10^2
Respiratory inorganics	kg $PM_{2.5}$ eq	16×10^{-2}
Non-carcinogens	kg C_2H_3Cl eq	3.0
Carcinogens	kg C_2H_3Cl eq	1.3

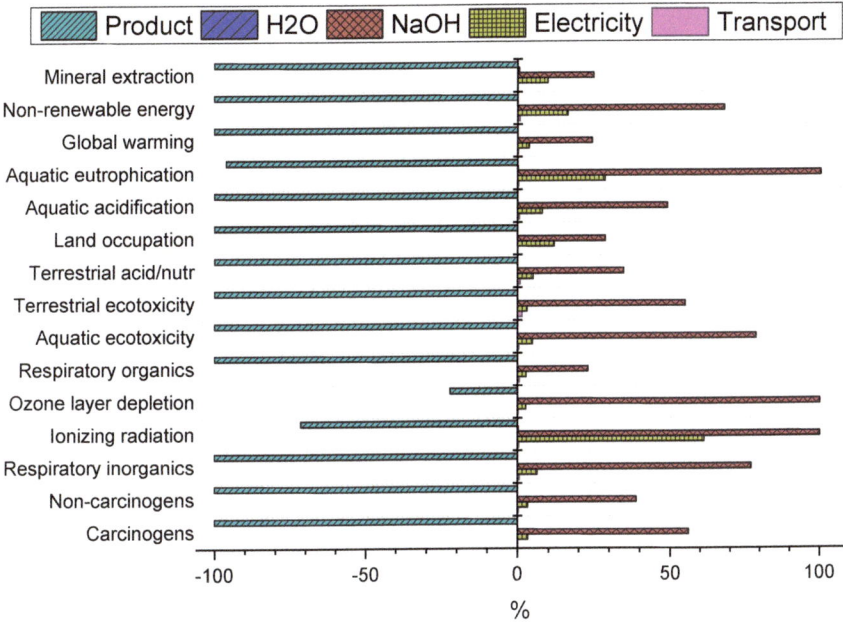

Figure 3. Comparative results per 1000 kg of waste glass for the different parts of the geopolymerization process in the midpoint damage categories.

In all of the midpoint impact categories, the process product had the highest absolute value, and in all cases, it was expressed as a negative harm (or environmental benefit). A negative impact value is strongly connected with the reduction in emissions to the ecosphere implementing the proposed methodology, avoiding the production of a conventional material [28]. In these midpoint categories, the addition of NaOH had the second highest absolute value, always expressed as damage (environmental impact). The environmental burden of NaOH addition outweighed the environmental benefit of the final product in three midpoint categories, namely aquatic eutrophication, ozone layer depletion, and ionizing radiation. The significance of these three midpoint categories will be clarified after their comparison and aggregation with the other relevant categories at the endpoint level. The third most significant stage of the process was the consumption of electric energy, especially in the ionizing radiation category. Conversely, water consumption and transportation had a negligible impact on the overall results.

3.2. Damage Assessment

The results of the LCI midpoint category aggregation were further aggregated into four different endpoint categories to provide a comprehensive interpretation of the results. The endpoint category results for the different sub-processes are shown in Table 4.

Table 4. Aggregated damage assessment results per 1000 kg of waste glass for the different sub-processes of geopolymerization.

Damage Category	Unit	Transport	Electricity	NaOH	H_2O	Product	Total
Human health	DALY	7.08×10^{-7}	7.52×10^{-6}	8.97×10^{-5}	3.67×10^{-8}	-1.2×10^{-4}	-2.2×10^{-5}
Ecosystem quality	PDF*m²*yr	0.5	1.3	17.7	0.01	−34	−14.5
Climate change	kg CO_2 eq	0.7	10	65	0.1	−265	−189
Resources	MJ primary	11	235	962	1	−1421	−212

The aggregation of damages into endpoint categories reiterates the significant contributions of the end product and NaOH addition to the overall impact of the process. At this level, the environmental benefits of the product outweigh the impact of NaOH addition in all four endpoint damage categories. Electricity consumption is again the third largest contributor, while transportation and water consumption have very small contributions to the overall results.

3.3. Normalization

A final normalization step was performed to aggregate the results in terms of the environmental impact of an average European citizen. The results of this step for the different sub-processes are shown in Figure 4. The addition of NaOH was identified as the most environmentally damaging process, as it has the highest impact in all categories of endpoint impact. On the other hand, the prevention of cement tile production was the process with the most positive impact (negative damage). Specifically, in the case of the human health damage category, the negative damage of the avoided product outweighs the positive damage of the chemical addition in the process.

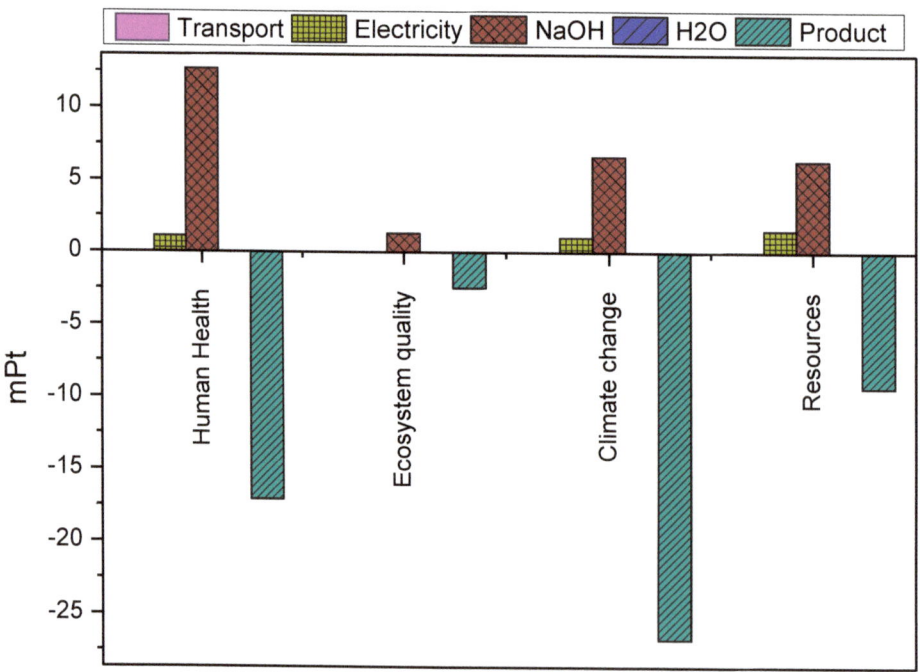

Figure 4. Normalized damage per 1000 kg of waste glass for the different parts of the geopolymerization process in the endpoint damage categories.

The proposed process was compared to the baseline scenario process of glass recycling (Figure 5). The geopolymerization process shows similar impacts to the recycling process in the human health and ecosystem quality damage categories, but there is a significant advantage of the geopolymerization process (about seven times less impact compared to the recycling process) in the climate change category. This difference between the two processes in the climate change category is due to the displacement of the production of cement tiles, as their production is very energy intensive. For recycling, the low impact in the Resource Damage category is related to the abundance of silica sand in the ecosphere, the displacement of which has little impact on the process. Also, the energy used to dry the raw material after washing may contribute to the increased impact in this impact category.

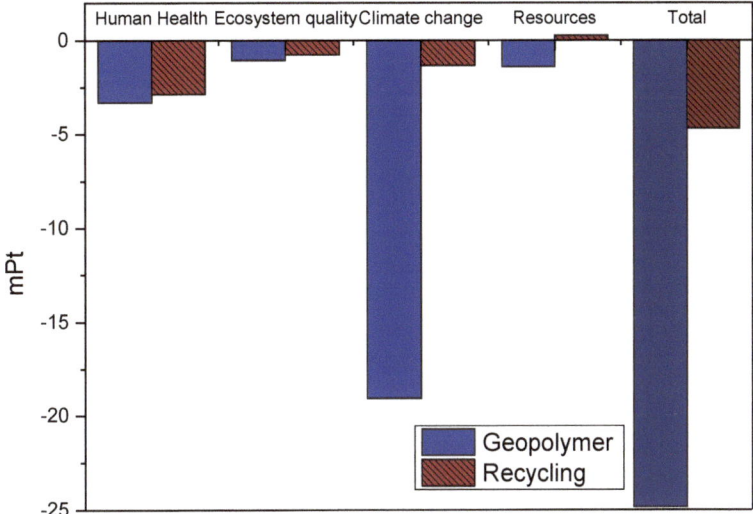

Figure 5. Comparison of geopolymerization and recycling process per 1000 kg of waste glass for the endpoint categories.

4. Interpretation

According to the evaluation of the results of the midpoint categories, the negative damage caused by the prevention of cement tile production proved to be satisfactory, since it can compensate for the environmental impact of the remaining process steps. High impact values were observed for the NaOH addition, which is consistent with similar studies in the existing literature [18].

The NaOH production process consists of several sub-processes (well drilling, brine extraction, etc.) that consume significant amounts of energy and fuel. The efficiency in energy and fuel consumption has been reported as a crucial parameter affecting the environmental impact of NaOH [29]. Therefore, NaOH production using a renewable energy mix can further reduce the geopolymerization environmental burden in the climate change impact category. Another alternative for impact reduction during the alkaline treatment is the use of combinations of different activators. Sodium silicate and fly ash and slag can be used in different concentrations alongside NaOH and KOH in order to optimize the process' environmental impact and product's characteristics [30]. According to the Ecoinvent database, sodium silicate (Na_2SiO_3) has a lower environmental impact across all categories compared to sodium hydroxide (NaOH) (5.27×10^{-6} DALY kg^{-1} Na_2SiO_3 instead of 1.41×10^{-5} DALY kg^{-1} NaOH and 4.05 PDF m^2 year kg^{-1} Na_2SiO_3 instead of 23.5 PDF m^2 year kg^{-1} NaOH). Thus, any admixture of this component to the alkali treatment can lead to less impacts in alkaline treatment.

A significant burden was attributed to the electricity needed for the geopolymerization process, while the water needed, and the transportation of waste glass do not significantly affect the process. This impact can also be reduced by using electricity from renewable energy sources. The use of this type of energy could decarbonize up to 5% of the total process impact in the climate change category [31]. To reduce the impact of the NaOH addition, several authors suggest replacing conventional NaOH with NaOH produced from solar salt. This can lead to an 18% reduction in the global warming category [32]. In another study by Mir et al. [33], the impact assessment of recycled ceramic tile and recycled brick waste-based geopolymers was addressed. The larger impacts in this process were also observed by the NaOH addition and electricity consumption (about 60% of the total impact). The same observation has been made by other authors in their analysis of the environmental impacts of alkali-activated concrete produced with a silicate activator derived from waste glass [34]. By converting the midpoint categories to endpoint damage categories, the three impact categories that show environmental impact (aquatic eutrophication, ozone layer depletion, and ionizing radiation) do not affect the overall endpoint result because the environmental damage avoided by the product outweighs the damage of these categories. In all four endpoint categories, the benefit of the product outweighs the burden of the rest of the process. The endpoint categories were reported as the final step in linking the LCA to the Sustainable Development Goals (SDGs) of Good Health and Well-being, Clean Water and Sanitation, Affordable and Clean Energy, Sustainable Cities, Climate Action, and Life on Land and Water [35].

Regarding the comparison of the geopolymerization process with the conventional recycling process, the impacts had similar values regarding the endpoint categories of ecosystem quality, human health, and resources. However, the geopolymerization process showed a significantly reduced impact in the category of climate change. This can be attributed to the avoided products of each process. Conventional cement tiles have a higher production impact than silica sand (avoided product of the recycling process) because the raw material (cement) has several environmental impacts from its production. It is clear that the geopolymerization process offers environmental benefits compared to conventional cement tile production. In the work of Samuel et al. [36], a sustainability comparison was made between geopolymerization and lime treatment, considering the environmental, economic, and social index. The geopolymerization process showed a reduced sustainability index of 10% compared to lime treatment, so there are other alternatives worth pursuing and investigating. Nevertheless, the geopolymerization of waste glass for the production of cement tiles during the periods of excessive waste glass generation seems to be a promising alternative to recycling. Moreover, feedstock material (solid precursors) can be a crucial factor for efficient geopolymerization in terms of raw materials consumption and energy accumulation. While Si-rich precursors require more energy but less chemical treatment compared to clayey materials (like kaolin) in the geopolymerization process, this study reveals that chemical treatment remains a significant impact factor for Si-rich materials [37]. Despite this, Si-rich materials like volcanic ash, and Si-rich fly ash are still suitable for geopolymerization due to their overall efficiency and reduced chemical dependency.

Summarizing the normalized results of the endpoint damage categories, the geopolymerization process shows improved results in the overall score (25 mPt avoided per ton of waste glass) compared to conventional glass recycling (4.7 mPt avoided per ton of waste glass). In addition, geopolymer materials can immobilize heavy metals. The safe consolidation of all these materials in a geopolymer matrix is far more preferable to landfilling, as the degradation of landfill cells can pose risks to human health, the surrounding soil, air quality, groundwater sources, and surface water [38].

The economic potential has been reported in the literature for the geopolymerization process for different materials. An increase in financial gain of 5% has been exhibited for the geopolymerization bricks compared to conventional fire bricks for a case study in the region of France [12]. In the same study, the lower production cost was estimated at EUR 114 t^{-1}. A major contribution in the total product cost can be attributed to the high market price of NaOH (EUR 490 t^{-1}); thus, the use of different alkaline precursors may lead to further cost reduction, enhancing the process's sustainability [39].

The proposed process presents a comprehensive strategy for waste valorization for the production of recyclable materials in the context of the circular economy and zero-waste politics. Thus, its implementation aligns with and contributes to the relevant SDGs of the 2030 Agenda [40]. By converting this waste into construction material, the process implementation can reduce the waste amount that ends up in landfills, which is aligned with the SDG 11, 'Sustainable Cities and Communities'. Geopolymerization also supports the recycling and reuse of materials, lowering the carbon footprint associated with conventional cement tile production, and contributing to SDG 12, 'Responsible Consumption and Production' and SDG 13, 'Climate Action'. Finally, an indirect connection can be identified with SDG 9, 'Industry, Innovation, and Infrastructure', since this process can foster the development of resilient infrastructure and alternatives in industrial practices.

5. Conclusions

The environmental impact of the waste glass geopolymerization process was evaluated through the application of the life cycle analysis methodology, which revealed a net positive impact. The primary factor contributing to this observation was the displacement of other materials with high environmental costs by the product of the process. The deployment of the geopolymerization process was validated as a supplementary process for seasonal fluctuations in the quantity of glass collected by a municipality. This method of waste treatment has the potential to further reduce the overall impact of waste remediation in comparison to conventional recycling. It is important to note that the geopolymerization process is not intended to compete with recycling. Rather, it is designed to address the accumulation of materials in sorting centers or end up in landfills. The proposed process offers a valuable alternative for reducing landfill use and advancing the sustainability goals set forth by the European Union for the transition to a sustainable and "green" future.

Author Contributions: Conceptualization, M.K., D.Z., and C.G.; methodology, G.M. and D.Z.; software, D.Z.; validation, G.M., D.Z., and C.G.; formal analysis, G.M. and D.Z.; investigation, G.M. and D.Z.; resources, M.K. and C.Z.; data curation, G.M. and D.Z.; writing—original draft preparation, G.M. and D.Z.; writing—review and editing, C.Z., C.G., and M.K.; visualization, G.M. and D.Z.; supervision, C.Z. and M.K.; project administration, C.G. and M.K.; funding acquisition, C.Z. and M.K. All authors have read and agreed to the published version of the manuscript.

Funding: This research has been funded by the Transnational Cooperation Programme Interreg V-B Balkan- Mediterranean 2014–2020: "Invalor 101—A network for joint valorization of material flows in tourist areas", BMP1/2.2/2131/2017 (MIS 5016108).

Data Availability Statement: Data can be provided on request.

Conflicts of Interest: Author Constantina Zafiri was employed by the company Green Technologies Ltd. The remaining authors declare that the research was conducted in the absence of any commercial or financial relationships that could be construed as a potential conflict of interest.

References

1. Mota, B.; Gomes, M.I.; Carvalho, A.; Barbosa-Povoa, A.P. Towards supply chain sustainability: Economic, environmental and social design and planning. *J. Clean. Prod.* **2015**, *105*, 14–27. [CrossRef]
2. Santoyo-Castelazo, E.; Azapagic, A. Sustainability assessment of energy systems: Integrating environmental, economic and social aspects. *J. Clean. Prod.* **2014**, *80*, 119–138. [CrossRef]
3. Jitmaneeroj, B. Reform priorities for corporate sustainability: Environmental, social, governance, or economic performance? *Manag. Decis.* **2016**, *54*, 1497–1521. [CrossRef]
4. Pahlevani, F.; Sahajwalla, V. From waste glass to building materials—An innovative sustainable solution for waste glass. *J. Clean. Prod.* **2018**, *191*, 192–206.
5. Eurostat. *Generation of Waste by Waste Category, Hazardousness and NACE Rev. 2 Activity*; Dispon. en ligne; Eurostat: Luxembourg, 2016.

6. Bignozzi, M.C.; Saccani, A.; Barbieri, L.; Lancellotti, I. Glass waste as supplementary cementing materials: The effects of glass chemical composition. *Cem. Concr. Compos.* **2015**, *55*, 45–52. [CrossRef]
7. Bisikirske, D.; Blumberga, D.; Vasarevicius, S.; Skripkiunas, G. Multicriteria analysis of glass waste application. *Environ. Clim. Technol.* **2019**, *23*, 152–167. [CrossRef]
8. Khale, D.; Chaudhary, R. Mechanism of geopolymerization and factors influencing its development: A review. *J. Mater. Sci.* **2007**, *42*, 729–746. [CrossRef]
9. Komnitsas, K.; Zaharaki, D. Geopolymerisation: A review and prospects for the minerals industry. *Miner. Eng.* **2007**, *20*, 1261–1277. [CrossRef]
10. Rao, F.; Liu, Q. Geopolymerization and its potential application in mine tailings consolidation: A review. *Miner. Process. Extr. Metall. Rev.* **2015**, *36*, 399–409. [CrossRef]
11. You, S.; Ho, S.W.; Li, T.; Maneerung, T.; Wang, C.-H. Techno-economic analysis of geopolymer production from the coal fly ash with high iron oxide and calcium oxide contents. *J. Hazard. Mater.* **2019**, *361*, 237–244. [CrossRef] [PubMed]
12. Youssef, N.; Lafhaj, Z.; Chapiseau, C. Economic analysis of geopolymer brick manufacturing: A french case study. *Sustainability* **2020**, *12*, 7403. [CrossRef]
13. Hauschild, M.Z.; Rosenbaum, R.K.; Olsen, S.I. *Life Cycle Assessment*; Springer: Berlin/Heidelberg, Germany, 2018.
14. Manthos, G.; Zagklis, D.; Zafiri, C.; Kornaros, M. Comparative life cycle assessment of anaerobic digestion, lagoon evaporation, and direct land application of olive mill wastewater. *Bioresour. Technol.* **2023**, *388*, 129778. [CrossRef]
15. Turner, L.K.; Collins, F.G. Carbon dioxide equivalent (CO_2-e) emissions: A comparison between geopolymer and OPC cement concrete. *Constr. Build. Mater.* **2013**, *43*, 125–130. [CrossRef]
16. Habert, G.; De Lacaillerie, J.B.D.; Roussel, N. An environmental evaluation of geopolymer based concrete production: Reviewing current research trends. *J. Clean. Prod.* **2011**, *19*, 1229–1238. [CrossRef]
17. Petrillo, A.; Cioffi, R.; Ferone, C.; Colangelo, F.; Borrelli, C. Eco-sustainable geopolymer concrete blocks production process. *Agric. Agric. Sci. Procedia* **2016**, *8*, 408–418. [CrossRef]
18. Salas, D.A.; Ramirez, A.D.; Ulloa, N.; Baykara, H.; Boero, A.J. Life cycle assessment of geopolymer concrete. *Constr. Build. Mater.* **2018**, *190*, 170–177. [CrossRef]
19. Curran, M.A. *Life Cycle Assessment Handbook: A Guide for Environmentally Sustainable Products*; John Wiley & Sons: Hoboken, NJ, USA, 2012; ISBN 1118099729.
20. Kazmi, D.; Williams, D.J.; Serati, M. Waste glass in civil engineering applications—A review. *Int. J. Appl. Ceram. Technol.* **2020**, *17*, 529–554. [CrossRef]
21. PRé Sustainability B.V., Simapro 8, 2010. Available online: https://simapro.com (accessed on 30 November 2024).
22. Wernet, G.; Bauer, C.; Steubing, B.; Reinhard, J.; Moreno-Ruiz, E.; Weidema, B. The ecoinvent database version 3 (part I): Overview and methodology. *Int. J. Life Cycle Assess.* **2016**, *21*, 1218–1230. [CrossRef]
23. Jolliet, O.; Margni, M.; Charles, R.; Humbert, S.; Payet, J.; Rebitzer, G.; Rosenbaum, R. IMPACT 2002+: A new life cycle impact assessment methodology. *Int. J. Life Cycle Assess.* **2003**, *8*, 324–330. [CrossRef]
24. Humbert, S.; Margni, M.; Jolliet, O. IMPACT 2002+: User guide. *Draft Version Q* **2012**, *2*.
25. Blengini, G.A.; Busto, M.; Fantoni, M.; Fino, D. Eco-efficient waste glass recycling: Integrated waste management and green product development through LCA. *Waste Manag.* **2012**, *32*, 1000–1008. [CrossRef] [PubMed]
26. Henao Rios, L.M.; Hoyos Triviño, A.F.; Villaquirán-Caicedo, M.A.; de Gutiérrez, R.M. Effect of the use of waste glass (as precursor, and alkali activator) in the manufacture of geopolymer rendering mortars and architectural tiles. *Constr. Build. Mater.* **2023**, *363*, 129760. [CrossRef]
27. Rivera, J.F.; Cuarán-Cuarán, Z.I.; Vanegas-Bonilla, N.; Mejía de Gutiérrez, R. Novel use of waste glass powder: Production of geopolymeric tiles. *Adv. Powder Technol.* **2018**, *29*, 3448–3454. [CrossRef]
28. Jeswani, H.K.; Saharudin, D.M.; Azapagic, A. Environmental sustainability of negative emissions technologies: A review. *Sustain. Prod. Consum.* **2022**, *33*, 608–635. [CrossRef]
29. Hong, J.; Chen, W.; Wang, Y.; Xu, C.; Xu, X. Life cycle assessment of caustic soda production: A case study in China. *J. Clean. Prod.* **2014**, *66*, 113–120. [CrossRef]
30. Rathee, M.; Singh, N. Reviewing geopolymer concrete: A possible sustainable structural material of future. *Environ. Dev. Sustain.* **2024**, 1–55. [CrossRef]
31. Osman, A.I.; Chen, L.; Yang, M.; Msigwa, G.; Farghali, M.; Fawzy, S.; Rooney, D.W.; Yap, P.-S. Cost, environmental impact, and resilience of renewable energy under a changing climate: A review. *Environ. Chem. Lett.* **2023**, *21*, 741–764. [CrossRef]
32. Munir, Q.; Abdulkareem, M.; Horttanainen, M.; Kärki, T. A comparative cradle-to-gate life cycle assessment of geopolymer concrete produced from industrial side streams in comparison with traditional concrete. *Sci. Total Environ.* **2023**, *865*, 161230. [CrossRef] [PubMed]
33. Mir, N.; Khan, S.A.; Kul, A.; Sahin, O.; Lachemi, M.; Sahmaran, M.; Koç, M. Life cycle assessment of binary recycled ceramic tile and recycled brick waste-based geopolymers. *Clean. Mater.* **2022**, *5*, 100116. [CrossRef]

34. Bianco, I.; Tomos, B.A.D.; Vinai, R. Analysis of the environmental impacts of alkali-activated concrete produced with waste glass-derived silicate activator—A LCA study. *J. Clean. Prod.* **2021**, *316*, 128383. [CrossRef]
35. Weidema, B.; Goedkoop, M.; Meijer, E.; Harmens, R. LCA-based assessment of the Sustainable Development Goals. Development update and preliminary findings of the Project "Linking the UN Sustainable Development Goals to life cycle impact pathway frameworks". *PRé Sustain.* **2020**, *2*, 1–55.
36. Samuel, R.; Puppala, A.J.; Radovic, M. Sustainability benefits assessment of metakaolin-based geopolymer treatment of high plasticity clay. *Sustainability* **2020**, *12*, 10495. [CrossRef]
37. Kamseu, E.; Alzari, V.; Nuvoli, D.; Sanna, D.; Lancellotti, I.; Mariani, A.; Leonelli, C. Dependence of the geopolymerization process and end-products to the nature of solid precursors: Challenge of the sustainability. *J. Clean. Prod.* **2021**, *278*, 123587. [CrossRef]
38. Shehata, N.; Mohamed, O.A.; Sayed, E.T.; Abdelkareem, M.A.; Olabi, A.G. Geopolymer concrete as green building materials: Recent applications, sustainable development and circular economy potentials. *Sci. Total Environ.* **2022**, *836*, 155577. [CrossRef]
39. Umer, M.; Ahmad, J.; Mukhtar, H. Innovative valorization of biomass waste-derived sodium silicate for geopolymer concrete synthesis: Sustainability assessment and circular economy potential. *J. Clean. Prod.* **2024**, *452*, 142181. [CrossRef]
40. Colglazier, W. Sustainable development agenda: 2030. *Science* **2015**, *349*, 1048–1050. [CrossRef]

Disclaimer/Publisher's Note: The statements, opinions and data contained in all publications are solely those of the individual author(s) and contributor(s) and not of MDPI and/or the editor(s). MDPI and/or the editor(s) disclaim responsibility for any injury to people or property resulting from any ideas, methods, instructions or products referred to in the content.

Article

Simulation Tool for the Techno-Economic Assessment of the Integrated Production of Polyhydroxyalkanoates as Value-Added Byproducts of a Wastewater Treatment Plant

Laura Pozo-Morales [1,*], Antonio Rosales Martínez [1], Enrique Baquerizo [2] and Germán del Valle Agulla [3]

[1] Department of Chemical Engineering, University of Seville, 41011 Sevilla, Spain; arosales@us.es
[2] Emasesa Metropolitan, 41003 Sevilla, Spain; ebaquerizo@emasesa.com
[3] Ollearis, S.A., 41410 Sevilla, Spain; german.delvalle@ollearis.org
* Correspondence: lauratar@us.es

Abstract: The polyhydroxyalkanoate (PHA) production process that uses mixed microbial cultures combined with main stream wastewater treatment plants (WWTPs) is a competitive integrated resource recovery process in which non-oxygen electron acceptors can be used to enrich the PHA producer. Trials carried out in operating plants are very scarce, and there are no simulation tools available to analyse the feasibility of integrating the two processes. This research presents a novel analysis tool for a techno-economic assessment of value-added biopolymers. A general model for a conventional WWTP has been designed and eventually validated using the operating data collected in the database of a fully operational plant. In the model, a simulation of a PHA production line based on thickened primary sludge as a substrate has been integrated. The assembly has been treated as a closed-loop system with an accuracy level of 0.1% with a limit of 1000 iterations. Two strategies based on internal (ADF) or external (AN/AD) limitations of some nutrients have been contrasted for the selection of a biomass capable of feast–famine PHA synthesis. The ADF strategy was found to be the most favourable system, with a production of 0.226 kg of $COD_{PHA} \cdot kg^{-1}$ COD. The calculated production cost was EUR $0.11 \cdot kg^{-1}$ COD_{PHA}. The sludge production was reduced by 6%.

Keywords: polyhydroxyalkanoates; wastewater treatment plant; techno-economic assessment; process element

1. Introduction

Global plastic production represents a substantial component of the global economy, exhibiting an exponential expansion with a clear tendency to continue rising in the future [1]. This is largely attributable to the advent of novel applications and the advancement of increasingly sophisticated products that incorporate plastic as the building material [2]. Yet, unfortunately, most plastics are derived from non-renewable sources, predominantly fossil fuels, which are becoming increasingly scarce. Additionally, the carbon emissions generated during the production of plastics contribute significantly to climate change. Finally, the high resistance of plastics to microbial degradation results in a high accumulation rate in the environment [3,4]. Therefore, it can be concluded that plastics production and waste management represent one of the most significant environmental challenges currently facing humanity.

The transition to environmentally friendly materials will be a crucial step in reducing the carbon footprint of plastics. In addition, the use of alternative raw materials to reduce the consumption of fossil resources and the achievement of green synthesis processes contribute to the fulfilment of principles 3, 4, 7 and 10 of Green Chemistry in favour of greater sustainability [5].

Biopolymers are regarded as potentially optimal substitutes for plastics derived from fossil resources [6], and their lifecycle analysis indicates that they have a very short biodegradation time on Earth's surface under standard conditions [7]. Polyhydroxyalkanoates, or PHAs, are renewable, bio-based plastics with properties similar to polypropylene and polystyrene [8] which, in comparison with standard plastics, offer a potential average of 2 kg less of CO_2 emissions and 30 MJ less in fossil fuel consumption per kg of PHA produced. They belong to the same family of thermoplastic, biodegradable polyesters as the well-established polylactic acid (PLA) and polybutylene succinate (PBS), widely regarded as among the most promising alternatives to conventional plastics for the foreseeable future [8]. The length of the chain of a given PHA polymer and the functional groups it contains are two factors with a large influence over their physical characteristics. Short-chain PHAs are highly crystalline, rigid materials, while a longer chain confers them elastomeric properties [8,9]. Regarding their mechanical properties, a longer chain is associated with a higher resistance [10]. Nevertheless, the economic viability of PHA production remains a challenge. Depending on its exact composition, its price oscillates between EUR 4 and 6 per Kg, which is to say at least five to six times that of petroleum-based polymers [11,12]. Nowadays, conventional production of PHA at an industrial level is mostly carried out from pure microbial cultures, whose sterility requirements and the high cost of the necessary substrates compound one of the main drawbacks associated with their industrial production. The synthesis of PHA by mixed microbial cultures (MMCs) using high-carbon-content byproducts as the substrate, offers a potential solution to this economic hurdle while providing a means to advance their industrial development in an environmentally sustainable manner [10,13]. MMCs can be used to ferment organic compounds, thus converting the latter into biopolymers through a natural metabolic pathway [9,14]. Third-generation feedstocks (provided that, for ethical reasons, they do not compete with human or animal food, arable land or freshwater [15]) provide not only an even more cost-effective alternative but also contribute to the development of a circular economy. This remains viable for as long as selective pressure is applied during the degradation of organic matter, allowing the promotion of microorganisms capable of storing PHA [16]. This accumulation of PHA is, in turn, a response to an imbalance in microbial growth caused by a lack of some nutrients accompanied by an excess source of carbon. It has been demonstrated that PHA biosynthesis occurs in the presence of a deficiency of nitrogen, phosphorus, magnesium or sulphate, regardless of whether oxygen is present or not [10]. The carbon sources used are based on carbohydrates, methanol, alkanes, fatty acids and their derivatives [17].

Consequently, integration strategies have been proposed to synthesise PHA with MMCs within urban WWTPs, where substrates with significant organic carbon contents are already present, as evidenced in [4,18,19]. Furthermore, this biosynthesis process contributes to a reduction in the volume of wastewater sludge generated by the WWTP, which becomes revalorised in the form of PHA. The upscaling of PHA production from wastewater sludge has the potential to contribute to waste management and resource recovery in a simultaneous and mutually reinforcing manner [20]. Nevertheless, industrial-scale installations remain scarce [14]. Despite the technical feasibility of producing biomass with the capacity to store PHA from urban wastewater sludge having been demonstrated on the laboratory scale, a lack of full-scale experience has been reported for the integration of PHA production lines with MMCs in urban WWTPs [4,18]. A number of challenges must be addressed in order to facilitate the implementation of these production lines. These include the handling of substrates and logistics, the absence of public policies to encourage the development of bioplastics, the limited social awareness regarding the environmental benefits of bioplastics, and the inconsistency of results when scaling up PHAs production [4]. It can be concluded that wastewater sludge-based PHA production shows great promise but still requires further research and development for its industrialisation. The promotion of biomaterials, the implementation of optimisation and analytical methodologies and the facilitation of the development of pilot plants are imperative components for the successful integration of these elements [4].

Currently, there is a lack of mathematical models and simulation tools that can accurately predict the production of PHA in a WWTP. The development of such tools could facilitate the assessment of the feasibility of this process while also providing valuable insights into strategies to improve productivity, enhance product quality and reduce costs. In this study, a model has been developed to simulate the operation of a WWTP in which a biological treatment by activated sludge with anaerobic digestion and codigestion of the sludge (eventually yielding PHA) takes place. To this end, a comprehensive process modelling tool was constructed using the model proposed by Mininni [21] as a starting point.

This model was then evaluated using real operational data from the WWTP El Copero (Seville, Spain), which has the necessary capacity for treating wastewater from a population equivalent of 950,000 by means of biological aerobic processes by activated sludge, anaerobic digestion and codigestion of the generated sludge as well as cogeneration systems.

Following the implementation of the necessary corrections to match the theoretical and the real parameters, a high degree of alignment was achieved. The objective was to develop a tool to simulate the installation of a polyhydroxyalkanoate production line integrated in the existing process line. To this effect, the thickened primary sludge was used as a raw material and the three-element method [18] was used to model PHA production.

Two biomass selection strategies were evaluated based on the dynamic substrate supply under aerobic conditions by internal growth limitation, namely, the aerobic dynamic feeding process (ADF), with low nutrient concentration, and the AN/AE strategy with external growth limitation, which involves alternating aerobic and anaerobic conditions in the absence of an electron acceptor (such as oxygen or nitrate) at the time of substrate supply [22]. Electron acceptors play an instrumental part in the production of PHAs. While under aerobic conditions oxygen is the usual electron acceptor, under anaerobic conditions, microorganisms must use an alternative for this role. These acceptors are reduced, generating energy (ATP) in the process as well as metabolic intermediates. ATP is later used to provide the necessary energy in the metabolic pathway leading to PHA generation [9,14].

It must be clearly stated that implementing a PHA production line within a given plant will have an impact on the sludge it generates, and thus, on the energy it is able to cogenerate [23]. It seems reasonable to conclude that the incorporation of a PHA production line into the sludge line of a WWTP implies sending smaller quantities of sludge to anaerobic digestion. In plants equipped with cogeneration systems, this reduction may lead to a potential reduction in the energy generated. Nevertheless, smaller amounts of sludge sent into the anaerobic digester will enhance the capacity of the plant to accept external substrates for codigestion, thereby mitigating the adverse impact on the plant's energy balance.

The main goal of this work is to produce a techno-economic assessment of MMC–based polyhydroxyalkanoate production in the WWTP EL Copero, using the sludges produced in the plant as feedstock. As a key part of this project, all mass and energy balances related to the proposed modification of the plant were calculated and contrasted with the volume of PHA that would be generated. This analysis has led us to build a modelling tool able to project the impacts on sludge and energy production (as well as their associated economical drawbacks) of a given WWTP in the case of implementing a PHA production line using the ADF or AN/AE process alternatives.

2. Materials and Methods

The simulation of the integration of a PHA production line by means of MMCs within WWTP El Copero included the following steps. Throughout the process, it was kept as a prerequisite not to undermine the normal function of the WWTP.

1. Modelling of the WWTP and adjustments to align this theoretical model with real parameter levels in order to obtain a reference scenario.
2. Modelling of the ADF and AN/AE alternative methods of PHA production.
3. Incorporation of the ADF and AN/AE models into the reference scenario described in point 1 using thickened primary sludge as a raw material.
4. Comparison and techno-economic assessment of both production alternatives.

2.1. WWTP Modelling and Reference Scenario

WWTP El Copero (Figure 1) is designed to treat an average flow of 255,000 $m^3 \cdot d^{-1}$ of urban wastewater via a conventional active sludge system operating at an OLR between 0.257 and 0.336 kg $COD \cdot kg^{-1}$ $MLSS \cdot d^{-1}$. The primary treatment in the water treatment line includes six 43 m-diameter clarifiers. The overall decantation surface area is 8713 m^2, with a usable volume of 30,204 m^3. Secondary treatment in the plant comprises 8 plug flow reactors with a volume of 6375 m^3 each as well as 8 50 m-diameter clarifiers. Each reactor has its own aeration system with fine bubble diffusers. Air supply capacity in this stage sits at 140,100 $m^3 \cdot h^{-1}$. Fifteen percent of the reactor's volume is occupied by an anoxic tank equipped with submersible mixers. The sludge line includes anaerobic digestion and codigestion and has the capacity to manage more than 10^5 annual t of waste. Primary sludge is screened and thickened by gravity in 4 tanks with a total volume of 1726 m^3. Secondary sludge is thickened in three 13 m-diameter flotation tanks. The plant also has 8 primary and 2 secondary anaerobic reactors. Anaerobic digestion occurs following a 2-part serial configuration, which allows treating the sludge in a process of thermal hydrolysis, furthering biogas production. A cogeneration system provides the plant with an energetic self-sufficiency of 95% owing to a production of between 1.80 and 2.20 $kWh \cdot m^{-3}$ of biogas.

Due to new legal standards regarding nutrient removal, a substitution of the present biological treatment for an EBPR system (Enhancing Biological Phosphorus Removal) is planned. Our WWTP model is based on the current activated sludge treatment, whereas the implementation simulation of PHA production systems takes into consideration the new EBPR biological treatment.

The WWTP model was laid out following the steps described by Mininni [21]. In particular, the WWTP flow diagram corresponds to reference case 3.2 in a conventional WWTP. Energy and mass balances were calculated for every step in the wastewater treatment.

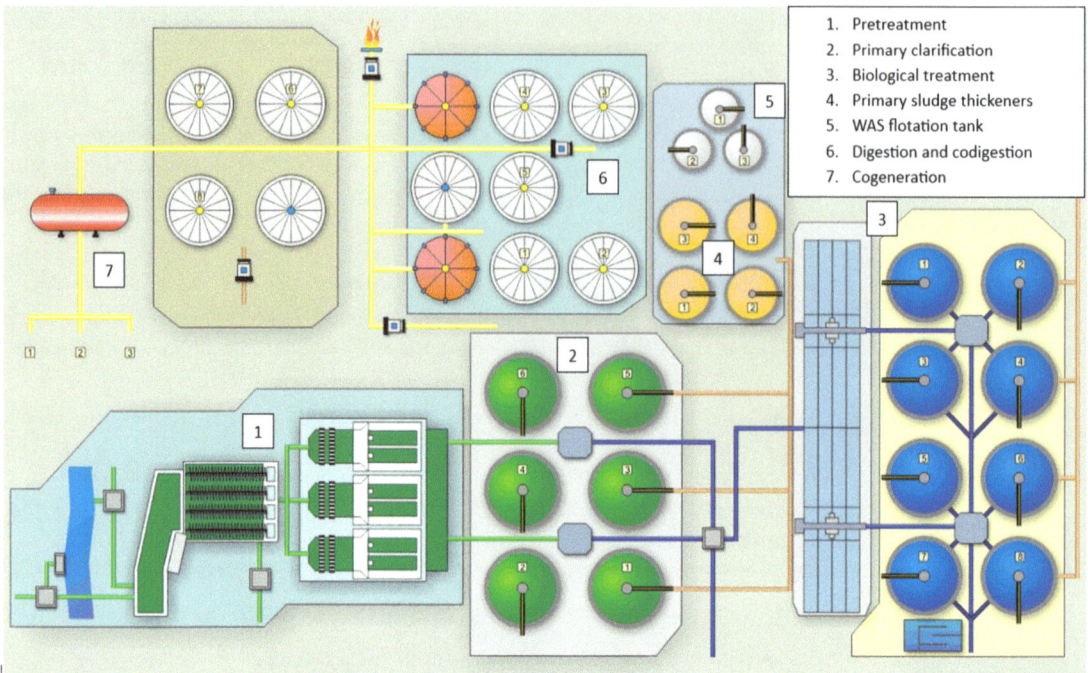

Figure 1. Ground plan of WWTP El Copero.

The inflow data required an initial adjustment to take into consideration the repercussions of the recollection of overflows, supernatants and drains back onto the overall plant influent. This was accomplished by first establishing a model, denominated as cycle 0, which contemplates only plant influents from the sewage network, for which all return flows were calculated. These were later added together with the initial inflow in a second cycle, cycle 1. The iterative process of inflow increases due to return flows was stabilized by the 5th cycle. Figures 4–6 include examples of mass balances from the WWTP (in particular, with data from November 2022), showing the main current flow as well as these returning flows.

Once this theoretical model of the WWTP was finally implemented, its validity was put to the test by feeding it with real inlet water quality and flow data. The results of the model were contrasted with actual mass and energy balances registered on site by each processing unit. The assembly was treated as a closed-loop system with an accuracy level of 0.1% with a limit of 1000 iterations.

The processing of all data produced by the plant by heterogeneous sources such as PLC and SCADA was handled by the operational intelligence system IDbox, which was already in use at the WWTP. These data include water flow and quality measurements between the years 2021 and 2023, a total of 913 days, as well as of the energy consumed by each plant process.

Our model was made in Microsoft Excel and consists of 13 worksheets, with 12 monitoring the plant's performance throughout each month of the year, with the aim of taking into consideration the influence of different ambient temperatures and general conditions as well as date-specific eventualities. Each of them uses a monthly average as per the IDbox monitoring. The upper and lower 5% values, as well as all extrema, were discarded by default. The 13th worksheet includes an annual analysis of all data and compares the outcomes of the ADF and AN/AE approaches.

All energy balances assume that 95% of the plant's energy consumption is cogenerated on site, with the remaining 5% supplied by the local grid, mimicking the plant's actual energy usage patterns.

CAPEX and OPEX were considered in the economic assessment. The cost of implementing the necessary infrastructure was calculated following the methodology developed by Gurieff and Lant [24].

Each data file includes a first worksheet where the IDbox data required for each process's mass balance are dumped into. The abbreviations used can be found in Table 1.

Table 1. List of abbreviations.

AD	Anaerobic digestion	OPEX	Operational expenditures
ADF	Aerobic dynamic feeding	PAO	Polyphosphate-accumulating organism
AIS	Acid-induced sludge	PE	Process element
AIW	Acid-induced water	PE1	Acidogenic fermentation
AN/AE	Anaerobic/aerobic	PE2	Enrichment and production of biomass with PHA-storing capacity
C1, C2	Primary/secondary clarifier	PE3	PHA accumulation
CapEx	Capital expenditures	PreW	Pretreated water
CCHS	Chemical conditionated hydrolysed sludge	S1	Primary sludge
DM	Dry matter	SF2	Waste-activated sludge flotation tank
DW	Dilution water	SRT	Solids retention time (d)
DWS	Dewatered sludge	ST1	Primary sludge thickener
DS	Digested sludge	TH	Thermal hydrolysis
GAO	Glycogen-accumulating organism	TS1	Thickened primary sludge
HRT	Hydraulic retention time (h)	TSS	Total suspended solids
HS	Hydrolysed sludge	TW	Treated water
inf	Influent	VFA	Volatile fatty acid
ISS	Inert suspended solids	VSS	Volatile suspended solids
OLR	Organic loading rate	WAS	Waste-activated sludge

Tables 2 and 3 include flow diagrams (for water and sludge, respectively) for each processing unit and characterization parameters as far as matter and energy balances are concerned.

The biological treatment includes biological reactors as well as secondary clarifiers. It is assumed that the TP is equal to the sum of P included in the TW plus the P_{WAS}.

Table 2. Flow diagrams and water characterisation parameters.

PRIMARY CLARIFICATION			
Flow Diagram	Parameters	Values/Units	
(diagram: Influent → C1 → Settled ww; S1 with TSS_{S1}, VSS_{S1}, ISS_{S1}, COD_{S1}, BOD_{S1})	$TSS_{S1} = TSS_{inf} \cdot \eta TSS_{C1}$ $TSS_{C1} = TSS_{inf} - TSS_{C1}$	ηTSS_{C1}: IDbox data	TSS_{C1} — % TSS_{S1} — $Kg \cdot m^{-3}$
	$VSS_{S1} = TSS_{S1} \cdot \%VM_{S1}$	$\%VM_{S1}$: IDbox data	$Kg \cdot m^{-3}$
	$ISS_{S1} = TSS_{S1} - VSS_{S1}$		$Kg \cdot m^{-3}$
	$COD_{S1} = COD_{inf} \cdot \eta COD_{C1}$ $COD_{C1} = COD_{inf} - COD_{S1}$	ηCOD_{inf}, ηCOD_{C1}: IDbox data	$Kg \cdot m^{-3}$
	$BOD_{S1} = BOD_{inf} \cdot \eta BOD_{C1}$ $BOD_{C1} = BOD_{inf} - BOD_{S1}$	ηBOD_{C1}: IDbox data	$Kg \cdot m^{-3}$

Average daily flow (derived from yearly quantity) = $m^3 \cdot d^{-1}$.
The TN quantity in S1 was determined by using the TN/VSS ratio registered in the WWTP.
10% of TP was considered to decantated with S1.

BIOLOGICAL REACTOR (BR). SECONDARY TREATMENT			
Flow Diagram	Parameters	Values/Units	
(diagram: Settled ww → BR → TW; WAS with TSS_{WAS}, VSS_{WAS}, ISS_{WAS}, COD_{WAS}, NT_{WAS}, PT_{WAS})	$TSS_{WAS} = Q_{WAS} \cdot WAS_{TSS}$	WAS_{TSS}: IDbox data	$Kg \cdot m^{-3}$
	$VSS_{WAS} = TSS_{WAS} \cdot \%VM_{WAS}$	$\%VM_{WAS}$: IDbox data	%
	$ISS_{WAS} = TSS_{WAS} - VSS_{WAS}$		
	$COD_{WAS} = VSS_{WAS} \cdot COD \cdot VSS_{WAS}^{-1}$	COD_{VSSWAS} [24]	$KgCOD_{WAS} \cdot KgVSS_{WAS}^{-1}$
	$TN_{WAS} = VSS_{WAS} \cdot TN \cdot VSS^{-1}$	TN_{VSS} [24]	$KgTN_{WAS} \cdot KgVSS_{WAS}^{-1}$
	$TP_{WAS} = TP_{S1} - TP_{TW}$		

The daily WAS flow was calculated from the ORL needed in the biological reactor.

Table 3. Flow diagrams and sludge characterization parameters.

PRIMARY SLUDGE THICKENER/WASTE ACTIVATED SLUDGE FLOTATION TANK	
Flow Diagram	Parameters
(diagram: S1/WAS → TS1/SF2 → SUPERNATANTS, TS1/FWAS)	The TS1 and FWAS flows were calculated according to the data gathered in IDbox, allowing, in turn, the supernatant flow to be calculated. The TS1 and FWAS flows were calculated according to the data gathered in IDbox. The predigested sludge COD was calculated from the SSV present in the former.

Table 3. Cont.

(MESOPHILIC) ANAEROBIC DIGESTION		
Flow Diagram	Parameters	Values/Units
[MS→AD→DS with VSS_DS, TSS_DS, COD_DS, TP_DS, Q_Biogas^AD]	$VSS_{DS} = VSS_{MS} \cdot (100 - \eta VSS_{MS})$	VSS_{MS} IDbox data $Kg \cdot m^{-3}$
	$TSS_{DS} = TSS_{MS} - (VSS_{MS} - VSS_{DS})$	$Kg \cdot m^{-3}$
	$COD_{DS} = VSS_{DS} \cdot COD \cdot SSV_{DS}^{-1}$	COD_{SSVDS} $Kg \cdot m^{-3}$
	$TP_{DS} = (COD_{MS} - COD_{DS}) PO_4^{3-} \cdot COD^{-1} + TP_{MS}$	$Kg \cdot m^{-3}$
	$Q_{BiogasAD} = (VSS_{MS} - VSS_{DS}) \cdot \eta_{Biogas}$	η_{Biogas} IDbox data m^3 biogas$\cdot kg^{-1}$ VSS_{elim}

Input and output flows are equal, as well as their SSI and TN.

DEWATERING	
Flow Diagram	Parameters
[DS→DW→DWS, DRAIN]	The DW performance was provided by IDbox. This performance translates into all quality parameters, which allows TSS in the sludge to be calculated (and by subtraction, also those in the drain).

THERMAL HYDROLYSIS	
Flow Diagram	Parameters
	Owing to the vapour injected during the sludge hydrolysis, HS concentration becomes lower than that of DS. HS now needs to be conditioned before being dehydrated again. CCHS concentration was established to need to reach a given level, which is accomplished by the addition of dilution water.

POST (MESOPHILIC) ANAEROBIC DIGESTION	
Flow Diagram	Parameters
[CCHS→PAD→DS2]	$QBiogas_{DS2} = (QBiogas_{DS} \cdot \eta Biogas^{-1} \cdot 15\% + VSS_{cosustrates}\ 85\%) \cdot \eta Biogas$ Gas production is a consequence of the elimination of 85% of VSS in the co-substrates and of 15% of VSS in AD.

2.2. Modelling of the PHA Production Process

Our modelling of two different PHA production alternatives is based on the process described by Morgan-Sagastume [18], consisting of three phases or process elements (PEs). The first one requires a substrate high in VFA content, which is obtained via acidogenic fermentation of the thickened primary sludge. This first process element (PE1) is common to both of the described process alternatives. PE2 involves the selection of biomass with the capacity to generate and accumulate PHA in a sufficient and homogeneous way as well as the development of this biomass inside a new reactor by means of internally or externally limiting its access to some nutrient, either ADF or AN/AE, depending on the process alternative. PE3 is responsible for the accumulation of PHA and requires aerobic working conditions and an uninterrupted supply of substrate. HRT and OLR are different in each alternative process.

2.2.1. PE1 Modelling

The adaptation of one of the WWTP's ST1s was considered for housing the PE1. This thickener has a volume of 428 m^3 and is operated with an HTR of 3 d, while the remaining flow of thickened sludge in the WWTP is further treated as it normally would be. An OLR of 6.7 kg COD m^{-3} d^{-1} was established for optimal fermentation, using the thickener overflow to keep the rate at the correct level. As a result of the fermentation, 5% of the SSV is estimated to have been eliminated.

TS1 was chosen as the substrate in PE1 for the following reasons:

1. A thickened sludge reduces the useable volume needed in the reactor and allows for a better control over the process via OLR_{COD} adjustments using dilution water [25].
2. Primary sludge reaches a higher acidification than WAS, providing a higher concentration of VFA in the feeding substrate, which, in turn, will translate into a higher yield of PHA [19,26].
3. N and P concentrations in TS1 are the lowest in the whole WWTP sludge line.
4. An eventual drop in performance due to the redissolution of the orthophosphate present in WAS is avoided.
5. The use of TS1 as a substrate for PE1 requires no previous biological adaptation [25].

Table 4 includes the design parameters defined for PE1.

Table 4. PE1 design parameters.

Parameter	Value	Unit	Reference
Volume	428	m^3	WWTP El Copero
HRT	3	d	[27]
OLR	6.7	$Kg\ COD \cdot m^{-3} \cdot d^{-1}$	[28]
VFA production	0.8	$Kg\ COD_{VFA} \cdot kg\ COD_{inf}^{-1}$	[27]
VSS elimination	5	%	WWTP El Copero
COD elimination	20	%	[28]
Power	0.25	$Kw \cdot t^{-1}$	[27]

Parameters such as the C/N ratio, pH and temperature have a very important impact on the VFA production but can be modified to better suit the composition of a given substrate [29], which is to say, a close monitoring of these parameters can have a heavy influence on productivity [30]. The C/N ratio needed to guarantee bacterial growth was found to be between 20 and 30 [29,31]. The combination of low pH levels, low temperatures and low HRT ensures a high level of acidification [20,28], yet the drop in pH caused by the increase in VFA concentration could bring the fermentation to a stop [29,32]; hence, pH levels are recommended to be kept between 5 and 12 [29,33].

2.2.2. Description of the ADF Process Alternative

The process of aerobic dynamic feeding (ADF) has been widely applied as a useful method of enrichment for PHA-accumulating bacteria. In PE2, the acid-induced sludge from PE1 is subjected to a feast–famine sequence under aerobic conditions [34]. In the feast phase, microorganisms accumulate PHA from the available carbon. In this phase, both the electron donor and acceptor are present, facilitating the accumulation of the biopolymer [22]. During the famine phase, only PHA-producing bacteria, where their accumulated PHA acts as their carbon source, are able to survive. The biomass of interest for this process is thus selected. This strategy is appropriate for the treatment of wastewaters with an excess of C and only limited concentrations of P and N [35], further justifying the use of TS1 as the raw material for PE1 feedstock.

The PE2 batch reactor was modelled as per the following sequence:

1. Feeding: 50% of the flow exiting from PE1 is mixed with dilution water until the required OLR is met.
2. Feast–famine cycle: extended feast periods facilitate microorganism growth. Long famine periods allow a larger accumulation of PHA-generating bacteria, but they must not be extended to the point where microbial mass becomes insufficient [36,37].
3. Sedimentation.
4. Extraction.

Table 5 includes the design parameters defined for the PE2–ADF process alternative.

Table 5. PE2 design parameters—ADF process alternative.

Parameter	Value	Unit	Reference
HRT	1	d	[38]
SRT	10	d	[38]
Nutrients demand	0.03	kg NH3·kgCOD$_{VFA}$$^{-1}$	[38]
OLR	1.9	kg COD·m^{-3}·d^{-1}	[28]
Biomass concentration	4	g VSS·L^{-1}	[27]
Oxygen demand	1.3	kg O$_2$·kg BOD^{-1}	[27]
Energy demand	3.5	Kg O$_2$·kWh^{-1}	[27]

The feeding of PE3 was modelled to be 50% of the flow from PE1 and the biomass selected during the famine phase of PE2. The OLR was adjusted by means of dilution water. In both stages, all provided VFAs were considered to have been fully consumed. The design parameters for the ADF process alternative are shown in Table 6.

Table 6. PE3 design parameters—ADF process alternative.

Parameter	Value	Unit	Reference
HRT	0.2	d	[28]
OLR	41	kg COD·m^{-3}·d^{-1}	[28]
PHA production	0.819	kg COD$_{PHA}$·kg COD$_{VFA}$	[27]
PHA contents	70	% VM	[27]
Oxygen demands	1.3	kg O$_2$·kgBOD^{-1}	[27]
Energy demands	3.5	kg O$_2$·kWh^{-1}	[27]

Figure 2 details the insertion of the described process within the WWTP main stream.

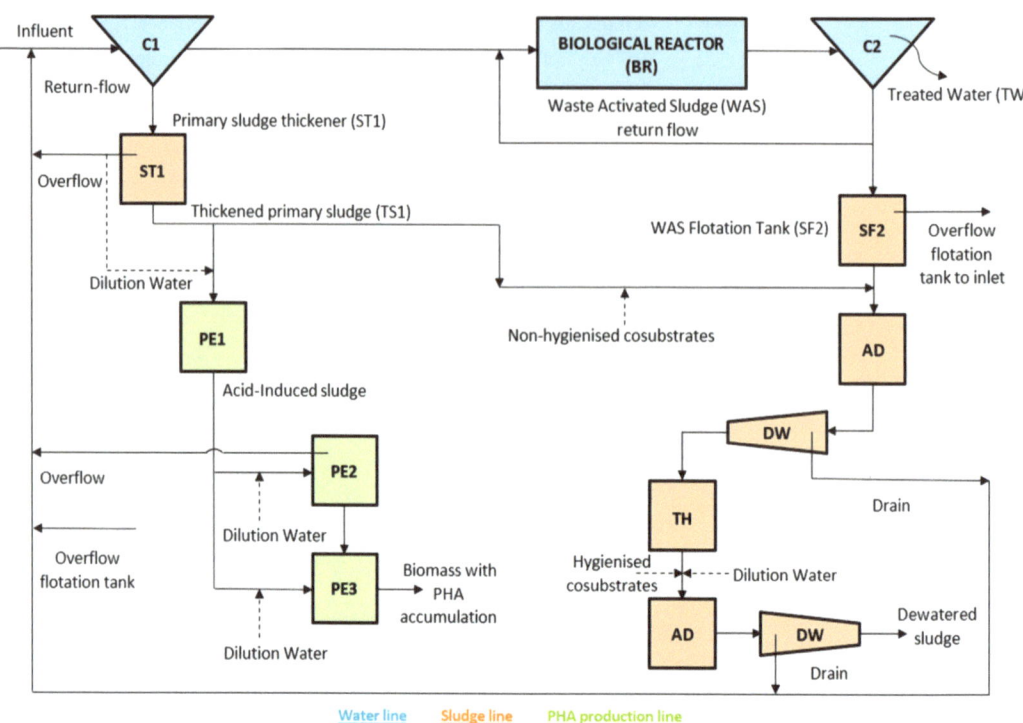

Figure 2. Process diagram—ADF process alternative.

2.2.3. Description of the AN/AE Process Alternative

The repeated switch between aerobic and anaerobic conditions introduces an external restriction in microbial growth, given that in the absence of oxygen there is no electron acceptor present [22]. This limits the capacity of the biomass to generate PHA. Organisms capable of storing PHA under these conditions are polyphosphate and glycogen accumulators (PAO and GAO, respectively).

The AN/AE offers the advantage of providing the WWTP with an EBPR system, where aerobic and anaerobic conditions are alternated. This allows the biomass selection to occur directly in the reactor itself, within the water line, removing the need to introduce an adipose infrastructure and skipping PE2 altogether. This process alternative is appropriate for wastewater with high C and P concentrations, as is the case in our WWTP of reference.

The process diagram in Figure 3 illustrates the sequence followed in the AN/AE process alternative:

1. Overflow from PE1 consists of acid-induced water where all COD has been transformed into VFA. This is directly fed into PE3 as a substrate.
2. Part of the WAS coming from the EBPR are directly fed into PE3.
3. PE3 processes the currents from both previous points under aerobic conditions. Dilution water is added to adjust the OLR_{COD}. VFAs are then considered to be totally consumed.

Table 7 shows the PE1 and PE2 design parameters for the AN/AE process alternative. Figure 3 details the insertion of the described process within the WWTP main stream.

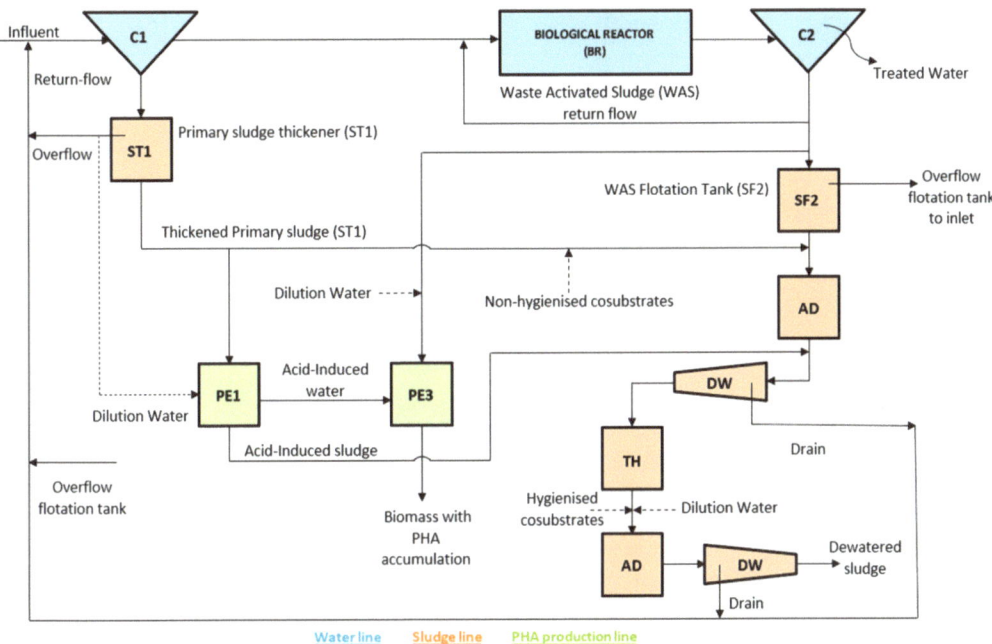

Figure 3. Process diagram—AN/AE process alternative.

Table 7. PE1 and PE3 design parameters—AN/AE process alternative.

Process	Parameter	Value	Unit	Reference
PE1	SRT	3	d	[39]
	Acidified sludge concentration	40	$g \cdot L^{-1}$	[39]
	HRT	0.29	d	[39]
PE3	OLR	1200	$mg\ COD \cdot L^{-1}$	[22,39]
	PHA production	0.94	$kg\ COD_{PHA} \cdot kg^{-1}\ COD_{VFA}$	[22,39]
	PHA contents	40	%MV	[22,39]
	PHA yield	0.23	$kg\ COD_{PHA} \cdot kg^{-1}\ COD \cdot h^{-1}$	[22,39]
	Oxygen demands	1.3	$kg\ O_2 \cdot kg^{-1}\ BOD$	[27]
	Energy demands	3.5	$kg\ O_2 \cdot kWh^{-1}$	[27]

3. Results and Discussion

When fed the plant's influent water flow and pollution data, our simulator was able to calculate the input and output, water and sludge flows for each step of the process in $m^3 \cdot h^{-1}$, as well as their COD, TSS and VSS in $mg \cdot L^{-1}$. Inflow water quality at the WWTP was characterized as follows: 119,139 $m^3 \cdot d^{-1}$; 293 $mg \cdot L^{-1}$ TSS; 608.9 $mg \cdot L^{-1}$ COD; 275 $mg \cdot L^{-1}$ BOD; 61 $mg \cdot L^{-1}$ N and 8.8 $mg \cdot L^{-1}$ P (monthly average).

Figures 4–6 include the results of the mass balance, showing the main current flow as well as the returning flows. In these figures, the values from the month of November were picked as an example. They are intended to illustrate how the overall procedures work rather than to provide relevant quantitative data.

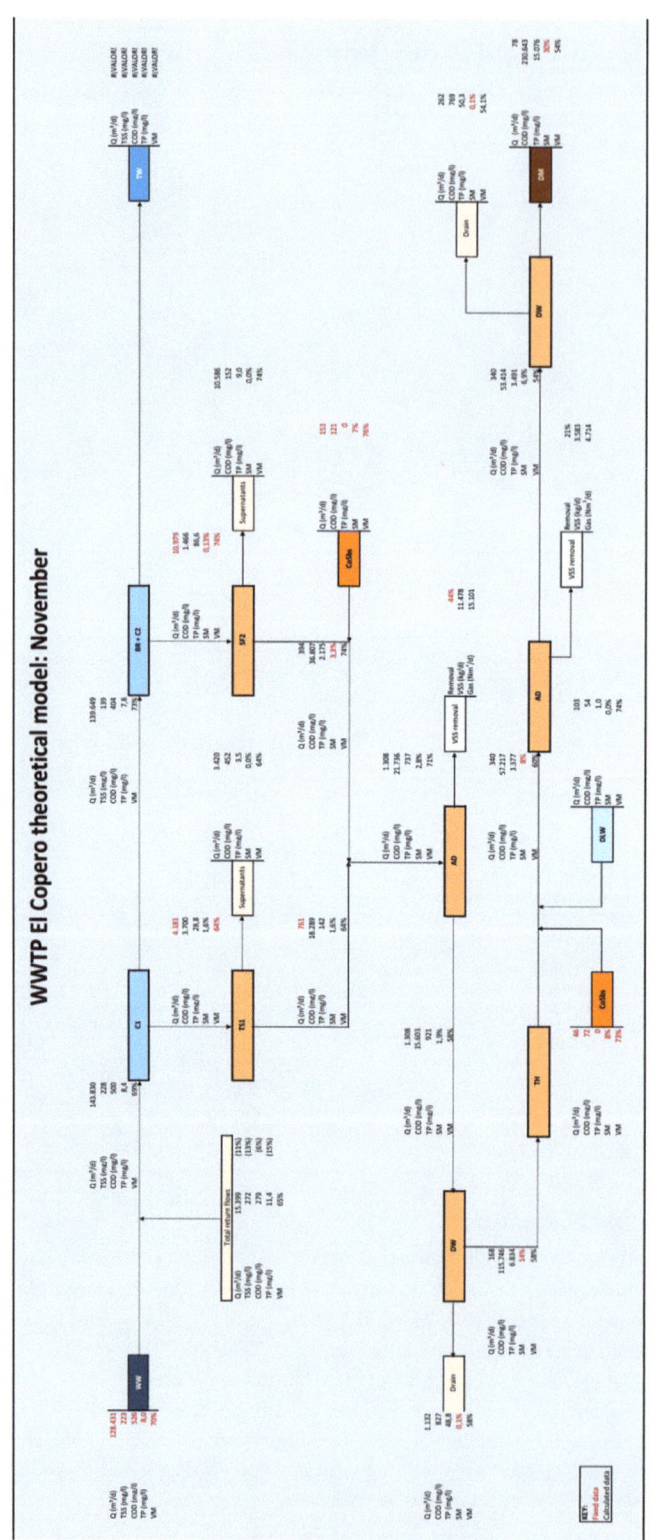

Figure 4. Mass balance at reference scenario.

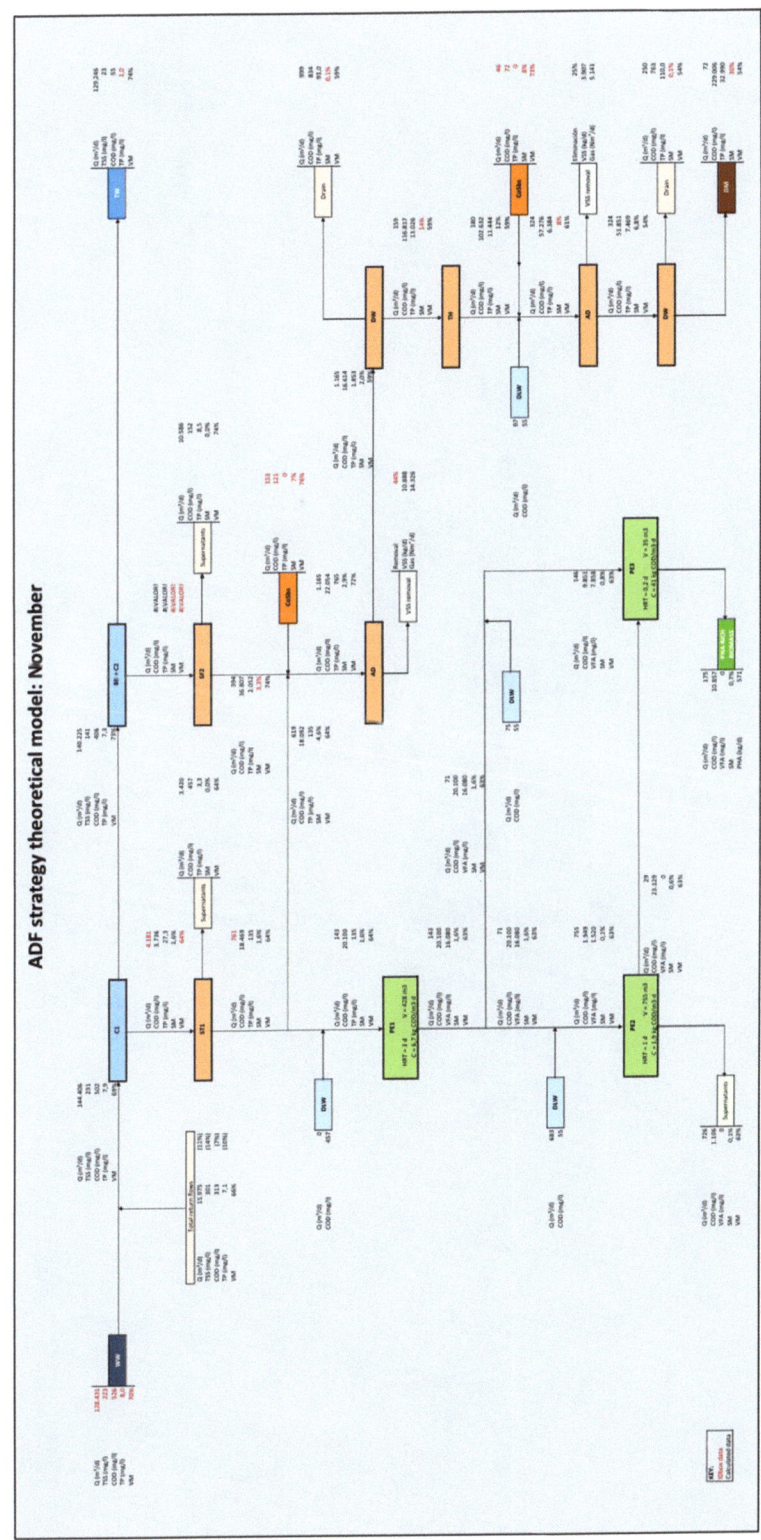

Figure 5. Mass balance in ADF process alternative.

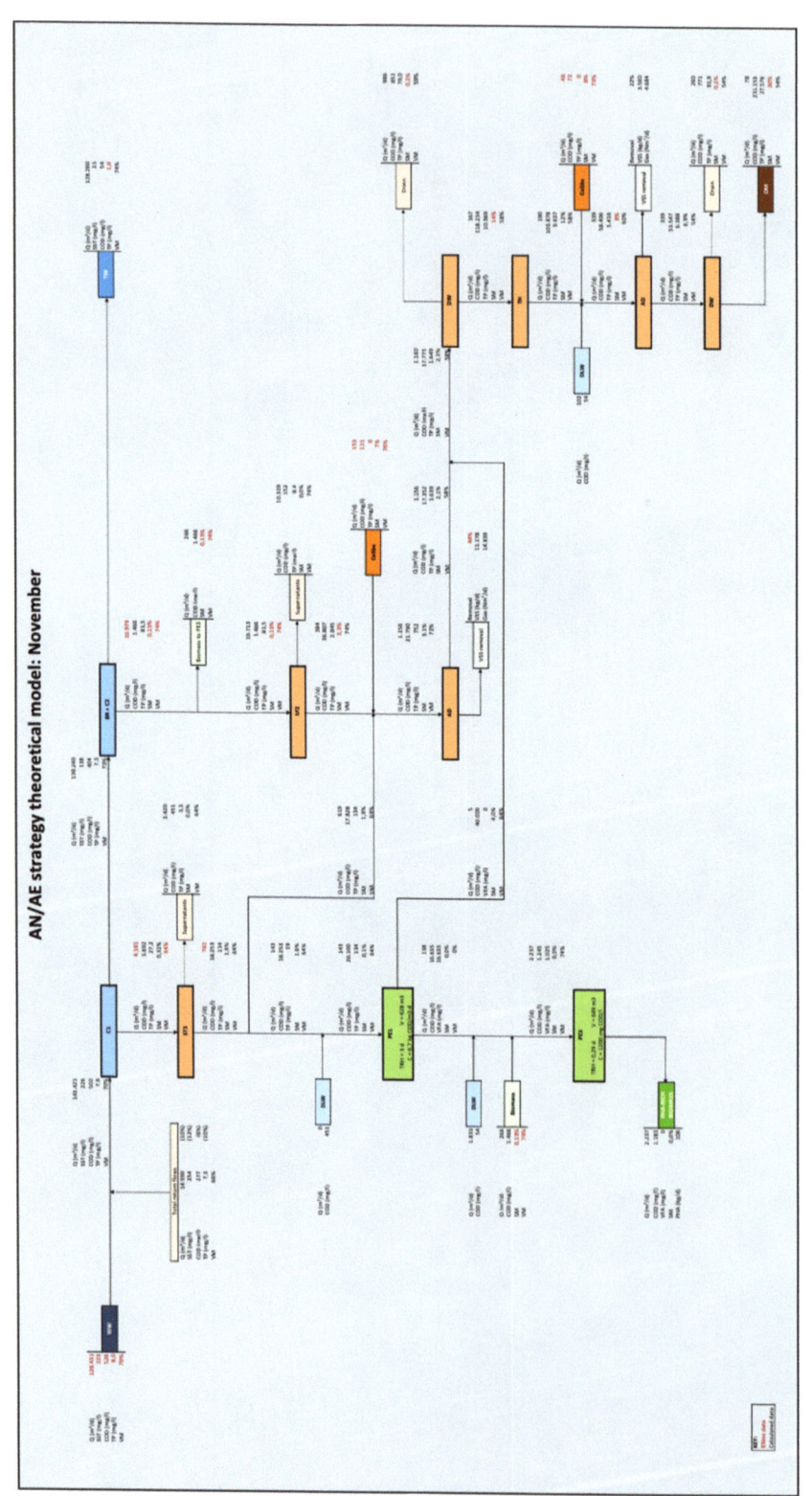

Figure 6. Mass balance in AN/AE process alternative.

The diagram in Figure 4 shows how our simulator obtains the input and output values for each step of the process after being fed the reference scenario mass and energy balances' data, which we calculated for these purposes.

The diagram displayed in Figures 5 and 6 shows how PHA production data are obtained using the ADF and AN/AE strategy, respectively. They also include water and sludge flow and quality data, as well as PHA production rates, at each stage of each process alternative.

After the data from a simulated 913 days of operation at the plant using both alternatives were gathered, the differences between results in each route's PHA production, the impact on sludge production, as well as the economic investments and energy consumption they require, can be discussed.

As a global result, we can assess that, in spite of a 35% increase in the OPEX generated by energy requirements of the WWTP, the ADF process was identified as the most favourable system. Simulations of the plant at full capacity, revealed that the feed flow of primary sludge was 143 $m^3 \cdot d^{-1}$ with an OLR_{COD} of 20.1 $g \cdot L^{-1}$. Under these conditions, a production of 651 kg of $COD_{PHA} \cdot d^{-1}$ using the ADF strategy was obtained. The calculated production cost was EUR 0.11 per kilogram of COD_{PHA}, and the quantity of sludge produced was reduced by 6% in the ADF model.

3.1. Required Investments

The ADF process alternative requires the installation of two separate reactors for PE2 and PE3, with 759 m^3 and 35 m^3 of required volume, respectively. This translates into a 1.4% increase in CAPEX and a 1.6% increase in OPEX in comparison with the reference scenario, or a total of EUR 494,238.77.

The AN/AE process alternative requires only the addition of one 653 m^3 reactor for PE3. In comparison with the reference scenario, this alternative requires a 1.3% increase in CAPEX and a 1.4% increase in OPEX, or a total of EUR 405,145.48.

It can be stated that neither of the proposals requires a particularly large investment for an infrastructure of the size of the studied WWTP.

Furthermore, both proposals lend themselves to a large degree of automation, with the presence of personnel needed only for the supervision of the processes from a control centre. Personnel represent the largest cost in all proposed models.

The AN/AE alternative is therefore economically superior. It also requires only one new reactor to be constructed on the site, which is especially relevant at plants where space is a limiting factor.

3.2. Sludge Production

Current dewatered sludge production in the studied WWTP stands at 92.93 $t \cdot d^{-1}$. While the ADF proposal would lower the sludge production to 87.43 $t \cdot d^{-1}$ due to the usage of thickened sludge to feed PE1, the AN/AE process alternative shows no relevant decrease in the sludge production (92.48 $t \cdot d^{-1}$), due to the fact that decanted sludge in PE1 is reintegrated into the WWTP sludge line, and only acid-induced water is used to feed PE3. The fact that the ADF alternative sends a lower quantity of sludge into digestion leads to a lower overall sludge quantity generated in the WWTP and, in turn, lower costs and fewer drawbacks associated with their appropriate handling, storage and logistics. In this regard, the ADF alternative can be regarded as superior.

3.3. Energy Consumption

The ADF proposal requires a slightly higher energy consumption than the current model the WWTP operates on, mainly due to the overflow return from PE2 to the starting point of the plant line. This higher overall energy consumption in the plant is reflected in the energy that needs to be imported into the process. Nevertheless, this does not have a significant economic impact, owing to the fact that these extra energy requirements can be met by means of cogeneration using the excess biogas already at the plant's disposal.

On the contrary, the AN/AE approach would impose a significant drop in consumption in comparison with the current digestion process while implying no major differences in dehydration levels, owing to the postdigestion treatment the acidified sludge is subjected to. In this case, the overall energy consumption was shown to be lower than in the reference scenario, in spite of the addition of further systems.

Table 8 illustrates the final energy consumption in detail, taking into consideration the limitation that 95% of the plant's electricity must be provided by cogeneration and only 5% can be obtained from the grid.

Table 8. Average daily electricity consumption in the WWTP under the three scenarios studied.

Process	Electricity Consumption (kWh·d^{-1})		
	Reference Scenario	ADF	AN/AE
Pretreatment and C1	6.231	6.259	6.213
Secondary treatment	7.793	7.830	7.771
Aeration	12.956	13.138	12.928
Digestion	2.690	2.320	2.087
Dewatering	3.693	3.402	3.425
Tertiary treatment	609	612	607
Deodorisation	1.000	1.004	997
PE1	--	17	17
PE2	--	249	---
PE3	--	356	522

In this case, it must be noted that both alternatives reduce the quantity of sludge sent into codigestion in comparison with the reference scenario, which translates into a lower overall energy production. This also has a negative economic impact on the plant.

Table 9 shows the economic and energetic assessments of the two proposed alternatives.

Table 9. Economic and energetic assessment of both proposed alternatives.

Parameter	WWTP El Copero	ADF	AN/AE
Total electricity consumption (kWh·d^{-1})	34,972	35,187	34,567
Total electricity production (kWh·d^{-1})	33,223	33,428	32,839
Energy from the grid (kWh·d^{-1})	1749	1759	1728
Energy not produced (kWh·d^{-1})		1728	309
Total energy consumption (kWh·d^{-1})	1749	3487	2037
Cost kw power (EUR·d^{-1})	191.78	191.78	191.78
Cost kwh energy (EUR·d^{-1})	104.92	209.24	122.24
OPEX (EUR·d^{-1})	296.70	401.02	317.02

While PE2 is skipped in the AN/AE process, PE3 requires more energy in this proposal than in the ADF scheme. Overall, the total OPEX energy-associated costs rose by 35.16% in the case of ADF, in stark comparison with the 6.84% increase associated with AN/AE.

Figure 7 shows the comparison between both models' energy consumption overall and by process unit.

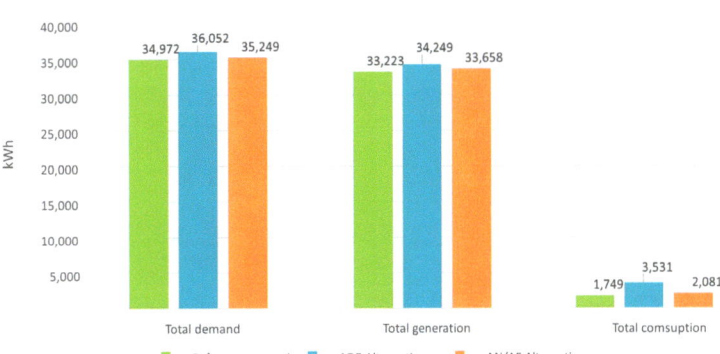

Figure 7. Comparison between both models' energy consumption overall.

The WWTP processes that have experienced the most modifications in comparison with the reference scenario are those of the sludge line, where energy consumption drops as a response to the lower volume of sludge being treated. In comparison with the reference scenario, the energy consumption of aeration remained the same in the case of the AN/AE alternative, while it slightly increased in the case of the ADF alternative.

Regarding the energy consumption of each stage of the ADF and AN/AE alternatives, PE1 remained similar in both cases. While the AN/AE strategy does not include a PE2, its energy consumption at the PE3 stage was higher than that registered for the ADF alternative. From a global perspective, however, the AN/AE associated processes have a lower overall energy consumption than those of the ADF strategy.

As a consequence of their energy consumption, both alternatives cause a drop in the available excess biogas present at the plant, which partly needs to be sent into cogeneration. Nevertheless, owing to the use of external substrates of high biodegradability, neither of the proposed alternatives' extra energy consumptions constitute a challenge for the plant.

3.4. PHA Production

Within our model, the ADF process had an average daily PHA production of 651 kg·d^{-1}, with an associated cost of production of EUR 0.11 kg^{-1}. Meanwhile, the AN/AE process reached an average daily PHA production of just 106 kg·d^{-1}, increasing production costs to EUR 1.15 kg^{-1}. With regards to PHA production, it is the ADF process that has a clear advantage in terms of production capacity as well as costs. It is important to clarify that the result of this process is PHA-rich biomass, which is to say, further industrial processing will be required for the extraction of the bioplastic. These additional processes will add to the final cost of PHA production and are beyond the scope of this study.

4. Conclusions

This work of research has brought about the development of a novel modelling tool suitable for predicting the suitability of implementing a PHA production line within a functioning WWTP with codigestion and cogeneration systems. This tool has enabled a contrast of two different approaches to PHA production (ADF vs. AN/AE) from a feedstock of WWTP thickened primary sludge, of which the ADF proposal was shown to be the better option owing to its higher PHA production rate and lower production cost. The impact of this additional process on the plant's performance on an economic and energetic level were also taken into consideration within our model. Moreover, this study further establishes the generation of PHA at a WWTP as a viable route for a large-scale production of this bioplastic, owing to the following two facts: Firstly, it allows the use of a raw material (wastewater-associated sludge) of essentially null cost, and secondly, the energy needed in the relatively power-hungry biomass selection and bioplastic accumulation phases can be sourced from the plant's internal production (no extra energy is required from the grid). Aside from this, the present approach has the added advantage of freeing up the plant's resources for the processing of external substrates.

Author Contributions: Conceptualization, L.P.-M. and A.R.M.; methodology, L.P.-M. and G.d.V.A.; software, L.P.-M., G.d.V.A. and E.B.; validation and formal analysis, E.B., G.d.V.A. and L.P.-M.; investigation, L.P.-M. and A.R.M.; writing, G.d.V.A. and L.P.-M.; supervision, G.d.V.A. and L.P.-M. All authors have read and agreed to the published version of the manuscript.

Funding: This research received no external funding.

Data Availability Statement: The original contributions presented in this study are included in the article. Further inquiries can be directed to the corresponding author.

Acknowledgments: Special thanks to our translator, D. Daniel Barea Pozo, for the English version of this article.

Conflicts of Interest: Author Enrique Baquerizo was employed by the company Emasesa Metropolitan. Author Germán del Valle Agulla was employed by the company Ollearis, S.A. The remaining authors declare that the research was conducted in the absence of any commercial or financial relationships that could be construed as a potential conflict of interest.

References

1. Williams, A.T.; Rangel-Buitrago, N. The past, present, and future of plastic pollution. *Mar. Pollut. Bull.* **2022**, *176*, 113429. [CrossRef] [PubMed]
2. Stublić, K.; Ranilović, J.; Bulatović, V.O.; Grgić, D.K. Advancing Sustainability: Utilizing Bacterial Polyhydroxyalkanoate for Food Packaging. *Processes* **2024**, *12*, 1886. [CrossRef]
3. Możejko-Ciesielska, J.; Kiewisz, R. Bacterial polyhydroxyalkanoates: Still fabulous? *Microbiol. Res.* **2016**, *192*, 271–282. [CrossRef] [PubMed]
4. de Mello, A.F.M.; Vandenberghe, L.P.d.S.; Machado, C.M.B.; Brehmer, M.S.; de Oliveira, P.Z.; Binod, P.; Sindhu, R.; Soccol, C.R. Polyhydroxyalkanoates production in biorefineries: A review on current status, challenges and opportunities. *Bioresour. Technol.* **2023**, *393*, 130078. [CrossRef] [PubMed]
5. Green Chemistry By Paul T. Anastas and John C. Warner. Oxford University Press: Oxford. 2000. Paperback. 135 pp. £14.99. ISBN 0-19-850698-9. *Org. Process Res. Dev.* **2000**, *4*, 437–438. [CrossRef]
6. Koller, M. Advances in Polyhydroxyalkanoate (PHA) Production, Volume 3. *Bioengineering* **2022**, *9*, 328. [CrossRef] [PubMed]
7. Hassan, M.A.; Bakhiet, E.K.; Ali, S.G.; Hussien, H.R. Production and characterization of polyhydroxybutyrate (PHB) produced by Bacillus sp. isolated from Egypt. *J. Appl. Pharm. Sci.* **2016**, *6*, 46–51. [CrossRef]
8. Akaraonye, E.; Keshavarz, T.; Roy, I. Production of polyhydroxyalkanoates: The future green materials of choice. *J. Chem. Technol. Biotechnol.* **2010**, *85*, 732–743. [CrossRef]
9. Albuquerque, P.B.; Malafaia, C.B. Perspectives on the production, structural characteristics and potential applications of bioplastics derived from polyhydroxyalkanoates. *Int. J. Biol. Macromol.* **2018**, *107*, 615–625. [CrossRef]
10. Mannina, G.; Presti, D.; Montiel-Jarillo, G.; Carrera, J.; Eugenia Suárez-Ojeda, M. Recovery of polyhydroxyalkanoates (PHAs) from wastewater: A review. *Bioresour. Technol.* **2020**, *297*, 122478. [CrossRef] [PubMed]
11. Tan, D.; Wang, Y.; Tong, Y.; Chen, G.-Q. Grand Challenges for Industrializing Polyhydroxyalkanoates (PHAs). *Trends Biotechnol.* **2021**, *39*, 953–963. [CrossRef] [PubMed]
12. Gholami, R.; Watson, R.; Hasan, H.; Molla, A.; Bjorn-Andersen, N. Information Systems Solutions for Environmental Sustainability: How Can We Do More? *J. Assoc. Inf. Syst.* **2016**, *17*, 521–536. [CrossRef]
13. Comisión Europea. *Comunicación de la Comisión al Parlamento Europeo, al Consejo, al Comité Económico y Social Europeo y al Comité de las Regiones. Una Estrategia Europea para el Plástico en una Economía Circular*; EU Law and Publications: Luxembourg, 2018; p. 20.
14. Gautam, S.; Gautam, A.; Pawaday, J.; Kanzariya, R.K.; Yao, Z. Current Status and Challenges in the Commercial Production of Polyhydroxyalkanoate-Based Bioplastic: A Review. *Processes* **2024**, *12*, 1720. [CrossRef]

15. Amadu, A.A.; Qiu, S.; Ge, S.; Addico, G.N.D.; Ameka, G.K.; Yu, Z.; Xia, W.; Abbew, A.-W.; Shao, D.; Champagne, P.; et al. A review of biopolymer (Poly-β-hydroxybutyrate) synthesis in microbes cultivated on wastewater. *Sci. Total. Environ.* **2021**, *756*, 143729. [CrossRef] [PubMed]
16. Vicent, S.C.; Clavijo, J.G.B.; Cuenca, R.M.; Agustina, J.C. *Depuración de Aguas Residuales: Digestión Anaerobia*; Publicacions de la Universitat Jaume I: Castellón de la Plana, Spain, 2018. [CrossRef]
17. Kamravamanesh, D.; Pflügl, S.; Nischkauer, W.; Limbeck, A.; Lackner, M.; Herwig, C. Photosynthetic poly-β-hydroxybutyrate accumulation in unicellular cyanobacterium *Synechocystis* sp. PCC 6714. *AMB Express* **2017**, *7*, 143. [CrossRef] [PubMed]
18. Morgan-Sagastume, F.; Heimersson, S.; Laera, G.; Werker, A.; Svanström, M. Techno-environmental assessment of integrating polyhydroxyalkanoate (PHA) production with services of municipal wastewater treatment. *J. Clean. Prod.* **2016**, *137*, 1368–1381. [CrossRef]
19. Valentino, F.; Moretto, G.; Lorini, L.; Bolzonella, D.; Pavan, P.; Majone, M. Pilot-Scale Polyhydroxyalkanoate Production from Combined Treatment of Organic Fraction of Municipal Solid Waste and Sewage Sludge. *Ind. Eng. Chem. Res.* **2019**, *58*, 12149–12158. [CrossRef]
20. Pittmann, T.; Steinmetz, H. Polyhydroxyalkanoate Production on Waste Water Treatment Plants: Process Scheme, Operating Conditions and Potential Analysis for German and European Municipal Waste Water Treatment Plants. *Bioengineering* **2017**, *4*, 54. [CrossRef] [PubMed]
21. Mininni, G.; Laera, G.; Bertanza, G.; Canato, M.; Sbrilli, A. Mass and energy balances of sludge processing in reference and upgraded wastewater treatment plants. *Environ. Sci. Pollut. Res.* **2015**, *22*, 7203–7215. [CrossRef]
22. Serafim, L.S.; Lemos, P.C.; Albuquwrque, M.G.E.; Reis, M.A.M. Strategies for PHA production by mixed cultures and renewable waste materials. *Appl. Microbiol. Biotechnol.* **2008**, *81*, 615–628. [CrossRef] [PubMed]
23. Valentino, F.; Gottardo, M.; Micolucci, F.; Pavan, P.; Bolzonella, D.; Rossetti, S.; Majone, M. Organic Fraction of Municipal Solid Waste Recovery by Conversion into Added-Value Polyhydroxyalkanoates and Biogas. *ACS Sustain. Chem. Eng.* **2018**, *6*, 16375–16385. [CrossRef]
24. Metcalf; Eddy; Tchobanoglous, G.; Stensel, H.D.; Tsuchihashi, R.; Burton, F.L. *Wastewater Engineering: Treatment and Resource Recovery*; MacGraw Hill: New York, NY, USA, 2013.
25. Pittmann, T.; Steinmetz, H. Influence of operating conditions for volatile fatty acids enrichment as a first step for polyhydroxyalkanoate production on a municipal waste water treatment plant. *Bioresour. Technol.* **2013**, *148*, 270–276. [CrossRef] [PubMed]
26. Valentino, F.; Karabegovic, L.; Majone, M.; Morgan-Sagastume, F.; Werker, A. Polyhydroxyalkanoate (PHA) storage within a mixed-culture biomass with simultaneous growth as a function of accumulation substrate nitrogen and phosphorus levels. *Water Res.* **2015**, *77*, 49–63. [CrossRef]
27. Gurieff, N.; Lant, P. Comparative life cycle assessment and financial analysis of mixed culture polyhydroxyalkanoate production. *Bioresour. Technol.* **2007**, *98*, 3393–3403. [CrossRef]
28. Valentino, F.; Morgan-Sagastume, F.; Campanari, S.; Villano, M.; Werker, A.; Majone, M. Carbon recovery from wastewater through bioconversion into biodegradable polymers. *New Biotechnol.* **2017**, *37*, 9–23. [CrossRef]
29. Vázquez-Fernández, A.; Suárez-Ojeda, M.E.; Carrera, J. Review about bioproduction of Volatile Fatty Acids from wastes and wastewaters: Influence of operating conditions and organic composition of the substrate. *J. Environ. Chem. Eng.* **2022**, *10*, 107917. [CrossRef]
30. Wang, J.; Liu, S.; Huang, J.; Qu, Z. A review on polyhydroxyalkanoate production from agricultural waste Biomass: Development, Advances, circular Approach, and challenges. *Bioresour. Technol.* **2021**, *342*, 126008. [CrossRef] [PubMed]
31. Nghiem, L.D.; Hai, F.I.; Price, W.E.; Wickham, R.; Ngo, H.H.; Guo, W. By-products of Anaerobic Treatment: Methane and Digestate from Manures and Cosubstrates. In *Current Developments in Biotechnology and Bioengineering: Biological Treatment of Industrial Effluents*; Elsevier: Amsterdam, The Netherlands, 2017; pp. 469–484. [CrossRef]
32. Latif, M.A.; Mehta, C.M.; Batstone, D.J. Influence of low pH on continuous anaerobic digestion of waste activated sludge. *Water Res.* **2017**, *113*, 42–49. [CrossRef]
33. Jie, W.; Peng, Y.; Ren, N.; Li, B. Volatile fatty acids (VFAs) accumulation and microbial community structure of excess sludge (ES) at different pHs. *Bioresour. Technol.* **2014**, *152*, 124–129. [CrossRef] [PubMed]
34. Kourmentza, C.; Plácido, J.; Venetsaneas, N.; Burniol-Figols, A.; Varrone, C.; Gavala, H.N.; Reis, M.A.M. Recent Advances and Challenges towards Sustainable Polyhydroxyalkanoate (PHA) Production. *Bioengineering* **2017**, *4*, 55. [CrossRef] [PubMed]
35. Rodgers, M.; Wu, G. Production of polyhydroxybutyrate by activated sludge performing enhanced biological phosphorus removal. *Bioresour. Technol.* **2010**, *101*, 1049–1053. [CrossRef] [PubMed]
36. Albuquerque, M.G.E.; Torres, C.A.V.; Reis, M.A.M. Polyhydroxyalkanoate (PHA) production by a mixed microbial culture using sugar molasses: Effect of the influent substrate concentration on culture selection. *Water Res.* **2010**, *44*, 3419–3433. [CrossRef]
37. Fu, X.; Xu, H.; Zhang, Q.; Xi, J.; Zhang, H.; Zheng, M.; Xi, B.; Hou, L. A review on polyhydroxyalkanoates production from various organic waste streams: Feedstocks, strains, and production strategy. *Resour. Conserv. Recycl.* **2023**, *198*, 107166. [CrossRef]

38. Serafim, L.S.; Lemos, P.C.; Oliveira, R.; Reis, M.A.M. Optimization of polyhydroxybutyrate production by mixed cultures submitted to aerobic dynamic feeding conditions. *Biotechnol. Bioeng.* **2004**, *87*, 145–160. [CrossRef] [PubMed]
39. Coats, E.R.; Loge, F.J.; Wolcott, M.P.; Englund, K.; McDonald, A.G. Synthesis of Polyhydroxyalkanoates in Municipal Wastewater Treatment. *Water Environ. Res.* **2007**, *79*, 2396–2403. [CrossRef] [PubMed]

Disclaimer/Publisher's Note: The statements, opinions and data contained in all publications are solely those of the individual author(s) and contributor(s) and not of MDPI and/or the editor(s). MDPI and/or the editor(s) disclaim responsibility for any injury to people or property resulting from any ideas, methods, instructions or products referred to in the content.

Review

Quaternary Treatment of Urban Wastewater for Its Reuse

Jakub Jurík, Barbora Jankovičová, Ronald Zakhar *, Nikola Šoltýsová and Ján Derco

Institute of Chemical and Environmental Engineering, Faculty of Chemical and Food Technology, Slovak University of Technology in Bratislava, Radlinského 9, 81237 Bratislava, Slovakia; jakub.jurik@stuba.sk (J.J.); barbora.jankovicova@stuba.sk (B.J.); jan.derco@stuba.sk (J.D.)
* Correspondence: ronald.zakhar@stuba.sk

Abstract: In today's ongoing rapid urban expansion, deforestation and climate changes can be observed mainly as unbalanced rain occurrence during the year, long seasons without any rain at all and unordinary high temperatures. These adverse changes affect underground water levels and the availability of surface water. In addition, quite a significant proportion of drinking water is used mainly for non-drinking purposes. With several EU countries increasingly suffering from droughts, reusing quaternary treated urban wastewater can help address water scarcity. At the European level, Regulation 2020/741 of the European Parliament and of the Council of 25 May 2020 on minimum requirements for water reuse was adopted. This regulation foresees the use of recycled wastewater mainly for agricultural irrigation. This article provides an overview of various processes, such as filtration, coagulation, adsorption, ozonation, advanced oxidation processes and disinfection, for quaternary treatment of urban wastewater in order to remove micropollutants and achieve the requirements for wastewater reuse. According to the literature, the most effective method with acceptable financial costs is a combination of coagulation, membrane filtration (UF or NF) and UV disinfection. These processes are relatively well known and commercially available. This article also helps researchers to identify key themes and concepts, evaluate the strengths and weaknesses of previous studies and determine areas where further research is needed.

Keywords: irrigation; micropollutants; wastewater reuse; water scarcity; quaternary treatment

Citation: Jurík, J.; Jankovičová, B.; Zakhar, R.; Šoltýsová, N.; Derco, J. Quaternary Treatment of Urban Wastewater for Its Reuse. *Processes* **2024**, *12*, 1905. https://doi.org/10.3390/pr12091905

Academic Editor: Dimitris Zagklis

Received: 24 July 2024
Revised: 28 August 2024
Accepted: 3 September 2024
Published: 5 September 2024

Copyright: © 2024 by the authors. Licensee MDPI, Basel, Switzerland. This article is an open access article distributed under the terms and conditions of the Creative Commons Attribution (CC BY) license (https://creativecommons.org/licenses/by/4.0/).

1. Introduction

Water has several unique functions. It is the source of ecosystem quality, ensures existence for all animals and humans on our planet and plays a key role in the production of food and energy. However, the long-term environmental degradation due to the development of the world economy and urbanization with climate and demographic changes is slowly depleting its quantity and thus water resources are being polluted and depleted [1]. In addition, quite a significant proportion of drinking water is used mainly for non-drinking purposes. It is clear that water scarcity and drought events are likely to be more severe and more frequent in the future. The so-called "water stress" is increasingly coming to the force and it is assumed that this issue will be one of the most significant challenges of the 21st century [2]. The water stress is intensified by deforestation which reduces the global forest cover where rainwater could be stored and then re-generated, thus reducing the global average temperature of the Earth. Due to the deforestation and the associated lack of precipitation on the planet, we are observing a gradual increase in dry periods, which prevail for a long time in the world. Generally, the dry season has increased by 29% since 2000 and for the European continent, the dry seasons during the last few years has been the worst in the last 500 years [3].

The number of people on our planet who live in a state of drinking water scarcity for a period of 1 month is estimated to be around 4 billion, and it is predicted that by 2050 it will reach about half of the world's population [4]. In terms of total water demand, it has increased threefold since 1950, to around 4 000 km^3/year, and is projected to reach around

6000 km^3/year by 2050. This is why water is also referred to as "the oil of the 21st century" by several economic and scientific journals [5].

The largest quantities of fresh water are used worldwide in the industrial and agricultural sectors. The growing human population is responsible for the global expansion of agricultural land that needs to be irrigated. Over the past half century, the global irrigated area has more than doubled, with agricultural irrigation accounting for more than 70% of freshwater consumption [6]. The World Bank warns that if a deep-water crisis occurs, regions such as the Middle East and North Africa could lose up to 6% of their GDP [7].

Based on this huge number of facts and predictions for the coming decades, the question of how to supplement and replace the missing water resources gradually arises. The answer is to look for non-traditional and new sources of water, represented by quaternary treated wastewater [8]. The European Commission defined quaternary treatment as the additional and advanced treatment of urban wastewater in order to eliminate the broadest possible spectrum of micropollutants.

This treatment reduces the risk of micropollutants uptake by plants and soils when the effluent is reused for crop irrigation [9].

The reuse of quaternary treated wastewater for agricultural irrigation is a market-driven activity based on the demands and needs of the agricultural sector, especially in countries facing a shortage of water resources. Irrigation with quaternary treated wastewater could reduce the "water stress" in the given location to a certain extent. In developed countries, it represents a strategy for improving the state of the environment and sustainable agricultural production. At the same time, it is assumed that the reuse of quaternary treated wastewater from urban wastewater treatment plants has less impact on the environment than other alternative methods of water supply, such as water transportation or seawater desalination [10]. The reuse of quaternary treated wastewater for agricultural irrigation can also contribute to the promotion of a circular economy by recovering nutrients (especially potassium, nitrogen and phosphorus) from recycled wastewater and applying them to crops through fertigation techniques. It could therefore potentially reduce the need for additional application of mineral fertilizer and thereby contribute to the recovery of nutrients. In this way, the environment would be less burdened by artificial fertilizers. For end users (farmers), the quaternary treated wastewater is a relatively cheap substitute for artificial fertilizers. For this reason, this type of water can be an interesting commodity in agriculture [11–13].

On the other hand, wastewater recycling poses concerns about microbial risk, the presence of resistant microorganisms (i.e., antibiotic resistant bacteria and genes (ARB&ARGs)) and the presence of micropollutants, such as pesticides, pharmaceuticals, illegal drugs, synthetic and natural hormones and personal care products [10]. The occurrence of these pollutants in the environment is related to various human and industrial activities and are associated with biologically adverse effects on living organisms, such as toxicity and endocrine disruption. The problem may be that some of them are persistent, bioaccumulative and toxic (PBT) or persistent, mobile and toxic (PMT) [14,15]. The current urban wastewater treatment plants are not designed to eliminate micropollutants and can remove many chemicals only to a limited extent, depending on the treatment conditions, but also depending on mobility and resistance to degradation. Then these micropollutants pass through wastewater treatment processes and they may end up in the aquatic environment, becoming threats to wildlife and problems for drinking water production and water reuse. In addition, in most urban wastewater treatment plants, monitoring actions for micropollutants have not been well established and the release of micropollutants and ARB&ARGs into the environment (except Switzerland) is not currently regulated, nor is their occurrence in wastewater for reuse in agriculture, so there are certain risks for public health. The main risk is related to the consumption of raw or undercooked vegetables contaminated with pathogenic microorganisms originating from the use of untreated or poorly treated wastewater for crop irrigation [16]. The monitoring of micropollutants in wastewater to reuse for crop irrigation is one of the main areas of discussion among scientists, legislators and stakeholders at the European Union (EU) level [17].

Legislation in the field of using treated wastewater for irrigation develops differently in individual countries [18]. At the European level, Regulation 2020/741 of the European Parliament and of the Council of 25 May 2020 on minimum requirements for water reuse was adopted in 2020. This regulation foresees the use of recycled wastewater mainly for agricultural irrigation and sets minimum requirements for the quality of recycled wastewater, which it divides into four quality classes (A to D), from crops consumed raw to technical and energy crops. At the same time, this regulation establishes the permitted methods of irrigation. The purpose of this regulation is to facilitate the implementation of water reuse wherever appropriate and cost effective, thus creating a supportive framework for those Member States that want or need to reuse wastewater. This Regulation lays down minimum requirements for water quality and monitoring and risk management provisions for the safe use of recycled wastewater in the context of integrated water management. Water reuse is a promising option for many Member States, but currently only a small number of them implement this practice and have adopted national legislation or standards in this regard. In addition, Member States may use treated wastewater for other purposes, such as water reuse in industry [19].

Adherence to the minimum requirements for water reuse should be in line with the EU's water policy and should contribute to the achievement of the Sustainable Development Goals set out in the United Nations 2030 Agenda for Sustainable Development, in particular the goal of ensuring the availability and sustainable management of water and sanitation for all, as well as substantially increasing water recycling and safe water reuse globally. The aim of this regulation should also be to ensure the application of Article 37 of the Charter of Fundamental Rights of the EU, which concerns environmental protection [20].

Despite these general requirements, there are still risks that need to be addressed individually depending on the sources of wastewater pollution, the rate of removal of specific pollutants, and the methods and goals of using recycled wastewater. Despite the legislative framework adopted above, the rate of water reuse in the EU is low, which results in high investments needed to modernize urban wastewater treatment plants and a lack of financial incentives for quaternary treated wastewater reuse in agriculture. Regarding agricultural products, the reason for the low rate of water reuse is the possible health and environmental risks and possible obstacles to the free movement of such products that have been irrigated with recycled water. These doubts should be resolved by promoting innovative systems and economic incentives that take into account the costs and socio-economic and environmental benefits of quaternary treated wastewater reuse [21].

The aim of this review article is to provide systematic insights into quaternary treatment of urban wastewater by different processes, such as filtration, coagulation, adsorption, ozonation, advanced oxidation processes and disinfection. This article contributes to a better understanding of the described processes with their advantages and disadvantages and also builds and maintains trust in wastewater reuse and promotes it as a possible alternative to reduce the risk of water scarcity for irrigation in the EU.

2. Filtration

One of the oldest methods of water treatment still in use around the world is filtration, which physically removes (separates) particles from the water. For the removal of suspended materials, granular media filters or membrane filters are used. The filtration efficiency depends on the size of the gaps between the filter media, or the pore size of the membrane used [22].

In filtration, depth or cake filtration can be distinguished. In depth filtration, particles are caught in the pore system of the medium through the attachment, whereas in cake filtration, a "cake" is formed on the surface of the medium, with most of the solids being removed at the surface [23].

2.1. Sand Filtration

Historically, the first filters used in water treatment were slow sand filters, which are still in use today. The slow sand filtration process provides treatment through physical filtration of particles and biological degradation in the sand bed [24]. This is followed by a process of adsorption, mechanical filtration and degradation, with the important physical factors that determine pollutant removal being the use of slow filtration rates (0.1–0.3 m/h) and fine sand [25]. Slow sand filtration techniques are characterized by their low capital cost and effectiveness in reducing pathogen load, removing turbidity, suspended solids, and toxic metals in treated water [26].

Rapid sand filtration is characterized by higher filtration rates between 5 and 15 m/h and also differs from slow sand filtration in the quality of the sand used. As in rapid sand filtration, much coarser sand is used with an effective grain size in the range 0.35–0.60 mm. The use of coarser sand results in the pores of the filter bed being relatively large and the impurities contained in the raw water penetrating deep into the filter bed [27].

2.2. Membrane Filtration

Membranes function as selective barriers, allowing the passage of components and retaining other components based on pore size, shape and chemical/physical properties. These membrane filtration systems are commonly known as pressure-driven processes [28].

These filtration processes can be classified as microfiltration (MF), ultrafiltration (UF), nanofiltration (NF) and reverse osmosis (RO). Microfiltration allows the separation of particles with an average size greater than 0.1 µm and varies the working pressure between 1 and 3 atm. Ultrafiltration membranes have pore diameters from 0.01 µm to 0.1 µm with working pressures from 2 to 7 atm. Nanofiltration membranes have pore diameters between 1 nm and 10 nm and working pressures of 5–20 atm. Reverse osmosis requires higher pressures of 30 to 50 atm as the pore size is 0.1 to 0.6 nm [29].

The process of membrane separation combined with activated sludge is referred to in wastewater treatment as a membrane bioreactor (MBR), while low-pressure membrane filtration, either microfiltration (MF) or ultrafiltration (UF), is used to separate the wastewater from the activated sludge [30]. As a biological unit for wastewater treatment, MBR has been proven to be effective in removing organic and inorganic matters [31]. MBR systems have several advantages including high performance compared to a conventional activated sludge precipitator (CASP) and no need for a secondary clarification, low workspace requirements, removal of micropollutants down to the discharge limits, complete retention of bacterial flakes by the membrane, and faster removal of persistent micropollutants [32].

Membrane technology is the advanced method of separation and water treatment, which is characterized by high efficiency, low energy cost, ease for continuous operation, and low footprint [33]. But one of the most challenging problems in membrane filtration is fouling, which reduces permeate flux, interferes with membrane selectivity or permeate quality, and increases membrane maintenance and replacement costs [34].

2.3. Applications of Filtration for Micropollutant Removals

Filtration as an effective water treatment method is applicable in quaternary wastewater treatment to remove micropollutants that are significantly present in the waters. Its removal efficiency can be demonstrated on selected significant micropollutants:

- Microplastics

More and more studies are devoted to the removing of microplastics as a global water pollutant. In the work published by Sembiring et al. [35], the effectiveness of rapid sand filtration (RSF) for the removal of microplastics (MPs) was determined. The MPs samples were made of plastic bags and flakes from tires ranging in size from 10 µm to more than 500 µm, and bentonite was added to represent turbidity in water. The removal efficiency using RSF with an effective size filter media of 0.39 mm and 0.68 mm was 85% to 97% [35].

Wolff et al. [36] showed that the efficiency of sand filtration as the final stage of treatment in municipal wastewater treatment plants was 99% in removing MPs.

The work of Bayo et al. [37] deals with the removal of MPs from the final effluent of an urban wastewater treatment plant by two methods, namely membrane (MBR) and rapid sand filtration (RSF). At influent, the mean MPs concentration was 4.40 ± 1.01 MP L^{-1} and the major isolated forms of microplastics were fibers with a concentration of 1.34 ± 0.23 items L^{-1}. Both methods were found to be effective for MPs removal, with MBR efficiency and RSF efficiency being 79% and 76%, respectively. Selective particle removal was confirmed here, as the removal efficiency of microplastic particulate forms was much higher (99% for MBR and 96% for RSF), as compared to microfiber removal (58% for MBR and 54% for RSF) [37]. Filtration has been shown to be effective in removing MPs, however, significant differences in removal efficiency were observed for smaller plastics that are not removed efficiently. It has also been shown that the filtration process can break down the particles, creating larger amounts of very small microplastics [38].

- Microbial pollution

The protozoa, bacteria and viruses that make up microbial water pollution vary greatly in size but can be removed using different types of filtrations. The following filtration methods are required for the complete physical removal of certain groups of microbial pathogens: rapid and slow sand filters with coagulation with a filter size of 4 μm for protozoa such as *Cryptosporidium* and *Giardia*; microfiltration with a filter size of 0.2 μm for bacteria such as *E. coli*, *Salmonella* and *Cholera*; and ultrafiltration with a filter size of 0.01 μm for viruses such as *Rotavirus*, *Norovirus*, and *Hepatitis-A* [22].

To successfully meet the drinking water specifications submitted by the respective countries, membrane filtration is effective in the removal of pathogens from water, either as a stand-alone unit or as a hybrid unit [39]. In Marsono et al.'s research [40], the overall immersed membrane microfiltration with a pore size of 0.05 μm had a removal efficiency of 100% for *E. coli* and with a pore size of 0.07 μm, the removal of *E. coli* was 99.8% [40].

Incorporation of antimicrobial nanoparticles into membranes can improve removal efficiency, as confirmed in the work of Kacprzyńska-Gołacka et al. [41], in which they achieved complete inhibition of cultured colonies of Gram-negative (*Escherichia coli*) and Gram-positive bacteria (*Bacillus subtilis*) when silver oxide (AgO) was coated on the surface of polyamide microfiltration membranes.

- Pharmaceuticals and endocrine disruptors

Numerous studies have also looked at the use of filtration methods to remove pharmaceuticals and endocrine-disrupting chemicals. In a study by Maryam et al. [42] a loose nanofiltration membrane was used to filter pharmaceutically active substances namely diclofenac, ibuprofen and paracetamol at different pH values as these drugs are the most common type of non-steroidal anti-inflammatory drugs recorded in drinking and treated waters. The highest removal efficiencies of the selected drugs were obtained as follows: 99.74% removal of diclofenac at pH 3, 80.54% removal of ibuprofen at neutral pH and 36.16% removal of paracetamol at pH 12 [42].

The study by Couto et al. [43] investigated the rejection of betamethasone and fluconazole as pharmaceutically active compounds by nanofiltration and reverse osmosis. The ability of nanofiltration and reverse osmosis membranes to reject pharmaceuticals decreased with increasing permeate recovery rate, with the first appearance of pharmaceuticals in the permeate occurring at 40% and 60% permeate recovery rates for nanofiltration and reverse osmosis, respectively [43].

Membrane processes have shown their applicability for the removal of the most common endocrine disruptors found in water and wastewater, especially high-pressure and denser membranes such as nanofiltration and reverse osmosis [44]. More than 90% removal efficiency of a steroid hormone micropollutant 17β-estradiol using an activated carbon fiber-ultrafiltration composite membrane is reported by Zhang et al. [45].

Nakada et al. [46] achieved more than 80% removal efficiency of various pharmaceutically active compounds such as phenolic antiseptics, acid analgesics, anti-inflammatory agents, antibiotics, endocrine disrupting phenolic chemicals, and natural estrogens using a combination of ozonation and sand filtration with activated sludge treatment.

- Pesticides

Membrane technologies can also be used as effective methods to remove pesticides from water [47]. The study by Mukherjee et al. [48] evaluated the removal efficiency of 43 pesticides from water using a thin-film composite polyamide membrane prepared by interfacial polymerization of 1,3-phenylenediamine and 1,3,5 trimesoyl chloride coated on asymmetric polysulfone support. Of the 43 selected pesticides, 33 were removed at more than 80%. The highest removal efficiencies were achieved for the persistent organochlorine insecticides, namely 100% endosulfan, 95% dichlorodiphenyltrichloroethane and 92% hexachlorocyclohexane [48].

Wang et al. [49] used macroporous membranes doped with micro-mesoporous β-cyclodextrin polymers for the separation of organic micropollutants including the pesticide 2,4-dichlorophenol and achieved removal efficiencies of more than 99.9%.

- Heavy metals

Technological advances in membrane development have promoted the increased use of membranes for the filtration and extraction of heavy metal ions from wastewater [50]. In the work of Qi et al. [51], using a positively charged NF membrane prepared by using 2-chloro-1-methyliodopyridine as an active agent to graft polyimide polymer onto the membrane surface achieved removal efficiencies of toxic heavy metal ions of 96% for $CuCl_2$, 95.8% for $NiCl_2$, and 98% for $CrCl_3$.

High efficiency removal of heavy metal ions by nanofiltration membrane was achieved by Morandi et al. [52] using a membrane prepared by incorporating boehmite nanoparticles functionalized with curcumin into a polyethersulfone membrane; the ejection of Fe^{2+}, Cu^{2+}, Pb^{2+}, Mn^{2+}, Zn^{2+} and Ni^{2+} was measured at 99.88, 98.72, 99.61, 99.31, 99.11 and 99.51%, respectively.

In a study by Rezaee et al. [53], they evaluated the use of polysulfone (PSF)/graphene oxide (GO) nanocomposite membranes in terms of arsenate rejection from water, and the maximum rejection was obtained for PSF/GO-2 type at 83.65% at 4 bar pressure. It has been confirmed by many other works that membrane filtration methods have promising potential for practical applications for heavy metal removal [54,55].

3. Coagulation

A physical-chemical method that could be used for the quaternary treatment of wastewater is coagulation. This treatment technology is effective for the removal of pollutants [56,57] as well as the reduction of colloidal turbidity and suspended solids [58]. Coagulation is useful in protecting the environment and human health, while being simple, efficient and low in energy consumption [59].

3.1. Mechanisms of Coagulation

Coagulation is generally encountered as an intact process with flocculation. While the basis of coagulation is the addition of coagulants with rapid mixing, which cause destabilization and neutralization of suspended particles [60], during flocculation, destabilized particles are aggregated through gentle agitation that leads to the formation of larger particles called flocs [61]. The formed flocs are subsequently separated by filtration or sedimentation [62].

The coagulation can be categorized into four mechanisms: simple charge neutralization, charge patching, bridging and sweeping [63].

- Simple charge neutralization

Since most of the colloidal particles dispersed in the water are negatively charged, the process of charge neutralization occurs by adsorption of positively charged cations or polymers. When a metal salt coagulant or cationic organic polymers are added to the water, they can be rapidly hydrolyzed to form various cations that interact with the negatively charged surface of the particles and neutralize them [61,64].

- Charge patching

The adsorption of polymers onto local sites of a particle causes patches of local charge reversal, resulting in a positive–negative attraction between the particles [65].

- Bridging

By adding non-ionic polymers or long-chain low-surface charge polymers alone or together with metal salts, they dissociate and form larger molecules. A particle attaches to the chain of one polymer, and other available active surface sites of other particles can attach to the remainder of the polymers since these polymers can have a linear or branched structure with high surface reactivity. A bridge is formed between the particles, as the polymer-colloidal groups can form an enmeshment, and thus the particles become heavier and that settles down the flocs [61].

- Sweeping

Adding a high concentration of metal salts to water causes the precipitate of amorphous metal hydroxides and forms heavier amorphous gelatin flocs [66].

3.2. Influencing Factors of Coagulation

The coagulation and flocculation processes are influenced by several factors, but in particular, they are influenced by speed and time of mixing, raw water properties, temperature, pH, type and dose of coagulant.

- Mixing

Mixing is an important factor in these processes as rapid mixing is required to promote the interaction of coagulants with suspended particles and the formation of microflocs, while slow mixing is required to promote the aggregation of microflocs into large flocs. The rate of floc formation may be reduced if the mixing speed is too low and the mixing time is too short. To achieve high flocs settling efficiency, it is necessary to form larger flocs, which may be limited if the mixing speed is too high and the mixing time too long [67].

- Coagulant type

Coagulants effective for pollutant removal can be classified into two main groups, namely chemical and natural coagulants. Chemical coagulants include hydrolyzing metallic salts (ferric chloride, ferric sulphate, magnesium chloride, and alum), pre-hydrolyzing metallic salts (poly aluminum chloride (PAC), poly ferric chloride (PFC), poly ferrous sulphate (PFS), poly aluminum ferric chloride) and synthetic cationic polymers (aminomethyl polyacrylamide, polyalkylene, polyethylenimine, polyamine). The most used coagulants in water and wastewater treatment worldwide are alum salts and PACs because they are considered to be widely available and have high treatment efficiency [68].

Due to their biodegradability and availability, natural coagulants represent an opportunity to improve nature and the ecosystem. The advantage of natural coagulants is that they are an environmentally friendly product, and their use does not have a negative impact on human health and the environment [69]. Natural coagulants include microorganisms (bacterial, microalgae, fungal), substances, seeds and plant extracts, starch, fruit waste, chitosan and isinglass [68,70,71].

- Coagulant dosage

For the effective removal of pollutants, a sufficient dose of coagulant is required to destabilize all the colloidal particles. However, with an excessive dose of coagulant, stabilization of suspended particles can occur, which reduces the efficiency of the process [72].

- pH

In the case of inorganic coagulants, pH directly influences the formation of existing hydrolysis product species because pH affects the hydrolysis and polymerization reaction of aluminum, iron ions, and charge density [63].

One important factor in assessing the suitability of using coagulation is the production of the voluminous sludge that is generated as a result of coagulation. The use of inorganic coagulants results in the production of large quantities of metal hydroxide toxic sludge, making it difficult to dispose of and causing an increase in the metal (e.g., aluminum) concentration in the treated water, which may have implications for human health [73].

Several studies have focused on regeneration of the coagulants from water treatment sludge and further reuse in water and wastewater treatment. Other sludge disposal alternatives are incineration, land application and landfilling [74].

3.3. Applications of Coagulation for Micropollutant Removals

- Microplastics

Coagulation has proven effective in removing microplastics from wastewater [75] and drinking water [76]. Ziembowicz et al. [77] investigated the removal efficiency of six different types of microplastics (three types of PE and three types of PVC) from tap water using $AlCl_3 \cdot 6H_2O$ and $FeCl_3 \cdot 6H_2O$ as coagulants. The microplastic removal effect reached its highest value at the initial neutral pH of tap water (pH 7) and when $AlCl_3 \cdot 6H_2O$ was used at the coagulant dose of 0.05 g/L, i.e., 28–44% for PE types and 89–100% for PVC types. Similarly, they investigated the removal efficiency of MP via detergent-assisted coagulation and found that the addition of SDBS (sodium dodecyl benzenesulfonate) surfactant to tap water prior to the coagulation process resulted in removal efficiencies greater than 95% (Al-coagulant) and 80% (Fe-coagulant) for each of the microplastics tested [77].

Similarly, high PE removal efficiency, 84.9%, was achieved by Li et al. [78] using magnesium hydroxide formed under alkaline conditions with anionic polyacrylamide (PAMAM) as a dual coagulant. Hu et al. [79] achieved high removal efficiency of 100 nm 5.0 μm polystyrene microplastics by using poly-aluminum silicate sulphate (PSiAS) and poly-titanium silicate sulphate (PSiTS).

According to Gong et al. [80], coagulation was shown to be effective for the removal of nanoplastics when the removal efficiency was 96.6% from 50 mg/L of nanoplastics of carboxyl-modified polystyrene using 10 mg/L of aluminum chloride as the coagulant.

- Disinfection by-products

Coagulation can also be used to remove disinfection byproducts (DBP) resulting from reactions between disinfectants and natural organic matter [81]. Lin and Ika [82] observed superior DBP formation potential reduction of PACl. Wang et al. [83] compared the coagulation efficiency of three Al-based coagulants, aluminum sulfate, poly-aluminum chloride and a novel type of covalently bonded hybrid coagulant (synthesized using $AlCl_3$) for controlling DBP formation and DBP-associated toxicity. The results showed that the highest removal (by 50%) of the aggregated DBP concentration was obtained by using polyaluminum chloride at a dose of 1.5 [Al]/[DOC] [83].

- Turbidity

In the work of Dahasahastra et al. [84], a regenerated coagulant from a byproduct of the coagulation–flocculation–sedimentation process of drinking water treatment was used as a coagulant to remove turbidity, as it contains a significant concentration of aluminum. A 74% turbidity removal was achieved when 1 mL/l of regenerated coagulant was added to synthetic turbid water with effluent turbidity concentration < 20 NTU [84].

Coagulation is also very effective when combined with other methods such as adsorption. For example, Zahmatkesh et al. [57] used $FeCl_3$ as a coagulant in combination with adsorption on activated carbon, and 99% elimination of NTU was achieved.

The use of plant-based coagulants has also been shown to be effective for turbidity removal [85]. The results of Zedan et al. [86] showed that the removal efficiency was 84.6, 95.2, and 97.8% at initial turbidities of 13, 54, and 194 NTU using walnut seed extract doses of 3.0 mL/L. Ahmad et al. [87] achieved turbidity removal of 24.2% by using the plant P. sarmentosum at an optimum dosage of 5 g/L.

- Pharmaceuticals

Numerous studies have also looked at the use of coagulation to remove pharmaceuticals. In Tahraoui et al.'s work [88], the coagulants copper sulfate, ferric chloride and a combination of cupric sulfate and ferric chloride in a ratio of 1:1 were used. The best results using these coagulants on pharmaceutical plant effluent were obtained using a mixed coagulant ($CuSO_4$ + $FeCl_3$) at pH = 5 and dose = 600 mg/L with a DOC reduction of 97.3%.

The use of natural coagulants for the removal of pharmaceuticals is a promising method for wastewater treatment [89]. According to Nonfodji et al. [90], the use of a natural coagulant from Moringa oleifera seeds in the treatment of hospital wastewater resulted in turbidity removal efficiencies of 64% and COD of 38%. In the work of Iloamaeke and Julius [91], Phoenix dactylifera was shown to be an effective natural coagulant in the treatment of pharmaceutical wastewater.

- Heavy metals

The removal of heavy metals from water has received a great deal of attention due to their adverse effects on aquatic organisms and even human health. Coagulation is one of the available technologies for the removal of heavy metals from waters [92]. In Johnson et al.'s work [93], dosing 40 mg/L ferric chloride and 0.5 mg/L polymer achieved metal removal efficiencies of 95% lead, 92% chromium, 79% copper, 57% zinc, and 17% nickel.

The use of a natural coagulant to remove heavy metals has also been investigated. In Skotta et al.'s work [94], the use of Lepidium sativum mucilage as a bioflocculent in water treatment yielded Cu^{2+} and Zn^{2+} removal at 87% and 71%, respectively.

4. Adsorption

As we have seen in the previous chapters of this review, advanced water treatment methods come in different forms. They can bear chemical, physical or even biological resemblance, while alternatively it is possible to be a combination of all, thus creating hybrid systems. This availability of various processes is necessary if we are to remove pollution, and harmful compounds released into waters by anthropogenic activities [95]. Pollution does not have to be physical only; it is defined as a release of unwanted amounts of any particles (chemicals) such as organics and inorganics, but even as a form of energy (such as noise and light) into the environment. Certain amounts of these pollutants in nature can cause destructive or long-term negative effects on the ecosystem and living organisms [96].

There are diverse ways of purifying treated wastewater to acceptable values, after which, the water will not impact the processes it would be used for. In specific cases, it can improve the recipient (be it water bodies, processes or soil etc.). The principle of purifying process can be destructive or separative, and adsorption is part of the latter. Adsorption can be also used as an emergency water treatment process in case of polluted effluents during breakdowns. It will also serve as filtration media in that case [97]. The adsorption process is widely known as an efficient method for the removal of pollutants from wastewaters thanks to its adaptability, simplicity, ability to use adsorbent material again, and low cost and quite importantly, adsorbents are safe and do not pose a threat to the environment. Moreover, other advantages include their origin, regenerative ability, economic aspect and they are easily accessible [98].

It is important to note the difference between absorption and adsorption. While they have the common word "sorption", they are inherently different. The former happens in the whole volume of another material (typically liquid or gas), while the latter takes action only on the surface of the solid media. The removed substance is called an adsorbate, while the solid material is an adsorbent [99].

Adsorbents should generally have many pores with a large specific surface area. The solids can have a uniform or diverse particle size, containing homogenous or heterogeneous pores. Adsorbents should be selective to certain substances contained in the purified fluid, while being inert to the bulk of the fluid [100]. According to IUPAC classi-

fication [101];,adsorbents as porous materials are separated according to the nature and structure of their pores in classes as follows [102]:
(a). macroporous materials with pores structure > 50 nm and d > 50 nm,
(b). mesoporous materials with pores structure 2–50 nm and d ≈ 2–50 nm,
(c). microporous materials with pores structure < 2 nm and d < 2 nm.

The shape or structure of pores can be understood better with nitrogen (N_2) adsorption, which creates isotherms and hysteresis as shown in Figure 1 [103]. Corresponding pore shapes are included in the figure.

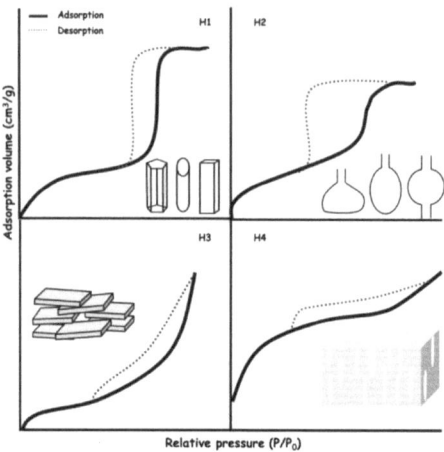

Figure 1. Adsorption according to pore shape [103].

We must remember that even in adsorption there is energy involved. Figure 2 [104] shows the possible interactions of adsorbate and adsorbent. In this regard, two possible options of adsorbate binding to the adsorbent surface are available. The nature of adhesion is reflected also in their names: physisorption and chemisorption.

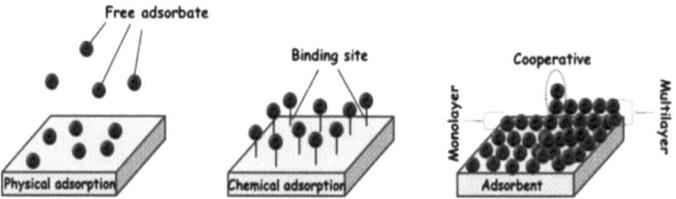

Figure 2. Difference between physisorption, chemisorption and mono/multilayer adsorption [104].

4.1. Physisorption and Chemisorption

As the name for physisorption suggests, the physical bonding is created by minimizing surface energy. Forces responsible for binding the adsorbate to the adsorbent could be Van der Waals, hydrogen bonding, electrostatic forces, and hydrophobic interactions with the first one being the most common [105]. Regarding the actual energy of adsorption, when we assume that these forces are similar to the ones of vapor condensation of the adsorbate, the released energy could be compared to adsorbate condensation energy at the given conditions. The overall nature of physisorption makes it possible for it to be a reversible process. The strength of a bond between the adsorbent and adsorbate is relatively weak, and the bond is easily disrupted by changing conditions, which leads to a release of a pollutant into the surrounding medium, generally labeled as desorption. Energy of adsorption in physisorption ranges usually between 8 and 40 kJ/mol, while in chemisorption it goes over, reaching as high as 800 kJ/mol. This fact gives away the nature of the bond in chemisorption. A covalent bond is created between the adsorbent and adsorbate, altering the structure of the latter and simultaneously limiting sorption to the monolayer. While the overall sorption capacity of the adsorbent is not maximized by filling the pores, the chemical reaction is more selective, thus making chemisorption valuable. Desorption becomes ineffective and unpractical due to chemical change in the structure of the adsorbate [106,107].

4.2. Characterization of Adsorbents and the Adsorbent Process

There are multiple mathematical ways to characterize the process of adsorption: adsorption isotherms, kinetics and thermodynamics. Parameters which are used in adsorbent characterization designing are in Table 1 [108–110]. Parameters and graphical interpretation of previous characterization depends on multiple specifications of adsorbent.

Table 1. Parameters used in adsorbent characterization and designing of technologies [108–110].

Parameter	Symbol	Unit
Iodine number	IN	mg/g
Ash		%
Porosity	ε_p	–
Skeletal density	ρ_{He}	kg/m^3
Geometrical density	ρ_{Hg}	kg/m^3
Bulk density	ρ_s	kg/m^3
Specific surface	S_{BET}	m^2/g
Particle size	d	mm
Pore size	d_p	Å
Moisture	–	%

Adsorption isotherm, as the name implies, is a quantitative measurement of equilibrium between free adsorbate in the fluid and bonded on the adsorbent. It is also useful in designing an adsorption system and helps to describe the interaction between the adsorbent and adsorbate [111]. The adsorption process itself must abide hydrodynamics in the solution, which means that adsorption happens as shown in Figure 3 [112].

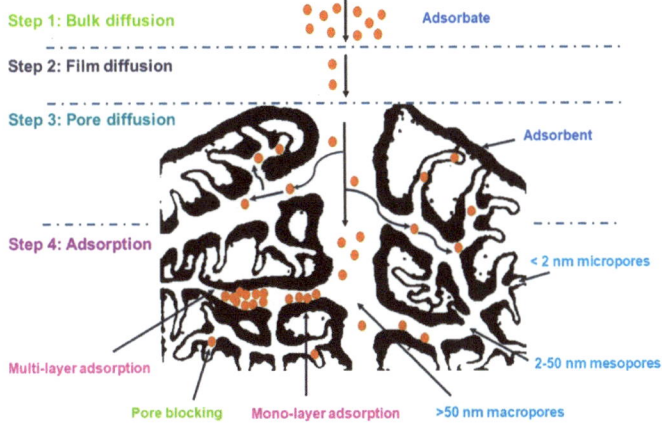

Figure 3. Adsorption mechanism of pollutants [112].

In simplicity, for adsorption to work, there needs to be 1. interparticle diffusion, 2. intraparticle diffusion, and 3. surface sorption [106,112]. As for the adsorption kinetics, commonly applied models are pseudo-first order (PFO), pseudo-second order (PSO),

Avrami and Elovich models [106]. An important note about calculation of kinetic equation parameters is inclusion of equilibrium data or close ones. Determining a better model for the process is biased, which is caused by a used method for the calculation. Because of this, PSO was leading as the most fitting model in numerous studies. First, the diffusion-controlled process is described by PSO more precisely than with PFO, although the former model cannot describe the steep rise in adsorption in a short time [113]. Moreover, the parameters in the PFO and PSO kinetic model do not have physical meaning, they are derived from multiple processes happening during the adsorption (for example combination of diffusion and adsorption). On the other hand, the parameters in the Elovich equation do have physical meaning [106,114].

As we have discussed in the previous text, adsorption seems like a simple process, but it has many applications in water treatment. We must always keep in mind that purifying water is needed and wanted, and as a result, we produce toxic or non-toxic solid waste. As a general consensus, materials used for adsorbents are cheap. Most of the carbon-based adsorbents can be prepared from waste materials such as tomato seeds, plum stones, coconut shell, and rice straw shell etc. Waste materials are not overlooked as before, environmental thinking affects research to look for alternative raw sorbent material sources. Activated alumina, zeolites, silica gel and activated carbon (from coal) are still commonly used for their specific uses, but their counterparts receive a lot of attention too [115,116]. One should always bear in mind the rules for a good adsorbent, which are the following [117]:

(a). high selectivity for specific pollutants,
(b). possibility of regeneration,
(c). non-toxicity to humans and the environment,
(d). non-corrosiveness to construction materials of the system,
(e). low cost,
(f). mechanical stability,
(g). market availability.

4.3. Adsorption as a Method for Removal of Organic Micropollutants

As concerns about water availability become more prevalent, so has monitoring expanded to a more specific pollutant. They also can be referred as contaminants of emerging concern (CECs) or organic micropollutants (OMPs), which are mostly unregulated chemicals in the environment and their biological effects are not yet studied in detail, but they definitely pose threat for the aquatic environment and human health [118,119]. Stopping the rise of an antibiotic presence in an environment is essential for the protection of aquatic life and limiting the ability of the microbial population to gain resistance [120,121]. Regular wastewater treatment plants (WWTP) are not designed to remove CECs, but they are still able to reach a removal efficiency ranging from 30% to 65%. In municipal wastewaters, CECs are also present, which consist of pharmaceuticals and personal care products, endocrine disrupting compounds, disinfection byproducts, and fluorinated organic chemical compounds such as perfluorooctanoic acid and perfluorooctane sulfonate [122–124]. The presence of these chemicals and their concentration levels are achieved by overconsumption of medications and their unresponsible disposal. It is possible to remove these compounds from wastewaters by adsorption. For example, from 18 monitored CECs, only 1,4-Dioxane, Sucralose, and Iohexol showed no concentration decline in a 1.5 m bed depth of granulated coconut shell-based media. Flow through filter bed was 54–65 m^3/d, which resulted in 45 min of contact time. A possible reason for the low removal efficiency of 1,4-Dioxane could be the low carbon partitioning coefficient, which in turn affects sorption [125]. For example, caffeine, carbamazepine, gemfibrozil, and sulfamethoxazole are documented to be removed to levels below detection limits [119,125].

Alternatively, modified adsorbent materials can be applied to treat wastewater containing pharmaceuticals. Sand filtration and a subsequent graphene-based nanoadsorbent reactor was studied. The reactor was patented under the name RECAM®. Used graphene had a bulk density of 1.05–1.80 g/cm^3 at 25 °C, mesoporous nanostructure with a surface area of 890 m^2/g and a carbon content of 97.5%. The operation pressure was in a range of 0.4–0.6 bar with a flowrate of 4.3–5.5 mL/min resulting in a contact time of 75 min. The process was in use for days, resulting in a measured breakthrough curve with a breakthrough point at the 45–55 days mark for carbamazepine, diclofenac and ibuprofen. Interestingly, it was not observed for caffeine. At the start-up phase, the process was different for each chemical, with diclofenac being the shortest (14 days) and caffeine the longest (50 days). Over the duration of the process, removal efficiencies reached higher than 95% [126].

Adsorption Mechanism of Organic Pollutants

Adsorption for organic pollutants follows mechanisms such as partitioning, pore filling, electrostatic interaction, electron donor and acceptor interaction, and hydrophobic interaction. Additionally, adsorption of pharmaceuticals on nanotubes is believed to follow physisorption as their main mechanism [127].

Partitioning happens when the adsorbate diffuses into the pores of the biochar that has not yet been carbonized. After this step, adsorption of the organic adsorbate can proceed by adhering to the adsorbent surface. Generally speaking, adsorbents (or biochar) have higher volatile content and organic contaminants [128].

Pore filling occurs when mesopores and micropores are present in the adsorbent, as well as polarity of organic contaminants. Prerequisites for a good pore filling mechanism is little volatile matter content in the biochar and a lower concentration of organic contaminants in the liquid [128].

Electrostatic interaction occurs with ionizable organic compounds to the positively charged surface of the adsorbent. It is dependent on the pH and ionic strength of the aqueous solution. Lower pH favors this mechanism, while higher pH hinders the efficiency of the process. It was also experimented that adding NaCl to a solution with methylene blue resulted in lowered adsorption for the dye from 4.5 to 3 mg/g [128].

An electron donor and acceptor interaction is common with aromatic compounds as is adsorbents having a graphene-like structure. For biochar to have electron-acceptor/donor capabilities is dependent on the pyrolysis temperature. Below 500 °C, biochar acts as an acceptor and above this temperature it behaves as a donor. Sulfamethoxazole adsorption was studied on π-electron graphene-enriched biochar and great adsorption capabilities were noted, especially with adsorbate aniline-protonated rings. Another interesting point regarding this mechanism is atrazine adsorption enhancement due to chlorine and aromatic carbon interaction on the biochar surface [128].

Hydrophobic interaction occurs during adsorption, when neutral compounds are present. Reported organic pollutants such as benzoic acid, o-chlorobenzene acid and p-chlorobenzene acid obey this type of adsorption mechanism. Higher pyrolysis temperature improves the sorption processes connected to this mechanism [128].

4.4. Heavy Metal Removal from Wastewaters by Adsorption

The presence of heavy metals in wastewater can also be natural, but in the last few centuries, it has been to a substantial extent achieved by anthropogenic activities. Mining, battery, nuclear, textile, and tannery are all industries which produce important materials or products we cannot live without, but their side effects are affecting human health and the environment [129]. Generally, activated carbons are used as adsorbents to treat water containing heavy metals. The ability to remove heavy metals is dependent on a microporous structure, large surface area and chemical complexity. For adsorption of heavy metals, regular activated carbon can be used, but alternative cheaper variants are studied. This includes biochar, byproducts, agricultural waste, seafood waste, food waste and soil particles. There is also the possibility to use natural zeolites, natural diatomite, and natural clay, etc. since they are economically viable [130–132].

4.4.1. Effect of pH

The effect of pH plays a key role in many chemical processes and the adsorption of heavy metals is not any different. It affects the ionization and solubility of metal ions and surface functional groups. For Cr^{6+} ion, a pH as low as 2 is preferred, but the exact process conditions depend on the metal ion speciation and functional groups situated on the adsorbent surface. A possible explanation is dichromate species being present at such low pHs [133,134]. Cr^{6+} can be also reduced to Cr^{3+} by electron donor groups on the adsorbent. Regarding Cr^{4+}, 95% adsorption potential was achieved with rice husk carbon. Adsorbent amount, temperature, time and optimal pH at 12 were observed. By applying coconut jute carbon for adsorption, 99.8% removal efficiency was reached. Optimal conditions were low Cr^{4+} concentration and low pH. Low pH also favors the adsorption of As^{3+}. Specifically, for hydrochars that were modified by KOH, cadmium adsorption efficiency was recorded best for pHs ranging from 4.0 to 8.0. Metallic ions like Cu^{2+}, Zn^{2+}, and Pb^{2+} have an optimal pH for adsorption ranging from 4.0 to 6.0. As for the adsorption capacity of metal ions, it increases in the following order: Zn^{2+}, Cd^{2+}, Cu^{2+}, Fe^{2+}, Pb^{2+} [133–135].

4.4.2. Effect of Temperature

The temperature effect on heavy metal adsorption is supported by multiple research papers to be positive at higher temperatures. This fact is probably linked with possible chemisorption and creation of multiple active sites, subsequently rising adsorption capacity. Keeping the previous information in mind, rising temperatures way too high would make the adsorption process worse. Heavy metal adsorption could also be an endothermic process, which would explain this behavior [136–138].

4.4.3. Effect of Contact Time

Rising contact time for heavy metal adsorption processes achieved better results for different adsorbents. It was noted that adsorption is quick at the start and reaches equilibrium gradually [138].

4.4.4. Adsorption Mechanisms of Heavy Metals

There are various variables such as specific areas of the adsorbent and surface-active functional groups, and the mechanism can vary from metal to metal. The most prominent adsorption mechanisms for heavy metals are physical adsorption, electrostatic adsorption, precipitation, ion exchange, complexation, and reduction [128,138].

It was demonstrated that physical adsorption is most common with heavy metals such as As, Cd, Zn and U, which are immobilized on the surface. Higher temperatures seem to provide better removal by altering the biochar structure [128,138].

Ion exchange is connected to negatively charged surface groups on the adsorbent and positively charged one on heavy metal ions. Contrary to physical adsorption, cation exchange capacity decreases with pyrolysis temperatures higher than 350 °C. The force that is responsible for the binding is called Coulombic. It was reported that heavy metal ions such as Cd^{2+} and K^+ in water solution abide this form of the mechanism. K^+ occurred on the deprotonated functional groups, while Cd^{2+} was affected by two different cation-π bonding mechanisms. Also, the adsorption between Hg^{2+} and Zn^{2+} was measured and compared and the former adsorbed much higher the latter. This type of adsorption mechanism has low adsorption capacity and is very pH dependent. Reports state that the higher iron oxide content in the adsorbent material, the better the cation exchange capacity [128,138].

The electrostatic adsorption mechanism is keen to take place in adsorbents with plenty of negatively charged active sites on them. The strength of this bond is related to the pH of the solution, ionic radius, valence state of the heavy metal, and zero potential of the biochar. It was reported multiple times that Hg followed this mechanism of adsorption on the biochar. The described mechanism is also connected with redox reactions, which can be seen with Cr^{6+} adsorbing to the surface thanks to electrostatic forces and then reduced to Cr^{3+} by elemental carbon [128,138].

There is also a possibility of the precipitation effect taking place during adsorption, which is caused by the presence of functional groups such as PO_4^{3-} and CO_3^{2-}. These groups are contained in larger numbers in animal-based biochar, compared to plant-based ones. Heavy metal ions such as Cd^{2+}, Pb^{2+} and others can form stable elements, for example, $CdCO_3$ and $PbCO_3$ [128,138].

Complexation was reported with adsorbents (biochar) made at lower pyrolysis temperatures, containing phenolic, lactonic and carboxyl functional groups. Oxidation of the adsorbent surface makes it easier for heavy metals to form complexes. Plant-based raw material is mentioned as being a better starting material for biochar production, due to greater content of the previously mentioned functional groups. Heavy metals which were observed to abide this mechanism are Cu, Cd, Ni, and Pb [128,138].

4.5. Control of Disinfection Byproducts Contained in Wastewaters with Adsorption

If we want to achieve highly purified water, disinfection is often needed. Generally, the water would be used as drinking water, but with recent environmental problems, water is used for different applications, which also demand disinfection. There are several ways to disinfect water and using chemicals is one of them.

The combination of ultraviolet (UV) light and chlorine or chloramine generates highly reactive molecules such as hydroxyl radicals, reactive chlorine species, chlorine radicals, dichlorine radical anions and chlorine monoxide. These species reliably destroy the ability of microorganisms to reproduce or outright kill them [139]. Albeit, using such methods can lead to the formation of halogenated disinfection byproducts (DBP) [140].

A study that applied ozonation and subsequent treatment of the sample (wastewater from municipal water reclamation plant, Singapore) to an adsorption column showed positive removal efficiency for possible halogenated precursors. The BAC column consisted of granulated activated carbon that had an effective particle size of 0.86–1.00 mm, apparent density of 0.5 g/cm^3 and uniformity coefficient of 1.7. Rinsed GAC was inoculated with activated sludge obtained from a water reclamation facility, with a mixed liquor suspended solids concentration of 3500 mg/L. After BAC treatment, wastewater parameters TOC, UVA$_{254}$, and SUV$_A$ were significantly lowered from 8.74 mg/L, 0.062 mg/L, and 0.71 mg/L to 3.85 mg/L, 0.014 mg/L, and 0.36 mg/L. Overall O$_3$-BAC treatment had great removal efficiency for aromatic compounds, nitrile organic matter and disinfection byproducts formation potential (DBPFP). Removal of DBPs achieved 46.0% efficiency in the raw wastewater. DBPFP, trihalomethanes (THMs) and haloacetic acids (HAAs) reached removal efficiencies of 81.5–97.5%. The process lowered the formation potential of THM by 87.6% and more than 99% for trichloronitromethane (TCNM), haloketones (HKs), and haloacetonitrils (HANs), while HAAs achieved only 29.7% reduction [141].

4.6. Removal of Micro/Nanoplastics by Adsorption

Activated carbon and graphene materials are used as adsorbents for microplastics and bioplastics removal to a significant extent; this is because of their availability and price [142,143]. Biochar was studied as an adsorbent material to remove polystyrene microbeads. Biochar was prepared from corn straw and hardwood feedstock and was directly applied into sand filtration to increase microplastics removal. The sand filtration removal efficiency increased from 60–80% to 95% by using the modified system. The mechanism showed that larger microplastics were stuck between particles and smaller ones were trapped in biochar pores. During the process it was reported that biochar formed larger particles (described as colloidal) and trapped even more microplastics, which made them immobile [144].

Modified biochar materials are also viable for microplastic removals, as it was presented in [145,146]. Biochar was modified by impregnating iron nanoparticles into the structure, which granted intensified magnetic and surface qualities to the material. Then it was tested for nanoplastics adsorption removal and the researchers' results showed that the process achieved 100% removal efficiency, which in comparison to 75% of raw biochar is a great difference. Moreover, they concluded the effect of solution pH on the process, which seemed to have almost none. Characteristics of the adsorption principle was discussed to be surface complexation and electrostatic interactions between the nanoplastics and nanoparticles. Regeneration was successful due to retainment of adsorption capacity.

Adsorption of microplastics with different shapes was experimentally tested by pyrolyzing pine and spruce bark at a temperature of 475 °C. Its morphology was subsequently modified through steam activation at 800 °C. The monitored microplastics species were spherical polyethylene microbeads (10 µm), cylindrical polyethylene pieces (2–3 mm), and fibers of a fleece shirt. The results show a more promising removal of larger particles, almost 100% retention for fleece shirt fibers and a complete one for cylindrical polyethylene particles. The negative outcome of the study is low removal efficiency for polyethylene microbeads [147].

5. Advanced Oxidation Processes (AOPs)

Advanced oxidation processes (AOPs) are new, highly effective technologies to eliminate persistent micropollutants by utilizing the oxidizing potential of reactive oxygen species (ROS) generated in situ via chemical or physical pathways. ROS are a group of radicals, ions or molecules that have at least one unpaired electron. There are two types of ROS–free oxygen radicals and non-radical ROS (Table 2) [148–152]. The hydroxyl radical ($^\bullet$OH) is the most commonly used in AOPs technology due to its advantages such as non-selectivity, high reactivity and ease of formation. It is also often considered a green harmless oxidant because non-toxic byproducts are formed when pollutants are oxidized [151]. The chemical AOPs method in the aqueous phase can initiate the formation of $^\bullet$OH radicals in the presence of chemical precursors such as O_3 or H_2O_2, with or without catalysts or promoters. Some physical methods of AOPs can directly initiate $^\bullet$OH radical formation in the aqueous phase without the presence of promoters. Such methods include photolysis, sonolysis, radiolysis or supercritical water oxidation [150].

Table 2. Example of ROS [148–152].

ROS as Free Oxygen Radicals	Non-Radical ROS
Hydroxyl radical $^\bullet$OH	Hydrogen peroxide H_2O_2
Superoxide anion radical $O_2^{\bullet-}$	Singlet oxygen $^1O_2$
Alkoxyl radical RO$^\bullet$	Ozone/trioxygen O_3
Peroxyl radical ROO$^\bullet$	Organic hydroperoxides ROOH
Hydroperoxide radical $^\bullet$OOH	Hypochloride HOCl
Nitric oxide NO$^\bullet$	Peroxynitrite ONO^-
Thiyl radicals RS$^\bullet$	Nitrocarbonate anion $O_2NOCO_2^-$
Sulphonyl radicals ROS$^\bullet$	Dinitrogen dioxide N_2O_2
Thiyl peroxyl RSOO$^\bullet$	Nitronium NO_2^+
Sulphate radicals $SO_4^{\bullet-}$	Highly reactive lipid- or carbohydrate-derived carbonyl compounds

In general, AOPs occur in two phases. In the first phase is the production of radicals and the second phase is the reaction of these radicals with micropollutants present in the wastewater [149,153]. Based on the in situ radical production, AOPs can be categorized into four groups (Figure 4). Chemical AOPs use a chemical reagent and a catalyst; photochemical ones are based on the use of a solar energy or a UV source. An electrical source is used to generate radicals in electrochemical methods of AOPs. Sonochemical AOPs use an ultrasound in the first phase to generate radicals [151,154].

Figure 4. Some types of AOPs by in situ radical production.

5.1. Chemical Types of AOPs

5.1.1. Fenton's Reaction Technique

The Fenton reaction is a type of chemical AOP. The principle is the use of hydrogen peroxide and ferrous ions to generate hydroxyl radicals at an acidic pH. The mechanism of formation of hydroxyl radicals in the Fenton reaction involves approximately 20 reactions. However, in general, the equation can be written according to Equation (1) [155].

$$Fe^{2+} + H_2O_2 + H^+ \rightarrow Fe^{3+} + H_2O + {}^\bullet OH \quad (1)$$

In the reaction mechanism, in addition to hydroxyl radicals, hydroperoxide radicals are also formed as intermediates (Equation (2)), which can subsequently react with hydrogen peroxide (Equation (3)), hydroxyl radicals (Equation (4)) or iron ions (Equations (5) and (6)) [156,157].

$$H_2O_2 + H^- \rightarrow H_2O + {}^\bullet OOH \quad (2)$$

$$^\bullet OOH + H_2O_2 \rightarrow {}^\bullet OH + H_2O + O_2 \quad (3)$$

$$^\bullet OOH + {}^\bullet OH \rightarrow H_2O + O_2 \quad (4)$$

$$^\bullet OOH + Fe^{2+} \rightarrow Fe^{3+} + HO_2^- \quad (5)$$

$$^\bullet OOH + Fe^{3+} \rightarrow Fe^{2+} + H^+ + O_2 \quad (6)$$

The efficiency of organic pollutant degradation in Fenton's reaction technique depends on several parameters such as pH, concentration of chemical reagent and initial organic pollutant content. pH is a key parameter for the Fenton reaction. The optimal pH range is 2–4 and is connected to the nature of the reagents. If the pH was neutral or alkaline, there would be risk of iron precipitating in a form of insoluble compounds and additionally, losing its catalytic abilities. At a lower pH than the previously mentioned range, the scavenging effect of $^\bullet OH$ by H^+ would be too prominent, which would result in inhibition of the Fenton degradation effect. However, most wastewaters have a pH value higher than the optimal range. For this reason, it is necessary to adjust the pH value of the wastewater before the Fenton reaction itself, but at the same time, it is necessary to adjust the pH value even after the treatment process in order to achieve suitable outlet pH of the treated wastewater. From this point of view, the Fenton reaction is an expensive process because large amounts of chemicals are required [158].

Zhao et al. [159] applied the Fenton reaction to remove recalcitrant dissolved organic matter. Their results show 77.7% removal efficiency at the optimal dosage of 11.5 g H_2O_2/L and Fe^{2+}/H_2O_2 ratio of 1:20.

In a review by Wang et al. [160], the removal of microplastics (MPs) and nanoplastics (NPs) by the Fenton reaction is mentioned. The Fenton reaction could change the chemical structures of MPs, reduce the particle size of MPs or mineralize MPs. This is mostly caused by •OH attacking the C−H bond to form a C−O bond and destabilizing the micro/nanoplastic structure. If the C−C bond is attacked, the chains become separated and the larger particles crumble into smaller ones, generating a greater reaction area for the radicals to attack [161].

According to [162], Fenton reactions are effective for the inactivation of pathogenic microorganisms in various types of wastewaters.

The electro-Fenton reaction is in situ generation of H_2O_2 in the medium on the electrode by a process called oxygen reduction reaction (ORR). Dissolved oxygen is the main part of H_2O_2 generation. As for the cations, Fe^{2+} is added to the system from external sources. Due to the electrochemical nature of the process, iron ions are regenerated during the reaction [163]. The electro-Fenton reaction, just as the classical homogeneous Fenton reaction, suffers from pH prerequisites, resulting in high chemical usage and creation of unwanted sludge [164].

Electrochemical peroxidation (EP) is based on in situ Fe^{2+} generation thanks to the iron (steel) anode while H_2O_2 is externally added to the reaction mixture. In a study there was direct comparison of a substance named Reactive Black 5 (RB5) with classical Fenton for dye removal. It was shown that in simulated wastewater, classical Fenton was faster and gave more satisfactory results compared to EP. This partially happened with coagulation, but effective azo bond destruction was still observed, which caused discoloration of the sample. In real wastewater fast discoloration happened too but this was probably caused by the conditions. Forty percent color removal was noted in the real wastewater. During the EP process, H_2O_2 was introduced in the sample from the beginning but the •OH creation lasted during the whole reaction time and Fe^{2+} needed for the reaction in both simulated and real wastewater, was available for the reaction thanks to slow release from the anode. The dye was gradually removed from the samples by degradation and not by coagulation [163].

The heterogeneous Fenton reaction consists of either iron minerals (for example magnetite–Fe_3O_4), iron-based composite catalysts, iron-based semiconductors, iron-modified porous materials and externally added H_2O_2. The huge advantage of this process is independence from pH, and it consumes less H_2O_2 than the classical Fenton reaction. The availability of iron minerals is high, and their cost is rather quite low. To some extent, the heterogeneous Fenton reaction is present even in soil because of iron minerals and H_2O_2 can be generated by photochemical reactions using iron oxides [165].

The heterogeneous electro-Fenton is a mix of the electro-Fenton and heterogeneous Fenton reaction, albeit without electro-Fenton disadvantages. Used iron carriers such as Fe_3O_4, support the mixture with Fe^{2+} and Fe^{3+} cations available for oxidation or reduction. It is not dependent on pH and its use of H_2O_2 is less intense due to lower iron abundance in the mixture. There is also a higher ability of the iron to regenerate due to the electrochemical nature of the process. Studies proved that modified iron carried by metal ions such as Ni can assist with H_2O_2 activation [164].

5.1.2. Ozone-Based Processes

Ozone-based processes are oxidative technologies that use a strong oxidizing agent, specifically ozone. Ozone reacts nonspecifically and easily with pollutants due to its high reduction potential (2.07 V vs. SHE) and reactivity. Ozone-based processes can be used to color and odor COD, nutrients or micropollutants removal. Ozone can react with pollutants through two reaction pathways—direct and indirect reaction. In the direct reaction, ozone molecules react directly with the pollutant. This reaction is also called ozonolysis [166–169].

Ozonolysis is a direct reaction of ozone with pollutants. In general, it is a selective reaction with a slow reaction rate. The unsaturated bond in pollutants is split by ozone according to the Criegee mechanism. Ozonolysis is technically and economically a feasible treatment process to eliminate micropollutants in wastewaters. For example, the removal efficiency of particular cytostatic compounds, antibiotics and other dissolved organics (like phenols, aniline, thioethers, aromatics, amines, pharmaceuticals) is more than 90% [169]. Ozonolysis is also effective in the elimination of organochlorine pesticides [170]. Tripathi and Hussain [168] indicated that ozonolysis is an attractive disinfectant for inactivation of both virus and bacteria. The elimination efficiency of different viruses and bacteria is between 78 and 99.9% by ozonolysis.

In the indirect reaction, reactive oxygen species are generated from ozone, which react with the pollutant. These two reaction pathways lead to different oxidation products. Indirect reaction belongs to AOPs and it is usually catalyzed by ozonolysis. For example, hydrogen peroxide, UV radiation, iron ions or an alkaline condition can be used as a catalyst [166–169].

Due to the fact that ozone is an unstable gas, it must be generate in situ. In situ generation of ozone can be from air, pure oxygen or water using some form of energy (Table 3).

Table 3. Different methods of ozone generation [166–169].

Method of Ozone Generation	Principle	Ozone Source
Electrical	Electrical discharge	Air or O_2
Electrochemical	Electrolysis	Water (highly purified)
Photochemical	Irradiation ($\lambda < 185$ nm)	Air, O_2, water
Radiation chemistry	X-rays, radioactive γ-rays	Water (highly purified)
Thermal	Light arc ionization	Water

The most widely used method of ozone generation is the electrical method via dielectric barrier discharge (DBD). In dielectric barrier discharge ozone generators, ozone is produced using energy from electrons in an electric field between two electrodes. At least one of the electrodes must be covered with a dielectric material. The electrodes are separated by a gas-containing space or gap. When a high voltage alternating current is created between two electrodes, the gas is ionized. The resulting ions act as charge carriers for the second electrode, and when they collide with an oxygen molecule, ozone molecules are formed. The formation of ozone molecules can be described by Figure 5 [169–172].

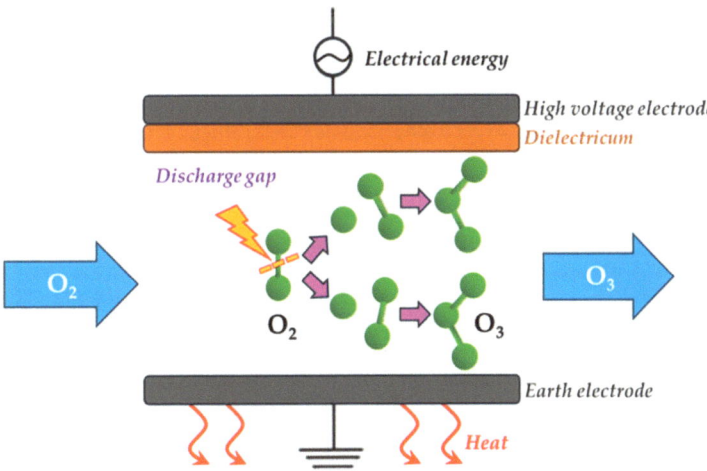

Figure 5. Principle of dielectric barrier discharge [171].

The combination of ozone and catalyst such as UV, H_2O_2 or iron ions belongs also to chemical AOPs due to the generation of reactive oxygen species (ROS).

The combination of ozone and UV is also defined as photochemical AOPs. The principle is using UV for the photodecomposition of ozone in aqueous media. Photolysis of ozone leads to hydroxyl radical formation (Equation (7)). Hydroxyl radicals can react not only with pollutants, but conversion to peroxyl radical occurs with the reaction of hydroxyl radicals with ozone molecules (Equation (8)) [151,173].

$$O_3 + H_2O + h\nu \rightarrow 2\,^\bullet OH + O_2 \qquad (7)$$

$$O_3 +\,^\bullet OH \rightarrow\,^\bullet OOH + O_2 \qquad (8)$$

The treatment process O_3/UV has benefits such as disinfection and toxicity reduction. O_3/UV can be used to abate ozone-resistant trace organic contaminants more efficiently and lead to less toxic byproducts formation in comparison with ozonation alone. The removal efficiency of some antibiotics such as carbamazepine, ciprofloxacin, clarithromycin, diclofenac, and sulfamethoxazole reach around 80–100% with the O_3/UV combination [166].

Presumido et al. [174] investigated a membrane ozone contactor for wastewater treatment. The application of a small dose of UV radiation had no effect on the oxidation of contaminants of emerging concern but had a positive effect on the reduction of microbial contamination. Despite the high reduction of potentially harmful bacteria, the reduction effect was transient. Microorganisms that survived the O_3/UV treatment process were able to grow back to their original concentrations. However, this process requires high energy to power the UV lamps and the ozone generator [173].

The peroxone technique combines ozone with hydrogen peroxide (H_2O_2). Supposedly, it is the most studied and implemented AOP based on ozonation [156,164]. The H_2O_2 molecule in aqueous media is dissociated into hydrogen cations and hydroperoxide anions (Equation (9)). Ozone reacts with hydroperoxide anions to formed hydroperoxide radical and ozonide ions (Equation (10)) [151,169].

$$H_2O_2 \rightarrow HO_2^- + H^+ \qquad (9)$$

$$O_3 + HO_2^- \rightarrow\,^\bullet OOH + O_3^- \qquad (10)$$

Ozone can also directly react with H_2O_2 to produce hydroxyl radical and ozonide ions (Equation (11)).

$$O_3 + 2H_2O_2 \rightarrow 2\,^\bullet OH + O_3^- \qquad (11)$$

In both reaction mechanisms of the peroxone technique, ozonide ions are formed. The reaction between the ozonide ions and the hydrogen cation leads to the production of more hydroxyl radicals (Equations (12) and (13)) [151,169].

$$O_3^- + H^+ \rightarrow HO_3^\bullet \rightarrow\,^\bullet OH + O_2 \qquad (12)$$

$$^\bullet OH + O_3 \rightarrow\,^\bullet OOH + O_2 \qquad (13)$$

The reaction rate and efficiency of the peroxone technique is higher than ozonation alone. However, an excessive amount of H_2O_2 acts as a radical scavenger, so it is necessary to find the optimal dose of H_2O_2 [173]. In [175], the removal of 70 organic micropollutants and microbial contamination by ozonation and peroxone technique in sewage effluent was studies. The peroxone technique significantly decreased bacteria/virus inactivation compared to ozonation and the impact of adding H_2O_2 was insignificant to organic micropollutants removal.

5.2. Photochemical Types of AOPs

5.2.1. Photodecomposition Technique

As the name suggests, photodecomposition techniques are classified as a photochemical AOP. The generation of ROS is usually based on the decomposition of precursors such as ozone, hydrogen peroxide, chlorine or peroxodisulphates via ultraviolet radiation.

The combination of UV (200–300 nm) and H_2O_2 is the most frequently used UV-AOPs at full-scale [176,177]. The presence of UV breaks the O-O bond, resulting in two hydroxyl radicals according to Equation (14). Subsequently, the hydroxyl radical can participate in the degradation of harmful substances or further react with hydrogen peroxide to form a hydroperoxide radical (Equation (15)) [151].

$$H_2O_2 + h\nu \rightarrow 2\,^{\bullet}OH \tag{14}$$

$$^{\bullet}OH + H_2O_2 \rightarrow H_2O + \,^{\bullet}OOH \tag{15}$$

Photodecomposition AOPs based on the UV/H_2O_2 are typically affected by pollutant type and concentration, light transmittance of solution, pH, temperature, and H_2O_2 concentration. H_2O_2 concentration affects the process most significantly. If there is an excess of H_2O_2, there is a decrease in the efficiency of pollutant degradation, because the H_2O_2 also acts as a radical scavenger. If the H_2O_2 concentration is too low, a small number of radicals is formed. For each type of wastewater, a sample is required to find the optimal dose of H_2O_2 [151,178].

Another photodecomposition AOPs technique is used the decomposed of free chlorine by UV (UV/chlorine). In water treatment, free chlorine consists of HOCl and OCl^- and it is usually used as an oxidant and disinfectant. Photolysis of these precursors produces not only ROS but also reactive chlorine species (Equations (16) and (17)).

$$HOCl + h\nu \rightarrow \,^{\bullet}OH + Cl^{\bullet} \tag{16}$$

$$OCl^- + h\nu \rightarrow \,^{-\bullet}O + Cl^{\bullet} \tag{17}$$

Miklos et al. [176] compared different UV–AOPs processes in municipal wastewater treatment. They focused on the removal of trace organic compounds and demonstrated that the combination UV/chlorine is more effective than UV/H_2O_2. Also, UV/chlorine has higher compound selectivity. However, negative oxidation byproducts might be produced by the UV/chloride technique, while negative byproducts have not yet resulted from the UV/H_2O_2 technique [166]. Similar results for total organic carbon (TOC) removal were presented in [179]. TOC removal efficiency was higher by UV/chlorine [179]. According to [180], the UV/chlorine combination is a more cost-effective process than UV/H_2O_2. The benefits of UV/chlorine are higher removal efficiency, lower energy consumption and easy construction [180].

5.2.2. Photocatalysis Technique

In general, photocatalysis is considered as the acceleration of a photoreaction by the presence of a semiconductor catalyst. Photocatalysis is based on the absorption of the photons by the semiconductor. Results of absorption is excitation of electrons (e^-) from the valence band to the conduction band and formed holes (h^+) in the valence band (Equation (18)). The formed holes scavenge molecules of water (Equation (19)) or hydroxide anions (Equation (20)) to generate hydroxyl radicals and the excited electron react with dissolved oxygen in water (Equation (21)) to generate a superoxide radical anion ($O_2^{\bullet -}$) [151,181].

$$semiconductor + h\nu \rightarrow e^- + h^+ \tag{18}$$

$$h^+ + H_2O \rightarrow H^+ + \,^{\bullet}OH \tag{19}$$

$$h^+ + OH^- \rightarrow \,^{\bullet}OH \tag{20}$$

$$e^- + O_2 \rightarrow O_2^{\bullet -} \tag{21}$$

Wide-band gap semiconductors based on metal oxide such as titanium dioxide (TiO_2), zinc oxide (ZnO) or bismuth-based oxides are usually used in wastewater treatment technologies. The preference of ZnO semiconductors is due to its chemical stability, high electrochemical coupling coefficient and high photostability. TiO_2 is the most preferred due to its stability, high activity, non-toxicity, low cost and chemical/biological inertness [151,170,182].

In a study by Martínez-Escudero et al. [183], the degradation of three antibiotics (erythromycin, larithromycin, sulfadiazine) was compared in a wastewater treatment plant effluent by photocatalysis using UV/TiO_2 and UV/ZnO. Results show that using UV/TiO_2 is more effective for the removal of these three antibiotics.

It is possible to use photocatalysis for micro/nanoplastics removal. About 25% removal efficiency was achieved using UV/TiO_2 [184,185].

The photocatalysis technique also includes methods such as the Photo-Fenton process, which is a combination of UV/Fe^{2+}/H_2O_2. In the basic Fenton reaction, sludge containing Fe^{3+} is formed, while in Photo-Fenton, Fe^{3+} is photolytically reduced to Fe^{2+}. Ultimately, this reaction regenerates the Fe^{2+} catalyst [151]. For example, Beyazit and Karaca [186] report that the combination of UV and the Fenton process causes an increase in COD removal efficiency compared to the Fenton process alone.

5.3. Electrochemical Types of AOPs

5.3.1. Anodic Oxidation Technique

The anodic oxidation technique (Figure 6) is the simplest and most popular electrochemical advanced oxidation process [187]. This is a surface-controlled process. Anodic oxidation is characterized by the generation of hydroxyl radicals (•OH) on the anode surface (M) by oxidation with water without using chemical reagents [151]. Based on the oxygen evolution potential, the anodes used in anodic oxidation are divided into active and inactive. The active anodes have low oxygen evolution potential and may interact strongly with the generated free radical and its oxidation to chemisorbed oxygen or superoxide is increased [188]. These anodes are constructed from mixed metal oxides (e.g., oxides of ruthenium, iridium and platinum) [189]. The inactive anode has a higher oxygen release potential and weak interactions with the radicals are formed, thus allowing them to react with pollutants [188]. Due to this fact, inactive anodes are considered as ideal anodes for the mineralization of organic pollutants [190].

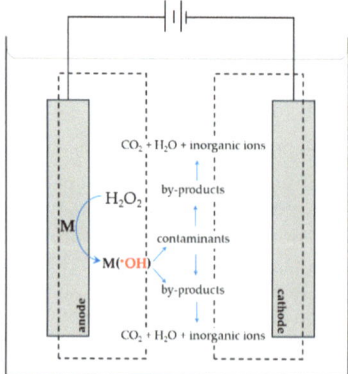

Figure 6. Schematic representation of the mechanism in anodic oxidation [189].

The boron-doped diamond electrode (BDD) is the strongest known inactive anode. It also has good stability and strong corrosion resistance. PbO_2 and SnO_2 are the two most common inactive metal oxide anodes for anoxic oxidation. Their advantages include strong oxidation ability, high oxygen evolution potential, excellent electrical conductivity and low cost [187,190]. Despite many advantages, the negatives probably outweigh the positives for active commercial use. There have been reports about optimization issues of the process and high manufacturing costs connected with the processing of gases and substrate materials which have not yet been solved. Another disadvantage is the worse measurement of samples due to mistakes made by permeate getting between the electrode and epoxy resin, which is often applied to protect the measurement surface [191].

The authors of [192] summarize dye, pharmaceuticals, and pesticide degradation by electro-AOPs. It is shown that anodic oxidation has more than 90% efficiency removal of these pollutants.

5.3.2. Electro-Fenton Technique

The Fenton reaction can be improved by using an electrical source (electrode). The electro-Fenton technique (Figure 7) is based on the continuous electrogeneration of hydrogen peroxide (H_2O_2) via an oxygen cathodic reduction acidic pH value (2.8–3.5). Injected oxygen is from air or pure gas [193]. There is also a reduction of Fe^{3+} on the surface of the cathode, which means that the Fe^{2+} used in the Fenton reaction is continuously regenerated. This maintains the activity of the Fe^{3+}/Fe^{2+} cycle to form homogeneous $^\bullet OH$ with minimum iron hydroxide sludge precipitation [194,195]

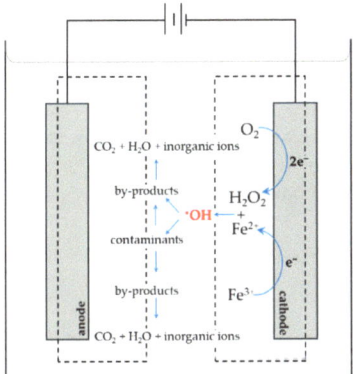

Figure 7. Schematic representation of the mechanism in the electro-Fenton technique [189].

Electro-Fenton is undeniably an efficient method for the degradation of persistent organic contaminants in various types of wastewaters [196].

5.4. Sonochemical Types of AOPs
Sonocatalysis

Sonolysis is considered to be a safe, clean and versatile technique. The principle of sonolysis is using ultrasound waves without the presence of catalysts, to produce radicals in aqueous media (Equations (22) and (23)) [197]. The propagation of ultrasound wave induces the acoustic cavitation, which involve the formation, growth, and violent implosion of micro-bubbles in a liquid [198].

$$H_2O+))) \rightarrow H^\bullet + {}^\bullet OH \qquad (22)$$

$$H^\bullet + O_2+))) \rightarrow {}^\bullet OOH \qquad (23)$$

Sonolysis alone does not produce a sufficient amount of hydroxyl radical. Therefore, sonolysis is often combined with other catalysts (e.g., UV, TiO_2), which increases the efficiency of the process. This process is called sonocatalysis or sonophotocatalysis depending on the used catalyst [151]

In a study by Hayati et al. [199], the combination of LED visible light and ultrasound waves to remove pharmaceutical (specifically sulfathiazole) from wastewater was studied. They confirmed the complete removal of sulfathiazole optimal conditions of sonophotocatalysis. The high efficiency of antibiotics removal was also reported by Calcio Gaufio et al. [200] when they applied ultrasound to conventional treatment processes.

The sono-Fenton technique is a Fenton reaction combined with ultrasound, where cavitation creates more •OH radicals and also accelerates Fe^{2+} regeneration [201]. •OH radicals are formed by sonolysis of water and hydrogen peroxide. The regeneration of Fe^{2+} occurs through the reaction of Fe^{3+} and H• (Equations (24)–(26)) [202].

$$H_2O+))) \rightarrow H^\bullet + {}^\bullet OH \qquad (24)$$

$$H_2O_2+))) \rightarrow 2{}^\bullet OH \qquad (25)$$

$$Fe^{3+} + H^\bullet \rightarrow Fe^{2+} + H^+ \qquad (26)$$

The benefits of the ultrasound and the Fenton reagents are aggregated, allowing a higher generation of HO• and more effective degradation of organic pollutants [202].

6. Disinfection

To overcome water shortages, reused treated wastewater effluent for crop irrigation is counted as one of the most optimal solutions [203]. Aside from physical and chemical pollution of the wastewaters, biological pollution is not to be taken lightly. Therefore, treated wastewater without additional quaternary treatment, might serve as a water-borne pathogenic microorganisms spawning ground. Due to this fact, microbial contamination has become a problem endangering public health. Disinfection should be the last step in wastewater treatment to ensure the effectiveness of the applied methods. Regardless of the disinfection nature, whether being physical or chemical, present organic and inorganic substances can react and consume applied disinfectants or physically affect the applied processes [204,205].

6.1. Chemical Disinfection

6.1.1. Sodium Hypochlorite

Use of sodium hypochlorite (NaClO) is widely spread in water treatment works. It is not technologically demanding; its disinfection properties last for a long period of time and it has a low dosing cost [206,207]. Compared to gaseous chlorine and calcium hypochlorite, NaClO is more stable. The mechanism of chlorine disinfection lies in breaking chemical bonds such as proteins and highly active enzymes on the outer layer of the bacteria. The reaction happens with the addition of chlorine gas in water and it undergoes hydrolysis as shown in Equations (27) and (28):

$$Cl_2 + H_2O \leftrightarrow H^+ + Cl^- + HOCl \qquad (27)$$

$$2NaClO + H_2O \leftrightarrow HOCl + 2NaCl + H^+ \qquad (28)$$

Due to the neutral nature of HClO, it attacks negatively charged parts of bacteria and enters inside bacteria easily, while negatively charged ions of ClO− serve as the main disinfectant at pHs higher than 7.5 [208]. The used phrase "free available chlorine" accounts for HClO and ClO−-. To study the disinfection ability, a solution of NaClO was prepared from stock solution (Sigma-Aldrich Saint-Louis, Missouri, USA) with an active chlorine ppm concentration range of 40,000–50,000. Solutions were standardized with diethylphenylenediamine (DPD). Studies about NaClO disinfection of secondary effluent concluded that acidic conditions of pH = 4 made chlorination most efficient. They monitored a real wastewater treatment plant and temperature fluctuations during the year had quite a significant effect on water pH. Rising temperatures during the summer months affected pH with the opposite trend and knowing that the correlation between pH and temperature was disproportionate, we can conclude an effect of low temperatures on pH. The experiment noted more than 3-log removal of coliforms at doses as low as 1.5 ppm of NaClO. Removal of total coliforms varied with dose and time. Log reduction of 0.45-log with a dose of 0.5 mg/L and a contact time of 15 min was the worst result, while a dose of 2.5–3 ppm over 15 min achieved 7.71-log reduction. Bacteria growth was noted to be asymptotical and at the concentration with the highest removal of bacteria, their growth followed a declining trend which confirmed their removal [209].

6.1.2. Peracetic Acid

Peracetic acid (PAA) is generally sold as a mixture of PAA, acetic acid (PA), hydrogen peroxide (H_2O_2) and water. At standard conditions, standard reduction potential of PAA is equal to 1.96 V, which is higher than regular disinfectants like Cl_2, HClO, ClO_2 and H_2O_2. The first use of PAA was noted in the early 1980s. PAA has a generally low risk of creating harmful substances and has high pathogen inactivation across species [210,211].

Studies proved that a concentration time of 30–60 mg·min/L seems to remove most of the enteric bacteria such as *E. coli*, total coliforms, and *E. faecium*, etc. On the other hand, Gram-positive intestinal bacterium *Enterococcus* spp., had inactivation efficiency 1–2 log lower compared to *Enterococci* or *E. coli*. For multidrug-resistant *E. coli*, 25.1 mg·min/L of PAA was needed to reach 4-log reduction. Removal efficiency regarding spores is concerning and unacceptable and should have attention for more studies. Reaction species generated during disinfection are hydroxyl radicals, peracetyl radical and also methyl radical which could be part of the degradation process [205,212]. The disinfection mechanism of PAA relies on reacting with sulfur and sulfhydryl bonds.

6.1.3. Performic Acid

Compared to PAA, performic acid (PFA) shows better inactivation abilities for *Escherichia coli*, *fecal coliform*, and *Enterococci*. In a bioreactor, inactivation efficiency of bacteria descended in the order of PFA, chlorine, and PAA [213].

For example, to achieve inactivation of *E. coli* and *Enterococci* in a sewer overflow, a PFA dose of 2–4 mg/L and 20 min of time was needed for a 3-log inactivation. The PAA time was 18 times longer for similar result. Regarding disinfection of the municipal secondary effluent, the concentration time for PFA was recorded to be 1.5 and 3.5 mg·min/L to achieve 1-log inactivation of *E. coli* and *Enterococci*. Disinfection of the tertiary effluent with PFA at a dose of 1.5 mg/L, which was already treated by filtration, showed inactivation of *E. coli* and *Enterococci* by 3-log and 2.8-log within 2 and 10 min, respectively. Additionally, degradation products of PFA are relatively harmless and do not pose a serious threat to water bodies [205].

6.2. Physical Means of Disinfection

6.2.1. UV Irradiation

Its disinfection ability affects a large spectrum of microorganisms with great efficiency, while not having the disadvantage of creating harmful byproducts which could greatly affect the receiving body. The wavelength range of UV irradiation lies between 10 and 400 nm. The principle of UV disinfection is to destroy the ability of microorganisms to reproduce by altering or degrading genetical material such as DNA and RNA (Figure 8) [214,215].

Negative aspects of UV disinfection are photoreactions of microorganisms, which may cause in certain cases a rise of active *E. coli* cells. This was observed at radiation conditions of 5 mJ/cm^2. Another important concern is the presence of other pollutants such as chroma, turbidity and organic matter. Reported results inform us that turbidity less than 4 NTU does not affect UV disinfection to a large extent. The problem arises when turbidity becomes higher than 4 NTU [214]. Additionally, the latest studies confirm that microplastics affect disinfection with UV in a negative way. The first research paper experimented with polyethylene and polyvinyl chloride microplastics, while the tested bacteria were multidrug-resistant *E. coli* and *Enterococci* in pure water with a pH around 6.0. A microplastics-free sample showed the expected inactivation trend of bacteria while for water containing microplastics, the inactivation was slower or completely halted. It is speculated that microplastics can either absorb UV light or bacteria grow on the particles which protect them. While microplastic-free samples achieved max log removal with UV fluence of 10 mJ/cm^2 and 15 mJ/cm^2 for *E. coli* and *Enterococci*, respectively, it was shown that there was almost no log removal for all microplastic types after application of the mentioned UV fluences [216]. The second research paper tested polyethylene affecting UV/H_2O_2, also in real secondary treated urban wastewater. The used equipment was a UVC 80 W lamp that emitted light with a wavelength of 254 nm. The dose of H_2O_2 was 30 mg/L and the concentration of microplastics were 0.25 g/L, 0.5 g/L, and 1.0 g/L. Log reduction according to time of disinfection is shown in Figure 9a,b. Note the efficiency of UV disinfection without microplastics, in this case one colony forming unit per 100 mL was achieved [204].

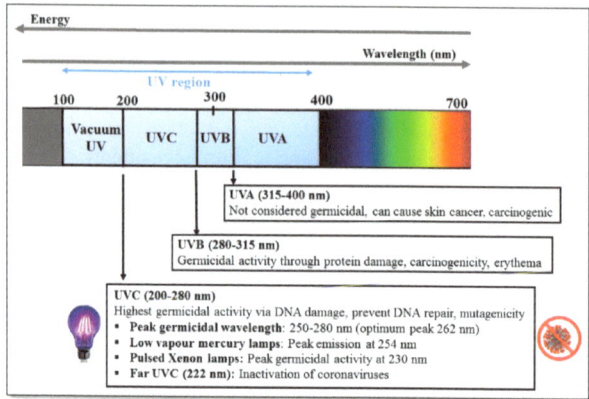

Figure 8. Spectrum of light and its disinfection capacities [214].

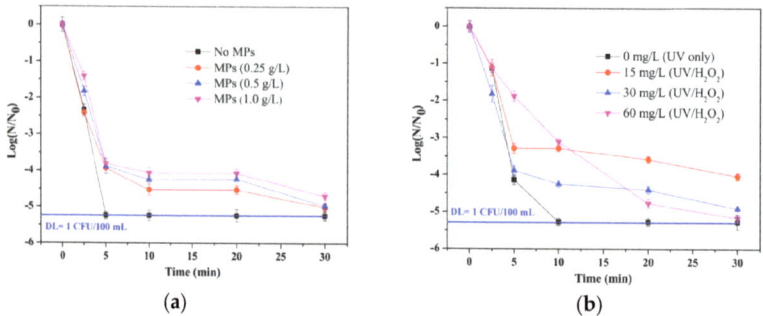

Figure 9. In the two graphs, there is shown dependence of log reduction of microorganisms from time. In graph (**a**) we see microplastics affecting ozonation and in graph (**b**), UV/H_2O_2 [204].

6.2.2. Sonolysis

The use of ultrasound (US) has been used for a long time in wastewater pollutant removal. Ultrasound is safe to use, has good distribution along water media and does not produce unwanted products. By applying a frequency of 16 kHz–100 MHz, we are able to inactivate microorganisms. In the wastewater, microbubbles are created in a process called cavitation, which triggers chemical reactions. The principle of disinfection by sonolysis depends on the type of radicals [217–219].

6.3. Use of AOPs as a Disinfection Method

Hydroxyl radicals (HO•) have been observed to destroy enzymes such as lysozyme and ribonuclease. Additionally, alteration of essential compounds takes place, amino acids are oxidized, modifications happen to sulfur groups, and crosslinking occurs which has the ability to make microorganisms to survive. Useful auto-reactions happen when unsaturated fatty acids are oxidized, which transform into lipid-peroxyl radicals [219].

Sulfate radicals ($SO_4^{\bullet-}$) mostly react with organics, which can offer many electrons. The negative charge present in $SO_4^{\bullet-}$ creates repulsion with the microorganism surface. Reported results of microorganism inactivation informs us about the generation of $SO_4^{\bullet-}$ from the peroxydisulfate system by natural magnetic pyrrhotite. Dissolution of cell casing is followed by degradation of intracellular substrates and the genome [219].

Superoxide radicals ($O_2^{\bullet-}$) are selective and have long-distance diffusion. $O_2^{\bullet-}$ radicals marginally affect the growth of *E. coli* while being at a low steady-state concentration of 1.5 nM. Compared to other ROS, it has higher efficiency. Again, the negative charge on the active substance generates repulsion with the cellular membrane. Moreover, $O_2^{\bullet-}$ could not react with peptides, carbohydrates, lipids and nucleic acids directly. Radicals were generated intracellularly and seemed to block biosynthetic enzymes with electrostatic interactions and acts selectively [219].

Singlet oxygen affects chains of amino acids, peptides, and proteins. $^1O_2$ attacks and destroys parts of tyrosine, tryptophan, and cysteine. The ability to disrupt enzymes makes it useful, even though it has quite a low redox capacity [219].

6.4. Electrochemical Disinfection

Electrochemical disinfection (ED) uses an external power supply to inactivate microorganisms present in the water. From a technical standpoint, it works based on direct oxidation, indirect oxidation and electric fields. Technologically, the effluent flows across electrochemical cell where the disinfection happens. Bacteria inactivation for different types of wastewaters or even tap waters is possible to a large extent completely. We need to remember that various conditions are applied at the studied inactivation potentials [220,221].

Direct oxidation happens when a multi-electron reaction is causing degradation of the proteins and functional groups inside a cell membrane. For this to happen, microorganisms need to get directly on the anode's surface. Applying low voltages causes dehydration and depression of the cells, while in a case of higher voltages, lipid peroxidation happens. Chain reactions take place, degrading microorganism function [220].

Indirect oxidation works by mediating compounds by reacting with an anode to produce intermediates which have oxidizing potential. Application of a milliampere (mA) electrical current produces reactive agents, which include reactive oxygen and chlorine [220,222].

The electric field can alone affect microorganism functions and in the end, completely inactivate bacteria. The mechanism for electrical field disinfection lies in membrane destruction and oxidative stress. Triggered reactions in lipids and modifications in membrane proteins affect its permeability [220].

7. Assessment of Reviewed Treatment Methods

The advantages and disadvantages of reviewed treatment methods are summarized in Table 4. The provided information is based on the recent literature and may be helpful to select suitable methods for wastewater quaternary treatment. The table mainly gives the qualitative assessment of reviewed methods and also gives information on which method is or is not commercially available. From an economic point of view, the reviewed methods were assessed as relatively low or high financial costs.

Table 4. Assessment of reviewed treatment methods [24–204].

Method	Advantages	Disadvantages
Sand filtration	Chemicals free, simple in operation, no harmful byproducts, relatively low financial costs, relatively well known and commercially available.	Very low removal efficiency for micropollutants and other contaminants, backwash is needed, and disposal of used sand.

Table 4. Cont.

Method	Advantages	Disadvantages
Membrane filtration	Well-defined and high removal efficiency of micropollutants, capable of removal of other contaminants and microorganisms, no toxic solid waste, chemicals free, no harmful byproducts and commercially available.	High energy demand, membrane fouling, disposal of concentrate, high water rejection, corrosive nature of the produced water, high-tech operation and maintenance, and relatively high financial costs.
Coagulation	Simple in operation, no harmful byproducts, relatively low financial costs, relatively well known and common chemicals are available.	Low removal efficiency for micropollutants, large amount of chemical sludge, introduction of coagulant salts in the aqueous phase, and sedimentation and filtration is needed.
Adsorption	High removal efficiency of micropollutants and other contaminants, simple in operation, chemical and sludge free, no harmful byproducts, relatively well known and commercially available.	Lower efficiency removal in the presence of NOMs, regeneration is needed, disposal of used carbon, production of toxic solid waste, desorption of sorbed contaminants, and relatively high financial costs.
Ozonation and other AOPs	Novel and promising technique, high removal efficiency of micropollutants, other contaminants and microorganisms, sludge free, ozonation is well known and commercially available.	High energy consumption, formation of harmful byproducts, interference of radical scavengers, strong developing is needed, focus on effective design and operation parameters is needed, other AOPs are not commercially available, and relatively high financial costs.
Chemical disinfection	Simple in operation, high removal efficiency of microorganisms, no toxic solid waste is produced, relatively low financial costs, relatively well known and commercially available.	Formation of harmful byproducts, not chemicals free, corrosive effects, requires understanding of principles of chemical disinfection, And does not prevent stored water from recontamination.
Physical disinfection (UV)	Simple in operation, high removal efficiency of microorganisms, no toxic solid waste, no harmful byproducts, chemicals free, relatively well known and commercially available.	Requires clear water, does not prevent stored water from recontamination, and relatively high financial costs.

8. Conclusions

- The existing literature is dominated by water scarcity and water stress, which are caused by rapid urban expansion, development of the world economy, demographic changes, deforestation and climate change.
- According to the predictions, the water scarcity and drought events are likely to be more frequent in the future. Due to these facts, the missing water resources must be replaced by a suitable water source.
- Quaternary treated urban wastewater has been proposed as an alternative water source for irrigation in Europe. For quaternary treatment, various additional processes

can be used, such as filtration, coagulation, adsorption, ozonation, advanced oxidation processes and disinfection. The choice of the specific process depends on various factors, including wastewater characteristics and treatment goals. According to the existing literature, we recommend for quaternary urban wastewater treatment, a combination of coagulation, membrane filtration (UF or NF) and UV disinfection. These processes are relatively well known and commercially available with high removal efficiencies of micropollutants and microorganisms.

- The quaternary treated wastewater reuse has the following innovativeness in the field of water management: an efficient use of water resources by citizens, industry and agriculture; promoting water saving and reuse; water-efficient technologies in all sectors; fitting in the context of the 2020 Circular Economy Action Plan; development of the huge potential for safe wastewater reuse in line with the new EU Regulation on water reuse; contribution to reduce greenhouse gas emissions; reduction the use of additional fertilizers resulting in savings for the environment, farmers and wastewater treatment; and the creation of green jobs in the water-related industry.
- Barriers to the reuse of quaternary treated urban wastewater are well characterized, and they mainly include concerns about microbial risk and presence of micropollutants; high investments for modernization of urban wastewater treatment plants; and a lack of financial incentives for quaternary treated wastewater reuse in agriculture.
- This review article serves as a basis for knowledge development, provides a comprehensive understanding of the current state of quaternary treatment of urban wastewater for its reuse, creates guidelines for practice, has the capacity to engender new ideas and serve as the grounds for future research directions. It helps researchers to identify key themes and concepts, evaluate the strengths and weaknesses of previous studies and determine areas where further research is needed.

Author Contributions: Conceptualization, R.Z., J.J., B.J., N.Š. and J.D.; R.Z., J.J., B.J. and N.Š.; software, R.Z., J.J., B.J. and N.Š.; validation, R.Z., J.J., B.J., N.Š. and J.D.; formal analysis, R.Z., J.J., B.J., N.Š. and J.D.; investigation, R.Z., J.J., B.J., N.Š. and J.D.; resources, R.Z., J.J., B.J. and N.Š.; data curation, R.Z., J.J., B.J. and N.Š.; writing—original draft preparation, R.Z., J.J., B.J., N.Š. and J.D.; writing—review and editing, R.Z., J.J., B.J. and N.Š.; visualization, R.Z., J.J., B.J. and N.Š.; supervision, R.Z.; project administration, R.Z., J.J., B.J. and N.Š.; funding acquisition, R.Z. and J.D. All authors have read and agreed to the published version of the manuscript.

Funding: This research was funded by the Slovak Research and Development Agency under the contracts No. APVV-22-0292; by the project BIN SGS02_2021_001 funded under the Norway Grants 2014–2021 and co-funded by state budget of the Slovak Republic; and by a Grant Scheme for the Support of the Young Researchers Under the Conditions of the SUT in Bratislava.

Data Availability Statement: Data are contained within the article.

Conflicts of Interest: The authors declare no conflicts of interest.

Abbreviations

•OH	hydroxyl radical
•OOH	hydroperoxide radical
AOPs	advanced oxidation processes
ARB&ARGs	antibiotic resistant bacteria and genes
BAC	biological activated carbon
BDD	boron-doped diamond electrode
CEC	contaminants of emerging concern
COD	chemical oxygen demand
DBD	dielectric barrier discharge
DBP	disinfection byproducts
DBPFP	disinfection byproducts formation potential
DNA	deoxyribonucleic acid

DOC	dissolved organic carbon
DPD	diethylphenylenediamine
e^-	electrons
ED	electrochemical disinfection
EU	European Union
GAC	granular activated charcoal
GDP	gross domestic product
GO	graphene oxide
h^+	holes
HAA	haloacetic acid
HAN	haloacetonitril
HK	haloketone
HOCl	hypochloride
IUPAC	international union of pure and applied chemistry
LED	light-emitting diode
MBR	membrane bioreactor
MF	microfiltration
MP	microplastic
NF	nanofiltration
$NO^\bullet$	nitric oxide
NOMs	natural organic matters
NTU	nephelometric turbidity unit
$O_2^{\bullet-}$	superoxide anion radical
OMP	organic micropollutant
PAA	peracetic acid
PAC	poly aluminum chloride
PBT	persistent, bioaccumulative and toxic
PE	polyethylene
PFA	performic acid
PFC	poly ferric chloride
PFO	pseudo-first order
PFS	poly ferrous sulphate
PMT	persistent, mobile and toxic
PSF	polysulfone
PSiAS	poly-aluminum silicate sulphate
PSiTS	poly-titanium silicate sulphate
PSO	pseudo-second order
PVC	polyvinyl chloride
RNA	ribonucleic acid
RO	reverse osmosis
$RO^\bullet$	alkoxyl radical
$ROO^\bullet$	peroxyl radical
ROOH	organic hydroperoxides
ROS	reactive oxygen species
$ROS^\bullet$	sulphonyl radicals
$RS^\bullet$	thiyl radicals
RSF	rapid sand filtration
$RSOO^\bullet$	thiyl peroxyl
SDBS	sodium dodecyl benzenesulfonate
SHE	standard hydrogen electrode
$SO_4^{\bullet-}$	sulphate radicals
SUV_A	specific ultraviolet absorbance
TCNM	trichloronitromethane
THM	trihalomethane
TOC	total organic carbon
UF	ultrafiltration
US	ultrasound
UV	ultraviolet

UVA$_{254}$	absorbance of light in the UV part of the light spectrum at 254 nm
WWTP	wastewater treatment plant

References

1. Khan, S.A.R.; Ponce, P.; Yu, Z.; Golpîra, H.; Mathew, M. Environmental technology and wastewater treatment: Strategies to achieve environmental sustainability. *Chemosphere* **2022**, *286*, 131532. [CrossRef]
2. Falco, C.; Galeotti, M.; Olper, A. Climate change and migration: Is agriculture the main channel? *Glob. Environ. Change* **2019**, *59*, 101995. [CrossRef]
3. International Decade for Action: Water for Life—United Nations. Available online: http://www.un.org/waterforlifedecade/scarcity.shtml (accessed on 15 June 2024).
4. The United Nations World Water Development Report 2020: Water and Climate Change—UNESCO. Available online: https://unesdoc.unesco.org/ark:/48223/pf0000372985 (accessed on 15 June 2024).
5. Capocelli, M.; Piemonte, V. Technologies for Water Reuse: Current status and future challenges. *Water* **2021**, *13*, 832. [CrossRef]
6. The United Nations World Water Development Report 2017—UNESCO. Available online: https://www.unwater.org/publications/un-world-water-development-report-2017 (accessed on 15 June 2024).
7. Water in Agriculture—World Bank Group. Available online: https://www.worldbank.org/en/news/infographic/2023/07/26/water-in-agriculture (accessed on 15 June 2024).
8. Kesari, K.K.; Soni, R.; Jamal, Q.M.S.; Tripathi, J.; Lal, J.A.; Jha, N.K.; Siddiqui, M.H.; Kumar, P.; Tripathi, V.; Ruokolainen, J. Wastewater treatment and Reuse: A review of its applications and health implications. *Water Air Soil Pollut.* **2021**, *232*, 208. [CrossRef]
9. Proposal for a Revised Urban Wastewater Treatment Directive—European Commission. Available online: https://environment.ec.europa.eu/publications/proposal-revised-urban-wastewater-treatment-directive_en (accessed on 15 June 2024).
10. Wang, H.; Wang, J.; Yu, X. Wastewater irrigation and crop yield: A meta-analysis. *J. Integr. Agric.* **2022**, *21*, 1215–1224. [CrossRef]
11. Rizzo, L.; Gernjak, W.; Krzeminski, P.; Malato, S.; McArdell, C.S.; Perez, J.A.S.; Schaar, H.; Fatta-Kassinos, D. Best available technologies and treatment trains to address current challenges in urban wastewater reuse for irrigation of crops in EU countries. *Sci. Total Environ.* **2020**, *710*, 136312. [CrossRef]
12. Hristov, J.; Barreiro-Hurle, J.; Salputra, G.; Blanco, M.; Witzke, P. Reuse of treated water in European agriculture: Potential to address water scarcity under climate change. *Agric. Water Manag.* **2021**, *251*, 106872. [CrossRef]
13. Duckett, D.; Troldborg, M.; Hendry, S.; Cousin, H. Making waves: Promoting municipal water reuse without a prevailing scarcity driver. *Water Res.* **2024**, *249*, 120965. [CrossRef]
14. Bilal, M.; Ashraf, S.S.; Barceló, D.; Iqbal, H.M. Biocatalytic degradation/redefining removal fate of pharmaceutically active compounds and antibiotics in the aquatic environment. *Sci. Total Environ.* **2019**, *691*, 1190–1211. [CrossRef]
15. Bilal, M.; Iqbal, H.M.; Barceló, D. Persistence of pesticides-based contaminants in the environment and their effective degradation using laccase-assisted biocatalytic systems. *Sci. Total Environ.* **2019**, *695*, 133896. [CrossRef]
16. Luo, Y.; Guo, W.; Ngo, H.H.; Nghiem, L.D.; Hai, F.I.; Zhang, J.; Liang, S.; Wang, X.C. A review on the occurrence of micropollutants in the aquatic environment and their fate and removal during wastewater treatment. *Sci. Total Environ.* **2014**, *473–474*, 619–641. [CrossRef] [PubMed]
17. Deng, S.; Yan, X.; Zhu, Q.; Liao, C. The utilization of reclaimed water: Possible risks arising from waterborne contaminants. *Env. Pollut* **2019**, *254*, 113020. [CrossRef] [PubMed]
18. Vojtěchovská Šrámková, M.; Diaz-Sosa, V.; Wanner, J. Experimental verification of tertiary treatment process in achieving effluent quality required by wastewater reuse standards. *J. Water Process Eng.* **2018**, *22*, 41–45. [CrossRef]
19. Regulation (EU) 2020/741 of the European Parliament and of the Council of 25 May 2020 on Minimum Requirements for Water Reuse. Available online: https://eur-lex.europa.eu/legal-content/EN/TXT/PDF/?uri=CELEX:32020R0741 (accessed on 15 June 2024).
20. The EU and the United Nations—Common Goals for a Sustainable Future. Available online: https://commission.europa.eu/strategy-and-policy/sustainable-development-goals/eu-and-united-nations-common-goals-sustainable-future_en (accessed on 15 June 2024).
21. Faour-Klingbeil, D.; Todd, E.C.D. The impact of climate change on treated and untreated wastewater use for agriculture, especially in arid regions: A Review. *Foodborne Pathog. Dis.* **2018**, *15*, 61–72. [CrossRef] [PubMed]
22. Gray, N.F. Filtration methods. In *Microbiology of Waterborne Diseases*; Academic Press: Cambridge, MA, USA, 2014; pp. 631–650. [CrossRef]
23. Cescon, A.; Jiang, J.Q. Filtration process and alternative filter media material in water treatment. *Water* **2020**, *12*, 3377. [CrossRef]
24. Guchi, E. Review on slow sand filtration in removing microbial contamination and particles from drinking water. *Am. J. Food Nutr.* **2015**, *3*, 47–55. [CrossRef]
25. Jaeel, A.J.; Abdulkathum, S. Sustainable pollutants removal from wastewater using sand filter: A review. In Proceedings of the 2018 International Conference on Advance of Sustainable Engineering and its Application (ICASEA) IEEE, Wasit, Iraq, 14–15 March 2018; pp. 179–183. [CrossRef]
26. Verma, S.; Daverey, A.; Sharma, A. Slow sand filtration for water and wastewater treatment—A review. *Environ. Technol. Rev.* **2017**, *6*, 47–58. [CrossRef]

27. Sabale, R.; Mujawar, S. Improved rapid sand filter for performance enhancement. *Int. J. Sci. Res.* **2014**, *3*, 1031–1033.
28. Hakami, M.W.; Alkhudhiri, A.; Al-Batty, S.; Zacharof, M.P.; Maddy, J.; Hilal, N. Ceramic microfiltration membranes in wastewater treatment: Filtration behavior, fouling and prevention. *Membranes* **2020**, *10*, 248. [CrossRef]
29. Cevallos-Mendoza, J.; Amorim, C.G.; Rodríguez-Díaz, J.M.; Montenegro, M.D.C.B. Removal of contaminants from water by membrane filtration: A review. *Membranes* **2022**, *12*, 570. [CrossRef]
30. Melin, T.; Jefferson, B.; Bixio, D.; Thoeye, C.; De Wilde, W.; De Koning, J.; van der Graaf, J.; Wintgens, T. Membrane bioreactor technology for wastewater treatment and reuse. *Desalination* **2006**, *187*, 271–282. [CrossRef]
31. Al-Asheh, S.; Bagheri, M.; Aidan, A. Membrane bioreactor for wastewater treatment: A review. *Case Stud. Chem. Environ. Eng.* **2021**, *4*, 100109. [CrossRef]
32. Goswami, L.; Kumar, R.V.; Borah, S.N.; Manikandan, N.A.; Pakshirajan, K.; Pugazhenthi, G. Membrane bioreactor and integrated membrane bioreactor systems for micropollutant removal from wastewater: A review. *J. Water Process Eng.* **2018**, *26*, 314–328. [CrossRef]
33. Rajbongshi, A.; Gogoi, S.B. Microfiltration, ultrafiltration and nanofiltration as a post-treatment of biological treatment process with references to oil field produced water of Moran oilfield of Assam. *Pet. Res.* **2024**, *9*, 143–154. [CrossRef]
34. Wang, J.; Cahyadi, A.; Wu, B.; Pee, W.; Fane, A.G.; Chew, J.W. The roles of particles in enhancing membrane filtration: A review. *J. Membr. Sci.* **2020**, *595*, 117570. [CrossRef]
35. Sembiring, E.; Fajar, M.; Handajani, M. Performance of rapid sand filter–single media to remove microplastics. *Water Supply* **2021**, *21*, 2273–2284. [CrossRef]
36. Wolff, S.; Weber, F.; Kerpen, J.; Winklhofer, M.; Engelhart, M.; Barkmann, L. Elimination of microplastics by downstream sand filters in wastewater treatment. *Water* **2020**, *13*, 33. [CrossRef]
37. Bayo, J.; López-Castellanos, J.; Olmos, S. Membrane bioreactor and rapid sand filtration for the removal of microplastics in an urban wastewater treatment plant. *Mar. Pollut. Bull.* **2020**, *156*, 111211. [CrossRef]
38. Conesa, J.A.; Ortuño, N. Reuse of water contaminated by microplastics, the effectiveness of filtration processes: A review. *Energies* **2022**, *15*, 2432. [CrossRef]
39. Goswami, K.P.; Pugazhenthi, G. Credibility of polymeric and ceramic membrane filtration in the removal of bacteria and virus from water: A review. *J. Environ. Manag.* **2020**, *268*, 110583. [CrossRef]
40. Marsono, B.D.; Yuniarto, A.; Purnomo, A.; Soedjono, E.S. Comparison performances of microfiltration and rapid sand filter operated in water treatment plant. *IOP Conf. Ser. Earth Environ. Sci.* **2022**, *1111*, 012048. [CrossRef]
41. Kacprzyńska-Gołacka, J.; Kowalik-Klimczak, A.; Woskowicz, E.; Wieciński, P.; Łożyńska, M.; Sowa, S.; Barszcz, W.; Kaźmierczak, B. Microfiltration Membranes Modified with Silver Oxide by Plasma Treatment. *Membranes* **2020**, *10*, 133. [CrossRef] [PubMed]
42. Maryam, B.; Buscio, V.; Odabasi, S.U.; Buyukgungor, H. A study on behavior, interaction and rejection of Paracetamol, Diclofenac and Ibuprofen (PhACs) from wastewater by nanofiltration membranes. *Environ. Technol. Innov.* **2020**, *18*, 100641. [CrossRef]
43. Couto, C.F.; Santos, A.V.; Amaral, M.C.S.; Lange, L.C.; de Andrade, L.H.; Foureaux, A.F.S.; Fernandes, B.S. Assessing potential of nanofiltration, reverse osmosis and membrane distillation drinking water treatment for pharmaceutically active compounds (PhACs) removal. *J. Water Process Eng.* **2020**, *33*, 101029. [CrossRef]
44. Vieira, W.T.; de Farias, M.B.; Spaolonzi, M.P.; da Silva, M.G.C.; Vieira, M.G.A. Removal of endocrine disruptors in waters by adsorption, membrane filtration and biodegradation. A review. *Environ. Chem. Lett.* **2020**, *18*, 1113–1143. [CrossRef]
45. Zhang, J.; Nguyen, M.N.; Li, Y.; Yang, C.; Schäfer, A.I. Steroid hormone micropollutant removal from water with activated carbon fiber-ultrafiltration composite membranes. *J. Hazard. Mater.* **2020**, *391*, 122020. [CrossRef]
46. Nakada, N.; Shinohara, H.; Murata, A.; Kiri, K.; Managaki, S.; Sato, N.; Takada, H. Removal of selected pharmaceuticals and personal care products (PPCPs) and endocrine-disrupting chemicals (EDCs) during sand filtration and ozonation at a municipal sewage treatment plant. *Water Res.* **2007**, *41*, 4373–4382. [CrossRef]
47. Jatoi, A.S.; Hashmi, Z.; Adriyani, R.; Yuniarto, A.; Mazari, S.A.; Akhter, F.; Mubarak, N.M. Recent trends and future challenges of pesticide removal techniques—A comprehensive review. *J. Environ. Chem. Eng.* **2021**, *9*, 105571. [CrossRef]
48. Mukherjee, A.; Mehta, R.; Saha, S.; Bhattacharya, A.; Biswas, P.K.; Kole, R.K. Removal of multiple pesticide residues from water by low-pressure thin-film composite membrane. *Appl. Water Sci.* **2020**, *10*, 244. [CrossRef]
49. Wang, Z.; Zhang, B.; Fang, C.; Liu, Z.; Fang, J.; Zhu, L. Macroporous membranes doped with micro-mesoporous β-cyclodextrin polymers for ultrafast removal of organic micropollutants from water. *Carbohydr. Polym.* **2019**, *222*, 114970. [CrossRef]
50. Qasem, N.A.A.; Mohammed, R.H.; Lawal, D.U. Removal of heavy metal ions from wastewater: A comprehensive and critical review. *npj Clean Water* **2021**, *4*, 36. [CrossRef]
51. Qi, Y.; Zhu, L.; Shen, X.; Sotto, A.; Gao, C.; Shen, J. Polyethyleneimine-modified original positive charged nanofiltration membrane: Removal of heavy metal ions and dyes. *Sep. Purif. Technol.* **2019**, *222*, 117–124. [CrossRef]
52. Moradi, G.; Zinadini, S.; Rajabi, L.; Derakhshan, A.A. Removal of heavy metal ions using a new high performance nanofiltration membrane modified with curcumin boehmite nanoparticles. *Chem. Eng. J.* **2020**, *390*, 124546. [CrossRef]
53. Rezaee, R.; Nasseri, S.; Mahvi, A.H.; Nabizadeh, R.; Mousavi, S.A.; Rashidi, A.; Jafari, A.; Nazmara, S. Fabrication and characterization of a polysulfone-graphene oxide nanocomposite membrane for arsenate rejection from water. *J. Environ. Health Sci. Eng.* **2015**, *13*, 61. [CrossRef] [PubMed]
54. Xiang, H.; Min, X.; Tang, C.J.; Sillanpää, M.; Zhao, F. Recent advances in membrane filtration for heavy metal removal from wastewater: A mini review. *J. Water Process Eng.* **2022**, *49*, 103023. [CrossRef]

55. Saleh, T.A.; Mustaqeem, M.; Khaled, M. Water treatment technologies in removing heavy metal ions from wastewater: A review. *Environ. Nanotechnol. Monit. Manag.* **2022**, *17*, 100617. [CrossRef]
56. El-Taweel, R.M.; Mohamed, N.; Alrefaey, K.A.; Husien, S.; Abdel-Aziz, A.B.; Salim, A.I.; Mostafa, N.G.; Said, L.A.; Fahim, I.R.; Radwan, A.G. A review of coagulation explaining its definition, mechanism, coagulant types, and optimization models; RSM, and ANN. *Curr. Res. Green Sustain. Chem.* **2023**, *6*, 100358. [CrossRef]
57. Zahmatkesh, S.; Karimian, M.; Chen, Z.; Ni, B.J. Combination of coagulation and adsorption technologies for advanced wastewater treatment for potable water reuse: By ANN, NSGA-II, and RSM. *J. Environ. Manag.* **2024**, *349*, 119429. [CrossRef]
58. Gautam, S.; Saini, G. Use of natural coagulants for industrial wastewater treatment. *Glob. J. Environ. Sci. Manag.* **2020**, *6*, 553–578. [CrossRef]
59. Precious Sibiya, N.; Rathilal, S.; Kweinor Tetteh, E. Coagulation treatment of wastewater: Kinetics and natural coagulant evaluation. *Molecules* **2021**, *26*, 698. [CrossRef]
60. Bahrodin, M.B.; Zaidi, N.S.; Hussein, N.; Sillanpää, M.; Prasetyo, D.D.; Syafiuddin, A. Recent advances on coagulation-based treatment of wastewater: Transition from chemical to natural coagulant. *Curr. Pollut. Rep.* **2021**, *7*, 379–391. [CrossRef]
61. Sonal, S.; Mishra, B.K. Role of coagulation/flocculation technology for the treatment of dye wastewater: Trend and future aspects. In *Water Pollution and Management Practices*; Springer: Singapore, 2021; pp. 303–331. [CrossRef]
62. Abujazar, M.S.S.; Karaağaç, S.U.; Amr, S.S.A.; Alazaiza, M.Y.; Bashir, M.J. Recent advancement in the application of hybrid coagulants in coagulation-flocculation of wastewater: A review. *J. Clean. Prod.* **2022**, *345*, 131133. [CrossRef]
63. Zhao, C.; Zhou, J.; Yan, Y.; Yang, L.; Xing, G.; Li, H.; Wu, P.; Wang, M.; Zheng, H. Application of coagulation/flocculation in oily wastewater treatment: A review. *Sci. Total Environ.* **2021**, *765*, 142795. [CrossRef]
64. Tang, W.; Li, H.; Fei, L.; Wei, B.; Zhou, T.; Zhang, H. The removal of microplastics from water by coagulation: A comprehensive review. *Sci. Total Environ.* **2022**, *851*, 158224. [CrossRef]
65. Hjorth, M.; Jørgensen, B.U. Polymer flocculation mechanism in animal slurry established by charge neutralization. *Water Res.* **2012**, *46*, 1045–1051. [CrossRef]
66. Sukmana, H.; Bellahsen, N.; Pantoja, F.; Hodur, C. Adsorption and coagulation in wastewater treatment–Review. *Prog. Agric. Eng. Sci.* **2021**, *17*, 49–68. [CrossRef]
67. Kurniawan, S.B.; Abdullah, S.R.S.; Imron, M.F.; Said, N.S.M.; Ismail, N.I.; Hasan, H.A.; Othman, A.R.; Purwanti, I.F. Challenges and opportunities of biocoagulant/bioflocculant application for drinking water and wastewater treatment and its potential for sludge recovery. *Int. J. Environ. Res. Public Health* **2020**, *17*, 9312. [CrossRef]
68. Al-Sahari, M.; Al-Gheethi, A.A.S.; Radin Mohamed, R.M.S. Natural coagulates for wastewater treatment; A review for application and mechanism. In *Prospects of Fresh Market Wastes Management in Developing Countries*; Springer: Cham, Germany, 2020; pp. 17–31. [CrossRef]
69. Othmani, B.; Rasteiro, M.G.; Khadhraoui, M. Toward green technology: A review on some efficient model plant-based coagulants/flocculants for freshwater and wastewater remediation. *Clean Technol. Environ. Policy* **2020**, *22*, 1025–1040. [CrossRef]
70. Ang, W.L.; Mohammad, A.W. State of the art and sustainability of natural coagulants in water and wastewater treatment. *J. Clean. Prod.* **2020**, *262*, 121267. [CrossRef]
71. Desta, W.M.; Bote, M.E. Wastewater treatment using a natural coagulant (Moringa oleifera seeds): Optimization through response surface methodology. *Heliyon* **2021**, *7*, e08451. [CrossRef]
72. Zhang, L.; Liu, X.; Zhang, M.; Wang, T.; Tang, H.; Jia, Y. The effect of pH/PAC on the coagulation of anionic surfactant wastewater generated in the cosmetic production. *J. Environ. Chem. Eng.* **2023**, *11*, 109312. [CrossRef]
73. Iwuozor, K.O. Prospects and challenges of using coagulation-flocculation method in the treatment of effluents. *Adv. J. Chem.-Sect. A* **2019**, *2*, 105–127. [CrossRef]
74. Ahmad, T.; Ahmad, K.; Ahad, A.; Alam, M. Characterization of water treatment sludge and its reuse as coagulant. *J. Environ. Manag.* **2016**, *182*, 606–611. [CrossRef]
75. Na, S.H.; Kim, M.J.; Kim, J.; Batool, R.; Cho, K.; Chung, J.; Lee, S.; Kim, E. J Fate and potential risks of microplastic fibers and fragments in water and wastewater treatment processes. *J. Hazard. Mater.* **2024**, *463*, 132938. [CrossRef]
76. Mao, Y.; Hu, Z.; Li, H.; Zheng, H.; Yang, S.; Yu, W.; Tang, B.; Yang, H.; He, R.; Guo, W.; et al. Recent advances in microplastic removal from drinking water by coagulation: Removal mechanisms and influencing factors. *Environ. Pollut.* **2024**, *349*, 123863. [CrossRef]
77. Ziembowicz, S.; Kida, M.; Koszelnik, P. Elimination of a Mixture of Microplastics Using Conventional and Detergent-Assisted Coagulation. *Materials* **2023**, *16*, 4070. [CrossRef] [PubMed]
78. Li, B.; Zhao, J.; Ge, W.; Li, W.; Yuan, H. Coagulation-flocculation performance and floc properties for microplastics removal by magnesium hydroxide and PAM. *J. Environ. Chem. Eng.* **2022**, *10*, 107263. [CrossRef]
79. Hu, P.; Ren, J.; Ren, W.; Sun, Y.; Yang, H. The feasibility and mechanism of poly-aluminum/titanium silicate composite coagulants for the efficient removal of nano-and micro-sized plastics. *Chem. Eng. J.* **2024**, *482*, 149095. [CrossRef]
80. Gong, Y.; Bai, Y.; Zhao, D.; Wang, Q. Aggregation of carboxyl-modified polystyrene nanoplastics in water with aluminum chloride: Structural characterization and theoretical calculation. *Water Res.* **2022**, *208*, 117884. [CrossRef] [PubMed]
81. Wang, P.; Ding, S.; Xiao, R.; An, G.; Fang, C.; Chu, W. Enhanced coagulation for mitigation of disinfection by-product precursors: A review. *Adv. Colloid Interface Sci.* **2021**, *296*, 102518. [CrossRef] [PubMed]

82. Lin, J.L.; Ika, A.R. Minimization of halogenated DBP precursors by enhanced PACl coagulation: The impact of organic molecule fraction changes on DBP precursors destabilization with Al hydrates. *Sci. Total Environ.* **2020**, *703*, 134936. [CrossRef] [PubMed]
83. Wang, P.; Ding, S.; An, G.; Qu, R.; Liu, X.; Fang, C.; Chu, W. Removal of disinfection by-product precursors by Al-based coagulants: A comparative study on coagulation performance. *J. Hazard. Mater.* **2021**, *420*, 126558. [CrossRef]
84. Dahasahastra, A.V.; Balasundaram, K.; Latkar, M.V. Turbidity removal from synthetic turbid water using coagulant recovered from water treatment sludge: A potential method to recycle and conserve aluminium. *Hydrometallurgy* **2022**, *213*, 105939. [CrossRef]
85. Okoro, B.U.; Sharifi, S.; Jesson, M.A.; Bridgeman, J. Natural organic matter (NOM) and turbidity removal by plant-based coagulants: A review. *J. Environ. Chem. Eng.* **2021**, *9*, 106588. [CrossRef]
86. Zedan, T.; Mossad, M.; Fouad, M.; Mahanna, H. Potential application of natural coagulant extraction from walnut seeds for water turbidity removal. *Water Pract. Technol.* **2022**, *17*, 684–698. [CrossRef]
87. Ahmad, A.; Abdullah, S.R.S.; Hasan, H.A.; Othman, A.R.; Ismail, N.I. Potential of local plant leaves as natural coagulant for turbidity removal. *Environ. Sci. Pollut. Res.* **2022**, *29*, 2579–2587. [CrossRef] [PubMed]
88. Tahraoui, H.; Belhadj, A.E.; Triki, Z.; Boudellal, N.R.; Seder, S.; Amrane, A.; Zhang, J.; Moula, N.; Tifoura, A.; Ferhat, R.; et al. Mixed coagulant-flocculant optimization for pharmaceutical effluent pretreatment using response surface methodology and Gaussian process regression. *Process Saf. Environ. Prot.* **2023**, *169*, 909–927. [CrossRef]
89. Alazaiza, M.Y.; Albahnasawi, A.; Ali, G.A.; Bashir, M.J.; Nassani, D.E.; Al Maskari, T.; Amr, S.S.A.; Abujazar, M.S.S. Application of natural coagulants for pharmaceutical removal from water and wastewater: A review. *Water* **2022**, *14*, 140. [CrossRef]
90. Nonfodji, O.M.; Fatombi, J.K.; Ahoyo, T.A.; Osseni, S.A.; Aminou, T. Performance of Moringa oleifera seeds protein and Moringa oleifera seeds protein-polyaluminum chloride composite coagulant in removing organic matter and antibiotic resistant bacteria from hospital wastewater. *J. Water Process Eng.* **2020**, *33*, 101103. [CrossRef]
91. Iloamaeke, I.M.; Julius, C.O. Treatment of pharmaceutical effluent using seed of phoenix dactylifera as a natural coagulant. *J. Basic Phys. Res.* **2019**, *9*, 91–100.
92. Liao, Z.L.; Zhao, Z.C.; Zhu, J.C.; Chen, H.; Meng, D.Z. Complexing characteristics between Cu (II) ions and dissolved organic matter in combined sewer overflows: Implications for the removal of heavy metals by enhanced coagulation. *Chemosphere* **2021**, *265*, 129023. [CrossRef] [PubMed]
93. Johnson, P.D.; Girinathannair, P.; Ohlinger, K.N.; Ritchie, S.; Teuber, L.; Kirby, J. Enhanced removal of heavy metals in primary treatment using coagulation and flocculation. *Water Environ. Res.* **2008**, *80*, 472–479. [CrossRef] [PubMed]
94. Skotta, A.; Jmiai, A.; Elhayaoui, W.; El-Asri, A.; Tamimi, M.; Assabbane, A.; El Issami, S. Suspended matter and heavy metals (Cu and Zn) removal from water by coagulation/flocculation process using a new Bio-flocculant: Lepidium sativum. *J. Taiwan Inst. Chem. Eng.* **2023**, *145*, 104792. [CrossRef]
95. Shekho, M.S.; Hassan, N.E. A Review on Techniques for the Cleaning of Wastewater. *GSC Adv. Res. Rev.* **2024**, *18*, 118–128. [CrossRef]
96. Manisalidis, I.; Stavropoulou, E.; Stavropoulos, A.; Bezirtzoglou, E. Environmental and Health Impacts of Air Pollution: A Review. *Front. Public Health* **2020**, *8*, 14. [CrossRef]
97. Hasan, F.; Kandhan, K.; Liu, Y.; Ren, M.; Jaleel, A.; Abdul, M. Wastewater Irrigation: A Promising Way for Future Sustainable Agriculture and Food Security in the United Arab Emirates. *Water* **2023**, *15*, 2284. [CrossRef]
98. Ighalo, J.O.; Omoarukhe, F.O.; Ojukwu, V.E.; Iwuozor, K.O.; Igwegbe, C.A. Cost of Adsorbent Preparation and Usage in Wastewater Treatment: A Review. *Clean. Chem. Eng.* **2022**, *3*, 100042. [CrossRef]
99. Mahmoodi, N.M.; Oveisi, M.; Taghizadeh, A.; Taghizadeh, M. Novel Magnetic Amine Functionalized Carbon Nanotube/Metal-Organic Framework Nanocomposites: From Green Ultrasound-Assisted Synthesis to Detailed Selective Pollutant Removal Modelling from Binary Systems. *J. Hazard. Mater.* **2019**, *368*, 746–759. [CrossRef] [PubMed]
100. Mahmoodi, N.M.; Oveisi, M.; Taghizadeh, A.; Taghizadeh, M. Synthesis of Pearl Necklace-like ZIF-8@Chitosan/PVA Nanofiber with Synergistic Effect for Recycling Aqueous Dye Removal. *Carbohydr. Polym.* **2020**, *227*, 115364. [CrossRef]
101. Mahmoodi, N.M.; Taghizadeh, M.; Taghizadeh, A. Mesoporous Activated Carbons of Low-Cost Agricultural Bio-Wastes with High Adsorption Capacity: Preparation and Artificial Neural Network Modeling of Dye Removal from Single and Multicomponent (Binary and Ternary) Systems. *J. Mol. Liq.* **2018**, *269*, 217–228. [CrossRef]
102. Sing, K.S.W.; Williams, R.T. Physisorption Hysteresis Loops and the Characterization of Nanoporous Materials. *Adsorpt. Sci. Technol.* **2004**, *22*, 773–782. [CrossRef]
103. Verma, C.; Aslam, J.; Khan, M.E. *Adsorption through Advanced Nanoscale Materials*; Elsevier: Amsterdam, The Netherlands, 2023; pp. 8–9.
104. Xiong, Q.; Li, K.; Yang, D.; Yu, H.; Pan, Z.; Song, Y. Characterizing Coal Pore Space by Gas Adsorption, Mercury Intrusion, FIB–SEM and μ-CT. *Environ. Earth Sci.* **2020**, *79*, 209. [CrossRef]
105. Zhang, P.; Chen, Y.-P.; Guo, J.-S. SPR for Water Pollutant Detection and Water Process Analysis. In *Comprehensive Analytical Chemistry*; Surface Plasmon Resonance in Bioanalysis; Elsevier: Amsterdam, The Netherlands, 2021; pp. 145–183. [CrossRef]
106. Tseng, R.-L.; Tran, H.N.; Juang, R.-S. Revisiting Temperature Effect on the Kinetics of Liquid–Phase Adsorption by the Elovich Equation: A Simple Tool for Checking Data Reliability. *J. Taiwan Inst. Chem. Eng.* **2022**, *136*, 104403. [CrossRef]
107. Mudoi, M.P.; Sharma, P.; Khichi, A.S. A Review of Gas Adsorption on Shale and the Influencing Factors of CH_4 and CO_2 Adsorption. *J. Pet. Sci. Eng.* **2022**, *217*, 110897. [CrossRef]
108. Tien, C. *Introduction to Adsorption*; Elsevier: Amsterdam, The Netherlands, 2018; pp. 8–11.

109. Markoš, J.; Steltenpohl, P. *Separation Processes II*; Slovak Chemical Library: Bratislava, Slovakia, 2017; p. 25.
110. Shukla, V.; Kumar, N. *Environmental Concerns and Sustainable Development. Volume 1, Air, Water and Energy Resources*; Springer: Singapore, 2020; p. 372.
111. Iftekhar, S.; Srivastava, V.; Sillanpää, M. Synthesis of Hybrid Bionanocomposites and Their Application for the Removal of Rare-Earth Elements from Synthetic Wastewater. In *Advanced Water Treatment*; Elsevier Ebooks; Elsevier: Amsterdam, The Netherlands, 2020; pp. 505–564. [CrossRef]
112. Chakhtouna, H.; Benzeid, H.; Zari, N.; Qaiss, A.e.K.; Bouhfid, R. Recent Advances in Eco-Friendly Composites Derived from Lignocellulosic Biomass for Wastewater Treatment. *Biomass Convers. Biorefinery* 2022, *14*, 12085–12111. [CrossRef]
113. Samadi, A.; Kong, L.; Guo, W.; Sillanpää, M.; Boztepe, I.; Song, C.; Zeng, Q.; Zhao, S. Standardized Methodology for Performance Evaluation in Using Polyaniline-Based Adsorbents to Remove Aqueous Contaminants. *J. Environ. Chem. Eng.* 2024, *12*, 112650. [CrossRef]
114. Zhang, J. Physical Insights into Kinetic Models of Adsorption. *Sep. Purif. Technol.* 2019, *229*, 115832. [CrossRef]
115. Alves, S.C.; Araújo, R.F.; Moura, T.A.; Sousa, H.; Beatriz, S.; Fregolente, L.G.; Ferreira, O.P.; Avelino, F. Coconut Shell-Based Biochars Produced by an Innovative Thermochemical Process for Obtaining Improved Lignocellulose-Based Adsorbents. *Int. J. Biol. Macromol.* 2024, *275*, 133685. [CrossRef]
116. Sharafian, A.; Bahrami, M. Assessment of Adsorber Bed Designs in Waste-Heat Driven Adsorption Cooling Systems for Vehicle Air Conditioning and Refrigeration. *Renew. Sustain. Energy Rev.* 2014, *30*, 440–451. [CrossRef]
117. Zhang, Y.; Palomba, V.; Frazzica, A. Understanding the Effect of Materials, Design Criteria and Operational Parameters on the Adsorption Desalination Performance—A Review. *Energy Convers. Manag.* 2022, *269*, 116072. [CrossRef]
118. Gutierrez, M.; Mutavdžić Pavlović, D.; Stipaničev, D.; Repec, S.; Avolio, F.; Zanella, M.; Verlicchi, P. A Thorough Analysis of the Occurrence, Removal and Environmental Risks of Organic Micropollutants in a Full-Scale Hybrid Membrane Bioreactor Fed by Hospital Wastewater. *Sci. Total Environ.* 2024, *914*, 169848. [CrossRef] [PubMed]
119. van der Hoek, J.P.; Deng, T.; Spit, T.; Luimstra, V.; de Kreuk, M.; van Halem, D. Bromate Removal in an Ozone—Granular Activated Carbon Filtration Process for Organic Micropollutants Removal from Wastewater. *J. Water Process Eng.* 2024, *58*, 104877. [CrossRef]
120. Qin, W.; Dong, Y.; Jiang, H.; Loh, W.H.; Imbrogno, J.; Swenson, T.M.; Garcia-Rodriguez, O.; Lefebvre, O. A New Approach of Simultaneous Adsorption and Regeneration of Activated Carbon to Address the Bottlenecks of Pharmaceutical Wastewater Treatment. *Water Res.* 2024, *252*, 121180. [CrossRef] [PubMed]
121. Wang, W.; Weng, Y.; Luo, T.; Wang, Q.; Yang, G.; Jin, Y. Antimicrobial and the Resistances in the Environment: Ecological and Health Risks, Influencing Factors, and Mitigation Strategies. *Toxics* 2023, *11*, 185. [CrossRef]
122. Deere, J.R.; Streets, S.; Jankowski, M.D.; Ferrey, M.L.; Chenaux-Ibrahim, Y.; Convertino, M.; Isaac, E.J.; Phelps, N.B.D.; Primus, A.; Servadio, J.L.; et al. A Chemical Prioritization Process: Applications to Contaminants of Emerging Concern in Freshwater Ecosystems (Phase I). *Sci. Total Environ.* 2021, *772*, 146030. [CrossRef] [PubMed]
123. Tiedeken, E.J.; Tahar, A.; McHugh, B.; Rowan, N.J. Monitoring, Sources, Receptors, and Control Measures for Three European Union Watch List Substances of Emerging Concern in Receiving Waters—A 20 Year Systematic Review. *Sci. Total Environ.* 2017, *574*, 1140–1163. [CrossRef]
124. Sousa, J.C.G.; Ribeiro, A.R.; Barbosa, M.O.; Pereira, M.F.R.; Silva, A.M.T. A Review on Environmental Monitoring of Water Organic Pollutants Identified by EU Guidelines. *J. Hazard. Mater.* 2018, *344*, 146–162. [CrossRef]
125. Guarin, T.C.; Li, L.; Haak, L.; Teel, L.; Pagilla, K.R. Contaminants of Emerging Concern Reduction and Microbial Community Characterization across a Three-Barrier Advanced Water Treatment System. *Sci. Total Environ.* 2024, *912*, 169637. [CrossRef]
126. Rizzo, L.; Fiorentino, A.; Grassi, M.; Attanasio, D.; Guida, M. Advanced Treatment of Urban Wastewater by Sand Filtration and Graphene Adsorption for Wastewater Reuse: Effect on a Mixture of Pharmaceuticals and Toxicity. *J. Environ. Chem. Eng.* 2015, *3*, 122–128. [CrossRef]
127. Emanuele, D.V.D.; Oliveira, M.G.; Spaolonzi, M.P.; Heloisa, P.S.C.; Thiago, L.S.; Melissa, G.A.V. Adsorption of Pharmaceutical Products from Aqueous Solutions on Functionalized Carbon Nanotubes by Conventional and Green Methods: A Critical Review. *J. Clean. Prod.* 2022, *372*, 133743. [CrossRef]
128. Ambaye, T.G.; Vaccari, M.; van Hullebusch, E.D.; Amrane, A.; Rtimi, S. Mechanisms and Adsorption Capacities of Biochar for the Removal of Organic and Inorganic Pollutants from Industrial Wastewater. *Int. J. Environ. Sci. Technol.* 2021, *18*, 3273–3294. [CrossRef]
129. Briffa, J.; Sinagra, E.; Blundell, R. Heavy Metal Pollution in the Environment and Their Toxicological Effects on Humans. *Heliyon* 2020, *6*, e04691. [CrossRef] [PubMed]
130. Qiu, B.; Tao, X.; Wang, H.; Li, W.; Ding, X.; Chu, H. Biochar as a Low-Cost Adsorbent for Aqueous Heavy Metal Removal: A Review. *J. Anal. Appl. Pyrolysis* 2021, *155*, 105081. [CrossRef]
131. Ghasaq, A.A.; Salih, M.; Ghsoon, A.F.; Fahim, R. Adsorption Technique for the Removal of Heavy Metals from Wastewater Using Low-Cost Natural Adsorbent. *IOP Conf. Ser. Earth Environ. Sci.* 2023, *1129*, 012012. [CrossRef]
132. ElSayed, E.E. Natural Diatomite as an Effective Adsorbent for Heavy Metals in Water and Wastewater Treatment (a Batch Study). *Water Sci.* 2018, *32*, 32–43. [CrossRef]

133. Chai, W.S.; Cheun, J.Y.; Kumar, P.S.; Mubashir, M.; Majeed, Z.; Banat, F.; Ho, S.-H.; Show, P.L. A Review on Conventional and Novel Materials towards Heavy Metal Adsorption in Wastewater Treatment Application. *J. Clean. Prod.* **2021**, *296*, 126589. [CrossRef]
134. Khushk, S.; Zhang, L.; Pirzada, A.M.; Irfan, M.; Li, A. Cr(VI) Heavy Metal Adsorption from Aqueous Solution by KOH Treated Hydrochar Derived from Agricultural Wastes. *AIP Conf. Proc.* **2019**, *2119*, 020003. [CrossRef]
135. Khanzada, A.K.; Al-Hazmi, H.E.; Kurniawan, T.A.; Majtacz, J.; Piechota, G.; Kumar, G.; Ezzati, P.; Saeb, M.R.; Rabiee, N.; Karimi-Maleh, H.; et al. Hydrochar as a Bio-Based Adsorbent for Heavy Metals Removal: A Review of Production Processes, Adsorption Mechanisms, Kinetic Models, Regeneration and Reusability. *Sci. Total Environ.* **2024**, *945*, 173972. [CrossRef]
136. Zhang, W.; Hu, L.; Hu, S.; Liu, Y. Optimized Synthesis of Novel Hydrogel for the Adsorption of Copper and Cobalt Ions in Wastewater. *RSC Adv.* **2019**, *9*, 16058–16068. [CrossRef]
137. Al-Senani, G.M.; Al-Fawzan, F.F. Adsorption Study of Heavy Metal Ions from Aqueous Solution by Nanoparticle of Wild Herbs. *Egypt. J. Aquat. Res.* **2018**, *44*, 187–194. [CrossRef]
138. Li, J.; Dong, X.; Liu, X.; Xu, X.; Duan, W.; Park, J.; Gao, L.; Lu, Y. Comparative Study on the Adsorption Characteristics of Heavy Metal Ions by Activated Carbon and Selected Natural Adsorbents. *Sustainability* **2022**, *14*, 15579. [CrossRef]
139. Teo, Y.S.; Jafari, I.; Liang, F.; Jung, Y.; Van der Hoek, J.P.; Ong, S.L.; Hu, J. Investigation of the Efficacy of the UV/Chlorine Process for the Removal of Trimethoprim: Effects of Operational Parameters and Artificial Neural Networks Modelling. *Sci. Total Environ.* **2022**, *812*, 152551. [CrossRef]
140. Zhong, Y.; Chen, Y.; Ong, S.L.; Hu, J.; Balakrishnan, V.; Ang, W.S. Disinfection By-Products Control in Wastewater Effluents Treated with Ozone and Biological Activated Carbon Followed by UV/Chlor(Am)Ine Processes. *Sci. Total Environ.* **2024**, *922*, 171317. [CrossRef]
141. Shao, B.; Shen, L.; Liu, Z.; Tang, L.; Tan, X.; Wang, D.; Zeng, W.; Wu, T.; Pan, Y.; Zhang, X.; et al. Disinfection Byproducts Formation from Emerging Organic Micropollutants during Chlorine-Based Disinfection Processes. *Chem. Eng. J.* **2023**, *455*, 140476. [CrossRef]
142. Al Bsoul, A.; Hailat, M.; Abdelhay, A.; Tawalbeh, M.; Al-Othman, A.; Al-kharabsheh, I.N.; Al-Taani, A.A. Efficient Removal of Phenol Compounds from Water Environment Using Ziziphus Leaves Adsorbent. *Sci. Total Environ.* **2021**, *761*, 143229. [CrossRef] [PubMed]
143. Vasseghian, Y.; Dragoi, E.-N.; Almomani, F.; Le, V.T. Graphene Derivatives in Bioplastic: A Comprehensive Review of Properties and Future Perspectives. *Chemosphere* **2022**, *286*, 131892. [CrossRef] [PubMed]
144. Wang, Z.; Sedighi, M.; Lea-Langton, A. Filtration of Microplastic Spheres by Biochar: Removal Efficiency and Immobilisation Mechanisms. *Water Res.* **2020**, *184*, 116165. [CrossRef] [PubMed]
145. Singh, N.; Khandelwal, N.; Ganie, Z.A.; Tiwari, E.; Darbha, G.K. Eco-Friendly Magnetic Biochar: An Effective Trap for Nanoplastics of Varying Surface Functionality and Size in the Aqueous Environment. *Chem. Eng. J.* **2021**, *418*, 129405. [CrossRef]
146. Ji, G.; Xing, Y.; You, T. Biochar as Adsorbents for Environmental Microplastics and Nanoplastics Removal. *J. Environ. Chem. Eng.* **2024**, *12*, 113377. [CrossRef]
147. Siipola, V.; Pflugmacher, S.; Romar, H.; Wendling, L.; Koukkari, P. Low-Cost Biochar Adsorbents for Water Purification Including Microplastics Removal. *Appl. Sci.* **2020**, *10*, 788. [CrossRef]
148. Giannakis, S.; Rtimi, S.; Pulgarin, C. Light-Assisted Advanced Oxidation Processes for the Elimination of Chemical and Microbiological Pollution of Wastewaters in Developed and Developing Countries. *Molecules* **2017**, *22*, 1070. [CrossRef] [PubMed]
149. Mukherjee, J.; Lodh, B.K.; Sharma, R.; Mahata, N.; Shah, M.P.; Mandal, S.; Ghanta, S.; Bhunia, B. Advanced Oxidation Process for the Treatment of Industrial Wastewater: A Review on Strategies, Mechanisms, Bottlenecks and Prospects. *Chemosphere* **2023**, *345*, 140473. [CrossRef] [PubMed]
150. Mahbub, P.; Duke, M. Scalability of Advanced Oxidation Processes (AOPs) in Industrial Applications: A Review. *J. Environ. Manag.* **2023**, *345*, 118861. [CrossRef]
151. Kumari, P.; Kumar, A. Advanced oxidation process: A Remediation Technique for Organic and Non-Biodegradable Pollutant. *Results Surf. Interfaces* **2023**, *11*, 100122. [CrossRef]
152. Rayaroth, M.P.; Aravindakumar, C.T.; Shah, N.S.; Boczkaj, G. Advanced Oxidation Processes (AOPs) Based Wastewater Treatment—Unexpected Nitration Side Reactions—A Serious Environmental Issue: A Review. *Chem. Eng. J.* **2021**, *430*, 133002. [CrossRef]
153. Ghime, D.; Ghosh, P. Advanced Oxidation Processes: A Powerful Treatment Option for the Removal of Recalcitrant Organic Compounds. In *Advanced Oxidation Processes—Applications, Trends, and Prospects*; IntechOpen: London, UK, 2020.
154. Oturan, N.; Oturan, M.A. Electro-Fenton Process: Background, New Developments, and Applications. In *Electrochemical Water and Wastewater Treatment*; Martínez-Huitle, C.A., Rodrigo, M.A., Scialdone, O., Eds.; Butterworth-Heinemann: Oxford, UK, 2018; pp. 193–221. [CrossRef]
155. Pliego, G.; Zazo, J.A.; Garcia-Muñoz, P.; Munoz, M.; Casas, J.A.; Rodriguez, J.J. Trends in the Intensification of the Fenton Process for Wastewater Treatment: An Overview. *Crit. Rev. Env. Sci. Technol.* **2015**, *45*, 2611–2692. [CrossRef]
156. Tang, J.; Wang, J. Metal Organic Framework with Coordinatively Unsaturated Sites as Efficient Fenton-like Catalyst for Enhanced Degradation of Sulfamethazine. *Environ. Sci. Technol.* **2018**, *52*, 5367–5377. [CrossRef] [PubMed]
157. Wang, J.; Wang, S. Reactive Species in Advanced Oxidation Processes: Formation, Identification and Reaction Mechanism. *Chem. Eng. J.* **2020**, *401*, 126158. [CrossRef]

158. Zhang, M.; Dong, H.; Zhao, L.; Wang, D.; Meng, D. A Review on Fenton Process for Organic Wastewater Treatment Based on Optimization Perspective. *Sci. Total Environ.* **2019**, *670*, 110–121. [CrossRef]
159. Zhao, X.; Huang, Z.; Sun, H.; Zhao, Q.; Huang, Z.; Zhang, C.; Wang, Y.; Yang, C.; Zhou, Z. Comparison on Molecular Transformation of Dissolved Organic Matter during Fenton and Activated Carbon Adsorption Processes for Chemical Cleaning Wastewater Treatment. *Sep. Purif. Technol.* **2024**, *344*, 127226. [CrossRef]
160. Wang, X.; Dai, Y.; Li, Y.; Yin, L. Application of Advanced Oxidation Processes for the Removal of Micro/Nanoplastics from Water: A Review. *Chemosphere* **2024**, *346*, 140636. [CrossRef]
161. Ortiz, D.; Munoz, M.; Nieto-Sandoval, J.; Romera-Castillo, C.; de Pedro, Z.M.; Casas, J.A. Insights into the Degradation of Microplastics by Fenton Oxidation: From Surface Modification to Mineralization. *Chemosphere* **2022**, *309*, 136809. [CrossRef]
162. Ziembowicz, S.; Kida, M. Limitations and Future Directions of Application of the Fenton-like Process in Micropollutants Degradation in Water and Wastewater Treatment: A Critical Review. *Chemosphere* **2022**, *296*, 134041. [CrossRef]
163. Sobczak, M.; Bujnowicz, S.; Bilińska, L. Fenton and Electro-Fenton Treatment for Industrial Textile Wastewater Recycling. Comparison of By-Products Removal, Biodegradability, Toxicity, and Re-Dyeing. *Water Resour. Ind.* **2024**, *31*, 100256. [CrossRef]
164. Zhang, M.; Li, Q.; Li, H.; Yang, P. Enhanced Heterogeneous Electro-Fenton Degradation of Salicylic Acid by Different Fe_3O_4 Loaded Carriers. *Desalination Water Treat.* **2024**, *320*, 100723. [CrossRef]
165. Zhu, Y.; Xie, Q.; Deng, F.; Ni, Z.; Lin, Q.; Cheng, L.; Chen, X.; Qiu, R.; Zhu, R. The Differences in Heterogeneous Fenton Catalytic Performance and Mechanism of Various Iron Minerals and Their Influencing Factors: A Review. *Sep. Purif. Technol.* **2023**, *325*, 124702. [CrossRef]
166. Liu, Z.; Demeestere, K.; Hulle, S.V. Comparison and Performance Assessment of Ozone-Based AOPs in View of Trace Organic Contaminants Abatement in Water and Wastewater: A Review. *J. Environ. Chem. Eng.* **2021**, *9*, 105599. [CrossRef]
167. Derco, J.; Gotvajn, A.Ž.; Čižmárová, O.; Dudáš, J.; Sumegová, L.; Šimovičová, K. Removal of Micropollutants by Ozone-Based Processes. *Processes* **2021**, *9*, 1013. [CrossRef]
168. Tripathi, S.C.; Hussain, T. Water and Wastewater Treatment through Ozone-Based Technologies. In *Development in Wastewater Treatment Research and Processes*; Shah, M., Rodriguez-Couto, S., Biswas, J., Eds.; Elsevier: Amsterdam, The Netherlands, 2022; pp. 139–172. [CrossRef]
169. Rekhate, C.V.; Srivastava, J.K. Recent Advances in Ozone-Based Advanced Oxidation Processes for Treatment of Wastewater- a Review. *Chem. Eng. J. Adv.* **2020**, *3*, 100031. [CrossRef]
170. Derco, J.; Dudáš, J.; Valičková, M.; Šimovičová, K.; Kecskés, J. Removal of Micropollutants by Ozone Based Processes. *Chem. Eng. Process. Process Intensif.* **2015**, *94*, 78–84. [CrossRef]
171. Deng, L.-Z.; Mujumdar, A.S.; Pan, Z.; Vidyarthi, S.K.; Xu, J.; Zielinska, M.; Xiao, H.-W. Emerging Chemical and Physical Disinfection Technologies of Fruits and Vegetables: A Comprehensive Review. *Crit. Rev. Food Sci. Nutr.* **2019**, *60*, 2481–2508. [CrossRef] [PubMed]
172. Gou, X.; Yuan, D.; Wang, L.; Xie, L.; Wei, L.; Zhang, G. Enhancing Ozone Production in Dielectric Barrier Discharge Utilizing Water as Electrode. *Vacuum* **2023**, *212*, 112047. [CrossRef]
173. Joseph, C.G.; Farm, Y.Y.; Taufiq-Yap, Y.H.; Pang, C.K.; Nga, J.L.H.; Li Puma, G. Ozonation Treatment Processes for the Remediation of Detergent Wastewater: A Comprehensive Review. *J. Environ. Chem. Eng.* **2021**, *9*, 106099. [CrossRef]
174. Presumido, P.H.; Ribeirinho-Soares, S.; Montes, R.; Quintana, J.B.; Rodil, R.; Ribeiro, M.; Neuparth, T.; Santos, M.M.; Feliciano, M.; Nunes, O.C.; et al. Ozone Membrane Contactor for Tertiary Treatment of Urban Wastewater: Chemical, Microbial and Toxicological Assessment. *Sci. Total. Environ.* **2023**, *892*, 164492. [CrossRef] [PubMed]
175. Lee, W.; Choi, S.; Kim, H.; Lee, W.; Lee, M.; Son, H.J.; Chang, H.L.; Cho, M.; Lee, Y. Efficiency of Ozonation and O_3/H_2O_2 as Enhanced Wastewater Treatment Processes for Micropollutant Abatement and Disinfection with Minimized Byproduct Formation. *J. Hazard. Mater.* **2023**, *454*, 131436. [CrossRef] [PubMed]
176. Miklos, D.B.; Wang, W.-L.; Linden, K.G.; Drewes, J.E.; Hübner, U. Comparison of UV-AOPs (UV/H_2O_2, UV/PDS and UV/Chlorine) for TOrC Removal from Municipal Wastewater Effluent and Optical Surrogate Model Evaluation. *Chem. Eng. J.* **2019**, *362*, 537–547. [CrossRef]
177. Miklos, D.B.; Hartl, R.; Philipp, M.; Linden, K.G.; Drewes, J.E.; Hübner, U. UV/H_2O_2 Process Stability and Pilot-Scale Validation for Trace Organic Chemical Removal from Wastewater Treatment Plant Effluents. *Water Res.* **2018**, *136*, 169–179. [CrossRef]
178. Collivignarelli, M.C.; Pedrazzani, R.; Sorlini, S.; Abbà, A.; Bertanza, G. H_2O_2 Based Oxidation Processes for the Treatment of Real High Strength Aqueous Wastes. *Sustainability* **2017**, *9*, 244. [CrossRef]
179. Gao, Y.; Zhang, J.; Li, C.; Tian, F.; Gao, N. Comparative Evaluation of Metoprolol Degradation by UV/Chlorine and UV/H_2O_2 Processes. *Chemosphere* **2020**, *243*, 125325. [CrossRef]
180. Farzanehsa, M.S.Z.; Vaughan, L.; Zamyadi, A.; Khan, S.J. Comparison of UV-Cl and $UV-H_2O_2$ Advanced Oxidation Processes in the Degradation of Contaminants from Water and Wastewater: A Review. *Water Environ. J.* **2023**, *37*, 633–643. [CrossRef]
181. Akerdi, A.T.; Bahrami, S.H. Application of Heterogeneous Nano-Semiconductors for Photocatalytic Advanced Oxidation of Organic Compounds: A Review. *J. Environ. Chem. Eng.* **2019**, *7*, 103283. [CrossRef]
182. Ahmaruzzaman, M.; Raha, S. ZnO Nanostructured Materials and Their Potential Applications: Progress, Challenges and Perspectives. *Nanoscale Adv.* **2022**, *8*, 1868–1925. [CrossRef]

183. Martínez-Escudero, C.M.; Garrido, I.; Contreras, F.; Hellín, P.; Flores, P.; León-Morán, L.O.; Arroyo-Manzanares, N.; Campillo, N.; Pastor, M.; Viñas, P.; et al. Photodecomposition of Antibiotics and Their Transformation Products in Wastewaters Using ZnO and TiO$_2$ with LED Lamps. *J. Photochem. Photobiol. A Chem.* **2024**, *454*, 115732. [CrossRef]
184. Allé, P.H.; Garcia-Muñoz, P.; Adouby, K.; Keller, N.; Robert, D. Efficient Photocatalytic Mineralization of Polymethylmethacrylate and Polystyrene Nanoplastics by TiO$_2$/β-SiC Alveolar Foams. *Environ. Chem. Lett.* **2020**, *19*, 1803–1808. [CrossRef]
185. Domínguez-Jaimes, L.P.; Cedillo-González, E.I.; Luévano-Hipólito, E.; Acuña-Bedoya, J.D.; Hernández-López, J.M. Degradation of Primary Nanoplastics by Photocatalysis Using Different Anodized TiO$_2$ Structures. *J. Hazard. Mater.* **2021**, *413*, 125452. [CrossRef]
186. Beyazıt, N.; Karaca, H. Performance comparison of UV, UV/H$_2$O$_2$, UV/Fe^{2+}, H$_2$O$_2$/Fe^{2+}, UV/H$_2$O$_2$/Fe^{2+} processes in the removal of COD and color from textile wastewater. *J. Sci. Rep.-A* **2020**, *45*, 236–252.
187. Moreira, F.C.; Boaventura, R.A.R.; Brillas, E.; Vilar, V.J.P. Electrochemical Advanced Oxidation Processes: A Review on Their Application to Synthetic and Real Wastewaters. *Appl. Catal. B Environ.* **2017**, *202*, 217–261. [CrossRef]
188. Ganiyu, S.O.; Martínez-Huitle, C.A.; Rodrigo, M.A. Renewable Energies Driven Electrochemical Wastewater/Soil Decontamination Technologies: A Critical Review of Fundamental Concepts and Applications. *Appl. Catal. B Environ.* **2020**, *270*, 118857. [CrossRef]
189. Xie, J.; Zhang, C.; Waite, T.D. Hydroxyl Radicals in Anodic Oxidation Systems: Generation, Identification and Quantification. *Water Res.* **2022**, *217*, 118425. [CrossRef]
190. Hu, Z.; Cai, J.; Song, G.; Tian, Y.; Zhou, M. Anodic Oxidation of Organic Pollutants: Anode Fabrication, Process Hybrid and Environmental Applications. *Curr. Opin. Electrochem.* **2021**, *26*, 100659. [CrossRef]
191. Kim, S.; Jeong, Y.; Park, M.-O.; Jang, Y.; Bae, J.-S.; Hong, K.-S.; Kim, S.; Song, P.; Yoon, J.H. Development of Boron Doped Diamond Electrodes Material for Heavy Metal Ion Sensor with High Sensitivity and Durability. *J. Mater. Res. Technol.* **2023**, *23*, 1375–1385. [CrossRef]
192. Vinayagam, V.; Palani, K.N.; Ganesh, S.; Rajesh, S.; Akula, V.V.; Avoodaiappan, R.; Kushwaha, O.S.; Pugazhendhi, A. Recent developments on advanced oxidation processes for degradation of pollutants from wastewater with focus on antibiotics and organic dyes. *Environ. Res.* **2024**, *240*, 117500. [CrossRef]
193. Brillas, E.; Garcia-Segura, S. Benchmarking Recent Advances and Innovative Technology Approaches of Fenton, Photo-Fenton, Electro-Fenton, and Related Processes: A Review on the Relevance of Phenol as Model Molecule. *Sep. Purif. Technol.* **2020**, *237*, 116337. [CrossRef]
194. Brillas, E. Fenton, Photo-Fenton, Electro-Fenton, and Their Combined Treatments for the Removal of Insecticides from Waters and Soils. A Review. *Sep. Purif. Technol.* **2022**, *284*, 120290. [CrossRef]
195. Monteil, H.; Péchaud, Y.; Oturan, N.; Oturan, M.A. A Review on Efficiency and Cost Effectiveness of Electro- and Bio-Electro-Fenton Processes: Application to the Treatment of Pharmaceutical Pollutants in Water. *Chem. Eng. J.* **2019**, *376*, 119577. [CrossRef]
196. Ismail, S.A.; Ang, W.L.; Mohammad, A.W. Electro-Fenton Technology for Wastewater Treatment: A Bibliometric Analysis of Current Research Trends, Future Perspectives and Energy Consumption Analysis. *J. Water Process Eng.* **2021**, *40*, 101952. [CrossRef]
197. Madhavan, J.; Theerthagiri, J.; Balaji, D.; Sunitha, S.; Choi, M.; Ashokkumar, M. Hybrid Advanced Oxidation Processes Involving Ultrasound: An Overview. *Molecules* **2019**, *24*, 3341. [CrossRef]
198. Serna-Galvis, E.A.; Porras, J.; Torres-Palma, R.A. A Critical Review on the Sonochemical Degradation of Organic Pollutants in Urine, Seawater, and Mineral Water. *Ultrason. Sonochem.* **2022**, *82*, 105861. [CrossRef]
199. Hayati, F.; Khodabakhshi, M.R.; Isari, A.A.; Moradi, S.; Kakavandi, B. LED-Assisted Sonocatalysis of Sulfathiazole and Pharmaceutical Wastewater Using N, Fe Co-Doped TiO$_2$@SWCNT: Optimization, Performance and Reaction Mechanism Studies. *J. Water Process Eng.* **2020**, *38*, 101693. [CrossRef]
200. Calcio Gaudino, E.; Canova, E.; Liu, P.; Wu, Z.; Cravotto, G. Degradation of Antibiotics in Wastewater: New Advances in Cavitational Treatments. *Molecules* **2021**, *26*, 617. [CrossRef]
201. Saleh, R.; Taufik, A. Degradation of Methylene Blue and Congo-Red Dyes Using Fenton, Photo-Fenton, Sono-Fenton, and Sonophoto-Fenton Methods in the Presence of Iron(II,III) Oxide/Zinc Oxide/Graphene (Fe$_3$O$_4$/ZnO/Graphene) Composites. *Sep. Purif. Technol.* **2019**, *210*, 563–573. [CrossRef]
202. Nicodemos, D.; Santana, C.S.; Silva, C.C.; Magalhães, F.; Aguiar, A. A Review on the Treatment of Textile Industry Effluents through Fenton Processes. *Process Saf. Environ. Prot.* **2021**, *155*, 366–386. [CrossRef]
203. Ofori, S.; Puškáčová, A.; Růžičková, I.; Wanner, J. Treated Wastewater Reuse for Irrigation: Pros and Cons. *Sci. Total Environ.* **2021**, *760*, 144026. [CrossRef] [PubMed]
204. Adeel, M.; Maniakova, G.; Rizzo, L. Tertiary/Quaternary Treatment of Urban Wastewater by UV/H$_2$O$_2$ or Ozonation: Microplastics May Affect Removal of E. Coli and Contaminants of Emerging Concern. *Sci. Total Environ.* **2024**, *907*, 167940. [CrossRef] [PubMed]
205. Ding, N.; Li, Z.; Jiang, L.; Liu, H.; Zhang, Y.; Sun, Y. Kinetics and Mechanisms of Bacteria Disinfection by Performic Acid in Wastewater: In Comparison with Peracetic Acid and Sodium Hypochlorite. *Sci. Total. Environ.* **2023**, *878*, 162606. [CrossRef] [PubMed]
206. Cheng, L.; Wei, X.; Gao, A.; Zhou, L.; Shi, X.; Zhou, X.; Bi, X.; Yang, T.; Huang, S. Performance and Mechanism of Sequential UV-NaClO Disinfection: Inactivation and Reactivation of Antibiotic-Resistant Bacteria, Disinfection Byproduct Formation and Microbial Community Variation. *J. Water Process Eng.* **2024**, *58*, 104824. [CrossRef]

207. Li, Q.; Cui, X.; Gao, X.; Chen, X.; Zhao, H. Intelligent Dosing of Sodium Hypochlorite in Municipal Wastewater Treatment Plants: Experimental and Modeling Studies. *J. Water Process Eng.* **2024**, *64*, 105662. [CrossRef]
208. Andrés, C.M.C.; Pérez de la Lastra, J.M.; Juan, C.A.; Plou, F.J.; Pérez-Lebeña, E. Hypochlorous Acid Chemistry in Mammalian Cells—Influence on Infection and Role in Various Pathologies. *Int. J. Mol. Sci.* **2022**, *23*, 10835. [CrossRef]
209. Kesar, S.; Bhatti, M.S. Chlorination of Secondary Treated Wastewater with Sodium Hypochlorite (NaOCl): An Effective Single Alternate to Other Disinfectants. *Heliyon* **2022**, *8*, e11162. [CrossRef]
210. Shi, C.; Li, C.; Wang, Y.; Guo, J.; Barry, S.; Zhang, Y.; Marmier, N. Review of Advanced Oxidation Processes Based on Peracetic Acid for Organic Pollutants. *Water* **2022**, *14*, 2309. [CrossRef]
211. Chen, G.-Y.; Lin, Y.-H.; Fu, C.-H.; Lin, C.-H.; Muthiah, B.; Espulgar, W.V.; Santos, G.N.; Yu, D.E.; Kasai, T. Quantification of Peracetic Acid (PAA) in the H_2O_2 + Acetic Acid Reaction by the Wavelength Shift Analysis in Near-UV/Visible Absorption Region. *Anal. Sci.* **2024**, *40*, 489–499. [CrossRef]
212. Lin, Y.; He, Y.; Sun, Q.; Ping, Q.; Huang, M.; Wang, L.; Li, Y. Underlying the Mechanisms of Pathogen Inactivation and Regrowth in Wastewater Using Peracetic Acid-Based Disinfection Processes: A Critical Review. *J. Hazard. Mater.* **2024**, *463*, 132868. [CrossRef] [PubMed]
213. Wang, J.; Chen, W.; Wang, T.; Reid, E.; Krall, C.; Kim, J.; Zhang, T.; Xie, X.; Huang, C.-H. Bacteria and Virus Inactivation: Relative Efficacy and Mechanisms of Peroxyacids and Chlor(Am)Ine. *Environ. Sci. Technol.* **2023**, *57*, 18710–18721. [CrossRef] [PubMed]
214. Zhang, Y.; Xiang, J.-L.; Wang, J.; Du, H.-S.; Wang, T.; Huo, Z.-Y.; Wang, W.; Liu, M.; Du, Y. Ultraviolet-Based Synergistic Processes for Wastewater Disinfection: A Review. *J. Hazard. Mater.* **2023**, *453*, 131393. [CrossRef] [PubMed]
215. Foschi, J.; Turolla, A.; Antonelli, M. Artificial Neural Network Modeling of Full-Scale UV Disinfection for Process Control Aimed at Wastewater Reuse. *J. Environ. Manag.* **2021**, *300*, 113790. [CrossRef] [PubMed]
216. Manoli, K.; Naziri, A.; Ttofi, I.; Michael, C.; Allan, I.J.; Fatta-Kassinos, D. Investigation of the Effect of Microplastics on the UV Inactivation of Antibiotic-Resistant Bacteria in Water. *Water Res.* **2022**, *222*, 118766. [CrossRef]
217. Sun, X.; Wang, Z.; Xuan, X.; Ji, L.; Li, X.; Tao, Y.; Boczkaj, G.; Zhao, S.; Yoon, J.Y.; Chen, S. Disinfection Characteristics of an Advanced Rotational Hydrodynamic Cavitation Reactor in Pilot Scale. *Ultrason. Sonochem.* **2021**, *73*, 105543. [CrossRef]
218. Suprakas, S.R.; Rashi, G.; Kumar, N. Water Purification Using Various Technologies and Their Advantages and Disadvantages. In *Carbon Nanomaterial-Based Adsorbents for Water Purification*; Elsevier: Amsterdam, The Netherlands, 2020; pp. 37–66. [CrossRef]
219. Chen, Y.; Duan, X.; Zhou, X.; Wang, R.; Wang, S.; Ren, N.; Ho, S.-H. Advanced Oxidation Processes for Water Disinfection: Features, Mechanisms and Prospects. *Chem. Eng. J.* **2021**, *409*, 128207. [CrossRef]
220. Li, Z.; Yang, D.; Li, S.; Yang, L.; Yan, W.; Xu, H. Advances on Electrochemical Disinfection Research: Mechanisms, Influencing Factors and Applications. *Sci. Total Environ.* **2024**, *912*, 169043. [CrossRef]
221. Mosquera-Romero, S.; Prévoteau, A.; Louage, F.; Dominguez-Granda, L.; Korneel, R.; Diederik, P.L. Rousseau Fouling and Energy Consumption Impede Electrochemical Disinfection of Constructed Wetland Effluents. *J. Environ. Chem. Eng.* **2024**, *12*, 113348. [CrossRef]
222. Li, H.; Dechesne, A.; He, Z.; Jensen, M.M.; Song, H.L.; Smets, B.F. Electrochemical Disinfection May Increase the Spread of Antibiotic Resistance Genes by Promoting Conjugal Plasmid Transfer. *Sci. Total Environ.* **2023**, *858*, 159846. [CrossRef] [PubMed]

Disclaimer/Publisher's Note: The statements, opinions and data contained in all publications are solely those of the individual author(s) and contributor(s) and not of MDPI and/or the editor(s). MDPI and/or the editor(s) disclaim responsibility for any injury to people or property resulting from any ideas, methods, instructions or products referred to in the content.

Article

Cobalt-Modified Biochar from Rape Straw as Persulfate Activator for Degradation of Antibiotic Metronidazole

Lei Hu [1], Lin Shi [1], Edwin Hena Dawolo [1], Ning Ding [2] and Hong Liu [1,*]

[1] School of Environmental Science and Engineering, Jiangsu Key Laboratory of Environmental Science and Technology, Suzhou University of Science and Technology, Suzhou 215009, China
[2] Department of Environmental Science and Engineering, Beijing Technology and Business University, Beijing 100048, China
* Correspondence: hong.liu@usts.edu.cn; Tel.: +86-18051902267

Abstract: A cobalt-loaded magnetic biochar (Co-MBC) catalyst was synthesized to enhance the removal of metronidazole (MNZ). Study explored the performance and mechanism of MNZ degradation by Co-MBC activated permonosulfate (PMS). Results showed that cobalt oxides were effectively deposited onto the biochar surface, new oxygen functional groups were added to the modified biochar, and the presence of the metallic element Co enhanced the efficiency of PMS activation in the composite. More than 90% of MNZ was removed after 60 min with a catalyst dosage of 0.2 g/L and a PS concentration of 1 mM. After four reuses, Co-MBC still showed excellent catalytic performance to degrade over 75% of MNZ. The reaction system performed well even in the presence of inorganic anions and organic macromolecules. However, the degradation rate was inhibited under alkaline conditions. The quenching experiment indicated that $\bullet SO_4^-$, $\bullet OH$, $^1O_2$, and $\bullet O_2^-$ synergistically degraded MNZ, and that $\bullet SO_4^-$ played a dominant role. LC-MS was applied to assess intermediate degradation products, in which CO_2, H_2O, and NO_3^- were the final degradation products, and potential degradation pathways were suggested. In conclusion, Co-MBC was an efficient and stable catalytic material, and its ability to activate PMS was improved to effectively degrade antibiotics, a typical priority pollutant.

Keywords: biochar; PMS; metronidazole; degradation

Citation: Hu, L.; Shi, L.; Dawolo, E.H.; Ding, N.; Liu, H. Cobalt-Modified Biochar from Rape Straw as Persulfate Activator for Degradation of Antibiotic Metronidazole. *Processes* **2024**, *12*, 1596. https://doi.org/10.3390/pr12081596

Academic Editors: Dimitris Zagklis and Georgios Bampos

Received: 23 June 2024
Revised: 23 July 2024
Accepted: 23 July 2024
Published: 30 July 2024

Copyright: © 2024 by the authors. Licensee MDPI, Basel, Switzerland. This article is an open access article distributed under the terms and conditions of the Creative Commons Attribution (CC BY) license (https://creativecommons.org/licenses/by/4.0/).

1. Introduction

Globally, the use of various antibiotic medicines is rapidly increasing, reaching 100,000 to 200,000 tons per year [1]. In aquatic environments, antibiotic resistance can be greatly enhanced by excess antibiotics and their derivatives [2]. Antibiotic contamination has become an issue of concern, presenting significant challenges to public safety and the ecological environment [3,4]. Metronidazole (MNZ) is a widely utilized antibiotic that may cause carcinogenic, mutagenic, and genotoxic effects in organisms. MNZ has great solubility in water, is difficult to biodegrade, has very slow absorption, and can persist in the environment for extended durations [5–7]. Hence, it is particularly important to control and treat MNZ contamination in aquatic environments.

Currently, advanced oxidation processes (AOPs) are extensively employed to degrade emerging organic pollutants in the environment, such as antibiotics [8–10]. AOPs can produce highly reactive oxygen species (ROS) to oxidize nonbiodegradable pollutants [11,12]. The ROS can be produced by advanced oxidation methods such as Fenton [13], ozone [14], activated persulfate [15], electrochemistry [16], ionizing radiation [17], and photocatalytic [18]. The activated persulfate method has been widely studied because of its high oxidizing power, wide pH range, and excellent water solubility [19,20]. Peroxydisulfate (PDS) and permonosulfate (PMS) are commonly used oxidizing agents in SR-AOPs [21]. Due to the asymmetry in the structure of the PMS molecule itself, PMS is easier to activate using a catalyst in the oxidizing system [22]. However, it is difficult for PMS to be used directly for the oxidative degradation of organic pollutants, and some methods are needed to activate PMS to degrade the pollutants.

UV light, transition metals, heat, and carbon-based materials can activate PMS to generate ROS, which degrade and mineralize organic contaminants. Among them, carbon-based materials have a wide range of applications in removing antibiotic contamination owing to their cost-effectiveness, economic viability, and environmentally benign nature [23]. Carbon materials, including graphene [24], carbon nanotubes [25], activated carbon [26], biochar [27], and aerogel [28], are extensively researched as a result of their low cost of use and strong biocompatibility [20]. Because of its enormous specific surface area, pore structure, and numerous oxygen-containing functional groups, biochar (BC) can efficiently catalyze PMS [4,29]. Magnetic biochar (MBC) materials are obtained by adding magnetic substances such as cobalt and iron to biochar, which retains the excellent properties of biochar and also has the property of being magnetizable and separable [30]. The surface of MBC holds persistent free radicals (PFRs), oxygenated functional groups (OFGs), magnetic compounds, and graphitic frameworks, enhancing its adsorption capabilities and catalytic qualities [31–33]. Therefore, MBC can boost PMS activation, contributing to more ROS generation and rapidly degrading organic pollutants.

The loading of metal materials on biochar can significantly modulate the surface properties of biochar, and through the covalent bonding interactions between the biochar carrier and the metal, it can help to improve the stability of the catalyst and further enhance the catalytic activity of the biochar catalysts [34,35]. The redox potential of Co^{3+}/Co^{2+} (E^0 = 1.92 V) is higher than that of Fe^{3+}/Fe^{2+} (E^0 = 0.77 V), Mn^{3+}/Mn^{2+} (E^0 = 1.54 V), and Cu^{2+}/Cu^{+} (E^0 = 0.153 V), which results in higher catalytic activity in cobalt-based catalysts [36]. In addition, the biochar carrier and cobalt active sites can form a synergistic effect by promoting electron transfer, which improves the catalytic activity and stability of the catalyst, effectively activates the PMS, and reduces the cost [36,37]. Therefore, cobalt-modified biochar was selected in this study to degrade an antibiotic. Yi et al. prepared cobalt-loaded water hyacinth biochar (Co-BC) as a catalyst to promote the degradation of norfloxacin (NOR) by effective activation of PS, and found that the Co-BC/PS system could remove 97.66% of NOR within 180 min [38]. In the present study, cobalt-loaded biochar was prepared using a simple method, and PMS was chosen as the oxidizing agent because it is more susceptible to catalyst activation, which leads to the efficient degradation of antibiotics in a shorter period of time.

Thie intention of this study was to prepare cobalt-loaded magnetic biochar (Co-MBC) to activate PMS for degrading MNZ and examine the degradation performance and mechanism. In this study, rapeseed straw biomass was selected for the preparation of Co-MBC by impregnation pyrolysis, which was magnetically modified in order to achieve the recovery and reuse of the catalyst. Meanwhile, the impact of factors such as catalyst dosage, PMS concentration, initial pH, and inorganic anions on degrading MNZ was explored. The active species connected to the degradation process was determined by quenching assays. Additionally, the degradation pathways of MNZ were investigated through employing liquid chromatography-mass spectrometry (LC-MS). This study promotes the recycling of waste biomass resources while degrading the targeted antibiotics.

2. Materials and Methods

2.1. Materials and Chemicals

Cobalt(II) nitrate hexahydrate ($Co(NO_3)_2 \cdot 6H_2O$) was obtained from Shanghai Epi Chemical Reagent Co., Ltd., Shanghai, China. Metronidazole (MNZ), permonosulfate (PMS), isopropyl alcohol (IPA), p-benzoquinone (BQ), humic acid, sodium hydroxide, sodium bicarbonate, sodium chloride, sodium dihydrogen phosphate, and anhydrous ethanol were obtained from Shanghai Aladdin Biochemical Technology Co., Ltd., Shanghai, China. Methanol (MeOH) was obtained from Wuxi Zhanwang Chemical Reagent Co., Ltd., Wuxi, China. L-Histidine (L-His) and tert-butanol (TBA) were purchased from Shanghai Macklin Biochemical Technology Co., Ltd., Shanghai, China. Nitric acid was obtained from

Sinopharm Chemical Reagent Co., Ltd., Shanghai, China. Nitrogen was provided by Wuxi Shengma Gas Co., Ltd., Wuxi, China. All reagents and chemicals were of analytical reagent grade without purification steps.

2.2. Preparing Rapeseed Straw Biomass

Rapeseed straw was obtained from rapeseed fields in a district of Jiangsu Province, China. The processing method was as follows: firstly, the rape straw was gathered, cleaned with deionized water, and then dried in an oven at 80 °C. Subsequently, the products were crushed by a wall breaker and passed through a 100-mesh sieve. The powdered biomass material obtained was labeled BC and collected for spare use.

2.3. Preparation of Cobalt Nitrate Modified Biochar

This experiment improved the preparation of biocarbon composites based on previous methods [39]. Co-MBC was prepared by the impregnation pyrolysis method. Five grams of rapeseed straw powder was added to 100 mL of cobalt nitrate solution (14 g/L) and stirred magnetically for 12 h to achieve a thorough mixing of rapeseed straw biomass and the cobalt nitrate solution. After mixing, the biomass was placed in a blower drying oven at 80 °C. After being completely dried, the biomass was placed in a mortar and ground into a powder. Subsequently, the cobalt-loaded rape straw powder was transferred to a volatile matter crucible to spread out, and then subjected to pyrolysis through a tube furnace at 700 °C for 2 h. The heating and pyrolysis procedure occurred in an N_2 environment with a temperature rise of 5 °C/min. After the furnace temperature dropped to room temperature, the magnetic biocarbon material was taken out, ground, and sieved. The material was repeatedly cleaned with ethanol and deionized water, then dried in the oven. After complete drying, the sample was taken out and labeled as Co-MBC.

2.4. Experimental Procedures

The experiments took place in 250 mL conical flasks containing 100 mL of MNZ solution (20 mg/L). The reactions took place at room temperature with a pH of 7. Appropriate amounts of PMS and Co-MBC were reacted with MNZ solution at 600 rpm for 60 min. A specific volume of the solution was withdrawn at 0, 5, 10, 15, 20, 30, 40, and 60 min. The samples were passed through a 0.45 μm filter and then transferred into the centrifugal tube. Additionally, 0.5 mL of methanol was included to stop the oxidation process. The UV spectrophotometer was applied to determine the concentration of MNZ at 320 nm.

The effectiveness of catalyst activation of PMS for degrading MNZ was studied in the impact factor tests. The effects of catalyst dosage (0.005 g, 0.01 g, 0.02 g, 0.03 g, and 0.04 g), PMS concentration (0.5 mM, 1 mM, 1.5 mM, and 2 mM), and initial pH (3, 5, 7, 9, and 11) on the degradation effectiveness of MNZ were investigated. The pH was modified by 1 M NaOH and 1 M HNO_3. The impact of anions (Cl^-, NO_3^-, HCO_3^-, $H_2PO_4^-$, and SO_4^{2-}) on the degrading efficiency of MNZ was investigated in distinct concentrations (1 mM, 5 mM, 10 mM, and 20 mM). Humic acid was added to the solution to investigate whether macromolecular organic matter impacted the entire reaction system. A degradation kinetic model was fitted to evaluate the degradation performance of Co-MBC on MNZ.

The reusability of Co-MBC catalysts for practical applications was explored through cycling experiments. Following the degradation experiment, the catalyst was recovered by the magnetic separation technique. The impurities were removed with deionized water and anhydrous ethanol, followed by drying and recycling for the next degradation experiment, in order to assess the stability and reproducibility of the catalyst.

2.5. Free Radical Identification Experiment

The active substances and their mechanisms of action that significantly contribute to the degrading reaction were identified by adding quenching agents. Tert-butanol (TBA) was employed to quench hydroxyl radicals (•OH), methanol (MeOH) was employed for hydroxyl radicals (•OH) and sulfate radicals (•SO_4^-), p-benzoquinone (BQ) was employed for superoxide radicals ($\bullet O_2^-$), and L-histidine was employed for singlet oxygen ($^1O_2$), respectively. In quenching experiments, the catalyst and oxidizer were introduced first, followed by the addition of the bursting agent. The MNZ concentration after the reaction was determined, the impacts of various quenching agents on MNZ removal were investigated, and the key active substances involved were analyzed.

3. Results and Discussions

3.1. Analysis of Morphological and Structural

Scanning electron microscopy (SEM, FEI Quanta FEG 250, FEI Company, Hillsboro, OR, USA) was implemented for analyzing the morphology and structure of Co-MBC in order to determine the existence of magnetic cobalt oxides. Figure 1 shows that Co-MBC retained the lamellar structure of BC, but due to pyrolysis, the structure of the MBC collapsed and fragmented to form faults and new pores. Additionally, a few scattered particles appeared on the original smooth surface, which indicates that cobalt oxides were successfully doped on the surface of Co-MBC. The cobalt oxide was uniformly dispersed throughout the loading process, contributing to the exposure of active sites on the catalyst surface [40].

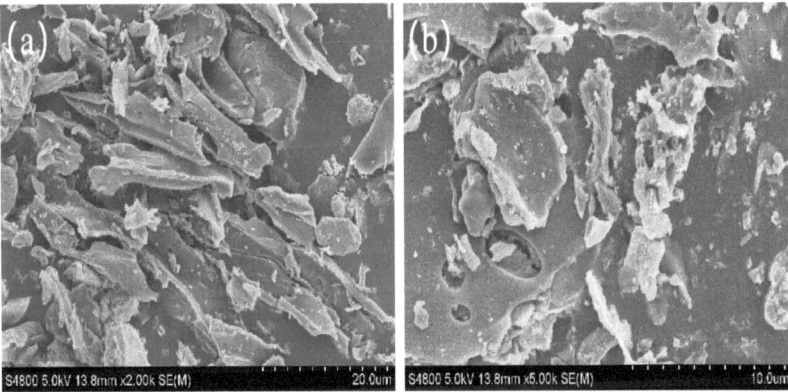

Figure 1. SEM of Co-MBC. (**a**) shows the morphological structure of Co-MBC at a magnification of 2000×, and (**b**) shows the morphological structure of Co-MBC at a magnification of 5000×.

3.2. Specific Surface Area and Pore Size Analysis

The specific surface area, pore size volume, and pore size distribution of BC and Co-MBC were determined using N_2 adsorption-desorption experiments employing a physical adsorption analyzer (BET, Micromeritics ASAP 2020 HD88, Micromeritics Instruments Corp, Atlanta, GA, USA). Figure 2 indicates the N_2 adsorption-desorption isotherms (a) and the distribution of pore sizes (b) of BC and Co-MBC. The samples had type IV adsorption isotherm features with distinct hysteresis loops, suggesting that the catalysts possessed micropore and mesopore structures [41].

The results show an inflection point at $P/P0 = 0.05$, followed by a significant rise in adsorption at low pressures, which implies a robust connection between the sample surface and nitrogen molecules, along with a notably high microporous content in the sample.

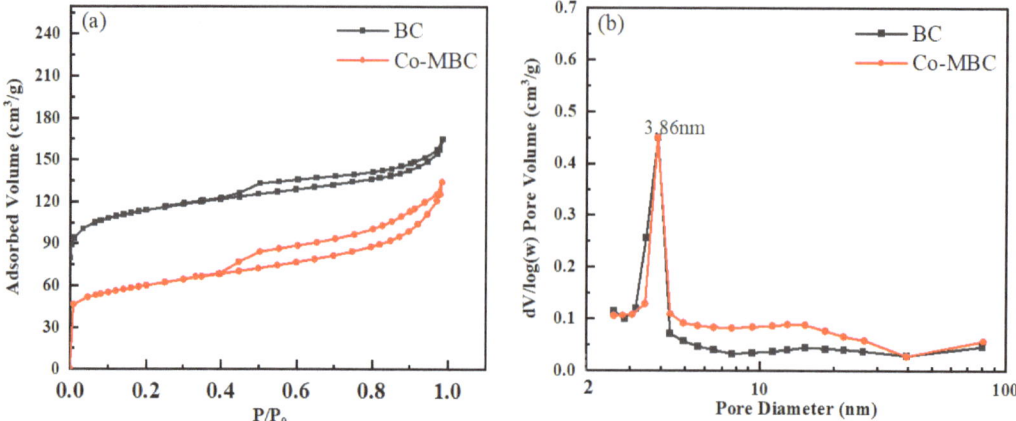

Figure 2. BET of BC and Co-MBC. (**a**) shows the nitrogen adsorption and desorption of the material, and (**b**) shows the pore size distribution of the material, both with corresponding descriptions in the text.

Table 1 shows that the micropore volume of biochar was three times greater than that of the modified biochar. The nitrogen adsorption isotherms proved that the highest adsorption capacity of Co-MBC at P/P0 (0.98) was notably lower compared to that of BC. The total pore volume declined by 17% after modification, probably due to cobalt oxides filling the pores and occupying many voids.

Table 1. Specific area and pore size parameters for BC and Co-MBC.

Samples	BET Specific Area (m²/g)	Average Pore Size (nm)	Micropore Volume (cm³/g)	Mesopore Volume (cm³/g)
BC	429.23	13.98	0.12	0.12
Co-MBC	218.57	27.45	0.05	0.16

Figure 2b illustrates that the mesoporous pore diameters of the samples, both before and after modification, mostly varied from 2 to 80 nm, with the highest pore volume observed at a mesoporous pore size of 3.86 nm. The mesopore pore volume in the modified samples increased, and the signal of micropore pore volume weakened, indicating that the mesopore porosity increased while the microporous pore volume decreased after modification. This may be due to the fact that the cobalt oxides mainly entered into micropores, and the cobalt oxides adsorbed on the surface of the samples formed more mesoporous pores, resulting in an increase in mesopore pore volume. In conclusion, in the modified biochar, the cobalt oxides mainly entered the microporous pore channels and increased the mesoporous porosity, thus providing more activation sites.

3.3. Crystal Structure of Analysis

The performance of catalysts is influenced by their crystal structure, which in this study, was determined and studied by X-ray diffraction (XRD, Rigaku Smartlab 3kwX, Rigaku Corporation, Tokyo, Japan).

Within a swept range of 10°–90°, the XRD diffractograms from BC and Co-MBC showed broader diffraction peaks at about $2\theta = 20-25°$ (Figure 3a), which indicates the presence of amorphous carbon in the material [42]. The crystallographic peaks occurring at diffraction angles of approximately 29.4°, 39.4°, and 47.6° are the characteristic peaks of the (104), (102), and (018) crystallographic planes of calcite ($CaCO_3$), according to standard chart card PDF#01-083-0578. The crystallographic peaks at diffraction angles of about 31.3°, 36.8°, and 59.4° are characteristic peaks of (220), (311), and (5111) crystallographic planes of Co_3O_4 in the cubic crystal system and are referenced to the standard atlas with the file number PDF#97-002-4210. The crystallographic peaks seen at a diffraction angle of about 42.4° correspond to the characteristic peaks of the (200) crystallographic plane of the cubic crystal structure of CoO, according to the standard atlas with the file number PDF#97-000-9865. The characteristic peaks at $2\theta = 60°$ are based on the (111) crystallographic plane of the Co metal CoO of the JCPDS#05-0727 card.

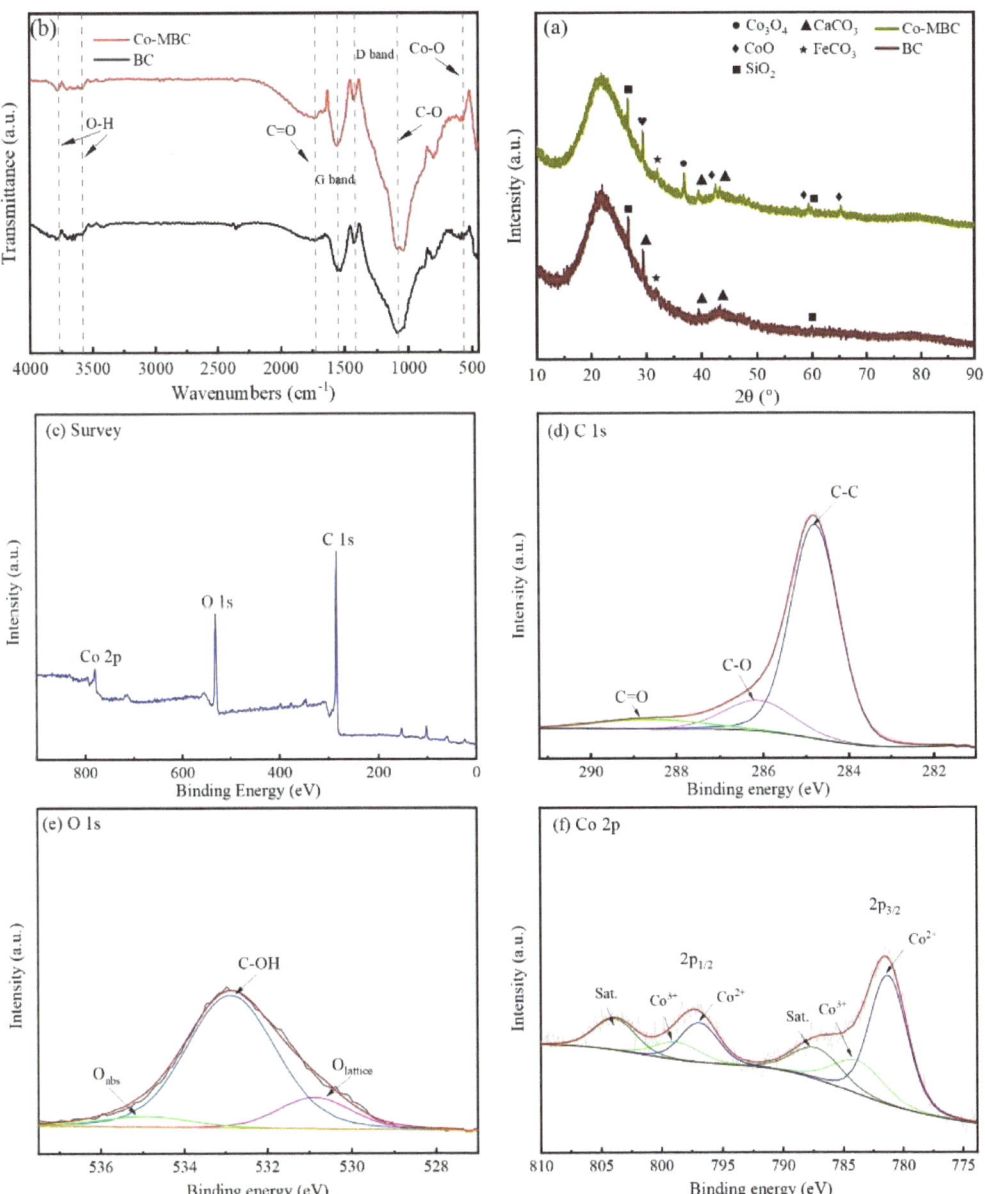

Figure 3. (**a**) XRD patterns of BC and Co-MBC. (**b**) Infrared spectra of BC and Co-MBC modified materials. XPS spectra of Co-MBC: (**c**) Full spectrum; (**d**) C 1S; (**e**) O 1S; and (**f**) Co 2p.

The XRD analysis indicated that the small width of the characteristic peaks of Co_3O_4 implied the high crystallinity of the synthesized Co-MBC [43]. The characterization results of Co-MBC proved the successful loading of cobalt oxides and the successful preparation of the material.

3.4. Identifying Functional Groups of a Catalyst

Fourier transform infrared (FT-IR, Thermo Scientific Nicolet iS20, Waltham, MA, USA) spectroscopy was utilized to ascertain the various functional groups of the catalyst. The FTIR spectra of Co-MBC and BC indicated that the primary absorption peaks of the two materials were seen at 1740, 1550, 1420, and 1080 cm^{-1}, respectively (Figure 3b). An absorption peak at 2350 cm^{-1} vanished as a result of high-temperature pyrolysis, causing the degradation of the structure of BC and the loss of its original functional groups.

A peak at 1725 cm^{-1} in the Co-MBC spectrum was caused by the C=O stretching vibration, indicating the presence of carboxyl groups within the catalyst, which is essential for PMS activation [44].

Both the BC and Co-MBC samples showed two characteristic peaks near 1420 cm^{-1} and 1550 cm^{-1}, correlating the D and G bands associated with disordered sp3 and ordered sp2 bonded carbon atoms, respectively. The band of absorption around 1080 cm^{-1} was caused by the C-O stretching vibration. More importantly, IR absorption peaks at 3580 and 3770 cm^{-1} were related to the O-H stretching vibration, indicating the existence of intermolecular hydrogen bonding in the samples [45]. Additionally, the peaks at 550–570 cm^{-1} were associated with the Co-O vibration of Co [46].

3.5. Analysis of Catalyst Bonding State and Elements

The bonding state and valence distribution of various elements in catalysts can be detected using X-ray photoelectron spectroscopy (XPS, Thermo Scientific K-Alpha, Thermo Fisher Scientific, Waltham, MA, USA).

Figure 3c shows peaks corresponding to C1s, O1s, and Co in the Co-MBC catalyst. Figure 3d shows the high-resolution C1s spectrum with three peaks near 284.86 eV, 286.26 eV, and 288.86 eV, representing C-C, C-O, and C=O, respectively [47]. Figure 3e shows that the O 1s spectrum of Co-MBC demonstrated the presence of three types of oxygen, with peaks located at 530.74 eV, 532.87 eV, and 535.16 eV, which belong to lattice oxygen (O_{lat}), surface hydroxyl group (O_{surf}), and surface adsorbed oxygen (O_{ads}), respectively [48]. Figure 3 shows the high-resolution XPS spectra of cobalt in Co-MBC. Depending on the valence state and binding energy, four peaks for Co^{2+} (781.36 eV and 796.96 eV) and Co^{3+} (784.16 eV and 798.86 eV) were observed by fitting Co $2P_{1/2}$ and Co $2P_{3/2}$. This correlates with the XRD spectrum analysis, confirming the presence of cobalt oxides in Co-MBC.

The signals of Co^{3+} corresponded with the XRD spectra analysis, indicating the presence of cobalt oxides in Co-MBC. The XPS results showed that the cobalt species in the crystals were both Co^{2+} and Co^{3+}, and that the cobalt oxides had been successfully loaded into biochar.

4. Catalytic Evaluation

4.1. Effect of Different Catalytic Systems on MNZ Degradation

Figure 4 points out the effect of different systems of BC, Co-MBC, BC+PMS, and Co-MBC+PMS on the degradation of MNZ.

When only BC was present within the reaction system, the MNZ removal efficiency was only 7.4%, while in the Co-MBC reaction system, the removal rate was elevated to 8.9%. Compared with the BC system, the enhancement of the adsorption effect was not obvious. This is because Co-MBC has a smoother surface and expanded pore structure compared to BC, but incorporating metal elements decreased the specific surface area of Co-MBC, restricting its interior pore structure.

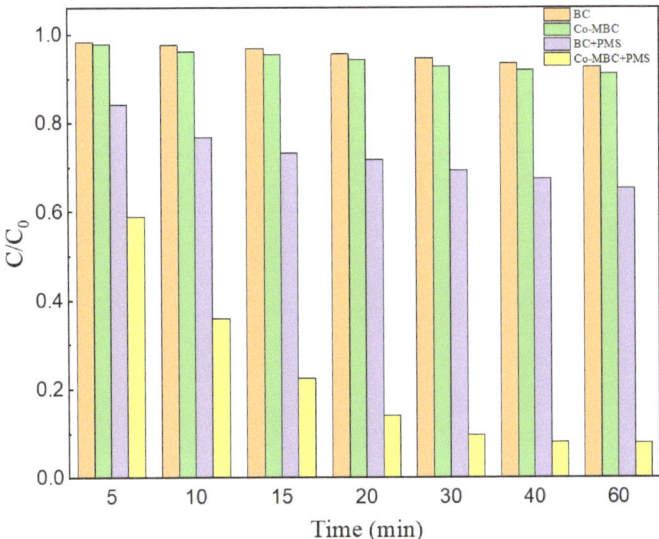

Figure 4. MNZ removal rate in different catalytic systems. Reaction conditions: [catalysts] = 0.3 g/L; [PMS] = 1 mM; [MNZ] = 20 mg/L; T = 25 ± 3 °C; initial pH = 7.

The Co-MBC+PMS system reached a 90.3% removal of MNZ within 60 min, which was much higher than that of other systems. This was due to the fact that more active spots were added to the surface of the modified biochar, and more active substances were generated to take part in the reaction during PMS activation, which enhanced the degradation of MNZ. Therefore, Co-MBC effectively triggered the activation of PMS, leading to the enhancement of MNZ degradation. The Co-MBC+PMS system was chosen for subsequent studies.

4.2. Effectiveness of Catalyst Dosage on MNZ Degradation

The dosage of catalyst applied significantly impacts the efficiency of the catalytic process. A catalyst dosage that is too small will lead to insufficient active sites in the reaction process, thus reducing the catalytic efficiency, while too much catalyst leads to difficulties in catalyst recovery, an increased risk of metal ion leaching, and greater disposal costs.

Therefore, the catalytic efficiency of the reaction system for MNZ degradation was studied by changing the degree of catalyst dosage. The degradation effects of different Co-MBC additions on MNZ are shown in Figure 5a. The degradation of MNZ exhibited a tendency of first rising and then decreasing as the addition of catalyst varied from 0 g/L to 0.4 g/L.

Specifically, when no catalyst was added, only PMS and MNZ were present in the reaction system, resulting in a little degradation of MNZ due to the activation of PMS by light. Expanding the catalyst amount from 0.05 g/L to 0.2 g/L resulted in the degradation rate of MNZ rising from 57.9% to 90.3%. Increasing the catalyst amount caused the quantity of active sites in the reaction process to rise, leading to quicker degradation of MNZ. Figure 5a shows that the degradation effect on MNZ did not increase significantly but instead decreased when the catalyst dosage was increased to 0.3 g/L and 0.4 g/L compared to the 0.2 g/L catalyst dosage. Owing to magnetic forces, excessive catalysts were drawn together and formed clusters, which covered their active sites and hindered their ability to catalyze PMS efficiently [49]. In addition, the excess catalyst may have activated PMS to produce high concentrations of •SO_4^-, which can lead to quenching reactions with the oxidizer, resulting in poor degradation [50]. Excessive catalyst use not only wastes resources, but also increases economic costs, and the removal effect on pollutants becomes less than ideal. When using catalyst amounts of 0.2 g/L and 0.3 g/L, the resultant reaction rates were 0.16411 min^{-1} and 0.15505 min^{-1}, respectively (Figure 5b), resulting in little change in reaction and degradation rates. Thus, a catalyst dosage of 0.2 g/L was selected for the next investigation.

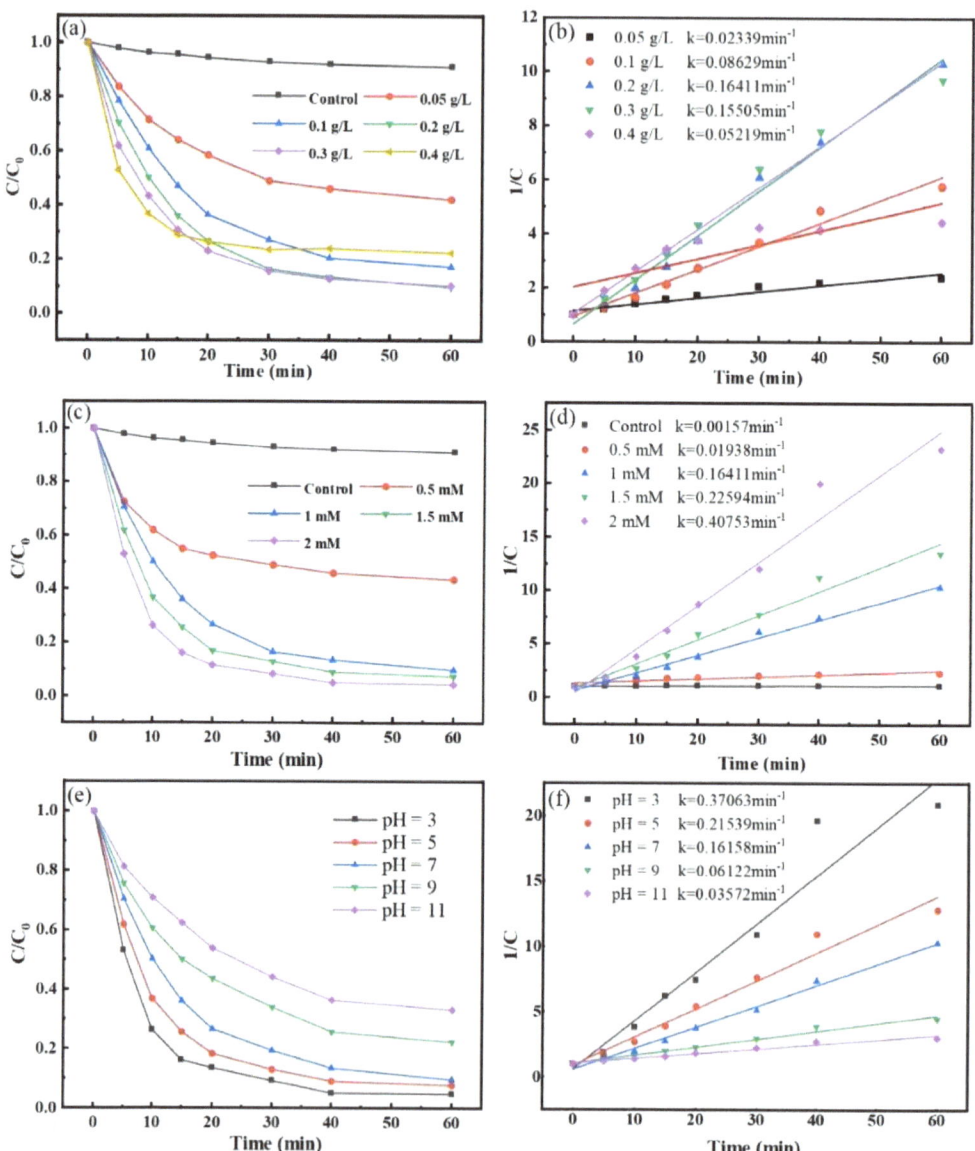

Figure 5. Influence of catalyst dosage. (**a**) (Reaction conditions: [PMS] = 1 mM; [MNZ] = 20 mg/L; T = 25 ± 3 °C; initial pH = 7), PS concentration; (**c**) (Reaction conditions: [Co-MBC] = 0.2 g/L; [MNZ] = 20 mg/L; T = 25 ± 3 °C; initial pH = 7), and pH; (**e**) (Reaction conditions: [Co-MBC] = 0.2 g/L; [PMS] = 1 mM; [MNZ] = 20 mg/L; T = 25 ± 3 °C). MNZ degradation kinetic curves (**b,d,f**) correspond to (**a,c,e**), respectively.

4.3. Effectiveness of PMS Concentration on MNZ Degradation

PMS can be activated to produce $•SO_4^-$; hence, the concentration of PMS directly influences the overall degradation process [51]. The previous study in this experiment showed that the removal of MNZ by Co-MBC without the addition of PMS was only 8.9% after 60 min. The effects of different concentrations of PMS on the degradation of MNZ were investigated. The degradation rates of MNZ after 60 min were 56.4%, 90.3%, 92.6%, and 95.7% at PMS concentrations of 0.5 mM, 1 mM, 1.5 mM, and 2 mM, respectively (Figure 5c). The result showed that an increased amount of oxidizing agent in the reaction system resulted in a more effective degradation of pollutants.

The possible reason for this is that when the concentration of the oxidizer is low, it cannot produce enough $•SO_4^-$, so the degradation effect of the whole reaction process is reduced. Increasing the concentration enhances the catalyst touch possibilities with PMS, contributing to the increased production of $•SO_4^-$ for the reaction, leading to steady degradation and a higher degradation rate. Once the concentration of PMS is excessive, the excess HSO_5^- in the solution is absorbed by the catalyst, saturating the reactive sites of Co-MBC and restrictedly generating free radicals. Furthermore, the $•SO_4^-$ in the reaction system experiences a self-quenching reaction, resulting in the creation of $S_2O_8^{2-}$, which consumes $•SO_4^-$ and influences the degradation reaction. Moreover, excessive $•SO_4^-$ is an environmental pollutant as it causes corrosive effects upon contact with basic surfaces, such as drainage pipes. Therefore, in this study, 1 mM PMS was selected due to the observation of enhanced degradation rates at other concentrations without a substantial enhancement in the final degradation.

4.4. Effectiveness of pH on MNZ Degradation

The initial pH has been shown in earlier research to impact the surface characteristics of catalytic materials and the production of free radicals, thereby influencing the removal of pollutants [52,53]. The pH was adjusted in accordance with the preceding section. Figure 5e reveals that altering the solution pH impacted the degradation of MNZ by Co-MBC+PMS, showing that the degradation efficiency was reduced as the pH increased.

From Figure 5e,f, it can be seen that when the pH = 3, the reaction rate was 0.37063 min^{-1}, and MNZ degradation by the Co-MBC+PMS system was as high as 95.2% after 60 min. When the pH = 11, the constant of reaction rate was 0.03572 min^{-1}; the reaction rate became slower, and the degradation rate decreased to 66.9%. The degradation effect was shown to reach a rate of more than 90% in neutral and acidic systems. In the alkaline system, the degradation rate was slowed down, but still had some effect. The results show that the modified biochar Co-MBC could work under different pH conditions and has good potential for practical applications. This happens because $•SO_5^-$, which has lower oxidizing capacity, replaces HSO_5^- as the predominant form present under alkaline conditions, and OH^- will interact with $•SO_4^-$ to generate less reactive $•OH$, which is unfavorable for the degradation of MNZ in the reaction system, as shown in Equations (1)–(3) [54]. The experimental findings demonstrated that Co-MBC proved efficient in treating MNZ wastewater throughout an extensive pH range in real environments.

$$HSO_5^- + •SO_4^- \rightarrow •SO_5^- + HSO_4^- \qquad (1)$$

$$•SO_4^- + OH^- \rightarrow •OH + SO_4^{2-} \qquad (2)$$

$$H_2O + •SO_4^- \rightarrow HSO_4^- + •OH \qquad (3)$$

4.5. Influence of Anions on MNZ Degradation

Anions present in natural bodies of water may influence the degradation of MNZ in a Co-MBC system. Degradation experiments were conducted to explore the influence of varying concentrations of inorganic anions (NO_3^-, HCO_3^-, $H_2PO_4^-$, and Cl^-) on the degradation process.

As can be seen in Figure 6, the coexisting anions mainly had a restricting impact on MNZ degradation. From Figure 6a,b, it is obvious that Cl⁻ and HCO₃⁻ exerted inhibitory effects on the reaction system with increasing anion concentrations. This could be because Cl⁻ and HCO₃⁻ reacted with •SO₄⁻, thus quenching •SO₄⁻ and •OH and generating minor active radicals •Cl and •O₂⁻ (Equations (4) and (5)) [55,56]. In reverse, the addition of H₂PO₄⁻ ions promoted the reaction system, as shown in Figure 6d, which was due to the fact that the phosphate anion itself had a certain activation effect on PMS [57].

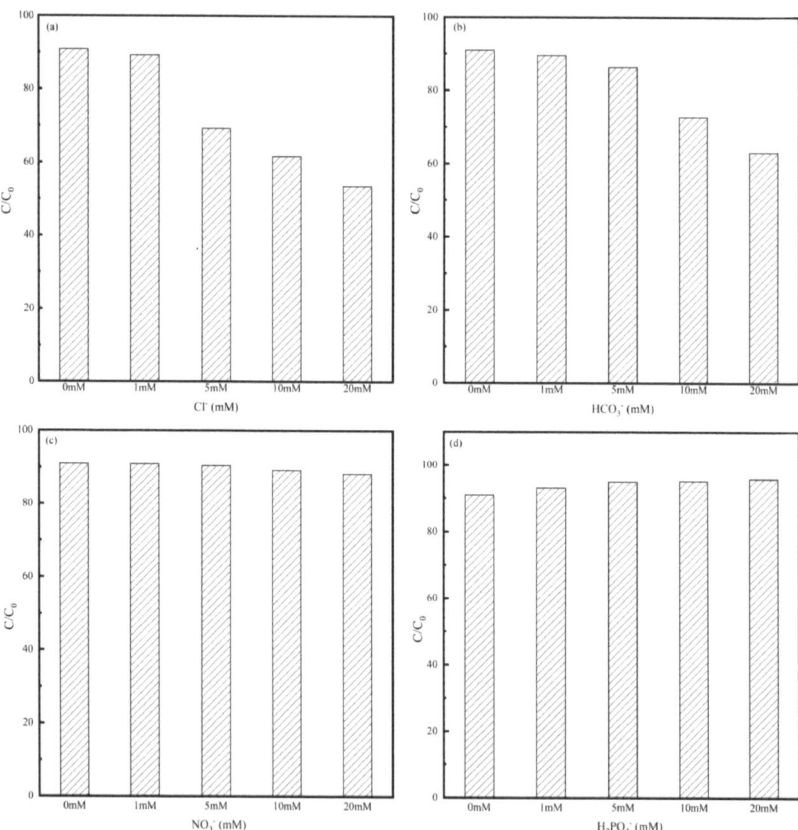

Figure 6. Effect of inorganic anions on MNZ degradation efficiency: (**a**) Cl⁻; (**b**) HCO₃⁻; (**c**) NO₃⁻; and (**d**) H₂PO₄⁻. Reaction conditions: [Co-MBC] = 0.2 g/L; [PMS] = 1 mM; [MNZ] = 20 mg/L; T = 25 ± 3 °C; initial pH = 7.

Figure 6c illustrates a 5% reduction in the MNZ degradation rate at the NO₃⁻ ionic concentration of 20 mM. The reason for this is that NO₃⁻ interacts with the free radicals in the system as shown in Equation (6), quenching a small portion of •SO₄⁻ and occupying the active site, and thus having a weak inhibitory effect on the reaction system [58]. Overall, the results showed that in the low concentration range of ionic concentration, interference did not have much of an effect on degradation.

$$Cl^- + \bullet SO_4^- \rightarrow \bullet Cl + SO_4^{2-} \tag{4}$$

$$Cl^- + \bullet OH + O_2 \rightarrow HOCl + \bullet O_2 \tag{5}$$

$$NO_3^- + \bullet SO_4^- \rightarrow \bullet NO_3^- + SO_4^{2-} \tag{6}$$

4.6. Effect of Humic Acid on MNZ Degradation

In this work, humic acid was introduced at various doses to examine the impact of macromolecular organic compounds on the Co-MBC/PMS system. Figure 7a suggests that the presence of 5 mg/L of humic acid did not significantly impact the degradation of MNZ. However, at HA levels of 50 mg/L, the degradation rate fell considerably compared to the system without HA.

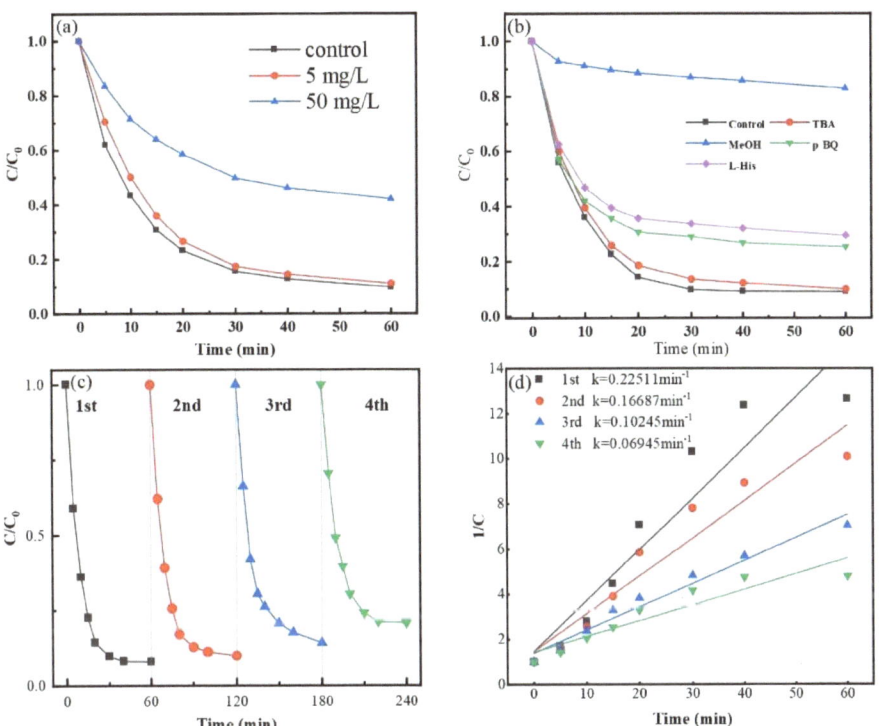

Figure 7. (**a**) Effect of organic matter on MNZ degradation efficiency. (**b**) Impact of various quenching agents on the Co-MBC/PMS system. Recurrent experiments with Co-MBC: (**c**) degradation efficiency; (**d**) kinetic curves. (Reaction conditions: [Co-MBC] = 0.2 g/L; [PMS] = 1 mM; [MNZ] = 20 mg/L; T = 25 ± 3 °C; initial pH = 7).

This situation may be caused by the quinone group in HA stimulating PMS to generate slightly activated free radicals in the reaction system while also quenching •SO_4^-. The low concentration of HA was adsorbed by Co-MBC, and the bursting effect was not obvious, but the excess of the large molecular HA could have acted as a radical cleaner in the system, which reduced the degradation effect [59].

4.7. Free Radical Quenching Experiment

An assessment was performed regarding the impact of various radicals on degrading MNZ in a Co-MBC/PMS system. Methanol was utilized to quench •SO_4^- and •OH, tert-butanol was used to quench •OH, p-benzoquinone was employed to quench •O_2^-, and L-histidine was applied to quench $^1O_2$ [60,61]. The concentrations of all of the quenchers employed were 0.05 M.

Figure 7b shows a substantial reduction in the rate of degradation of MNZ after methanol was added to the reaction system during a 60 min period. In contrast, the addition of tert-butanol slightly inhibited MNZ degradation, which suggests that the dominant role is played by •SO$_4^-$ instead of •OH. At the same time, the degradation rate reduced correspondingly following the addition of p-benzoquinone and L-histidine, indicating that the burst of •O$_2^-$ and ^{1}O$_2$ also had an inhibiting effect on the reaction system.

4.8. Recurrent Experiment

Whether a catalyst can be reused is one of the necessary prerequisites for determining its potential in future practical applications. Since the cobalt nitrate-modified biochar itself had strong magnetism, the catalyst material could be recovered after use by using an applied magnetic field. The recovered material was washed, dried, and then used in a cyclic experiment.

As shown in Figure 7c, the degradation effect of Co-MBC on MNZ was reduced by 13% after four re-uses, indicating that the material still showed good degradation performance. However, the reaction rate tended to decrease as the experiment was repeated, as shown in Figure 7d. This is because the small molecule intermediates generated by MNZ decomposition bind to the catalyst, diminishing the functionality of the active site and hindering the production of •SO$_4^-$, resulting in reduced degradation efficiency.

4.9. Degradation Pathway of MNZ

The intermediates of MNZ degradation were analyzed by LC-MS. Figure 8 displays the major mass peaks appearing at m/z = 142 (P2), 145 (P3), 159 (P4), 103 (P5), 187 (P6), 99 (P7), 118 (P8), 88 (P9), 158 (P10), 116 (P11), and 90 (P12), and the information about these intermediates is summarized in Table 2. Among them, P2, P6, and P10 were weighted more heavily, and it was speculated that these three substances may be the main intermediates that formed during the reaction.

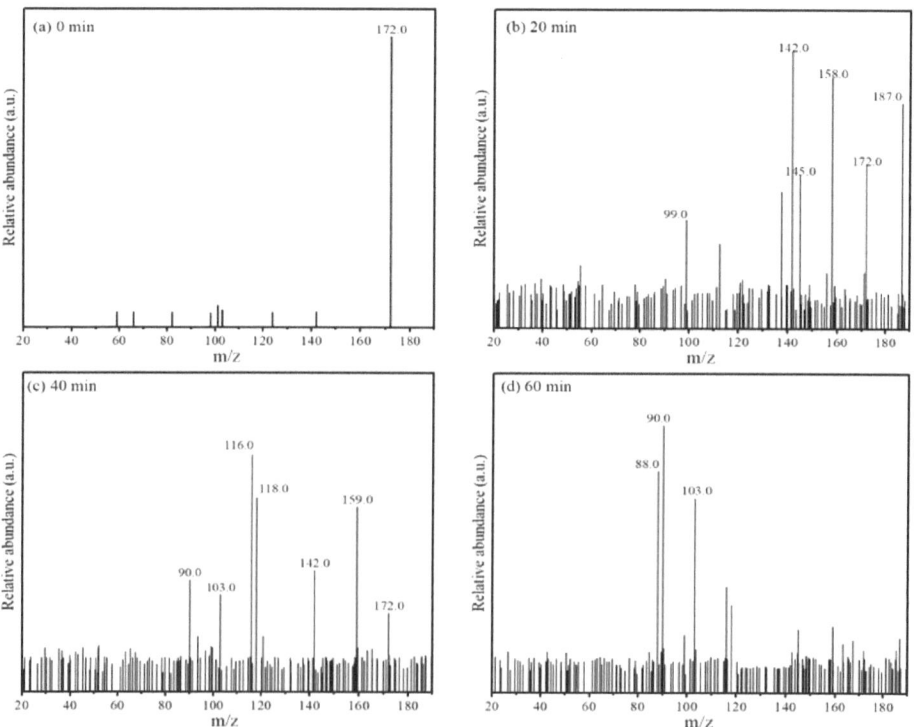

Figure 8. Mass spectrum of MNZ degraded by Co-MBC/PMS system.

Table 2. Intermediates of MNZ degradation.

Product Serial Number	Relative Molecular Mass (g/mol)	Molecular Formula	Preliminary Structure	Intermediates
P1	172	$C_6H_9N_3O_3$		Metronidazole
P2	142	$C_6H_{10}N_2O_2$		1-(2-Hydroxyethyl)-2-methyl-1H-imidazol-5-ol
P3	145	$C_5H_8N_2O_3$		1-(2-hydroxyethyl)-1H-imidazole-2,5-diol
P4	159	$C_5H_6N_2O_4$		2-(2,5-dihydroxy-1H-imidazol-1-yl) acetic acid
P5	103	$C_3H_6N_2O_2$		(E)-N'-((E)-2-hydroxyethenyl) carbamic acid
P6	187	$C_5H_5N_3O_5$		2-(2-hydroxy-5-nitro-1H-imidazol-1-yl) acetic acid
P7	99	$C_3H_5N_3O$		5-amino-1H-imidazol-2-ol
P8	118	$C_3H_6N_2O_3$		Carbamoylglycine
P9	88	$C_2H_4N_2O_2$		(Z)-N-methyl-1-nitrosimidic acid
P10	158	$C_5H_6N_2O_4$		2-(2,5-dihydroxy-1H-imidazol-1-yl) acetic acid
P11	116	$C_3H_4N_2O_3$		1H-imidazole-2,4,5-triol
P12	90	$C_2H_2O_4$		Ethanedioic acid

With the increase in degradation time, the MNZ signal gradually disappeared, and the signal of small molecules was enhanced. Combined with the compounds produced by degradation, it can be concluded that ring-opening oxidation, denitrohydroxylation, demethylation, and decarboxylation are the main pathways for the degradation of MNZ. A potential degradation pathway for MNZ was indicated by the identification of intermediates.

Figure 9 shows the three pathways of MNZ degradation, with an initial m/z of 171 for MNZ. In pathway I, free radicals attacked the C-N bond of MNZ through denitrohydroxylation to generate 1-(2-hydroxyethyl)-2-methyl-1H-imidazol-5-ol (P2, m/z = 142). P2 underwent hydroxylation to produce 1-(2-hydroxyethyl)-1H-imidazole-2,5-diol (P3, m/z = 144) [62]. P3 was oxidized to 2-(2,5-dihydroxy-1H-imidazol-1-yl) acetic acid (P4, m/z = 159) by reactive oxygen species. Finally, P4 was degraded to (E)-N'-((E)-2-hydroxyethenyl) carbamic acid (P5, m/z = 102) through C-N bond cleavage [63]. In pathway II, MNZ underwent direct oxidation by reactive oxygen species to form 2-(2-hydroxy-5-nitro-1H-imidazol-1-yl) acetic acid (P6, m/z = 187), which was subsequently transformed into 5-amino-1H-imidazol-2-ol (P7, m/z = 99) through nitro reduction and cleavage. This was further converted to carbamoylglycine (P8, m/z = 118) by breaking the C=C bond of P7, and then dehydrogenated through the hydroxylamino function to yield (Z)-N-methyl-1-nitrosimidic acid (P9, m/z = 88). In pathway III, MNZ underwent hydroxylation to produce 2-(2,5-dihydroxy-1H-imidazol-1-yl) acetic acid (P10, m/z = 158), followed by decarboxylation to generate 1H-imidazole-2,4,5-triol (P11, m/z = 116), and then experienced a ring-opening process to yield ethanedioic acid (P12, m/z = 90). Finally, P5, P9, and P12 were oxidized to CO_2, H_2O, and NO_3^- by the active substances [64,65].

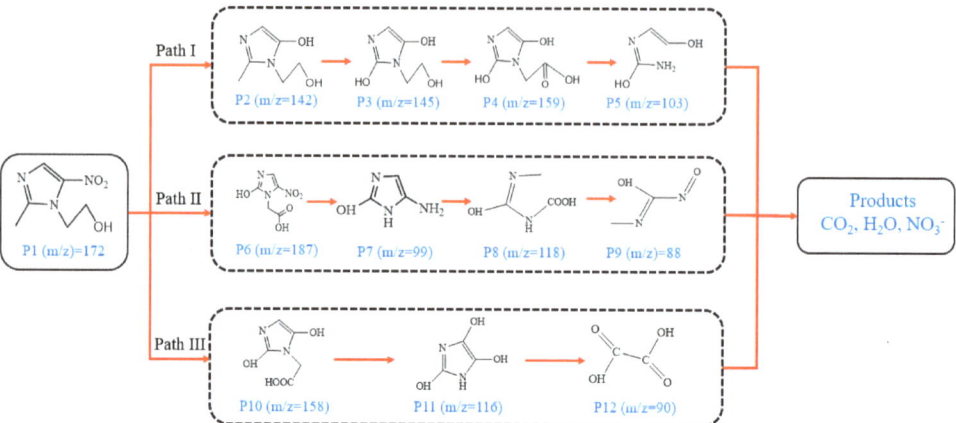

Figure 9. MNZ degradation pathways.

5. Conclusions

A cobalt-loaded magnetic biochar (Co-MBC) catalyst was successfully synthesized in this study, and it was shown that this material can be used to enhance the removal of the antibiotic pollutant metronidazole (MNZ). The degradation process conformed to the proposed secondary reaction kinetics, resulting in the degradation rate of MNZ reaching 90% after 60 min of reaction in the Co-MBC/PMS system under optimal conditions. The active species, including •OH, $•SO_4^-$, $•O_2^-$, and $^1O_2$, cooperated together to degrade MNZ, but $•SO_4^-$ was the main participant throughout the whole reaction process, attacking the MNZ macromolecules through the processes of ring-opening oxidation, dinitro-hydroxylation, demethylation, and decarboxylation. In addition, the Co-MBC/PMS reaction system was shown to be highly resistant to interference, and was able to degrade MNZ well even across an extensive pH range and in the presence of different anions. In conclusion, this study demonstrated that the high redox potential and magnetic properties of cobalt are favorable for expanding the specific surface area and increasing the active sites in cobalt-loaded biochar, which can promote electron transfer. The cobalt-loaded magnetic biochar material was shown to efficiently activate PMS and exhibit good catalytic performance in degrading the antibiotic MNZ while also realizing the effective recycling of biochar materials. The material had high reusability and stability. The resource utilization of waste biomass was realized while effectively removing pollutants. This research offers a reference for preparing effective, reusable, and environmentally friendly catalysts for the degradation of non-biodegradable pollutants.

Author Contributions: Formal analysis, L.S.; Writing—original draft, L.H.; Writing—review & editing, E.H.D.; Supervision, H.L.; Funding acquisition, N.D. All authors have read and agreed to the published version of the manuscript.

Funding: This research received funding from the National Natural Science Foundation of China (No. 52100071).

Data Availability Statement: The original contributions presented in the study are included in the article, further inquiries can be directed to the corresponding author.

Conflicts of Interest: The authors declare no conflict of interest.

References

1. Ahankar, H.; Ramazani, A.; Ślepokura, K.; Lis, T.; Kinzhybalo, V. Magnetic cobalt ferrite nanoparticles functionalized with citric acid as a green nanocatalyst for one-pot three-component sonochemical synthesis of substituted 3-pyrrolin-2-ones. *Res. Chem. Intermed.* **2019**, *45*, 5007–5025. [CrossRef]
2. Alamgir; Talha, K.; Wang, B.; Liu, J.-H.; Ullah, R.; Feng, F.; Yu, J.; Chen, S.; Li, J.-R. Effective adsorption of metronidazole antibiotic from water with a stable Zr(IV)-MOFs: Insights from DFT, kinetics and thermodynamics studies. *J. Environ. Chem. Eng.* **2020**, *8*, 103642. [CrossRef]
3. Arast, N.; Farhadian, M.; Tangestaninejad, S.; Navarchian, A.H. Efficient photocatalytic performance of $BiVO_4$/ZIF-8/Cu_2S/Ag_2S incorporated in solar driven-cleaning ABS/MWCNT membrane applied in metronidazole decontamination. *Process Saf. Environ. Prot.* **2023**, *176*, 87–100. [CrossRef]
4. Cao, J.; Li, J.; Chu, W.; Cen, W. Facile synthesis of Mn-doped BiOCl for metronidazole photodegradation: Optimization, degradation pathway, and mechanism. *Chem. Eng. J.* **2020**, *400*, 125813. [CrossRef]
5. Cha, J.S.; Choi, J.-C.; Ko, J.H.; Park, Y.-K.; Park, S.H.; Jeong, K.-E.; Kim, S.-S.; Jeon, J.-K. The low-temperature SCR of NO over rice straw and sewage sludge derived char. *Chem. Eng. J.* **2010**, *156*, 321–327. [CrossRef]
6. Chen, C.; Sun, H.; Zhang, S.; Su, X. Non-metal activated peroxydisulfate by straw biochar for tetracycline hydrochloride oxidative degradation: Catalytic activity and mechanism. *Environ. Sci. Pollut. Res.* **2023**, *30*, 50815–50828. [CrossRef] [PubMed]
7. Chen, G.; Yu, Y.; Liang, L.; Duan, X.; Li, R.; Lu, X.; Yan, B.; Li, N.; Wang, S. Remediation of antibiotic wastewater by coupled photocatalytic and persulfate oxidation system: A critical review. *J. Hazard. Mater.* **2021**, *408*, 124461. [CrossRef] [PubMed]
8. Coha, M.; Farinelli, G.; Tiraferri, A.; Minella, M.; Vione, D. Advanced oxidation processes in the removal of organic substances from produced water: Potential, configurations, and research needs. *Chem. Eng. J.* **2021**, *414*, 128668. [CrossRef]
9. Crofts, T.S.; Gasparrini, A.J.; Dantas, G. Next-generation approaches to understand and combat the antibiotic resistome. *Nat. Rev. Microbiol.* **2017**, *15*, 422–434. [CrossRef]
10. Dang, T.T.; Do, V.M.; Trinh, V.T. Nano-Catalysts in Ozone-Based Advanced Oxidation Processes for Wastewater Treatment. *Curr. Pollut. Rep.* **2020**, *6*, 217–229. [CrossRef]
11. Ding, J.; Zhang, Y.; Lu, S.; Zhang, X.; Li, Y.; Zhong, Y.; Zhang, H. A novel strategy using persulfate activated with thiosulfate for strong enhancement of trace 2,2′-dichlorobiphenyl removal: Influencing factors, and mechanisms. *Chem. Eng. J.* **2021**, *415*, 128969. [CrossRef]
12. Ding, Y.; Zhu, L.; Wang, N.; Tang, H. Sulfate radicals induced degradation of tetrabromobisphenol A with nanoscaled magnetic $CuFe_2O_4$ as a heterogeneous catalyst of peroxymonosulfate. *Appl. Catal. B Environ.* **2013**, *129*, 153–162. [CrossRef]
13. Dong, C.; Fang, W.; Yi, Q.; Zhang, J. A comprehensive review on reactive oxygen species (ROS) in advanced oxidation processes (AOPs). *Chemosphere* **2022**, *308*, 136205. [CrossRef] [PubMed]
14. Fan, J.; Gu, L.; Wu, D.; Liu, Z. Mackinawite (FeS) activation of persulfate for the degradation of p-chloroaniline: Surface reaction mechanism and sulfur-mediated cycling of iron species. *Chem. Eng. J.* **2018**, *333*, 657–664. [CrossRef]
15. Feng, Y.; Song, Q.; Lv, W.; Liu, G. Degradation of ketoprofen by sulfate radical-based advanced oxidation processes: Kinetics, mechanisms, and effects of natural water matrices. *Chemosphere* **2017**, *189*, 643–651. [CrossRef] [PubMed]
16. Feng, Z.; Yuan, R.; Wang, F.; Chen, Z.; Zhou, B.; Chen, H. Preparation of magnetic biochar and its application in catalytic degradation of organic pollutants: A review. *Sci. Total Environ.* **2021**, *765*, 142673. [CrossRef] [PubMed]
17. Gao, B.; Yap, P.S.; Lim, T.M.; Lim, T.-T. Adsorption-photocatalytic degradation of Acid Red 88 by supported TiO_2: Effect of activated carbon support and aqueous anions. *Chem. Eng. J.* **2011**, *171*, 1098–1107. [CrossRef]
18. Gao, J.; Han, D.; Xu, Y.; Liu, Y.; Shang, J. Persulfate activation by sulfide-modified nanoscale iron supported by biochar (S-nZVI/BC) for degradation of ciprofloxacin. *Sep. Purif. Technol.* **2020**, *235*, 116202. [CrossRef]
19. Gao, Y.; Wang, Q.; Ji, G.; Li, A. Degradation of antibiotic pollutants by persulfate activated with various carbon materials. *Chem. Eng. J.* **2022**, *429*, 132387. [CrossRef]
20. Hou, J.; He, X.; Zhang, S.; Yu, J.; Feng, M.; Li, X. Recent advances in cobalt-activated sulfate radical-based advanced oxidation processes for water remediation: A review. *Sci. Total Environ.* **2021**, *770*, 145311. [CrossRef]
21. Huang, Y.; Tian, X.; Nie, Y.; Yang, C.; Wang, Y. Enhanced peroxymonosulfate activation for phenol degradation over MnO_2 at pH 3.5–9.0 via Cu(II) substitution. *J. Hazard. Mater.* **2018**, *360*, 303–310. [CrossRef] [PubMed]
22. Jin, Q.; Liu, W.; Dong, Y.; Lu, Y.; Yang, C.; Lin, H. Single atom catalysts for degradation of antibiotics from aqueous environments by advanced oxidation processes: A review. *J. Clean. Prod.* **2023**, *423*, 138688. [CrossRef]
23. Karkman, A.; Do, T.T.; Walsh, F.; Virta, M.P.J. Antibiotic-Resistance Genes in Waste Water. *Trends Microbiol.* **2018**, *26*, 220–228. [CrossRef]
24. Kumar, A.; Pal, D. Antibiotic resistance and wastewater: Correlation, impact and critical human health challenges. *J. Environ. Chem. Eng.* **2018**, *6*, 52–58. [CrossRef]
25. Li, M.-F.; Liu, Y.-G.; Zeng, G.-M.; Liu, N.; Liu, S.-B. Graphene and graphene-based nanocomposites used for antibiotics removal in water treatment: A review. *Chemosphere* **2019**, *226*, 360–380. [CrossRef] [PubMed]
26. Liu, J.; Jiang, J.; Wang, M.; Kang, J.; Zhang, J.; Liu, S.; Tang, Y.; Li, S. Peroxymonosulfate activation by cobalt particles embedded into biochar for levofloxacin degradation: Efficiency, stability, and mechanism. *Sep. Purif. Technol.* **2022**, *294*, 121082. [CrossRef]

27. Liu, S.; Zhao, C.; Wang, Z.; Ding, H.; Deng, H.; Yang, G.; Li, J.; Zheng, H. Urea-assisted one-step fabrication of a novel nitrogen-doped carbon fiber aerogel from cotton as metal-free catalyst in peroxymonosulfate activation for efficient degradation of carbamazepine. *Chem. Eng. J.* **2020**, *386*, 124015. [CrossRef]
28. Liu, Y.; Chen, M.; Yongmei, H. Study on the adsorption of Cu(II) by EDTA functionalized Fe_3O_4 magnetic nano-particles. *Chem. Eng. J.* **2013**, *218*, 46–54. [CrossRef]
29. Liu, Y.; Chen, X.; Yang, Y.; Feng, Y.; Wu, D.; Mao, S. Activation of persulfate with metal–organic framework-derived nitrogen-doped porous Co@C nanoboxes for highly efficient p-Chloroaniline removal. *Chem. Eng. J.* **2019**, *358*, 408–418. [CrossRef]
30. Liu, Z.; Shi, X.; Yan, Z.; Sun, Z. Activation of peroxymonosulfate by biochar in-situ enriched with cobalt tungstate and cobalt: Insights into the role of rich oxygen vacancies and catalytic mechanism. *Chem. Eng. J.* **2023**, *475*, 146124. [CrossRef]
31. Lou, X.; Wu, L.; Guo, Y.; Chen, C.; Wang, Z.; Xiao, D.; Fang, C.; Liu, J.; Zhao, J.; Lu, S. Peroxymonosulfate activation by phosphate anion for organics degradation in water. *Chemosphere* **2014**, *117*, 582–585. [CrossRef] [PubMed]
32. Luo, J.; Yi, Y.; Ying, G.; Fang, Z.; Zhang, Y. Activation of persulfate for highly efficient degradation of metronidazole using Fe(II)-rich potassium doped magnetic biochar. *Sci. Total Environ.* **2022**, *819*, 152089. [CrossRef]
33. Martins, P.M.; Salazar, H.; Aoudjit, L.; Gonçalves, R.; Zioui, D.; Fidalgo-Marijuan, A.; Costa, C.M.; Ferdov, S.; Lanceros-Mendez, S. Crystal morphology control of synthetic giniite for enhanced photo-Fenton activity against the emerging pollutant metronidazole. *Chemosphere* **2021**, *262*, 128300. [CrossRef] [PubMed]
34. Meng, F.; Song, M.; Wei, Y.; Wang, Y. The contribution of oxygen-containing functional groups to the gas-phase adsorption of volatile organic compounds with different polarities onto lignin-derived activated carbon fibers. *Environ. Sci. Pollut. Res.* **2019**, *26*, 7195–7204. [CrossRef]
35. Mirzaee, R.; Darvishi Cheshmeh Soltani, R.; Khataee, A.; Boczkaj, G. Combination of air-dispersion cathode with sacrificial iron anode generating $Fe^{2+}Fe^{3+}{}_2O_4$ nanostructures to degrade paracetamol under ultrasonic irradiation. *J. Mol. Liq.* **2019**, *284*, 536–546. [CrossRef]
36. Muttakin, M.; Mitra, S.; Thu, K.; Ito, K.; Saha, B.B. Theoretical framework to evaluate minimum desorption temperature for IUPAC classified adsorption isotherms. *Int. J. Heat Mass Transf.* **2018**, *122*, 795–805. [CrossRef]
37. Peng, L.; Shang, Y.; Gao, B.; Xu, X. Co_3O_4 anchored in N, S heteroatom co-doped porous carbons for degradation of organic contaminant: Role of pyridinic N-Co binding and high tolerance of chloride. *Appl. Catal. B Environ.* **2021**, *282*, 119484. [CrossRef]
38. Priyadarshini, M.; Das, I.; Ghangrekar, M.M.; Blaney, L. Advanced oxidation processes: Performance, advantages, and scale-up of emerging technologies. *J. Environ. Manag.* **2022**, *316*, 115295. [CrossRef] [PubMed]
39. Qi, Y.; Ge, B.; Zhang, Y.; Jiang, B.; Wang, C.; Akram, M.; Xu, X. Three-dimensional porous graphene-like biochar derived from Enteromorpha as a persulfate activator for sulfamethoxazole degradation: Role of graphitic N and radicals transformation. *J. Hazard. Mater.* **2020**, *399*, 123039. [CrossRef]
40. Ren, F.; Zhu, W.; Zhao, J.; Liu, H.; Zhang, X.; Zhang, H.; Zhu, H.; Peng, Y.; Wang, B. Nitrogen-doped graphene oxide aerogel anchored with spinel $CoFe_2O_4$ nanoparticles for rapid degradation of tetracycline. *Sep. Purif. Technol.* **2020**, *241*, 116690. [CrossRef]
41. Sinha, R.; Kumar, R.; Sharma, P.; Kant, N.; Shang, J.; Aminabhavi, T.M. Removal of hexavalent chromium via biochar-based adsorbents: State-of-the-art, challenges, and future perspectives. *J. Environ. Manag.* **2022**, *317*, 115356. [CrossRef]
42. Thomas, N.; Dionysiou, D.D.; Pillai, S.C. Heterogeneous Fenton catalysts: A review of recent advances. *J. Hazard. Mater.* **2021**, *404*, 124082. [CrossRef] [PubMed]
43. Tian, J.; Wei, L.; Hu, J.; Lu, J. Boosting reactive oxygen species generation over $Bi_3O_4Br/CuBi_2O_4$ by activating peroxymonosulfate under visible light irradiation. *Sep. Purif. Technol.* **2022**, *289*, 120794. [CrossRef]
44. Wang, B.; Wang, Y. A comprehensive review on persulfate activation treatment of wastewater. *Sci. Total Environ.* **2022**, *831*, 154906. [CrossRef]
45. Wang, C.; Liu, H.; Wang, G.; Huang, W.; Wei, Z.; Fang, H.; Shen, F. Visible light driven S-scheme heterojunction $Zn_3In_2S_6/Bi_2MoO_6$ for efficient degradation of metronidazole. *J. Alloys Compd.* **2022**, *917*, 165507. [CrossRef]
46. Wang, J.; Wang, S. Activation of persulfate (PS) and peroxymonosulfate (PMS) and application for the degradation of emerging contaminants. *Chem. Eng. J.* **2018**, *334*, 1502–1517. [CrossRef]
47. Wang, J.; Zhuan, R.; Chu, L. The occurrence, distribution and degradation of antibiotics by ionizing radiation: An overview. *Sci. Total Environ.* **2019**, *646*, 1385–1397. [CrossRef] [PubMed]
48. Wang, W.; Chen, M. Catalytic degradation of sulfamethoxazole by peroxymonosulfate activation system composed of nitrogen-doped biochar from pomelo peel: Important roles of defects and nitrogen, and detoxification of intermediates. *J. Colloid Interface Sci.* **2022**, *613*, 57–70. [CrossRef]
49. Wang, W.; Chen, M.; Wang, D.; Yan, M.; Liu, Z. Different activation methods in sulfate radical-based oxidation for organic pollutants degradation: Catalytic mechanism and toxicity assessment of degradation intermediates. *Sci. Total Environ.* **2021**, *772*, 145522. [CrossRef]
50. Wei, Z.; Liu, J.; Shangguan, W. A review on photocatalysis in antibiotic wastewater: Pollutant degradation and hydrogen production. *Chin. J. Catal.* **2020**, *41*, 1440–1450. [CrossRef]
51. Wu, D.; Song, W.; Chen, L.; Duan, X.; Xia, Q.; Fan, X.; Li, Y.; Zhang, F.; Peng, W.; Wang, S. High-performance porous graphene from synergetic nitrogen doping and physical activation for advanced nonradical oxidation. *J. Hazard. Mater.* **2020**, *381*, 121010. [CrossRef] [PubMed]

52. Wu, S.; Hu, Y.H. A comprehensive review on catalysts for electrocatalytic and photoelectrocatalytic degradation of antibiotics. *Chem. Eng. J.* **2021**, *409*, 127739. [CrossRef]
53. Yan, Y.; Zhang, H.; Wang, W.; Li, W.; Ren, Y.; Li, X. Synthesis of Fe^0/Fe_3O_4@porous carbon through a facile heat treatment of iron-containing candle soots for peroxymonosulfate activation and efficient degradation of sulfamethoxazole. *J. Hazard. Mater.* **2021**, *411*, 124952. [CrossRef] [PubMed]
54. Yang, Q.; Chen, Y.; Duan, X.; Zhou, S.; Niu, Y.; Sun, H.; Zhi, L.; Wang, S. Unzipping carbon nanotubes to nanoribbons for revealing the mechanism of nonradical oxidation by carbocatalysis. *Appl. Catal. B Environ.* **2020**, *276*, 119146. [CrossRef]
55. Yao, C.; Zhang, Y.; Du, M.; Du, X.; Huang, S. Insights into the mechanism of non-radical activation of persulfate via activated carbon for the degradation of p-chloroaniline. *Chem. Eng. J.* **2019**, *362*, 262–268. [CrossRef]
56. Yi, Y.; Fu, Y.; Wang, Y.; Cai, Y.; Liu, Y.; Xu, Z.; Diao, Z. Persulfate oxidation of norfloxacin by cobalt doped water hyacinth biochar composite: The key role of cobalt and singlet oxygen. *J. Water Process Eng.* **2024**, *59*, 104967. [CrossRef]
57. Yi, Y.; Huang, Z.; Lu, B.; Xian, J.; Tsang, E.P.; Cheng, W.; Fang, J.; Fang, Z. Magnetic biochar for environmental remediation: A review. *Bioresour. Technol.* **2020**, *298*, 122468. [CrossRef] [PubMed]
58. You, Y.; Shi, Z.; Li, Y.; Zhao, Z.; He, B.; Cheng, X. Magnetic cobalt ferrite biochar composite as peroxymonosulfate activator for removal of lomefloxacin hydrochloride. *Sep. Purif. Technol.* **2021**, *272*, 118889. [CrossRef]
59. Zeng, H.; Yang, B.; Shi, W.; Huang, K.; Ye, C.; Ma, X.; Wang, Z.; Huang, F.; Li, X.; Deng, J. Peroxymonosulfate activation by sulfur doped $CoFe_2O_4$ rod for arsanilic acid removal: Performance and arsenic enrichment. *J. Environ. Chem. Eng.* **2023**, *11*, 111044. [CrossRef]
60. Zhang, H.; Zhu, Y.; Nutakki, T.U.K.; Alghassab, M.A.; Alkhalaf, S.; Islam, S.; Elmasry, Y. Preparation of CeO_2-WO_3 binary heterojunction photocatalyst for sustainable tetracycline degradation: Optimization of synthesis and degradation conditions, characterization, transformation pathway, and dominant reactive species. *Surf. Interfaces* **2024**, *44*, 103793. [CrossRef]
61. Zhang, X.; Wei, J.; Wang, C.; Wang, L.; Guo, Z.; Song, Y. Recent advance of Fe-based bimetallic persulfate activation catalysts for antibiotics removal: Performance, mechanism, contribution of the key ROSs and degradation pathways. *Chem. Eng. J.* **2024**, *487*, 150514. [CrossRef]
62. Zhong, Q.; Lin, Q.; Huang, R.; Fu, H.; Zhang, X.; Luo, H.; Xiao, R. Oxidative degradation of tetracycline using persulfate activated by N and Cu codoped biochar. *Chem. Eng. J.* **2020**, *380*, 122608. [CrossRef]
63. Zhu, K.; Wang, X.; Geng, M.; Chen, D.; Lin, H.; Zhang, H. Catalytic oxidation of clofibric acid by peroxydisulfate activated with wood-based biochar: Effect of biochar pyrolysis temperature, performance and mechanism. *Chem. Eng. J.* **2019**, *374*, 1253–1263. [CrossRef]
64. Zhu, L.; Yang, F.; Lin, X.; Zhang, D.; Duan, X.; Shi, J.; Sun, Z. Highly efficient catalysts of polyoxometalates supported on biochar for antibiotic wastewater treatment: Performance and mechanism. *Process Saf. Environ. Prot.* **2023**, *172*, 425–436. [CrossRef]
65. Zhu, M.P.; Yang, J.-C.E.; Duan, X.; Zhang, D.-D.; Wang, S.; Yuan, B.; Fu, M.-L. Interfacial $CoAl_2O_4$ from ZIF-67@γ-Al_2O_3 pellets toward catalytic activation of peroxymonosulfate for metronidazole removal. *Chem. Eng. J.* **2020**, *397*, 125339. [CrossRef]

Disclaimer/Publisher's Note: The statements, opinions and data contained in all publications are solely those of the individual author(s) and contributor(s) and not of MDPI and/or the editor(s). MDPI and/or the editor(s) disclaim responsibility for any injury to people or property resulting from any ideas, methods, instructions or products referred to in the content.

Article

Efficient Enzymatic Hydrolysis and Polyhydroxybutyrate Production from Non-Recyclable Fiber Rejects from Paper Mills by Recombinant *Escherichia coli*

Linjing Jia [1], Ankita Juneja [1], Erica L.-W. Majumder [2], Bandaru V. Ramarao [1] and Deepak Kumar [1,*]

[1] Department of Chemical Engineering, State University of New York College of Environmental Science and Forestry, Syracuse, NY 13210, USA
[2] Department of Bacteriology, University of Wisconsin-Madison, Madison, WI 53706, USA
* Correspondence: dkumar02@esf.edu; Tel.: +1-315-470-6503

Abstract: Non-recyclable fiber rejects from paper mills, particularly those from recycled linerboard mills, contain high levels of structural carbohydrates but are currently landfilled, causing financial and environmental burdens. The aim of this study was to develop efficient and sustainable bioprocess to upcycle these rejects into polyhydroxybutyrate (PHB), a biodegradable alternative to degradation-resistant petroleum-based plastics. To achieve high yields of PHB per unit biomass, the specific objective of the study was to investigate various approaches to enhance the hydrolysis yields of fiber rejects to maximize sugar recovery and evaluate the fermentation performance of these sugars using *Escherichia coli* LSBJ. The investigated approaches included size reduction, surfactant addition, and a chemical-free hydrothermal pretreatment process. A two-step hydrothermal pretreatment, involving a hot water pretreatment (150 °C and 15% solid loading for 10 min) followed by three cycles of disk refining, was found to be highly effective and resulted in an 83% cellulose conversion during hydrolysis. The hydrolysate obtained from pretreated biomass normally requires a detoxification step to enhance fermentation efficiency. However, the hydrolysate obtained from the pretreated biomass contained minimal to no inhibitory compounds, as indicated by the efficient sugar fermentation and high PHB yields, which were comparable to those from fermenting raw biomass hydrolysate. The structural and thermal properties of the extracted PHB were analyzed using various techniques and consistent with standard PHB.

Keywords: polyhydroxybutyrate; fiber rejects; pretreatment; recombinant *Escherichia coli*

Citation: Jia, L.; Juneja, A.; Majumder, E.L.-W.; Ramarao, B.V.; Kumar, D. Efficient Enzymatic Hydrolysis and Polyhydroxybutyrate Production from Non-Recyclable Fiber Rejects from Paper Mills by Recombinant *Escherichia coli*. Processes 2024, 12, 1576. https://doi.org/10.3390/pr12081576

Academic Editors: Dimitris Zagklis and Georgios Bampos

Received: 8 July 2024
Revised: 22 July 2024
Accepted: 23 July 2024
Published: 27 July 2024

Copyright: © 2024 by the authors. Licensee MDPI, Basel, Switzerland. This article is an open access article distributed under the terms and conditions of the Creative Commons Attribution (CC BY) license (https://creativecommons.org/licenses/by/4.0/).

1. Introduction

Plastic is a ubiquitous polymer derived from petroleum. Since the 1950s, global plastic production has increased at an average rate of around 9% annually. It is projected that worldwide production will reach 540 million metric tons by 2040 [1]. Its high rate of consumption and resistance to natural degradation would result in approximately 11,000 million metric tons of non-biodegradable plastics accumulating in landfills and in the natural environment by 2025, leading to plastic pollution and threatening land and marine ecosystems [2,3]. As environmental concerns escalate, there is a growing push to replace traditional petroleum-based plastics with non-toxic, biosynthetic, and biodegradable alternatives. Polyhydroxyalkanoates (PHAs) are regarded as one of the most promising alternatives to conventional, non-biodegradable petroleum-based plastics, with desirable eco-friendly characteristics.

PHAs are aliphatic polyesters that can be synthesized by a variety of microorganisms as intracellular carbon and energy reservoirs in the form of cytoplasmic granules under nutrient-limiting conditions and are fully biodegradable [1,4,5]. Polyhydroxybutyrate (PHB), the most prevalent and earliest recognized type of PHA, has garnered significant attention due to its promising physical and mechanical properties, making it a potential substitute for traditional plastics [6]. However, the relatively high cost of production of PHBs in comparison to petrochemical-derived plastics hinders their widespread production and commercialization. Since the cost of the feedstock contributes as much as 50% in the PHB production, utilizing zero/low-cost waste materials, especially agro-industrial waste, as a substrate is one method to lower production costs [1,7]. Most of these waste streams are rich in carbohydrates (mostly structural carbohydrates) that can be hydrolyzed to produce fermentable sugars and subsequently fermented to PHAs [8–10]. These waste streams provide a sustainable zero/negative-cost alternative to currently used food-based feedstock for PHB production and also address the waste management issue for agro-processing industries. Non-recyclable fiber rejects from paper mills, especially from recycled linerboard mills, contain high amounts of structural carbohydrates and are one such high potential feedstock for PHB production.

During the production of recycled paper, the bonding tendency between fibers may decrease in the repulping or de-inking unit operation. In order to compensate for the reduced bonding tendency, paper mills usually apply compression and shear forces to the pulp in the refining process. Although most recycled fibers have been refined, this measure generates a large number of short fibers [11]. Retention of these short fibers reduces the dewatering performance of the paper, impacting drying efficiency and productivity. The short fibers also contribute to decreased strength properties, such as tear strength and fold resistance. Therefore, these short fibers are unsuitable for recycling and are rejected by paper mills [12]. Due to the shortage of paper raw materials and the need to protect forests, the recycling and utilization of wastepaper have been strongly encouraged. In the past decades, the amount of recycled paper has increased, with the recovery rate rising from 33.5% in 1990 to 66.2% in 2019, peaking at 68% during this period. In 2014, recovered paper consumption amounted to 257 million tons worldwide (57.9% of the total paper production). Approximately 15–20% of the reused fiber becomes too short to be useful after the repulping process and is rejected from recycled paper mills, leading to about 34 to 46 million tons of fiber rejects produced very year. Therefore, the disposal of these fibers has placed a significant burden on the pulp and paper industry. Currently, these rejected fibers are sent to landfills. Landfill disposal can be expensive and contributes to land use challenges and methane emissions as organic materials decompose anaerobically [13]. Upcycling these fiber rejects into PHB could offer several benefits, including reducing PHB production costs, eliminating waste management issues, and promoting a circular economy within the paper industry.

Similar to any lignocellulosic biomass, utilization of fiber rejects for PHB production is constrained by low sugar recoveries during enzymatic hydrolysis [13]. This is primarily because of the recalcitrant structure of biomass consisting of cellulose, hemicellulose, and lignin, which are tightly intertwined and bound to each other by covalent or non-covalent bonds to form the lignocellulosic matrix [14]. The structural complexity of lignocellulosic biomass makes it highly resistant to enzymes, resulting in the relatively low digestibility of raw lignocellulosic feedstocks [15]. High ash content due to the presence of inorganics is another challenge in utilizing fiber rejects. To overcome this recalcitrance and make polysaccharides readily accessible for enzyme digestion, an appropriate pretreatment approach is needed, such as grinding, microwaving, steam explosion, hydrothermal pretreatment, ammonia fiber/freeze explosion, acid pretreatment, alkali pretreatment, organosolv processes, and biological pretreatment [16–19]. Although these pretreatments enhance the subsequent enzymatic hydrolysis efficiency, most of these suffer from the limitations of harsh operating conditions, need for expensive reactors, and production of compounds that are inhibitory to microbial fermentation [20].

This study intended to demonstrate the feasibility of using fiber reject hydrolysate as the sole carbon source for PHB production. To achieve high productivity from biomass, the first objective of this study was to investigate three approaches to enhance the hydrolysis yields of fiber rejects. Firstly, the effect of size reduction on the enzymatic hydrolysis efficiency was investigated because it is hypothesized that smaller fibers will be more labile to enzymatic degradation. Secondly, the addition of surfactants was explored to mitigate the negative effects of paper fillers, such as calcium carbonate, by preventing non-productive enzyme adsorption. The third approach to enhance hydrolysis efficiency focused on using a chemical-free two-step hydrothermal pretreatment process. This process uses a combination of hot water pretreatment and disk milling/refining to reduce biomass recalcitrance, solubilize hemicellulose, and increase the specific surface area of biomass predicted to lead to efficient enzymatic hydrolysis [20–23]. Various pretreatment conditions were investigated to determine the optimal conditions for maximum cellulose conversion. In the second objective of study, the hydrolysate obtained from the optimal process was used as the fermentation medium for PHB bioproduction using recombinant *Escherichia coli* LSBJ. It was hypothesized that the sugars obtained from the hydrolysis of pretreated biomass would ferment efficiently and yield PHB yields similar to those from the hydrolysate obtained from raw biomass. The fermentation performance (cell dry weight, PHB inclusion level in the bacterial cells, and PHB yields) of the optimized fiber reject hydrolysate was also compared to the fermentation yields from pure sugars. The structural and thermal properties of the PHB produced in this study were analyzed and compared with standard PHB.

2. Materials and Methods

2.1. Biomass Collection

Fiber reject samples were collected from a local paper mill (WestRock Paperboard Mill, Syracuse, NY, USA). The biomass was dried at 50 °C for about 48 h to reduce the moisture content below 10%. The samples were then stored in a refrigerator at 4 °C until needed for experimentation.

2.2. Chemical Composition

The chemical composition (cellulose, hemicellulose, lignin, extractives) of biomass was determined using the standard Laboratory Analytical Procedure (LAP) from the National Renewable Energy Laboratory (NREL) [24,25]. In the first step of the process, the extractives were removed by sequential water and ethanol-based extraction using the Soxhlet apparatus [24]. Carbohydrates and lignin in the extractive-free biomass were determined using a two-step acid hydrolysis method [25]. In brief, 0.3 g of biomass was mixed with 3 mL of 72% sulfuric acid and stirred in a water bath at 30 °C for 1 h. The acid concentration was then diluted to 4% by adding 84 mL of deionized water, and the slurry was autoclaved at 121 °C for 1 h. The hydrolyzed samples were vacuum filtered using the ashed Pyrex filter crucibles (ASTM 10–15 M) to separate the solid and liquid fractions. The acid-insoluble lignin (AIL) in the solid fractions was determined using gravimetric analysis. The filter crucible was dried in an oven at 105 °C for 24 h, followed by combusting the dry residues in a muffle furnace at 575 °C for 24 h. The AIL was calculated based on the weight of dry solids and ash weight after burning. The filtrate was spectrophotometrically analyzed for acid-soluble lignin (ASL) at a wavelength of 240 nm and for sugar content by high-performance liquid chromatography (HPLC). All experiments were performed in triplicate.

2.3. Hot Water Pretreatment

Hot water pretreatment was conducted in a 300-mL stainless-steel Parr reactor vessel (Parr Instrument Company, Moline, IL, USA) at a 15% solid loading and 150 mL working volume [20]. In each run, 22.5 g biomass was mixed with a pre-calculated amount of water (based on the moisture in biomass) to achieve 15% solids. The pretreatment was conducted at different temperatures, 140, 150, 160, 170, and 180 °C, for a residence time of 10 min. After the incubation time, the reactor was immersed in chilled water (2–3 min) to quickly reduce temperature and pressure [20,21]. The pretreated slurry was collected and carried over into the disk milling treatment/hydrolysis [20–22].

2.4. Disk Milling

The mechanical refining of biomass was conducted using a lab-scale disk mill (Quaker City Mill model 4E, Philadelphia, PA, USA). The mill was coupled with two nonporous disks, one stationary and the other rotating at a speed of 89 rpm [21]. The width between the two plates was reduced to nearly zero [21,22]. In the case of two-stage pretreatment, the recovered slurry from hot water pretreatment was directly processed in the disk mill, without any washing neutralization or separation. For the refining of untreated fiber rejects, a slurry was prepared by mixing 30 g biomass and 170 mL water, and the slurry was processed in the disk mill. Based on previous studies [20,21], milling was restricted to three consecutive cycles in all cases to optimize electricity usage, cost, and heat dissipation. The moisture content of the samples after disk refining was determined using gravimetric analysis.

2.5. Enzymatic Hydrolysis

Enzymatic hydrolysis of the untreated and pretreated biomass was performed using a modified NREL/TP-5100-63351 procedure [20,21]. The hydrolysis was performed at 10% solid loading at a 50 mL working volume in 125 mL flasks. The pH of the biomass slurry was adjusted to 5.0 by the addition of glacial acetic acid. A sodium acetate buffer (pH 5, 1 M) was added to obtain a final concentration of 50 mM to maintain pH 5.0 during the hydrolysis. The commercial cellulase and hemicellulase cocktails Cellic®Ctec2 and Cellic®Htec2 (Novozymes North America, Inc., Franklinton, NC, USA) were added to each flask at dosages of 0.17 mL/g biomass (15 FPU/g biomass) and 0.04 mL/g biomass (one-fourth the volume of cellulase). Sodium azide was added at a concentration of 0.002% sodium to inhibit microbial growth. The hydrolysis was carried out in a shaking incubator maintained at 50 °C controlled with an agitation rate of 200 rpm for 72 h. Samples were withdrawn at 0, 4, 8, 24, 48, and 72 h for determination of sugar release during hydrolysis. Samples were heated in a heating block at 95 °C for 6 min to deactivate the enzymes and centrifuged at $10,000\times g$ for 5 min. The supernatant was filtered through a 0.22 µm nylon syringe filter into 2 mL microcentrifuge tubes for HPLC analysis. All experiments were performed in triplicate. In the case of hydrolysate generation for the PHB fermentation, hydrolysis was performed at a 100 mL working volume, and sodium azide was not added. At the end of the hydrolysis (72 h), the slurry was filtered with Wattman No. 4 cellulose filter paper to remove the solids, and the filtrate was sterile filtered and stored at 4 °C until used for fermentation. All experiments were performed in triplicate.

2.6. HPLC Analysis

The concentrations of sugars, organic acids, and furan compounds in the samples collected during composition analysis and hydrolysis experiments were analyzed by HPLC (LC-20AD; Shimadzu, Kyoto, Japan) coupled with a refractive index detector (RID-10A). The analyses were conducted using the Aminex HPX-87H column (Bio-Rad, Hercules, CA, USA) operating at 60 °C using 5 mM H_2SO_4 as mobile phase at a rate of 0.6 mL/min [20–22].

2.7. Cellulose Conversion Efficiency

Cellulose conversion efficiency is defined as the ratio of glucose produced from the biomass conversion (at the end of hydrolysis) to the theoretical maximum glucose based on the cellulose content in the biomass (Equation (1)).

$$\text{Cellulose Conversion } (\%) = \frac{G \times V}{M_b \times C \times 1.11} * 100 \qquad (1)$$

where "G" refers to adjusted glucose concentration (g/L) at the end of hydrolysis; "V" represents the volume of hydrolysate; "M_b" refers to the mass of the biomass; "C" represents the cellulose content in the biomass; and "1.11" represents the hydrolytic gain during cellulose to glucose conversion

It is important to note that the adjusted glucose concentration (G) value used in Equation (1) was calculated by subtracting the glucose concentration in the blank (because of sugars in enzymes) from the glucose concentration in the hydrolysate at the end of hydrolysis. To determine the hydrolysate volume (V), at the conclusion of the hydrolysis, the slurry was filtered using a pre-weighed Whatman No. 4 cellulose filter paper, and the filtrate density was calculated from the measured volume and weight. The solids retained on the filter were washed with 50 mL of water and then dried in an oven to determine the weight of the insoluble solids. The hydrolysate (liquid only) weight was determined by subtracting the solids' weight from the slurry weight, and the hydrolysate volume was calculated by dividing this value by the density of hydrolysate [21].

2.8. PHB Production Using Hydrolysate by Recombinant E. coli LSBJ

The fermentation of pure sugars and hydrolysate was conducted using recombinant *E. coli* LSBJ containing PHB biosynthesis plasmid (pBBRSTQKAB) [20,26,27]. Information about the strain's origin and its PHB synthesis pathway was already provided in previous chapters and published studies [27]. The growth medium was an LB medium (10 g/L tryptone, 5/L g yeast extract, and 5 g/L sodium chloride) adjusted to pH 7 and containing 50 mg/L of the antibiotic kanamycin (Km), when needed. For each experiment, cultures were freshly prepared by streaking the freezer stock onto solid LB agar plates (15 g/L) supplemented with 50 mg/L Km. These plates were incubated at 37 °C for 16 h to allow for colony formation. Individual colonies were then used to inoculate the seed culture in 10 mL test tubes containing the LB medium with Km. The seed culture was incubated in a shaking incubator at 37 °C and 200 RPM for 16 h to prepare the inoculum for subsequent shake flask experiments. Fermentation was carried out at a 100 mL scale in 500 mL baffled shake flasks containing the LB medium supplemented with 50 mg/L Km, the carbon source from hydrolysate or pure sugars, and a 1% (v/v) inoculation of seed culture. The carbon source was either hydrolysate from raw or pretreated biomass, glucose, xylose, and a mixture of glucose and xylose, all adjusted to a fixed total sugar concentration of 20 g/L at the start of fermentation. The flasks were cultivated in a shaking incubator at 30 °C, with an agitation rate of 200 rpm for 72 h. At the end of fermentation, the cells were harvested by centrifugation at 4000 rpm (3820× g relative centrifugal force) for 20 min. After decanting the supernatant, the cell pellets were washed with 35% ethanol followed by water and subsequently lyophilized for 48 h [27]. The cell dry weight was measured gravimetrically. All experiments were performed in triplicate.

In the case of kinetic experiments, to determine fermentation performance (biomass growth, PHB inclusion, substrate consumption, pH) at various time points, we employed the strategy of sacrificing flasks at every time point. Multiple flasks were set up initially, and at each specified time point during the fermentation, two flasks (as replicate) were dedicated solely for analysis purposes to determine pH, optical density (at 600 nm), cell dry weight, and PHB inclusions. Sampling was performed at 6 h, 12 h, 18 h, 24 h, 30 h, 36 h, 48 h, and 72 h.

2.9. Analytical Methods for PHB Extraction and Quantification

The PHB content within the cells was measured using a gas chromatograph equipped with a flame ionization detector (Shimadzu, Kyoto, Japan). In the first step of PHB extraction, about 15 mg of lyophilized cells were added to 2 mL of 15% (v/v) H_2SO_4 in methanol and 2 mL of chloroform in Kimble™ KIMAX™ tubes and vortexed. The tubes were heated to a temperature of 100 °C in a dry heating bath and incubated for 140–150 min. After cooling the tubes to room temperature, 1 mL of ultrapure water and 0.5 mL of 0.25% (v/v) methyl octanoate in chloroform (internal standard) were added to the tube. The tubes were briefly vortexed and then centrifuged at 700 rpm (equivalent to a relative centrifugal force of 85× g) for 5 min. The organic layer was filtered with 0.2 μm PTFE filters in GC vials. The samples were analyzed using GC with a Rtx®-5 column and flame ionization detector in triplicate [20,27]. Then, 1 μL of samples was injected at 280 °C in split mode (40:1) and run with a detector temperature of 310 °C and the following oven heating profile: after holding at 100 °C for 7 min, ramp 8 °C/min to 280 °C holding for 2 min, and then ramp 20 °C/min to 310 °C holding for another 2 min. The data were analyzed using Shimadzu's GCsolution Version 2.31 software [28].

2.10. PHB Characterization

2.10.1. Extraction and Purification of PHB

PHB purification was performed according to the protocol adapted from previous studies [29]. Briefly, 5–10 g of lyophilized cells were subjected to a Whatman cellulose extraction thimble and refluxed using 125 mL chloroform for 6 h by Soxhlet extraction. The polymer was concentrated via rotary evaporation and precipitated in ice-cold methanol (1:10, v/v CHCl3: MeOH) under continuous stirring. Methanol was removed by centrifuging at $7000 \times g$ for 10 min at 4 °C to collect the polymer pellet. The pellet was then redissolved in chloroform, and the methanol purification step was repeated two more times. The purified polymer was dried by rotor evaporation.

2.10.2. Nuclear Magnetic Resonance (NMR) Spectroscopy

Approximately 10 mg of the purified PHB was dissolved in 1 mL of deuterated chloroform and analyzed with a Bruker AVANCE III HD 600 MHz NMR (Bruker, Billerica, MA, USA) to perform ^{1}H and ^{13}C NMR analyses [30]. Spectra were analyzed by Bruker TopSpin v4.4.1 software.

2.10.3. Fourier-Transform Infrared Spectroscopy with Attenuated Total Reflectance (FTIR-ATR)

FTIR spectra were recorded for the extracted PHB samples in the IR region between 4000 and 500 cm^{-1} with a resolution of 4 cm^{-1} and 32 scans using a spectrophotometer (IR Affinity-1, M/s Shimadzu, Kyoto, Japan). This setup was provided with an Attenuated Total Reflectance accessory, which allowed for the dried powders' analysis by directly placing them over the probe window (crystal) [31].

2.10.4. Thermogravimetric Analysis (TGA)

TGA of extracted PHB samples was performed on a TGA Q500 (TA instruments, Waltham, MA, USA) from room temperature to 600 °C at a heating rate of 10 °C/min in a nitrogen atmosphere with a flow rate of 40 mL/min [32]. The reported decomposition temperature (onset) was obtained from the thermogravimetric curve using ASTM E2550.

2.10.5. Differential Scanning Calorimetry (DSC)

The thermal transitions of the purified polymer were determined with DSC Q200 equipment (TA Instruments, Waltham, MA, USA). The sample was packed in an aluminum pan and heated in the temperature range of −25 °C to 200 °C at a heating and cooling rate of 10 °C/min in a nitrogen environment and then heated again [33]. The crystallization temperature (T_c) and melting temperature (T_m) were obtained from thermograms using the TA universal analysis software.

2.11. Statistical Analysis

The collected data were analyzed using a one-way analysis of variance (ANOVA) followed by Tukey's HSD test, with the analysis carried out using SPSS v29 software. A confidence level of 95.00% was set to evaluate differences between the means.

3. Results and Discussion

3.1. Composition of Fiber Rejects

The composition of fiber rejects is summarized in Table 1. It was comprised of about 45% carbohydrates (35.5% glucan, 9.0% xylan) and 16.6% lignin. The high carbohydrate content, with about an 80% glucose fraction, indicated that the feedstock is a high potential candidate for fermentation sugar production. Ash and extractive contents were estimated to be 25.0% and 9.7%, respectively. The ash content was significantly high compared to that observed in the woody biomass but in agreement with the ash content reported in the waste streams from paper mills [13,34,35]. Min et al. observed more than 40% ash in the waste fines rejects from an old corrugated containerboard (OCC) paper mill. They reported that ash originated from the minerals as fillers in the original pulp, with calcium carbonate ($CaCO_3$) accounting for about half [34]. Similar results were reported by Rauzi and Tschirner, who conducted a characterization of various paper mill reject streams and reported that the ash content could be as high as 70% in some samples. The rejects from an OCC mill contained about 18% ash content [13]. Jeffries and Schartman characterized three types of recycled waste fines and reported 22–33% ash and 45–65% carbohydrates, which is in agreement with the current study [35].

Table 1. Fiber rejects composition.

Composition	Dry Matter (%)
Glucan	35.5 ± 1.4
Xylan	9.0 ± 0.3
Lignin	16.7 ± 0.3
Ash	25.0 ± 1.3
Extractives	9.7 ± 0.7
Others (by difference)	4.2

Mean values and standard deviations of three determinations.

3.2. Effects of Biomass Size Reduction on Enzymatic Hydrolysis

Size reduction is an effective physical pretreatment to improve substrate accessibility to enzymes for efficient hydrolysis. Biomass particle size reduction could boost the affinity between the cellulose and enzyme, leading to an increase in the hydrolysis rate [36]. To investigate the effect of size reduction, fiber rejects were ground using a Wiley mill to pass through 0.5 mm, 1 mm, or 2 mm screens. The enzymatic hydrolysis experiments for all samples were performed under the same process conditions as described in Section 2.5. The glucose concentration obtained at the end of hydrolysis (72h) from the 2 mm ground fiber rejects was 31.8 g/L, increased significantly by 22% compared to unground fiber rejects (26.0 g/L) (Figure 1). Correspondingly, the cellulose conversion was increased from 51.8% to 65.1%, which indicated that particle size reduction is necessary for fiber reject conversion.

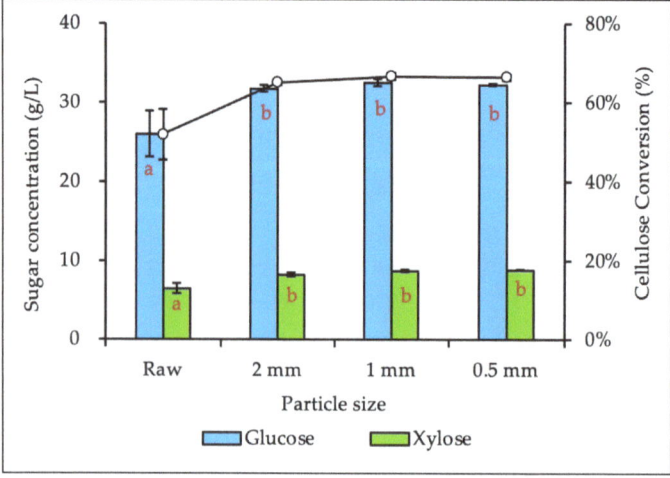

Figure 1. Effect of size reduction on the final sugar concentrations and cellulose conversion during hydrolysis of fiber rejects. Bars labeled by same letter in the same category are not significantly different ($p > 0.05$).

However, further reduction in the particle sizes (1 mm and 0.5 mm) did not show any significant improvement in sugar production as shown in Figure 1. This type of size reduction was categorized as a Class I size reduction because it does not significantly compromise the structural integrity of the plant cell wall. Typically, reaching the level of the fibers and fiber bundles only increases the substrate's external surface area without notably altering the fiber pore structure by breaking down the cell wall [37]. To hydrolyze the untreated lignocellulosic biomass efficiently, it is critical to improve the external surface since the majority of pores of the untreated lignocellulosic biomass are too small to be accessible to cellulase. However, a Class I size reduction is not able to increase saccharification by more than 20% based on the study, which is consistent with our experimental results [37].

3.3. Effects of Surfactant Addition on Enzymatic Hydrolysis

Non-ionic surfactants have been considered efficient additives to improve the mass transfer during enzymatic hydrolysis and are also believed to alter the lignocellulosic structure to promote cellulose accessibility, inhibit enzymes from adhering to lignin, and shield enzymes from denaturing by forming reverse micelles [38]. For this study, the surfactants Tween 80 and PEG 4000 were selected due to their proven effectiveness in enhancing enzymatic hydrolysis of lignocellulosic biomass, including waste from paper mills [34,39,40]. PEG 4000 and Tween 80 were added during the enzymatic hydrolysis of 2 mm grounded fiber rejects to evaluate their abilities to improve sugar production and hydrolysis efficiency. The addition of 3% Tween 80 did not significantly improve the glucose release, whereas the hydrolysis efficiency was improved by 15% with the addition of 2.5% PEG 4000 (Figure 2). Numerous studies have explored the mechanisms through which PEG enhances the efficiency of lignocellulosic materials' hydrolysis. Huang et al. indicated that PEG 4000 has the capacity to diminish the non-productive adsorption of lignin on cellulase enzymes by occupying ineffective lignin adsorption sites through hydrophobic interactions [39]. Hou et al. proposed that PEG can augment enzymatic hydrolysis by mitigating cellulase deactivation, which is induced by shear forces and interactions at the air–liquid interface [40].

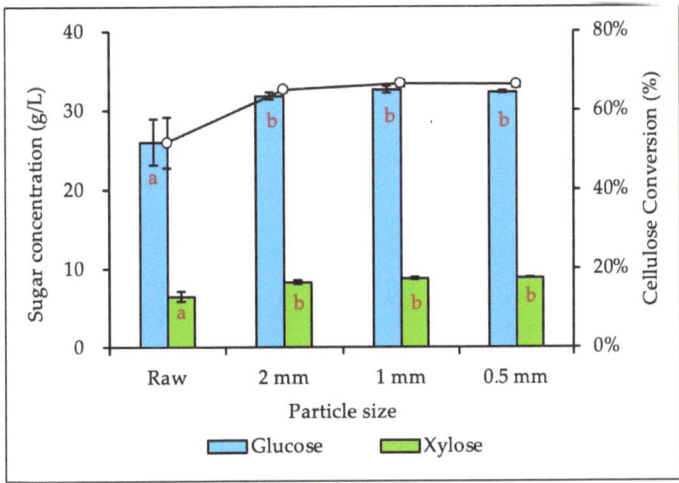

Figure 2. Effect of surfactant addition on the final glucose release and cellulose conversion during hydrolysis of fiber rejects. Bars labeled by same letter in the same category are not significantly different ($p > 0.05$).

3.4. Effect of Hydrothermal-Mechanical Pretreatment on Enzymatic Hydrolysis

Pretreatment is a key factor to increase the efficiency of lignocellulosic hydrolysis by reducing the biomass recalcitrance. This work involved the investigation of three pretreatment approaches: disk milling of wet slurry, also known as wet disk milling; hot water pretreatment; and hot water pretreatment followed by disk milling (two-step hydrothermal pretreatment). The total sugar production and cellulose conversions after 72 h of enzymatic hydrolysis for all scenarios are shown in Table 2. Compared to raw samples, glucose concentration increased from 31.8 to 33.1 g/L, resulting in an improvement by 4% after one cycle of wet disk milling. Wet disk milling pretreatment has proven to be an effective and promising pretreatment method to enhance sugar release during enzymatic hydrolysis [41]. Wet disk milling is mechanical grinding, which not only results in a size reduction of Class I but also a further size reduction of Class II. Shear pressures enhance fiber external surface area in class I size reduction by fiber separation, cutting, fragmentation, and external fibrillation (delamination). In Class II size reduction, microfibril cross-connections are broken, and internal fibrillation is generated to break down cell walls [42–45]. During the investigation of disk-milling-only pretreatment, the effect of increasing milling cycles to three was also evaluated. The milling cycle represents one pass through the machine. Increasing the milling cycles to three further enhanced the glucose yield to 34.7 g/L. Correspondingly, the cellulose conversion was estimated at 73.5%, which was 12.9% and 6.4% higher compared to that of untreated and single-cycle disk-milled treated biomass, respectively. The xylose concentration was found to be similar among the samples milled one time and three times. The number of cycles was limited to three because previous studies have reported that three disk milling cycles were optimal considering the constraints of process costs, energy use, moisture loss, and heat generation [23].

Table 2. Effect of different pretreatment conditions on the sugar released during hydrolysis.

Pretreatment	Residence Time during Hot Water Pretreatment (min)	Sugar Concentration (g/L)		Cellulose Conversion (%)
		Glucose	Xylose	
Untreated	NA	31.8 ± 0.4	8.2 ± 0.2	65.1 ± 0.6
Disk milling only (1 cycle)	NA	33.1 ± 0.2	7.5 ± 0.2	69.1 ± 0.7
Disk milling only (3 cycle)	NA	34.7 ± 0.1	7.7 ± 0.0	73.5 ± 0.9
Hot water pretreatment (180 °C)	10	33.7 ± 0.7	7.9 ± 0.1	67.8 ± 1.4
Hot water pretreatment 180 °C and disk milling	10	37.2 ± 0.3	9.0 ± 0.2	77.7 ± 1.8

Mean ± standard deviation.

To investigate the effect of hot water pretreatment, biomass was pretreated in water at 15% solids at 180 °C for 10 min. The glucose concentration at the end of hydrolysis for the pretreated biomass was observed to be 5.9% higher (33.7 vs. 31.8 g/L) compared to the untreated biomass. Correspondingly, the cellulose conversion was estimated to be 67.8%. Hot water pretreatment enhances the enzyme accessibility to cellulose, with minimal to no generation of inhibitory compounds. Water serves as a catalyst and solvent in the pretreatment process together with organic acids generated from biomass to help break down the plant cell wall matrix. According to reports, the elimination of hemicellulose by hot water pretreatment causes cellulose microfibril bundles to develop microscopic holes, which can weaken the network structure of the polymer matrix, resulting in higher hydrolysis efficiency [23]. However, hot water pretreatment alone is not considered sufficient to significantly enhance cellulose conversion, but the combination of hot water pretreatment with a mechanical treatment (e.g., disk milling) could lead to high cellulose conversions [20–22]. Similar observations were made in the current study: the use of only hot water pretreatment increased cellulose conversion by 4.1% (65.1 to 67.8%), whereas the use of disk milling (three cycles) followed by hot water pretreatment (HWDM) resulted in a 16.2% higher cellulose conversion (77.7%) compared to untreated biomass. This synergistic effect of hydrothermal and mechanical pretreatment results in a higher degree of defibrillation and specific surface area, resulting in high sugar yields during hydrolysis, as has been reported by several studies for a variety of feedstocks [20–23]. Weiqi et al. reported a significant improvement in the enzymatic hydrolysis of eucalyptus by using the combination of liquid hot water pretreatment (180 °C for 20 min) and disk milling, yielding maximum xylose and glucose recovery rates of 91.6% and 88.1%, respectively [46]. Kim et al. reported that the use of the HWDM of corn stover resulted in an up to 89% glucose yield [23]. Most of the previous studies that investigated HWDM reported that temperature during hot water pretreatment plays a critical role in the final sugar concentrations at the end of hydrolysis. The use of high-severity pretreatment (high temperature) could result in a breakdown of sugars, especially xylose [20,21].

To investigate the effect of pretreatment temperature, fiber rejects were pretreated from 140 to 180 °C temperature and subsequently disk milled (three cycles), and the corresponding results are presented in Figure 3. It was interesting to observe that the combination of hot water pretreatment and disk milling significantly improved sugar yields even at low temperatures. Application of 140 °C temperature during HWDM resulted in 37.5 g/L glucose at the end of hydrolysis, compared to 31.8 g/L for untreated biomass, with the difference being statistically significant. Correspondingly, the cellulose conversion was increased significantly by about 22% (65.1 to 79.3%). With a change in pretreatment temperature from 140 °C to 150 °C, the glucose concentration was further enhanced to 39.6 g/L, and the cellulose conversion increased to 83.2%. With a further increase in temperature up to 170 °C, the sugar yield did not change significantly. However, glucose recovery was observed to be lower at 180 °C. This behavior has been reported in several previous studies where a high temperature led to the degradation of sugars [20,21,47]. Based on the results illustrated in Figure 3, it could be concluded that HWDM pretreatment at 150 °C would be the best choice for fiber rejects, resulting in 39.6 g/L glucose, 8.3 g/L xylose, and 83.2% cellulose conversions. The cellulose conversion in the current study was higher than the cellulose conversion (69%) observed from the hydrolysis of dilute acid (0.5% sulfuric acid) pretreated fiber rejects [13] Several other studies using various feedstock have reported similar observations of achieving the same or higher cellulose conversion using HWDM compared to chemical pretreatments, leading to significant environmental benefits [20–22].

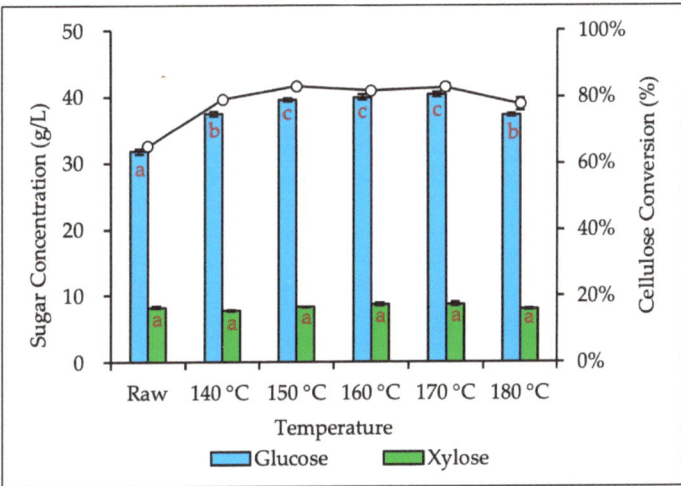

Figure 3. Effect of hot water pretreatment conditions and disk milling on sugar production and cellulose conversion. Bars labeled by same letter in the same category are not significant different ($p > 0.05$).

The glucose production profile for untreated samples and those pretreated at 150 °C are shown in Figure 4. The production of sugars increased rapidly within the first four hours for both raw fiber rejects and pretreated fiber rejects; however, the hydrolysis rate of pretreated fiber rejects was higher. The difference is that the non-pretreated fiber rejects continued to release glucose from the 4th to 48th hours of the hydrolysis process and then leveled off. For the fiber rejects after hydrothermal pretreatment at 150 °C and disk milling pretreatment, the conversion of glucan to glucose stopped at 24 h. This result could be explained by the fact that the pretreated fiber rejects were more easily liquefied, leading to a rapid increase in sugar production [48]. The final sugar yield of pretreated biomass was statistically (24.44%) higher than the untreated biomass.

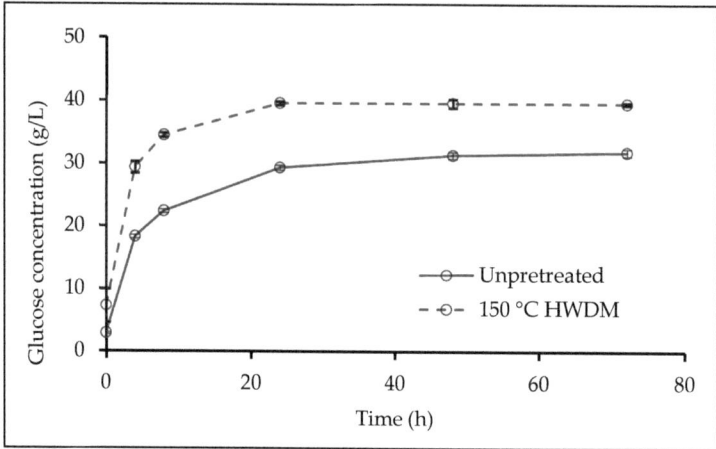

Figure 4. Glucose production profile during hydrolysis of raw biomass and biomass pretreated at 180 °C and 10 min with disk milling (HWDM).

3.5. PHB Production

The hydrolysate obtained from enzymatic hydrolysis of fiber rejects pretreated using the HWDM process at 150 °C for 10 min was investigated as a sole carbon source to produce PHB by recombinant *E. coli* LSBJ. It is commonly observed that although the pretreatment process enhances the sugar recovery, the generation of some inhibitory compounds, such as furans, affects microbial fermentation processes and results in lower fermentation yields. The generation of inhibitory compounds is more frequently observed with the increase in severity (pretreatment temperature and time) or chemical use [22]. Nonetheless, to investigate the effect of pretreatment on the fermentation of hydrolysate, both raw and pretreated fiber reject hydrolysates were assessed for PHB production in this study. All fermentations were performed at an initial reducing sugar (glucose and xylose) concentration (20 g/L). Pure laboratory-grade glucose, xylose, and mixed glucose/xylose were used as pure carbon sources as reference values.

The PHB titers from the fermentation of raw and pretreated fiber reject hydrolysates were found to be 6.27 and 5.99 g/L, respectively (Figure 5). Although the PHB inclusion (PHB mass fraction in cell mass; 33.3 and 33.7%) was similar among both conditions, a relatively lower cell dry weight (17.8 vs. 18.83 g/L) resulted in a slightly lower (4.4%) PHB yield for pretreated biomass hydrolysate compared to raw biomass hydrolysate. However, this difference was not statistically significant and was much lower compared to the effect of pretreatment on fermentation yield observed in previous studies. In a study on PHB production from brewers' spent grains using *E. coli* LSBJ, Thomas et al. [26] observed that while the sugars released increased by 27% (49.7 vs. 39.2 g/L reducing sugars) using hot water pretreatment, the PHA yield from the pretreated hydrolysate was 47% lower (2.39 g/L) compared to that from the untreated hydrolysate (3.53 g/L), potentially due to the presence of inhibitory compounds generated during pretreatment. The obtained PHB production from pretreated fiber rejects in this study is within the range of PHB yields obtained from various feedstocks in the literature [1,26,30]. The PHB yields in the current study were significantly higher compared to PHB yields reported for native producers *Burkholderia sacchari* (2.7 g/L) and *Burkholderia cepacia* (4.4 g/L), which were isolated from soil and utilized detoxified sugarcane bagasse hydrolysate as a substrate [49]. Compared to those native PHB-producing soil bacteria, *E. coli* LSBJ demonstrated greater efficiency in utilizing monosaccharide carbon sources. This capability may be attributed to the natural biological niche of *E. coli* in the mammalian intestinal gut, where it relies on carbohydrate metabolism for colonization and persistence [50]. Another advantage of *E. coli* LSBJ is its lack of PHA degradation pathways. This ensures that once the maximum PHB production is achieved, the PHB levels remain stable over time [26].

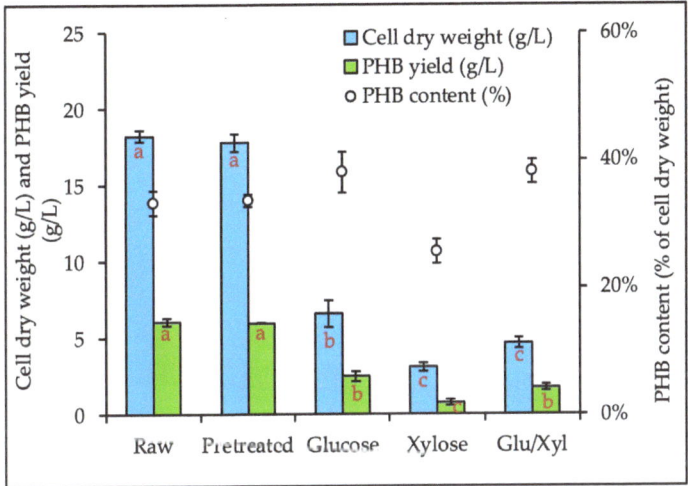

Figure 5. Comparison of PHB production during fermentation of fiber rejects hydrolysate and pure sugars. Bars labeled by same letter in the same category are not significantly different ($p > 0.05$).

It is important to note that most of the studies utilizing lignocellulosic hydrolysate as a carbon source employed an additional detoxification process following the pretreatment process to reduce or eliminate inhibitory compounds such as hydroxymethylfurfural (HMF), furfural, and phenolic compounds [51,52]. It is noteworthy that even without any detoxification or neutralization step employed in the current study, the hydrolysate did not contain a detectable number of furans, common inhibitors found in the hydrolysates of pretreated biomass, and this was further validated by the high PHB yields during fermentation. High cellulose conversion (83%) was achieved along with similar PHB yields.

The yields of PHB from fiber reject hydrolysate were higher than any other pure sugar carbon source, despite having the same sugar concentrations (20 g/L) at the start of fermentation as shown in Figure 5. The PHB yields from the fermentation of pure glucose, xylose, and sugar mix were 2.6 g/L, 0.8 g/L, and 1.8 g/L, respectively. The corresponding PHB inclusions were 40.0%, 25.6%, and 38.1%, respectively. The PHB yields while using xylose as the carbon source were significantly lower compared to using glucose as the carbon source. Similar results were reported by Paul et al. [2]. Even though *E. coli* can convert C5 sugars such as xylose into Acetyl Co-A via the pentose phosphate pathway (PPP), the efficiency of the PPP in terms of xylose utilization is enhanced in the presence of glucose [20,53]. The findings of higher PHB yields from biomass hydrolysate compared to pure sugars were also reported in previous studies [26,54,55]. Scheel et al. reported that the PHB yield obtained from waste fines' (a specific fraction of fiber rejects) hydrolysate was twice as high as those obtained from purified sugars using the same recombinant *E. coli* LSBJ. Similarly, Thomas et al. observed up to a 2.43-fold PHB yield (3.43 vs. 1.41 g/L) from the fermentation of hydrolysate compared to pure glucose at a 10 g/L initial sugar concentration [26]. As speculated by these authors, the increase in PHB yield when using hydrolysate as the carbon source is attributed to the presence of various important metal ions in the hydrolysate that promote bacterial growth [54]. Dietrich et al. suggested that the presence of supplementary nutrients in the hydrolysate, including polypeptides and amino acids obtained from denatured enzymes used during hydrolysis, extended the duration of acetyl-CoA flow into the citric acid cycle, consequently promoting enhanced cell growth [55]. Since our experiments used LB as the base medium for all conditions, the potential contribution of peptides present in LB is accounted for in the control conditions. The major reason for higher cell dry weight in the case of fermentation of fiber reject hydrolysate could be attributed to the high acetic acid concentration (~10 g/L) in the hydrolysate, which acts as an additional carbon source for *E. coli* LSBJ during fermentation. A high amount of acetic acid was observed because of the addition of acetic acid to change the pH to 5.0 at the start of enzymatic hydrolysis [56].

To gain a deeper understanding of the assimilation of the sugars originating from the hydrothermal-mechanical pretreated fiber rejects into PHB through microbial fermentation, biomass growth, PHB accumulation, and substrate consumption were monitored throughout the fermentation process, and the results are illustrated in Figure 6a,b. As per our knowledge, this is the first study to investigate the kinetics during fermentation of biomass hydrolysate using *E. coli* LSBJ.

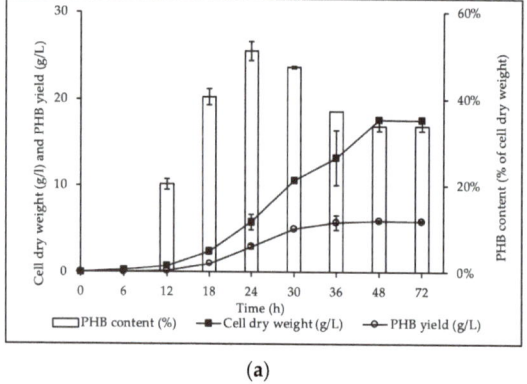 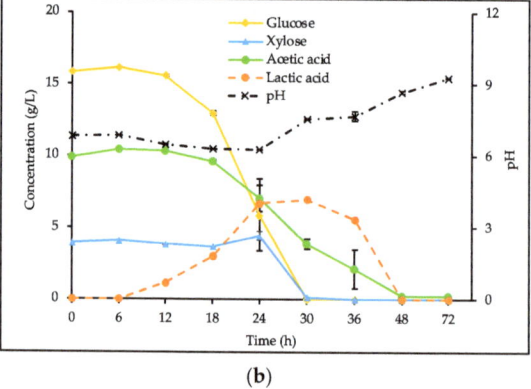

(a) (b)

Figure 6. Time evolution of (**a**) cell dry weight, PHB inclusion, and PHB yield and (**b**) substrate consumption and intermediate concentration during PHB production on 20 g/L of pure FR hydrolysate.

The bacteria exhibited a lag phase from 0 to 12 h followed by an exponential growth phase starting at 12 h characterized by a swift increase in cell growth, PHB accumulation, and glucose consumption. The cell dry weight continued to increase until it reached a maximum of 17.6 g/L in 48 h, coinciding with the complete depletion of all carbon sources. Similarly, PHB yield followed a comparable trend to cell dry weight, steadily increasing and peaking at 48 h (5.9 g/L) before stabilizing. Xylose consumption increased at 24 h, while glucose concentrations approached zero. This trend was expected because glucose is the preferred carbon source of *E. coli* [57]. Only after the depletion of glucose does the consumption of xylose begin due to carbon catabolite repression (CCR), a phenomenon observed in many microorganisms [58]. PHB accumulation was observed to commence at 12 h, peaking at 51% of CDW at the 24 h mark, subsequently declining to 34% by 48 h when CDW increased, and remaining stable until the end of the 72 h fermentation process. This indicates that after glucose was depleted, the cells redirected their metabolic focus from PHB synthesis to biomass production, using xylose and acetate more for cell growth rather than for PHB biosynthesis. *E. coli* can metabolize both glucose and acetate when there is an excess of acetate in the medium [59]. Acetate is metabolized via the Pta-AckA pathway [59]. Once the glucose and xylose are consumed, residual acetate in the medium, albeit at lower concentrations, is taken up by the cells and converted to acetyl-CoA by acetyl-CoA synthetase, which is subsequently utilized in the TCA cycle to generate cellular energy in the form of reduced cofactors [5]. Additionally, acetyl-CoA can contribute to biomass synthesis in the absence of glucose through some of the carbon flux being directed through the glyoxylate shunt [60]. Sun et al. reported significantly high cell density with the supplementation of 5–15 g/L of acetate to a minimal medium culture containing 10 g/L of glucose compared to cultures with only glucose [57]. The decrease in PHB inclusions from 30 to 36 h indicates that after the depletion of glucose, the residual acetate was primarily utilized for cell growth rather than PHB accumulation (Figure 6a,b). To balance the use of precursor metabolites after glucose depletion, cells employ tight regulation mechanisms that prioritize sugars for cell growth, homeostasis, and maintenance. This tight regulation explains why the consumption of acetate and xylose primarily supports cell growth rather than PHB production [61].

Another observation of carbon flux regulation was that the consumption of glucose coincided with a significant accumulation of lactate (7.0 g/L), a metabolic by-product, in the culture medium (Figure 6b). It has been reported that during PHB synthesis, cells may produce excess reducing equivalents, which can result in the secretion of lactate to alleviate this stress [62]. This observation is consistent with findings reported by Sekar and Tyo, which suggest that enhanced PHB synthesis is associated with increased substrate consumption and lactate secretion, accompanied by decreased secretion of formate and acetate [62]. In our results, cell growth continued after 30 h, primarily supported by the metabolism of acetate and lactate, which contributed more to cell growth than PHB accumulation. As a result, an increase in CDW and a reduction in PHB content were observed, leading to no significant increase in PHB yield after that. The PHB production remained stable after it reached its maximum due to the lack of genes responsible for PHA depolymerization in *E. coli* LSBJ [26].

3.6. PHB Characterization

3.6.1. Nuclear Magnetic Resonance (NMR) Analysis

The chemical structures of the extracted PHB produced by *Escherichia coli* LSBJ pB-BRSTQKAB using fiber reject hydrolysate were verified using ^{1}H and ^{13}C NMR spectroscopy as shown in Figure 7a,b. The ^{1}H NMR spectrum revealed the doublet signals at 1.21 ppm corresponding to the methyl group (-CH$_3$). The multiple signals between 2.39 and 2.56 are attributed to the diastereotopic methylene group (-CH$_2$). Additionally, multiple signals between 5.16 and 5.21 ppm were assigned to the methane group (-CH) with chiral carbon [63]. The peak at 7.2 ppm corresponded to chloroform used as the solvent. The ^{13}C NMR spectrum showed the methyl group (-CH$_3$) at 19.78 ppm, methylene group (-CH$_2$) at 40.8 ppm, methane group (-CH) at 67.62 ppm, and carbonyl group (-C=O) at 169.15 ppm. The triplet signals at 76.82–77.24 ppm are attributed to CDCl$_3$. The chemical shift signals of ^{1}H and ^{13}C NMR spectroscopy obtained in this study agreed with the commercial PHB characterization reported by Oliveira et al. and Prabisha et al., confirming that the material synthesized by this recombinant *E. coli* strain was PHB [63,64].

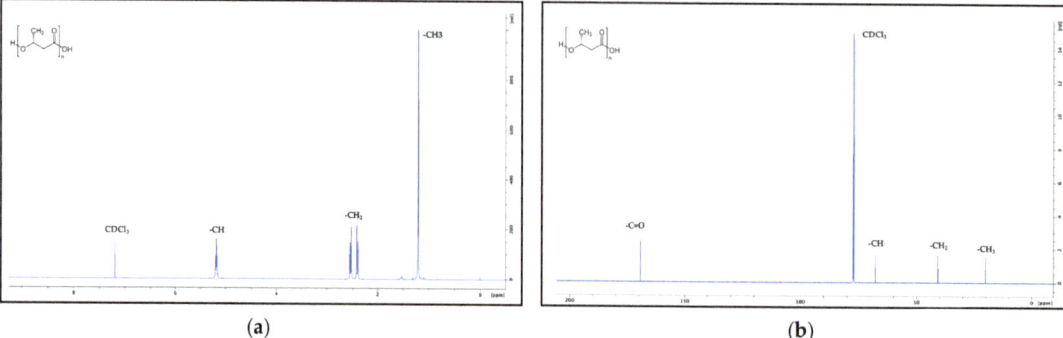

Figure 7. (a) ^{1}H NMR and (b) ^{13}C NMR spectrum of extracted PHB sample.

3.6.2. Fourier Transform InfraRed (FTIR) Spectroscopy

The functional groups of the extracted PHB produced by *Escherichia coli* LSBJ pB-BRSTQKAB using fiber reject hydrolysate were investigated by FTIR spectroscopy, as shown in Figure 8. The minor peak at 3431 cm^{-1} corresponded to the terminal OH group of PHB [65]. The peaks at 2977 and 2930 cm^{-1} represented the presence of C-H stretching of the methyl and methylene groups, respectively [66]. The sharp absorption peak at 1722 cm^{-1} corresponded to carbonyl (C=O) stretching vibrations [65]. The peak at 1278 cm^{-1} represented the carbonyl group (C–O), while the peak at 978 cm^{-1} was attributed to the amorphous component of PHB [67]. The results correlated well with published reports [65,67]. Therefore, the obtained biopolymer from *E. coli* with FR was PHB.

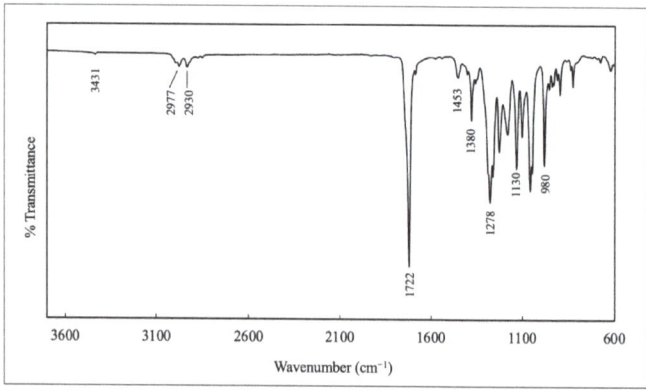

Figure 8. FTIR spectroscopy spectrum of extracted PHB sample.

3.6.3. Thermogravimetric Analysis (TGA) and Differential Scanning Calorimetry (DSC)

Thermal properties of PHB synthesis were investigated using DSC and TGA analyses (Figure 9). TGA was performed to observe the thermal stability of PHB synthesis. The material's thermal stability was evaluated and measured by the degradation temperature (T_d) corresponding to the mass loss of 5%. As shown in Figure 9a, the Td of the extracted PHB in this study was 265 °C. This T_d value obtained denotes considerable thermal stability, making it suitable for applications requiring high-temperature resistance. The observed T_d is consistent with other studies where PHB was synthesized by microbial fermentation, reporting T_d values for PHB ranging from 250 °C to 275 °C [68,69].

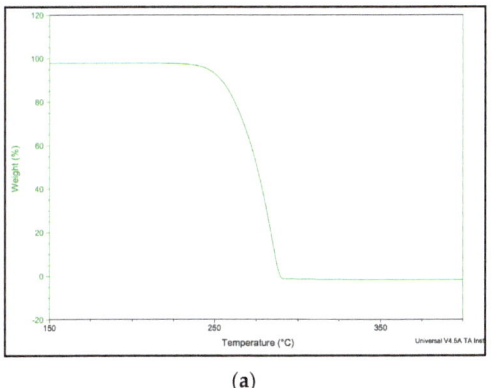 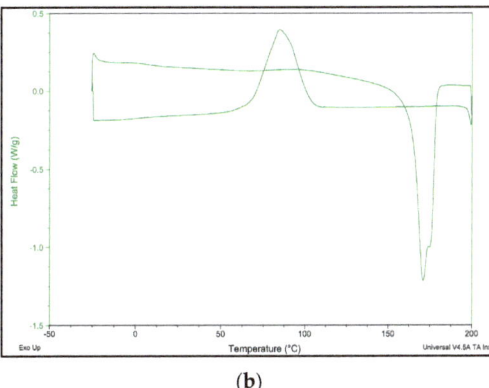

(a) (b)

Figure 9. (a) TGA and (b) DSC thermographs of extracted PHB sample.

DSC analysis was performed to elucidate the thermal transitions that a polymer undergoes as the sample is heated. The thermal transitions are manifested mainly in terms of melting point (T_m) and crystallization temperature (T_c). The T_c of extracted PHB was found to be 84 °C (Figure 9b). The extracted PHB exhibited dual melting temperatures (T_m) at 171 and 176 °C, which is close to that of polypropylene [70]. The dual melting point inferred that re-crystallization takes place followed by cross-linking isomerization reactions [71]. Overall, the combination of high degradation temperature and favorable DSC characteristics indicates that the PHB synthesized by *E. coli* LSBJ pBBRSTQKAB is a promising candidate for various industrial applications.

4. Conclusions

This study aimed to investigate the potential of utilizing fiber rejects, a waste stream from recycled paper mills, as a sustainable feedstock for cost-effective PHB production. This is the first comprehensive study to focus on developing efficient and sustainable bioprocess to maximize sugar recovery from this waste and utilize those sugars for PHB production. Three different approaches, including size reduction, the addition of surfactants, and the use of a chemical-free hydrothermal pretreatment, were investigated to improve the hydrolysis efficiency for high sugar recovery. Size reduction and the addition of PEG 4000 improved the enzymatic hydrolysis efficiency to some extent. A pretreatment including a hot water pretreatment followed by disk milling had synergistic effects on increasing sugar yields in enzymatic hydrolysis, achieving the highest reduction in sugar production (48 g/L) and cellulose conversion up to 83% without using any chemicals. Without performing any detoxification process (a major challenge associated with conventional thermo-chemical pretreatments), the hydrolysate obtained from pretreated biomass in this study fermented efficiently and yielded high PHB yields (6.0 g/L), which was similar to that observed (6.2 g/L) from the fermentation of the hydrolysate of raw biomass. The PHB yields were observed to be higher than those from the fermentation of pure sugars due to the presence of important metal ions and additional carbon sources in the hydrolysate. The fermentation kinetics provided important insights into the rates of substrate consumption, byproduct formation, and PHB synthesis, which are essential for scaling up the process and achieving consistent performance. The structural and thermal properties of the extracted PHB were consistent with standard PHB. Further research needs to be carried out to enhance PHB productivity through the optimization of fermentation parameters and to scale up this process in bioreactor systems.

Author Contributions: L.J.: Conceptualization, methodology, formal analysis, investigation, writing—original draft. A.J.: Methodology, writing—review & editing. E.L.-W.M.: Methodology, writing—review & editing. B.V.R.: Methodology, writing—review & editing, and funding acquisition. D.K.:

Conceptualization, resources, supervision, validation, writing, review and editing, and funding acquisition. All authors have read and agreed to the published version of the manuscript.

Funding: This work was supported by the New York State Center for Sustainable Materials Management (NYCSMM) at SUNY-ESF. The center funding was provided by the Environmental Protection Fund administered by the New York State Department of Environmental Conservation. Any opinions, findings, and/or interpretations of data contained herein are the responsibility of the NYCSMM and do not necessarily represent the opinions, interpretations, or policy of the state.

Data Availability Statement: Data will be made available on request.

Acknowledgments: Authors are thankful to WestRock Paperboard Mill, Syracuse, NY, for providing fiber reject samples for this study.

Conflicts of Interest: The authors declare no conflicts of interest. The funder had no role in the design of the study; in the collection, analyses, or interpretation of data; in the writing of the manuscript; or in the decision to publish the results.

References

1. Zytner, P.; Kumar, D.; Elsayed, A.; Mohanty, A.K.; Ramarao, B.; Misra, M. A review on cost-effective polyhydroxyalkanoate (PHA) production through the use of lignocellulosic biomass. *RSC Sustain.* **2023**, *1*, 2120–2134. [CrossRef]
2. Thushari, G.G.N.; Senevirathna, J.D.M. Plastic pollution in the marine environment. *Heliyon* **2020**, *6*, e04709. [CrossRef] [PubMed]
3. Adnan, M.; Siddiqui, A.J.; Ashraf, S.A.; Snoussi, M.; Badraoui, R.; Ibrahim, A.M.; Alreshidi, M.; Sachidanandan, M.; Patel, M. Characterization and Process Optimization for Enhanced Production of Polyhydroxybutyrate (PHB)-Based Biodegradable Polymer from Bacillus flexus Isolated from Municipal Solid Waste Landfill Site. *Polymers* **2023**, *15*, 1407. [CrossRef] [PubMed]
4. Steinbüchel, A. Perspectives for biotechnological production and utilization of biopolymers: Metabolic engineering of polyhydroxyalkanoate biosynthesis pathways as a successful example. *Macromol. Biosci.* **2001**, *1*, 1–24. [CrossRef]
5. Thomas, C.M.; Kumar, D.; Scheel, R.A.; Ramarao, B.; Nomura, C.T. Production of Medium Chain Length polyhydroxyalkanoate copolymers from agro-industrial waste streams. *Biocatal. Agric. Biotechnol.* **2022**, *43*, 102385. [CrossRef]
6. McAdam, B.; Brennan Fournet, M.; McDonald, P.; Mojicevic, M. Production of polyhydroxybutyrate (PHB) and factors impacting its chemical and mechanical characteristics. *Polymers* **2020**, *12*, 2908. [CrossRef] [PubMed]
7. Reis, M.; Serafim, L.; Lemos, P.; Ramos, A.; Aguiar, F.; Van Loosdrecht, M. Production of polyhydroxyalkanoates by mixed microbial cultures. *Bioprocess Biosyst. Eng.* **2003**, *25*, 377–385. [CrossRef] [PubMed]
8. Zabed, H.; Sahu, J.; Boyce, A.N.; Faruq, G. Fuel ethanol production from lignocellulosic biomass: An overview on feedstocks and technological approaches. *Renew. Sustain. Energy Rev.* **2016**, *66*, 751–774. [CrossRef]
9. Bhatia, S.K.; Jagtap, S.S.; Bedekar, A.A.; Bhatia, R.K.; Rajendran, K.; Pugazhendhi, A.; Rao, C.V.; Atabani, A.; Kumar, G.; Yang, Y.-H. Renewable biohydrogen production from lignocellulosic biomass using fermentation and integration of systems with other energy generation technologies. *Sci. Total Environ.* **2021**, *765*, 144429. [CrossRef] [PubMed]
10. Liu, H.; Kumar, V.; Jia, L.; Sarsaiya, S.; Kumar, D.; Juneja, A.; Zhang, Z.; Sindhu, R.; Binod, P.; Bhatia, S.K. Biopolymer polyhydroxyalkanoates (PHA) production from apple industrial waste residues: A review. *Chemosphere* **2021**, *284*, 131427. [CrossRef] [PubMed]
11. Hubbe, M.A.; Venditti, R.A.; Rojas, O.J. What happens to cellulosic fibers during papermaking and recycling? A Review. *BioResources* **2007**, *2*, 739–788.
12. Laivins, G.; Scallan, A. The influence of drying and beating on the swelling of fines. *J. Pulp Pap. Sci.* **1996**, *22*, J178–J184.
13. Rauzi, J.; Tschirner, U. Enzymatic Glucose and Xylose Production from Paper Mill Rejects. *Recycling* **2022**, *7*, 24. [CrossRef]
14. Kirui, A.; Zhao, W.; Deligey, F.; Yang, H.; Kang, X.; Mentink-Vigier, F.; Wang, T. Carbohydrate-aromatic interface and molecular architecture of lignocellulose. *Nat. Commun.* **2022**, *13*, 538. [CrossRef] [PubMed]
15. Zhao, X.; Zhang, L.; Liu, D. Biomass recalcitrance. Part I: The chemical compositions and physical structures affecting the enzymatic hydrolysis of lignocellulose. *Biofuels Bioprod. Biorefining* **2012**, *6*, 465–482. [CrossRef]
16. Merino-Pérez, O.; Martínez-Palou, R.; Labidi, J.; Luque, R. Microwave-assisted pretreatment of lignocellulosic biomass to produce biofuels and value-added products. In *Production of Biofuels and Chemicals with Microwave*; Springer: Berlin/Heidelberg, Germany, 2015; pp. 197–224.
17. Sarker, T.R.; Pattnaik, F.; Nanda, S.; Dalai, A.K.; Meda, V.; Naik, S. Hydrothermal pretreatment technologies for lignocellulosic biomass: A review of steam explosion and subcritical water hydrolysis. *Chemosphere* **2021**, *284*, 131372. [CrossRef] [PubMed]
18. Nitsos, C.K.; Matis, K.A.; Triantafyllidis, K.S. Optimization of hydrothermal pretreatment of lignocellulosic biomass in the bioethanol production process. *ChemSusChem* **2013**, *6*, 110–122. [CrossRef] [PubMed]
19. Behera, S.; Arora, R.; Nandhagopal, N.; Kumar, S. Importance of chemical pretreatment for bioconversion of lignocellulosic biomass. *Renew. Sustain. Energy Rev.* **2014**, *36*, 91–106. [CrossRef]

20. Paul, A.; Jia, L.; Majumder, E.L.-W.; Yoo, C.G.; Rajendran, K.; Villarreal, E.; Kumar, D. Poly (3-hydroxybuyrate) production from industrial hemp waste pretreated with a chemical-free hydrothermal process. *Bioresour. Technol.* **2023**, *381*, 129161. [CrossRef] [PubMed]
21. Juneja, A.; Kumar, D.; Singh, V.K.; Singh, V. Chemical free two-step hydrothermal pretreatment to improve sugar yields from energy cane. *Energies* **2020**, *13*, 5805. [CrossRef]
22. Wang, Z.; Dien, B.S.; Rausch, K.D.; Tumbleson, M.; Singh, V. Fermentation of undetoxified sugarcane bagasse hydrolyzates using a two stage hydrothermal and mechanical refining pretreatment. *Bioresour. Technol.* **2018**, *261*, 313–321. [CrossRef] [PubMed]
23. Kim, S.M.; Dien, B.S.; Tumbleson, M.; Rausch, K.D.; Singh, V. Improvement of sugar yields from corn stover using sequential hot water pretreatment and disk milling. *Bioresour. Technol.* **2016**, *216*, 706–713. [CrossRef] [PubMed]
24. Sluiter, A.; Ruiz, R.; Scarlata, C.; Sluiter, J.; Templeton, D. Determination of extractives in biomass. *Lab. Anal. Proced.* **2005**, *1617*, 1–16.
25. Sluiter, A.; Hames, B.; Ruiz, R.; Scarlata, C.; Sluiter, J.; Templeton, D.; Crocker, D. Determination of structural carbohydrates and lignin in biomass. *Lab. Anal. Proced.* **2008**, *1617*, 1–16.
26. Thomas, C.M.; Scheel, R.A.; Nomura, C.T.; Ramarao, B.; Kumar, D. Production of polyhydroxybutyrate and polyhydroxybutyrate-co-MCL copolymers from brewer's spent grains by recombinant *Escherichia coli* LSBJ. *Biomass Convers. Biorefinery* **2021**, 1–12. [CrossRef]
27. Hou, L.; Jia, L.; Morrison, H.M.; Majumder, E.L.-W.; Kumar, D. Enhanced polyhydroxybutyrate production from acid whey through determination of process and metabolic limiting factors. *Bioresour. Technol.* **2021**, *342*, 125973. [CrossRef] [PubMed]
28. Tappel, R.C.; Wang, Q.; Nomura, C.T. Precise control of repeating unit composition in biodegradable poly (3-hydroxyalkanoate) polymers synthesized by Escherichia coli. *J. Biosci. Bioeng.* **2012**, *113*, 480–486. [CrossRef] [PubMed]
29. Scheel, R.A. Enhancing polyhydroxyalkanoate biosynthesis in Escherichia coli: A genetic engineering and process optimization approach towards functionalized polymeric nanomedicine. *State Univ. N.Y. Coll. Environ. Sci. For.* **2020**. Available online: https://experts.esf.edu/esploro/outputs/graduate/Enhancing-polyhydroxyalkanoate-biosynthesis-in-Escherichia-coli/99870875704826 (accessed on 7 July 2024).
30. Thomas, C.M. Brewer's Spent Grains as a Substrate for Recombinant *E. coli* LSBJ to Produce Bioplastic Polyhydroxybutyrate and Medium Chain Length Polyhydroxyalkanoate Copolymers. Ph.D. Thesis, College of Environmental Science, Syracuse, NY, USA, 2021.
31. Manikandan, N.A.; Pakshirajan, K.; Pugazhenthi, G. Preparation and characterization of environmentally safe and highly biodegradable microbial polyhydroxybutyrate (PHB) based graphene nanocomposites for potential food packaging applications. *Int. J. Biol. Macromol.* **2020**, *154*, 866–877. [CrossRef]
32. de Sousa Junior, R.R.; Dos Santos, C.A.S.; Ito, N.M.; Suqueira, A.N.; Lackner, M.; Dos Santos, D.J. PHB processability and property improvement with linear-chain polyester oligomers used as plasticizers. *Polymers* **2022**, *14*, 4197. [CrossRef]
33. Borisova, I.; Stoilova, O.; Manolova, N.; Rashkov, I. Modulating the mechanical properties of electrospun PHB/PCL materials by using different types of collectors and heat sealing. *Polymers* **2020**, *12*, 693. [CrossRef] [PubMed]
34. Min, B.C.; Bhayani, B.; Jampana, V.; Ramarao, B. Enhancement of the enzymatic hydrolysis of fines from recycled paper mill waste rejects. *Bioresour. Bioprocess.* **2015**, *2*, 40. [CrossRef]
35. Jeffries, T.W.; Schartman, R. Bioconversion of secondary fiber fines to ethanol using counter-current enzymatic saccharification and co-fermentation. *Appl. Biochem. Biotechnol.* **1999**, *78*, 435–444. [CrossRef] [PubMed]
36. Cowling, E.B.; Kirk, T.K. Properties of Cellulose and Lignocellulosie Materials as Substrates for Enzymatic Conversion Processes. In Proceedings of the Biotechnology and Bioengineering Symposium, New York, NY, USA, 1 January 1976.
37. Zhu, J.; Wang, G.; Pan, X.; Gleisner, R. Specific surface to evaluate the efficiencies of milling and pretreatment of wood for enzymatic saccharification. *Chem. Eng. Sci.* **2009**, *64*, 474–485. [CrossRef]
38. Li, J.; Li, S.; Fan, C.; Yan, Z. The mechanism of poly (ethylene glycol) 4000 effect on enzymatic hydrolysis of lignocellulose. *Colloids Surf. B Biointerfaces* **2012**, *89*, 203–210. [CrossRef] [PubMed]
39. Huang, C.; Zhao, X.; Zheng, Y.; Lin, W.; Lai, C.; Yong, Q.; Ragauskas, A.J.; Meng, X. Revealing the mechanism of surfactant-promoted enzymatic hydrolysis of dilute acid pretreated bamboo. *Bioresour. Technol.* **2022**, *360*, 127524. [CrossRef] [PubMed]
40. Lou, H.; Zeng, M.; Hu, Q.; Cai, C.; Lin, X.; Qiu, X.; Yang, D.; Pang, Y. Nonionic surfactants enhanced enzymatic hydrolysis of cellulose by reducing cellulase deactivation caused by shear force and air-liquid interface. *Bioresour. Technol.* **2018**, *249*, 1–8. [CrossRef] [PubMed]
41. Hideno, A.; Inoue, H.; Tsukahara, K.; Fujimoto, S.; Minowa, T.; Inoue, S.; Endo, T.; Sawayama, S. Wet disk milling pretreatment without sulfuric acid for enzymatic hydrolysis of rice straw. *Bioresour. Technol.* **2009**, *100*, 2706–2711. [CrossRef] [PubMed]
42. Kerekes, R.J. Characterizing refining action in PFI mills. *Tappi J.* **2005**, *4*, 9–14.
43. Uetani, K.; Yano, H. Nanofibrillation of wood pulp using a high-speed blender. *Biomacromolecules* **2011**, *12*, 348–353. [CrossRef] [PubMed]
44. Wang, Q.; Zhu, J.; Gleisner, R.; Kuster, T.; Baxa, U.; McNeil, S. Morphological development of cellulose fibrils of a bleached eucalyptus pulp by mechanical fibrillation. *Cellulose* **2012**, *19*, 1631–1643. [CrossRef]
45. Leu, S.-Y.; Zhu, J. Substrate-related factors affecting enzymatic saccharification of lignocelluloses: Our recent understanding. *Bioenergy Res.* **2013**, *6*, 405–415. [CrossRef]

46. Weiqi, W.; Shubin, W.; Liguo, L. Combination of liquid hot water pretreatment and wet disk milling to improve the efficiency of the enzymatic hydrolysis of eucalyptus. *Bioresour. Technol.* **2013**, *128*, 725–730. [CrossRef] [PubMed]
47. Sediawan, W.B.; Sulistyo, H.; Hidayat, M. Kinetics of sequential reaction of hydrolysis and sugar degradation of rice husk in ethanol production: Effect of catalyst concentration. *Bioresour. Technol.* **2011**, *102*, 2062–2067.
48. Kadhum, H.J.; Mahapatra, D.M.; Murthy, G.S. A novel method for real-time estimation of insoluble solids and glucose concentrations during enzymatic hydrolysis of biomass. *Bioresour. Technol.* **2019**, *275*, 328–337. [CrossRef] [PubMed]
49. Silva, L.; Taciro, M.; Michelin Ramos, M.; Carter, J.; Pradella, J.; Gomez, J. Poly-3-hydroxybutyrate (P3HB) production by bacteria from xylose, glucose and sugarcane bagasse hydrolysate. *J. Ind. Microbiol. Biotechnol.* **2004**, *31*, 245–254. [CrossRef] [PubMed]
50. Le Bouguénec, C.; Schouler, C. Sugar metabolism, an additional virulence factor in enterobacteria. *Int. J. Med. Microbiol.* **2011**, *301*, 1–6. [CrossRef] [PubMed]
51. Kovalcik, A.; Kucera, D.; Matouskova, P.; Pernicova, I.; Obruca, S.; Kalina, M.; Enev, V.; Marova, I. Influence of removal of microbial inhibitors on PHA production from spent coffee grounds employing Halomonas halophila. *J. Environ. Chem. Eng.* **2018**, *6*, 3495–3501. [CrossRef]
52. Pan, W.; Perrotta, J.A.; Stipanovic, A.J.; Nomura, C.T.; Nakas, J.P. Production of polyhydroxyalkanoates by Burkholderia cepacia ATCC 17759 using a detoxified sugar maple hemicellulosic hydrolysate. *J. Ind. Microbiol. Biotechnol.* **2012**, *39*, 459–469. [CrossRef] [PubMed]
53. Walfridsson, M.; Hallborn, J.; Penttil, M.; Kernen, S.; Hahn-Hgerdal, B. Xylose-metabolizing Saccharomyces cerevisiae strains overexpressing the TKL1 and TAL1 genes encoding the pentose phosphate pathway enzymes transketolase and transaldolase. *Appl. Environ. Microbiol.* **1995**, *61*, 4184–4190. [CrossRef]
54. Scheel, R.A.; Fusi, A.D.; Min, B.C.; Thomas, C.M.; Ramarao, B.V.; Nomura, C.T. Increased production of the value-added biopolymers poly (R-3-hydroxyalkanoate) and poly (γ-glutamic acid) from hydrolyzed paper recycling waste fines. *Front. Bioeng. Biotechnol.* **2019**, *7*, 409. [CrossRef] [PubMed]
55. Dietrich, K.; Oliveira-Filho, E.R.; Dumont, M.-J.; Gomez, J.G.; Taciro, M.K.; da Silva, L.F.; Orsat, V.; Del Rio, L.F. Increasing PHB production with an industrially scalable hardwood hydrolysate as a carbon source. *Ind. Crops Prod.* **2020**, *154*, 112703. [CrossRef]
56. Min, B.; Jampana, S.N.; Thomas, C.M.; Ramarao, B.V. Study of buffer substitution using inhibitory compound $CaCO_3$ in enzymatic hydrolysis of paper mill waste fines. *J. TAPPI* **2018**, *50*, 77–82. [CrossRef]
57. Sun, S.; Ding, Y.; Liu, M.; Xian, M.; Zhao, G. Comparison of glucose, acetate and ethanol as carbon resource for production of poly (3-hydroxybutyrate) and other acetyl-CoA derivatives. *Front. Bioeng. Biotechnol.* **2020**, *8*, 833. [CrossRef] [PubMed]
58. Dañez, J.C.A.; Requiso, P.J.; Alfafara, C.G.; Nayve Jr, F.R.P.; Ventura, J.-R.S. Optimization of fermentation factors for polyhydroxybutyrate (PHB) production using Bacillus megaterium PNCM 1890 in simulated glucose-xylose hydrolysates from agricultural residues. *Philipp. J. Sci. USA* **2020**, *149*, 163–175. [CrossRef]
59. Enjalbert, B.; Millard, P.; Dinclaux, M.; Portais, J.-C.; Létisse, F. Acetate fluxes in *Escherichia coli* are determined by the thermodynamic control of the Pta-AckA pathway. *Sci. Rep.* **2017**, *7*, 42135. [CrossRef] [PubMed]
60. Bernal, V.; Castaño-Cerezo, S.; Cánovas, M. Acetate metabolism regulation in Escherichia coli: Carbon overflow, pathogenicity, and beyond. *Appl. Microbiol. Biotechnol.* **2016**, *100*, 8985–9001. [CrossRef] [PubMed]
61. Nielsen, J.; Keasling, J.D. Engineering cellular metabolism. *Cell* **2016**, *164*, 1185–1197. [CrossRef] [PubMed]
62. Sekar, K.; Tyo, K.E. Regulatory effects on central carbon metabolism from poly-3-hydroxybutyrate synthesis. *Metab. Eng.* **2015**, *28*, 180–189. [CrossRef] [PubMed]
63. Prabisha, T.P.; Sindhu, R.; Binod, P.; Sankar, V.; Raghu, K.G.; Pandey, A. Production and characterization of PHB from a novel isolate *Comamonas* sp. from a dairy effluent sample and its application in cell culture. *Biochem. Eng. J.* **2015**, *101*, 150–159. [CrossRef]
64. Oliveira, F.C.; Dias, M.L.; Castilho, L.R.; Freire, D.M. Characterization of poly (3-hydroxybutyrate) produced by *Cupriavidus necator* in solid-state fermentation. *Bioresour. Technol.* **2007**, *98*, 633–638. [CrossRef] [PubMed]
65. Kansiz, M.; Billman-Jacobe, H.; McNaughton, D. Quantitative determination of the biodegradable polymer poly (β-hydroxybutyrate) in a recombinant *Escherichia coli* strain by use of mid-infrared spectroscopy and multivariate statistics. *Appl. Environ. Microbiol.* **2000**, *66*, 3415–3420. [CrossRef] [PubMed]
66. Martínez-Herrera, R.E.; Alemán-Huerta, M.E.; Almaguer-Cantú, V.; Rosas-Flores, W.; Martínez-Gómez, V.J.; Quintero-Zapata, I.; Rivera, G.; Rutiaga-Quiñones, O.M. Efficient recovery of thermostable polyhydroxybutyrate (PHB) by a rapid and solvent-free extraction protocol assisted by ultrasound. *Int. J. Biol. Macromol.* **2020**, *164*, 771–782. [CrossRef] [PubMed]
67. Sirohi, R. Sustainable utilization of food waste: Production and characterization of polyhydroxybutyrate (PHB) from damaged wheat grains. *Environ. Technol. Innov.* **2021**, *23*, 101715. [CrossRef]
68. Martínez-Herrera, R.E.; Alemán-Huerta, M.E.; Flores-Rodríguez, P.; Almaguer-Cantú, V.; Valencia-Vázquez, R.; Rosas-Flores, W.; Medrano-Roldán, H.; Ochoa-Martínez, L.A.; Rutiaga-Quiñones, O.M. Utilization of Agave durangensis leaves by Bacillus cereus 4N for polyhydroxybutyrate (PHB) biosynthesis. *Int. J. Biol. Macromol.* **2021**, *175*, 199–208. [CrossRef] [PubMed]
69. Wang, B.; Sharma-Shivappa, R.R.; Olson, J.W.; Khan, S.A. Production of polyhydroxybutyrate (PHB) by Alcaligenes latus using sugarbeet juice. *Ind. Crops Prod.* **2013**, *43*, 802–811. [CrossRef]

70. Chaijamrus, S.; Udpuay, N. Production and characterization of polyhydroxybutyrate from molasses and corn steep liquor produced by Bacillus megaterium ATCC 6748. *Agric. Eng. Int. CIGR J.* **2008**, 1–12.
71. Kerketta, A.; Vasanth, D. Madhuca indica flower extract as cheaper carbon source for production of poly (3-hydroxybutyrate-co-3-hydroxyvalerate) using *Ralstonia eutropha*. *Process Biochem.* **2019**, *87*, 1–9. [CrossRef]

Disclaimer/Publisher's Note: The statements, opinions and data contained in all publications are solely those of the individual author(s) and contributor(s) and not of MDPI and/or the editor(s). MDPI and/or the editor(s) disclaim responsibility for any injury to people or property resulting from any ideas, methods, instructions or products referred to in the content.

Article

Investigations on Amoxicillin Removal from Aqueous Solutions by Novel Calcium-Rich Biochars: Adsorption Properties and Mechanisms Exploration

Salah Jellali [1,*], Wissem Hamdi [2], Majida Al-Harrasi [3], Malik Al-Wardy [1], Jamal Al-Sabahi [4], Hamed Al-Nadabi [1], Ahmed Al-Raeesi [1] and Mejdi Jeguirim [5]

[1] Centre for Environmental Studies and Research, Sultan Qaboos University, Al-Khoud, Muscat 123, Oman; hamed@squ.edu.om (H.A.-N.); aalraeesi@squ.edu.om (A.A.-R.)
[2] Higher Institute of the Sciences and Techniques of Waters, University of Gabes, Gabes 6029, Tunisia; wissemhemdi@yahoo.fr
[3] Department of Plant Sciences, College of Agricultural and Marine Sciences, Sultan Qaboos University, Al-Khoud, Muscat 123, Oman; mageda502@gmail.com
[4] Central Instrumentation Laboratory, College of Agricultural and Marine Sciences, Sultan Qaboos University, Al-Khoud, Muscat 123, Oman; jamal@squ.edu.om
[5] The Institute of Materials Science of Mulhouse (IS2M), University of Haute Alsace, University of Strasbourg, CNRS, UMR 7361, F-68100 Mulhouse, France; mejdi.jeguirim@uha.fr
* Correspondence: author: s.jelali@squ.edu.om

Abstract: This study investigates the synthesis, characterization, and environmental application for amoxicillin (AMX) removal in batch mode of three novel calcium-rich biochars. These biochars were produced from the co-pyrolysis of poultry manure, date palm wastes, and waste marble powder at temperatures of 700 °C (Ca-B-700), 800 °C (Ca-B-800), and 900 °C (Ca-B-900). Characterization results show that increasing the pyrolysis temperature results in improved structural, textural, and surface chemistry properties. For instance, the BET surface area of the Ca-B-900 was assessed to be 52.3 m^2 g^{-1}, which is 14.1 and 3.1 times higher than those observed for Ca-B-700 and Ca-B-800, respectively. Moreover, the Ca-B-900 shows higher AMX removal ability (56.2 mg g^{-1}) than Ca-B-800 (46.8 mg g^{-1}), Ca-B-700 (14.6 mg g^{-1}), and numerous other engineered biochars. The AMX removal process by these biochars is favorable under wide experimental conditions of initial pH and AMX concentrations. Additionally, the experimental and modeling data show that the AMX adsorption process includes both physical and chemical mechanisms. This study confirms that Ca-rich biochars can perform significant removal of AMX in batch mode.

Keywords: wastes management; engineered biochars; pharmaceuticals removal; adsorption characteristics; mechanism

Citation: Jellali, S.; Hamdi, W.; Al-Harrasi, M.; Al-Wardy, M.; Al-Sabahi, J.; Al-Nadabi, H.; Al-Raeesi, A.; Jeguirim, M. Investigations on Amoxicillin Removal from Aqueous Solutions by Novel Calcium-Rich Biochars: Adsorption Properties and Mechanisms Exploration. *Processes* **2024**, *12*, 1552. https://doi.org/10.3390/pr12081552

Academic Editors: Dimitris Zagklis and Georgios Bampos

Received: 4 July 2024
Revised: 23 July 2024
Accepted: 24 July 2024
Published: 25 July 2024

Copyright: © 2024 by the authors. Licensee MDPI, Basel, Switzerland. This article is an open access article distributed under the terms and conditions of the Creative Commons Attribution (CC BY) license (https://creativecommons.org/licenses/by/4.0/).

1. Introduction

Studies on emerging contaminants have attracted significant attention over the last two decades [1]. These substances, including herbicides, pesticides, micro- and nano-plastics, new organic dyes, and pharmaceuticals, have been increasingly detected in water ecosystems [2]. Even at very low concentrations, these compounds may have serious adverse impacts on both aquatic systems and also human health [3]. Special attention has been given to the pharmaceutical compounds due to their significant usage and the rising concentrations detected in water resources [4]. This presence is attributed to uncontrolled discharges from the pharmaceutical industry and the excretion of these substances in urine and feces by humans in hospitals and animals on farms [5]. Active pharmaceutical substances are highly resistant to biodegradation and thus persist in aquatic ecosystems. This persistence can adversely affect aquatic organisms and subsequently affect human health through the food chain [4]. Amoxicillin is an active compound that belongs to the penicillin family. It is one of the most widely used antibiotics in the majority of European countries [6]. Moreover, around 80% of the orally ingested AMX is excreted into the urine in a non-metabolized form and consequently transferred to wastewater treatment plants [7].

Numerous technologies have been tested for the removal of pharmaceuticals from aquatic environments. They mainly include membrane advanced oxidation processes, membrane filtration, and biological degradation [8]. However, the real application of these methods can be challenging due to the required stringent experimental conditions, high energy consumption, and the possible production of toxic by-products [9]. Adsorption methods have been pointed out as an attractive and promising approach for removing pharmaceuticals due to their simple design and operation, minimal energy requirements, eco-friendliness, and high effectiveness [10]. Numerous materials, such as raw agricultural wastes [11], activated carbons [12], molecular organic frameworks [13], and biochars [10] have been applied to purify water from pharmaceuticals. However, biochar constitutes a more cost-effective option for the elimination of pharmaceutical residues, valued by its environmental benefits and sustainability, low cost, and adaptability for large-scale use [14,15]. For instance, on the environmental side, the production of 1 kg of biochar requires only 6.1 MJ and has net negative greenhouse gas emissions (-0.9 kg CO_2 eq). These values are much more attractive when compared to those corresponding to the generation of 1 kg of activated carbon: 97 MJ and $+ 6.6$ kg CO_2 eq [9].

Calcium-rich biochars are novel materials that are typically synthesized from the pyrolysis of pre-impregnated biomasses or post-impregnated biochars with calcium chloride chemical reagents ($CaCl_2$) [16,17]. In this last decade, to reduce the use of chemicals and to boost sustainability and circular economy concepts, various Ca-rich biochars were produced from the co-pyrolysis of biomasses mixed with calcium-based wastes such as powder marble [18], oyster shell [19], crab shells [20], eggshell [21], and dolomite [22]. The characteristics of the synthesized biochars depend mainly on the percentage of the mineral waste and also the pyrolysis conditions [23–25]. Usually, improved textural properties (i.e., surface area and porosity) are obtained when increasing the pyrolysis temperature and the pyrolysis contact time or decreasing the percentage of the Ca-based wastes [25–28]. For instance, Wang et al. [24] showed that increasing the corn straw/eggshell mass ratio from 1:0 to 1:4 and 2:3 decreased the BET surface area of the related biochars from 179.7 to 67.5 and only 23.6 $m^2\ g^{-1}$, respectively. Moreover, Xu et al. [19] showed that increasing the pyrolysis temperature from 700 to 900 °C of a mixture of rice husk and oyster shells (at a mass ratio of 1:2) increased the BET surface area and the total pore volume from 21.3 $m^2\ g^{-1}$ and 0.025 $cm^3\ g^{-1}$ to 46.2 $m^2\ g^{-1}$ and 0.019 $cm^3\ g^{-1}$, respectively. A similar trend was observed for $Ca(OH)_2$-modified wood biochar [29].

In addition, most of the previous valorization studies of Ca-rich biochars for wastewater treatment have been concerned with nutrient recovery from wastewater (i.e., phosphorus (P)) [17,30]. In this regard, these biochars were found to be excellent materials for P recovery, even under challenging conditions [16]. However, only rare studies have investigated the use of Ca-rich biochars, which are synthesized from the co-pyrolysis of biomasses with Ca-based industrial wastes, for pharmaceuticals removal from aqueous solutions [29,31]. For instance, in the study of Zen and Kan [29], tetracycline removal by $Ca(OH)_2$-modified wood biochar was found to be moderately removed in batch mode (20.9 mg g^{-1}) and not removed in column mode. To the best of our knowledge, the only preliminary study regarding the use of Ca-rich biochar for AMX removal was recently carried out by our research work [31]. In this study, we synthesized a novel biochar at 900 °C from two abundant organic feedstocks and a mineral industrial waste: (i) an animal organic waste: poultry manure (PM), (ii) lignocellulosic biomass: date palm waste (DPW), and (iii) a Ca-based industrial waste: marble powder (WMP). Results of this study showed that this Ca-rich biochar (Ca-B-900) selectively recovered P, and no significant AMX removal was observed under dynamic conditions (both column and reactors). While this study provides valuable insights into the general behavior of AMX removal by Ca-B-900 in batch mode, a detailed and comprehensive understanding of the effect of pyrolysis temperature as well as the adsorption experimental conditions (i.e., contact time, initial pH, initial AMX concentration, etc.) on AMX removal efficacy is still lacking. Moreover, the involved mechanisms in this pharmaceutical removal by Ca-rich biochars were not yet appropriately illustrated [29,31]. Further investigations are needed in order to overcome this knowledge gap and also to facilitate the future upscaling process for real-site conditions application.

Therefore, the present research work aims to (i) synthesize Ca-rich biochars from the co-pyrolysis of poultry manure, date palm waste, and waste marble powder at three different temperatures: 700, 800, and 900 °C, (ii) characterize these biochars by using various analytical methods, (iii) study the AMX removal efficiency in batch mode and under different experimental situations encompassing contact time, initial pH, adsorbent dosage, ionic strength, and initial AMX concentration, and (iv) explore the main involved mechanisms in this removal process.

2. Materials and Methods

2.1. Feedstock Preparation and Biochars Synthesis

Three feedstocks were used during this work: PM, DPW, and WMP. The PM and dry DPW were provided from a local farm in Muscat, Oman. They were air-dried until they reached a nearly constant weight, then ground using a mechanical grinder and sieved. The fraction with a dimension lower than 1 mm was selected and used hereafter for the production of the biochars. The WMP was collected from an industrial site in Oman in a slurry form. It was air-dried until a constant weight and used without any modification. A feedstock mass of 100 g was prepared by a manual mixing of 45 g of PM, 10 g of DPW, and 45 g of WMP, respectively, and used for the production of the biochars. The chosen WMP percentage should permit the formation of enough contents of CaO and $Ca(OH)_2$. It is in line with previous works [21,32].

The Ca-rich biochars synthesis was performed using an electric tubular furnace (Carbolite, TF1-1200, Neuhausen, Germany) under an N_2 atmosphere. The heating gradient and residence time were kept constant at 5 °C min^{-1} and 2 h, respectively. Three biochars were synthesized at final pyrolysis temperatures of 700, 800, and 900 °C. They were labelled Ca-B-700, Ca-B-800, and Ca-B-900, respectively. These pyrolysis temperatures were chosen in order to elucidate the effect of WMP carbonization degree and the biochars' calcium oxide contents on AMX removal efficiency. They are in line with previous studies [18,19]. These biochars were kept in plastic airtight containers and used for AMX removal assays from aqueous solutions. The biochars production yields at a given temperature pyrolysis 'T' (Y_T (%)) were calculated as follows:

$$Y_T\ (\%) = \frac{M_{f,T}}{M_{0,T}} \times 100 \qquad (1)$$

where $M_{0,T}$ and $M_{f,T}$ are the feedstock mixture masses before and after the pyrolysis process at a fixed pyrolysis temperature.

2.2. Biochars Characterization

During this work, the three synthesized biochars were characterized through the analysis of their (i) surface morphology and elemental composition by a scanning electron microscope (SEM) coupled with energy dispersive X-ray (EDS) (Jeol, Jsm-7800F, Tokyo, Japan), (ii) mineral composition by X-ray fluorescence device (XRF) (Rigaku, Nexqc, Tokyo, Japan), (iii) crystallinity through X-ray diffraction (XRD) (Rigaku, Miniflex 600, Tokyo, Japan), (iv) pores properties (BET surface areas, total pore volumes (TPV), and average pore sizes (APS) by a Micrometrics instrument (ASAP-2020, Ottawa, ON, Canada), (v) functional groups richness by Fourier Transform Infrared (FTIR) (Perkin Elmer, Frontier, MA, USA), and (vi) the surface charge versus pH on the basis of the pH drift method [33].

2.3. Amoxicillin Adsorption Experiments

2.3.1. Chemicals

The AMX reagent used in this work (chemical formula: $C_{16}H_{19}N_3O_5S$; molecular weight: 365.4 g mol^{-1}) was purchased from Sigma-Aldrich, St. Louis, MO, USA. It was employed for the preparation of a stock solution of 1000 mg L^{-1}, which has been used throughout this study. This solution was diluted by using distilled water to obtain the desired synthetic solution concentrations. Moreover, NaOH and HCl (from Sigma-Aldrich) were used for the adjustment of the prepared solutions' pH values. These values were measured by a dedicated pH meter (Mettler Toledo, Columbus, OH, USA).

2.3.2. Batch Assays Experimental Protocol and Data Analysis

The efficiency of the three Ca-rich biochars in removing AMX from aqueous solutions was performed under static conditions (batch mode). This step was ensured through controlled shaking adsorbent within AMX solutions in 120 mL glass flasks by a multi-position magnetic stirrer (Gallenkamp, Cambridge, UK) at 600 rpm. The biochars' effectiveness in removing AMX was assessed through sample analyses before and after adsorption. These samples were first filtrated through 0.22 µm PVDF filters (Whatman, Buckinghamshire, UK) and then analyzed by high-performance liquid chromatography (HPLC, Shimadzu, Kyoto, Japan). The effect of various parameters (i.e., contact time, initial pH, biochar dosage, and initial concentration) on AMX removal by the three biochars was studied under the conditions given in Table 1. The interval variation of these parameters was fixed on the basis of our previous study [34] and also preliminary investigations.

Table 1. Experimental conditions used for AMX removal by the Ca-rich biochars.

Experimental Set	Contact Time (h)	pH	Biochar Dosage (g L^{-1})	Dissolved NaCl/Na$_2$SO$_4$ (mM L^{-1})	Initial Concentration (mg L^{-1})
Effect of contact time	From 1 min to 24 h	6.8	1	0/0	100
Effect of pH	24	4–10	1	0/0	100
Effect of dose	24	6.8	0.1–40	0/0	100
Effect of ionic strength	24	6.8	1	14–42/0	100
	24	6.8	1	1–5.2/0	100
Effect of initial concentration	24	6.8	1	0/0	5–100

The adsorbed AMX amount after a desired contact time 't' (q$_t$), and the corresponding removal yield (R$_t$) were assessed as follows:

$$q_t = \frac{(C_0 - C_t) * V}{Mb} \quad (2)$$

$$R_t(\%) = \frac{(C_0 - C_t)}{C_0} \times 100 \quad (3)$$

where C_0 and C_t (mg L^{-1}) are the AMX concentrations before adsorption and after a contact time of 't', respectively. Mb and V are the mass of the biochar (g) and the volume of the solutions (L), respectively.

To obtain a better understanding of the AMX kinetic adsorption process by the three biochars, the related experimental data were fitted to three famous models, namely pseudo-first-order (PFO), pseudo-second-order (PSO), and diffusion models (WM). Similarly, Freundlich, Langmuir, and Dubinin-Radushkevich (D-R) models were used to fit the experimental isotherm data. The equations of these kinetic and isotherm models, as well as the definition of the included parameters, are provided in the Supplementary Materials

(Table S1). The agreement between the experimental and these models-calculated curves was assessed by estimating the related correlation coefficients (R^2) as well as the mean absolute percentage errors (MPAE) as follows:

$$MAPE_{kinetic} = \frac{\sum \left| \frac{q_{t,exp} - q_{t,pred}}{q_{t,exp}} \right|}{N} * 100 \qquad (4)$$

$$MAPE_{isotherm} = \frac{\sum \left| \frac{q_{e,exp} - q_{e,pred}}{q_{e,exp}} \right|}{N} * 100 \qquad (5)$$

where $MAPE_{kinetic}$ and $MAPE_{isotherm}$ are the mean absolute percentage errors between the experimental and predicted kinetic and isotherm data, respectively. The $q_{t,exp}$, $q_{t,pred}$ and $q_{e,exp}$ and $q_{e,pred}$ denote the experimental and predicted adsorbed AMX quantity at time 't' and at equilibrium, respectively. N represents the number of experimental runs.

All the cited above batch experimental data were carried out at least in triplicate. The experimental results given in this work represent the average values.

2.3.3. Statistical Analysis

Excel 2016 was used for figure plotting and the regression analysis of the experimental and predicted data. The error bars in the plots are the standard deviation that is estimated from the triplicate batch assays.

3. Results

3.1. Biochars Characterization

The biochar production yields were assessed to be 63.9%, 57.5%, and 42.6% for Ca-B-700, Ca-B-800, and Ca-B-900, respectively (Table 2). The decrease of this yield production with the increase of the temperature is expected and is imputed to a higher decomposition rate of the volatile matter contained in the used feedstocks [35]. It is important to mention that these yields are much higher than those usually reported for lignocellulosic, animal, or even sludge biomasses [35–37]. This is mainly due to the mineral nature of the WMP, which is only slightly carbonized even at high pyrolysis temperatures [38,39].

Table 2. Main properties of the three synthesized calcium-rich biochars (BET SA: Brunauer–Emmett–Teller Surface area; TPV: total pore volume, APS: average pore size).

Biochar	Yield (%)	Mineral Contents (mg g^{-1})									Textural Properties			pHzpc
		Ca	K	P	Fe	Mn	Ni	Zn	Cu	Cd	BET SA (m^2 g^{-1})	TPV (cm^3 g^{-1})	APS (nm)	
Ca-B-700	63.9	219.0	10.8	9.4	0.76	0.25	0.18	0.15	0.04	0.01	3.7	0.013	35.1	10.89
Ca-B-800	57.5	245.0	11.4	9.4	0.87	0.26	0.19	0.16	0.05	0.01	16.9	0.018	15.1	13.30
Ca-B-900 [31]	42.6	324.0	12.3	12.4	1.03	0.34	0.22	0.12	0.06	0.08	52.3	0.032	9.4	13.46

The SEM images of the Ca-B-700, Ca-B-800, and Ca-B-900 are given in Figure S1. It can be clearly seen that the three biochars present irregular surfaces and a sponge-like structure containing pores with different dimensions. The Ca-B-900 seems to have a better structure with finer aggregates due to the fact that higher pyrolysis temperatures induce more volatilization of organic matter present in the mixed organic feedstocks and also a larger transformation yield of waste marble powder into calcium oxides/hydroxides [40,41]. The latter assumption is in line with the semi-qualitative EDS analyses, which indicate that the Ca peaks increase with the rise of the pyrolysis temperature (Figure S1). Additionally, the XRD analyses (Figure 1a–c) clearly show that at 700 °C, no significant transformation of $CaCO_3$ was observed (Figure 1a). However, as the pyrolysis temperature increases, the $CaCO_3$ transformation into CaO and Ca(OH)$_2$ is favored (Figure 1b–c). The highest transformation rate was observed at a temperature of 900 °C, where more Ca-based oxide contents were observed (Figure 1c). At this temperature, non-negligible peaks of CaO; and Ca(OH)$_2$ are detected at 2θ of 32.4°, 37.5°, 54.2°, 64.3°, and 67.5°; and at 18.1°, 28.4°, 28.8°, 34.2°, 51.0°, 62.5°, and 64.3°, respectively. This result is in concordance with that of [38], who studied the pyrolysis of marble originating from Turkey. They showed that its carbonization process occurs between around 650 and 850 °C with a maximum mass loss of 41.3% at 1000 °C. Moreover, Ca-based nanoparticles (CaO/Ca(OH)$_2$) detection was reported for Ca-rich biochars generated from the co-pyrolysis of eggshells mixed with corn straw [21] or with peanut shells [42], and oyster shells mixed with peanut shells [43] or ground coffee waste [32]. A similar finding was also reported for Ca-rich biochar generated from the pyrolysis of pure crab shells [26].

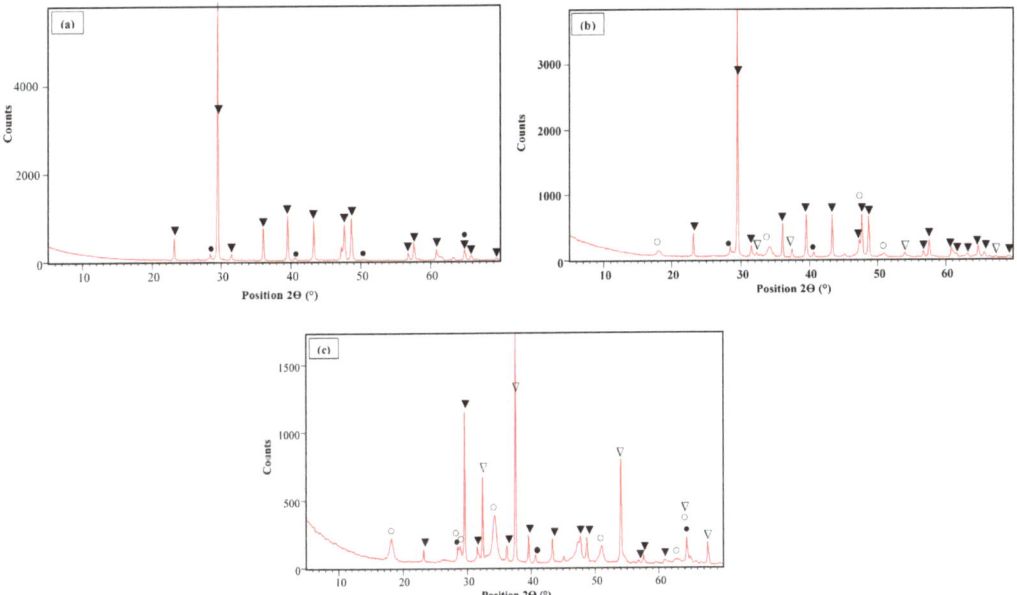

Figure 1. XRD analyses of Ca-B-700 (**a**), Ca-B-800 (**b**), and Ca-B-900 (**c**) [31] (▲: CaCO$_3$; •: KCl; Δ: CaO; ○: Ca(OH)$_2$).

The WMP carbonization and conversion into Ca-based oxides are further confirmed by the XRF analyses (Table 2). Indeed, the Ca contents increased from 219 mg g^{-1} for Ca-B-700 by 11.9% and 47.9% for Ca-B-800 and Ca-B-900 [31], respectively. These Ca contents increases are due to the higher volatilization rate of the organic matter contained in the PM and DPW feedstocks and also the better calcination of the WMP. The same increase trend was observed for the majority of the minerals such as P, K, Fe, Mn, etc. (Table 2). For instance, the potassium content observed at 700 °C has increased by around 5.6% and 13.9% in Ca-B-800 and Ca-B-900 [31], respectively. Moreover, most of the toxic heavy metals in the three synthesized biochars have relatively low contents (Table 2). Other heavy metals presented contents lower than the detection limit of the used ICP/MS apparatus: As, Al, Hg, and Co.

In addition, the textural properties of the synthesized biochars were significantly improved with the increase of the pyrolysis temperature (Table 2 and Figure 2). Indeed, compared to Ca-B-700, the BET surface areas and 'TPV' of Ca-B-800 and Ca-B-900 have increased by 356.8% and 1313.5%, and '38.5%' and '146.2%', respectively. This indicates that the deposition of Ca-based nanoparticles on the biochars' surface did not contribute to the clogging of the biochars' pores. This can be explained by the fact that all the biochars have mesoporous structures with average pore sizes varying in the range of 2 and 50 nm (Table 2). However, it is clear that the biochars' average pore sizes have decreased with the increase in temperature, tending to be microporous (Table 2). A comparable trend was observed for biochars derived from the co-pyrolysis of commercial wood biochar and Ca(OH)$_2$ at 100 and 300 °C [29]. However, some other studies have underlined that at high pyrolysis temperatures, biochars' structure may collapse, which can result in a significant decrease in the BET surface areas and the total pore volumes [44,45]. The enhanced textural properties of our Ca-rich biochars, especially Ca-B-900, may contribute to better AMX removal through physical adsorption processes [46].

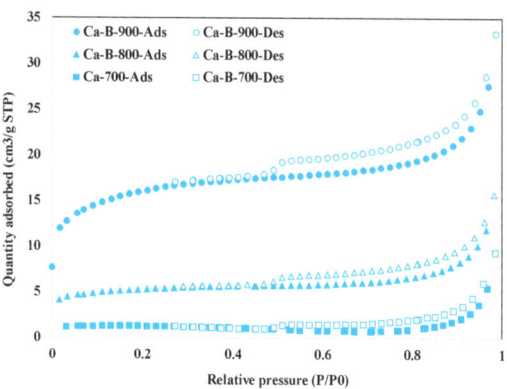

Figure 2. N$_2$ adsorption and desorption isotherms of the three synthesized Ca-rich biochars.

Finally, the pyrolysis temperature has an important effect on the surface chemistry of the synthesized biochars. Indeed, the FTIR spectra of these biochars (Figure 3) showed that they contain various functional groups such as hydroxyl, ketones, and carboxylic [26,40,45]. Furthermore, for all the synthesized biochars, Ca–O functional groups were observed at wavenumbers of 712, 875, and 2510 cm^{-1} [40,47]. This confirms the synthesized biochars richness in calcium that was observed in XRD (Figure 1) and XRF analyses (Table 2). Moreover, a narrow and strong peak of –OH groups was observed for Ca-B-800 and Ca-B-900 at 3643 cm^{-1} [31] (Figure 3) [48,49]. This observation confirms the XRD results, which indicated that Ca(OH)$_2$ nanoparticle formation was detected for only Ca-B-800 and Ca-B-900 [31] (see Figure 1). Such a peak was reported for Ca-rich biochars produced at 800 °C from the co-pyrolysis of bagasse waste mixed with marble powder [40] and also peanut shells mixed with oyster shells at 800 °C [43]. Finally, FTIR analyses showed the presence of P–O peaks at 566 and 1047 cm^{-1} [18], which confirms the high P contents (9.4–12.4 mg g^{-1}) observed with XRF analyses (see Table 2). The functional groups richness of the three synthesized biochars may favor the AMX adsorption through a complexation mechanism [50].

Moreover, the values of the pHzpc were evaluated to 10.89, 13.30, and 13.46 for Ca-B-700, Ca-B-800, and Ca-B-900 [31], respectively. The relatively high values observed at temperatures of 800 and 900 °C confirm the high transformation rates of WMP into CaO and Ca(OH)$_2$ that were pointed out by the XRD analyses. This indicates that the synthesized biochars surface will be positively charged for a large aqueous pH interval (lower than the corresponding pHzpc) and may retain negatively charged pollutants (i.e., AMX) through electrostatic interactions [50]. High alkaline pH values (11.9–12.0) were reported for Ca(OH)$_2$-modified biochars produced at temperatures varying between 100 and 500 °C [29].

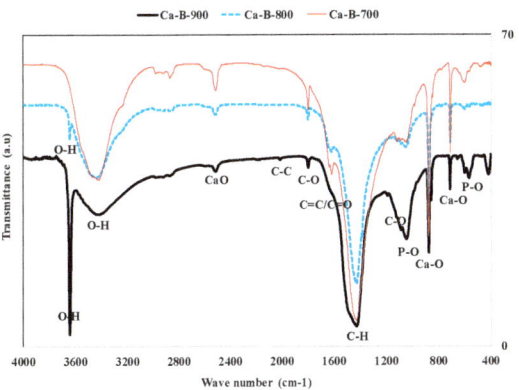

Figure 3. FTIR analyses of the three synthesized Ca-rich biochars.

3.2. Batch Adsorption Study

3.2.1. Impact of Contact Time—Kinetic Study

The AMX removal efficiency by the three synthesized Ca-rich biochars (Figure 4) shows that it is highly dependent on the contact time. Indeed, three kinetic phases can be distinguished. A first phase, where the kinetic rate is relatively rapid (until 8 h), followed by a slower one (until 20 h), then an equilibrium phase (between 20 and 24 h), where the AMX removed amounts remain quasi-constants. These three phases correspond to [34,51]: (i) diffusion through the boundary layer around the biochars particles, (ii) intraparticle diffusion where AMX is removed inside the mesoporous structure of the biochars, and (iii) the active sites of the biochars are saturated with AMX and no further adsorption is possible. For all biochars, the first phase seems to be the limiting step in the overall process because, for all the synthesized biochars, the corresponding diffusion coefficients (D_f) are lower than those of the intraparticle diffusion (D_{ip}) (Table 3). Similar findings were reported in previous studies related to pharmaceuticals removal by sludge-derived biochars [34,52]. The time required to reach the equilibrium state is evaluated to be around 20 h which is equivalent to those reported for sludge-derived biochars post-treated with Al, Fe, or Mn [53]. However, this time is higher than those reported for biochars generated from the pyrolysis of modified lignocellulosic biomasses such as a KOH-pretreated-cellulose fibers rejects (2 h) [54], a Zn-pretreated ginger waste (5 h) [46], and a Zn-pretreated corn cob (5–6 h) [51]. It is worth mentioning that the use of long contact times is not recommended in real applications due to the related high energetic expenses (i.e., pumping). In our case, a contact time of only 8 h can be suggested since it permits a relatively high removal percentage (Figure 4). Moreover, the PSO model fits better the experimental data for both Ca-B-800 and Ca-B-900 with rate constants of 2.2×10^{-4} and 4.6×10^{-4} g mg^{-1} min^{-1}, respectively (Table 3). Indeed, this model presents higher correlation coefficients and lower MAPE between the experimental and theoretical kinetic curves (Table 3). This suggests that the AMX removal process by these two biochars may involve chemical processes [53]. A similar finding was reported for AMX removal by biochars derived from sewage sludge [53] and from corn cobs [51]. The Ca-B-700 kinetic experimental data were better fitted with the PFO model, suggesting that the adsorption rate is mainly controlled by the diffusion process [55]. Additionally, the Ca-B-900 exhibits higher AMX removal efficiency in comparison with Ca-B-800 and Ca-B-700 (Figure 4). This is mainly attributed to its improved physico-chemical properties [29].

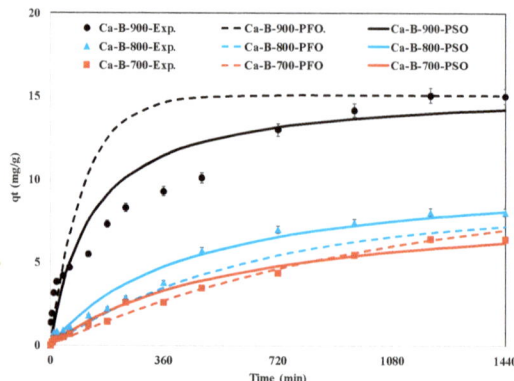

Figure 4. Experimental and predicted kinetic data of AMX removal by the synthesized calcium-rich biochars at 700, 800, and 900 °C.

Table 3. Parameters of the PFO and PSO kinetic models used for the AMX removal by Ca-rich biochars produced at 700, 800, and 900 °C.

	Parameter	Ca-B-700	Ca-B-800	Ca-B-900
PFO model	$q_{e,exp}$ (mg g^{-1})	6.4	8.0	15.1
	k_1 (min^{-1})	0.0009	0.0016	0.0096
	R^2	0.991	0.989	0.813
	MAPE (%)	18.0	26.7	43.1
PSO model	k_2 (g mg^{-1} min^{-1})	0.00019	0.00022	0.00046
	$q_{e,pred}$ (mg g^{-1})	8.8	10.5	15.9
	R^2	0.978	0.975	0.928
	MAPE (%)	21.7	20.5	28.9
Diffusion model	D_f ($\times 10^{-13}$ m^2 s^{-1})	0.39	0.52	1.45
	R^2	0.948	0.931	0.960
	D_{ip} ($\times 10^{-13}$ m^2 s^{-1})	1.56	1.87	1.57
	R^2	0.957	0.990	0.960

3.2.2. Impact of pH

The effect of pH on AMX removal by the three synthesized biochars was investigated for pH values varying between 4 and 10 while maintaining the contact time, the initial concentration, and the adsorbent dosage constants at 24 h, 100 mg L^{-1}, and 1 g L^{-1}, respectively. This wide pH interval was chosen because the electrical properties of both the adsorbent and the AMX are dependent on the aqueous pH values. Indeed, the AMX has three pKa values depending on its three possible ionizable forms [56]: carboxylic acid (pKa$_1$ = 2.7), primary amine group (pKa$_2$ = 7.5), and hydroxyl group (pKa$_3$ = 9.63). AMX is positively charged, zwitterionic (exists in two ionic forms AMX±), and negatively charged for pH values lower than pKa$_1$, between pKa$_1$ and pKa$_2$, and higher than pKa$_3$, respectively. Regarding our synthesized biochars, the Ca-B-700, Ca-B-800, and Ca-B-900 have pHzpc values of 10.89, 13.30, and 13.46 (see Table 2), indicating that for the studied pH range, their surface will be positively charged. Therefore, the adsorption of the negatively charged forms of AMX (observed for pH values higher than pKa1) will be well favored across the whole pH range studied through electrostatic interactions. In our case, for all the biochars, the AMX adsorbed amounts were almost constant for the tested pH range (Figure 5). The average AMX removed masses were quantified to 6.6, 8.4, and 15.3 mg g^{-1} for Ca-B-700,

Ca-B-800, and Ca-B-900, respectively. Relatively similar behavior was observed for AMX removal by a biochar derived from palm oil bunch waste [57].

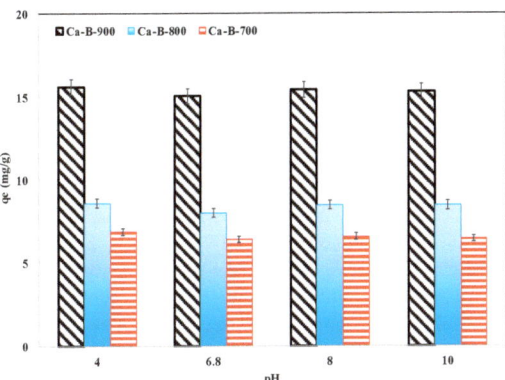

Figure 5. pH effect on AMX removal by Ca-B-700, Ca-B-800, and Ca-B-900.

3.2.3. Impact of Adsorbent Dose

The impact of the synthesized Ca-rich biochars in removing AMX from aqueous solutions was carried out for an initial concentration of 100 mg L^{-1}, a natural pH of 6.8 (without adjustment), and a contact time of 24 h. Results (Figure 6) show that for all biochars, the AMX removal yields increase with the increase of the adsorbent dose. Indeed, for a small dose of 0.1 g L^{-1}, the AMX removal yields were assessed to be only 3.7%, 6.4%, and 11.3% for Ca-B-700, Ca-B-800, and Ca-B-900, respectively. These yields gradually increase with the increase of the dose to reach quasi-constant performances, with the highest removal yields evaluated to be 68.6%, 86.7%, and 94.7% for Ca-B-700, Ca-B-800, and Ca-B-900, respectively. This behavior is due to the presence of more active adsorption sites for increased doses that can react with AMX molecules. In addition, as specified above, owing to its better physicochemical properties, the Ca-B-900 exhibits the highest AMX removal yield for the lowest required dose (10 g L^{-1}) to reach the performance plateau. For Ca-B-700, a much higher dose (30–40 g L^{-1}) is needed to reach this state (Figure 6). Similar trends were observed in numerous previous studies dealing with AMX removal by engineered biochars [34,46,54].

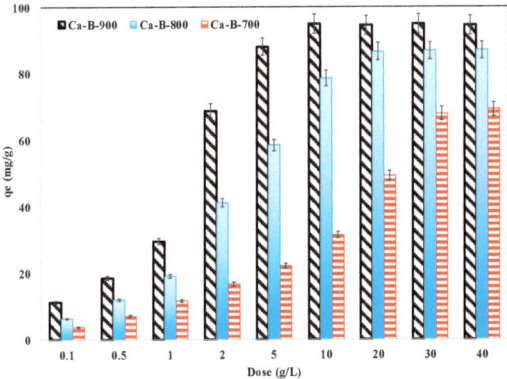

Figure 6. Effect of the tested biochars dose on AMX removal from aqueous solutions.

3.2.4. Impact of Ionic Strength

Since actual wastewater usually contains various ions at different contents, we studied the effect of the presence of dissolved NaCl and Na_2SO_4 on AMX removal for an initial AMX concentration of 100 mg L^{-1}, a non-adjusted pH, and a contact time of 24 h. Results (Figure 7a,b) show that adding Na_2SO_4 at concentrations varying between 1 and 5.2 mM significantly increased the AMX removed amounts (Figure 7a). The largest increase was observed for the highest Na_2SO_4 concentration of 5.2 mM and was evaluated to be 4.1%, 22.3%, and 11.1% for Ca-B-700, Ca-B-800, and Ca-B-900, respectively (Figure 7a). A similar trend was also observed when adding NaCl at concentrations in the range of 14–42 mM. The highest increase of AMX removed amount (30.8%) was observed for Ca-B-900 for a NaCl concentration of 42 mM (Figure 7b). This result indicates that the presence of Na$^+$ and Cl$^-$ has favored the adsorption of AMX by the synthesized Ca-rich biochars. This finding can be attributed to an improvement in the activity coefficient of AMX [58]. This leads to a decline of AMX solubility and, therefore, can favor its adsorption by the Ca-rich biochars. A comparable trend was reported by Varela et al. [51] when exploring AMX removal by a Zn-modified biochar. These authors reported that increasing NaCl contents from 0.0 to 0.1 M raised the AMX removed amount by 14.9%. Contrarily, other previous studies have shown that an important increase in the ionic strength may result in a non-negligible decrease in AMX removal capacity [59,60].

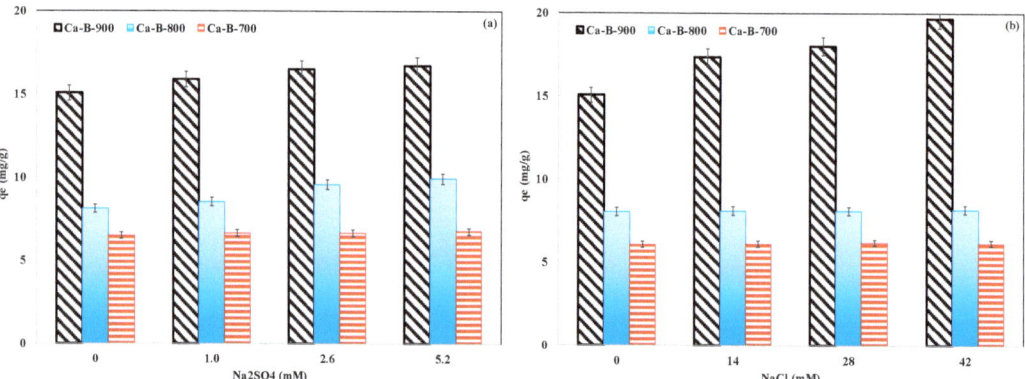

Figure 7. Effect of the presence of Na_2SO_4 (**a**) and NaCl (**b**) on AMX removal by the tested Ca-rich biochars.

3.2.5. Impact of Initial Concentration—Isotherm Study

The effect of the AMX initial concentration on its removal efficiency by the three synthesized biochars is given in Figure 8. It clearly shows that the AMX adsorbed amounts increase when the initial concentration is raised. The highest AMX removed amounts were observed for an initial concentration of 100 mg L^{-1} and were assessed to 8.9, 15.5, and 27.8 mg g^{-1} for Ca-B-700, Ca-B-800, and Ca-B-900, respectively (Figure 8). This is attributed to the fact that higher AMX initial concentrations result in larger concentration gradients between the aqueous and solid media and consequently greater diffusion fluxes in the biochars porosity and, thus, more chances for AMX to be removed [46]. The results of the experimental data fitting to Langmuir, Freundlich, and D-R results are displayed in Figure 8 and Table 4. For Ca-B-700 and Ca-B-800, the D-R and Langmuir models fit the best to the experimental data since the corresponding R^2 and MAPE are respectively higher and lower than those observed for the Freundlich model (Table 4). This suggests that the adsorption of AMX molecules occurs on a monolayer at the surface of these adsorbents with the presence of a finite number of energetically equivalent adsorption sites [49,53,54]. Regarding the Ca-B-900, the Freundlich model is the most suitable, with the highest R^2 (0.962) and the lowest MAPE (7.9%) (Table 4). This indicates that AMX adsorption onto this adsorbent occurs heterogeneously and on multilayers [61,62]. In addition, for the three biochars, the AMX adsorption is favorable since all the calculated Langmuir's constants $(R_L = \frac{1}{1+K_L*C_0})$ were lower than 1, and the Freundlich coefficient (n) is higher than 1 (Table 4). The Langmuir's adsorption capacities of AMX onto Ca-B-700, Ca-B-800, and Ca-B-900 were assessed to be 13.6, 46.8, and 56.2 mg g^{-1}. The increase of this parameter with the rising pyrolysis temperature is mainly ascribed to the enhancement of the textural properties of the biochars. For instance, the BET surface area of the Ca-B-900 was evaluated to be 14.1 and 3.1 times higher than those of Ca-B-700 and Ca-B-800 (see Table 2).

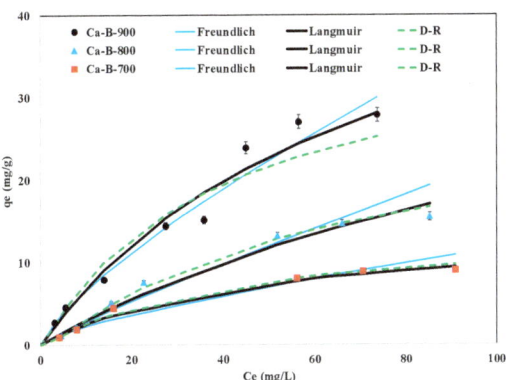

Figure 8. Isotherm experimental data of AMX removal by the synthesized Ca-rich biochars and their fitting with Freundlich, Langmuir, and D-R models.

Table 4. Calculated isotherms parameters for AMX removal by the synthesized Ca-rich biochars.

Isotherm	Parameter	Ca-B-700	Ca-B-800	Ca-B-900
Langmuir	K_L (L mg^{-1})	0.019	0.007	0.0136
	$q_{m,L,pred}$ (mg g^{-1})	14.6	46.8	56.2
	R^2	0.982	0.975	0.962
	MAPE (%)	9.8	12.1	11.4
Freundlich	n	1.38	1.10	1.31
	K_F	0.409	0.346	1.134
	R^2	0.941	0.947	0.962
	MAPE (%)	13.7	14.8	7.9
D-R	$q_{m,D-R,pred}$ (mg g^{-1})	13.6	26.3	37.1
	E (kJ mol^{-1})	4.75	4.24	4.96
	R^2	0.986	0.998	0.941
	MAPE (%)	6.0	4.3	13.8

It is important to underline that the adsorption capacity of Ca-B-900 is about 1.8 and 1.5 times larger than those given for biochars produced from the pyrolysis of Zn-modified sludge [34] and olive stone waste [63] (Table 5). It is comparable to the efficiency of a H$_3$PO$_4$-modified biochar from waste coffee grounds [61]. However, the Ca-B-900 efficiency is much lower than biochars derived from the pyrolysis of KOH-modified sludge: 204.0 mg g^{-1} [64], a KOH-pretreated sludge: 305.0 mg g^{-1} [65], and NaOH-pretreated guava seeds: 570.5 mg g^{-1} [66] (Table 5). These latter materials have more interesting physico-chemical properties than our Ca-rich biochars. For instance, the synthesized

NaOH-guava seeds-derived biochar has exceptionally high BET surface area and total pore volume of 2573.6 m^2 g^{-1} and 1.26 cm^3 g^{-1} [66].

Table 5. Comparison of AMX removal capacity of the Ca-rich biochars with other engineered biochars (T: pyrolysis temperature; G: heating gradient; t: residence time; RT: room temperature; -: not given).

Feedstock, Provenance	Pretreatment	Pyrolysis Conditions	Post-Treatment	Adsorption Experimental Conditions	Langmuir's Adsorption Capacity (mg g^{-1})	Reference
Vine wood, Iran	-	T = 600 °C; G = -; t = 2 h	Impregnation with NaOH at a mass ratio of 5%	C_0 = 20–200 mg L^{-1}; pH = 2; D = 0.4 g L^{-1}; t = 8 h; T = 25 °C	2.7	[67]
Industrial sludge, Oman			-		22.6	[34]
	Impregnation with 1 M ZnCl$_2$	T = 750 °C; G = 5 °C min^{-1}; t = 2 h	-	C_0 = 20–120 mg L^{-1}; pH = 6.8; D = 1 g L^{-1}; t = 3 h; T = RT	31.9	
	Impregnation with 1 M FeCl$_3$				32.1	
Olive stone, Tunisia	Impregnation with phosphoric acid (50%, by weight) at 110 °C for 9 h	T = 170 °C; G = -; t = 0.5 h, then T = 380 °C; G = -; t = 2.5 h	-	C_0 = 12.5–100 mg L^{-1}; pH = not adjusted; D = 1 g L^{-1}; t = 10 h; T = 20 °C	38.7	[63]
Coffee grounds, South Korea	Impregnation with phosphoric acid at 110 °C for 36 h	T = 600 °C; G = -; t = 2 h	-	C_0 = 0–200 mg L^{-1}; pH = not adjusted; D = 1 g L^{-1}; t = 24 h; T = RT	54.6	[61]
Paper mill sludge, Portugal	Impregnation with KOH at a ratio (KOH/sludge) of 1:5 (w/w), then sonication for 1 h in an ultrasonic batch	T = 800 °C; G = 15 °C min^{-1}; t = 20 min	-	C_0 = 0–5 mg/L; pH = not adjusted; D = 15 mg L^{-1}; t = 15 h; T = 25 °C	204.0	[64]
Pulp and paper mill sludge, Sweeden	Impregnation with KOH at a mass ratio of 1:1	T = 800 °C; G = 10 °C min^{-1}; t = 3 h	-	C_0 = 0–1000 mg L^{-1}; pH = 6; D = 1.5 g L^{-1}; t = 4 h; T = 25 °C	305.0	[65]
Guava seeds, Brazil	-	T= 500 °C; G = 20 °C min^{-1}; t = 2 h	Impregnation with NaOH at a mass ratio of 3:1 (NaOH/biomass), then pyrolysis for: T= 750 °C; G = - °C min^{-1}; t = 1.5 h	C_0 = 50–800 mg L^{-1}; pH = 4; D = 1 g L^{-1}; t = 4 h; T = 25 °C	570.5	[66]
Mixture of poultry manure and date palm waste, Oman	Mixing with waste marble powder	T = 700 °C; G = 5 °C min^{-1}; t = 2 h	-	C_0 = 5–100 mg L^{-1}; pH = 6.8; D = 1 g L^{-1}; t = 20 h; T = RT	14.6	This study
		T = 800 °C; Idem.			46.8	
		T = 900 °C; Idem.			56.2	

Additionally, for all tested biochars, the calculated free energy (E) by the D-R model is lower than 8 kJ mol^{-1} (Table 4), suggesting that AMX adsorption would also involve physical processes [66]. This result is in agreement with that presented by Meghani et al. [46] and Varela et al. [51] regarding AMX removal by biochars derived from ginger waste and corn cobs, respectively.

The main mechanisms involved in AMX removal by the Ca-rich biochars were explored by combining the experimental results (pH effect), the numerical studies (both kinetic and isotherm), and previously published data. Indeed, on the basis of the pH effect and the kinetic and isotherm studies, it seems that the AMX adsorption by the synthesized biochars involves both physical and chemical processes. The physical mechanisms may include low-energy interactions such as pore filling, Van Der Waals, and hydrogen bonds [36]. The chemical processes may encompass electrostatic interactions between the positively charged biochars' particles and the negative forms of AMX (above the pKa_1 of 2.7). Moreover, according to FTIR spectra of the biochars before and after AMX adsorption, only the hydroxyl groups might be involved in the adsorption process. Indeed, for all biochars, the –OH, the narrow peak observed at 3643 cm^{-1} (see Figure 3), has completely disappeared for the three biochars. Moreover, the second O-H peak observed before the adsorption at 3427 cm^{-1} was shifted by +6, +5, and +20 cm^{-1} for Ca-B-700, Ca-B-800, and Ca-B-900, respectively. Besides that, AMX adsorption could also involve π-π interactions between π electrons existing in the aromatic rings of the biochars, the conjugated aromatic rings of AMX [68].

3.3. Challenges and Opportunities

This study shows that Ca-rich biochar may be considered an interesting material for AMX removal from aqueous solutions under static conditions. The precise assessment of AMX and other pharmaceuticals removal for wider experimental conditions under dynamic mode (columns and reactors) is crucial for future work. These dynamic assays have the main advantages of using large-scale plants where the pollutant can be continuously injected through the adsorbent bed in column mode, and either the adsorbate or the adsorbent can be continuously fed to the CSTR system. Such a study should be compared with the related rare previous works [29,31]. Moreover, the management of the pharmaceutical-loaded biochars is another challenge to be ascertained. Nowadays, various chemical reagents have been tested for the effective regeneration of AMX-loaded biochars. They showed that the regenerated biochars could be used for several cycles without a significant decrease in their adsorption capacities [10,69]. The desorbed and concentrated solutions with AMX can be treated by using advanced oxidation processes [70]. Therefore, the optimization of the desorption process and the treatment of the desorbed solution by adapted technologies (i.e., advanced oxidation processes) have to be intensively investigated in the future. Besides these technical challenges, the economic side has to be seriously considered. In this context, the energy consumption during the pyrolysis process should be absolutely reduced. Moreover, important work has to be undertaken regarding the social perception constraints of biochar production and use. Finally, policy challenges concerning solid waste conversion into biochars and their use for wastewater treatment have to be accounted for [71]. In this regard, the implementation of biochar use specific incentives for concerned end users' encouragement could significantly contribute to its widespread application.

Nevertheless, biochar production and use is currently gaining high worldwide attention [15]. According to the latest report of the International Biochar Initiative (IBI), more than 350,000 metric tons of biochar were produced in 2023, and a 91% compound annual growth (CAGR) was estimated for 2021 [72]. Moreover, it is projected that by 2025, biochar revenues will grow further to around USD 3.3 billion [72]. Biochar is usually presented as an interesting alternative to activated carbons (for wastewater treatment) and synthetic fertilizers (for agricultural soil amendment). In our case, the Ca-rich biochars production and use for pharmaceuticals removal and nutrient recovery present remarkable advantages, including (i) better management of huge amounts of poultry manure and date palm waste, as well as industrial marble waste, (ii) preservation of surface water against pollution and eutrophication due to the presence of high contents of nutrients and also pharmaceuticals, (iii) greenhouse gases emission reduction, and (iv) promotion of sustainability and circular economy concepts that is highly recommended by international initiatives such as the United Nations Sustainable Development Goals and also specific future national visions in several countries.

4. Conclusions

This paper demonstrates that Ca-rich biochars generated from the co-pyrolysis of poultry manure, date palm fronds, and waste marble powder can be considered promising materials for amoxicillin removal under wide experimental conditions in batch mode. High AMX removal ability can be obtained through the increase of the pyrolysis temperature, which significantly improves the biochars' structural, textural, and surface chemical properties. The highest AMX removal capacity was observed for Ca-B-900 (56.2 mg g^{-1}), which is relatively high in comparison with some other engineered biochars. The experimental and modeling study shows that the AMX removal process may involve both physical and chemical mechanisms, such as pore filling, π-π interactions, Van Der Waals and hydrogen bonds, electrostatic interactions, and complexation with hydroxyl groups. Further dynamic investigations using laboratory columns and/or reactors are needed in order to confirm these results. Moreover, the management of the AMX-loaded biochars should be explored in the future.

Supplementary Materials: The following supporting information can be downloaded at: https://www.mdpi.com/article/10.3390/pr12081552/s1, Figure S1: SEM/EDS analyses of Ca-B-700 (a), Ca-B-800 (b), and Ca-B-900 (c); Table S1: Kinetic and isotherm model equations used for the fitting of experimental data.

Author Contributions: Conceptualization, S.J., M.A.-H., J.A.-S. and M.J.; methodology, S.J., M.A.-H., J.A.-S., A.A.-R. and M.J.; software, S.J. and W.H.; validation, S.J., W.H. and M.J.; formal analysis, S.J. and W.H.; investigation, M.A.-H., H.A.-N. and A.A.-R.; resources, S.J. and M.A.-W.; data curation, S.J. and W.H.; writing—original draft preparation, S.J. and W.H.; writing—review and editing, W.H., M.A.-W., J.A.-S. and M.J.; visualization, S.J., M.A.-W., H.A.-N. and A.A.-R.; supervision, S.J. and J.A.-S.; project administration, S.J.; funding acquisition, S.J. All authors have read and agreed to the published version of the manuscript.

Funding: This research was funded by Sultan Qaboos University, grant number CL/SQU/QU/CESR/23/01.

Data Availability Statement: Data may be available on request.

Acknowledgments: The authors would like to thank Ibrahim Al-Khusaibi from CAARU for his valuable help on XRD analyses.

Conflicts of Interest: The authors declare no conflicts of interest.

References

1. Yu, Y.; Wang, S.; Yu, P.; Wang, D.; Hu, B.; Zheng, P.; Zhang, M. A bibliometric analysis of emerging contaminants (ECs) (2001–2021): Evolution of hotspots and research trends. *Sci. Total Environ.* **2024**, *907*, 168116. [CrossRef] [PubMed]
2. Omeka, M.E.; Ezugwu, A.L.; Agbasi, J.C.; Egbueri, J.C.; Abugu, H.O.; Aralu, C.C.; Ucheana, I.A. A review of the status, challenges, trends, and prospects of groundwater quality assessment in Nigeria: An evidence-based meta-analysis approach. *Environ. Sci. Pollut. Res.* **2024**, *31*, 22284–22307. [CrossRef] [PubMed]
3. Wang, F.; Xiang, L.; Sze-Yin Leung, K.; Elsner, M.; Zhang, Y.; Guo, Y.; Pan, B.; Sun, H.; An, T.; Ying, G.; et al. Emerging contaminants: A One Health perspective. *Innovation* **2024**, *5*, 100612. [CrossRef] [PubMed]
4. Sumpter, J.P.; Johnson, A.C.; Runnalls, T.J. Pharmaceuticals in the Aquatic Environment: No Answers Yet to the Major Questions. *Environ. Toxicol. Chem.* **2024**, *43*, 589–594. [CrossRef]
5. Rathi, B.S.; Kumar, P.S.; Show, P.L. A review on effective removal of emerging contaminants from aquatic systems: Current trends and scope for further research. *J. Hazard. Mater.* **2021**, *409*, 124413. [CrossRef] [PubMed]
6. Litskas, V.D.; Karamanlis, X.N.; Prousali, S.P.; Koveos, D.S. Effects of the Antibiotic Amoxicillin on Key Species of the Terrestrial Environment. *Bull. Environ. Contam. Toxicol.* **2018**, *100*, 509–515. [CrossRef] [PubMed]
7. Kovalakova, P.; Cizmas, L.; McDonald, T.J.; Marsalek, B.; Feng, M.; Sharma, V.K. Occurrence and toxicity of antibiotics in the aquatic environment: A review. *Chemosphere* **2020**, *251*, 126351. [CrossRef]
8. Nasir, A.; Saleh, M.; Aminzai, M.T.; Alary, R.; Dizge, N.; Yabalak, E. Adverse effects of veterinary drugs, removal processes and mechanisms: A review. *J. Environ. Chem. Eng.* **2024**, *12*, 111680. [CrossRef]
9. Akintola, A.T.; Ayankunle, A.Y. Improving Pharmaceuticals Removal at Wastewater Treatment Plants Using Biochar: A Review. *Waste Biomass Valorization* **2023**, *14*, 2433–2458. [CrossRef]
10. Hama Aziz, K.H.; Mustafa, F.S.; Hassan, M.A.; Omer, K.M.; Hama, S. Biochar as green adsorbents for pharmaceutical pollution in aquatic environments: A review. *Desalination* **2024**, *583*, 117725. [CrossRef]

11. Homem, V.; Alves, A.; Santos, L. Amoxicillin removal from aqueous matrices by sorption with almond shell ashes. *Int. J. Environ. Anal. Chem.* **2010**, *90*, 1063–1084. [CrossRef]
12. Mansour, F.; Al-Hindi, M.; Yahfoufi, R.; Ayoub, G.M.; Ahmad, M.N. The use of activated carbon for the removal of pharmaceuticals from aqueous solutions: A review. *Rev. Environ. Sci. Biotechnol.* **2018**, *17*, 109–145. [CrossRef]
13. Du, C.; Zhang, Z.; Yu, G.; Wu, H.; Chen, H.; Zhou, L.; Zhang, Y.; Su, Y.; Tan, S.; Yang, L.; et al. A review of metal organic framework (MOFs)-based materials for antibiotics removal via adsorption and photocatalysis. *Chemosphere* **2021**, *272*, 129501. [CrossRef]
14. Yu, S.; Zhang, W.; Dong, X.; Wang, F.; Yang, W.; Liu, C.; Chen, D. A review on recent advances of biochar from agricultural and forestry wastes: Preparation, modification and applications in wastewater treatment. *J. Environ. Chem. Eng.* **2024**, *12*, 111638. [CrossRef]
15. Prochnow, F.D.; Cavali, M.; Dresch, A.P.; Belli, I.M.; Libardi, N.J.; de Castilhos, A.B.J. Biochar: From Laboratory to Industry Scale-An Overview Brazilian Context, and Contributions to Sustainable Development. *Processes* **2024**, *12*, 1006. [CrossRef]
16. Samaraweera, H.; Palansooriya, K.N.; Dissanayaka, P.D.; Khan, A.H.; Sillanpää, M.; Mlsna, T. Sustainable phosphate removal using Mg/Ca-modified biochar hybrids: Current trends and future outlooks. *Case Stud. Chem. Environ. Eng.* **2023**, *8*, 100528. [CrossRef]
17. Jellali, S.; Hadroug, S.; Al-Wardy, M.; Al-Nadabi, H.; Nassr, N.; Jeguirim, M. Recent developments in metallic-nanoparticles-loaded biochars synthesis and use for phosphorus recovery from aqueous solutions. A critical review. *J. Environ. Manag.* **2023**, *342*, 118307. [CrossRef] [PubMed]
18. Jellali, S.; Khiari, B.; Al-balushi, M.; Al-sabahi, J.; Hamdi, H.; Bengharez, Z.; Al-abri, M.; Al-nadabi, H.; Jeguirim, M. Use of waste marble powder for the synthesis of novel calcium-rich biochar: Characterization and application for phosphorus recovery in continuous stirring tank reactors. *J. Environ. Manag.* **2024**, *351*, 119926. [CrossRef]
19. Xu, C.; Liu, R.; Chen, L. Removal of Phosphorus from Domestic Sewage in Rural Areas Using Oyster Shell-Modified Agricultural Waste–Rice Husk Biochar. *Processes* **2023**, *11*, 2577. [CrossRef]
20. Xu, Z.C.; Zhang, B.; Wang, T.; Liu, J.; Mei, M.; Chen, S.; Li, J. Environmentally friendly crab shell waste preparation of magnetic biochar for selective phosphate adsorption: Mechanisms and characterization. *J. Mol. Liq.* **2023**, *385*, 122436. [CrossRef]
21. Li, S.; Wang, N.; Chen, S.; Sun, Y.; Li, P.; Tan, J.; Jiang, X. Enhanced soil P immobilization and microbial biomass P by application of biochar modified with eggshell. *J. Environ. Manag.* **2023**, *345*, 118568. [CrossRef] [PubMed]
22. Li, J.; Li, B.; Huang, H.; Lv, X.; Zhao, N.; Guo, G.; Zhang, D. Removal of phosphate from aqueous solution by dolomite-modified biochar derived from urban dewatered sewage sludge. *Sci. Total Environ.* **2019**, *687*, 460–469. [CrossRef] [PubMed]
23. Wang, K.; Peng, N.; Zhang, D.; Zhou, H.; Gu, J.; Huang, J.; Liu, C.; Chen, Y.; Liu, Y.; Sun, J. Efficient removal of methylene blue using Ca(OH)$_2$ modified biochar derived from rice straw. *Environ. Technol. Innov.* **2023**, *31*, 103145. [CrossRef]
24. Wang, L.; Wang, J.; Wei, Y. Facile synthesis of eggshell biochar beads for superior aqueous phosphate adsorption with potential urine P-recovery. *Colloids Surfaces A Physicochem. Eng. Asp.* **2021**, *622*, 126589. [CrossRef]
25. Liao, Y.; Chen, S.; Zheng, Q.; Huang, B.; Zhang, J.; Fu, H.; Gao, H. Removal and recovery of phosphorus from solution by bifunctional biochar. *Inorg. Chem. Commun.* **2022**, *139*, 109341. [CrossRef]
26. Cao, L.; Ouyang, Z.; Chen, T.; Huang, H.; Zhang, M.; Tai, Z.; Long, K.; Sun, C.; Wang, B. Phosphate removal from aqueous solution using calcium-rich biochar prepared by the pyrolysis of crab shells. *Environ. Sci. Pollut. Res.* **2022**, *29*, 89570–89584. [CrossRef] [PubMed]
27. Yang, F.; Chen, Y.; Nan, H.; Pei, L.; Huang, Y.; Cao, X.; Xu, X.; Zhao, L. Metal chloride-loaded biochar for phosphorus recovery: Noteworthy roles of inherent minerals in precursor. *Chemosphere* **2021**, *266*, 128991. [CrossRef] [PubMed]
28. Santos, A.F.; Lopes, D.V.; Alvarenga, P.; Gando-Ferreira, L.M.; Quina, M.J. Phosphorus removal from urban wastewater through adsorption using biogenic calcium carbonate. *J. Environ. Manag.* **2024**, *351*, 119875. [CrossRef] [PubMed]
29. Zeng, S.; Kan, E. Sustainable use of Ca(OH)$_2$ modified biochar for phosphorus recovery and tetracycline removal from water. *Sci. Total Environ.* **2022**, *839*, 156159. [CrossRef]
30. Jin, X.; Guo, J.; Hossain, M.F.; Lu, J.; Lu, Q.; Zhou, Y.; Zhou, Y. Recent advances in the removal and recovery of phosphorus from aqueous solution by metal-based adsorbents: A review. *Resour. Conserv. Recycl.* **2024**, *204*, 107464. [CrossRef]
31. Jellali, S.; Khiari, B.; Al-balushi, M.; Al-harrasi, M.; Al-sabahi, J. Novel calcium-rich biochar synthesis and application for phosphorus and amoxicillin removal from synthetic and urban wastewater: Batch, columns, and continuous stirring tank reactors investigations. *J. Water Process Eng.* **2024**, *58*, 104818. [CrossRef]
32. Shin, J.; Kwak, J.; Son, C.; Kim, S.; Lee, Y.-G.; Kim, H.-J.; Rho, H.; Lee, S.-H.; Park, Y.; Hwa Cho, K.; et al. Oyster shell-doped ground coffee waste biochars for selective removal of phosphate and nitrate ions from aqueous phases via enhanced electrostatic surface complexations: A mechanism study. *J. Environ. Chem. Eng.* **2024**, *12*, 112154. [CrossRef]
33. Jellali, S.; Azzaz, A.A.; Jeguirim, M.; Hamdi, H.; Mlayah, A. Use of lignite as a low-cost material for cadmium and copper removal from aqueous solutions: Assessment of adsorption characteristics and exploration of involved mechanisms. *Water* **2021**, *13*, 164. [CrossRef]
34. Jellali, S.; Khiari, B.; Al-Harrasi, M.; Charabi, Y.; Al-Sabahi, J.; Al-Abri, M.; Usman, M.; Al-Raeesi, A.; Jeguirim, M. Industrial sludge conversion into biochar and reuse in the context of circular economy: Impact of pre-modification processes on pharmaceuticals removal from aqueous solutions. *Sustain. Chem. Pharm.* **2023**, *33*, 101114. [CrossRef]

35. Altıkat, A.; Alma, M.H.; Altıkat, A.; Bilgili, M.E.; Altıkat, S. A Comprehensive Study of Biochar Yield and Quality Concerning Pyrolysis Conditions: A Multifaceted Approach. *Sustainability* **2024**, *16*, 937. [CrossRef]
36. Jellali, S.; Khiari, B.; Usman, M.; Hamdi, H.; Charabi, Y.; Jeguirim, M. Sludge-derived biochars: A review on the influence of synthesis conditions on pollutants removal efficiency from wastewaters. *Renew. Sustain. Energy Rev.* **2021**, *144*, 111068. [CrossRef]
37. Tomczyk, A.; Sokołowska, Z.; Boguta, P. Biochar physicochemical properties: Pyrolysis temperature and feedstock kind effects. *Rev. Environ. Sci. Biotechnol.* **2020**, *19*, 191–215. [CrossRef]
38. Sutcu, M.; Alptekin, H.; Erdogmus, E.; Er, Y.; Gencel, O. Characteristics of fired clay bricks with waste marble powder addition as building materials. *Constr. Build. Mater.* **2015**, *82*, 1–8. [CrossRef]
39. Kwon, E.E.; Lee, T.; Ok, Y.S.; Tsang, D.C.W.; Park, C.; Lee, J. Effects of calcium carbonate on pyrolysis of sewage sludge. *Energy* **2018**, *153*, 726–731. [CrossRef]
40. Deng, W.; Zhang, D.; Zheng, X.; Ye, X.; Niu, X.; Lin, Z.; Fu, M.; Zhou, S. Adsorption recovery of phosphate from waste streams by Ca/Mg-biochar synthesis from marble waste, calcium-rich sepiolite and bagasse. *J. Clean. Prod.* **2021**, *288*, 125638. [CrossRef]
41. Liu, Y.; Wang, S.; Huo, J.; Zhang, X.; Wen, H.T.; Zhang, D.; Zhao, Y.; Kang, D.; Guo, W.; Ngo, H.H. Adsorption recovery of phosphorus in contaminated water by calcium modified biochar derived from spent coffee grounds. *Sci. Total Environ.* **2024**, *909*, 168426. [CrossRef] [PubMed]
42. Liu, X.; Lv, J. Efficient Phosphate Removal from Wastewater by Ca-Laden Biochar Composites Prepared from Eggshell and Peanut Shells: A Comparison of Methods. *Sustainability* **2023**, *15*, 1778. [CrossRef]
43. Xu, Y.; Liao, H.; Zhang, J.; Lu, H.; He, X.; Zhang, Y.; Wu, Z.; Wang, H.; Lu, M. A Novel Ca-Modified Biochar for Efficient Recovery of Phosphorus from Aqueous Solution and Its Application as a Phosphorus Biofertilizer. *Nanomaterials* **2022**, *12*, 2755. [CrossRef] [PubMed]
44. Qin, J.; Zhang, C.; Chen, Z.; Wang, X.; Zhang, Y.; Guo, L. Converting wastes to resource: Utilization of dewatered municipal sludge for calcium-based biochar adsorbent preparation and land application as a fertilizer. *Chemosphere* **2022**, *298*, 134302. [CrossRef] [PubMed]
45. Choi, Y.K.; Jang, H.M.; Kan, E.; Wallace, A.R.; Sun, W. Adsorption of phosphate in water on a novel calcium hydroxide-coated dairy manure-derived biochar. *Environ. Eng. Res.* **2019**, *24*, 434–442. [CrossRef]
46. Meghani, R.; Lahane, V.; Kotian, S.Y.; Lata, S.; Tripathi, S.; Ansari, K.M.; Yadav, A.K. Valorization of Ginger Waste-Derived Biochar for Simultaneous Multiclass Antibiotics Remediation in Aqueous Medium. *ACS Omega* **2023**, *8*, 11065–11075. [CrossRef] [PubMed]
47. Hadroug, S.; Jellali, S.; Jeguirim, M.; Kwapinska, M.; Hamdi, H.; Leahy, J.J.; Kwapinski, W. Static and dynamic investigations on leaching/retention of nutrients from raw poultry manure biochars and amended agricultural soil. *Sustainability* **2021**, *13*, 1212. [CrossRef]
48. Mitrogiannis, D.; Psychoyou, M.; Baziotis, I.; Inglezakis, V.J.; Koukouzas, N.; Tsoukalas, N.; Palles, D.; Kamitsos, E.; Oikonomou, G.; Markou, G. Removal of phosphate from aqueous solutions by adsorption onto $Ca(OH)_2$ treated natural clinoptilolite. *Chem. Eng. J.* **2017**, *320*, 510–522. [CrossRef]
49. Shan, G.N.M.; Rafatullah, M.; Siddiqui, M.R.; Kapoor, R.T.; Qutob, M. Calcium oxide from eggshell wastes for the removal of pharmaceutical emerging contaminant: Synthesis and adsorption studies. *J. Indian Chem. Soc.* **2024**, *101*, 101174. [CrossRef]
50. Jellali, S.; Azzaz, A.A.; Al-Harrasi, M.; Charabi, Y.; Al-Sabahi, J.N.; Al-Raeesi, A.; Usman, M.; Al Nasiri, N.; Al-Abri, M.; Jeguirim, M. Conversion of Industrial Sludge into Activated Biochar for Effective Cationic Dye Removal: Characterization and Adsorption Properties Assessment. *Water* **2022**, *14*, 2206. [CrossRef]
51. Varela, C.F.; Moreno-Aldana, L.C.; Agámez-Pertuz, Y.Y. Adsorption of pharmaceutical pollutants on $ZnCl_2$-activated biochar from corn cob: Efficiency, selectivity and mechanism. *J. Bioresour. Bioprod.* **2024**, *9*, 58–73. [CrossRef]
52. Ma, Y.; Li, P.; Yang, L.; Wu, L.; He, L.; Gao, F.; Qi, X.; Zhang, Z. Iron/zinc and phosphoric acid modified sludge biochar as an efficient adsorbent for fluoroquinolones antibiotics removal. *Ecotoxicol. Environ. Saf.* **2020**, *196*, 110550. [CrossRef] [PubMed]
53. Fan, X.; Qian, Z.; Liu, J.; Geng, N.; Hou, J.; Li, D. Investigation on the adsorption of antibiotics from water by metal loaded sewage sludge biochar. *Water Sci. Technol.* **2021**, *83*, 739–750. [CrossRef] [PubMed]
54. Grimm, A.; Chen, F.; Simões dos Reis, G.; Dinh, V.M.; Khokarale, S.G.; Finell, M.; Mikkola, J.P.; Hultberg, M.; Dotto, G.L.; Xiong, S. Cellulose Fiber Rejects as Raw Material for Integrated Production of *Pleurotus* spp. Mushrooms and Activated Biochar for Removal of Emerging Pollutants from Aqueous Media. *ACS Omega* **2023**, *8*, 5361–5376. [CrossRef] [PubMed]
55. Wang, T.; Jiang, M.; Yu, X.; Niu, N.; Chen, L. Application of lignin adsorbent in wastewater Treatment: A review. *Sep. Purif. Technol.* **2022**, *302*, 122116. [CrossRef]
56. Chakhtouna, H.; Benzeid, H.; Zari, N.; el kacem Qaiss, A.; Bouhfid, R. Functional $CoFe_2O_4$-modified biochar derived from banana pseudostem as an efficient adsorbent for the removal of amoxicillin from water. *Sep. Purif. Technol.* **2021**, *266*, 118592. [CrossRef]
57. Allwar, A.; Herawati, M.; Wardana, F.S.; Khoirunnisa, A.; Anugrah, Z.M. Composite of Ag_2O-CuO/biochar as an adsorbent for removal of amoxicillin and paracetamol from aqueous solution. *Int. J. Environ. Sci. Technol.* **2023**, *20*, 13411–13422. [CrossRef]
58. Zhang, Y.; Zhu, C.; Liu, F.; Yuan, Y.; Wu, H.; Li, A. Effects of ionic strength on removal of toxic pollutants from aqueous media with multifarious adsorbents: A review. *Sci. Total Environ.* **2019**, *646*, 265–279. [CrossRef]
59. Yunusa, U.; Umar, U.; Idris, S.A.; Kubo, A.I.; Abdullahi, T. Experimental and DFT computational insights on the adsorption of selected pharmaceuticals of emerging concern from water systems onto magnetically modified biochar. *J. Turkish Chem. Soc. Sect. A Chem.* **2021**, *8*, 1179–1196. [CrossRef]

60. Wu, Q.; Zhang, Y.; Cui, M.-h.; Liu, H.; Liu, H.; Zheng, Z.; Zheng, W.; Zhang, C.; Wen, D. Pyrolyzing pharmaceutical sludge to biochar as an efficient adsorbent for deep removal of fluoroquinolone antibiotics from pharmaceutical wastewater: Performance and mechanism. *J. Hazard. Mater.* **2022**, *426*, 127798. [CrossRef]
61. Choi, S.W.; Hong, J.; Youn, S.; Kim, I. Removal of amoxicillin by coffee grounds biochar with different pretreatment methods. *Environ. Adv.* **2023**, *14*, 100446. [CrossRef]
62. Herrera, K.; Morales, L.F.; López, J.E.; Montoya-Ruiz, C.; Muñoz, S.; Zapata, D.; Saldarriaga, J.F. Biochar production from tannery waste pyrolysis as a circular economy strategy for the removal of emerging compounds in polluted waters. *Biomass Convers. Biorefinery* **2023**. [CrossRef]
63. Limousy, L.; Ghouma, I.; Ouederni, A.; Jeguirim, M. Amoxicillin removal from aqueous solution using activated carbon prepared by chemical activation of olive stone. *Environ. Sci. Pollut. Res.* **2017**, *24*, 9993–10004. [CrossRef] [PubMed]
64. Sousa, É.; Rocha, L.; Jaria, G.; Gil, M.V.; Otero, M.; Esteves, V.I.; Calisto, V. Optimizing microwave-assisted production of waste-based activated carbons for the removal of antibiotics from water. *Sci. Total Environ.* **2021**, *752*, 141662. [CrossRef] [PubMed]
65. Simões Dos Reis, G.; Bergna, D.; Tuomikoski, S.; Grimm, A.; Lima, E.C.; Thyrel, M.; Skoglund, N.; Lassi, U.; Larsson, S.H. Preparation and Characterization of Pulp and Paper Mill Sludge-Activated Biochars Using Alkaline Activation: A Box-Behnken Design Approach. *ACS Omega* **2022**, *7*, 32620–32630. [CrossRef] [PubMed]
66. Pezoti, O.; Cazetta, A.L.; Bedin, K.C.; Souza, L.S.; Martins, A.C.; Silva, T.L.; Santos Júnior, O.O.; Visentainer, J.V.; Almeida, V.C. NaOH-activated carbon of high surface area produced from guava seeds as a high-efficiency adsorbent for amoxicillin removal: Kinetic, isotherm and thermodynamic studies. *Chem. Eng. J.* **2016**, *288*, 778–788. [CrossRef]
67. Pouretedal, H.R.; Sadegh, N. Effective removal of Amoxicillin, Cephalexin, Tetracycline and Penicillin G from aqueous solutions using activated carbon nanoparticles prepared from vine wood. *J. Water Process Eng.* **2014**, *1*, 64–73. [CrossRef]
68. Tan, X.; Liu, Y.; Zeng, G.; Wang, X.; Hu, X.; Gu, Y.; Yang, Z. Application of biochar for the removal of pollutants from aqueous solutions. *Chemosphere* **2015**, *125*, 70–85. [CrossRef] [PubMed]
69. Krasucka, P.; Pan, B.; Sik Ok, Y.; Mohan, D.; Sarkar, B.; Oleszczuk, P. Engineered biochar—A sustainable solution for the removal of antibiotics from water. *Chem. Eng. J.* **2021**, *405*, 126926. [CrossRef]
70. Azzaz, A.A.; Jellali, S.; Akrout, H.; Assadi, A.A.; Bousselmi, L. Dynamic investigations on cationic dye desorption from chemically modified lignocellulosic material using a low-cost eluent: Dye recovery and anodic oxidation efficiencies of the desorbed solutions. *J. Clean. Prod.* **2018**, *201*, 28–38. [CrossRef]
71. Pathy, A.; Ray, J.; Paramasivan, B. Challenges and opportunities of nutrient recovery from human urine using biochar for fertilizer applications. *J. Clean. Prod.* **2021**, *304*, 127019. [CrossRef]
72. Gray, M.; Smith, L.B.; Maxwell-Barton, W.L. *Global Biochar Market Report*. 2023, pp. 1–30. Available online: https://biochar-international.org/2023-global-biochar-market-report/ (accessed on 2 July 2024).

Disclaimer/Publisher's Note: The statements, opinions and data contained in all publications are solely those of the individual author(s) and contributor(s) and not of MDPI and/or the editor(s). MDPI and/or the editor(s) disclaim responsibility for any injury to people or property resulting from any ideas, methods, instructions or products referred to in the content.

Article

Recycling PVC Waste into CO$_2$ Adsorbents: Optimizing Pyrolysis Valorization with Neuro-Fuzzy Models

Emilia A. Jiménez-García, Salvador Pérez-Huertas *, Antonio Pérez *, Mónica Calero and Gabriel Blázquez

Department of Chemical Engineering, Faculty of Science, University of Granada, 18071 Granada, Spain; ejimenezg@correo.ugr.es (E.A.J.-G.); mcaleroh@ugr.es (M.C.); gblazque@ugr.es (G.B.)
* Correspondence: shuertas@ugr.es (S.P.-H.); aperezm@ugr.es (A.P.)

Abstract: Nowadays, the environmental challenges associated with plastics are becoming increasingly prominent, making the exploitation of alternatives to landfill disposal a pressing concern. Particularly, polyvinyl chloride (PVC), characterized by its high chlorine content, poses a major environmental risk during degradation. Furthermore, PVC recycling and recovery present considerable challenges. This study aims to optimize the PVC pyrolysis valorization process to produce effective adsorbents for removing contaminants from gaseous effluents, especially CO$_2$. For this purpose, PVC waste was pyrolyzed under varied conditions, and the resulting solid fraction was subjected to a series of chemical and physical activations by means of hydroxides (NaOH and KOH) and nitrogen. Characterization of the PVC-based activated carbons was carried out using surface morphology (SEM), N$_2$ adsorption/desorption, elemental analysis, and FTIR, and their capacity to capture CO$_2$ was assessed. Finally, neuro-fuzzy models were developed for the optimization of the valorization technique. The resulting activated carbons exhibited excellent CO$_2$ adsorption capabilities, particularly those activated with KOH. Optimal activation conditions include activations at 840 °C with NaOH at a ratio of 0.66 and at 760 °C using either NaOH or KOH with ratios below 0.4. Activations under these experimental conditions resulted in a significant increase in the adsorption capacity, of up to 25%, in the resulting samples.

Keywords: PVC; CO$_2$ capture; activated carbon; plastic waste; neuro-fuzzy model

1. Introduction

Plastics are essential materials that play a vital role in modern times. These materials have become an integral part of our daily lives, serving in a wide array of industries and applications, ranging from packaging and construction to healthcare and electronics. However, these materials also pose a significant environmental challenge due to their non-biodegradable nature, especially single-use plastics. Global plastics production increased from 280 Mt in 2011 to nearly 390 Mt in 2021 and is expected to continue to grow firmly over the coming years [1]. This excessive use of plastic has resulted in an enormous generation of waste, exceeding our capacity for its proper management. Despite there having been significant progress in recycling and energy recovery technologies to effectively utilize and recycle waste, these methods may not always be suitable or economically viable for managing all plastic waste. Indeed, only a minor fraction of this waste is recycled (≈18%), while the majority is either incinerated (25%) or disposed of in landfills (57%), hindering its potential for profitable utilization [2]. In this way, the exploration of alternative methods for utilizing plastic waste and reducing landfill disposal is highly desirable. One promising alternative is the pyrolysis valorization technique. Pyrolysis is a chemical recycling process that involves the thermochemical degradation of plastic waste by the application of heat and pressure, typically in the absence of oxygen [3]. During this process, three main products can be obtained, i.e., liquid (or oil), gas, and solid (also called char), that can be used for both materials and energy purposes. For example, the liquid fraction obtained from the pyrolysis of plastic waste can be refined into fuel or chemicals [4], while the gas fraction is usually used to feed the pyrolysis process. Furthermore, the solid product can serve as a solid fuel [5] or as a precursor to produce adsorbents [6]. While significant attention has been given to the liquid and gaseous fractions, research on the applications of char is comparatively scarce [7]. Thus, the present study aims to approach to the integral exploitation of plastic pyrolysis by-products, focusing particularly on the solid fraction.

Polyvinyl chloride (PVC) is among the most extensively used plastics; it accounts for 12% of the worldwide plastic demand, with an annual production of around 45 Mt [8]. PVC holds paramount importance in material science for its remarkable characteristics, including high durability, reusability, cost-efficiency, versatility, and low thermal conductivity [9]. Additionally, PVC can be provided with specific functional properties by means of incorporating various additives such as plasticizers, lubricants, and stabilizers [2]. In contrast, this material is considered one of the most environmentally harmful plastics because of its high chlorine content (~56 wt%) and high levels of hazardous additives. Consequently, recycling and valorization of PVC waste currently represents a great challenge.

In general, plastics have been widely studied for pyrolysis processes to make use of their fractions. For instance, Zhang et al. [10] obtained a methane-rich gas from the pyrolysis of polyethylene terephthalate (PET) waste and used the solid fraction to produce activated carbons for use as electrode material in supercapacitors. Kalargaris et al. [11] successfully produced high-quality bio-oil from the pyrolysis of mixed plastic waste, consisting of styrene-butadiene and polyester. The obtained bio-oils were found to have similar properties to those of diesel fuels. In another work, H_2 and carbon nanotubes were produced from the pyrolysis and catalytic decomposition of polypropylene waste [12]. Saeaung et al. [13] used the liquid fraction derived from the thermal decomposition of polypropylene, polylactide, and high- and low-density polyethylene waste to produce valuable chemicals. However, the pyrolysis of PVC waste has been historically problematic due to the formation of toxic compounds (hydrochloric (HCl-) species), and low thermal stability [14]. In contrast to other polymers, such as PET, PE, or PP, which undergo thermal degradation in a single step, PVC degradation occurs in two distinct stages. During the first step, the main process is the dechlorination of PVC, wherein the highly polarized C-Cl bonds are readily broken at relatively low temperatures. This results in the release of chlorine, primarily as gaseous HCl, along with other volatile compounds (benzenes, hydrocarbons, etc.). This stage occurs at temperatures ranging from 250 to 350 °C, depending on the types of stabilizers and additives present in the PVC. In the second step, the free chlorine polymer undergoes further degradation, resulting in its breakdown and decomposition. The second degradation step occurs at temperatures between 350 and 500 °C [15]. Qureshi et al. [16] reported that the by-products of PVC thermal degradation can have a detrimental effect on the pyrolysis process and its resulting products, as it generates chlorine-containing organics that may cause reactor corrosion and lead to liquid fraction degradation. To tackle this challenge, dechlorination units can be used in order to remove chlorine species and purify the pyrolysis products; however, this involves additional costs [17]. Thus, testing and optimization of the PVC pyrolysis process are required to gain a deeper insight into the management of this waste and progress toward the integral valorization of its by-products.

On the other hand, the liquid, gas, and char yields obtained from the pyrolysis process vary depending on the polymer's nature. For instance, PVC produces the lowest oil yield among the most commonly used plastics; however, a high percentage of solid residue (up to 25 wt%) can be obtained [18]. This is significantly higher compared to the less than 1 wt% yielded by other widely used polymers, such as PP or PS, in the same process [7]. Thus, PVC waste can serve as an excellent precursor for the production of char-based materials due to its capacity to yield a significant solid residue during the pyrolysis process; nevertheless, its use to produce activated carbons has scarcely been studied.

In light of the above-mentioned concerns, this study aims to valorize the pyrolysis PVC waste by-products, with a special focus on the solid fraction. For that, the pyrolysis solid by-products will be used as precursors to obtain high-value products, particularly CO_2 adsorbents. A complete set of characterizations including SEM, textural properties (N_2 adsorption/desorption isotherms), elemental analysis, FTIR, and CO_2 adsorption was carried out. Additionally, neuro-fuzzy models were designed to optimize the performance of the adsorbents by finely tuning the experimental variables involved in their synthesis process. Research on PVC valorization techniques will contribute to reducing its continuous disposal in landfills, which would otherwise cause irreversible environmental issues [19] and severe impacts on human beings' health [20].

2. Materials and Methods

2.1. PVC-Based Char Production

Char production was carried out using PVC piping waste supplied by a municipal solid waste treatment plant in Granada, Spain. Firstly, 40 g of PVC pipe was crushed and sieved to a particle size lower than 0.5 mm. Pyrolysis of PVC was carried out in a reactor (Nabertherm, Lilienthal, Germany) at a temperature of 500 °C, with a residence time of 2 h, a heating rate of 20 °C/min, and a nitrogen flow rate of 100 L/h. The products of pyrolysis were cooled to room temperature and then removed from the holding crucible and condensable collectors to measure their masses. Finally, the product yields were calculated based on the mass of PVC fed. The pyrolysis product yields were 5.93% liquid, 33.73% char, and 60.34% gas. The resulting solid fraction (char) was ground and subjected to the activation process.

2.2. PVC-Based Char Activation

Five grams of char was mixed with the activating agent, i.e., NaOH or KOH, according to the defined ratio. A two-step activation process was then carried out in the pyrolysis reactor. In the first step, the mixture was heated up to 300 °C with a heating rate of 10 °C/min, a residence time of 1 h, and a N_2 flow rate of 12 L/h. In the second step, the temperature was raised to 760, 800, or 840 °C and maintained for 1 h under the same environmental conditions as in the first step. These activation conditions were selected based on previous studies [21]. Finally, the sample was cooled to room temperature, i.e., 23 °C. After activation, samples were washed with 1 M HCl and dried at 120 °C for 24 h. Furthermore, untreated char was thermally activated (nitrogen physical activation) under the same conditions as described above. The resulting samples were labeled as follows: agent-activation temperature-ratio, e.g., Na-800-1:1 or N_2-840. All chemicals, i.e., hydroxides and HCl, were obtained from Sigma Aldrich, St. Louis, MO, USA.

2.3. Activated Carbon Characterization

Elemental analysis was conducted to determine the carbon, hydrogen, nitrogen, and sulfur content. Oxygen content was calculated by the difference between the total content and the sum of the other elements. This analysis was performed using the Thermo Scientific Flash 2000 device (Thermo Fisher Scientific, Waltham, MA, USA). FTIR analysis was carried out using a Perkin-Elmer spectrophotometer, specifically the Spectrum-65 model (PerkinElmer, Waltham, MA, USA), equipped with an Attenuated Total Reflectance (ATR) device. Spectra were recorded over a wavelength range of 4000–400 cm^{-1}, with a spectral resolution of 0.5 cm^{-1}. Textural properties were assessed using N_2 adsorption–desorption isotherms at 77 K with an ASAP 2010 Micromeritics apparatus (Micromeritics, Norcross, GA, USA). The total specific surface area (S_{BET}) was calculated by means of the BET method, while the total pore volume was determined based on the N_2 uptake at p/p0~0.99. The specific surface of micropores and the volume of micropores were estimated using the t-plot method. Additionally, the average pore size was determined through the BJH method from the adsorption step. The morphological characterization was performed using scanning electron microscopy (SEM) with Energy Dispersive X-ray (EDX) analysis (Oxford Instruments, Abingdon, UK) in an Auriga (FIB-FESEM) device (Zeiss, Oberkochen, Germany).

2.4. CO₂ Adsorption Tests

CO_2 adsorption tests were conducted in a thermogravimetric analyzer (Perkin-Elmer, STA 6000) (Waltham, MA, USA) in three stages. Firstly, a drying step was conducted to eliminate any moisture and other species that might be adsorbed onto the sample surface. For that, the sample was heated from room temperature to 200 °C and held for 1 h in an inert atmosphere with an N_2 flow rate of 50 mL/min. Secondly, the sample was cooled from 200 °C to the adsorption temperature, i.e., 20 °C, under the same environmental conditions. Finally, isothermal CO_2 adsorption was carried out. During this stage, the N_2 flow rate was switched to 50 mL/min of CO_2 and maintained for 2 h. After the latter step, there should be an increase in the sample mass due to CO_2 adsorption. If so, the difference between the initial and the final mass of the sample would determine the amount of CO_2 adsorbed.

2.5. Mathematical Modeling of CO₂ Adsorption: Factorial Design

A mathematical model for the optimization of the CO_2 adsorption process was designed. The model was based on a factorial design with three input variables (chemical agent (A), agent/char ratio (D), and activation temperature (T)), one response variable (CO_2 uptake (ye)), and a central point (with three repetitions). Each variable was assigned three levels, i.e., low, intermediate, and high, coded as −1, 0, and 1, respectively. Thus, the experimental design was a model with three factors (variables), three levels, one response variable, and one central point. In order to develop an optimal experimental design, the following parameters were considered:

- k, number of studied variables.
- n_c, number of central points.
- p, constant for values of k < 5 (p = 0).

The number of experiments required was estimated by the following equation:

$$n = 2^{k-p} + 2k + n_c \quad (1)$$

where n is the number of experiments and k is the number of independent variables (if k < 5; p = 0, if k > 5, p = 1), so:

$$n = 2^{3-0} + 2 \cdot 3 + 1 = 15$$

Thus, fifteen experiments, including the three repetitions of the central point, were required to develop an optimal experimental design. Table 1 displays the experimental design proposed for the study and the coding assigned to each variable.

Table 1. Proposed experimental design and codification.

Experiment No.	Activation	Temperature °C	Ratio	Code
1	NaOH	760	1:1	0, −1, 0
2 *	NaOH	800	1:1	0, 0, 0
3	NaOH	800	1:2	0, 0, 1
4	NaOH	800	2:1	0, 0, −1
5	NaOH	840	1:1	0, 1, 0
6	KOH	760	2:1	1, −1, −1
7	KOH	760	1:2	1, −1, 1
8	KOH	800	1:1	1, 0, 0
9	KOH	840	1:2	1, 1, 1
10	KOH	840	2:1	1, 1, −1
11	N_2	760	-	−1, −1
12	N_2	800	-	−1, 0
13	N_2	840	-	−1, 1
14 *	NaOH	800	1:1	0, 0, 0
15 *	NaOH	800	1:1	0, 0, 0

* Central points.

The response variable (y_e) was determined using the following equation:

$$y_e = \frac{\sum_{l=1}^{12} al \cdot FRl}{\sum_{l=1}^{12} FRl} \quad (2)$$

where y_e is the estimated value of the variable to be modeled, al represents the constants calculated by the model for each variable and level (see Supplementary Materials, Script S1), and FRl refers to the fuzzy rules of the model (12 in this study), which corresponds to each possible combination of levels. For instance, the calculation of the first three model rules would be as follows [22]:

$$FR1 = \mu_A(\text{low}) \cdot \mu_B(\text{low}) \cdot \mu_C(\text{low}) \quad (3)$$

$$FR2 = \mu_A(\text{low}) \cdot \mu_B(\text{low}) \cdot \mu_C(\text{medium}) \quad (4)$$

$$FR3 = \mu_A(\text{low}) \cdot \mu_B(\text{low}) \cdot \mu_C(\text{high}) \quad (5)$$

L represents the width of the Gaussian function and μ (low), μ (medium), and μ (high) correspond to the values of each level. Finally, the function to calculate the response variable is as follows:

$$y_e = \frac{a_1 \cdot FR_1 + a_2 \cdot FR_2 + \cdots + a_{12} \cdot FR_{12}}{FR_1 + FR_2 + \cdots + FR_{12}} \quad (6)$$

The full expression is detailed in the Supplementary Materials.

Mathematical Modeling of CO_2 Adsorption: Neuro-Fuzzy Models

To develop the neuro-fuzzy models, the experimental adsorption results were introduced in the ANFIS edit tool (Adaptive Neural Fuzzy Inference System). For that, the variables were coded as follows: activating agent: N_2 (0), NaOH (1), and KOH (2); agent/char ratio: 1:2 (0.33); 1:1 (0.5), and 2:1 (0.66); temperature: the same as Celsius degrees, e.g., 760 (760); and central point: A (activated agent) = 1; D (ratio) = 0.5; T (temperature) = 800. The results of the three central point experiments were averaged (Exp. 2, 14, and 15; Table 1) and the final value was used. Therefore, 13 (12 + 1 central point) experiments were used to perform the model. These experiments are detailed in Table S1, Supplementary Materials.

From the 12 fuzzy rules of the model (FR1-12), it is possible to generate models that include three levels for one of the variables, and two levels for the other two variables. This means that each model can work with a maximum of one variable in three levels because $2 \times 2 \times 3 = 12$, which is the maximum number of rules. Optimization was performed using the model with the most accurate predictive results, which is the model with the lowest error (E = 0.0063). In this model, data from the 13 experiments were fitted to a Gaussian dependence of $2 \times 3 \times 2$. For optimization, a script was developed based on ANFIS results (see Supplementary Materials). The model designed provides valuable insights into which variable has the most significant influence on the response variable and how the effect of one variable changes with varying levels of the other.

3. Results and Discussion

3.1. CO_2 Adsorption Tests

Table 2 shows the experimental CO_2 uptakes of PVC-based activated carbons, measured in milligrams of CO_2 retained per gram of activated carbon, and the activation conditions.

The results show that the alkaline activation played a critical role in the CO_2 adsorption capacity of the resulting samples. For instance, NaOH-activated samples increased their adsorption capacity more than seven-fold compared to the untreated sample, i.e., the solid fraction resulting from the pyrolysis of PVC waste. Particularly, the adsorption capacity increased from 5.1 mg/g for untreated char to 33–37 mg/g for NaOH-treated samples. The sample activated by KOH at 760 °C with an agent/char ratio of 2:1 exhibited the highest adsorption capacity of 45.6 mg/g. The adsorption capacities achieved in this study are comparable to those reported in the literature by other plastic-based activated carbons. For instance, Singh et al. [23] prepared activated carbons using polyacrylonitrile waste as a precursor and various chemical agents, including NaOH, KOH, and K_2CO_3, and studied their CO_2 adsorption capacity under dynamic conditions. The sample activated by KOH at 800 °C for 2 h using an agent/precursor ratio of 3:1 exhibited the highest adsorption capacity of 52 mg/g at 30 °C. In another study, PET household waste was used as a precursor to prepare porous carbons via KOH activation, and the resulting carbons exhibited a CO_2 adsorption capacity of 101 mg/g [24]. Choma et al. [25] reported a CO_2 adsorption capacity of 3.3 mmol/g at 25 °C using char derived from CDs and DVDs waste activated with KOH. Yuan et al. [26] synthesized carbon adsorbents from PET plastic bottles through KOH and NaOH activations and reported a CO_2 adsorption capacity of 194 and 169 mg/g, respectively. The larger adsorption capacities obtained in the latter study can be attributed to the different nature of the precursor and the specific activation conditions applied. According to Lian et al. [27], PET is a more suitable precursor to develop efficient adsorbents than PVC due to its aromatic structure. This may explain the limited use of PVC waste as a precursor to produce carbonaceous materials in comparison with other widely used plastics.

Table 2. CO_2 uptakes of PVC-based carbons.

Act. Agent	Act. Temperature	Ratio (A/C)	CO_2 Uptake (mg/g)
-	-	-	5.1
NaOH	760	1:1	37.3
NaOH	800	1:1	37.4
NaOH	800	1:2	32.7
NaOH	800	2:1	36.4
NaOH	840	1:1	35.3
KOH	760	2:1	45.6
KOH	760	1:2	14.8
KOH	800	1:1	37.6
KOH	840	1:2	22.7
KOH	840	2:1	35.1
N_2	760	-	26.4
N_2	800	-	11.7
N_2	840	-	6.4

On the other hand, reducing the agent/char ratio or increasing activation temperature both led to a decrease in CO_2 adsorption capacity, regardless of the chemical agent used (Table 2). This negative impact on the adsorption capacity is presumably related to the unfavorable porous structure formed under these activation conditions. It is well-known that the porosity of the activated carbons can be tuned by tailoring the activation conditions. Additionally, the CO_2 adsorption capacity is directly related to the formation of narrow micropores suitable for capturing the CO_2 molecules. Thus, the decreased CO_2 adsorption capacity can be attributed to a reduction in microporosity, probably induced by the pore-widening effect under those activation conditions, resulting in fewer channels available for CO_2 diffusion and a lower number of active sites for CO_2 uptake [7]. Regarding the physically activated samples, the CO_2 adsorption capacity tended to increase as the activation temperature decreased. The sample activated at 760 °C achieved the highest adsorption capacity of 26.4 mg/g. Similar findings were reported by Lee and Park [28] in their study on the activation of poly(vinylidene fluoride) with N_2. The most favorable adsorption capacities were achieved when carbons were activated at low temperatures, approximately 600 °C. However, the adsorption values reported by these researchers were higher than those of this work, i.e., around 130 mg/g. This difference may be attributed to the different nature of the precursor. Finally, the N_2-based activated carbons showed the lowest CO_2 adsorption capacities among all treated samples, which can be also attributed to the unsuitable porosity formed on the sample surfaces. Thus, surface morphology as well as surface textural properties should reflect these changes. This will be discussed in the following sections.

3.2. N_2 Adsorption/Desorption Isotherms

The key goal in the synthesis of any effective CO_2 adsorbent is to obtain a tailored pore structure. The desired structure should have a significant surface area and an abundance of pores with the ideal size to fit CO_2 molecules. Table 3 summarizes the textural properties of PVC-based carbons obtained from the N_2 sorption isotherms.

Table 3. Textural properties of PVC-based carbons.

Sample	S_{BET} m^2/g	V_{TOTAL} cm^3/g	V_{MICRO} cm^3/g	A_{MICRO} m^2/g	MicroP$_{DIAMETER}$ nm
Char	3.5	0.015	0.000	0.0	0.998
Na-760-1:1	152.3	0.113	0.056	112.4	0.812
Na-800-1:1	135.0	2.831	0.043	92.1	0.791
Na-800-1:2	82.0	0.077	0.026	50.7	0.766
Na-800-2:1	46.3	0.071	0.005	10.4	0.831
Na-840-1:1	79.8	0.077	0.024	47.2	0.786
K-760-2:1	886.2	0.531	0.252	528.2	0.824
K-760-1:2	117.8	0.093	0.035	76.9	0.840
K-800-1:1	530.6	0.302	0.214	447.0	0.818
K-840-1:2	123.8	2.764	0.033	70.4	0.789
K-840-2:1	461.5	0.297	0.192	371.8	0.859
N_2-760	7.2	0.028	0.000	0.0	0.884
N_2-800	7.4	0.020	0.000	0.0	0.817
N_2-840	23.8	0.050	0.000	0.0	0.825

As expected, alkali activation impacted the textural properties of the activated carbons. The surface area (S_{BET}), total pore volume (V_{TOTAL}), and micropore area (A_{MICRO}) of untreated char increased dramatically for the samples activated with hydroxides. For instance, the S_{BET} of untreated char increased from 3.5 m^2/g to 886.2 and 530.6 m^2/g for K-760-2:1 and K-800-1:1 samples, respectively. Regarding the NaOH-activated samples, the S_{BET} increased up to 152.3 m^2/g. Furthermore, the total pore volume increased from 0.0015 cm^3/g to 2.831 and 2.764 cm^3/g for the Na-800-1:1 and K-840-1:2 samples, respectively. While it has been suggested that larger surface areas and total pore volumes can enhance the CO_2 adsorption process, there is no strict correlation between the CO_2 adsorption capacity and an increase in the surface area and pore volume. Large surface area values may be achieved due to pores that are suitable for N_2 adsorption but not for CO_2 adsorption [7]. In this study, the highest values of micropore volume are aligned with the largest CO_2 adsorption capacities (Tables 2 and 3). The K-760-2:1 sample showed the largest volume of micropores, i.e., 0.252 cm^3/g, as well as the best adsorption capacity. Likewise, the NaOH-activated sample with the largest micropore volume exhibited the highest CO_2 uptake of all the NaOH-activated samples. This indicates that the formation of micropore structures dominated the CO_2 adsorption capability of PVC-based carbons. In particular, micropores with diameters ranging from 0.791 nm to 0.831 nm exhibited the highest adsorption capacities (Table 3). This can be achieved by finely tuning the activation conditions, e.g., temperature, chemical agent, and agent/precursor ratio. For instance, the largest micropore volume was obtained for the samples activated at the lowest temperature, i.e., 760 °C; thus, increasing the activation temperature had a detrimental effect on the microporosity development of both NaOH- and KOH-activated samples. Furthermore, increasing the agent/precursor ratio enhanced the microporosity of the KOH-activated samples, whereas the opposite effect was observed for the samples activated with NaOH. Lastly, the nitrogen activation was not effective in obtaining micropores and, consequently, producing efficient PVC-based

CO_2 adsorbents. To gain a better understanding of this phenomenon, the most efficient CO_2 adsorbents, i.e., Na-800-1:1, and K-760-2:1, were subjected to further characterization.

3.3. Characterization of PVC-Based AC

The elemental composition of Na-800-1:1, K-760-2:1, and untreated char is presented in Table 4.

Table 4. Elemental analysis of most efficient PVC-based adsorbents.

Sample	Element (%)			
	N	C	H	O
Char	0	19.05	1.75	79.20
Na-800-1:1	0.08	42.32	1.12	56.48
K-760-2:1	0	48.36	0.98	50.66

In general, very low nitrogen and high oxygen and carbon contents were found in the elemental analysis of the char derived from PVC waste, which is characteristic of hydrocarbon-based materials. The large O content can be ascribed to both the carbonization process and the volatile compounds decomposition [21]. It is interesting to note that no chlorine content was found in the char. During the thermal degradation of PVC, the dechlorination of PVC occurs. Most of the chlorine present in the PVC is released as HCl in gaseous form, with less than 1% remaining in the liquid fraction [15]. Zhou et al. (2016) [29] reported a chlorine loss from 55% to less than 1% during the PVC pyrolysis process. They concluded that the primary cause of the PVC total mass loss was the dechlorination of the polymer during pyrolysis. In a prior study, the chlorine content in the PVC pyrolysis by-products was measured. It was found that the chlorine content in the oil fraction was ~0.16% [30].

Chemical activation led to a decrease in the O and H content and an increase in the C content of the resulting samples. This can be explained by the removal of their respective functional groups, which could be released during the decomposition reactions [31]. Finally, the KOH treatment produced a larger carbon yield than the NaOH treatment, which can be attributed to the larger agent/precursor ratio employed for the activation of the former sample. Therefore, the hydroxide activations caused significant chemical changes in the resulting materials, which contributed to the development of their porosity (Table 3).

The surface morphologies of selected PVC-based carbons examined by SEM at different magnifications are given in Figure 1.

The porosity development of the hydroxide-treated samples is evident from the SEM images. It is clearly seen that the microstructure of both activated carbons is granular with a relatively narrow particle size distribution (e, f, h, and i), whilst the microstructure of untreated char is non-porous (a–c). Another notable observation is that the activated samples developed a randomly dispersed roughness on the surface, which was manifested by the huge increase in the surface area compared to the untreated char (Table 3). Meanwhile, the KOH-activated sample exhibits a more porous structure and a denser porous network compared to the NaOH-treated sample, i.e., f vs. y, which can be attributed to the larger agent/precursor ratio of the former sample. Probably, the larger agent/precursor ratio promoted the formation of more pores and expanded the porous network through various chemical reactions between KOH and carbon species during the activation process [7]. Therefore, the morphology analysis evidenced that hydroxide activations create a porous network on the carbon surface, which is consistent with the textural properties discussed above. The development of these surface structures impacted their CO_2 adsorption capacity.

The interaction of the PVC-based carbons with infrared light was analyzed to assess the potential alterations in the samples' chemical structures. FTIR spectra of the PVC-based activated carbons are presented in Figure 2.

Figure 1. High-magnification SEM images of PVC-based carbons: (**a–c**) untreated char; (**d–f**) K-770-2:1; (**g–i**) Na-800-1:1.

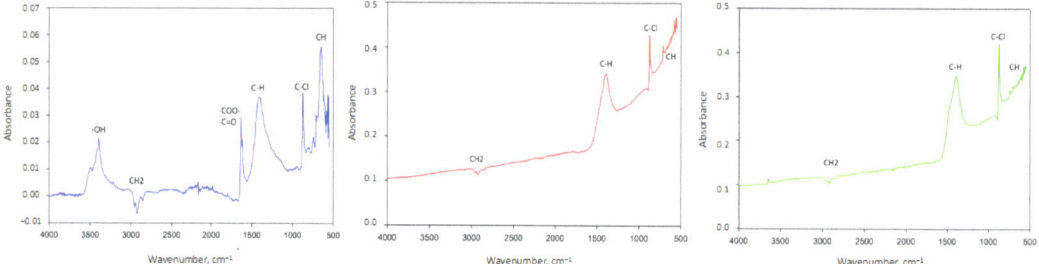

Figure 2. Spectra of untreated char (**left**), K-760-2:1 (**middle**), and Na-800-1:1 (**right**) samples.

The untreated char spectra show a characteristic band at the wavelength of 2970 cm^{-1}, corresponding to the -CH$_2$ asymmetric stretching vibration of the -CH$_2$- group. This band can also be observed for the KOH- and NaOH-activated carbons at 3002 and 3006 cm^{-1}, respectively. Vibrations of the aliphatic bond (C-H) are also visible at the frequencies of 1412, 1319 cm^{-1}, and 1392 cm^{-1} for the untreated char, KOH-, and NaOH-activated carbons, respectively [32]. The characteristic PVC peaks at 600–950 cm^{-1} attributed to the oscillations of trans and cis of the CH group are also observable in all samples [33]. Furthermore, it is possible to observe peaks at 850 and 650 cm^{-1}, corresponding to the C-Cl stretching vibrations [34].

The influence of the chemical activation can be easily seen when comparing the spectra of untreated and treated samples. For example, the broad wavelength band between 3100 and 3400 cm^{-1}, corresponding to the OH stretching of carboxy and phenols, is only observable in the untreated char spectra [35]. This band may be attributed to the presence of some additives, which were ostensibly removed during the HCl washing procedure. Similarly, the absorption band at the wavelength of 1629 cm^{-1} is only visible for the untreated char sample. This peak is assigned to the different conformations of carbonyl groups, i.e., -COO- and -C=O, derived from different organic compounds, which are generally introduced during the polymer manufacturing process. As seen, chemical activation induced important chemical changes in the treated carbons. This is reflected by the absence of several peaks, along with the variations in the absorption intensities of the activated samples.

3.4. Optimization of the CO_2 Adsorption Process

Mathematical modeling of the parameters involved in the synthesis of CO_2 adsorbents is essential for the optimization of their adsorption capacities. It allows a throughout interpretation of the effects of operating conditions on system behavior, avoiding the need to perform a large number of experiments [36]. Table 5 presents the experiments conducted to optimize the CO_2 adsorption process, the neuro-fuzzy model prediction results, and the relative error.

Table 5. CO_2 adsorption capacity of PVC-based carbons; experimental and prediction model results.

Sample	Activation (A)	Act. Temperature °C (T)	Ratio (D)	CO_2 Uptake mg/g (qe)	CO_2 Uptake Model mg/g (ye)	Error
Na-760-1:1	1	760	0.5	37.29	37.28	0.004
Na-800-1:1	1	800	0.5	37.34	35.49	1.851
Na-800-1:2	1	800	0.66	32.65	33.51	0.890
Na-800-2:1	1	800	0.33	36.36	37.32	0.959
Na-840-1:1	1	840	0.5	35.26	35.26	0.001
K-760-2:1	2	760	0.33	45.59	45.58	0.013
K-760-1:2	2	760	0.66	14.74	14.73	0.007
K-800-1:1	2	800	0.5	37.52	37.52	0.003
K-840-1:2	2	840	0.66	22.70	22.70	0.003
K-840-2:1	2	840	0.33	35.03	35.03	0.001
N_2-760	0	760	0	26.33	26.33	0.000
N_2-800	0	800	0	11.65	11.65	0.000
N_2-840	0	840	0	6.38	6.38	0.003

Overall, there was a minimal difference between the experimental values and those estimated by the neuro-fuzzy model (error rate < 5%), indicating that the values fitted accurately to those predicted by the neuro-fuzzy model. This suggests that the proposed model accurately predicts values and can be effectively utilized for accurate predictions. The response surfaces were plotted as a function of the activating agent, agent/precursor ratio, activation temperature, and CO_2 adsorption capacity.

Figure 3 shows the three-dimensional representation of the impact of each input variable, i.e., activating agent, and agent/precursor ratio, on the output variable, i.e., CO_2 adsorption capacity, at various activation temperatures. At 760 °C, the CO_2 adsorption capacity of the KOH-activated samples decreased with increasing the ratio, reaching maximum adsorption points at ratios lower than 0.4. In contrast, the adsorption capacity of NaOH-activated samples increased with increasing the ratio, reaching the greatest adsorptions of 40–44 mg/g at ratios larger than 0.5 (Figure 3a). Furthermore, at a ratio of 0.33, the type of chemical agent employed in the activation did not influence the adsorption capacity of the resulting samples, as their CO_2 adsorption capacities remained virtually constant. However, at higher ratios (around 0.66), the type of activating agent was relevant. The adsorption capacity was minimal for the KOH-activated samples and maximal for the NaOH-activated samples. The response surface obtained at 800 °C was very similar to the previous one. For the NaOH-activated samples, the CO_2 adsorption capacity increased with increasing the ratio; however, an opposite trend was observed for the samples activated by KOH. The greatest CO_2 adsorption capacity was obtained for the carbons activated by KOH using a ratio of 0.33 (Figure 3b). At 840 °C, the most favorable activation conditions were obtained using NaOH as an activating agent and ratios larger than 0.6. Under these experimental conditions, the CO_2 adsorption capacity was approximately 44 mg/g. Consequently, optimal activation conditions include activations at 840 °C with NaOH at a ratio of 0.66 and at 760 °C using either NaOH or KOH with ratios below 0.4. Activations under these experimental conditions resulted in a significant increase in the adsorption capacity of up to 25% in the resulting samples.

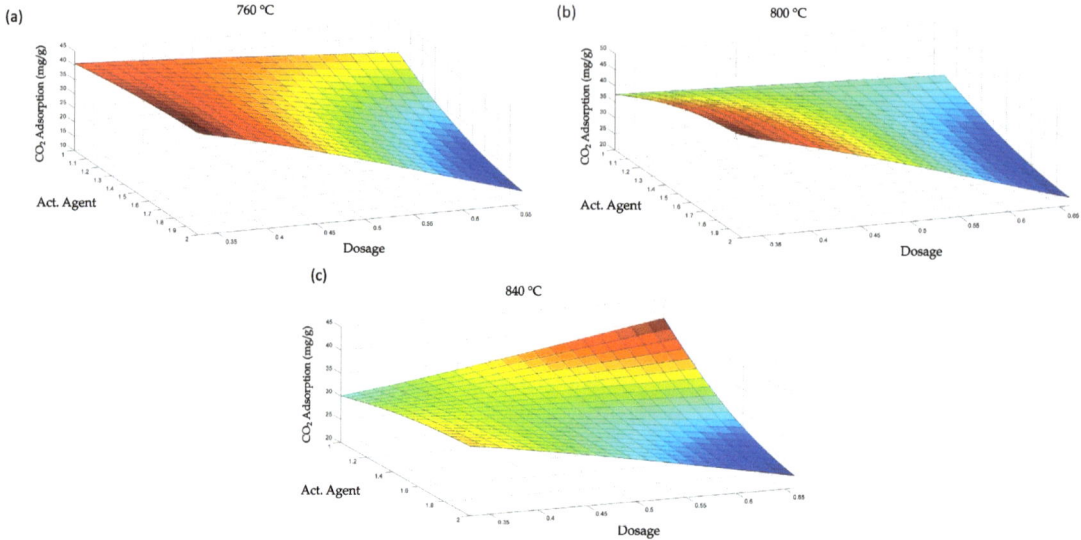

Figure 3. Response surfaces as a function of the activated conditions at (**a**) 760 °C, (**b**) 800 °C, and (**c**) 840 °C.

For the optimization of the activation temperature, Figure 4a,b presents the three-dimensional representation of the impact of each input variable, i.e., activation temperature and agent/precursor ratio, on the output variable, i.e., CO_2 adsorption capacity, for different activation agents.

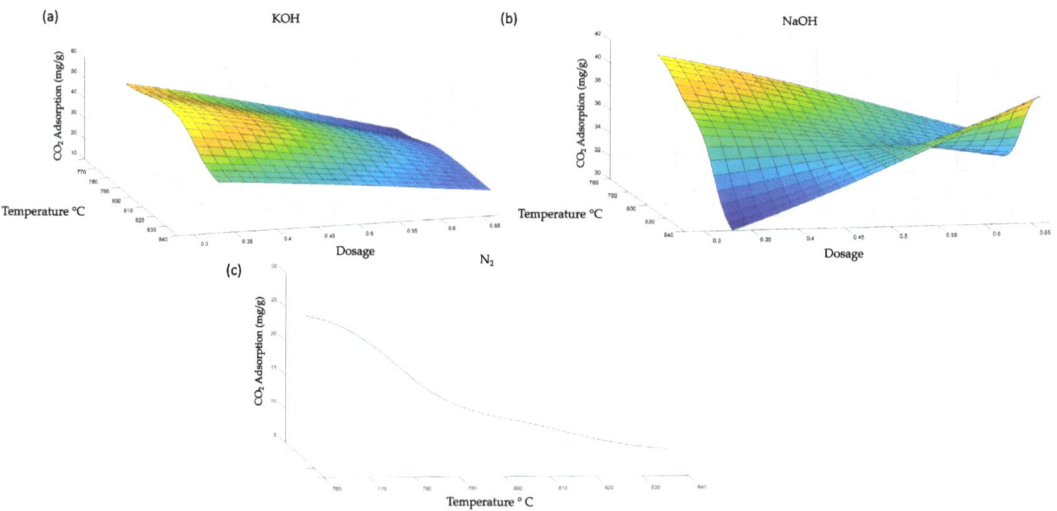

Figure 4. Response surfaces of (**a**) KOH-activated carbons, (**b**) NaOH-activated carbons, and (**c**) N_2-activated carbons as a function of the activated conditions.

The adsorption capacity of the samples activated with KOH at the highest ratio (0.66) was not significantly affected by the activation temperature. The maximum adsorption point was observed at 800 °C for the samples activated with a ratio of 0.37. The CO_2 adsorption capacity of the NaOH-activated samples varied greatly with temperature. For example, the maximum CO_2 adsorption was observed at temperatures below 780 °C, and the adsorption capacity decreased significantly as the activation temperature increased. An opposite behavior was observed for the samples activated at a ratio of 0.6, as the maximum adsorption points corresponded to the highest activation temperature (Figure 4b). Finally, the response surface for the physically activated samples (N_2) is presented as a 2D plot (Figure 4c), where only the activation temperature was monitored. The CO_2 adsorption capacity decreased with increasing the activation temperature, reaching the maximum adsorption point at the lowest activation temperature, i.e., 760 °C.

4. Conclusions

The CO_2 adsorption capacity of PVC-based activated carbons was optimized by finely tuning the activation conditions. The chemical activation proved to be more effective than the physical activation in developing PVC-based CO_2 adsorbents. Carbons activated by KOH with a 2:1 agent/precursor ratio at 760 °C exhibited the highest CO_2 adsorption capacity of 45 mg/g. The use of KOH was more effective than NaOH. The largest surface area and pore volume values do not necessarily correlate with a greater CO_2 adsorption capacity. The development of microporous structures was the key factor in the CO_2 adsorption. All fittings were perfectly fitted to the neuro-fuzzy model and the proposed model accurately predicted the most optimal activation conditions for the CO_2 uptake.

Supplementary Materials: The following supporting information can be downloaded at: https://www.mdpi.com/article/10.3390/pr12030431/s1, Table S1. Operating parameters introduced in ANFIS edit tool; Script S1. Script designed from the experimental results, and neuro-fuzzy variables. This script was used to carry out CO_2 adsorption predictions.

Author Contributions: Conceptualization, A.P. and G.B.; methodology, E.A.J.-G.; software, A.P.; validation, A.P., S.P.-H. and G.B.; formal analysis, A.P.; investigation, E.A.J.-G.; resources, M.C.; writing—original draft preparation, E.A.J.-G. and S.P.-H.; writing—review and editing, S.P.-H. and M.C.; supervision, G.B.; project administration, M.C. funding acquisition, M.C. All authors have read and agreed to the published version of the manuscript.

Funding: This work belongs to the project PDC2022-133808-I00, funded by MCIN/AEI/10.13039/501100011033 and the European Union "NextGeneration EU"/PRTR. S.P.-H. is funded by a Juan de la Cierva Fellowship (FJC2021-048044-I, funded by MCIN/AEI/10.13039/501100011033 and the EU "NextGenerationEU/PRTR").

Data Availability Statement: Data will be made available on request.

Conflicts of Interest: The authors declare no conflicts of interest.

References

1. Plastic Europe. Plastics—The facts 2022. *PlasticEurope* **2022**, *1*, 1–17.
2. Yu, J.; Sun, L.; Ma, C.; Qiao, Y.; Yao, H. Thermal Degradation of PVC: A Review. *Waste Manag.* **2016**, *48*, 300–314. [CrossRef]
3. Chen, S.; Liu, Z.; Jiang, S.; Hou, H. Carbonization: A feasible route for reutilization of plastic wastes. *Sci. Total Environ.* **2020**, *710*, 136250. [CrossRef]
4. Scott, D.S.; Czernik, S.R.; Piskorz, J.; Radlein, D.S.A. Fast pyrolysis of plastic wastes. *Energy Fuels* **1990**, *4*, 407–411. [CrossRef]
5. Kunwar, B.; Chen, H.N.; Chandrashekaran, S.; Sharma, B. Plastics to fuel: A review. *Renew. Sustain. Energy Rev.* **2016**, *54*, 421–428. [CrossRef]
6. Zhang, H.; Pap, S.; Taggart, M.A.; Boyd, K.G.; James, N.A.; Gibb, S.W. A review of the potential utilisation of plastic waste as adsorbent for removal of hazardous priority contaminants from aqueous environments. *Environ. Pollut.* **2020**, *258*, 113698. [CrossRef]

7. Peréz-Huertas, S.; Calero, M.; Ligero, A.; Pérez, A.; Terpiłowski, K.; Martín-Lara, M.A. On the use of plastic precursors for preparation of activated carbons and their evaluation in CO_2 capture for biogas upgrading: A review. *Waste Manag.* **2023**, *161*, 116–141. [CrossRef]
8. PlasticsEurope EP. *Plastics—The Facts 2019. An Analysis of European Plastics Production, Demand and Waste Data*; PlasticEurope: Bruxelles, Belgium, 2019.
9. Miliute-Plepiene, J.; Fråne, A.; Almasi, A.M. Overview of polyvinyl chloride (PVC) waste management practices in the Nordic countries. *Clean. Eng. Technol.* **2021**, *4*, 100246. [CrossRef]
10. Zhang, H.; Zhou, X.L.; Shao, L.M.; Lü, F.; He, P.J. Upcycling of PET waste into methane-rich gas and hierarchical porous carbon for high-performance supercapacitor by autogenic pressure pyrolysis and activation. *Sci. Total Environ.* **2021**, *772*, 145309. [CrossRef] [PubMed]
11. Kalargaris, I.; Tian, G.; Gu, S. The utilisation of oils produced from plastic waste at different pyrolysis temperatures in a DI diesel engine. *Energy* **2017**, *131*, 179–185. [CrossRef]
12. Yao, D.; Wang, C.H. Pyrolysis and in-line catalytic decomposition of polypropylene to carbon nanomaterials and hydrogen over Fe- and Ni-based catalysts. *Appl. Energy* **2020**, *265*, 114819. [CrossRef]
13. Saeaung, K.; Phusunti, N.; Phetwarotai, W.; Assabumrungrat, S.; Cheirsilp, B. Catalytic pyrolysis of petroleum-based and biodegradable plastic waste to obtain high-value chemicals. *Waste Manag.* **2021**, *127*, 101–111. [CrossRef] [PubMed]
14. Buekens, A.; Cen, K. Waste incineration, PVC, and dioxins. *J. Mater. Cycles Waste Manag.* **2011**, *13*, 190–197. [CrossRef]
15. Ye, L.; Li, T.; Hong, L. Understanding Enhanced Char Formation in the Thermal Decomposition of PVC Resin: Role of Intermolecular Chlorine Loss. *Mater. Today Commun.* **2021**, *26*, 102186. [CrossRef]
16. Qureshi, M.S.; Oasmaa, A.; Pihkola, H.; Deviatkin, I.; Tenhunen, A.; Mannila, J.; Minkkinen, H.; Pohjakallio, M.; Laine-Ylijoki, J.J. Pyrolysis of plastic waste: Opportunities and challenges. *Anal. Appl. Pyrolysis* **2020**, *152*, 104804. [CrossRef]
17. Zhang, Y.; Zhang, H.; Liu, T.; Zhou, Y.; Li, Z.; Deng, S.; Li, Y.; Liang, P. Synergistic removal of HCl and Hg0 in pyrolytic waste plastic gas on Ca and Co loaded carbon aerogel at room temperature. *Fuel Process. Technol.* **2022**, *238*, 107497. [CrossRef]
18. Sharuddin, S.; Abnisa, F.; Daud, W.; Aroua, M. A review on pyrolysis of plastic wastes. *Energy Convers. Manag.* **2016**, *115*, 308–326. [CrossRef]
19. Zheng, J.; Suh, S. Strategies to reduce the global carbon footprint of plastics. *Nat. Clim. Chang.* **2019**, *9*, 374–378. [CrossRef]
20. Almroth, B.C.; Eggert, H. Marine Plastic Pollution: Sources, Impacts, and Policy Issues. *Rev. Environ. Econ. Policy* **2019**, *13*, 317–326. [CrossRef]
21. Ligero, A.; Calero, M.; Pérez, A.; Solís, R.R.; Muñoz-Batista, M.J.; Martín-Lara, M.A. Low-cost activated carbon from the pyrolysis of post-consumer plastic waste and the application in CO_2 capture. *Process Saf. Environ.* **2023**, *173*, 558–566. [CrossRef]
22. Calero, M.; Iáñez-Rodríguez, I.; Pérez, A.; Martín-Lara, M.A.; Blázquez, G. Neural Fuzzy Modelization of Copper Removal from Water by Biosorption in Fixed-Bed Columns Using Olive Stone and Pinion Shell. *Bioresour Technol.* **2018**, *252*, 100–109. [CrossRef]
23. Singh, J.; Basu, S.; Bhunia, H. Dynamic CO_2 adsorption on activated carbon adsorbents synthesized from polyacrylonitrile (PAN): Kinetic and isotherm studies. *Microporous Mesoporous Mater.* **2019**, *280*, 357–366. [CrossRef]
24. Kaur, B.; Singh, J.; Gupta, R.K.; Bhunia, H. Porous carbons derived from polyethylene terephthalate (PET) waste for CO_2 capture studies. *J. Environ. Manag.* **2019**, *242*, 68–80. [CrossRef] [PubMed]
25. Choma, J.; Marszewski, M.; Osuchowski, L.; Jagiello, J.; Dziura, A.; Jaroniec, M. Adsorption Properties of Activated Carbons Prepared from Waste CDs and DVDs. *ACS Sustain. Chem. Eng.* **2015**, *3*, 733–742. [CrossRef]
26. Yuan, X.; Lee, J.G.; Yun, H.; Deng, S.; Kim, Y.J.; Lee, J.E.; Kwak, S.K.; Lee, K.B. Solving two environmental issues simultaneously: Waste polyethylene terephthalate plastic bottle-derived microporous carbons for capturing CO_2. *Chem. Eng. J.* **2020**, *397*, 125350. [CrossRef]
27. Lian, F.; Xing, B.; Zhu, L. Comparative study on composition, structure, and adsorption behavior of activated carbons derived from different synthetic waste polymers. *J. Colloid Interface Sci.* **2011**, *360*, 725–730. [CrossRef]
28. Lee, S.Y.; Park, S.J. Carbon dioxide adsorption performance of ultramicroporous carbon derived from poly(vinylidene fluoride). *J. Anal. Appl. Pyrol.* **2014**, *106*, 147–151. [CrossRef]
29. Zhou, J.; Gui, B.; Qiao, Y.; Zhang, J.; Wang, W.; Yao, H.; Yu, Y.; Xu, M. Understanding the Pyrolysis Mechanism of Polyvinylchloride (PVC) by Characterizing the Chars Produced in a Wire-Mesh Reactor. *Fuel* **2016**, *166*, 526–532. [CrossRef]
30. Calero, M.; Solís, R.R.; Muñoz-Batista, M.J.; Pérez, A.; Blázquez, G.; Martín-Lara, M.Á. Oil and gas production from the pyrolytic transformation of recycled plastic waste: An integral study by polymer families. *Chem. Eng. Sci.* **2023**, *271*, 118569. [CrossRef]
31. López, A.; de Marco, I.; Caballero, B.M.; Laresgoiti, M.F.; Adrados, A. Influence of time and temperature on pyrolysis of plastic wastes in a semi-batch reactor. *Chem. Eng. J.* **2011**, *173*, 62–71. [CrossRef]
32. Islam, I.; Sultana, S.; Kumer Ray, S.; Parvin Nur, H.; Hossain, M.T.; Md. Ajmotgir, W. Electrical and Tensile Properties of Carbon Black Reinforced Polyvinyl Chloride Conductive Composites. *C* **2018**, *4*, 15. [CrossRef]
33. Rajendran, S.; Uma, T. Effect of ZrO_2 on conductivity of PVC–$LiBF_4$–DBP polymer electrolytes. *Mater. Lett.* **2000**, *44*, 208–214. [CrossRef]
34. Pandey, M.; Joshi, G.M.; Mukherjee, A.; Thomas, P. Electrical Properties and Thermal Degradation of Poly(Vinyl Chloride)/Polyvinylidene Fluoride/ZnO Polymer Nanocomposites. *Polym. Int.* **2016**, *65*, 1098–1106. [CrossRef]

35. Pezoti, O.; Cazetta, A.L.; Bedin, K.C.; Souza, L.S.; Martins, A.C.; Silva, T.L.; Santos, O.; Visentainer, J.V.; Almeida, V.C. NaOH-activated carbon of high surface area produced from guava seeds as a high-efficiency adsorbent for amoxicillin removal: Kinetic, isotherm and thermodynamic studies. *Chem. Eng. J.* **2016**, *288*, 778–788. [CrossRef]
36. Ravikumar, K.; Krishnan, S.; Ramalingam, S.; Balu, K. Optimization of process variables by the application of response surface methodology for dye removal using a novel adsorbent. *Dyes Pigm.* **2007**, *72*, 66–74. [CrossRef]

Disclaimer/Publisher's Note: The statements, opinions and data contained in all publications are solely those of the individual author(s) and contributor(s) and not of MDPI and/or the editor(s). MDPI and/or the editor(s) disclaim responsibility for any injury to people or property resulting from any ideas, methods, instructions or products referred to in the content.

Article

Optimal Mesh Pore Size Combined with Periodic Air Mass Load (AML) for Effective Operation of a Self-Forming Dynamic Membrane BioReactor (SFD MBR) for Sustainable Treatment of Municipal Wastewater

Senouci Boulerial [1,2,†], Carlo Salerno [1,*,†], Fabiano Castrogiovanni [1], Marina Tumolo [1], Giovanni Berardi [1], Abdelkader Debab [2], Boumediene Haddou [3], Abdellah Benhamou [3] and Alfieri Pollice [1]

[1] CNR IRSA (National Research Council of Italy, Water Research Institute), V.le F. De Blasio 5, 70132 Bari, Italy; senouci.boulerial@univ-usto.dz (S.B.); fabiano.castrogiovanni@ba.irsa.cnr.it (F.C.); marina.tumolo@ba.irsa.cnr.it (M.T.); giovanni.berardi@ba.irsa.cnr.it (G.B.); alfieri.pollice@cnr.it (A.P.)

[2] Laboratory of Process Engineering and Environment, University of Science and Technology of Oran, BP 1505, Elmnouar, Oran 31000, Algeria; abdelkader.debab@univ-usto.dz

[3] Laboratory of Physical Chemistry of Materials, Catalysis and Environment, University of Science and Technology of Oran, BP 1505, Elmnouar, Oran 31000, Algeria; boumeddiene.haddou@univ-usto.dz (B.H.); abdellah.benhamou@univ-usto.dz (A.B.)

* Correspondence: carlo.salerno@cnr.it
† These authors contributed equally to this work.

Citation: Boulerial, S.; Salerno, C.; Castrogiovanni, F.; Tumolo, M.; Berardi, G.; Debab, A.; Haddou, B.; Benhamou, A.; Pollice, A. Optimal Mesh Pore Size Combined with Periodic Air Mass Load (AML) for Effective Operation of a Self-Forming Dynamic Membrane BioReactor (SFD MBR) for Sustainable Treatment of Municipal Wastewater. *Processes* 2024, 12, 323. https://doi.org/10.3390/pr12020323

Academic Editors: Dimitris Zagklis and Georgios Bampos

Received: 10 January 2024
Revised: 26 January 2024
Accepted: 31 January 2024
Published: 2 February 2024

Copyright: © 2024 by the authors. Licensee MDPI, Basel, Switzerland. This article is an open access article distributed under the terms and conditions of the Creative Commons Attribution (CC BY) license (https://creativecommons.org/licenses/by/4.0/).

Abstract: A self-forming dynamic membrane bioreactor (SFD MBR) is a cost-effective alternative to conventional MBR, in which the synthetic membrane is replaced by a "cake layer," an accumulation of the biological suspension over a surface of inert, low-cost support originated by filtration itself. Under optimized conditions, the cake layer is easy to remove and quick to form again, resulting a "dynamic membrane." The permeate of the SFD MBR has chemo-physical characteristics comparable to those of conventional ultrafiltration-based MBR. In this paper, two nylon meshes with pore sizes of 20 and 50 µm, respectively, were tested in a bench-scale SFD MBR in which an air mass load (AML) was periodically supplied tangentially to the filtration surface to maintain filtration effectiveness. The SFD MBR equipped with 20 µm nylon mesh coupled with 5 min of AML every 4 h showed the best performance, ensuring both a permeate with turbidity values always below 3 NTU and revealing no increases in transmembrane pressure (TMP) with manual maintenance needs. A benchmark test with the only difference of a suction break (relaxation) instead of AML was conducted under identical operating conditions for validation with an already known maintenance strategy. This latter test produced a permeate of very good quality, but it needed frequent TMP increases and consequent manual cleanings, showing that a periodic AML coupled with the use of a 20 µm mesh can be an optimal strategy for long-term operation of SFD MBR.

Keywords: biological membrane; SFD MBR; trans-membrane pressure; dynamic membrane; turbidity; air mass load

1. Introduction

The membrane bioreactor (MBR) is an established technology for the treatment and reuse of domestic and industrial wastewater [1–3]. It is based on solid/liquid activated sludge separation through synthetic membranes made of different materials and operated by positive or negative (suction) force. The membrane filtration pore size range for MBR includes micro- and ultra-filtration [4]. In MBR, the role of the membrane is to separate the supernatant from the suspended solids, and this may be obtained by adopting mainly two possible configurations: (i) membranes submerged in the bioreactor (submerged MBR), (ii) membranes immersed in the secondary clarifier or in another separate vessel (sidestream MBR). MBR technology offers several advantages with respect to conventional activated sludge (CAS) systems, including a significantly reduced footprint and improved degradation of pollutants. This is mostly due to the possibility of operating the system with higher concentrations of suspended solids in the mixed liquor (MLSS) and to the absence of a secondary clarifier. Submerged MBR allows for the adsorption, biodegradation, and membrane separation in the same biological tank [5]. Moreover, wastewater treatment plants (WWTPs) based on MBR technology usually produce permeates of excellent quality with very low levels of total suspended solids (TSS), turbidity, chemical oxygen demand (COD), biological oxygen demand (BOD), and pathogens [6]. In specific situations, MBR can be coupled with or integrated into other technologies to ameliorate wastewater treatment performance [7].

Nevertheless, a limitation of the application of MBR is the occurrence of membrane fouling and pore clogging, which deteriorate the system's performance, require maintenance efforts, and may shorten the membrane's service life. Both phenomena are detectable by monitoring the resistance to filtration imposed by the materials that tend to accumulate over the membrane surface or into the membrane structure, called transmembrane pressure (TMP) [8]: when the TMP (in absolute values) rapidly increases, the membrane is fouling/clogging, leading to a decrease in permeate flux. The mechanisms of fouling are: (i) adsorption of soluble microbial products (SMP), extracellular polymeric substances (EPS), colloids, and other particles into/on the membranes; (ii) deposition of sludge flocs on the membrane surface with consequent formation of a "cake" layer on the membrane surface; (iii) changes in membrane and/or mixed liquor composition during long-term operation (e.g., changes in bacterial community and biopolymer components in the cake layer, degradation of membrane composition) [9].

Periodic maintenance of MBR systems is often accomplished either by backwashing the membranes, i.e., temporarily reversing the permeate flow, or by cyclic relaxation from suction, which simply involves stopping permeate extraction for a defined time interval. These techniques do not influence the ordinary functionality of the bioreactor, as they are conventionally incorporated into most MBR designs as standard operational strategies for fouling control, and normally do not require chemical reagents, preventing any risk of membrane degradation/damage [10,11].

When the TMP thresholds determining significant and critical reductions in flux are passed despite periodic maintenance, the membrane needs to be removed from the biological tank to be manually cleaned [12–14]. For MBR in treating municipal wastewater, water jet rinsing is ordinarily enough to remove the pore clogging and excess sludge accumulation and to recover the initial set flux. If the flux is not recovered due to a deep fouling of membrane pores, a chemical treatment is needed [15]. On the contrary, when the TMP does not tend to increase and the quality of permeate decreases, the integrity of the membrane should be tested, with its possible (partial or complete) replacement [16]. This may imply a relevant burden in terms of investment cost.

In the last decade, self-forming dynamic membrane bioreactors (SFD MBRs) were developed as a cost-effective alternative to conventional ultrafiltration (UF)-based MBR, and their application in wastewater treatment has been studied [17,18]. The SFD MBR is a particular MBR in which inert materials (meshes, nets) with medium-large pore-size (in the range of 10–500 µm) are used as supports for the formation of cake layers, these becoming the real biological membrane [19]. Different studies have revealed that the main chemical and physical characteristics of the SFD MBR permeate can be similar to those of conventional MBR permeate, apart from the microbiological quality indicators, so a post-disinfection step is still required, especially in the case of effluent reuse. An advantage of SFD MBR with respect to classical MBR is that chemical or other deep cleaning procedures are rarely used because the medium-large pore-size support media are less exposed to critical clogging than the UF membranes used in MBR, and a physical cleaning is usually enough to remove the cake layer from the support surface. In conventional MBR, the gel layers that may develop over the long term can clog the membrane pores [17]. To solve this, the modules are submitted to chemical treatment for the oxidation and removal of the sticky and colloidal substances that pass inside the small pores. In SFD MBR, controlling and limiting the clogging gel layer is easier due to the larger pore size, and often physical methods, such as water jet rinsing, surface air sparging, permeate backwashing, and flux relaxation, are efficient [20]. Afterwards, the filtration system can soon be restored so that the biological membrane can form again. The easy removal and then reforming of the biological membrane explain why it is also called "dynamic membrane" (DM) [21].

In a green economy context, SFD MBR is a lower-pollutant and energy-saving technology because no chemicals are used for cleaning and lower pressure is required for filtration (in the range of a few hundred mbar, also achievable by gravity) with respect to conventional UF-based MBR.

In a previous paper, Salerno and co-authors showed the effectiveness of SFD MBR for the treatment of municipal wastewater and with limited maintenance needs in tests with low sludge retention time (SRT) [20]. The purpose of the present paper is to evaluate the performance of a bench-scale SFD MBR in treating real municipal sewage with a medium-high SRT of 30 days, having support media with two different pore sizes, and with a maintenance strategy based on a periodic air mass load (AML, large bubbles causing turbulence at the filtration surface). In the first experiment, called test A, a 50 μm nylon mesh was used as the support material for the development of DM with a periodic cleaning of the mesh using a high air mass flow rate in short time. The second test, named test B, was identical to the first but used a 20 μm nylon mesh. Test B had better performance than test A, so it was finally compared to a benchmark test, called test C, under the same conditions and mesh as test B, but with a different and already known maintenance strategy based on periodic relaxation from permeate suction. Finally, the best performance, both in terms of permeate quality and support cleaning requirements, was shown by test B (20 μm SFD MBR coupled with an AML of 5 min every 4 h).

2. Materials and Methods

All bench-scale SFD MBR plants, the features of which are summarized in Table 1, were operated at room temperature, continuously aerated, and under the same operating conditions, except for the pore size of the support mesh and the strategy of periodic maintenance.

Table 1. Main characteristics and operating conditions of the bench-scale SFD MBR plants.

Parameter	Test A	Test B	Test C
SRT	30 days	30 days	30 days
Volume	16.0 L	16.0 L	16.0 L
Filtering area	0.0072 m^2	0.0072 m^2	0.0072 m^2
Target flux	73 L m^{-2} h^{-1}	73 L m^{-2} h^{-1}	73 L m^{-2} h^{-1}
Mesh pore size	50 μm	20 μm	20 μm
Periodic maintenance *	AML	AML	relaxation
No suction time distribution	3′ break + 5′ AML + 3′ break	3′ break + 5′ AML + 3′ break	11′ break

* every 4 h.

In the bench-scale SFD MBR, two filtration modules were positioned vertically and face-to-face, at a distance of about 3 cm from one another, and every single module had a 6 × 6 cm filtration surface, for a total surface of 72 cm^2. Aeration was provided in the reactors by four external air pumps (M2K3, Schego, Frankfurt am Main, Germany), respectively connected to four fine-bubble diffusers placed on the reactor bottom. The pumped air also ensured the necessary mixing of sludge to achieve homogeneity of the suspended biomass. For every test, permeate suction was ensured by a peristaltic pump connected to the filtration modules with a set flow rate of 12.6 L d^{-1}. The TMP was measured by an analogic manometer placed between DM and the suction pump and recorded at least every hour between 9:00 A.M. and 5:00 P.M. from Monday to Friday. In test A, a support nylon mesh with a pore size of 50 μm was used, while a 20 μm nylon mesh was employed in tests B and C. When the TMP overcame the threshold of −200 mbar, the modules were temporarily removed from the bioreactor, washed by tap water jet rinsing, and finally reassembled to restart. As summarized in Table 1, all systems had a periodic 4-h cycle consisting of 229 min of suction and 11 min of no suction. In tests A and B, the no suction time was organized as follows: 3 min of simple suction break, 5 min of AML with an air flow rate of 42.0 L_{air} min^{-1} supplied tangentially to the filtration surface (still without any permeate suction), and another 3 min of suction break, as described by Salerno and colleagues [20]. In Test C, the whole 11 min period was in simple no suction mode, called relaxation. The bioreactor's operating volume was maintained constant through a level control switch connected to the feed pump. The latter was turned on as the level control detected a decrease in the reactor's operating volume, and it was turned off when the volume had been restored. The general scheme for all plants is illustrated in Figure 1.

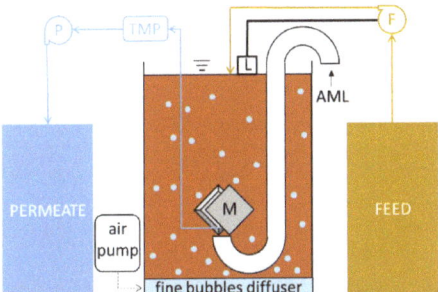

Figure 1. Plant scheme common to all tests. F is the feed pump; L is the level control that activates F; M is the couple of filtration modules; TMP is the manometer measuring transmembrane pressure; P is the permeate suction pump; AML is the periodic air mass load pipeline (not present in test C).

Real pre-settled municipal wastewater was collected twice per week from the municipal wastewater treatment plant of Giovinazzo (41°10′39.6″ N 16°41′04.5″ E, Area Metropolitana di Bari, Italy), managed by Acquedotto Pugliese S.p.A. (Bari, Italy). The wastewater was characterized, diluted to the target value of 460 mg COD L^{-1}, and finally given as feed to the SFD MBR. Table 2 shows the average characteristics of the feed.

Table 2. Main conventional parameters of the wastewater feeding the SFD MBR.

Parameter	Unit	Average ± St.Dev.
TSS	mg L^{-1}	248.8 ± 103.6
VSS	mg L^{-1}	243.2 ± 95.9
COD	mg L^{-1}	460.0 ± 22.6
soluble COD	mg L^{-1}	112.3 ± 49.0
TN	mg L^{-1}	65.5 ± 17.3
$N-NH_4^+$	mg L^{-1}	42.0 ± 11.1
$N-NO_2^-$	mg L^{-1}	0.1 ± 0.0
$N-NO_3^-$	mg L^{-1}	0.2 ± 0.2
pH	-	7.4 ± 0.2
Electr. conductivity	mS cm^{-1}	1.3 ± 0.5
Tot. coliforms	MPN 100 mL^{-1}	2.5×10^7 (median); 2.0×10^6 (min); 7.9×10^7 (max)
E. coli	MPN 100 mL^{-1}	7.9×10^6 (median); 3.0×10^5 (min); 2.9×10^7 (max)

Both the feeding wastewater and the produced permeate were characterized twice per week in terms of total and volatile suspended solids (TSS and VSS, respectively), chemical oxygen demand (COD), total nitrogen (TN), ammonium, nitrite, and nitrate, according to standard methods [22]. Electrical conductivity and pH were measured with an InnoLab® Multi 9420 IDS (WTW, Weilheim, Germany), while permeate turbidity was determined by a 2100P turbidimeter (HACH, Loveland, CO, USA). The activated sludge was characterized on the same days as the feed and permeate. The mixed liquor suspended solids (MLSS) and the sludge volume index at 30 min (SVI_{30}) of the SFD MBR activated sludge were measured according to standard methods [22]. Conventionally, the SVI_{30} is an evaluation test of sludge settling capacity [23]. A phase-contrast microscope BX50 (Olympus, Tokyo, Japan) was used to evaluate the morphological characteristics of the activated sludge.

3. Results

3.1. Activated Sludge Characteristics

The activated sludge features during the three tests are displayed in Table 3.

Table 3. Activated sludge characteristics during the different tests.

Parameter	Unit	Test A	Test B	Test C
MLSS	g L^{-1}	3.4 ± 1.2	4.4 ± 1.3	2.9 ± 1.6
MLVSS	g L^{-1}	3.0 ± 1.0	3.8 ± 1.1	2.6 ± 1.4
SVI$_{30}$	mL g^{-1}	64.3 ± 14.1	92.1 ± 8.6	43.9 ± 9.9
Temperature	°C	20.0 ± 0.6	20.2 ± 0.2	22.5 ± 0.8
DO	mg L^{-1}	6.3 ± 1.1	4.1 ± 1.2	6.2 ± 1.8
ORP	mV	305.5 ± 39.1	294.6 ± 6.2	314.8 ± 9.7
pH	-	6.8 ± 0.5	7.1 ± 0.5	7.0 ± 0.8

Generally, all of the SFD MBR tests had average concentrations of mixed liquor suspended solids (MLSS) between 3 and 4.5 g L^{-1}, with about 90% volatile suspended solids (MLVSS). The SVI$_{30}$ values of the tests never approached the threshold of 150 mL g^{-1}, after which sludge bulking generally occurs [24]. The pumped oxygen ensured aerobic conditions in all experiments, achieving dissolved oxygen (DO) values always well above 3 mg L^{-1}, and the redox potential (ORP) and pH average values were always around 300 mV and 7.0, respectively. Images of fresh activated sludge taken by a phase-contrast microscope at 100× magnification and related to four different moments for each test are shown in Figure 2.

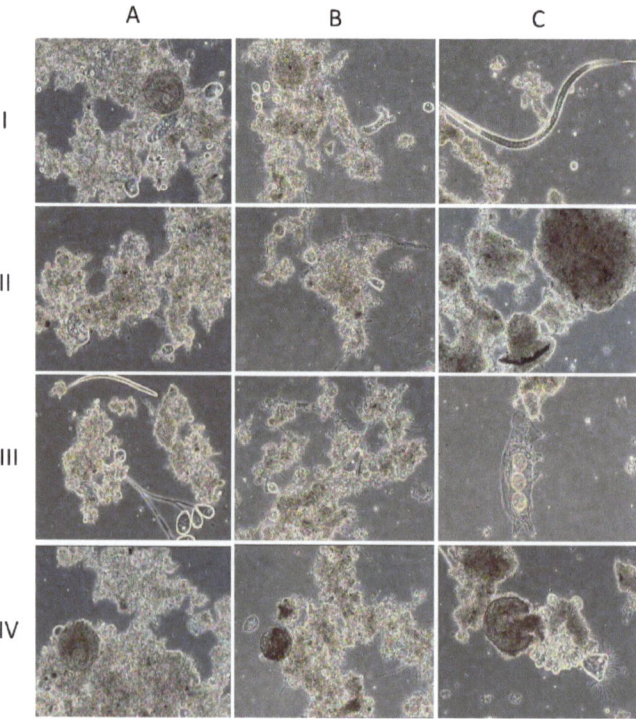

Figure 2. Activated sludge samples under phase-contrast microscopy at 100× magnification. The three tests are reported in columns (**A–C**), each one represented by four pictures in each column (**I–IV**).

3.2. Performance of the SFD MBR Tests

Figure 3 shows the trends in permeate turbidity, flux, and wash events for every test.

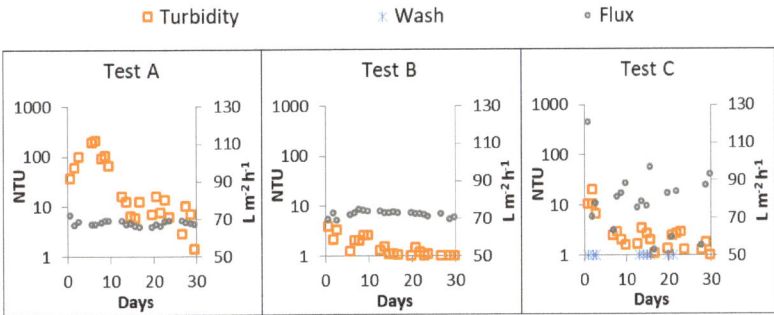

Figure 3. Trends in permeate turbidity, flux, and wash events of Tests A, B and C, respectively. Turbidity values are expressed in terms of nephelometric turbidity unit (NTU), while flux values are expressed in terms of liters per square meter per hour (L m^{-2} h^{-1}).

Tests A and B maintained the set flux over time, while test C was revealed to be more problematic and the flux was more heavily affected by the filtration efficiency. Indeed, the higher frequency of TMP increase observed in test C caused a decrease in permeate flux and was only temporarily solved with module washing. On the contrary, in tests A and B, the TMP did not tend to increase over time, and consequently no module washing was required. Moreover, test C showed some fluctuations in the permeate turbidity, but still with an average value of around 5 NTU. Test B always produced an effluent with turbidity values even below 3 NTU. Generally, when the mesh with 20 µm pore size was adopted (tests B and C), the permeate turbidity was consistently under 10 NTU. On the contrary, in test A (equipped with 50 µm mesh), the permeate turbidity was always higher than 50 NTU during the first 10 days (with a peak of 211 NTU), which decreased to lower values around 10 NTU in the following 20 days, reaching values below 5 NTU toward the end of the test. In Table 4, the main quality parameters of the three permeates are compared. The total coliforms and *Escherichia coli* contents in all permeates showed median, minimum, and maximum values between 4 and 5 Log and between 3 and 5 Log, respectively.

Table 4. Comparison of the produced permeates from every SFD MBR.

Parameter	Unit	Test A	Test B	Test C
TSS	mg L^{-1}	366.7 ± 78.5	4.7 ± 1.9	6.4 ± 6.2
COD	mg L^{-1}	103.0 ± 86.7	30.4 ± 5.0	32.8 ± 6.2
TN	mg L^{-1}	98.7 ± 52.1	55.1 ± 5.3	41.3 ± 8.8
N-NH$_4^+$	mg L^{-1}	1.0 ± 2.3	0.1 ± 0.1	0.3 ± 0.3
N-NO$_2^-$	mg L^{-1}	0.0 ± 0.0	0.0 ± 0.0	1.6 ± 0.9
N-NO$_3^-$	mg L^{-1}	24.7 ± 5.1	35.7 ± 6.7	27.1 ± 7.3
Electr. conductivity	mS cm^{-1}	1.0 ± 0.1	0.8 ± 0.0	1.1 ± 0.0
pH	-	7.1 ± 0.8	7.4 ± 0.3	7.3 ± 0.3
Tot. coliforms	MPN 100 mL^{-1}	1.6 × 10^5 (median)	4.4 × 10^5 (median)	1.6 × 10^4 (median)
		1.3 × 10^5 (min)	5.0 × 10^4 (min)	1.0 × 10^4 (min)
		1.9 × 10^5 (max)	4.6 × 10^5 (max)	2.2 × 10^4 (max)
E. coli	MPN 100 mL^{-1}	6.0 × 10^4 (median)	1.0 × 10^5 (median)	8.2 × 10^3 (median)
		5.8 × 10^4 (min)	2.0 × 10^4 (min)	6.3 × 10^3 (min)
		6.3 × 10^4 (max)	2.2 × 10^5 (max)	1.0 × 10^4 (max)

4. Discussion

4.1. Activated Sludge Characteristics

The characteristics of the activated sludge were evaluated applying the microscopy methods indicated by Jenkins and colleagues [25]. Generally, the phase-contrast microscopy revealed very similar morphological features among the activated sludges sampled during the three tests. Particularly, all three bioreactors had an average floc size in the range of 150–500 µm. Moreover, in all cases, the flocs appeared to be irregular but compact, with the presence of eukaryotic organisms typical of activated sludge (e.g., both swimming and stalked ciliates, nematodes, tardigrades, or rotifers). The bacterial filaments/floc ratio was also monitored, always resulting in the range of 2–5, as normally expected. The whole of these observations indicated that all sludges had a general state of good health.

The relatively lower DO concentration of test B (still well above the normal threshold recommended for aerobic activated sludge bioreactors) with respect to the other two tests may have depended on the higher average MLSS concentration observed, considering that all three plants had the same air flow rates. The SVI_{30} values revealed a higher settling capacity of the sludge of test C, followed by those of tests A and B. Moreover, the SVI_{30} average value of test B was twice that of test C, while the average value of test A was more or less halfway between tests B and C, highlighting some differences in the physical properties of the three sludges. Figure 3 showed that test C faced several stops for mesh cleaning with removal of the DM from the mesh, its recovery, and re-entry of the sludge cake material in the suspended activated sludge. This may have affected the sludge settling ability. Similarly, also in Figure 3, test A showed the loss of part of the suspended biomass in the permeate during the first weeks, possibly influencing the sludge settling. The SVI_{30} can also give indications about the possible bulking phenomenon due to the presence of filamentous bacteria, about the sludge density, and about the presence of sticky substances in the supernatant of the mixed liquor [26–28]. Nevertheless, the bulking threshold was not exceeded in any test, and the physiological features of all three sludges appeared similar, as already described above. Therefore, further functional investigations of the effects of activated sludge imbalances or disturbances on the settling ability, such as those shown in the described tests, are suggested for future research.

4.2. Permeate Quality in the Different SFD MBR Tests

The 20 µm SFD MBR tests produced permeates with very low turbidity values (Figure 3). Besides turbidity, the lower quality of the permeate of test A (50 µm) was also confirmed by other parameters. Lower solid retention was clearly revealed by the permeate TSS value, which was on average one order of magnitude higher with respect to tests B and C, but also by the permeate COD and TN average values, which were three and two times higher than the other two tests, respectively. This suggested that under the applied operating conditions, the 50 µm mesh had lower efficiency in supporting the cake layer than the 20 µm mesh, as shown in the other two tests. The aerobic conditions ensured very good nitrification for all SFD MBR tests, considering the average values of ammonium, nitrite, and nitrate in the permeates. The average ammonium value in the permeate of test A was affected by a high punctual value of 6.6 mgN L^{-1} on day 7, when a peak in solids in the permeate was also detected. In the rest of test A, the ammonium measured in the permeate was always less than 1 mgN L^{-1}. In terms of nitrite content, the permeate of test C had an average value of nitrite equal to 1.6 mgN L^{-1}, while under the applied aerobic conditions, it was expected to be almost null (Table 3). This could be explained by the low MLVSS concentration, which represents an estimate of the active bacterial content [29], and the relatively high concentration of ammonium in the feeding wastewater (Table 2). These results suggested that ammonium oxidation may have tended toward its maximum rate, which was higher than the maximum rate of nitrite oxidation, leading to a slight residual nitrite accumulation [30].

The total coliforms and *E. coli* assays in all SFD MBR permeates showed the relative independence of these microbiological indicators from physical determinations such as turbidity and TSS of permeates, confirming the need for further disinfection steps of the

SFD MBR permeates in case of reuse. In this sense, the use of already tested on demand UV disinfection systems could be recommended [3]. As a possible alternative, direct exposure to solar light could represent an easy and green solution [31].

4.3. Effects of the Mesh Pore Size and the AML on SFD MBR Performance

The pore size of the support material was demonstrated to play a relevant role during the initial formation phase of dynamic membranes and after cleaning of the support itself [32]. In the same paper, the authors asserted that the mesh pore size had negligible effects on the cleaning requirements and a small influence on the effluent quality under their tested conditions (overall a permanent slight air scouring), i.e., a stop for TMP increase at least once every 5 days, in their best case. In the present paper, the choice of 20 or 50 μm was demonstrated to be relevant when coupled with AML. As matter of fact, differently from "50 μm mesh + AML", the combination "20 μm mesh + AML" was revealed to be optimal for better permeate quality and quicker formation of a new DM after the periodic manual cleaning of the support. Cai and colleagues demonstrated that a larger pore size of the support material can cause a significant loss of biomass in the early phase of cake formation [33]. In the same paper, before the formation of the self-forming dynamic membrane (SFDM), the turbidity obtained using a 50 μm mesh could be higher than 250 NTU, similar to the turbidity peak of test A (50 μm) described herein. Adopting two other meshes with 25 and 10 μm pore sizes, the same authors obtained turbidity values lower than 40 and 10 NTU, respectively. Nevertheless, once the SFDM was formed and stable operations were achieved, no correlation between the pore size of the support material and the quality of the permeate was observed. Saleem and coworkers [34] reported that using a 50 μm pore size support net, although it contributed to improving the SFDM effluent quality in terms of turbidity values with respect to the 200 μm net, accelerated the mesh clogging, resulting in a faster TMP increase, and therefore in more frequent cleanings. Another study from Sreeda and coworkers [35] reported that the pore size of the support medium did not affect the formation of the SFDM, and that the bacterial composition of an SFDM grown on a support with a pore size of 2 mm was similar to the one observed on other much smaller pore size nets. In a previous work by Chuang and colleagues [36], the use of a 14 μm support material led to a supernatant with more than 95% of particles between 0.2 and 6.4 μm in size, and large particles (>10 μm) accounted for less than 1%. Nevertheless, some particles accumulated inside the pores and caused clogging. Moreover, in a work by most of the authors of the present paper [37], a continuous slight air scouring was used to control the excess DM growth. Those conditions were observed to be effective at relatively high MLSS values. In the tests described in the current manuscript, the combination of "20 μm mesh + AML" showed no TMP increases (on the contrary of Vergine and colleagues, wherein even the best experiment required at least one manual cleaning per week), suggesting good control of the excess DM growth over time and very low effluent turbidity.

There are different possible approaches to mesh cleaning in order to resume the filtration performance. As previously described, water jet rinsing proved to be effective when the sludge was sufficiently dense and in "good health" (i.e., not subject to stress conditions due to feed or operation). Nevertheless, physical mesh cleaning usually has temporary effects on the system's filtration performance, with losses of suspended solids through the mesh and a decrease in overall effluent quality during the transient phase of new DM formation [21]. When the activated sludge faces stress, it can produce bioproducts such as soluble microbial products (SMP), extracellular polymeric substances (EPS), or other classes with colloidal characteristics that could reduce the pore size, stick on the support surface, and make physical cleaning less effective. Under these conditions, water jet rinsing should be integrated with chemical cleaning. Weak acids, bases, and oxidants are typical cleaning reagents, while metal-chelating chemicals, surfactants, and formulated detergents may also be used [38]. Guan and colleagues [39] compared the cleaning effects of sodium dodecylsulfate (SDS), NaOH, and NaClO on three identical fouled modules. Their results showed that the main fouling of SFD MBR was a complex mixture of bacterial flocs and EPS, and that NaClO was the best performing reagent for SFD MBR chemical cleaning in terms of TMP, flux recovery, and total resistance reduction, successfully oxidizing both the EPS and the bacterial flocs. The authors also found that SDS and NaOH were effective in removing the EPS, but they were not effective in removing mixed fouling as well as β-polysaccharides.

The use of air sparging for mesh cleaning is well known in the literature [19]. Rezvani and colleagues [40] adopted an SFD MBR with a similar configuration as that proposed in this paper, except for the use of synthetic wastewater, a lower suction flux for long-term operation (30 L m^{-2} h^{-1}), and overall continuous permeate suction until TMP reached the value of 26 kPa (equal to 260 mbar, to use the same unit of the present paper). At that moment, an air flow rate of 0.3 m^3 h^{-1} (5 L min^{-1}) was applied for 30 min to clean the mesh. This means that a total of 150 L of air was sparged for cleaning the mesh when the TMP had reached the threshold. In the present paper, an air flow rate of 42 L min^{-1} adopted for 5 min (i.e., 210 L of air) was used for periodic preventive air cleaning. Nevertheless, the permeate quality of the best combination reported in this paper (20 μm mesh + AML) was better than the one obtained by Rezvani and co-workers in terms of filtration performance. Anyway, it must be taken into account that the same authors used synthetic wastewater, different from the real wastewater used in the present paper. As matter of fact, it is very likely that the activated sludge of Rezvani's test and those described here had different compositions, possibly influencing the quality of DM. Further investigations of the air cleaning flow rate and time for AML to optimize preventive fouling control of SFD MBR in treating real wastewater shall be conducted. Indeed, a preventive, quick, intense, and periodic air mass load for mesh cleaning coupled with the more appropriate pore size to achieve a very performant SFD MBR has not yet been optimized. The results of the present research have shown that the SFD MBR plants having mesh supports with 50 μm and 20 μm pore sizes operated under the same operating conditions, including a stable working flux of more than 70 L m^{-2} h^{-1}, had different permeate quality trends from the first days. This can be attributed to the speed of sludge cake formation and DM development. In particular, the 20 μm mesh demonstrated more efficiency in rapid DM build-up, with consequent production of permeates with turbidity always lower than 3 NTU. A second important finding was the demonstration that a periodic air mass load with a flow rate of 42.0 L$_{air}$ min^{-1} for 5 min every 4 h achieved and kept the stability of the system with no need of washing the mesh support on site. Test B was compared to the benchmark (test C) and confirmed the effectiveness of the combination of 20 μm with AML with respect to a conventional maintenance strategy based on simple periodic interruption of filtration (relaxation). Other studies are required to investigate the optimal air mass load flow rate and duration to achieve the best cleaning efficiency and most sustainable operation for meshes of different pore sizes in order to optimize the overall system performance.

5. Conclusions

Two different nylon meshes of 20 and 50 μm pore sizes were used as corresponding supports for the development of a biological DM in three parallel SFD MBR tests for the treatment of real municipal wastewater. In two tests, the nylon meshes had different pore sizes, but both were periodically cleaned through an AML (air mass load, i.e., large bubbles causing turbulence) with a flow rate of 42.0 L$_{air}$ min^{-1} for 5 min every 4 h. The third test was equipped with the 20 μm pore size and operated with periodic interruption of filtration for DM relaxation. The SFD MBR with 20 μm nylon mesh was revealed to be more efficient in the production of a high-quality permeate in comparison with the larger 50 μm pores. The maintenance strategy based on an intense AML of 5 min every 4 h was effective in controlling the excessive build-up of the cake layer and maintaining a relatively stable DM. On the other hand, relaxation during the maintenance breaks was not very efficient in controlling the excessive DM growth under the experimental conditions tested. Optimization of the AML in terms of flow rate and time will require further investigation, also depending on the mesh pore size adopted, the sludge characteristics, and the operating conditions. Nevertheless, the present results confirm the sustainability and effectiveness of the approach proposed for long-term operation of SFD MBR for municipal wastewater treatment.

Author Contributions: Conceptualization, C.S.; methodology, C.S., F.C. and A.P.; software, M.T.; validation, A.D., B.H. and A.B.; formal analysis, G.B. and F.C.; investigation, S.B. and G.B; resources, A.P.; data curation G.B., F.C. and M.T.; writing—original draft preparation, S.B. and C.S.; writing—review and editing, S.B., C.S. and A.P.; visualization, A.D., B.H. and A.B.; supervision, A.P.; project administration, A.P.; funding acquisition, A.P. All authors have read and agreed to the published version of the manuscript.

Funding: This research was partially supported by the EU-India project "Pavitra Ganga" funded by the EC with contract n. 821051, call H2020 SC5-12-2018.

Data Availability Statement: The data presented in this study are available upon request from the corresponding author.

Conflicts of Interest: The authors declare no conflicts of interest.

References

1. Friha, I.; Karray, F.; Feki, F.; Jlaiel, L.; Sayadi, S. Treatment of cosmetic industry wastewater by submerged membrane bioreactor with consideration of microbial community dynamics. *Int. Biodeterior. Biodegrad.* **2014**, *88*, 125–133. [CrossRef]
2. Hoinkis, J.; Gukelberger, E.; Atiye, T.; Galiano, F.; Figoli, A.; Gabriele, B.; Mancuso, R.; Mamo, J.; Clough, S.; Hoevenaars, K. Membrane Bioreactor (MBR) Treated Domestic Wastewater for Reuse in a Recirculating Aquaculture System (RAS). In *Water-Energy-Nexus in the Ecological Transition: Natural-Based Solutions, Advanced Technologies and Best Practices for Environmental Sustainability*; Naddeo, V., Choo, K.-H., Ksibi, M., Eds.; Advances in Science, Technology & Innovation; Springer International Publishing: Cham, Switzerland, 2022; pp. 153–155. [CrossRef]
3. Vergine, P.; Amalfitano, S.; Salerno, C.; Berardi, G.; Pollice, A. Reuse of ultrafiltered effluents for crop irrigation: On-site flow cytometry unveiled microbial removal patterns across a full-scale tertiary treatment. *Sci. Total Environ.* **2020**, *718*, 137298. [CrossRef] [PubMed]
4. Asif, M.B.; Zhang, Z.; Vu, M.T.; Mohammed, J.A.H.; Pathak, N.; Nghiem, L.D.; Nguyen, L.N. Membrane Bioreactor for Wastewater Treatment: Current Status, Novel Configurations and Cost Analysis. In *Cost-Efficient Wastewater Treatment Technologies: Engineered Systems*; Nasr, M., Negm, A.M., Eds., The Handbook of Environmental Chemistry; Springer International Publishing: Cham, Switzerland, 2023; pp. 147–167. [CrossRef]
5. Judd, S.J.; Le-Clech, P.; Taha, T.; Cui, Z.F. Theoretical and experimental representation of a submerged membrane bio-reactor system. *Membr. Technol.* **2001**, *2001*, 4–9. [CrossRef]
6. Wu, Y.; Huang, X.; Wen, X.; Chen, F. Function of dynamic membrane in self-forming dynamic membrane coupled bioreactor. *Water Sci. Technol.* **2005**, *51*, 107–114. [CrossRef] [PubMed]
7. Borea, L.; Castrogiovanni, F.; Ferro, G.; Hasan, S.W.; Belgiorno, V.; Naddeo, V. Hydrogen Production in Electro Membrane Bioreactors. In *Frontiers in Water-Energy-Nexus—Nature-Based Solutions, Advanced Technologies and Best Practices for Environmental Sustainability*; Naddeo, V., Balakrishnan, M., Choo, K.-H., Eds.; Advances in Science, Technology & Innovation; Springer International Publishing: Cham, Switzerland, 2020; pp. 85–87.
8. Hasan, S.W.; Elektorowicz, M.; Oleszkiewicz, J.A. Correlations between trans-membrane pressure (TMP) and sludge properties in submerged membrane electro-bioreactor (SMEBR) and conventional membrane bioreactor (MBR). *Bioresour. Technol.* **2012**, *120*, 199–205. [CrossRef] [PubMed]
9. Meng, F.; Chae, S.-R.; Drews, A.; Kraume, M.; Shin, H.-S.; Yang, F. Recent advances in membrane bioreactors (MBRs): Membrane fouling and membrane material. *Water Res.* **2009**, *43*, 1489–1512. [CrossRef]
10. Le-Clech, P.; Chen, V.; Fane, T.A.G. Fouling in membrane bioreactors used in wastewater treatment. *J. Membr. Sci.* **2006**, *284*, 17–53. [CrossRef]
11. Judd, S.; Judd, C. (Eds.) *The MBR Book*, 2nd ed.; Butterworth-Heinemann: Oxford, UK, 2011. [CrossRef]
12. Field, R.W.; Pearce, G.K. Critical, sustainable and threshold fluxes for membrane filtration with water industry applications. *Adv. Colloid Interface Sci.* **2011**, *164*, 38–44. [CrossRef]
13. Stoller, M.; Bravi, M.; Chianese, A. Threshold flux measurements of a nanofiltration membrane module by critical flux data conversion. *Desalination* **2013**, *315*, 142–148. [CrossRef]
14. Xie, W.; Li, J.; Sun, F.; Dong, W.; Dong, Z. Strategy study of critical flux/threshold flux on alleviating protein fouling of PVDF-TiO$_2$ modified membrane. *J. Environ. Chem. Eng.* **2021**, *9*, 106148. [CrossRef]
15. Wei, C.-H.; Huang, X.; Ben Aim, R.; Yamamoto, K.; Amy, G. Critical flux and chemical cleaning-in-place during the long-term operation of a pilot-scale submerged membrane bioreactor for municipal wastewater treatment. *Water Res.* **2011**, *45*, 863–871. [CrossRef]

16. Moattari, R.M.; Mohammadi, T.; Rajabzadeh, S.; Dabiryan, H.; Matsuyama, H. Reinforced hollow fiber membranes: A comprehensive review. *J. Taiwan Inst. Chem. Eng.* **2021**, *122*, 284–310. [CrossRef]
17. Mohan, S.M.; Nagalakshmi, S. A review on aerobic self-forming dynamic membrane bioreactor: Formation, performance, fouling and cleaning. *J. Water Process Eng.* **2020**, *37*, 101541. [CrossRef]
18. Xiao, T.; Zhu, Z.; Li, L.; Shi, J.; Li, Z.; Zuo, X. Membrane fouling and cleaning strategies in microfiltration/ultrafiltration and dynamic membrane. *Sep. Purif. Technol.* **2023**, *318*, 123977. [CrossRef]
19. Ersahin, M.E.; Ozgun, H.; Dereli, R.K.; Ozturk, I.; Roest, K.; Van Lier, J.B. A review on dynamic membrane filtration: Materials, applications and future perspectives. *Bioresour. Technol.* **2012**, *122*, 196–206. [CrossRef] [PubMed]
20. Salerno, C.; Berardi, G.; Casale, B.; Pollice, A. Comparison of fine bubble scouring, backwash, and mass air load supply for dynamic membrane maintenance and steady operation in SFD MBR for wastewater treatment. *J. Water Process Eng.* **2023**, *53*, 103846. [CrossRef]
21. How, S.W.; Kang, C.; Min, S.; Carrera, P.; Siddiqui, M.A.; Chen, G.; Wu, D. 13 – Self-Forming Dynamic Membrane BioReactors (SFDMBRs) for wastewater treatment. In *Current Developments in Biotechnology and Bioengineering: Membrane Technology for Sustainable Water and Energy Management*; Bui, X.-T., Guo, W., Chiemchaisri, C., Pandey, A., Eds.; Elsevier: Amsterdam, The Netherlands, 2023; pp. 293–311. [CrossRef]
22. American Public Health Association (APHA); American Water Works Association (AWWA); Water Environment Federation (WEF). *Standard Methods for the Examination of Water and Wastewater*, 24th ed.; Lipps, W., Braun-Howland, E., Baxter, T., Eds.; APHA Press: Washington, DC, USA, 2023; Available online: https://www.standardmethods.org/ (accessed on 16 November 2023).
23. Kim, Y.; Yeom, H.; Choi, S.; Bae, H.; Kim, C. Sludge settleability detection using automated SV30 measurement and comparisons of feature extraction methods. *Korean J. Chem. Eng.* **2010**, *27*, 886–892. [CrossRef]
24. Han, H.; Wu, X.; Ge, L.; Qiao, J. A sludge volume index (SVI) model based on the multivariate local quadratic polynomial regression method. *Chin. J. Chem. Eng.* **2018**, *26*, 1071–1077. [CrossRef]
25. Jenkins, D.; Richard, M.G.; Daigger, G.T. *Manual on the Causes and Control of Activated Sludge Bulking, Foaming, and Other Solids Separation Problems*, 3rd ed.; CRC Press: Boca Raton, FL, USA, 2003. [CrossRef]
26. Chen, X.; Kong, F.; Fu, Y.; Si, C.; Fatehi, P. Improvements on activated sludge settling and flocculation using biomass-based fly ash as activator. *Sci. Rep.* **2019**, *9*, 14590. [CrossRef]
27. Maltos, R.A.; Holloway, R.W.; Cath, T.Y. Enhancement of activated sludge wastewater treatment with hydraulic selection. *Sep. Purif. Technol.* **2020**, *250*, 117214. [CrossRef]
28. Nittami, T.; Batinovic, S. Recent advances in understanding the ecology of the filamentous bacteria responsible for activated sludge bulking. *Lett. Appl. Microbiol.* **2022**, *75*, 759–775. [CrossRef]
29. Gerardi, M.H. Appendix I: F/M, HRT, MCRT, MLVSS, Sludge Age, SVI. In *Settleability Problems and Loss of Solids in the Activated Sludge Process*; John Wiley & Sons, Ltd.: Hoboken, NJ, USA, 2002; pp. 153–156. [CrossRef]
30. Zhao, W.; Bi, X.; Bai, M.; Wang, Y. Research advances of ammonia oxidation microorganisms in wastewater: Metabolic characteristics, microbial community, influencing factors and process applications. *Bioprocess Biosyst. Eng.* **2023**, *46*, 621–633. [CrossRef]
31. Vivar, M.; Fuentes, M.; Torres, J.; Rodrigo, M.J. Solar disinfection as a direct tertiary treatment of a wastewater plant using a photochemical-photovoltaic hybrid system. *J. Water Process Eng.* **2021**, *42*, 102196. [CrossRef]
32. Vergine, P.; Salerno, C.; Casale, B.; Berardi, G.; Pollice, A. Role of Mesh Pore Size in Dynamic Membrane Bioreactors. *Int. J. Environ. Res. Public. Health* **2021**, *18*, 1472. [CrossRef]
33. Cai, D.; Huang, J.; Liu, G.; Li, M.; Yu, Y.; Meng, F. Effect of support material pore size on the filtration behavior of dynamic membrane bioreactor. *Bioresour. Technol.* **2018**, *255*, 359–363. [CrossRef]
34. Saleem, M.; Masut, E.; Spagni, A.; Lavagnolo, M.C. Exploring dynamic membrane as an alternative for conventional membrane for the treatment of old landfill leachate. *J. Environ. Manag.* **2019**, *246*, 658–667. [CrossRef]
35. Sreeda, P.; Sathya, A.B.; Sivasubramanian, V. Novel application of high-density polyethylene mesh as self-forming dynamic membrane integrated into a bioreactor for wastewater treatment. *Environ. Technol.* **2018**, *39*, 51–58. [CrossRef]
36. Chuang, S.-H.; Lin, P.-K.; Chang, W.-C. Dynamic fouling behaviors of submerged nonwoven bioreactor for filtration of activated sludge with different SRT. *Bioresour. Technol.* **2011**, *102*, 7768–7776. [CrossRef] [PubMed]
37. Vergine, P.; Salerno, C.; Berardi, G.; Pollice, A. Self-Forming Dynamic Membrane BioReactors (SFD MBR) for municipal wastewater treatment: Relevance of solids retention time and biological process stability. *Sep. Purif. Technol.* **2021**, *255*, 117735. [CrossRef]
38. Wang, Z.; Ma, J.; Tang, C.Y.; Kimura, K.; Wang, Q.; Han, X. Membrane cleaning in membrane bioreactors: A review. *Membr. Clean. Membr. Bioreact. Rev.* **2014**, *468*, 276–307. [CrossRef]
39. Guan, D.; Dai, J.; Ahmar Siddiqui, M.; Chen, G. Comparison of different chemical cleaning reagents on fouling recovery in a Self-Forming dynamic membrane bioreactor (SFDMBR). *Sep. Purif. Technol.* **2018**, *206*, 158–165. [CrossRef]
40. Rezvani, F.; Mehrnia, M.R.; Poostchi, A.A. Optimal operating strategies of SFDM formation for MBR application. *Sep. Purif. Technol.* **2014**, *124*, 124–133. [CrossRef]

Disclaimer/Publisher's Note: The statements, opinions and data contained in all publications are solely those of the individual author(s) and contributor(s) and not of MDPI and/or the editor(s). MDPI and/or the editor(s) disclaim responsibility for any injury to people or property resulting from any ideas, methods, instructions or products referred to in the content.

Article

Apple Pomace-Derived Cationic Cellulose Nanocrystals for PFAS Removal from Contaminated Water

Luis A. Franco [1,†], T. Dwyer Stuart [1,†], Md Shahadat Hossain [1], Bandaru V. Ramarao [1], Charlene C. VanLeuven [2], Mario Wriedt [3], Michael Satchwell [4] and Deepak Kumar [1,*]

[1] Department of Chemical Engineering, SUNY College of Environmental Science and Forestry, Syracuse, NY 13210, USA
[2] Department of Chemistry & Biomolecular Science, Clarkson University, Potsdam, NY 13699, USA
[3] Department of Chemistry and Biochemistry, University of Texas at Dallas, Richardson, TX 75080, USA
[4] Analytical and Technical Services, SUNY College of Environmental Science and Forestry, Syracuse, NY 13210, USA
* Correspondence: dkumar02@esf.edu; Tel.: +1-(315)-470-6503
† These authors contributed equally to this work.

Abstract: Per- and poly-fluoroalkyl substances (PFAS) are concerning contaminants due to their ubiquity, persistence, and toxicity. Conventional PFAS water treatments such as granular activated carbon are limited by low adsorption rates and capacities. Carbon-based nano-adsorbents with enhanced surface areas address these limitations but are hindered by their high cost and toxicity. Cellulose nanocrystals (CNC) are promising PFAS adsorbents due to sustainable sourcing, large surface areas, and amenable surface properties. In this study, CNC was synthesized from the agro-food waste, apple pomace (APCNC), and coated with *Moringa oleifera* cationic protein (MOCP) aqueous extract to produce MOCP/APCNC for the removal of perfluorooctanoic acid (PFOA) from water. APCNC and MOCP/APCNC were manufactured, characterized, and utilized in PFOA batch adsorption kinetics and equilibrium trials. APCNC was successfully produced from apple pomace (AP) and determined through characterization and comparison to commercial CNC (CCNC). APCNC and MOCP/APCNC exhibited rapid PFOA adsorption, approaching equilibrium within 15 min. MOCP coatings inverted the MOCP/CNC surface charge to cationic (−15.07 to 7.38 mV) and enhanced the PFOA adsorption rate (2.65×10^{-3} to 5.05×10^{-3} g/mg/s), capacity (47.1 to 61.1 mg/g), and robustness across varied water qualities. The sustainable sourcing of APCNC combined with a green surface coating to produce MOCP/CNC provides a highly promising environmentally friendly approach to PFAS remediation.

Keywords: PFAS adsorption; cellulose nanocrystals; agro-food processing waste valorization; *Moringa oleifera*; biodegradable coatings

Citation: Franco, L.A.; Stuart, T.D.; Hossain, M.S.; Ramarao, B.V.; VanLeuven, C.C.; Wriedt, M.; Satchwell, M.; Kumar, D. Apple Pomace-Derived Cationic Cellulose Nanocrystals for PFAS Removal from Contaminated Water. *Processes* **2024**, *12*, 297. https://doi.org/10.3390/pr12020297

Academic Editors: Dimitris Zagklis and Georgios Bampos

Received: 5 January 2024
Revised: 24 January 2024
Accepted: 26 January 2024
Published: 30 January 2024

Copyright: © 2024 by the authors. Licensee MDPI, Basel, Switzerland. This article is an open access article distributed under the terms and conditions of the Creative Commons Attribution (CC BY) license (https://creativecommons.org/licenses/by/4.0/).

1. Introduction

Per- and poly-fluoroalkyl substances (PFAS) have been used extensively since the 1950s for various industrial and commercial applications [1]. The high durability and water solubility of PFAS cause aquatic environmental persistence [2]. PFAS is released into the environment through industrial discharges, landfills, and consumer products [3]. PFAS exposure, specifically to perfluorooctanesulfonic acid (PFOS) and perfluorooctanoic acid (PFOA), has been associated with cancer, immunotoxicity, liver damage, and neurodevelopmental effects [4]. These growing health concerns have stimulated national efforts to remove PFAS from drinking water. In March 2023, the Biden administration announced the first-ever national PFAS regulations mandating public water utilities to test the concentration levels for six different PFAS chemicals and warn the public if these levels exceed the set limits (four parts per trillion (ppt) for PFOA). Increased awareness of the presence and risks of PFAS-contaminated water has spurred the development of PFAS remediation technologies.

Various technologies have been investigated for aqueous PFAS remediation. There is an urgent need to develop scalable, cost-effective, and sustainable PFAS water treatments. Adsorption technologies using activated carbon, biomaterials, minerals, ion exchange resins, and nanomaterials are widely explored [5–7]. Granular activated carbon (GAC) and anion exchange resins (AEX) are the most common adsorbents because of high removal efficiencies due to elevated specific surface areas [8]. Adsorption is used for PFAS-contaminated water due to low energy demand, simple operation, and economic feasibility [9]. Nanomaterials are excellent adsorbents due to their high specific surface area and reactivities [10,11]. However, the implementation of nanomaterials to remove PFAS is hindered by high costs, toxicities, and low biodegradability [12]. Cellulose nanocrystals (CNC) represent a sustainable alternative with a comparatively negligible carbon footprint and toxicity [13]. CNCs have unique mechanical, optical, and chemical properties, including high surface area, high aspect ratio (lengths from 150–300 nm and widths from 5–10 nm), and modifiable surface groups that make them attractive water treatment [14].

While wood is the most common source material for CNC, alternatives such as agro-food processing waste can also be used to lower the production cost and simultaneously address the issue of waste management for agro-food processing industries [15]. Several million tons of organic waste and low-value co-products are generated annually by agro-food industries. Most of these streams are rich in carbohydrates, proteins, and other nutrients but are currently underutilized. Conventionally, these streams are used as animal feed or are disposed of at landfills [16]. Disposal of these waste streams is an economic burden to food industries and at the same time causes several environmental problems, such as greenhouse gas emissions and groundwater contamination. These waste streams can be processed using a biorefinery approach where the cellulose fraction can be used for CNC production and the remaining fractions can be used for other applications. This provides a low/zero cost feedstock for CNC production, economic benefits to the industry, and addresses environmental issues associated with waste disposal [17].

Apple pomace (AP), a waste stream produced from the processing of apples into juices, ciders, and jellies, is a promising feedstock for CNC production. AP consists of the left-over seeds, stems, skins, and pulp from the juicing process and contains up to 25% cellulose [18]. AP accounts for up to 30% of the input apple mass and only about 20% of pomace is used for animal feed; the remainder is sent for composting [16]. A significant cellulose content in AP makes it a cost-effective substrate for CNC production, which can be used for aqueous PFAS remediation in an environmentally friendly manner. Like other cellulosic nanomaterials, APCNC derived from sustainable resources (AP) tends to be biodegradable. When APCNC is used in PFAS remediation, it can break down naturally over time, minimizing the persistence of materials in the environment. Sustainable sourcing of AP also involves practices that reduce the carbon footprint of the entire supply chain. This includes using eco-friendly cultivation methods, minimizing energy-intensive processing, and opting for transportation methods with lower emissions. A lower carbon footprint of APCNC further contributes to the overall environmental sustainability of PFAS remediation.

To enhance PFAS removal capacity, CNC surfaces are grafted or coated with synthetic chemicals, reducing material sustainability, and increasing material costs and toxicity. For water treatments, CNC surface modifications enhance the electrostatic affinity of the targeted pollutant to the adsorbent. While synthetic coatings are highly effective, more sustainable and cost-effective CNC surface modification agents are needed. Here, PFAS retention on CNC derived from AP (APCNC) was tested. In a novel approach, the surface charge of APCNC was inverted using *Moringa oleifera* cationic protein (MOCP) extracted from *Moringa oleifera* (MO) seeds as a sustainable CNC coating. The MOCP non-covalently bonded with the negative surface charges (hydroxyl and sulfonate groups) present in APCNC, making the MOCP-coated APCNC adsorbent (MOCP/APCNC) cationic. The cationic surface charge of MOCP/APCNC adsorbent induces electrostatic interactions between the targeted PFAS and adsorbent during water treatment. Previous studies reported the use of MOCP in decentralized water treatments as a cationic coagulant to reduce turbidity and remove bacteria [19]. Unlike conventional synthetic cationic CNC coating agents, MOCP is naturally occurring and biodegradable. This study investigates the application of MOCP coatings onto APCNC for PFAS remediation. The specific objectives of this study were to synthesize APCNC from AP, functionalize APCNC with MOCP extract to produce MOCP/APCNC, and characterize the batch adsorption behavior of PFOA onto APCNC and MOCP/APCNC at various environmental conditions.

The novelty of the study is the demonstration of nanocellulose-based adsorbents for PFAS remediation. Fast PFAS uptake at high capacities alongside sustainable sourcing makes CNC-based adsorbents highly competitive against existing technologies. This was also the first-ever demonstration of MOCP coatings on nanocellulose to enhance target solute affinity, highlighting a safe, sustainable, and environmentally friendly alternative to synthetic cationic polyelectrolyte coatings. MOCP coatings were shown to enhance PFOA surface retention, exhibiting the potential for bio-based adsorbent coatings to enhance PFAS treatment efficiencies. APCNC was produced from AP following a protocol that can be successfully applied to a wide variety of agro-food waste products, enabling potential large-scale implementation with diverse feedstock for PFAS remediation in an environmentally friendly way.

2. Materials and Methods

2.1. Materials

AP was procured from Beak and Skiff 1911 Distillery in Lafayette, NY. AP was dried in a convection oven set at 50 °C to reduce the moisture below 10%. Dried AP was ground to pass through a 10-mesh (2 mm sieve opening) using a Wiley mill. AP powder was stored at 4 °C until further processing. MO seeds were obtained from Vedic Secrets (East Brunswick, NJ, USA). Commercial cellulose nanocrystals (CCNC) in powder form were obtained from CelluForce (Windsor, QC, Canada).

Reagent-grade hydrochloric acid (HCl), sodium hydroxide (NaOH), sodium hypochlorite (NaOCl), and sulfuric acid (H_2SO_4) were purchased from Sigma-Aldrich (St. Louis, MO, USA). Perfluorooctanoic acid (PFOA), 96% purity, CAS No. 335-67-1, was purchased from Sigma-Aldrich (St. Louis, MO, USA) and prepared into stock solutions using Milli-Q water. Reagent-grade sodium chloride and humic acid were used to spike PFOA solution ionic strength and dissolved organic matter, respectively. Protein quantification was conducted using the Bradford protein assay (Bradford Reagent) with bovine serum albumin (BSA) standards purchased from Thermo Fisher Scientific (Waltham, MA, USA).

2.2. Isolation of Cellulose from AP

AP contains cellulose, hemicellulose, and lignin, along with soluble sugars, inorganics, extractives, and moisture. To synthesize CNC from AP (APCNC), cellulose was first isolated. To extract cellulose from AP, the protocols of Melikoğlu et al. (2020) and Szymanska-Chargot et al. (2019) were followed with small alterations [20,21]. An overall schematic for the extraction of cellulose and CNC from AP is given in Figure 1.

First, soluble sugars from milled AP were extracted using a hydrothermal washing step. In total, 100 g of dry-milled AP was added to 0.002 m^3 of DI water heated to 95 °C and mixed for 30 min. The aqueous-extracted AP was recovered by vacuum filtration. The sugar content of the filtrate was determined using high-performance liquid chromatography (HPLC). Aqueous-extracted AP was subjected to two rounds of mild acid hydrolysis (1 M HCl followed by 0.5 M HCl held at 95 °C for 30 min, each) to remove acid-soluble hemicellulose and pectin. After mild acid hydrolysis, lignin and remaining hemicelluloses were removed from acid-pretreated AP by the alkali pretreatment step (1 M NaOH heated to 95 °C for 30 min, repeated three times). Finally, bleaching was conducted to remove residual lignin from alkali-pretreated AP (1% NaOCl heated to 95 °C for 60 min, repeated twice). The washed cellulose was dried for 24 h at 50 °C in a convection oven. Afterward, the final weight of AP-cellulose was measured to determine the overall yield.

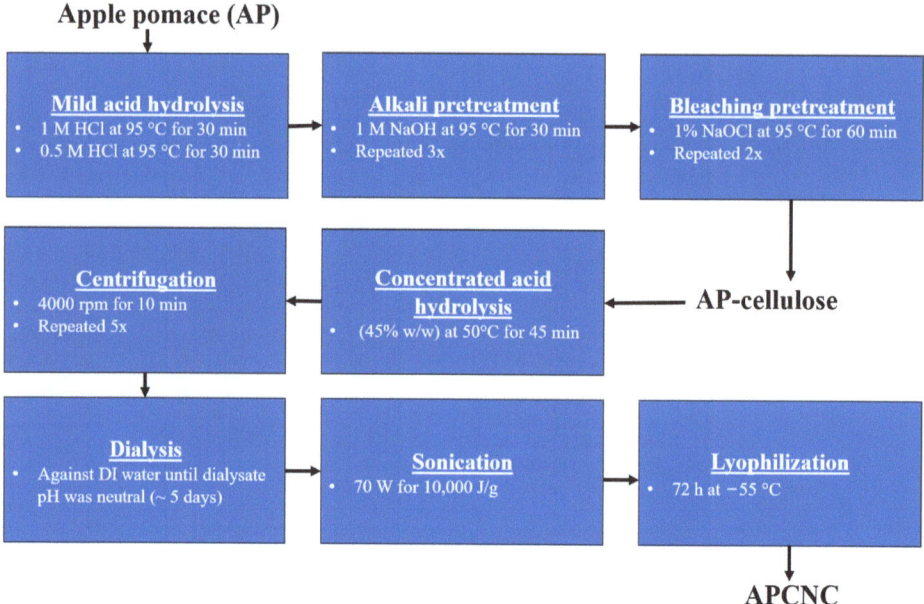

Figure 1. Process flow diagram for the isolation of APCNC from AP.

2.3. Synthesis of APCNC from AP-Cellulose

The cellulose extracted from apple pomace was ground into a fine powder using a coffee grinder to increase the surface area available for the subsequent treatment. APCNC was produced following the protocol listed by Melikoğlu et al. (2019) [21]. AP-cellulose (10 g) was added to a 0.0002 m^3 solution of H$_2$SO$_4$ (45% w/w) heated to 50 °C and mixed for 45 min. APCNC was removed from the acidic solution by a series of centrifugation and washing steps, followed by membrane dialysis (Figure 1). The neutralized suspension was placed in a beaker inside an ice bath and sonicated using a Misonix sonicator (Farmingdale, NY, USA) at 70% amplitude for 10,000 J/g [22], to disaggregate/fully disperse APCNC. Following sonication, the suspension was frozen at −20 °C overnight and then lyophilized at −55 °C for 72 h. The final weight of APCNC was measured to determine the extraction yield.

2.4. MOCP Extraction and Coating onto CCNC and APCNC

MO cationic protein (MOCP) aqueous extracts were coated onto APCNC to enhance PFOA removal efficiency by cationizing APCNC. The extraction procedure and process conditions were chosen based on previous studies using MO [23–26]. The MO seeds were manually dehulled, ground, and extracted in DI water. Jung et al. (2018) observed that the cationic charge of MOCP decreased with increasing extraction time [23]. Therefore, to maximize MOCP extract cationic charge, a quick extraction time of 5 min was applied in this study. After extraction, MOCP suspensions were clarified by sequential filtration through a glass fiber filter (1.5 µm) and a 0.2 µm cellulose acetate membrane [25]. APCNC or CCNC were added to MOCP extracts and mixed for 15 min, separated by centrifugation at 4000 rpm for 10 min, washed with DI water, re-separated by centrifugation to remove unbound MOCP, and lyophilized to recover MOCP/CCNC or MOCP/APCNC. No study has directly investigated the effect of MO extract loading mass on MOCP surface coating. In this study, loading ratios of 5–100 mg MO/mL demineralized (DI) water were applied.

To coat APCNC, MOCP was extracted at the highest loading level of 100 mg/mL in 40 mL of DI water and coated onto APCNC, using the previously described method.

Analysis of the Equilibrium Uptake of MOCP onto CCNC

To investigate the effect of MOCP concentration on APCNC coating, a series of experiments were conducted using CCNC as a model substrate. MO seeds were extracted at loading ratios of 5, 10, 25, 30, 40, 50, 60, 70, and 100 mg MO/mL DI water. After clarification, the protein concentration of the suspension was analyzed. MOCP extracts (40 mL) from varying MO loading levels were introduced to 0.4 g of CCNC, mixed for 15 min, and separated following the previously described protocol. An aliquot of supernatant was taken to assess the final (equilibrium) solution concentration of MOCP after adsorption. Adsorption efficiency was quantified by the uptake ratio given in Equation (1).

$$q_e = \frac{V(c_i - c_e)}{m_{ads}} \tag{1}$$

where the adsorption uptake ratio at equilibrium (q_e) was calculated in terms of the solution volume (V), initial (c_i) and equilibrium (c_e) adsorbate concentrations, and adsorbent mass (m_{ads}). Initial and equilibrium MOCP extract concentrations were quantified using the Bradford assay [27].

Equilibrium MOCP adsorption onto CCNC was studied using the Langmuir and Freundlich equilibrium models. The Langmuir model assumes adsorbates and adsorbents interact in an ideal manner on a homogenous surface and in a reversible fashion. The Langmuir adsorption equilibrium equation and its linearized form are given by Equations (2) and (3), respectively.

$$q_e = \frac{q_{max} K_L\, c_e}{1 + K_L c_e} \tag{2}$$

$$\frac{1}{q_e} = \frac{1}{K_L q_m}\frac{1}{c_e} + \frac{1}{q_m} \tag{3}$$

where q_{max} is the maximum theoretical adsorption capacity and K_L is the Langmuir equilibrium rate constant. The Freundlich model was developed to study adsorption on rough and multi-site surfaces by describing the degree of adsorbent surface heterogeneity. The Freundlich adsorption equilibrium model and its linearized form are given by Equations (4) and (5), respectively.

$$q_e = K_f C_e^{1/n} \tag{4}$$

$$ln(q_e) = ln(K_f) + \frac{1}{n}ln(C_e) \tag{5}$$

where K_f is the Freundlich equilibrium rate constant and the fitted constant $1/n$ represents the degree of surface heterogeneity. Model constants were obtained by fitting the experimental data from MOCP adsorption onto CCNC to the linear form of adsorption isotherm Equations (3) and (5). Experimental MOCP/CCNC adsorption data were fitted to equilibrium models to predict the maximum adsorption capacity and equilibrium adsorption rate constant of MOCP onto CNC-based adsorbents.

2.5. Characterization of AP, AP-Cellulose, APCNC, and MOCP/APCNC

2.5.1. Chemical Composition of AP

The chemical composition (cellulose, hemicellulose, lignin, and extractives) of AP and AP-cellulose were analyzed following the NREL Laboratory Analytical Procedure [28]. The moisture and ash contents of AP were determined gravimetrically. The extractive content was determined using the Soxhlet extraction apparatus and samples were first extracted for 8 h using DI water, followed by 16 h using ethanol (95%). The extractive content was gravimetrically determined by the change in sample mass after extraction. Two-step sulfuric acid hydrolysis was conducted to quantify the acid-soluble lignin (UV absorbance at 205 nm), acid-insoluble lignin (gravimetric analysis), and structural sugars (HPLC analysis of the hydrolysate) in the samples [28].

2.5.2. HPLC Analysis

The sugar content of AP, AP-cellulose, and AP hydrothermal extract was determined by HPLC with HyperREZ™ XP Carbohydrate H + LC column (Thermo Fisher Scientific, MA, USA) at 50 °C with 5 mM sulfuric acid at 0.6 mL/min, the refractive index at 35 °C, and UV detection at 210 nm [29]. Glucose and xylose quantification were conducted through a comparison of the sample to the external standard peak areas.

2.5.3. Scanning Electron Microscopy (SEM)

The morphological/structural changes in AP through pretreatment and APCNC extraction from AP-cellulose were visually investigated by scanning electron microscopy (SEM) with a JSM-IT100 (JOEL, Tokyo, Japan). AP, AP-cellulose, and APCNC were dispersed into separate 0.1% DI water suspensions by sonication, deposited onto small circles of aluminum foil, and vacuum dried at 50 °C overnight [30]. Samples were initially sputter-coated with gold before imaging. A constant 11 mm working distance and high vacuum were maintained during the SEM analysis.

2.5.4. Fourier-Transform Infrared Spectroscopy (FTIR)

The surface chemical functional groups of AP, AP-cellulose, APCNC, MOCP/APCNC, and CCNC were analyzed by FTIR. FTIR was used to assess the effect of AP treatment on AP-cellulose composition and to compare the surface functional groups of CCNC, APCNC, and MOCP/APCNC. The FTIR spectra were obtained by a PerkinElmer Frontier (Waltham, MA, USA) using the attenuated total reflectance (ATR) technique operating between wavenumbers of 4000–500 cm^{-1}. Samples were obtained after 64 scans.

2.5.5. Powder X-ray Diffraction (PXRD)

The change in sample crystallinity was used to assess the efficacy of AP-cellulose and APCNC extraction. The X-ray diffraction patterns of AP, AP-cellulose, APCNC, MOCP/APCNC, and CCNC were obtained at room temperature using a D2 Phaser diffractometer (Bruker, Bremen, Germany). The instrument was equipped with a copper-sealed tube that emitted X-rays with a wavelength of 1.54178 Å. To conduct the analysis, powdered samples were evenly spread on low-background discs. The crystallinity index (CrI) was calculated from the ratio of the 002 peak height (I_{002}) to the minimum height (I_{AM}) [31].

$$\text{CrI}(\%) = \frac{I_{002} - I_{AM}}{I_{002}} * 100\% \qquad (6)$$

I_{002} is the maximum intensity of the (002) lattice diffraction peak and I_{AM} is the intensity scattered by the amorphous regions of the sample.

2.5.6. Thermogravimetric analysis (TGA)

The thermal stabilities of AP, AP-cellulose, APCNC, MOCP/APCNC, and CCNC were tested by TGA using a Q50 thermogravimetric analyzer (TA Instruments, Newcastle, DE, USA). TGA was conducted under a nitrogen atmosphere with a temperature profile between 20–500 °C. Platinum crucibles were used for TGA in a dynamic nitrogen atmosphere (50 mL/min) under a rate of heating of 3 °C/min.

2.5.7. Brunauer–Emmet–Teller (BET) Surface

The specific surface areas of AP, AP-cellulose, APCNC, MOCP/APCNC, and CCNC were estimated through a collection of N_2 adsorption isotherms using a Micromeritics ASAP2020 surface area and pore analyzer (Norcross, GA, USA) and application of the BET adsorption model. To obtain reasonable isotherms, samples were activated at 30,

50, or 120 °C for 10, 12, or 15 h before data collection. Adsorption under the pressure of 0.005–0.2 bar was used for the calculation of the BET surface area.

2.5.8. Dynamic Light Scattering (DLS) and Zeta Potential Analysis

The hydrodynamic diameter and zeta potential of APCNC, MOCP/APCNC, and CCNC were analyzed to confirm the nanoscale dimensions of APCNC and the cationic surface charge of MOCP/APCNC [32]. DLS estimated the hydrodynamic diameter and zeta potential analysis estimated the colloidal particle surface charge. DLS and zeta potential analysis was performed using a Malvern Zetasizer (Malvern, Malvern Hills, UK). Zeta potential was calculated by the Smoluchowski equation in Malvern software v7.01. Samples were dispersed in a 0.1% suspension through sonication for 10,000 J/g [22]. Before analysis, samples were filtered through a 0.2 μm cellulose acetate membrane to remove debris. DLS and zeta potential analysis was conducted in triplicate for each sample at 25 °C and around pH of 7.0.

2.6. Batch Adsorption on PFOA onto APCNC and MOCP/APCNC

PFOA was chosen as a model PFAS solute due to its widespread usage and its recognition as one the most studied/regulated PFAS species [33]. Stock solutions of 1500 ppm (mg/L) PFOA were prepared using Milli-Q water and stored at room temperature in a high-density polyethylene (HDPE) container. All experimental measurements were conducted with triplicate controls and samples. The adsorbent dosage in all experiments was 5 mg APCNC or MOCP/APCNC/mL of PFOA solution. For adsorption kinetics trials, the working volume was 40 mL Inside 50 mL centrifuge tubes, otherwise, the working volume was set to 1.6 mL inside 2 mL microcentrifuge tubes. After the introduction of the adsorbent into PFOA solutions, samples were mixed end-over-end in a rotating incubator set to 25 °C. At chosen time points, samples were collected for PFOA analysis through centrifugation (10,000 rpm for 5 min) followed by filtration through a 0.2 μm nylon membrane.

The samples were analyzed following EPA Method 537.1 [34]. Samples were prepared by dilution to within the linear range of the PFOA standard curve, which was between 0.2 and 480 ppb. After dilution, 20 μL of internal standard (100 ppb PFOA) was added and then samples were vortexed to ensure homogeneity before measurement by HPLC coupled with triple quadrupole mass spectroscopy (HPLC-MS system).

2.6.1. Batch PFOA Adsorption Kinetics

Adsorption kinetics experiments were conducted to analyze the adsorption rate of PFOA onto APCNC and MOCP/APCNC. Adsorbents were added to a 500 ppm PFOA solution, agitated, and sampled at 0, 0.25, 0.5, 1, 2, 4, and 24 h to assess the dynamics of PFOA adsorption onto APCNC and MOCP/APCNC.

Adsorption kinetics of PFOA onto APCNC and MOCP/APCNC were studied using the pseudo-second order (PSSO) rate model. The PSSO model assumes that the adsorption rate is controlled by chemical adsorption and that adsorption capacity is proportional to the number of available adsorption sites. The PSSO model in its differential and linear form are given in Equations (7) and (8), respectively.

$$\frac{dq_t}{dt} = k_2(q_e - q_t)^2 \tag{7}$$

$$\frac{t}{q_t} = \frac{1}{k_2 q_e^2} + \frac{1}{q_e}t \tag{8}$$

where q_t is the uptake ratio at a given time point, q_e is the uptake ratio at equilibrium, t is the time point, and k_2 is the PSSO adsorption rate constant. The constants were obtained by fitting the experimental data from the PFOA adsorption kinetics studies using APCNC or MOCP/APCNC to the linearized PSSO model Equation (8).

2.6.2. Batch PFOA Equilibrium Adsorption and Isotherm Experiments

The equilibrium uptake ratio of PFOA to APCNC or MOCP/APCNC was determined for starting PFOA concentrations ranging from 10 ppb to 1500 ppm. The starting concentrations tested included 10, 50, 250, and 500 ppb, as well as 5, 100, 300, 500, 750, 1250, and 1500 ppm PFOA. The previously described Freundlich equilibrium model Equation (4) was fitted to the PFOA equilibrium adsorption data. Due to the linear nature of the reported results, the Henry equilibrium adsorption model was also employed [35]. The Henry adsorption equilibrium model is a simplification of the Freundlich model for a completely homogenous surface $((1/n) = 1)$, where adsorption equilibrium coverage is directly correlated to equilibrium solution concentration. The Henry adsorption model is given by Equation (9).

$$q_e = K_H c_e \tag{9}$$

where K_H is the Henry law adsorption equilibrium constant, which was fitted through simple linear regression to the experimental data after setting the y-intercept to zero. Alongside the equilibrium uptake ratio, the PFOA removal efficiency under different starting conditions was calculated for comparison purposes using Equation (10).

$$R\% = \frac{c_i - c_e}{c_i} * 100\% \tag{10}$$

2.6.3. Effects of Ionic Strength and Dissolved Organic Matter on PFOA Adsorption

To analyze the robustness of APCNC adsorbents in more realistic water conditions, PFOA solutions were spiked with sodium chloride (NaCl) or humic acid to represent elevated solution ionic strength or dissolved organic matter, respectively. For investigations into the effect of ionic strength on PFOA adsorption, 500 ppb PFOA solutions were spiked with 10 mM and 100 mM NaCl. For investigations into the effect of dissolved organic matter on PFOA adsorption, humic acid was used as a model solute [36] and was spiked into 500 ppb PFOA solutions up to concentrations of 5, 10, 20, and 50 mg/L. Spiked samples were mixed with 5 mg/mL APCNC or MOCP/APCNC for 24 h before separation and analysis of residual PFOA concentration.

3. Results and Discussion

3.1. Synthesis of APCNC from AP

The high extractive content of AP (42.5%) was attributed to the presence of pectin and soluble sugars [20]. Most of these extractives are recovered in the hot water washing step of the cellulose extraction process which could serve as a potential feedstock in a biorefinery context [16]. The cellulose content in the AP was 14.6%. AP cellulose content has been reported to be as low as 8% [16] or as high as 34% [21]. The hemicellulose and lignin contents (8.2% and 16.3%) were found within the range reported in the literature [20,21]. The diverse composition of AP suggested the potential co-production of multiple value-added bioproducts alongside APCNC.

The first step in the AP-cellulose extraction process was hydrothermal washing to remove soluble components. The mass loss after hot water washing was 47.05%, which closely matched the AP extractives content. The total reducing sugars in the hot water extract were 12.40 g/L. After hot water washing, mild acid, alkali, and bleaching pretreatments were conducted in sequence. The AP-cellulose yield on an extractive-free AP was 23.94%. Based on the AP cellulose content, the cellulose recovery was estimated as 86.8%, which closely matched the yield (86.1%) reported by Melikoğlu et al. (2019) [21].

During the APCNC production process, the yield after the sulfuric acid hydrolysis of the AP-cellulose was 49.1%, which is similar to the yield reported for other agro-food waste: passion fruit skins (58.1%), onion skins (48.6%), and grape pomace (20.96%) [37–39]. Differences in CNC yield could be attributed to the varied extraction conditions applied.

3.2. Cationization of CNC with MOCP Coating

The effect of MOCP extraction conditions on protein concentration was studied by varying the mass ratio of ground MO to DI water [37]. To control MOCP extraction concentration and maintain a cationic surface charge, the MO loading ratio was varied instead of the extraction time. The effect of the MO loading ratio on the MOCP extract protein concentration is shown in Figure 2a. MOCP concentration steadily increased with the increasing loading ratio. The maximum MOCP protein concentration obtained was 6.2 mg/mL from a loading level of 100 mg/mL DI water. At the maximum MOCP concentration, the extraction yield in terms of the mass of protein in the suspension to the initial mass of MO seed extracted was 49.6 mg/g, significantly higher than the previously reported value of 14.6 mg/g [40]. Variations in the reported MOCP concentration can be attributed to the extraction solvent, extraction time, MO pretreatment, and MO composition. The mean protein content of MO seeds was given as 19% [41], indicating that a protein extraction efficiency of around 33% was achieved. The surface charge of the 100 mg/mL MOCP extract was confirmed as cationic (8.53 ± 0.99 mV) by zeta potential analysis. MOCP extract concentrations were shown to strongly correlate to the MO loading ratio, providing significant insight into the selection of coating conditions for MOCP attachment onto APCNC and other adsorbent surfaces.

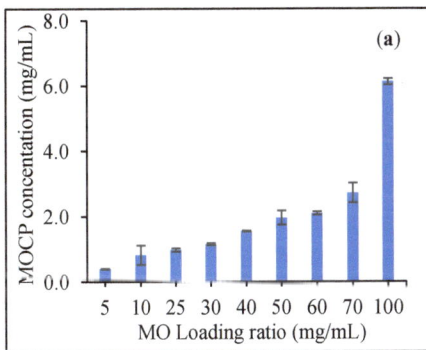
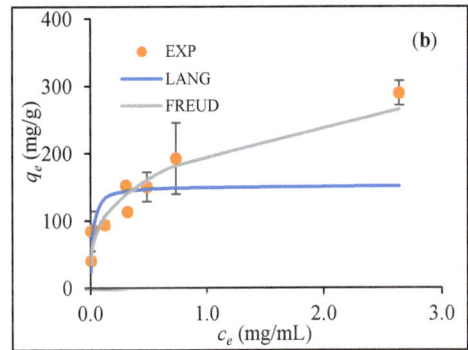

Figure 2. MOCP adsorption onto CCNC. (**a**) The effect of the MO loading ratio on the extract protein concentration and (**b**) adsorption equilibrium concentration of MOCP (C_e) vs. MOCP equilibrium uptake ratio onto CCNC (q_e), fitted with the Langmuir (LANG) and Freundlich (FREUD) equilibrium models.

MOCP was previously coated onto clay [42], sand [24,26], and cellulose fibers [43], as a cost-effective and sustainable treatment to enhance the retention of water pollutants during packed bed filtration. MOCP coatings were shown to enhance solute retention by adjusting the adsorbent's surface charge [24,26]. However, no investigation focused on the effect of extraction conditions on MOCP uptake onto adsorbent surfaces. In this study, set amounts of CCNC were coated with MOCP extracts of varying initial concentrations. Figure 2b illustrates the equilibrium MOCP concentration against the equilibrium MOCP uptake ratio onto CCNC. The maximum reported equilibrium uptake ratio was 289.5 mg/g. Experimental equilibrium MOCP uptake onto CCNC data was fitted by the Langmuir and Freundlich equilibrium models, which were plotted alongside the experimental results. The Langmuir model significantly underestimated the MOCP equilibrium uptake ratios at elevated initial concentrations (151.5 vs. 289.5 mg/g). The Freundlich model yielded smaller deviations at elevated starting concentrations (265.1 vs. 289.5 mg/g). Significant MOCP adsorption was reported onto CCNC surfaces due to the high surface area and electrostatic interactions between anionic CCNC and cationic MOCP.

Table 1 lists the fitted Langmuir and Freundlich equilibrium model constants for MOCP adsorption onto CCNC. The Langmuir maximum equilibrium adsorption uptake value (152.54 mg/g) was lower than multiple experimental equilibrium uptake ratios, indicating that the maximum equilibrium adsorption capacity of MOCP onto CCNC was not reached. The Freundlich model better predicted equilibrium uptake values at higher starting concentrations and possessed a slightly higher R^2 (0.934) than the Langmuir model (0.915). Since the value of the Freundlich fitted constant n (3.382) was significantly larger than 1, the data did not behave like a linear adsorption isotherm, where $n = 1$. In future studies, the maximum equilibrium adsorption capacity of MOCP onto CCNC can be determined by reducing the CCNC loading ratio and maintaining the MOCP initial concentration. Maximum MOCP adsorption capacity was not ascertained here but modeling the MOCP adsorption equilibrium onto CCNC can be applied to optimize surface coating conditions.

Table 1. Adsorption isotherm parameters for MOCP adsorption onto CCNC.

Langmuir			Freundlich		
q_{max} (mg/g)	K_L (L/mg)	R^2	K_f (mg/g) (mg/mL)$^{(1/n)}$	n	R^2
152.54	57.98	0.9152	199.084	3.382	0.9335

3.3. Characterization of AP, AP-Cellulose, APCNC, and MOCP/APCNC

The effects of pretreatment and acid hydrolysis on the morphology of AP, cellulose-AP, and APCNC were visualized using SEM imaging, shown in Figure S1 (Supplementary Information). The impact of treatments on particle size was apparent, as the diameter of AP reduced from 300 μm to ~10 μm for AP-cellulose and to <1 μm for APCNC. AP had a heterogeneous surface due to the presence of cellulose, hemicelluloses, lignin, and pectin. After pretreatment removed the non-cellulosic components of the biomass, the visibility of the high aspect ratio fibers increased. Further reduction in particle size is evident, which can be attributed to the degradation of the amorphous regions through the acid-catalyzed breakdown of the β-1,4-glucopyranose linkage [44]. The lack of clarity in APCNC structure from SEM images was previously reported [21,32] and attributed to small particle dimensions and the effect of sample preparation conditions. The larger crystals present in APCNC were caused by drying-induced agglomeration [45]. SEM imaging confirmed the production of APCNC from AP-cellulose and AP-cellulose from AP.

The surface chemical functional groups of AP, AP-cellulose, APCNC, CCNC, and MOCP/APCNC were analyzed through FTIR, with the superimposed spectrums provided in Figure S2 (Supplementary Information). Melikoğlu et al. (2019) reported spectral bands for AP at 3350, 2860–2927, 1748, 1650, 1530, 1259, 1160, and 900 cm^{-1}. Here, AP exhibited peaks at 3325, 2825–2925, 1745, 1660, 1605, 1225, and 1030 cm^{-1}, showing a high degree of similarity in chemical functionality with the previously studied sample. The primary lignocellulosic components of AP are cellulose, hemicellulose, and lignin. FTIR was used to validate the overarching objective of pretreatment: the removal of non-cellulosic components from biomass. Characteristic bands of cellulose functional groups were previously reported at the following wavelengths: OH (4000–2995 cm^{-1}), H-C-H (2890 cm^{-1}), Fiber-OH (1640 cm^{-1}), and C-O-C (1270–1232 cm^{-1} and 1170–1082 cm^{-1}) [46]. The OH, C-H-H, Fiber-OH, and C-O-C bands were visible in all samples, indicating that cellulose structure was preserved through the pretreatment, extraction, and coating. The characteristic bands of hemicelluloses were reported as: OH (1108 cm^{-1}, 4000–2995 cm^{-1}), H-C-H (2890 cm^{-1}), and C=O (1765–1715 cm^{-1}) [21]. For lignin, characteristic peaks were identified at 1730–1700, 1632, 1613, 1450, 1430, 1270-1232, and 700–900 cm^{-1} [21]. From Figure S2 (Supplementary Information), the peaks were observed in AP spectra at 1748 and 1259 cm^{-1} and the stretching at 1530 cm^{-1} indicated the presence of cellulose, hemicellulose, and lignin [21], respectively. For APCNC, peaks were observed at 3300, 2920-2815, 1660, 1310, and 1020 cm^{-1}. Similar spectra were produced by APCNC and CCNC, indicating a high degree of similarity in surface composition. For MOCP/APCNC, no discernable new peaks were detected. Previously, MOCP extract was reported to display

FTIR peaks at 1635 and 3472 cm^{-1} from the -OH, and -NH protein functional groups [47]. The presence of MOCP on MOCP/APCNC could not be confirmed by FTIR analysis. Successful isolation of AP-cellulose from AP and successful production of APCNC were affirmed by FTIR analysis.

The effect of pretreatment, CNC extraction, and MOCP coating on material crystallinity was analyzed by PXRD and compared against CCNC, shown in Figure 3. The XRD patterns are displayed in Figure 3a. Crystalline peaks were exhibited for all samples at 2-theta = 16.1°, 22°, and 34.7°, which were attributed to the cellulose I structure present in all samples [32]. The CrI values of AP, AP-cellulose, APCNC, CCNC, and MOCP/APCNC were 24, 58, 61, 66, and 59%, respectively, plotted in Figure 3b. Crystallinity increased after the removal of non-cellulosic components and further increased when amorphous regions of cellulose were dissolved during acid hydrolysis to produce APCNC. The crystallinity index of APCNC was comparable but slightly lower than CCNC. MOCP coating slightly reduced the crystallinity of APCNC. Reduction in the crystallinity of MOCP/APCNC provided evidence of the successful change in surface morphology after coating [42]. Increased crystallinity after pretreatment and APCNC extraction corroborated findings in the literature [21,31]. However, the increase in crystallinity after APCNC extraction was less significant here than what was previously reported. Melikoğlu et al. (2019) reported CrI values of 45, 67, and 78% for AP, AP-cellulose, and APCNC, respectively [21]. Differences in crystallinity can be attributed to differences in starting material and treatment conditions. Szymanska-Chargot et al. (2017) tested the crystallinity of cellulose derived from various feedstocks and reported the following values of CrI: apple (51.34%), tomato (48.97%), cucumber (53.61%), and carrot pomace (68.73) [16]. PXRD analysis verified the successful removal of non-crystalline components of biomass during pretreatment and the successful coating of MOCP onto APCNC.

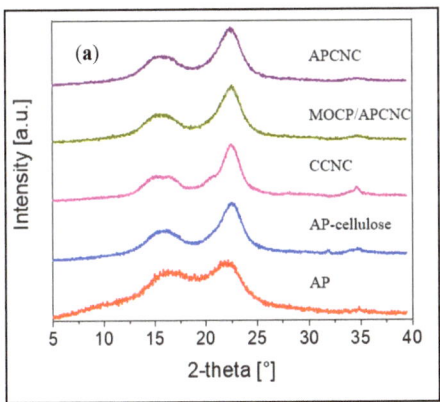 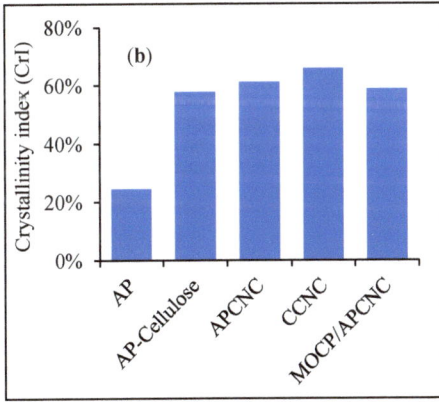

Figure 3. (a) X-ray diffractograms and (b) crystallinity indexes of AP, AP-cellulose, APCNC, CCNC, and MOCP/APCNC.

The thermal stabilities of AP, AP-cellulose, APCNC, CCNC, and MOCP/APCNC were analyzed using TGA, with the resulting mass loss curves shown superimposed in Figure S3 (Supplementary Information). The corresponding curves represented the sample weight loss during continuous heating. The initial weight loss at around 100–120 °C can be attributed to the evaporation of moisture. Yang et al. (2007) performed TGA on samples of cellulose, hemicellulose, and lignin and found that hemicellulose decomposition occurred gradually between 220–315 °C, cellulose decomposed sharply between 315–400 °C, and lignin slowly decomposed throughout the entire temperature range up to 900 °C [48]. The greater levels of mass loss at lower temperatures but lower levels of mass loss at higher temperatures for AP can be attributed to the presence of lignin and hemicelluloses which were mostly removed by the subsequent pretreatment. Cellulose degradation starting at around 300 °C was reported for all samples, with the sharpest mass loss occurring for CCNC, indicating its high purity and that residual lignocellulosic impurities may be present in APCNC. Similar thermal stability profiles were produced for AP-cellulose and APCNC, with the mass loss occurring slightly more sharply for APCNC than AP-cellulose, which can be attributed to the degradation of the less thermally stable amorphous regions of cellulose. Figure S3 (Supplementary Information) shows a high degree of similarity in the thermal degradation profile of AP-cellulose, APCNC, and MOCP/APCNC, which exhibited less sharp mass losses than CCNC. This was an indicator of the incomplete removal of non-cellulosic components from AP. MOCP coatings were not shown to significantly impact the thermal stability of APCNC but slightly reduced the mass loss beyond 500 °C. TGA confirmed the successful removal of non-cellulosic components from AP by pretreatment and enabled the comparison in purity between APCNC and CCNC.

The specific surface areas of APCNC, CCNC, and MOCP/APCNC were analyzed by fitting the BET isotherm onto N_2 adsorption data, under varied activation conditions, given in Figure S4 (Supplementary Information). N_2 adsorption isotherms were not suitably produced for AP or cellulose-AP, so the specific surface areas for those materials were not reported. APCNC exhibited a lower specific surface area (0.74 m^2/g) than CCNC (1.35 m^2/g), which could be attributed to differences in fiber source and treatment conditions [49]. Coating MOCP onto APCNC increased the material's specific surface area (1.06 m^2/g) relative to unmodified APCNC (0.74 m^2/g). The values of the specific surface area of APCNC and CCNC fall within the range reported in the literature [50,51]. Brinkmann et al. (2016) analyzed the specific surface area of CNC through BET, NMR, TEM, and AFM. The reported dimensions of CNC derived from AFM yielded a significantly larger specific surface area (419 m^2/g) than what was reported by N_2 adsorption isotherms (1.29 m^2/g), exemplifying the limitations of the BET isotherm approach for estimating CNC specific surface area. This can be attributed to the drying effects of CNC causing nanoparticle agglomeration. However, N_2 adsorption isotherms provided a comparative analysis for the effect of surface treatments on the available surface area. APCNC possessed a smaller specific surface area than CCNC, possibly due to the source material and extraction conditions. MOCP coating enhanced the specific surface area of APCNC.

The hydrodynamic diameters and the apparent surface charges of CCNC, APCNC, and MOCP/APCNC were analyzed through DLS and zeta potential analysis, with results shown in Table 2. CCNC possessed a smaller hydrodynamic diameter than APCNC, which can be attributed to different source materials and extraction conditions. However, DLS did confirm the production of nano-scale APCNC from AP [52]. MOCP coatings increased the size of MOCP/APCNC relative to APCNC, as previously demonstrated by polymer coatings onto CNC [53]. For CNC, hydrodynamic diameters can be only used on a comparative rather than an absolute basis [32], due to the high aspect ratio of CNC failing the assumptions of spherical particles given in the Stokes–Einstein diffusivity equation. In the literature, CNC hydrodynamic diameters are reported in the range of 100–500 nm [51]. The negative zeta potentials of CCNC and APCNC were attributed to the formation of sulfate groups during concentrated acid hydrolysis [44]. The charge of the MOCP extract used for APCNC coating was verified as cationic by zeta potential, with an average value of 8.53 ± 0.99 mV, confirming previous reports in the literature [27]. Zeta potential analysis verified the successful inversion of CNC surface charge through coating with cationic protein extract MOCP. CNC surface charge has previously been inverted by the coating of synthetic polymers or surfactants [22,54]. The primary advantage of MOCP extract coating in comparison to synthetic polymers is its biodegradability, cost-effective procurement, and nontoxicity [55]. DLS confirmed the nanoscale dimensions of APCNC and zeta potential confirmed the inversion of AP surface charge after MOCP coating.

Table 2. Hydrodynamic diameter and zeta potential of CCNC, APCNC, and MOCP/APCNC.

	Hydrodynamic Diameter (nm)	Zeta Potential (mV)
CCNC	92.2	−25.27
APCNC	230.8	−15.07
MOCP/APCNC	427.6	7.38

3.4. Batch Adsorption Studies of PFOA onto CNC-Based Adsorbents

The adsorption rate of PFOA onto unmodified APCNC and MOCP/APCNC was analyzed through modeling batch adsorption kinetic trials for a starting PFOA concentration of 500 ppm and an adsorbent dosage of 5000 mg/L, illustrated in Figure 4. Rapid PFOA uptake was observed with equilibrium being reached in both cases within 15 min. The uptake ratio at equilibrium was on average 27 mg/g for MOCP/APCNC and 10 mg/g for APCNC. This demonstrated both the rapid uptake of PFAS onto CNC-based adsorbents and the ability of MOCP coatings to enhance PFAS adsorption capacity. Conventional PFAS adsorbents such as GAC and IEX suffer from long equilibrium times, on the order of several days [56]. Therefore, significant efforts have been focused on developing PFAS adsorbents with shorter equilibrium times, such as with polyaniline polymers, where the PFOA equilibrium was reached within 5 h [57], or powdered activated carbon, where PFOA equilibrium was reached within 60 min [58]. Rapid PFAS adsorption was also observed on polyethyleneimine-coated cellulose microcrystals, where equilibrium was reached within 30 min for a wide range of PFAS tested in pure and lake water [59]. The adsorption rate of microporous adsorbents is diffusion-limited, which led to interest in nanostructured materials such as CNC, due to their high external surface areas [60]. APCNC and MOCP/APCNC offered rapid PFOA adsorption with significantly shorter equilibrium times than those reported for conventional PFAS adsorbents.

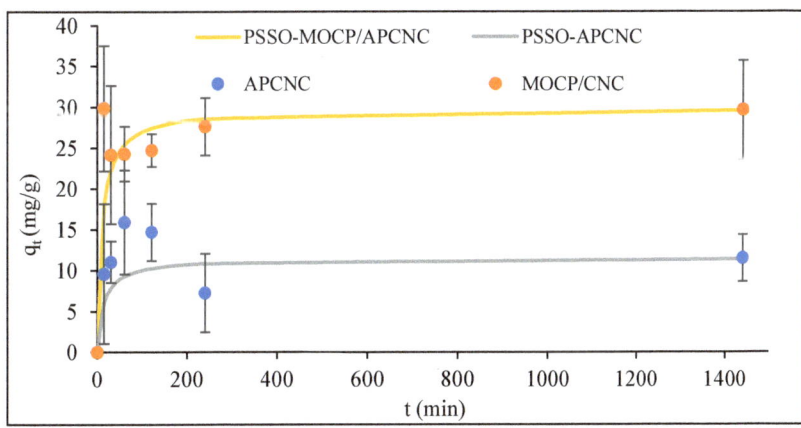

Figure 4. Adsorption kinetics of PFOA onto APCNC and MOCP/APCNC.

The fitted PSSO rate model parameters for PFOA uptake kinetics onto APCNC and MOCP/APCNC are given in Table 3. PFOA adsorption in both cases was well-described by the PSSO rate model with coefficients of variation (R^2) of 0.988 and 1.000, respectively. Modeling the adsorption kinetics was necessary to evaluate the experimental results and to extrapolate findings beyond the experimental conditions. PSSO is a widely used empirical kinetic model for batch adsorption studies due to its ability to describe the approach to the uptake ratio at equilibrium [61]. Zhang et al. (2021) applied PSSO and the interparticle diffusion model (IDM) to fit experimental PFAS adsorption kinetic data for GAC and biochar [62]. It is important to note that the adsorbent amounts (50 mg/L vs. 5000 mg/L) and the initial PFOA concentration (1 mg/L vs. 500 mg/L) were significantly lower in the

Zhang et al. (2021) [62] study. For all studied PFAS compounds (PFOA, PFOS, PFBA, and PFBS), the PSSO better described the experimental data than the intraparticle diffusion model, exemplified by the reported R^2. Since PFAS adsorption data fit the PSSO better than the IDM model, this indicated that intraparticle diffusion was not the rate-limiting step during PFAS adsorption. For GAC and biochar, the PSSO adsorption rate constant was reported as 9.59×10^{-6} and 6.64×10^{-6} g/mg/s, respectively, which was multiple orders of magnitude smaller than the PSSO constants derived by fitting PFOA adsorption kinetic data for APCNC (2.65×10^{-3}) and MOCP/APCNC (5.05×10^{-3}). This indicated that PFAS adsorption rates onto CNC-based adsorbents were significantly faster than PFAS adsorption rates of conventional adsorbents.

Table 3. PSSO rate model parameters for PFOA adsorption onto APCNC and MOCP/APCNC.

	q_e (mg/g)	k_2 (g/mg/s)	R^2
APCNC	11.49	2.65×10^{-3}	0.988
MOCP/APCNC	29.85	5.05×10^{-3}	1.000

Equilibrium PFOA adsorption experiments were conducted for starting PFOA concentrations ranging from 10 ppb (μg/L) to 1250 ppm (mg/L). Figure 5a,b shows the equilibrium PFOA concentration plotted against the equilibrium uptake ratio on APCNC and MOCP/APCNC modeled by the Freundlich and Henry model. Since no plateau in the equilibrium uptake ratio was found at elevated starting PFOA concentrations, the system was considered within the linear range. This allowed for evaluation using the Henry equilibrium model, which was compared against the Freundlich isotherm model, with the fitted parameters given in Table 4. Through visual inspection, it can be determined that for both APCNC and MOCP/APCNC, the equilibrium uptake ratio had not plateaued and the collected data fell within the linear region of the isotherm shape. Therefore, the maximum adsorption capacity cannot be determined by fitting this data to the Langmuir isotherm. The Freundlich model's best fit to the experimental data yielded a heterogeneity constant (n) near 1, indicating that the Henry model for linear adsorption would better describe the equilibrium uptake at the tested concentrations and adsorbent dosage. The Henry model was previously used in cases where the equilibrium uptake plateau was not reached for PFOA adsorption onto carbon nanotubes [63]. Plotting the equilibrium PFOA concentration against equilibrium uptake showed that MOCP/APCNC retained a larger quantity of PFOA than APCNC and that maximum adsorption was not reached for either adsorbent given the starting PFOA concentrations and adsorbent dosages tested.

Table 4. Fitted parameters for the Henry and Freundlich model for PFOA adsorption onto APCNC and MOCP/APCNC.

		APCNC	MOCP/APCNC
Henry	K_h	2.65×10^{-2}	4.70×10^{-2}
	R^2	0.938	0.933
Freundlich	K_f	6.30×10^{-3}	6.78×10^{-2}
	n	0.839	1.071
	R^2	0.885	0.872

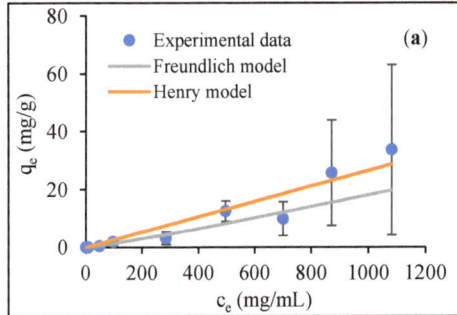
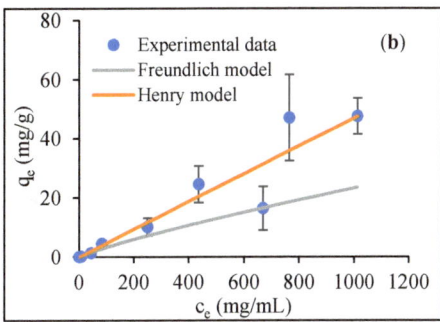
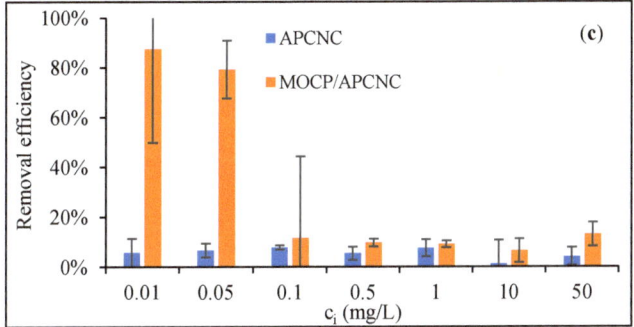

Figure 5. Adsorption equilibrium study for PFOA onto (**a**) APCNC, (**b**) MOCP/APCNC, and (**c**) PFOA removal efficiency for APCNC and MOCP/APCNC.

While PFOA adsorption was analyzed in the ppm (mg/L) range in this study, in the actual contaminated water, the PFOA is often detected in the low ppb or high ppt range (ng/L, μg/L) [64]. Therefore, to determine the efficacy of MOCP coatings on PFOA retention under relevant conditions, the removal efficiency of PFOA onto APCNC and MOCP/APCNC was plotted for different starting PFOA concentrations, ranging from 10 ppb to 50 ppm, shown in Figure 5c. At a starting concentration of 10 ppb, the average removal efficiency was 6% for APCNC and 87% for MOCP/APCNC, demonstrating the significant enhancement in PFAS retention for MOCP-coated APCNC compared to unmodified APCNC. Son et al. (2020) determined the removal efficiencies of various PFAS onto numerous types of powdered activated carbon by adding 50 mg/L of adsorbent to a 100 ng/L PFAS solution and mixing until equilibrium was reached [65]. The average removal efficiency was reported as 80%. Although the actual adsorbent dosage (5000 mg/L) and initial PFOA concentration (10,000 ng/L) conditions used in this study are different compared to the conditions used by Son et al. (2020) [65], the ratio of adsorbent dosage to solution PFOA concentration was similar (0.5 mg/ng). Considering adsorbent performance based on adsorbent dosage to solution PFOA concentration, MOCP/APCNC removed PFOA at a similar high efficiency as powdered activated carbon, a high-performing GAC-based alternative. At lower tested starting concentrations, MOCP/APCNC removed a significantly larger percentage of PFOA compared to APCNC. A schematic of the model PFAS removal (PFOA in this study) by the *Moringa oleifera*-based MOCP/APCNC adsorbent is shown in Figure 6. MO seeds contain high amounts of soluble proteins (MOCP) possessing net positive surface charges, which undergo electrostatic interactions with the negatively charged head groups of PFAS such as PFOA during batch adsorption. Moringa-based adsorbents have also been used previously for PFAS removal from water [66,67]. *Moringa oleifera* seeds outperformed all adsorbents but one of the non-activated carbon-based PFAS adsorbents, which corroborated previous evidence of MOCP efficacy against other organic pollutants [66]. Militao et al. (2022) encapsulated MO seed powder into alginate beads at different ratios and tested their PFOS removal efficiency from a 100 ppb PFOS solution dosed with 1.5 g/L of adsorbent after 24 h of contact time [67]. The maximum removal efficiency was observed at the highest MO bead dosage. While MO seeds have demonstrated high PFAS affinity, their application is hindered by the release of excessive organic matter leading to bacterial growth in water over time [24]. Therefore, it is noteworthy that this was the first study where MOCP-coated surfaces were shown to enhance PFAS retention since extracting the cationic protein and coating it onto adsorbent surfaces eliminates the issue of excessive organic matter.

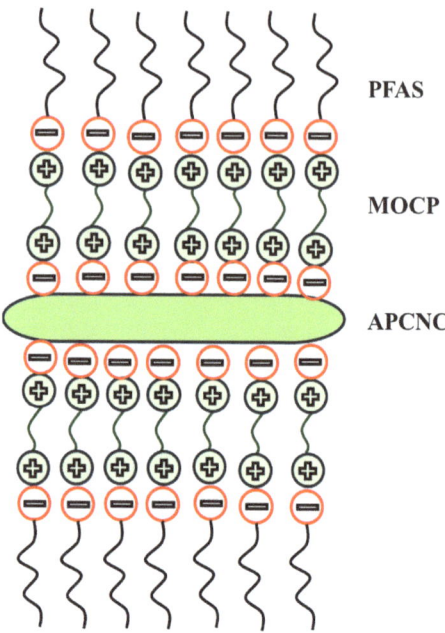

Figure 6. Schematic of the PFAS adsorption mechanism onto *Moringa oleifera*-derived MOCP/APCNC adsorbent.

Henry and Freundlich model constants, fitted by linear regression to experimental data, are given in Table 4. For both models, MOCP/APCNC possessed a higher adsorption rate constant, indicating that MOCP coatings led to elevated PFOA equilibrium adsorption capacity. In the range of PFOA concentrations tested, both APCNC and MOCP/APCNC adsorption equilibrium uptake ratios were better fitted by the Henry model than the Freundlich. This indicated that a significant amount of additional surface area was still available on the adsorbent and the maximum adsorption capacity was not closely approached. However, comparisons between this novel adsorbent and conventional PFAS adsorption technology were still able to be made. The maximum reported adsorption capacity from a starting concentration of 1250 ppm was 47.1 mg/g for APCNC and 61.1 mg/g for MOCP/APCNC, demonstrating that MOCP coatings enhanced the PFOA adsorption capacity. Both APCNC and MOCP/APCNC displayed a higher PFOA adsorption capacity than polyethyleneimine grafted cellulose microcrystals (2.32 mg/g) but a lower Freundlich adsorption rate constant (11.46 $(mg/g)(L/mg)^{1/n}$) [59]. Zhang et al. (2021) performed equilibrium experiments to test the adsorption capacity of various PFAS including PFOA on GAC and biochar and fitted the experimental data to the Langmuir and Freundlich isotherms [62]. From the Langmuir isotherm model, the theoretical maximum PFOA adsorption capacity was estimated to be 35.7 and 21.6 mg/g, respectively. The maximum adsorption uptake ratios observed for APCNC and MOCP/APCNC exceeded both adsorbents' theoretical maximum adsorption capacity, indicating a relatively high PFOA loading capacity. APCNC adsorbed PFOA at levels exceeding conventional adsorbents and MOCP coating was shown to enhance PFOA retention onto APCNC.

The kinetics and equilibrium studies reported so far were undertaken with model PFOA-contaminated aqueous solutions in DI water. However, the presence of ions or dissolved organic matter often negatively impacts adsorption performance in practice. Therefore, to test the robustness of MOCP coatings for PFOA adsorption onto APCNC, the effects of ionic strength and dissolved organic matter on PFOA uptake onto APCNC and MOCP/APCNC were studied and the results are illustrated in Figure 7a,b, respectively. In all cases, 500 ppb solutions of PFOA were challenged with 5 mg/L of adsorbent. For both APCNC and MOCP/APCNC, PFOA uptake increased with increasing ionic strength. However, at elevated solution ionic strength (100 mM), a much larger difference in adsorption uptake was observed between APCNC and MOCP/APCNC (0.013 vs. 0.029 mg/g) than in DI Water (0.006 vs. 0.010 mg/g). Liu et al. (2018) studied the effect of ionic strength on PFOA adsorption onto carbon nanotubes and found little influence [63]. To enhance PFAS retention, Ramos et al. (2022) coated poly(diallyldimethylammonium chloride) (PDADMAC) onto GAC [68]. Ramos et al. (2022) studied the effect of competing ions and organic matter on PFAS adsorption, finding that increasing ionic strength did not lead to a significant increase in the percentage increase in adsorption capacity between unmodified GAC and PDADMAC coated GAC. This trend was not observed in this study as elevated ionic strength increased the proportional difference in PFOA adsorption capacity between APCNC and MOCP/APCNC. One possible cause could be the differences in the chemical composition between MOCP vs PDADMAC. Unlike PDADMAC, which is a cationic polyelectrolyte, MOCP is a mostly cationic protein that contains some hydrophobic moieties [69]. PFAS adsorption can be driven by either electrostatic interaction between cationic surfaces and anionic PFAS head groups or by hydrophobic interactions between hydrophobic surfaces and hydrophobic PFAS tails [70]. It is well known that hydrophobic surface interactions increase with increasing salinity as nonpolar particles become less soluble in aqueous media at elevated conductivities [71]. Therefore, the hydrophobic regions of MOCP may be driving the enhanced adsorption rate observed for MOCP/APCNC at high ionic strengths.

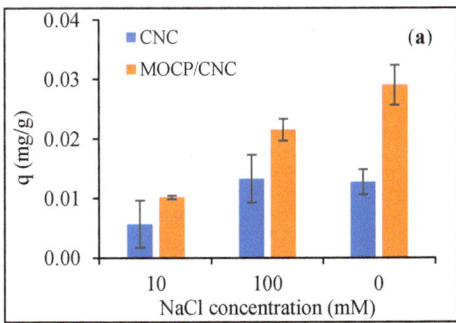 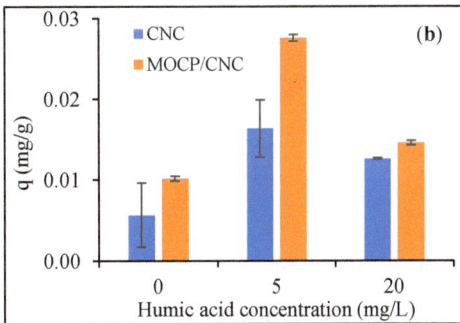

Figure 7. The effect of solution conditions on PFOA uptake on APCNC and MOCP/APCNC. (a) The effect of solution ionic strength and (b) the effect of solution dissolved organic carbon concentration.

To investigate the impact of dissolved organic matter, humic acid was spiked into solutions of 500 ppb PFOA as a model solute representative of natural organic matter found in surface water. Humic acid is a complex mixture of organic compounds derived from the decomposition of plant and animal matter. It shares some similarities with natural organic matter found in water. In addition, humic acid contains various functional groups, such as carboxylic, phenolic, and hydroxyl groups, which are representative of the types of interactions that can occur between PFAS and natural organic matter in the environment. Thus, using humic acid as a model solute allows PFAS adsorption in the presence of a complex and diverse organic matrix, similar to what is encountered in environmental systems. The effect of spiking PFOA solutions with 0–50 mg/L of humic acid on adsorption uptake onto APCNC and MOCP/APCNC is shown in Figure 7b. At elevated humic acid concentrations (50 mg/L), no quantifiable PFOA adsorption was reported, indicating that the dissolved organic carbon outcompeted PFOA for space on the adsorbent surface. From DI water to the lowest humic acid dosage (5 mg/L), the PFOA adsorption capacity increased from 0.006 to 0.016 mg/g for APCNC and from 0.010 to 0.027 mg/g for MOCP/APCNC. Low dissolved organic matter concentrations have been associated with increased PFOA uptake due to co-adsorption [72]. However, elevated humic acid concentrations have been shown to lower PFOA uptake [73]. Since the dissolved organic matter concentration in the surface water is typically between 0–20 mg/L [74], MOCP/APCNC PFOA adsorption performances were robust against variation in dissolved organic carbon concentrations in water within the range of realistic values.

4. Conclusions

This study investigated the potential of using apple pomace-derived cellulose nanocrystals cationized with protein extracted from *Moringa oleifera* seeds for the effective removal of PFOA from water. On a water extractive-free dry weight basis, the cellulose yield was 23.94% and the APCNC sulfuric acid hydrolysis yield was found to be 49.1%. The MO loading ratio directly correlated to MOCP protein concentration, with a maximum MOCP protein concentration of 6.2 mg/mL reported at a MO seed loading level of 100 mg MO/mL DI water. The surface charge of MOCP was confirmed as cationic (8.53 mV) by zeta potential analysis. PFOA adsorption equilibrium onto APCNC and MOCP/APCNC was reached within 15 min, significantly faster than conventional PFAS adsorbents. The maximum PFOA adsorption capacities onto APCNC and MOCP/APCNC were 47.1 and 61.1 mg/g, respectively, demonstrating that MOCP coatings enhanced PFAS retention. The linear relationship displayed between the equilibrium concentration and uptake ratio led to the successful fitting of the Henry linear adsorption model with an R^2 of 0.94 and 0.93 for APCNC and MOCP/APCNC, respectively. Henry law equilibrium rate constants showed that APCNC (2.65×10^{-2} L/g) had lower PFOA adsorption affinity than MOCP/APCNC (4.70×10^{-2} L/g). At low starting PFOA concentrations, MOCP/APCNC almost completely removed PFOA from the solution (87%), compared to only 6% removal by APCNC. Increasing the ionic strength of 500 ppb PFOA solutions was shown to enhance MOCP/APCNC adsorption capacity (0.010 to 0.029 mg/g) to a greater extent than APCNC (0.006 to 0.013 mg/g) due to the presence of hydrophobic groups in MOCP. At the dissolved organic matter content levels reported in groundwater, the PFOA adsorption capacity onto MOCP/APCNC increased. Successful coating of MOCP onto APCNC led to enhanced adsorption rates, capacities, and robustness against variation in water quality. Compared to conventional PFAS adsorbents, MOCP/APCNC offered more rapid uptake at elevated capacities, making it highly competitive as a replacement to or supplement for existing PFAS water treatments.

Supplementary Materials: The following supporting information can be downloaded at https://www.mdpi.com/article/10.3390/pr12020297/s1. Figure S1: SEM images of (a) AP, (b) AP-cellulose, and (c) APCNC; Figure S2: Superimposed FTIR spectra of AP, AP-cellulose, APCNC, MOCP/APCNC, and CCNC; Figure S3: TGA curve for AP, AP-cellulose, APCNC, MOCP/APCNC, and CCNC; Figure S4: Nitrogen adsorption–desorption isotherm for (a) APCNC, (b) MOCP/APCNC, and (c) CCNC.

Author Contributions: L.A.F.: Investigation and writing—original draft. T.D.S.: Conceptualization, investigation, and writing—original draft. M.S.H.: Investigation and writing—original draft. B.V.R.: Conceptualization and funding acquisition. C.C.V.: Investigation. M.W.: Investigation and editing. M.S.: Investigation. D.K.: Conceptualization, resources, supervision, writing, review and editing, and funding acquisition. All authors have read and agreed to the published version of the manuscript.

Funding: This work was financially supported by SyracuseCOE Faculty Fellows Program.

Data Availability Statement: The data presented in this study are within the article and supplementary file.

Conflicts of Interest: The authors declare no conflicts of interest. The funder had no role in the design of the study; in the collection, analyses, or interpretation of data; in the writing of the manuscript; or in the decision to publish the results.

References

1. Park, S.; Zenobio, J.E.; Lee, L.S. Perfluorooctane Sulfonate (PFOS) Removal with Pd0/NFe0 Nanoparticles: Adsorption or Aqueous Fe-Complexation, Not Transformation? *J. Hazard. Mater.* **2018**, *342*, 20–28. [CrossRef]
2. Wanninayake, D.M. Comparison of Currently Available PFAS Remediation Technologies in Water: A Review. *J. Environ. Manag.* **2021**, *283*, 111977. [CrossRef]
3. Gomis, M.I.; Vestergren, R.; Borg, D.; Cousins, I.T. Comparing the Toxic Potency in Vivo of Long-Chain Perfluoroalkyl Acids and Fluorinated Alternatives. *Environ. Int.* **2018**, *113*, 1–9. [CrossRef] [PubMed]
4. Sunderland, E.M.; Hu, X.; Dassuncao, C. A Review of Pathways of Human Exposure to PFAS. *Physiol. Behav.* **2019**, *173*, 665–676. [CrossRef]
5. Ross, I.; Mcdonough, J.; Miles, J.; Storch, P.; Kochunarayanan, P.T.; Kalve, E.; Hurst, J.; Dasgupta, S.S.; Burdick, J. A Review of Emerging Technologies for Remediation of PFASs. *Remediat. J.* **2018**, *28*, 101–126. [CrossRef]
6. Xu, B.; Liu, S.; Zhou, J.L.; Zheng, C.; Jin, W.; Chen, B.; Zhang, T.; Qiu, W. PFAS and Their Substitutes in Groundwater: Occurrence, Transformation and Remediation. *J. Hazard. Mater.* **2021**, *412*, 125159. [CrossRef] [PubMed]
7. Vu, C.T.; Wu, T. Recent Progress in Adsorptive Removal of Per- and Poly-Fluoroalkyl Substances (PFAS) from Water/Wastewater. *Crit. Rev. Environ. Sci. Technol.* **2022**, *52*, 90–129. [CrossRef]
8. Pauletto, P.S.; Bandosz, T.J. Activated Carbon versus Metal-Organic Frameworks: A Review of Their PFAS Adsorption Performance. *J. Hazard. Mater.* **2022**, *425*, 127810. [CrossRef] [PubMed]
9. Militao, I.M.; Roddick, F.A.; Bergamasco, R.; Fan, L. Removing PFAS from Aquatic Systems Using Natural and Renewable Material-Based Adsorbents: A Review. *J. Environ. Chem. Eng.* **2021**, *9*, 105271. [CrossRef]
10. Tan, K.B.; Vakili, M.; Horri, B.A.; Poh, P.E.; Abdullah, A.Z.; Salamatinia, B. Adsorption of Dyes by Nanomaterials: Recent Developments and Adsorption Mechanisms. *Sep. Purif. Technol.* **2015**, *150*, 229–242. [CrossRef]
11. Janusz, W.; Kowalska, K.; Skwarek, E. Research on Deposition of Silver Nanoparticles at the Cellulose/NaNO$_3$ Interface. *Physicochem. Probl. Miner. Process.* **2023**, *59*, 173554. [CrossRef]
12. Jia, G.; Wang, H.; Yan, L.; Wang, X.; Pei, R.; Yan, T.; Zhao, Y.; Guo, X. Cytotoxicity of Carbon Nanomaterials: Single-Wall Nanotube, Multi-Wall Nanotube, and Fullerene. *Environ. Sci. Technol.* **2005**, *39*, 1378–1383. [CrossRef] [PubMed]
13. Carpenter, A.W.; De Lannoy, C.F.; Wiesner, M.R. Cellulose Nanomaterials in Water Treatment Technologies. *Environ. Sci. Technol.* **2015**, *49*, 5277–5287. [CrossRef] [PubMed]
14. Kargarzadeh, H.; Mariano, M.; Gopakumar, D.; Ahmad, I.; Thomas, S.; Dufresne, A.; Huang, J.; Lin, N. *Advances in Cellulose Nanomaterials*; Springer: Dordrecht, The Netherlands, 2018; Volume 25, ISBN 1057001817235.
15. Vincent, S.; Kandasubramanian, B. Cellulose Nanocrystals from Agricultural Resources: Extraction and Functionalisation. *Eur. Polym. J.* **2021**, *160*, 110789. [CrossRef]
16. Liu, H.; Kumar, V.; Jia, L.; Sarsaiya, S.; Kumar, D.; Juneja, A.; Zhang, Z.; Sindhu, R.; Binod, P.; Bhatia, S.K.; et al. Biopolymer Poly-Hydroxyalkanoates (PHA) Production from Apple Industrial Waste Residues: A Review. *Chemosphere* **2021**, *284*, 131427. [CrossRef]
17. Padhi, S.; Singh, A.; Routray, W. Nanocellulose from Agro-Waste: A Comprehensive Review of Extraction Methods and Applications. *Rev. Environ. Sci. Biotechnol.* **2023**. [CrossRef]
18. Qin, S.; Shekher Giri, B.; Kumar Patel, A.; Sar, T.; Liu, H.; Chen, H.; Juneja, A.; Kumar, D.; Zhang, Z.; Kumar Awasthi, M.; et al. Resource Recovery and Biorefinery Potential of Apple Orchard Waste in the Circular Bioeconomy. *Bioresour. Technol.* **2021**, *321*, 124496. [CrossRef] [PubMed]
19. Skaf, D.W.; Punzi, V.L.; Rolle, J.T.; Cullen, E. Impact of Moringa Oleifera Extraction Conditions on Zeta Potential and Coagulation Effectiveness. *J. Environ. Chem. Eng.* **2021**, *9*, 104687. [CrossRef]
20. Szymanska-Chargot, M.; Chylinska, M.; Gdula, K.; Koziol, A.; Zdunek, A. Isolation and Characterization of Cellulose from Different Fruit and Vegetable Pomaces. *Polymers* **2017**, *9*, 495. [CrossRef]
21. Melikoğlu, A.Y.; Bilek, S.E.; Cesur, S. Optimum Alkaline Treatment Parameters for the Extraction of Cellulose and Production of Cellulose Nanocrystals from Apple Pomace. *Carbohydr. Polym.* **2019**, *215*, 330–337. [CrossRef]
22. Ranjbar, D.; Raeiszadeh, M.; Lewis, L.; MacLachlan, M.J.; Hatzikiriakos, S.G. Adsorptive Removal of Congo Red by Surfactant Modified Cellulose Nanocrystals: A Kinetic, Equilibrium, and Mechanistic Investigation. *Cellulose* **2020**, *27*, 3211–3232. [CrossRef]
23. Jung, Y.; Jung, Y.; Kwon, M.; Kye, H.; Abrha, Y.W.; Kang, J.W. Evaluation of Moringa Oleifera Seed Extract by Extraction Time: Effect on Coagulation Efficiency and Extract Characteristic. *J. Water Health* **2018**, *16*, 904–913. [CrossRef]
24. Jerri, H.A.; Adolfsen, K.J.; McCullough, L.R.; Velegol, D.; Velegol, S.B. Antimicrobial Sand via Adsorption of Cationic Moringa Oleifera Protein. *Langmuir* **2012**, *28*, 2262–2268. [CrossRef]

25. Nordmark, B.A.; Przybycien, T.M.; Tilton, R.D. Comparative Coagulation Performance Study of Moringa Oleifera Cationic Protein Fractions with Varying Water Hardness. *J. Environ. Chem. Eng.* **2016**, *4*, 4690–4698. [CrossRef]
26. Samineni, L.; Xiong, B.; Chowdhury, R.; Pei, A.; Kuehster, L.; Wang, H.; Dickey, R.; Soto, P.E.; Massenburg, L.; Nguyen, T.H.; et al. 7 Log Virus Removal in a Simple Functionalized Sand Filter. *Environ. Sci. Technol.* **2019**, *53*, 12706–12714. [CrossRef] [PubMed]
27. Abdul Hamid, S.H.; Lananan, F.; Khatoon, H.; Jusoh, A.; Endut, A. A Study of Coagulating Protein of Moringa Oleifera in Microalgae Bio-Flocculation. *Int. Biodeterior. Biodegrad.* **2016**, *113*, 310–317. [CrossRef]
28. Sluiter, A.; Hames, B.; Ruiz, R.O.; Scarlata, C.; Sluiter, J.; Templeton, D.; Crocker, D. Determination of Structural Carbohydrates and Lignin in Biomass. *Lab. Anal. Proced.* **2008**, *1617*, 1–16.
29. Hou, L.; Jia, L.; Morrison, H.M.; Majumder, E.L.-W.; Kumar, D. Enhanced Polyhydroxybutyrate Production from Acid Whey through Determination of Process and Metabolic Limiting Factors. *Bioresour. Technol.* **2021**, *342*, 125973. [CrossRef]
30. Sai Prasanna, N.; Mitra, J. Isolation and Characterization of Cellulose Nanocrystals from Cucumis Sativus Peels. *Carbohydr. Polym.* **2020**, *247*, 116706. [CrossRef] [PubMed]
31. Zhu, S.; Sun, H.; Mu, T.; Li, Q.; Richel, A. Preparation of Cellulose Nanocrystals from Purple Sweet Potato Peels by Ultrasound-Assisted Maleic Acid Hydrolysis. *Food Chem.* **2023**, *403*, 134496. [CrossRef] [PubMed]
32. Foster, E.J.; Moon, R.J.; Agarwal, U.P.; Bortner, M.J.; Bras, J.; Camarero-Espinosa, S.; Chan, K.J.; Clift, M.J.D.D.; Cranston, E.D.; Eichhorn, S.J.; et al. Current Characterization Methods for Cellulose Nanomaterials. *Chem. Soc. Rev.* **2018**, *47*, 2609–2679. [CrossRef]
33. Hossain, S.; Stuart, T.D.; Ramarao, B.V.; VanLeuven, C.C.; Wriedt, M.; Kiemle, D.; Satchwell, M.; Kumar, D. Investigation into Cationic Surfactants and Polyelectrolyte-Coated B Zeolites for Rapid and High-Capacity Adsorption of Short- and Long-Chain PFAS. *Ind. Eng. Chem. Res.* **2023**, *62*, 8373–8384. [CrossRef]
34. Shoemaker, J.A.; Tettenhorst, D.R. *EPA Method 537.1 Determination of Selected per- and Polyfluorinated Alkyl Substances in Drinking Water by Solid Phase Extraction and Liquid Chromatography/Tandem Mass Spectroscopy (LC/MS/MS)*; US EPA: Washington, DC, USA, 2018; Volume 1.
35. Mozaffari Majd, M.; Kordzadeh-Kermani, V.; Ghalandari, V.; Askari, A.; Sillanpää, M. Adsorption Isotherm Models: A Comprehensive and Systematic Review (2010–2020). *Sci. Total Environ.* **2022**, *812*, 151334. [CrossRef]
36. Appleman, T.D.; Dickenson, E.R.V.; Bellona, C.; Higgins, C.P. Nanofiltration and Granular Activated Carbon Treatment of Perfluoroalkyl Acids. *J. Hazard. Mater.* **2013**, *260*, 740–746. [CrossRef]
37. Coelho, C.C.S.; Michelin, M.; Cerqueira, M.A.; Gonçalves, C.; Tonon, R.V.; Pastrana, L.M.; Freitas-Silva, O.; Vicente, A.A.; Cabral, L.M.C.; Teixeira, J.A. Cellulose Nanocrystals from Grape Pomace: Production, Properties and Cytotoxicity Assessment. *Carbohydr. Polym.* **2018**, *192*, 327–336. [CrossRef]
38. Rhim, J.W.; Reddy, J.P.; Luo, X. Isolation of Cellulose Nanocrystals from Onion Skin and Their Utilization for the Preparation of Agar-Based Bio-Nanocomposites Films. *Cellulose* **2015**, *22*, 407–420. [CrossRef]
39. Wijaya, C.J.; Saputra, S.N.; Soetaredjo, F.E.; Putro, J.N.; Lin, C.X.; Kurniawan, A.; Ju, Y.H.; Ismadji, S. Cellulose Nanocrystals from Passion Fruit Peels Waste as Antibiotic Drug Carrier. *Carbohydr. Polym.* **2017**, *175*, 370–376. [CrossRef] [PubMed]
40. Dezfooli, S.M.; Uversky, V.N.; Saleem, M.; Baharudin, F.S.; Hitam, S.M.S.; Bachmann, R.T. A Simplified Method for the Purification of an Intrinsically Disordered Coagulant Protein from Defatted Moringa Oleifera Seeds. *Process Biochem.* **2016**, *51*, 1085–1091. [CrossRef]
41. Saa, R.W.; Fombang, E.N.; Ndjantou, E.B.; Njintang, N.Y. Treatments and Uses of Moringa Oleifera Seeds in Human Nutrition: A Review. *Food Sci. Nutr.* **2019**, *7*, 1911–1919. [CrossRef] [PubMed]
42. Tukki, O.H.; Barminas, J.T.; Osemeahon, S.A.; Onwuka, J.C.; Donatus, R.A. Adsorption of Colloidal Particles of Moringa Oleifera Seeds on Clay for Water Treatment Applications. *J. Water Supply Res. Technol.-AQUA* **2016**, *65*, 75–86. [CrossRef]
43. Samineni, L.; De Respino, S.; Tu, Y.; Chowdhury, R.; Mohanty, R.P.; Oh, H.; Geitner, M.; Alberg, C.H.; Roman-white, A.; Mckinzie, S.; et al. Effective Pathogen Removal in Sustainable Natural Fiber Moringa Filters. *NPJ Clean. Water* **2022**, *5*, 27. [CrossRef]
44. Habibi, Y.; Lucia, L.A.; Rojas, O.J. Cellulose Nanocrystals: Chemistry, Self-Assembly, and Applications. *Chem. Rev.* **2010**, *110*, 3479–3500. [CrossRef]
45. Mariano, M.; El Kissi, N.; Dufresne, A. Cellulose Nanocrystals and Related Nanocomposites: Review of Some Properties and Challenges. *J. Polym. Sci. B Polym. Phys.* **2014**, *52*, 791–806. [CrossRef]
46. Morán, J.I.; Alvarez, V.A.; Cyras, V.P.; Vázquez, A. Extraction of Cellulose and Preparation of Nanocellulose from Sisal Fibers. *Cellulose* **2008**, *15*, 149–159. [CrossRef]
47. Nisha, R.R.; Jegathambal, P.; Parameswari, K.; Kirupa, K. Biocompatible Water Softening System Using Cationic Protein from Moringa Oleifera Extract. *Appl. Water Sci.* **2017**, *7*, 2933–2941. [CrossRef]
48. Yang, H.; Yan, R.; Chen, H.; Lee, D.H.; Zheng, C. Characteristics of Hemicellulose, Cellulose and Lignin Pyrolysis. *Fuel* **2007**, *86*, 1781–1788. [CrossRef]
49. Babaei-Ghazvini, A.; Acharya, B. The Effects of Aspect Ratio of Cellulose Nanocrystals on the Properties of All CNC Films: Tunicate and Wood CNCs. *Carbohydr. Polym. Technol. Appl.* **2023**, *5*, 100691. [CrossRef]
50. Wang, G.; Zhang, J.; Lin, S.; Xiao, H.; Yang, Q.; Chen, S.; Yan, B.; Gu, Y. Environmentally Friendly Nanocomposites Based on Cellulose Nanocrystals and Polydopamine for Rapid Removal of Organic Dyes in Aqueous Solution. *Cellulose* **2020**, *27*, 2085–2097. [CrossRef]

51. Brinkmann, A.; Chen, M.; Couillard, M.; Jakubek, Z.J.; Leng, T.; Johnston, L.J. Correlating Cellulose Nanocrystal Particle Size and Surface Area. *Langmuir* **2016**, *32*, 6105–6114. [CrossRef] [PubMed]
52. Verma, C.; Chhajed, M.; Gupta, P.; Roy, S.; Maji, P.K. Isolation of Cellulose Nanocrystals from Different Waste Bio-Mass Collating Their Liquid Crystal Ordering with Morphological Exploration. *Int. J. Biol. Macromol.* **2021**, *175*, 242–253. [CrossRef]
53. Gicquel, E.; Martin, C.; Heux, L.; Jean, B.; Bras, J. Adsorption versus Grafting of Poly(N-Isopropylacrylamide) in Aqueous Conditions on the Surface of Cellulose Nanocrystals. *Carbohydr. Polym.* **2019**, *210*, 100–109. [CrossRef]
54. Brockman, A.C.; Hubbe, M.A. Charge Reversal System with Cationized Cellulose Nanocrystals to Promote Dewatering of a Cellulosic Fiber Suspension. *Cellulose* **2017**, *24*, 4821–4830. [CrossRef]
55. Nouhi, S.; Kwaambwa, H.M.; Gutfreund, P.; Rennie, A.R. Comparative Study of Flocculation and Adsorption Behaviour of Water Treatment Proteins from Moringa Peregrina and Moringa Oleifera Seeds. *Sci. Rep.* **2019**, *9*, 17945. [CrossRef] [PubMed]
56. Phong Vo, H.N.; Ngo, H.H.; Guo, W.; Hong Nguyen, T.M.; Li, J.; Liang, H.; Deng, L.; Chen, Z.; Hang Nguyen, T.A. Poly-and Perfluoroalkyl Substances in Water and Wastewater: A Comprehensive Review from Sources to Remediation. *J. Water Process Eng.* **2020**, *36*, 101393. [CrossRef]
57. He, J.; Gomeniuc, A.; Olshansky, Y.; Hatton, J.; Abrell, L.; Field, J.A.; Chorover, J.; Sierra-Alvarez, R. Enhanced Removal of Per- and Polyfluoroalkyl Substances by Crosslinked Polyaniline Polymers. *Chem. Eng. J.* **2022**, *446*, 137246. [CrossRef]
58. Qu, Y.; Zhang, C.; Li, F.; Bo, X.; Liu, G.; Zhou, Q. Equilibrium and Kinetics Study on the Adsorption of Perfluorooctanoic Acid from Aqueous Solution onto Powdered Activated Carbon. *J. Hazard. Mater.* **2009**, *169*, 146–152. [CrossRef]
59. Ateia, M.; Attia, M.F.; Maroli, A.; Tharayil, N.; Alexis, F.; Whitehead, D.C.; Karanfil, T. Rapid Removal of Poly- and Perfluorinated Alkyl Substances by Poly(Ethylenimine)-Functionalized Cellulose Microcrystals at Environmentally Relevant Conditions. *Environ. Sci. Technol. Lett.* **2018**, *5*, 764–769. [CrossRef]
60. Köse, K.; Mavlan, M.; Youngblood, J.P. Applications and Impact of Nanocellulose Based Adsorbents. *Cellulose* **2020**, *27*, 2967–2990. [CrossRef]
61. Kostoglou, M.; Karapantsios, T.D. Why Is the Linearized Form of Pseudo-Second Order Adsorption Kinetic Model So Successful in Fitting Batch Adsorption Experimental Data? *Colloids Interfaces* **2022**, *6*, 55. [CrossRef]
62. Zhang, D.; He, Q.; Wang, M.; Zhang, W.; Liang, Y. Sorption of Perfluoroalkylated Substances (PFASs) onto Granular Activated Carbon and Biochar. *Environ. Technol.* **2021**, *42*, 1798–1809. [CrossRef]
63. Liu, L.; Li, D.; Li, C.; Ji, R.; Tian, X. Metal Nanoparticles by Doping Carbon Nanotubes Improved the Sorption of Perfluorooctanoic Acid. *J. Hazard. Mater.* **2018**, *351*, 206–214. [CrossRef] [PubMed]
64. Barisci, S.; Suri, R. Occurrence and Removal of Poly/Perfluoroalkyl Substances (PFAS) in Municipal and Industrial Wastewater Treatment Plants. *Water Sci. Technol.* **2021**, *84*, 3442–3468. [CrossRef] [PubMed]
65. Son, H.; Kim, T.; Yoom, H.; Zhao, D.; An, B. And Polyfluoroalkyl Substances (PFASs) from Surface Water Using Powder-Activated Carbon. *Water* **2020**, *12*, 3287. [CrossRef]
66. Sörengård, M.; Östblom, E.; Köhler, S.; Ahrens, L. Adsorption Behavior of Per- And Polyfluoroalkyl Substances (PFASs) to 44 Inorganic and Organic Sorbents and Use of Dyes as Proxies for PFAS Sorption. *J. Environ. Chem. Eng.* **2020**, *8*, 103744. [CrossRef]
67. Militao, I.M.; Roddick, F.; Bergamasco, R.; Fan, L. Rapid Adsorption of PFAS. Application of Moringa Oleifera Seed Powder Encapsulated in Alginate Beads. *Environ. Technol. Innov.* **2022**, *28*, 102761. [CrossRef]
68. Ramos, P.; Singh Kalra, S.; Johnson, N.W.; Khor, C.M.; Borthakur, A.; Cranmer, B.; Dooley, G.; Mohanty, S.K.; Jassby, D.; Blotevogel, J.; et al. Enhanced Removal of Per- and Polyfluoroalkyl Substances in Complex Matrices by PolyDADMAC-Coated Regenerable Granular Activated Carbon. *Environ. Pollut.* **2022**, *294*, 118603. [CrossRef] [PubMed]
69. Kwaambwa, H.M.; Maikokera, R. A Fluorescence Spectroscopic Study of a Coagulating Protein Extracted from Moringa Oleifera Seeds. *Colloids Surf. B Biointerfaces* **2007**, *60*, 213–220. [CrossRef] [PubMed]
70. Gagliano, E.; Sgroi, M.; Falciglia, P.P.; Vagliasindi, F.G.A.; Roccaro, P. Removal of Poly- and Perfluoroalkyl Substances (PFAS) from Water by Adsorption: Role of PFAS Chain Length, Effect of Organic Matter and Challenges in Adsorbent Regeneration. *Water Res.* **2020**, *171*, 115381. [CrossRef]
71. Makowski, M.; Bogunia, M. Influence of Ionic Strength on Hydrophobic Interactions in Water: Dependence on Solute Size and Shape. *J. Phys. Chem. B* **2020**, *124*, 10326–10336. [CrossRef]
72. Qi, Y.; Cao, H.; Pan, W.; Wang, C.; Liang, Y. The Role of Dissolved Organic Matter during Per- and Polyfluorinated Substance (PFAS) Adsorption, Degradation, and Plant Uptake: A Review. *J. Hazard. Mater.* **2022**, *436*, 129139. [CrossRef]
73. Lei, X.; Yao, L.; Lian, Q.; Zhang, X.; Wang, T.; Holmes, W.; Ding, G.; Gang, D.D.; Zappi, M.E. Enhanced Adsorption of Perfluorooctanoate (PFOA) onto Low Oxygen Content Ordered Mesoporous Carbon (OMC): Adsorption Behaviors and Mechanisms. *J. Hazard. Mater.* **2022**, *421*, 126810. [CrossRef] [PubMed]
74. Evans, C.D.; Monteith, D.T.; Cooper, D.M. Long-Term Increases in Surface Water Dissolved Organic Carbon: Observations, Possible Causes and Environmental Impacts. *Environ. Pollut.* **2005**, *137*, 55–71. [CrossRef] [PubMed]

Disclaimer/Publisher's Note: The statements, opinions and data contained in all publications are solely those of the individual author(s) and contributor(s) and not of MDPI and/or the editor(s). MDPI and/or the editor(s) disclaim responsibility for any injury to people or property resulting from any ideas, methods, instructions or products referred to in the content.

Article

The Crucial Impact of Microbial Growth and Bioenergy Conversion on Treating Livestock Manure and Antibiotics Using *Chlorella sorokiniana*

Hee-Jun Kim [1,2,†], Sangjun Jeong [1,3,†], YeonA Lee [4], Jae-Cheol Lee [5,6] and Hyun-Woo Kim [1,4,*]

1. Department of Environmental Engineering, Soil Environment Research Center, Jeonbuk National University, 567 Baekje-daero, Deokjin-gu, Jeonju-si 54896, Republic of Korea; heejun.kim@kitox.re.kr (H.-J.K.); tkdwns1264@naver.com (S.J.)
2. Environmental Fate and Exposure Research Group, Korea Institute of Toxicology, Jinju-si 52834, Republic of Korea
3. Water Environmental Research Center, Jeonbuk National University, 109, Ballyong-ro, Deokjin-gu, Jeonju-si 54896, Republic of Korea
4. Department of Environment and Energy (BK21 Four), Jeonbuk National University, 567 Baekje-daero, Deokjin-gu, Jeonju-si 54896, Republic of Korea; lee98@jbnu.ac.kr
5. Division of Environmental Materials, Honam National Institute of Biological Resources (HNIBR), Mokpo 58762, Republic of Korea; jc.lee@hnibr.re.kr
6. Department of Environmental Engineering, School of Architecture, Civil and Environmental Engineering, Mokpo National University, Mokpo 58554, Republic of Korea
* Correspondence: hyunwoo@jbnu.ac.kr; Tel.: +82-63-270-2446
† These authors contributed equally and are considered joint co-first authors.

Abstract: The residual antibiotics in livestock excreta (LE) have been regarded as a potential threat to the ecosystem and human society. Some photoautotrophic microalgae, however, were found to metabolize them during active biomass photosynthesis. This study investigates how the strength of the antibiotics impacts the overall biodiesel yield and composition of the harvested microalgal biomass grown from LE. The microalgal growth results demonstrate that increasing the concentration of residual antibiotics suppresses the microalgal growth rate from 0.87 d^{-1} to 0.34 d^{-1}. This 61% lower biomass production rate supports the proposition that the kinetic impact of antibiotics may slow lipid synthesis. Moreover, the analytical results of fatty acid methyl ester (FAME) demonstrate that amoxicillin substantially reduces the C16:0 content by over 96%. This study evidences that the functional group similarity of amoxicillin may competitively inhibit the esterification reaction by consuming methanol. This explanation further highlights that residual antibiotics interfere with microalgal lipid synthesis and its transesterification. Moreover, it was confirmed that the presence of residual antibiotics may not affect the major nutrient removal (total nitrogen: 74.5~78.0%, total phosphorus: 95.6~96.8%). This indicates that residual antibiotics inhibit the metabolism associated with carbon rather than those associated with nitrogen and phosphorus, which is connected to the decrease in the biodiesel yield. Overall, these results reveal that the frequent abuse of antibiotics in livestock may harm the eco-friendly conversion of waste-into-bioenergy strategy.

Keywords: livestock excreta; microalgae; antibiotics; biodiesel; bioenergy conversion

Citation: Kim, H.-J.; Jeong, S.; Lee, Y.; Lee, J.-C.; Kim, H.-W. The Crucial Impact of Microbial Growth and Bioenergy Conversion on Treating Livestock Manure and Antibiotics Using *Chlorella sorokiniana*. *Processes* **2024**, *12*, 252. https://doi.org/10.3390/pr12020252

Academic Editors: Dimitris Zagklis and Georgios Bampos

Received: 23 December 2023
Revised: 12 January 2024
Accepted: 22 January 2024
Published: 24 January 2024

Copyright: © 2024 by the authors. Licensee MDPI, Basel, Switzerland. This article is an open access article distributed under the terms and conditions of the Creative Commons Attribution (CC BY) license (https://creativecommons.org/licenses/by/4.0/).

1. Introduction

In recent decades, factory farming has caused various environmental problems in the development of the livestock industry because it is inevitably associated with the large-scale generation of livestock excreta (LE) [1,2]. In addition, the feed can influence not only the quality of the livestock but also the characteristics of the LE [3,4]. The LE contains not only well-known environmental pollutants but also residual pharmaceuticals that can be harmful to the ecosystem and human health [5]. Due to the continuous abuse of antibiotics, they enter receiving water in the form of point or non-point source pathways [6]. Unlike other pollutants, they are present at very low concentrations, but even at the parts per billion (ppb) levels, they may cause bioaccumulation and toxicity in living organisms [6,7]. Moreover, LE treatment cannot be free from problems such as eutrophication, antibiotic-resistant bacteria, antibiotic-resistant gene transfer, greenhouse gases, and odor [8,9].

Antibiotics are commonly overused on most farms for excessive disease prevention, growth promotion, and efficient management of livestock's productivity [10,11]. Among the well-known antibiotics, amoxicillin (AMX) is a penicillin antibiotic with significant broad-spectrum and semi-synthetic characteristics [12]. AMX belongs to the beta-lactam group of antibiotics, which is active against a wide spectrum of Gram-positive bacteria [13]. AMX in the ecosystem, however, may increase the spread of antibacterial-resistant genes and ultimately result in the reproduction of beta-lactam-resistant bacteria [14]. Furthermore, long-time exposure to AMX may lead to liver injury, which is stimulated by amoxicillin-clavulanate-acid-secreted IFN-γ [15]. If AMX remains in the water environment, it poses a potential threat to both the ecosystem and human health [16–18]. Therefore, it is necessary to eliminate AMX in a highly efficient and sustainable way to minimize its potential hazard to humans. Additionally, antibiotics may potentially reduce the treatment efficiency of pollutants in the wastewater treatment process [19]. Moreover, due to their complex chemical structures, physico-chemical processes may be necessary for effective treatment [20].

From a viewpoint of waste-into-energy conversion and the circular economy, however, LE may be a valuable resource for renewable and sustainable energy that can contribute to replacing fossil fuels [21,22]. Thus, intensive research on biofuel (e.g., biodiesel, biogas, and bio-alcohols) generation from LE has been conducted internationally [23,24].

Although using microalgae could significantly remove both the total nitrogen and total phosphorus from LE while recovering the resources of bioenergy and biomass [25,26], traditional wastewater treatment facilities have shown a limited capability to treat residual pharmaceuticals [27]. Previous reports on microalgal treatment suggest that bioremediation of antibiotics is possible as an ecologically broad and sustainable approach which is gaining scientific attention [28].

Among various microalgae, *Chlorella* spp. are suitable species that can treat LE and antibiotics; however, the previous focus has been to verify biomass productivity [29]. In contrast to the effect of antibiotics on biomass, their impact on the bioenergy yield or components remains largely unknown. Hence, this study tests a microalgal treatment using *C. sorokiniana* to reduce the contaminants in LE together with antibiotics. Experiments were designed to confirm how the strength of the antibiotics affects the photosynthesis of *C. sorokiniana* and what factors causes the deterioration in the biodiesel potential. Specifically, the experiments were designed to evaluate the growth kinetic constants of *C. sorokiniana* according to the amount of AMX, to reveal the inhibitory mechanisms associated with AMX affecting nutrient and antibiotic removal, and to identify the causes that change the biodiesel yield and its components according to the antibiotics dose.

2. Materials and Methods

2.1. Inoculum and Culture Conditions

This study used *C. sorokiniana* as the inoculum, which was obtained from the Korean Collection for Type Cultures (KCTC). It has been reported that *C. sorokiniana* easily adapts to various environmental conditions and reduces the total nitrogen and total phosphorus significantly in wastewater [30]. The medium used for culturing the microalgae was BG-11, which is an artificial medium commonly used for culturing microalgae [31]. The composition of BG-11 is as follows based on 1.0 L: 1 mg EDTA disodium salt, 40 mg $K_2HPO_4 \cdot 3H_2O$, 6 mg citric acid, 1.5 g $NaNO_3$, 36 mg $CaCl_2 \cdot 2H_2O$, 75 mg $MgSO_4 \cdot 7H_2O$, 6 mg ferric ammonium citrate, 20 mg $NaCO_3$, and 1 mL mixed trace metal solution. Each liter of trace metal solution contained 49 mg $Co(NO_3)_2 \cdot 6H_2O$, 2.9 g H_3BO_3, 1.8 g $MnCl_2 \cdot 4H_2O$, 0.39 g $NaMoO_4 \cdot 2H_2O$, 79 mg $CuSO_4 \cdot 5H_2O$, and 0.22 g $ZnSO_4 \cdot 7H_2O$.

Th microalgae culture was carried out under the following conditions: the temperature was 28 °C, the light cycle ratio was light/dark = 16:8, the light intensity was 180 µmol/s·m², and it was incubated for a total of 6 days in a batch reaction. The cultured microalgae biomass was harvested using centrifugation at 8000 rpm for 10 min using a centrifuge. The harvested biomass was lyophilized for 96 h at −40 °C and 5 m Torr using lyophilization because the moisture content reached about 80 wt%.

2.2. Livestock Excreta Characteristics and Antibiotics

The LE used for the microalgae cultivation was obtained from a pig farm in K-City of Korea. The LE was sourced from a factory pig farming facility with a liquid manure handling system. We performed the collection of the livestock excreta (20 L) on a clear day with a temperature of approximately 25 °C. The initial characteristics of the LE are shown in Table 1. The antibiotic, used to achieve the purpose of this study, was ≥900 µg/mg AMX (Sigma-Aldrich, St. Louis, MO, USA). In this study, a large amount of amoxicillin (0.01 to 20 ppm) was tested to confirm its negative effects on the biological treatment of the LE according to the microalgal growth kinetics, biomass yield, and composition of biodiesel.

Table 1. Initial characteristics of LE.

Characteristics	Unit	Value
pH	-	7.5
CODcr (Chemical Oxygen Demand)	mg COD/L	280
T-N (Total Nitrogen)	mg N/L	120
T-P (Total Phosphorus)	mg P/L	1.5

2.3. Biodiesel Production from the Microalgae Biomass

The experimental method used for the biodiesel production in this study is direct transesterification (DT). First, lipids are extracted from the microalgae biomass by destroying the cell walls using physical, chemical, and biological methods [32]. Next, the extracted lipid is transesterified with alcohol in the presence of a catalyst to obtain methyl ester and glycerol. Finally, the final reactant is centrifuged to produce high-purity free fatty acid methyl ester (FAME).

In this study, two homogeneous catalysts (HCl and NaOH) were used to produce high-quality biodiesel of the same concentration (0.5 M based on methanol). The applied temperature varied based on the characteristics of the catalysts reported previously, meaning the acid catalyst (HCl) was optimized at a higher temperature (90 °C), while the base catalyst (NaOH) was optimized at a lower temperature (25 °C) [33]. The ratio of the biomass, catalysts, and n-hexane was adjusted to 1 g, 10 mL, and 10 mL, respectively. For the biomass, the microalgae were cultured using artificial growth medium (BG-11), the LE, and the LE containing antibiotics. At each temperature condition, the catalyst and the microalgal biomass were put into a test tube and mixed for 1 h for the DT reaction. After the reaction was completed, the FAME was extracted from the n-hexane layer. A flow chart of the overall DT process is shown in Figure 1.

The yield of FAME was calculated by dividing the total mass of the FAME by the total mass of the dried microalgae biomass. The yield of FAME was calculated using Equation (1) below [34].

$$\text{FAME yield } (\%) = \frac{\text{Total mass of FAME (g)}}{\text{Total mass of dried microalgae biomass (g)}} \quad (1)$$

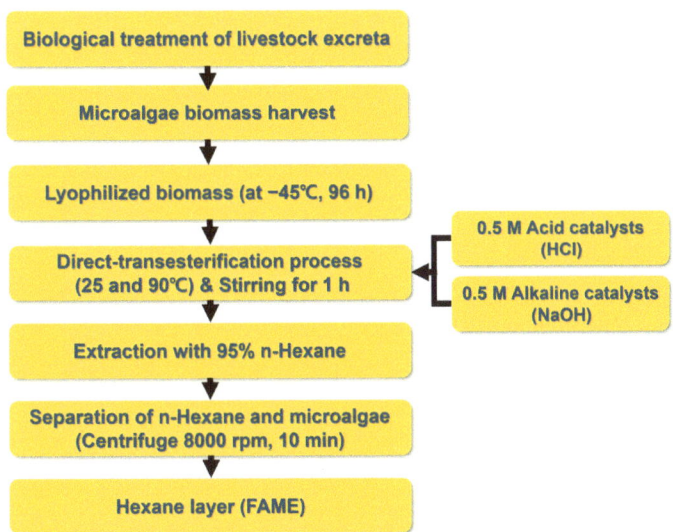

Figure 1. Experimental procedures of biodiesel production.

2.4. Analytical Methods for Water Quality and Fatty Acid Methyl Ester (FAME)

The water quality characteristics of the wastewater influent and effluent were analyzed following the standard methods. We employed the Standard Methods for the determination of total nitrogen (T-N) and total phosphorus (T-P): 4500 NC (persulfate digestion) and 4500 PE (ascorbic acid), respectively [35]. The chlorophyll-a (chl-a) concentrations were analyzed using a method based on acetone extraction using spectrophotometry.

The analytical parameters for the LC-ESI/MS/MS analysis of amoxicillin were established employing an LC-ESI/MS/MS Triple Quadrupole (6410 LC/MS/MS, Agilent, Santa Clara, CA, USA) equipped with HPLC and an electrospray ionization source (Agilent Technologies). The mobile phase comprised a blend of 0.1% formic acid in distilled water and 0.1% formic acid in acetonitrile (ACN), employed on a Synergi Hydro-RP 80 Å (150 × 2 mm) (97:3, v/v) and introduced into the system at a flow rate of 0.2 mL/min. The column oven temperature was 30 °C and the sample injection volume was 5.0 µL. Mass spectrometric detection was performed using a series 6410 LC-MS/MS Triple Quadrupole (Agilent Technologies) using multiple reaction monitoring.

The yield and composition of the extracted FAME were analyzed using a gas chromatograph (GC) (GC 2020, Shimadzu, Kyoto, Japan). The GC was equipped with a flame ionization detector (FID) and an SPTM-2330 capillary column (30 m × 0.25 mm × 0.20 µm; Sigma-Aldrich, USA). The methods used for the analysis are as follows: (1) Helium was used as the carrier gas (constantly 1 mL/min and the split ratio was 10:1); (2) The temperature of the FID detector and injector was set to 240 °C; (3) The oven temperature was programmed from 140 °C to 220 °C at a rate of 4 °C/min. The peak was interpreted based on the FAME mixture (CRM 18918, Supelco, Bellefonte, PA, USA) from C8:0 to C24:0.

3. Results and Discussion

3.1. Negative Effect on the Microalgae Growth of AMX

Figure 2 presents the change in chl-a, T-N, and T-P at the various concentrations of AMX while treating the LE. It was observed that the control experiment with no AMX showed an exponential growth pattern for chl-a. When the residual AMX concentration varied from 0.01 to 20 mg/L, the amount of chl-a was higher than the control for 4 days. On the fifth day, that of the control exceeded all the reactors due to the active exponential growth phase. This higher chl-a content in the initial startup periods implies that AMX might stimulate the growth of *C. sorokiniana*, which uptakes AMX according to bioaccumulation and bioadsorption mechanisms [36], and the transferred AMX must have caused a hormetic effect [37]. It seems that the stimulation may not last longer than 5 days, possibly due to the increasing oxidative stress within algal cells induced by AMX, which leads to the overturn in the chl-a content [38,39].

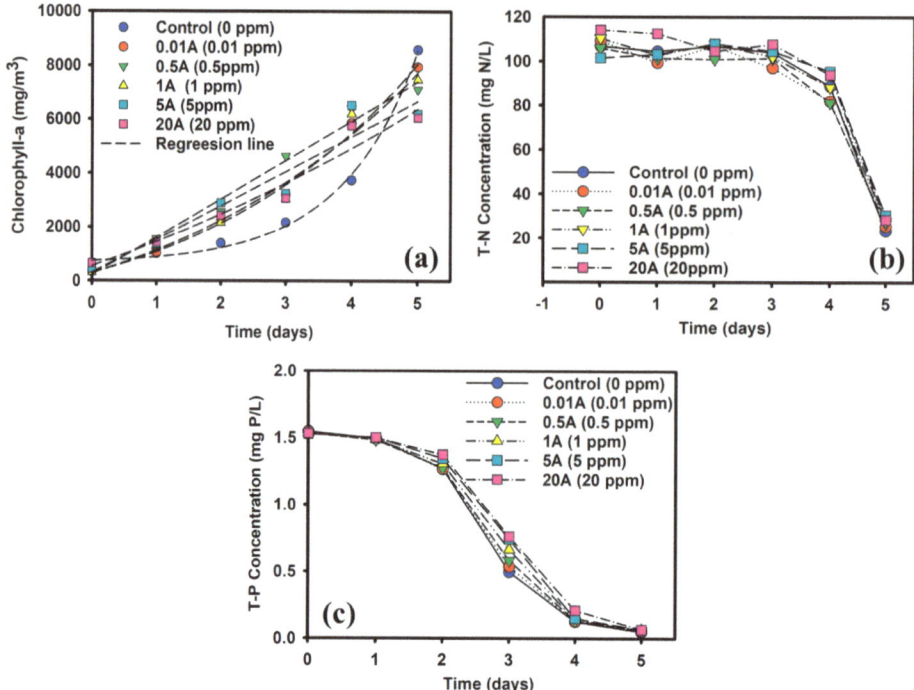

Figure 2. Variations in (**a**) chlorophyll-a, (**b**) T-N, and (**c**) T-P according to the change in antibiotic concentration in the microalgal treatment of LE.

Table 2 compares the final chl-a content, average daily growth rate, and specific growth rate of each experiment quantitatively after 5 days of culturing. The chl-a content of the control increased from 327.7 mg/m^3 to 8583 mg/m^3 while that of 0.01~20 ppm AMX increased to 7947~6052 mg/m^3. Compared to the control, the results evidence that the photosynthesis is inhibited more significantly by the end as the concentration of residual antibiotics increases. This is consistent with a previous study that revealed the metabolic inhibition of AMX in microalgae [40]. The specific growth rate obtained from a regression of growth pattern further supports the overall inhibitory effect of AMX. In the control, the specific growth rate was 0.87 days^{-1}. However, the rates gradually reduced to as low as 0.34 days^{-1} as the concentration of residual AMX increased from 0.01 to 20 ppm.

AMX, known as a beta-lactam antibiotic, can disrupt penicillin-binding proteins and interfere in the biosynthesis of the cell walls, causing osmotic rupture of the microalgae [41]. Also, beta-lactams significantly inhibit the growth and physiological processes of the algae by disturbing the primary photochemistry, photophosphorylation, electron transport, and carbon assimilation [42], which can lead to a reduction in biomass growth, a reduction in various syntheses [43,44], and even cell death [45]. Thus, the experimental results evidence that as the concentration of residual antibiotics increases, this reduces the microalgal growth rate by ~26.1% according to the prescribed inhibition mechanisms. These decreasing trends are consistent with those of other studies, which presented more significant inhibition by 25.6~79.9% in the biomass growth due to AMX [40,46].

Table 2. Chl-a concentration and specific growth rate according to residual AMX strength.

AMX Strength (mg/L)	Initial Chl-a (mg/m^3)	Final Chl-a (mg/m^3)	Average Daily Microalgae Growth (mg/m^3/Day)	Specific Growth Rate (Days^{-1})
0		8583	1651	0.87
0.01		7947	1519	0.46
0.5	328 [1]	7108	1345	0.35
1		7475	1435	0.43
5		6194	1150	0.34
20		6052	1080	0.35

[1] Initial average chl-a value of control experiment. Standard deviation was ±56 mg/m^3.

Overall, despite the initial growth stimulation, these results indicate that residual AMX may deteriorate the treatment performance of LE due to unavoidable inhibition, leading to decreased photoautotrophic cell synthesis.

3.2. Nutrient and AMX Removal in Microalgae Treatment

3.2.1. Effect of AMX on T-N Removal

Figure 2b shows the T-N reduction according to the residual antibiotic concentration. Table 3 tabulates the initial and final contents of T-N and the corresponding T-N removal efficiency in each experiment. The monitored T-N removal efficiency ranges from 78.0 to 74.5%. It was revealed that variation in the residual AMX concentration demonstrated no significant change in the removal efficiency. This indicates that *C. sorokiniana* actively assimilates nitrogen via its photoautotrophic metabolism despite the existence of AMX [47]. This non-correlated T-N removal means that AMX has little impact on the microalgal absorption of T-N despite the restriction of microalgal growth, and the free ammonia level of this study seems much lower than that of the inhibition level. This is consistent with previous batch studies which demonstrated an approximate 98% nitrogen removal, a result achieved without the influence of specific antibiotic inhibition [48,49]. Previous studies have also indicated that existing co-substrates, which are plentiful in livestock excreta, may enhance the degradation of AMX and promote the synthesis of proteins associated with T-N absorption [41].

Table 3 compares the nitrogen removal efficiency according to the microalgal species and the existence of antibiotics. Despite the presence of antibiotics, the T-N removal efficiency of the microalgae was maintained higher than seen in the literature [50]. Other studies showed a high nitrogen treatment efficiency even when wastewater contained the antibiotics AMX and sulfamethoxazole (SMX) but showed a longer operation period (7~18 days), and the initial concentration (45~55.4 mg N/L) was also lower than our study [43,49]. Also, microalgae without antibiotics presented a relatively similar or lower removal efficiency (29.4~70.4%) although the treatment time was longer (7~10 days) [50–53]. Overall, T-N removal by *C. sorokiniana* is not significantly affected by AMX even at a concentration of 20 mg/L. It seems that the interactions related to the co-substrates influence the maintenance of photosynthetic activity if the free ammonia level is kept below the inhibition level [47,54].

3.2.2. Effect of AMX on T-P Removal

Figure 2c shows the T-P reduction for each AMX concentration. And Table 4 shows the initial, final, and corresponding removal efficiency according to the experimental conditions. The exact initial T-P concentrations were 1.53~1.55 mg P/L and the final concentrations were 0.04~0.07 mgP/L. The T-P removal efficiency reached as high as 95.6~96.8%. Although a slight decrease (about 1.2%) in the overall T-P removal efficiency was seen, AMX seems to have an effect on the T-P removal because the maximum removal rate of T-P at around day 2~3 decreased from 0.77 to 0.61 mg P/L/day. This seems to be associated with microalgae growth inhibition, but the consequences on the whole seem negligible.

Table 3. T-N concentration and removal efficiency according to residual antibiotic concentration.

Microalgae	Antibiotic Type	Antibiotic Strength (mg/L)	Initial T-N (mg N/L)	Effluent T-N (mg N/L)	Removal Efficiency (%)	Operation Period	Reference
Chlorella sorokiniana	AMX	0	106.9	23.5	78.0	5	This study
		0.01	109.4	25.5	77.0		
		0.5	106.0	27.0	76.0		
		1	110.4	28.0	75.2		
		5	101.7	30.5	74.6		
		20	114.2	28.5	74.5		
Chlorella vulgaris and Scenedesmus dimorphus	-	-	-	-	70.4	10	[51]
Chlorella vulgaris and Scenedesmus dimorphus	-	-	-	-	64.5	10	[52]
Chlorella sorokiniana	-	-	214.9	150.3	29.4	7	[50]
Chlorella vulgaris	-	-	113.3	51.8	54.3	7	[53]
Chlorella vulgaris	SMX	0.5	55.4	0.84	98.5	7	[49]
Chlorella regularis	AMX	3	45	7.92	82.4	18	[43]

Table 4 compares the T-P treatment results with previous studies to confirm the applicability of the microalgal leachate treatment. Including the results of this study, antibiotic application cases (95.6~98.7%) [43,49] show a better T-P removal efficiency than those without antibiotics (37.0~79.7%) [51,55–57]. The better removal of nutrients seems to be attributed to either the rapid absorption for the initial stimulation of growth or the enhanced photosynthesis of existing co-substrates, even though we admit that the microalgae, wastewater source, and antibiotics used were different.

Table 4. T-P concentration and removal efficiency according to residual antibiotic concentration.

Microalgae	Antibiotic Type	Antibiotic Strength (mg/L)	Initial T-P (mg P/L)	Effluent T-P (mg P/L)	Highest Removal Rate (mg P/L/day)	Removal Efficiency (%)	Operation Periods	Reference
Chlorella sorokiniana	AMX	0	1.55	0.04	0.77	96.8	5	This study
		0.01	1.54	0.05	0.73	96.5		
		0.5	1.54	0.06	0.69	96.1		
		1	1.53	0.06	0.64	95.8		
		5	1.53	0.06	0.60	95.8		
		20	1.53	0.07	0.61	95.6		
Chlorella sp.	-	-	57.3	18.1	0.89	68.4	45	[56]
Asterarcys quadricellulare	-	-	0.40	0.20	-	50.0	8	[55]
Neochloris aquatica	-	-	0.40	0.25	-	37.0		
Chlorella vulgaris and Scenedesmus dimorphus	-	-	-	-	-	79.7	10	[51]
Chlorella vulgaris and Ganoderma lucidum	-	-	-	-	-	70.3	10	[57]
Chlorella vulgaris	SMX	0.5	27.2	0.41	3.82	98.5	7	[49]
Chlorella regularis	AMX	3	9.1	0.12	-	98.7	18	[43]

3.2.3. Reduction of Amoxicillin

Figure 3 shows the variation in AMX according to different initial concentrations. Regardless of the concentrations, the AMX content rapidly decreased down to the detection limit (0.001 mg/L) within a day. It is well known that antibiotics can be removed by microalgae via various mechanisms, which include adsorption [58], bioaccumulation [59], biodegradation [60], photolysis [61], and hydrolysis [62]. Not only is the main removal mechanism known as adsorption [37] but also *Chlorella* spp. are famous for the effective removal of various antibiotics, including AMX [28]. The results of *C. sorokiniana* are consistent with other *Chlorella* studies demonstrating an almost complete removal of AMX.

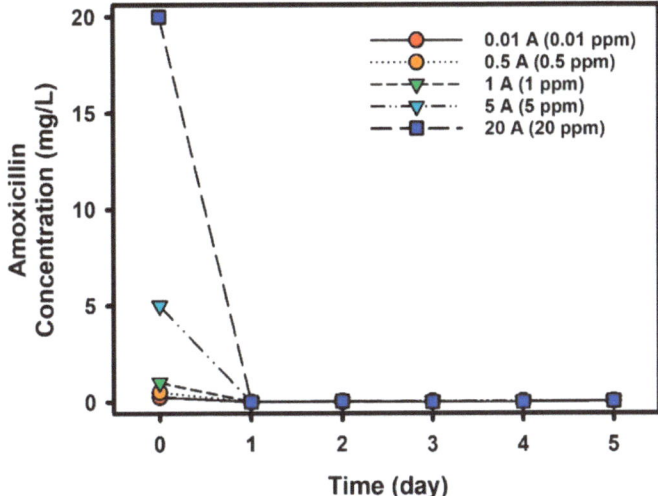

Figure 3. Antibiotic reduction according to different AMX concentrations in LE by microalgae.

In addition, because natural photoautotrophic growth uses light as an energy source, this could make photolysis contribute to AMX removal because intensive light can increase the dissolved oxygen and pH, which creates favorable conditions for photolysis. These reaction conditions may be able to induce reactive oxygen species that can support antibiotic clearance [61]. Overall, the results demonstrate that the microalgae can remove antibiotics from the water body appropriately. However, the statistical correlation and degradation mechanisms should be further demonstrated.

3.3. Inhibitory Effect of AMX on Biodiesel Production

3.3.1. Negative Effect of AMX Inhibition in Transesterification

In this study, biodiesel (FAME) was recovered from the microalgae biomass that was grown while treating LE with residual AMX according to the experimental design. Figure 4 presents the FAME yield obtained from the direct transesterification of the microalgal biomass using HCl and NaOH catalysts. It was observed that the yield decreases as the concentration of antibiotics increases. This negative correlation was more significant in the case of the HCl catalyst. The FAME yield reduced from 4.3% to 1.5%, while that of NaOH catalyst decreased from 4.3% to 2.9%. The cause of the decrease in the FAME yield must be associated with AMX's inhibition of the microalgal growth. A previous study confirmed that the higher the concentration of antibiotics, the more the microalgal photosynthesis was inhibited [28]. The results of this study were consistent with this and verify that the base catalyst might be preferable to prevent severe losses in the overall biodiesel recovery.

3.3.2. Changes in FAME Composition of Biodiesel Due to AMX

Figure 5 illustrates the variation in the FAME composition according to the residual AMX concentration and catalyst type. As a fuel, important FAME components are palmitic acid (C16:0) and stearic acid (C18:0) [63].

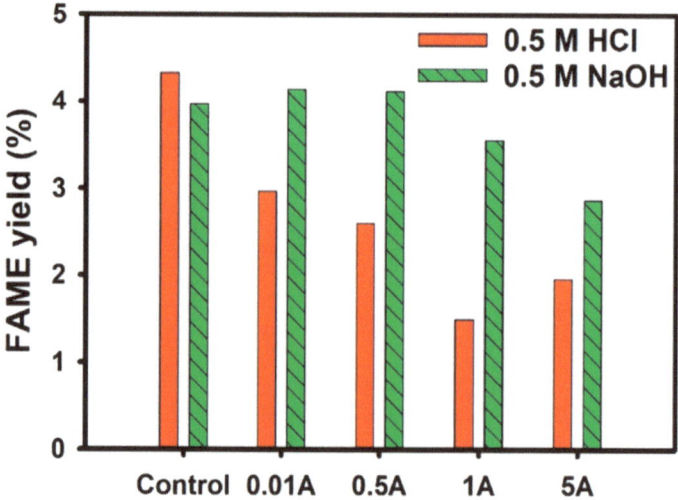

Figure 4. Effect of antibiotic concentration on FAME yield.

In the case of transesterification using HCl, the palmitic acid (C16:0) presented a drastic decrease as the residual AMX increased, while little change was observed in the case of the base catalyst. For the HCl catalyst, major elements of the FAME composition were transitioning from C16:0 to C18:2 (Figure 5b–e) and C18:3 (Figure 5b–d).

The cause of this change might be found in the esterification reaction. As shown in Equation (2), free fatty acids react with methanol and produce water through the esterification reaction.

$$\text{HOOC-R (free fatty acid)} + CH_3OH \leftrightarrow \text{R-COOCH}_3 \text{ (FAME)} + H_2O \tag{2}$$

Figure 6 compares the molecular structure of AMX with those of free fatty acids. It was observed that both AMX and free fatty acids similarly contain a carboxylic functional group (RCOOH). The carboxylic functional group of AMX also can be esterified by methanol [64]. This fact can reasonably explain why the FAME yields decrease in this study as the residual AMX concentration increases. Moreover, transesterification using an acid catalyst usually uses a temperature of 90 °C for optimal FAME recovery [65]. This high temperature may accelerate the reaction rate between the methanol and AMX, which results in methanol consumption due to this unnecessary reaction. Furthermore, Equation (2) also shows the production of water. Because the presence of water and the remaining free fatty acids may trigger soap formation, which consumes the catalyst, water also results in a low conversion rate. From these analyses, it can be confirmed that the presence of antibiotics in the transesterification process deteriorates the biodiesel yield and composition.

3.4. Limitations and Implications

This study primarily focuses on the effects of AMX in LE on microalgal growth, as well as the yield and composition of the biodiesel generated. Cultivating microalgae using LE is an eco-friendly method of converting waste into biofuel, effectively removing N and P. Additionally, the AMX in LE is degraded by microalgal metabolism, indicating that microalgae-based LE treatment can manage not only the nutrient levels but also the levels of antibiotics such as AMX.

With a continuous increase in antibiotic usage in the livestock industry, consideration of the type and concentration of antibiotics used is important. Not only AMX but various other antibiotics are used, including tetracyclines, quinolones, penicillin, cephems, ionophores, and sulfonamide [66–68]. Investigating the detailed interactions between these antibiotics and microalgal growth, as well as optimizing the conditions of cultivation, is essential. Additionally, evaluating the efficiency of continuous cultivation is essential for the industrial application of LE treatment.

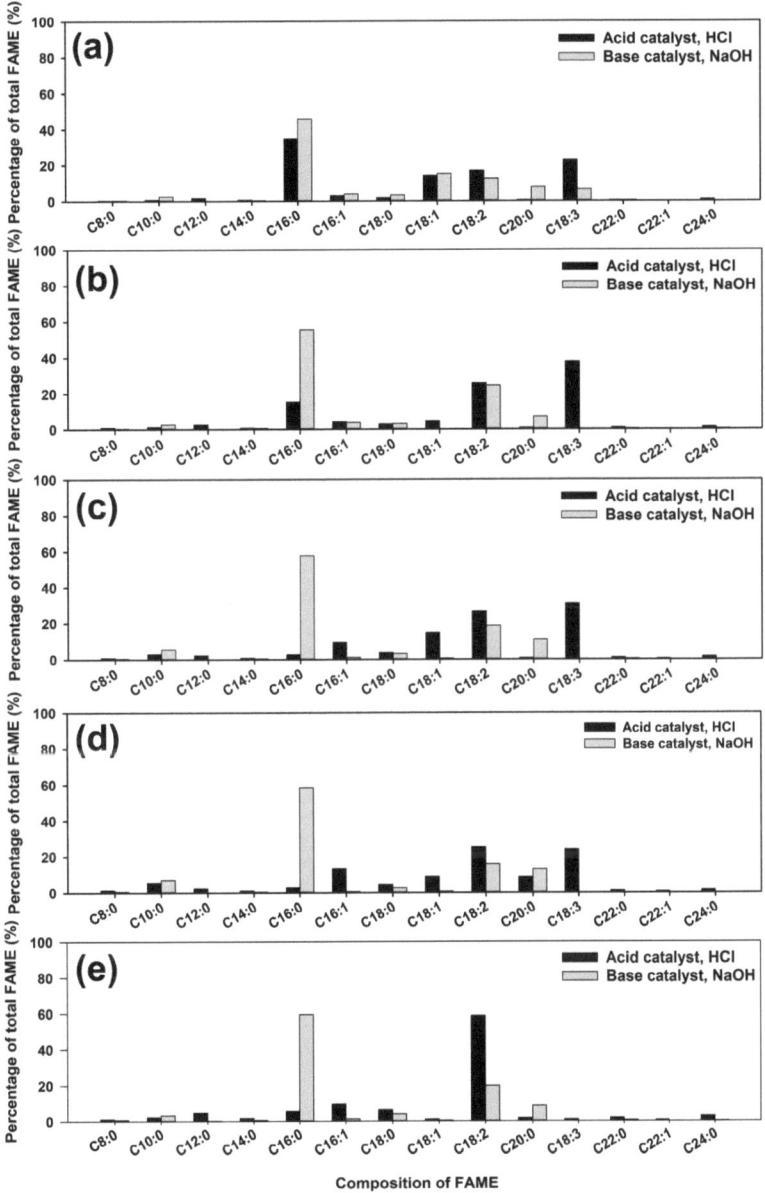

Figure 5. Change in FAME compositions according to antibiotic concentration: (**a**) control, (**b**) 0.01 ppm, (**c**) 0.5 ppm, (**d**) 1 ppm, (**e**) 5 ppm.

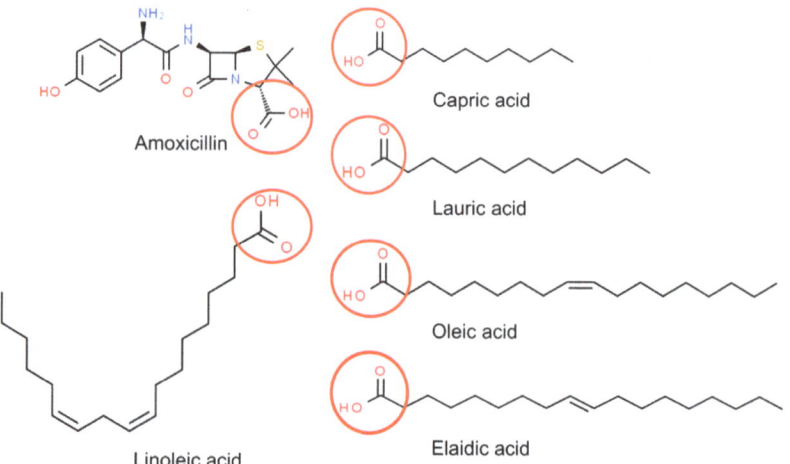

Figure 6. Comparative analysis of functional groups similarities between AMX and free fatty acids. Red circles denotes carboxylic functional group (RCOOH).

4. Conclusions

This study confirms that the presence of AMX while treating LE with microalgae leads to negative consequences in terms of the microalgal growth kinetics, biomass yield, and biodiesel composition. Specifically, an increase in the AMX concentration from 0.01 to 20 ppm resulted in a reduction in the average microalgal productivity from 1651 mg/m^3/day to 1080 mg/m^3/day and the growth kinetics from 0.87 days^{-1} to 0.35 days^{-1}. The overall biodiesel yield from the produced biomass significantly decreased from 4.3% to 1.5% with the acid catalyst and 4.0% to 2.9% with the base catalyst. The similarity in molecular structure between AMX and free fatty acids explains how methanol is consumed unnecessarily, leading to a low biodiesel yield while altering the FAME composition, in transesterification. The results show that residual AMX is strongly associated with a decrease in the C16:0 content in the FAME composition, which is an important constituent of biodiesel. Importantly, the findings of this study can be utilized to manage LE in animal breeding facilities using effective AMX controls. The harvested microalgae biomass resulting from this process can be effectively converted into biodiesel, offering an eco-friendly solution in waste-into-bioenergy conversion strategies.

Author Contributions: Conceptualization, H.-W.K.; methodology, S.J. and Y.L.; validation, H.-J.K. and J.-C.L.; formal analysis, S.J. and H.-J.K.; investigation, S.J. and J.-C.L.; resources, S.J. and Y.L.; data curation, S.J. and H.-J.K.; writing—original draft preparation, S.J. and H.-J.K.; writing—review and editing, H.-W.K.; visualization, H.-W.K.; supervision, H.-W.K.; project administration, H.-W.K.; funding acquisition, H.-W.K. All authors have read and agreed to the published version of the manuscript.

Funding: This research was supported by a grant (22-04-10-16-09) from the 2022 Research Development Program, funded by the Jeonbuk Green Environment Center. Additionally, this work was supported by the National Research Foundation of Korea (NRF) grant funded by the Korean government (MSIT) (No. 2022R1F1A1073198). Financial support from the Korean Ministry of Environment (MOE) as 「Waste to Energy-Recycling Human Resource Development Project (YL-WE-23-001)」 is also gratefully acknowledged.

Data Availability Statement: The data are contained within the article.

Conflicts of Interest: The authors declare no conflicts of interest.

Abbreviations

LE	Livestock excreta
FAME	Fatty acid methyl ester
ppb	Parts per billion
AMX	Amoxicillin
COD	Chemical oxygen demand
T-N	Total nitrogen
T-P	Total phosphorus
DT	Direct transesterification
Chl-a	Chlorophyll-a

References

1. Wei, Z.; Chen, X.; Huang, Z.; Jiao, H.; Xiao, X. Insights into the removal of gaseous oxytetracycline by combined ozone and membrane biofilm reactor. *Environ. Eng. Res.* **2022**, *27*, 210469. [CrossRef]
2. He, L.; Wang, D.; Wu, Z.; Li, S.; Lv, Y. Co-pyrolysis of pig manure and magnesium-containing waste residue and phosphorus recovery for planting feed corn. *J. Water Process Eng.* **2022**, *49*, 103146. [CrossRef]
3. Ossowski, M.; Wlazło, Ł.; Nowakowicz-Dębek, B.; Florek, M. Effect of natural sorbents in the diet of fattening pigs on meat quality and suitability for processing. *Animals* **2021**, *11*, 2930. [CrossRef] [PubMed]
4. Muszyński, S.; Dajnowska, A.; Arciszewski, M.B.; Rudyk, H.; Śliwa, J.; Krakowiak, D.; Piech, M.; Nowakowicz-Dębek, B.; Czech, A. Effect of Fermented Rapeseed Meal in Feeds for Growing Piglets on Bone Morphological Traits, Mechanical Properties, and Bone Metabolism. *Animals* **2023**, *13*, 1080. [CrossRef]
5. Li, C.; Li, Y.; Li, X.; Ma, X.; Ru, S.; Qiu, T.; Lu, A. Veterinary antibiotics and estrogen hormones in manures from concentrated animal feedlots and their potential ecological risks. *Environ. Res.* **2021**, *198*, 110463. [CrossRef] [PubMed]
6. Seibert, D.; Zorzo, C.F.; Borba, F.H.; de Souza, R.M.; Quesada, H.B.; Bergamasco, R.; Baptista, A.T.; Inticher, J.J. Occurrence, statutory guideline values and removal of contaminants of emerging concern by Electrochemical Advanced Oxidation Processes: A review. *Sci. Total Environ.* **2020**, *748*, 141527. [CrossRef] [PubMed]
7. Egea-Corbacho, A.; Ruiz, S.G.; Alonso, J.M.Q. Removal of emerging contaminants from wastewater using nanofiltration for its subsequent reuse: Full-scale pilot plant. *J. Clean. Prod.* **2019**, *214*, 514–523. [CrossRef]
8. Zubair, M.; Wang, S.; Zhang, P.; Ye, J.; Liang, J.; Nabi, M.; Zhou, Z.; Tao, X.; Chen, N.; Sun, K. Biological nutrient removal and recovery from solid and liquid livestock manure: Recent advance and perspective. *Bioresour. Technol.* **2020**, *301*, 122823. [CrossRef]
9. Lou, E.G.; Harb, M.; Smith, A.L.; Stadler, L.B. Livestock manure improved antibiotic resistance gene removal during co-treatment of domestic wastewater in an anaerobic membrane bioreactor. *Environ. Sci. Water Res. Technol.* **2020**, *6*, 2832–2842. [CrossRef]
10. Xiao, G.; Chen, J.; Show, P.L.; Yang, Q.; Ke, J.; Zhao, Q.; Guo, R.; Liu, Y. Evaluating the application of antibiotic treatment using algae-algae/activated sludge system. *Chemosphere* **2021**, *282*, 130966. [CrossRef]
11. Ma, Z.; Li, M.; Wang, X.; Wang, Q.; Li, Q.; Wang, Y.; Zhang, Z.; Gao, J.; Gao, X.; Yuan, H. Selective and high-efficient removal of tetracycline from antibiotic-containing aqueous solution via combining adsorption with membrane pre-concentration. *J. Water Process Eng.* **2022**, *50*, 103281. [CrossRef]
12. Chan, R.; Chiemchaisri, C.; Chiemchaisri, W. Effect of sludge recirculation on removal of antibiotics in two-stage membrane bioreactor (MBR) treating livestock wastewater. *J. Environ. Health Sci. Eng.* **2020**, *18*, 1541–1553. [CrossRef] [PubMed]
13. Sodhi, K.K.; Kumar, M.; Singh, D.K. Insight into the amoxicillin resistance, ecotoxicity, and remediation strategies. *J. Water Process Eng.* **2021**, *39*, 101858. [CrossRef]
14. Khan, W.; Nam, J.-Y.; Byun, S.; Kim, S.; Han, C.; Kim, H.-C. Emerging investigator series: Quaternary treatment with algae-assisted oxidation for antibiotics removal and refractory organics degradation in livestock wastewater effluent. *Environ. Sci. Water Res. Technol.* **2020**, *6*, 3262–3275. [CrossRef]
15. Waddington, J.C.; Meng, X.; Naisbitt, D.J.; Park, B.K. Immune drug-induced liver disease and drugs. *Curr. Opin. Toxicol.* **2018**, *10*, 46–53. [CrossRef]
16. Nam, J.-H.; Shin, J.-H.; Kim, T.-H.; Yu, S.; Lee, D.-H. Comparison of biological and chemical assays for measuring the concentration of residual antibiotics after treatment with gamma irradiation. *Environ. Eng. Res.* **2020**, *25*, 614–621. [CrossRef]
17. Aryee, A.A.; Han, R.; Qu, L. Occurrence, detection and removal of amoxicillin in wastewater: A review. *J. Clean. Prod.* **2022**, *368*, 133140. [CrossRef]
18. Saldarriaga, J.F.; Montoya, N.A.; Estiati, I.; Aguayo, A.T.; Aguado, R.; Olazar, M. Unburned material from biomass combustion as low-cost adsorbent for amoxicillin removal from wastewater. *J. Clean. Prod.* **2021**, *284*, 124732. [CrossRef]
19. Hazra, M.; Durso, L.M. Performance efficiency of conventional treatment plants and constructed wetlands towards reduction of antibiotic resistance. *Antibiotics* **2022**, *11*, 114. [CrossRef]
20. Lee, D.; Lee, J.-C.; Nam, J.-Y.; Kim, H.-W. Degradation of sulfonamide antibiotics and their intermediates toxicity in an aeration-assisted non-thermal plasma while treating strong wastewater. *Chemosphere* **2018**, *209*, 901–907. [CrossRef]

21. Park, J.-G.; Lee, B.; Lee, U.-J.; Jun, H.-B. An anaerobic digester with microbial electrolysis cell enhances relative abundance of methylotrophic methanogens in bulk solution. *Environ. Eng. Res.* **2022**, *27*, 210666. [CrossRef]
22. Jung, S.; Shetti, N.P.; Reddy, K.R.; Nadagouda, M.N.; Park, Y.-K.; Aminabhavi, T.M.; Kwon, E.E. Synthesis of different biofuels from livestock waste materials and their potential as sustainable feedstocks—A review. *Energy Convers. Manag.* **2021**, *236*, 114038. [CrossRef]
23. Simsek, S.; Uslu, S. Comparative evaluation of the influence of waste vegetable oil and waste animal oil-based biodiesel on diesel engine performance and emissions. *Fuel* **2020**, *280*, 118613. [CrossRef]
24. Vishwakarma, R.; Dhaka, V.; Ariyadasa, T.U.; Malik, A. Exploring algal technologies for a circular bio-based economy in rural sector. *J. Clean. Prod.* **2022**, *354*, 131653. [CrossRef]
25. Daneshvar, E.; Zarrinmehr, M.J.; Koutra, E.; Kornaros, M.; Farhadian, O.; Bhatnagar, A. Sequential cultivation of microalgae in raw and recycled dairy wastewater: Microalgal growth, wastewater treatment and biochemical composition. *Bioresour. Technol.* **2019**, *273*, 556–564. [CrossRef] [PubMed]
26. Kurniawan, S.B.; Ahmad, A.; Imron, M.F.; Abdullah, S.R.S.; Othman, A.R.; Hasan, H.A. Potential of microalgae cultivation using nutrient-rich wastewater and harvesting performance by biocoagulants/bioflocculants: Mechanism, multi-conversion of biomass into valuable products, and future challenges. *J. Clean. Prod.* **2022**, *365*, 132806. [CrossRef]
27. da Silva Rodrigues, D.A.; da Cunha, C.C.R.F.; Freitas, M.G.; de Barros, A.L.C.; e Castro, P.B.N.; Pereira, A.R.; de Queiroz Silva, S.; da Fonseca Santiago, A.; Afonso, R.J.d.C.F. Biodegradation of sulfamethoxazole by microalgae-bacteria consortium in wastewater treatment plant effluents. *Sci. Total Environ.* **2020**, *749*, 141441. [CrossRef]
28. Leng, L.; Wei, L.; Xiong, Q.; Xu, S.; Li, W.; Lv, S.; Lu, Q.; Wan, L.; Wen, Z.; Zhou, W. Use of microalgae based technology for the removal of antibiotics from wastewater: A review. *Chemosphere* **2020**, *238*, 124680. [CrossRef]
29. Deng, X.; Li, D.; Xue, C.; Chen, B.; Dong, J.; Tetteh, P.A.; Gao, K. Cultivation of *Chlorella sorokiniana* using wastewaters from different processing units of the silk industry for enhancing biomass production and nutrient removal. *J. Chem. Technol. Biotechnol.* **2020**, *95*, 264–273. [CrossRef]
30. Gatidou, G.; Anastopoulou, P.; Aloupi, M.; Stasinakis, A.S. Growth inhibition and fate of benzotriazoles in *Chlorella sorokiniana* cultures. *Sci. Total Environ.* **2019**, *663*, 580–586. [CrossRef]
31. Kim, H.W.; Vannela, R.; Zhou, C.; Harto, C.; Rittmann, B.E. Photoautotrophic nutrient utilization and limitation during semi-continuous growth of *Synechocystis* sp. PCC6803. *Biotechnol. Bioeng.* **2010**, *106*, 553–563. [CrossRef] [PubMed]
32. Chen, Z.; Wang, L.; Qiu, S.; Ge, S. Determination of microalgal lipid content and fatty acid for biofuel production. *BioMed. Res. Int.* **2018**, *2018*, 1503126. [CrossRef] [PubMed]
33. Lee, J.-C.; Kim, H.-W. Convergence of direct-transesterification and anaerobic digestion for improved bioenergy potentials of microalgae. *J. Clean. Prod.* **2018**, *178*, 749–756. [CrossRef]
34. Guo, J.; Sun, S.; Liu, J. Conversion of waste frying palm oil into biodiesel using free lipase A from *Candida antarctica* as a novel catalyst. *Fuel* **2020**, *267*, 117323. [CrossRef]
35. Rice, E.W.; Bridgewater, L. *Standard Methods for the Examination of Water and Wastewater*; American Public Health Association: Washington, DC, USA, 2012; Volume 10.
36. Anjali, R.; Shanthakumar, S. Insights on the current status of occurrence and removal of antibiotics in wastewater by advanced oxidation processes. *J. Environ. Manag.* **2019**, *246*, 51–62. [CrossRef] [PubMed]
37. Yu, Y.; Zhou, Y.; Wang, Z.; Torres, O.L.; Guo, R.; Chen, J. Investigation of the removal mechanism of antibiotic ceftazidime by green algae and subsequent microbic impact assessment. *Sci. Rep.* **2017**, *7*, 4168. [CrossRef] [PubMed]
38. Hom-Diaz, A.; Jaén-Gil, A.; Rodríguez-Mozaz, S.; Barceló, D.; Vicent, T.; Blánquez, P. Insights into removal of antibiotics by selected microalgae (*Chlamydomonas reinhardtii*, *Chlorella sorokiniana*, *Dunaliella tertiolecta* and *Pseudokirchneriella subcapitata*). *Algal Res.* **2022**, *61*, 102560. [CrossRef]
39. Ricky, R.; Chiampo, F.; Shanthakumar, S. Efficacy of Ciprofloxacin and Amoxicillin Removal and the Effect on the Biochemical Composition of *Chlorella vulgaris*. *Bioengineering* **2022**, *9*, 134. [CrossRef]
40. Zhong, X.; Zhu, Y.; Wang, Y.; Zhao, Q.; Huang, H. Effects of three antibiotics on growth and antioxidant response of *Chlorella pyrenoidosa* and *Anabaena cylindrica*. *Ecotoxicol. Environ. Saf.* **2021**, *211*, 111954. [CrossRef]
41. Zhang, C.; Zhang, Q.; Dong, S.; Zhou, D. Could co-substrate sodium acetate simultaneously promote *Chlorella* to degrade amoxicillin and produce bioresources? *J. Hazard. Mater.* **2021**, *417*, 126147. [CrossRef]
42. Chai, W.S.; Tan, W.G.; Munawaroh, H.S.H.; Gupta, V.K.; Ho, S.-H.; Show, P.L. Multifaceted roles of microalgae in the application of wastewater biotreatment: A review. *Environ. Pollut.* **2020**, *269*, 116236. [CrossRef] [PubMed]
43. Zhao, Z.; Xue, R.; Fu, L.; Chen, C.; Ndayisenga, F.; Zhou, D. Carbon dots enhance the recovery of microalgae bioresources from wastewater containing amoxicillin. *Bioresour. Technol.* **2021**, *335*, 125258. [CrossRef] [PubMed]
44. Wang, G.; Zhang, Q.; Li, J.; Chen, X.; Lang, Q.; Kuang, S. Combined effects of erythromycin and enrofloxacin on antioxidant enzymes and photosynthesis-related gene transcription in *Chlorella vulgaris*. *Aquat. Toxicol.* **2019**, *212*, 138–145. [CrossRef] [PubMed]
45. Kawai, Y.; Mickiewicz, K.; Errington, J. Lysozyme counteracts β-lactam antibiotics by promoting the emergence of L-form bacteria. *Cell* **2018**, *172*, 1038–1049.e10. [CrossRef]
46. Du, Y.; Wang, J.; Li, H.; Mao, S.; Wang, D.; Xiang, Z.; Guo, R.; Chen, J. The dual function of the algal treatment: Antibiotic elimination combined with CO_2 fixation. *Chemosphere* **2018**, *211*, 192–201. [CrossRef] [PubMed]

47. Ahmed, S.F.; Mofijur, M.; Parisa, T.A.; Islam, N.; Kusumo, F.; Inayat, A.; Badruddin, I.A.; Khan, T.Y.; Ong, H.C. Progress and challenges of contaminate removal from wastewater using microalgae biomass. *Chemosphere* **2021**, *286*, 131656. [CrossRef]
48. Xiong, Q.; Hu, L.-X.; Liu, Y.-S.; Zhao, J.-L.; He, L.-Y.; Ying, G.-G. Microalgae-based technology for antibiotics removal: From mechanisms to application of innovational hybrid systems. *Environ. Int.* **2021**, *155*, 106594. [CrossRef]
49. Xie, B.; Tang, X.; Ng, H.Y.; Deng, S.; Shi, X.; Song, W.; Huang, S.; Li, G.; Liang, H. Biological sulfamethoxazole degradation along with anaerobically digested centrate treatment by immobilized microalgal-bacterial consortium: Performance, mechanism and shifts in bacterial and microalgal communities. *Chem. Eng. J.* **2020**, *388*, 124217. [CrossRef]
50. Li, D.; Amoah, P.K.; Chen, B.; Xue, C.; Hu, X.; Gao, K.; Deng, X. Feasibility of growing *Chlorella sorokiniana* on cooking cocoon wastewater for biomass production and nutrient removal. *Appl. Biochem. Biotechnol.* **2019**, *188*, 663–676. [CrossRef]
51. Zhu, L.; Li, S.; Hu, T.; Nugroho, Y.K.; Yin, Z.; Hu, D.; Chu, R.; Mo, F.; Liu, C.; Hiltunen, E. Effects of nitrogen source heterogeneity on nutrient removal and biodiesel production of mono-and mix-cultured microalgae. *Energy Convers. Manag.* **2019**, *201*, 112144. [CrossRef]
52. Hu, D.; Zhang, J.; Chu, R.; Yin, Z.; Hu, J.; Nugroho, Y.K.; Li, Z.; Zhu, L. Microalgae *Chlorella vulgaris* and *Scenedesmus dimorphus* co-cultivation with landfill leachate for pollutant removal and lipid production. *Bioresour. Technol.* **2021**, *342*, 126003. [CrossRef]
53. Deng, X.-Y.; Gao, K.; Zhang, R.-C.; Addy, M.; Lu, Q.; Ren, H.-Y.; Chen, P.; Liu, Y.-H.; Ruan, R. Growing *Chlorella vulgaris* on thermophilic anaerobic digestion swine manure for nutrient removal and biomass production. *Bioresour. Technol.* **2017**, *243*, 417–425. [CrossRef]
54. Wang, J.; Zhou, W.; Chen, H.; Zhan, J.; He, C.; Wang, Q. Ammonium Nitrogen Tolerant *Chlorella* Strain Screening and Its Damaging Effects on Photosynthesis. *Front. Microbiol.* **2019**, *9*, 3250. [CrossRef]
55. Odjadjare, E.C.; Mutanda, T.; Chen, Y.-F.; Olaniran, A.O. Evaluation of pre-chlorinated wastewater effluent for microalgal cultivation and biodiesel production. *Water* **2018**, *10*, 977. [CrossRef]
56. Gao, F.; Peng, Y.-Y.; Li, C.; Yang, G.-J.; Deng, Y.-B.; Xue, B.; Guo, Y.-M. Simultaneous nutrient removal and biomass/lipid production by *Chlorella* sp. in seafood processing wastewater. *Sci. Total Environ.* **2018**, *640*, 943–953. [CrossRef]
57. Zhang, W.; Zhao, C.; Liu, J.; Sun, S.; Zhao, Y.; Wei, J. Effects of exogenous GR24 on biogas upgrading and nutrient removal by co-culturing microalgae with fungi under mixed LED light wavelengths. *Chemosphere* **2021**, *281*, 130791. [CrossRef]
58. Daneshvar, E.; Zarrinmehr, M.J.; Hashtjin, A.M.; Farhadian, O.; Bhatnagar, A. Versatile applications of freshwater and marine water microalgae in dairy wastewater treatment, lipid extraction and tetracycline biosorption. *Bioresour. Technol.* **2018**, *268*, 523–530. [CrossRef]
59. Bai, X.; Acharya, K. Algae-mediated removal of selected pharmaceutical and personal care products (PPCPs) from Lake Mead water. *Sci. Total Environ.* **2017**, *581*, 734–740. [CrossRef]
60. Chen, J.; Xie, S. Overview of sulfonamide biodegradation and the relevant pathways and microorganisms. *Sci. Total Environ.* **2018**, *640*, 1465–1477. [CrossRef] [PubMed]
61. Norvill, Z.N.; Toledo-Cervantes, A.; Blanco, S.; Shilton, A.; Guieysse, B.; Muñoz, R. Photodegradation and sorption govern tetracycline removal during wastewater treatment in algal ponds. *Bioresour. Technol.* **2017**, *232*, 35–43. [CrossRef] [PubMed]
62. Guo, W.-Q.; Zheng, H.-S.; Li, S.; Du, J.-S.; Feng, X.-C.; Yin, R.-L.; Wu, Q.-L.; Ren, N.-Q.; Chang, J.-S. Removal of cephalosporin antibiotics 7-ACA from wastewater during the cultivation of lipid-accumulating microalgae. *Bioresour. Technol.* **2016**, *221*, 284–290. [CrossRef]
63. Braun, J.V.; dos Santos, V.O.; Fontoura, L.A.; Pereira, E.; Napp, A.; Seferin, M.; Lima, J.; Ligabue, R.; Vainstein, M.H. GC-FID methodology validation for the fatty esters content determination in biodiesel with hexadecyl acetate as the internal standard. *Quim. Nova* **2017**, *40*, 1111–1116. [CrossRef]
64. Chaudhary, N.K.; Mishra, P. Spectral Investigation and In Vitro Antibacterial Evaluation of NiII and CuI Complexes of Schiff Base Derived from Amoxicillin and α-Formylthiophene (αft). *J. Chem.* **2015**, *2015*, 136285. [CrossRef]
65. Cheng, J.; Qiu, Y.; Huang, R.; Yang, W.; Zhou, J.; Cen, K. Biodiesel production from wet microalgae by using graphene oxide as solid acid catalyst. *Bioresour. Technol.* **2016**, *221*, 344–349. [CrossRef]
66. Lee, J.-C.; Jang, J.K.; Kim, H.-W. Sulfonamide degradation and metabolite characterization in submerged membrane photobioreactors for livestock excreta treatment. *Chemosphere* **2020**, *261*, 127604. [CrossRef]
67. Gao, J.; Cui, Y.; Tao, Y.; Huang, L.; Peng, D.; Xie, S.; Wang, X.; Liu, Z.; Chen, D.; Yuan, Z. Multiclass method for the quantification of 92 veterinary antimicrobial drugs in livestock excreta, wastewater, and surface water by liquid chromatography with tandem mass spectrometry. *J. Sep. Sci.* **2016**, *39*, 4086–4095. [CrossRef]
68. Lee, H.-J.; Ryu, H.-D.; Chung, E.G.; Kim, K.; Lee, J.K. Characteristics of veterinary antibiotics in intensive livestock farming watersheds with different liquid manure application programs using UHPLC-q-orbitrap HRMS combined with on-line SPE. *Sci. Total Environ.* **2020**, *749*, 142375. [CrossRef]

Disclaimer/Publisher's Note: The statements, opinions and data contained in all publications are solely those of the individual author(s) and contributor(s) and not of MDPI and/or the editor(s). MDPI and/or the editor(s) disclaim responsibility for any injury to people or property resulting from any ideas, methods, instructions or products referred to in the content.

Article

The Conversion of Pistachio and Walnut Shell Waste into Valuable Components with Subcritical Water

Maja Čolnik, Mihael Irgolič, Amra Perva and Mojca Škerget *

Laboratory for Separation Processes and Product Design, Faculty of Chemistry and Chemical Engineering, University of Maribor, Smetanova 17, SI-2000 Maribor, Slovenia; maja.colnik@um.si (M.Č.); mihael.irgolic@um.si (M.I.); amra.perva@um.si (A.P.)
* Correspondence: mojca.skerget@um.si

Abstract: Pistachio and walnut shells accumulate in large quantities as waste during food processing and represent a promising lignocellulosic biomass for the extraction of valuable components. Subcritical water technology was used as an environmentally friendly technique to study the extraction of active ingredients and other valuable degradation products from walnut and pistachio waste. Subcritical water extraction (SWE) was carried out under different process conditions (temperature (150–300 °C) and short reaction times (15–60 min)) and compared with conventional extraction using different organic solvents (acetone, 50% acetone and ethanol). The extracts obtained from pistachio and walnut shell waste are rich in various bioactive and valuable components. The highest contents of total phenols (127.08 mg GA/g extract at 300 °C for 15 min, from walnut shells), total flavonoids (10.18 mg QU/g extract at 200 °C for 60 min, from pistachio shells), total carbohydrates (602.14 mg TCH/g extract at 200 °C for 60 min, from walnut shells) and antioxidant activity (91% at 300 °C, for 60 min, from pistachio shells) were determined when the extracts were obtained via subcritical water. High contents of total phenols (up to 86.17 mg GA/g extract) were also determined in the conventional extracts obtained with ethanol. Using the HPLC method, sugars and their valuable derivatives were determined in the extracts, with glucose, fructose, furfurals (5-hydroxymethylfurfural (5-HMF) and furfural) and levulinic acid being the most abundant in the extracts obtained by subcritical water. The results show that subcritical water technology enables better exploitation of biowaste materials than conventional extraction methods with organic solvents, as it provides a higher yields of bioactive components such as phenolic compounds and thus extracts with high antioxidant activity, while at the same time producing degradation products that are valuable secondary raw materials.

Keywords: pistachio shells; walnut shells; subcritical water extraction; conventional extraction; waste biomass; valuable compounds; sugars; furfurals

Citation: Čolnik, M.; Irgolič, M.; Perva, A.; Škerget, M. The Conversion of Pistachio and Walnut Shell Waste into Valuable Components with Subcritical Water. *Processes* 2024, 12, 195. https://doi.org/10.3390/pr12010195

Academic Editor: Agnieszka Zgoła-Grześkowiak

Received: 17 December 2023
Revised: 11 January 2024
Accepted: 14 January 2024
Published: 16 January 2024

Copyright: © 2024 by the authors. Licensee MDPI, Basel, Switzerland. This article is an open access article distributed under the terms and conditions of the Creative Commons Attribution (CC BY) license (https://creativecommons.org/licenses/by/4.0/).

1. Introduction

Recently, due to the depletion of natural resources, increasing greenhouse gas emissions and ever-growing amounts of waste, there is a growing interest in finding the best way to convert waste biomass into valuable components and energy. The potential of discarded food and agricultural biomass in terms of the variety of natural compounds that can be obtained from it is very broad and includes many markets (including pharmaceuticals, food industry, cosmetics, etc.). Obtaining various chemical compounds from sustainable sources is an interesting research goal from both an environmental and economic point of view. This contributes to the development of a circular economy that focuses on minimizing waste and tends to replace raw materials from non-renewable synthetic sources with raw materials from natural renewable sources [1].

The fruits of the pistachio (*Pistacia vera* L.) and the walnut (*Juglans regia* L.) contain many nutrients, but only the kernel is edible, the outer shell, which represents more than 50% of the entire fruit, is considered waste and discarded. The total global production of pistachios and walnuts (in-shell) in 2022/2023 is estimated to be 747.31 thousand tons [2] and 2.6 million tons [3], respectively. The shell of walnuts consists of 22.2–30.2% hemicellulose, 25.5–27.9% cellulose and 39.1–52.3% lignin [4,5], while the shell of pistachios consists of 20–32% hemicellulose, 30–55% cellulose and 12–38% lignin [6,7]. Usually agricultural biomass waste (walnut and pistachio shells) is incinerated to generate heat. This method of disposing of biomass waste is energy inefficient and pollutes the air. Walnut and pistachio shells, which are among the most important wastes in the nut processing industry, have become very interesting for various researches. The shells of various nuts are often used to produce activated carbon [8,9], to isolate cellulose nanocrystals [7,10], as fillers in polymer composites [11,12] and as adsorbents for the removal of dyes [13,14] and heavy metals from water [15,16]. As the demand for natural antioxidants in the food industry is dynamically increasing, agricultural and food wastes are becoming an ideal material for obtaining phenolic compounds as natural antioxidants [4,17,18].

Due to their high lignin content, walnut and pistachio shells are rich in polyphenols, which have numerous health-promoting effects [19,20]. Some studies confirm that pistachio and walnut shells contain many valuable bio-compounds (polyphenols), which can be obtained from pistachio and walnut shells using various techniques (ultrasonic extraction, standard shaking method [4], microwave [21], conventional extraction and Soxhlet extraction) and various organic solvents (methanol, acetone, ethanol, chloroform, n-butanol and water). Han et al. [4] extracted polyphenolic compounds from walnut shells with ethanol/water as a solvent using an ultrasonic bath, an ultrasonic probe and a standard shaking method. The highest content of total phenolic compounds (52.8 mg gallic acid equivalents (GAE)/g dry weight (DW)) was obtained with the ultrasonic extraction when the particle size of the shells was between 45 and 100 mesh [4]. In the following, autohydrolysis assisted by microwave processes was used to depolymerize hemicellulose and amorphous cellulose in walnut shells to xylose, glucose, acetic acid, levulinic acid, 5-HMF and furfural [22]. Cardullo et al. [23] prepared extracts from pistachio shells with various alcohols and water. The extracts with very low yields (0.37–2.21% w/w) contained phenolic acids and their derivatives, flavonoids and hydrolysable tannins [23].

Subcritical water extraction (SWE) is an environmentally friendly method that uses subcritical water as a solvent and represents an alternative to conventional extraction using organic solvents [24]. Water is non-toxic, non-flammable and produces less greenhouse gases and waste that would need to be disposed of separately, which is a major advantage over organic solvents, which are toxic (harmful) [25]. SWE is most commonly used for the extraction of bioactive compounds from environmental, food and plant sources. The most important parameter of SWE is temperature, as it strongly influences the chemical and physical properties of water. By reducing polarity at elevated temperatures, high extraction yields can be achieved with subcritical water extraction technology. The reduction in surface tension enables better wetting of the extraction material with water and faster dissolution of the compounds. The reduced viscosity of the water increases its penetration into the extraction material, which also accelerates extraction [26,27]. The ionic product of subcritical water increases with temperature, reaches a maximum at approx. 300 °C and by further increase of the temperature it decreases again [17]. Subcritical water is therefore a highly reactive medium. In general, when biomass is processed in subcritical or supercritical water, numerous reactions (hydrolysis, dehydration, decarboxylation, aromatization, condensation, polymerization/depolymerization, hydrogenation/dehydrogenation, isomeric reactions, gasification) [28,29] can take place, degrading normally insoluble biomass and its compounds to degradation products such as carbohydrates, furfurals, organic acids [30], gasses and bio-oil [31]. Extractives such as phenolic compounds (phenolic glycosides, high molecular weight polyphenols) can be hydrolyzed to aglycones or further degraded. The course of the reactions is highly dependent on the reaction temperature and time, which can be manipulated to increase the selectivity of the reaction to desired products. SWE is used to extract components such as antioxidants, essential oils and especially phenolic compounds, which are in principle poorly soluble in water at atmospheric pressure, but soluble in subcritical water [32,33]. By changing the temperature and pressure of the subcritical water, the extraction of the components can be regulated depending on whether they are polar, semi-polar, low-polar or non-polar components. In addition, SWE enables effective extraction in a short time, in contrast to some conventional methods which often take longer. Natural materials already contain water, so primary drying of the material before SWE is generally not necessary, as water acts as a solvent in this case, which is a major advantage over conventional extractions [34]. In addition to grinding the material, many extraction techniques that use organic solvents often require drying as a pre-treatment step. This is because the water present in the material prevents the organic solvent from penetrating the material effectively, so additional energy must be invested in the process to achieve a satisfactory extraction yield. Furthermore, in some cases, the drying process reduces the content of bioactive compounds in the material [35].

In previous studies, various valuable components (methylxanthines, antioxidants, phenols) were separated from cocoa [36], chestnut [37], horse chestnut [38], peanut [39] and pecan [40] shells using subcritical water. However, there is a lack of studies using subcritical water for the extraction and/or decomposition of pistachio and walnut shells into valuable components. Erşan et al. [20] investigated the extraction of pistachio shells in a semi-continuous reactor in the temperature range of 110 to 190 °C at a flow rate of 4 mL/min through the column. It was found that pistachio shell extract contains various phenols (gallic acid and its derivatives), flavonoids (quercetin hexosides) and other components (5-HMF). Through hydrothermal process catalyzed by two bases (KOH and Na_2CO_3) and an acid (HCl) the walnut shells were converted into liquefied organic compounds. The main compounds from the hydrothermal process catalyzed by bases were phenol derivatives. Small amounts of cyclopentene derivatives and C_{12}-C_{18} fatty acids were also detected. HCl as a catalyst promoted the formation of levulinic acid, but the conversion rates were very low [41]. In another few studies, the shells of pistachios, walnuts and other nuts were used to generate hydrogen-rich gas with supercritical water as a medium [42–44].

The aim of this work was to investigate the conversion of waste walnut and pistachio shells to bioactive and valuable compounds with subcritical water as a green solvent. The influence of the process conditions (temperature, reaction time) on the extraction yield and their influence on the content of the analyzed compounds in the extracts was investigated. The content of total phenols, total flavonoids and total carbohydrates was determined in the extracts, and the antioxidant activity was determined using the DPPH method. The content of various sugars and their valuable derivatives (levulinic acid, furfurals), which were generated at higher temperatures, was determined using the HPLC method. The electricity consumption for the conversion of waste biomass via SWE into valuable products on a laboratory scale was also estimated. Moreover, in the present study, the extraction efficiency of phenolic compounds and antioxidant activity of extracts obtained with subcritical water under different process conditions were compared with that of conventional extraction using acetone, ethanol and 50% aqueous acetone solution as solvent.

2. Materials and Methods

2.1. Materials

The biowaste (pistachio and walnut shells) was provided by a local grocery store (Maribor, Slovenia). D-(+)-glucose (99.5%), lactose, 1,6-anhydroglucose (99%), levulinic acid (98%), D-(-)-fructose ($\geq$98%), furfural (99%), 5-hydrohymethylfurfural ($\geq$99%), 5-methylfurfural (99%), (phenol ($\geq$96%), trifluoroacetic acid, Folin-Ciocalteu's phenol reagent, sodium carbonate (Na_2CO_3), 2,2-diphenyl1-picrylhydrazyl (DPPH), gallic acid, quercetin and sodium acetate (CH_3COONa) were purchased from Sigma Aldrich (Steinheim, Germany). Cellobiose (99%) and aluminum chloride hexahydrate 98% ($AlCl_3 \cdot 6H_2O$) were obtained from Merck (Darmstadt, Germany). Absolute ethanol (EtOH, $\geq$99.9%), n-hexane ($\geq$98.5%), 96% sulfuric acid (H_2SO_4) and methanol (MeOH, $\geq$99.9%) were purchased from Carlo Erba Reagents (Val de Reuil, France) and LabExpert Kefo (Ljubljana, Slovenia). Nitrogen (99.5%) as inert gas was supplied by Messer (Ruše, Slovenia). Methanol ($\geq$99.9%)

and trifluoroacetic acid were used for HPLC analysis and purchased from J.T. Baker and Sigma-Aldrich. All standards and solvents were of analytical grade and were used without further purification.

2.2. Methods

2.2.1. The Characterization of Pistachio and Walnut Shells with TGA/DSC and Elemental Analysis

Thermal gravimetric analysis (TGA) with Differential Scanning Calorimetry (DSC) analysis (TGA/DSC1 STAR, Mettler Toledo, Columbus, OH, USA) were performed to identify the thermal behavior of pistachio and walnut shells. The samples (about 40 mg) were analyzed in a temperature range from 30 to 600 °C under air atmosphere using a heating rate of 10 °C/min [45].

The elemental analyses of pistachio and walnut shells before SWE were performed using a Perkin Elmer 2400 Series II System Analyzer (Waltham, MA, USA) and the content of carbon, hydrogen, nitrogen and sulphur was determined [46].

2.2.2. Biomass Waste Treatment with Subcritical Water

The extraction of pistachio and walnut shells in subcritical water was carried out in a 75 mL high-pressure, high-temperature batch reactor (Parr Instruments, Moline, IL, USA) (Figure 1), which can operate up to 538 °C and 545 bar, respectively. The shells were selected, washed with deionized water to remove impurities, dried at 105 °C for 24 h to remove water, and then ground to obtain a product with a particle size of 2–3 mm. For SWE, 2 g of the shells were weighed, and 20 mL of distilled water was added to obtain a material to solvent ratio of 1:10 (g/mL). The reaction mixture (shells and distilled water) and the magnetic stirrer were placed in the reactor and sealed. The reactor was then placed on a stand and connected to a pressure gauge and a digital thermocouple for temperature measurement. The heating wire was wrapped around the reactor and a magnetic stirrer was placed underneath. Before starting the experiment, the reaction mixture was flushed three times with inert gas (nitrogen) to prevent the oxidation of the products. The initial pressure in the reactor was set to 40 bar. The reaction mixture was then heated to the desired temperature (31 °C/min to 150 °C, 30 °C/min to 200 °C, 24 °C/min to 250 °C, 21 °C/min to 300 °C) and the pressure in the reactor was simultaneously increased (53 bar at 150 min, 60 bar at 200 °C, 74 bar at 250 °C and 89 bar at 300 °C). As soon as the desired temperature was reached, the reaction time was measured (15 min, 30 min and 60 min). After the completion of the hydrothermal reaction, the reactor was immediately immersed in cold water and cooled to room temperature. The gas was then released from the gas valve and the reactor was opened. The contents of the reactor were filtered. The experiments were carried out three times under the same conditions and the data given are the average values of three repetitions.

2.2.3. Conventional Extraction

5 g of ground material (particle size $\cong$ 0.5 mm) was extracted with 100 mL of different solvents (acetone, ethanol, and 50% aqueous acetone solution) at 40 °C and atmospheric pressure for 2 h. The extraction solution was then cooled and filtered. The solvent was evaporated using rotavapor, and the extraction yield was calculated and expressed in wt.%. The extracts were stored for further analysis.

2.2.4. The Determination of Antioxidant Activity of Dry Extract

The antioxidant activity of the extracts was determined with the radical method using the radical 2,2 diphenyl-1-picrylhydrazyl (DPPH), as explained in a previous work [36]. An aliquot of the extract (77 µL, concentration 1 mg/mL) was mixed with 3 mL of DPPH solution and incubated in the dark for 15 min. The absorbance of the samples was measured at 515 nm using a UV-VIS spectrophotometer (Cary 50, Varian, Palo Alto, CA, USA). All measurements were done in triplicate. The antioxidant activities were expressed in %.

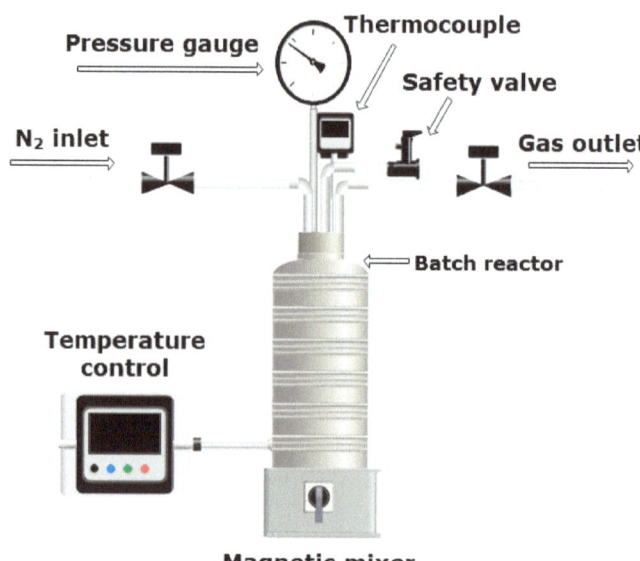

Figure 1. Scheme of apparatus for batch SWE.

2.2.5. The Determination of Total Phenolic Content in Dry Extract

The content of total phenols in the obtained extracts was determined spectrophotometrically using the Folin-Ciocalteu method, which is based on the oxidation reaction of the phenolic compounds with a reagent [36]. A total of 0.5 mL of the extract was mixed with 2.5 mL of the Folin-Ciocalteu reagent (diluted 1:10 in water) and 2 mL of Na_2CO_3 solution (75 mg/mL). The samples were incubated for 5 min at 50 °C in a water bath. They were then cooled at room temperature for 30 min. The absorbance was measured using a UV-VIS spectrophotometer (Cary 50, Varian, Palo Alto, CA, USA) at a wavelength of 760 nm. All measurements were performed in triplicate. The total amount of phenolic compounds was calculated using a standard curve for gallic acid (y = 9.8636x + 0.0396; R^2 = 0.9990) and expressed as mg gallic acid (GA) per g extract.

2.2.6. The Determination of Total Flavonoids in Dry Extract

The total flavonoids content in the extracts was determined using the aluminium chloride colorimetric method [47]. A total of 1.5 mL of a 96% alcohol solution, 0.5 mL of a 10% $AlCl_3 \cdot 6H_2O$ solution, 0.1 mL of 1M CH_3COONa and 2.8 mL of distilled water were added to 0.5 mL of the extract solution. The samples were then mixed and incubated at room temperature for 40 min. The absorbance of the samples was measured at a wavelength of 415 nm. All measurements were done in triplicate. The total amount of flavonoids was calculated using a standard curve of quercetin (QU) (y = 6.2872x + 0.0112; R^2 = 0.9986) and expressed as mg QU/g extract.

2.2.7. The Determination of Total Carbohydrates in Dry Extract

The content of total carbohydrates (TCH) in the extracts was determined using the phenol-sulfur colorimetric method, which is described in more detail in study [36]. A total of 1 mL of the extract was mixed with 0.5 mL of a 5% aqueous phenol solution and 2.5 mL of concentrated H_2SO_4. The samples were then placed in an ultrasonic bath for 10 min and then left to stand at room temperature for 20 min to develop color. In hot acidic medium, glucose is dehydrated to hydroxymethylfurfural, which forms a green color product with phenol and has an absorption maximum at 490 nm [30]. All measurements were done in triplicate. Total carbohydrates were calculated using a standard curve of glucose (y = 11.392x + 0.0458; R^2 = 0.9986) and expressed as mg TOH/g extract.

2.2.8. HPLC Analysis

The determination of 5-HMF, furfural and 5-MF in the extract solution was carried out using an Agilent HPLC, 1200 series system (Waldbronn, Germany), equipped with a binary pump, an autosampler, a column heater, a variable wavelength detector and an Agilent ZORBAX Eclipse XBD C18 column (4.6 × 150 mm; 3.5 µm) at a temperature of 25 °C. The mobile phase consisted of solvent A and solvent B. Solvent A was methanol and solvent B was a mixture of water and 0.1% trifluoroacetic acid. The gradients of the method were as follows: 0 min 90% B, 18 min 65% B and 20 min 90% B. The flow rate through the column was set to 1 mL/min. The volume of the injected extract sample was 10 µL. The detection of 5-HMF, furfural and 5-MF was carried out at a wavelength of 280 nm.

The aqueous extract solutions were also analyzed using a Shimadzu Nexera HPLC system (Shimadzu, Kyoto, Japan) equipped with a DGU-20A SR degasser, an LC-20AD XR pump, a SIL-20AC XR autosampler and a CTO-20AC column heater. The sugars and sugar derivatives were detected with the RI detector. The separation was performed isocratically on the chromatography column Rezex RHM Monosaccharide H+ (300 × 7.8 mm) at 80 °C with a flow rate of 0.55 mL/min and 5 mM H_2SO_4 in water as the mobile phase. The products obtained were quantified using the calibration curves of standards. The results were expressed in mg compound/g extract [48].

2.2.9. The Assessment of the Energy Costs of the Laboratory Process

The costs for the conversion of pistachio and walnut shells into active ingredients and other valuable products in subcritical water at a temperature of 200 °C and 300 °C and a reaction time of 15 and 60 min (maximum extraction yield, high content of valuable compounds) were roughly estimated for the experimental batch reactor on a laboratory scale. In addition, the energy consumption for a pilot process with a reactor capacity of 200 L and for an industrial-scale process with a capacity of 10,000 L was also calculated. The energy required to heat the material in the laboratory reactor was calculated based on the heat transfer power (0.15–0.30 kW for the laboratory reactor, 54–108 kW for the pilot reactor and 1800–3600 kW for the industrial reactor) and the heating time. Heat losses during heating were neglected.

3. Results and Discussion

3.1. The Elemental Analysis of Raw Material

The results of the elemental analysis of pistachio and walnut shells are presented in Table 1, where the content of oxygen was calculated by the mass balance.

Table 1. Ultimate analysis of pistachio and walnut shells.

	Elemental Composition (wt.%)				
Biomass Waste	C	H	N	S	O [1]
Pistachio shells	44.98	6.34	0.20	0.45	48.03
Walnut shells	47.72	6.41	0.56	0.30	45.01

[1] Obtained by mass balance.

As expected, the elemental composition of both shells consisted mainly of carbon and oxygen, since lignocellulosic biomass is composed of three basic macromolecular components, namely cellulose, hemicellulose and lignin. It was found that walnut shells contain slightly more carbon than pistachio shells. The reason for this could be the high content of lignin (up to 52%) [4] in walnut shells.

3.2. The TGA/DSC Properties of Raw Material

The thermal behavior of pistachio and walnut shells waste was monitored with TGA and DSC analysis (Figure 2). In both materials, the main constituents are cellulose, hemicellulose, and lignin. The first mass loss (5–6%) of pistachio and walnut shell materials starts at 40 °C and ends at 230 °C and corresponds to the loss of physically bound water [49]. This mass loss appears as an endothermic peak on the DSC curve and the enthalpy is 189.8 J/g in the case of walnut shells and 175 J/g in the case of pistachio shells. In the following, the second mass loss started at 230 °C and ended at 380 °C, with weight losses between 52 and 59%. In this range, two exothermic peaks can be seen on the DSC curve, which probably correspond to the complete degradation of hemicellulose and cellulose. As known from the literature, the decomposition range of hemicellulose is between 210 and 325 °C, of cellulose between 310 and 400 °C and of lignin between 160 °C and 900 °C [50]. In this study, the first peak is in the range between 240 and 325 °C (ΔH = 56 J/g) in the case of walnut shells and between 240 and 335 (ΔH = 119 J/g) in the case of pistachio shells and corresponds to the degradation of hemicellulose. The second exothermic peak appears in the range between 330 °C and 355 °C for walnut shells (ΔH = 30.13 J/g) and between 335 °C and 390 °C for pistachio shells (ΔH = 33.18 J/g) and corresponds to cellulose/lignin degradation [51]. The results of this study are consistent with the results from the literature [51,52]. The maximum weight loss (48% for walnut shells, 56% for pistachio shells) was observed in a temperature range between 240 °C and 360 °C. Minor weight losses were observed at higher temperatures up to 600 °C (about 13% in both cases).

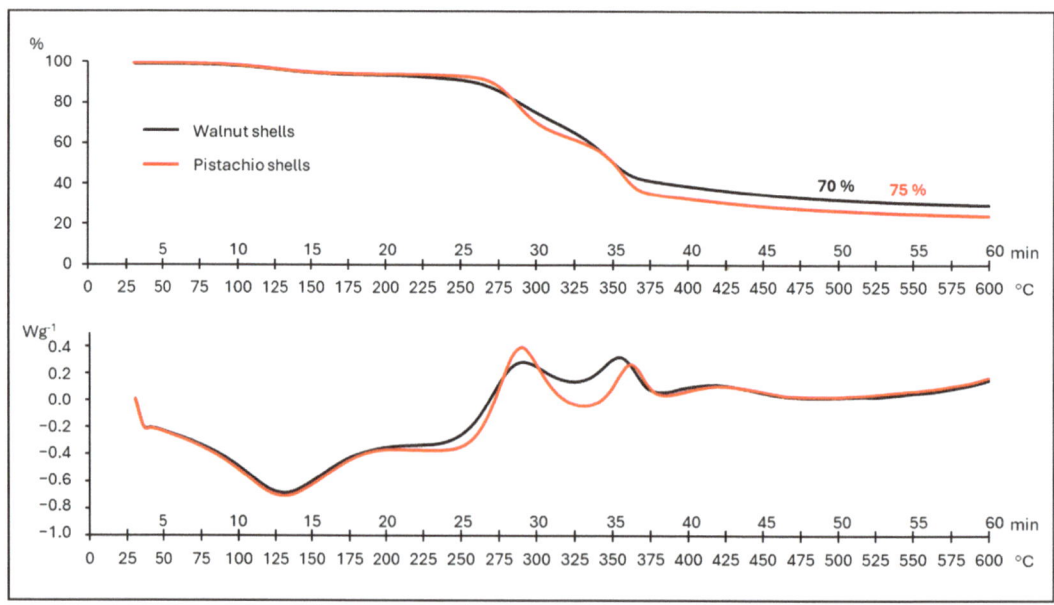

Figure 2. TGA/DSC thermogram of pistachio and walnut shells.

3.3. Extraction Yield

Figure 3 shows the maximum yields obtained in the extraction with subcritical water under different conditions and in the conventional extraction with acetone, ethanol and 50% acetone. At the lowest temperature (150 °C) and a reaction time of 60 min, the extraction yield was 8.17% for walnut shells and 26.18% for pistachio shells. Under these conditions, a lot of undegraded material remained in the reaction mixture (91% for walnut shells and 73% for pistachio shells). In order to achieve better conversion of the waste material, the temperature was increased to 200 °C. At this temperature, the maximum extraction yield was obtained in both cases, namely after 15 min (41.05%) for pistachio shells and after 60 min (31.61%) for walnut shells. The yield of the SWE (Figure 3a) decreased with increasing temperature from 200 °C to 300 °C in almost all cases, indicating that further decomposition of the products most likely occurred during the extraction of the material. However, when walnut shells were extracted at 200 °C, an increase in yield was observed with an increasing reaction time of up to 60 min. When comparing the results for both raw materials, it can be seen that processing with subcritical water led to a slightly earlier decomposition of the pistachio shells. This finding can also be confirmed with the TGA analysis, where a slightly earlier mass loss is observed in the case of pistachio shells, which is probably due to the degradation of a possibly higher content of hemicellulose (which decomposes faster with temperature) in the pistachio shells. In addition, walnut shells contain more lignin, which is reflected in the higher hardness of the material [53], and as a result they tend to decompose later than pistachio shells. Erşan et al. [20] extracted pistachio hulls with subcritical water in a semi-continuous reactor and achieved the highest yield of extraction at 150 °C and 30 min; the yield was quite high (70.9 g extract/100 g pistachio shells) and decreased with increasing temperature [20]. The difference in extraction yield is most likely due to the different size of the shell particles extracted, which was smaller in the case of Erşan et al. [20] (0.5–1 mm) than in our case (2–3 mm), resulting in earlier decomposition of the material. In our case, the lowest extraction yield was obtained at 300 °C and 60 min (8% for pistachio shells, 15% for walnut shells). The results indicate that high temperatures and longer reaction times promote the formation of volatile decomposition products [20] or char formation via the condensation and re-polymerization of liquid products [54].

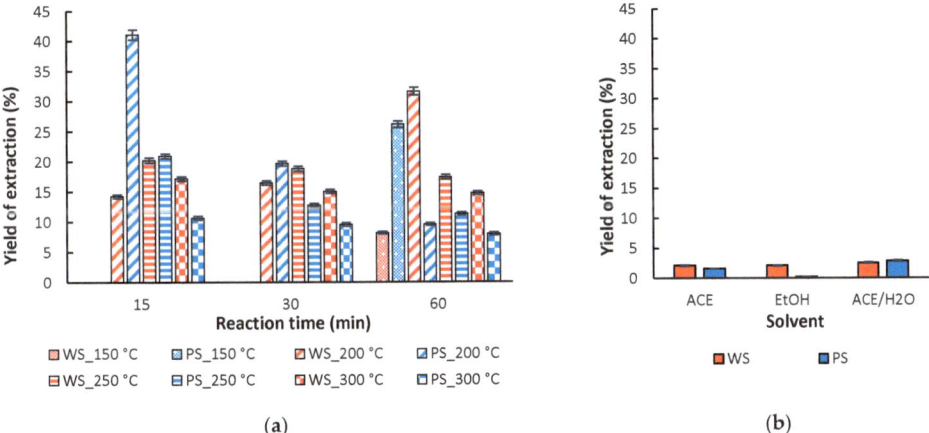

Figure 3. The yield of extraction of pistachio and walnut shells (PS-pistachio shells; WS-walnut shells) obtained via (a) subcritical water at different conditions and (b) conventional extraction with different solvents (ACE-acetone, EtOH-ethanol, ACE/H_2O-50% acetone).

The yields of the conventional extractions (Figure 3b) are significantly lower compared to the results of the extraction with subcritical water. The low yield after the conventional extraction of pistachio shells with different solvents was also reported by Cardullo et al. [23], where the highest yield of extraction (2.21%) was obtained with water and the lowest with ethanol (0.94%). In our case, the highest extraction yield was obtained using a 50% aqueous acetone solution as the solvent, 2.85% in the case of pistachio shells and 2.52% in the case of walnut shells. The lowest yield of conventional extraction was obtained for pistachio shells when ethanol (0.23%) was also used as a solvent. Thus, compared to SWE, the yield of conventional extraction was much lower and it required a longer extraction time. This could be a consequence of hydrolysis during processing in subcritical water, whereby more water-soluble compounds (carbohydrates, various sugars) were extracted from the shells.

3.4. The Antioxidant Activity of Extracts

Pistachio and walnut shells contain a high proportion of lignin. Lignin is a natural phenolic macromolecule [53]. The antioxidant activity of lignin is directly related to the ability of its phenolic group to scavenge and neutralize free radicals. In addition, the antioxidant capacity of lignin is determined by its structure and total phenolic content, especially by its molecular weight and polydispersity, methoxide content and aliphatic content [55,56]. In our study, high antioxidant activities of the dry extracts were observed, which increased with temperature and reaction time (Figure 4a). The highest antioxidant activity of the pistachio shell extract (90%) was determined at a temperature of 300 °C and 60 min, while the activity of the walnut shell extract (72%) was slightly lower and was determined at 300 °C and 30 min. The increase in antioxidant activity with temperature and reaction time was also reported by Jokić et al. [36], where the maximum antioxidant activity of cocoa shell extract was determined at 220 °C and 75 min (91.69%). Similarly, high antioxidant activity (90.54%) was determined for the extract of chestnut seed shells obtained under subcritical water conditions (250 °C, 30 min), which was significantly higher than that of the extracts of chestnut seeds (54.15%) and chestnut leaves (40.39%) [38].

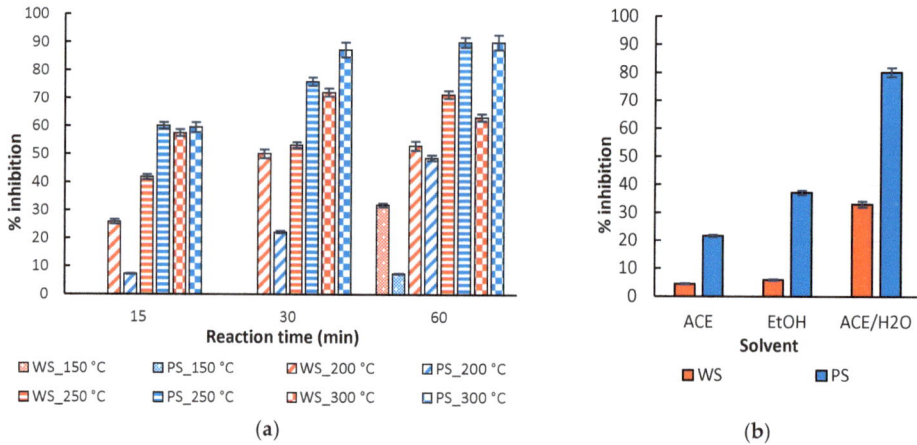

Figure 4. Antioxidant activity of pistachio and walnut shells (PS-pistachio shells; WS-walnut shells) extracts under different conditions, using (**a**) subcritical water and (**b**) conventional extraction (ACE-acetone, EtOH-ethanol, ACE/H$_2$O-50% acetone).

At lower temperatures and shorter reaction times, much lower antioxidant activity was observed, which can be attributed to poorer extraction of the phenolic components from the material. The lowest antioxidant activity was determined at 200 °C and 15 min and amounted to only 7.26% for pistachio shells and 26% for walnut shells. A slightly higher antioxidant activity was observed in the extracts (31.98% walnut shells and 7.38% pistachio shells) obtained at 150 °C and the longest reaction time (60 min). At higher temperatures (250 °C and 300 °C) and an extension of the reaction time to 30 or 60 min, the hydrolysis of the phenolic glycosides probably took place and phenolic aglycones were formed in the extracts, which have a higher antioxidant activity than phenolic glycosides [38].

The extracts obtained via conventional extraction generally showed lower antioxidant activities than the extracts obtained with subcritical water. Similar to the extraction with subcritical water, the extracts from pistachio shells obtained via conventional extraction (Figure 4b) showed significantly higher antioxidant activity, ranging from 20 to 80%, compared to the activity of the conventionally obtained extracts from walnut shells, where it was only between 4 and 33%. The highest antioxidant activities (80% for pistachio shells and 33% for walnut shells) were found for extracts with a 50% aqueous solution of acetone as solvent, while the lowest values (21.7% for pistachio shells and 4.5% for walnut shells) were found for extracts obtained with acetone. A comparison of the results with published data shows that dry extracts of pistachio shells obtained via conventional extraction with 50% methanol had lower antioxidant activities (ABTS radical scavenging assay) (0.51 mmol Trolox equivalents (TE)/g dry matter (DM) of shells) than the extracts of pistachio shells obtained via extraction with subcritical water (0.68–1.2 mmol TE/g DM of shells) [20]. Meng et al. [57] also found that an extract of peanut shells obtained with 80% methanol had a high antioxidant effect (96.68%) (DPPH radical scavenging assay).

3.5. Total Phenols Content

As can be seen in Figure 5a, the content of total phenols in the extracts generally increases with increasing temperature and reaction time. The higher content of phenolic compounds in the extract could be due to the release of various phenols (gallic acid and its derivatives, flavonoids) or other bioactive components with increasing temperature [20,58]. The highest concentration of total phenols from pistachio shells was achieved at a temperature of 250 °C and a reaction time of 60 min and amounted to 31.68 mg GA/g extract (3.58 mg GA/g pistachio shells). The hydrolysis of walnut shells at 300 °C and 15 min resulted in the highest content of total phenols in the extract, namely 127.08 mg GA/g extract (21.82 mg GA/g walnut shells), but the content decreases with increasing reaction time, which probably indicates the degradation of phenolic compounds. A similar content of total phenols (130.33 mg GAE/g extract) was also found in cocoa shell extract obtained with subcritical water at 220 °C and 75 min [36].

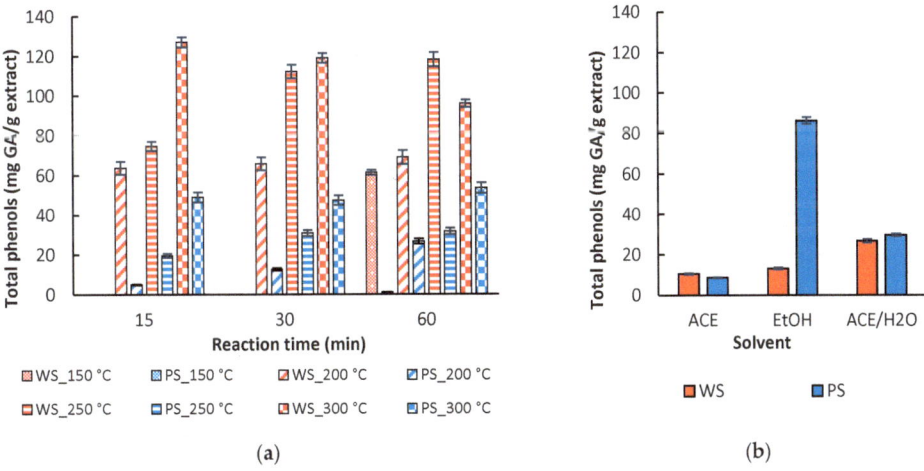

Figure 5. Content of total phenols in extracts of pistachio and walnut shells (PS-pistachio shells; WS-walnut shells) obtained via (**a**) SWE at various temperatures and reaction times and (**b**) conventional extraction with ACE-acetone, EtOH-ethanol, ACE/H$_2$O-50% acetone.

The lowest concentration of total phenols (Figure 5a) was determined in the extracts obtained at 150 °C and 60 min, where the content of total phenols in pistachio shell extracts was 1.05 mg GA/g extract (0.27 mg GA/g pistachio shells), while it was much higher in walnut shell extracts, amounting to 61.48 mg GA/g extract (5.02 mg GA/g walnut shells). As already known, walnut shells consist of more lignin than pistachio shells, and due to the aromatic/phenolic polymeric structure of lignin [59], the hydrolysis of the material could lead to a higher concentration of phenols than in pistachio shells. For walnut shells, it was also found that extending the reaction time from 15 to 60 min at 250 °C resulted in a significant increase in total phenolic content, from 74.74 mg GA/g extract to 118.23 mg GA/g extract.

The highest content of total phenols in pistachio shell extract obtained via conventional extraction was found when ethanol was used as a solvent and amounted to 86.17 mg GA/g extract (0.20 mg GA/g pistachio shells). In this case, the content of total phenols in extracts (expressed in mg GA/g extract) from conventional ethanol extraction was significantly higher than in extracts obtained with subcritical water. However, due to the much lower yield of conventional extraction, the isolation efficiency of phenolic compounds (expressed in mg GA/g shells) from pistachio shells was more than 20 times lower than that of SWE. Cardullo et al. [23] determined a two times higher amount of total phenols isolated from pistachio shells when ethanol was used as a solvent (189 mg GAE/g extracts) compared to our results [23]. These results could be due to a longer contact time of the material with the solvent (16 h) than in our case (2 h). In general, the lowest content of total phenols in extracts (pistachio shells −8.6 mg GA/extract (0.14 mg GA/g pistachio shells) and walnut shells −10.6 mg GA/extract (0.23 mg GA/g walnut shells) was detected in both cases when acetone was used as solvent.

3.6. Total Flavonoids Content

The content of total flavonoids in the pistachio shell extract obtained with subcritical water (Figure 6a) increased at 200 and 250 °C with increasing reaction time, while it decreased at 300 °C with increasing reaction time. The highest content of total flavonoids was determined at a temperature of 200 °C and a reaction time of 60 min and amounted to 10.18 mg QU/g extract (0.98 mg QU/g pistachio shells). A similar content of total flavonoids (0.7 g/kg DM of hulls) in the extract obtained with subcritical water at 190 °C and 30 min in a semi-continuous reactor was also found in the study by Erşan et al. [20]. They also reported that the dry extract mainly contained various flavonoids such as quercetin hexosides, pentosides, glucuronides and galloylated hexcosides [20]. In our study, the content of total flavonoids in pistachio shell extract increases at 250 °C up to a reaction time of 60 min, reaching a slightly lower concentration of flavonoids (9.24 mg QU/g extract) than at 200 °C and 60 min. With a further increase in temperature to 300 °C, the content of total flavonoids in the dry extract started to decrease. Similar findings were also reported in the study of Erşan et al. [20], where the flavonoid content in subcritical water extracts of pistachio shells decreased when the temperature was increased. [20]. It is likely that further decomposition of flavonoids into other unknown products occurs at higher temperatures and longer reaction times.

The lowest content of total flavonoids in pistachio shell extract (0.34 mg QU/g extract) was determined at a temperature of 150 °C and a reaction time of 60 min. Flavonoids are a group of phenolic compounds [60], so it is to be expected that the lowest content of total flavonoids is also the lowest content of total phenols (Figure 5). A similar content of total flavonoids was found in dry extracts of walnut shells, with the exception that the content of total flavonoids decreased with increasing temperature at a constant reaction time, and at 200 °C and 300 °C it decreased with increasing reaction time at constant temperature. The highest content (8.9 mg QU/g extract) was found at 200 °C and 15 min, while the lowest content was obtained at 300 °C and 60 min (2.57 mg QU/g extract). At the lowest reaction conditions (150 °C and 60 min) the content of total flavonoids was 7.99 mg QU/g extract. The extraction of walnut shells with ethanol (7.9 mg QU/g extract) and 50% acetone solution (8.8 mg QU/g extract) resulted in a similar content of total flavonoids in the dry extract compared to extraction with subcritical water at low temperature (150–200 °C). Ethanol has already proven to be a good solvent for the extraction of flavonoids from walnut shells (Figure 6b). Yang et al. [61] determined a slightly higher yield of total flavonoids (18.97 mg rutin equivalents (REs)/mg extract), which is probably due to the higher extraction temperature (50 °C) compared to our study.

Sultanova et al. [62] reported that 90% ethanol contributes to a higher concentration of flavonoids (quercetin and catechin).

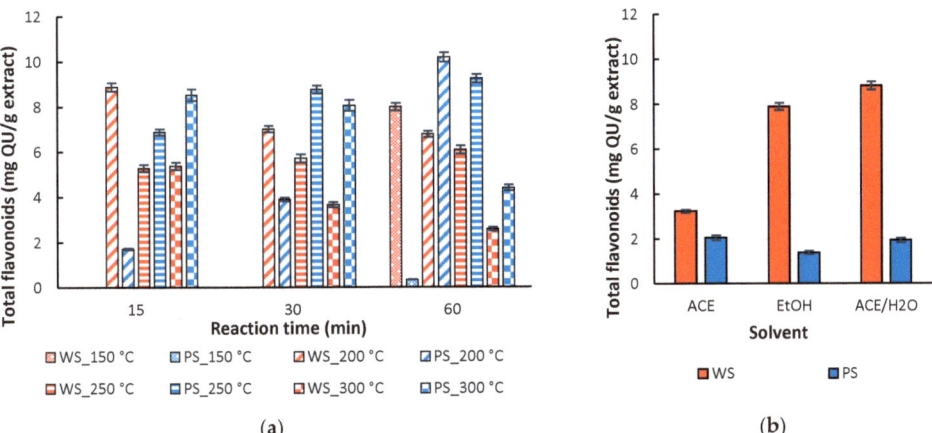

Figure 6. Content of total flavonoids in extracts of pistachio and walnut shells (PS-pistachio shells; WS-walnut shells) obtained via (**a**) SWE at various temperatures and reaction times and (**b**) conventional extraction with ACE-acetone, EtOH-ethanol, ACE/H$_2$O-50% acetone.

3.7. Total Carbohydrates Content

Carbohydrates can be completely dissolved in subcritical water due to the similar polarity of the medium, but this requires close monitoring of the reaction parameters, especially the temperature [30,63]. Using water as a medium, the hemicellulose in the biomass can be degraded to carbohydrates at low temperatures (190–210 °C) [64]. At this temperature, the hemicellulose in the biomass is completely decomposed. The residue after hydrolysis is rich in cellulose and lignin, which can be further utilised. Yang et al. [5] reported that the optimal conditions for the recovery of carbohydrates (about 400 mg TCH/g walnut shells) from walnut shells with subcritical water are 200 °C and 15 min. The residue from the walnut shells was used to produce a biodegradable foam by mixing it with corn starch. The biodegradable foam thus produced was a promising material that could take the place of plastic products in the future [5]. Gagić et al. also reported that the amount of carbohydrates (87.22 mg TCH/g shells) extracted from the shells of chestnut seeds was the highest at 200 °C and 15 min [38].

In our study, the total carbohydrate content in the extracts obtained from pistachio and walnut shells at 150 °C and 60 min was 250.13 mg TCH/g extract for walnut shells and 308.54 mg TCH/g extract for pistachio shells. At the temperature of 200 °C the total carbohydrate content in the extracts increased with increasing reaction time up to 60 min (Figure 7a), while it decreased with increasing reaction time at higher temperatures. Thus, the maximum content of total carbohydrates in dry extracts was determined at 200 °C after 60 min and amounted to 595 mg TCH/g extract in the case of the pistachio shells and 602 mg TCH/g extract in the case of the walnut shells. The highest isolation efficiency of carbohydrates for walnut shells was also achieved at 200 °C and 60 min and amounted to 190.34 mg TCH/g walnut shells, while in the case of pistachio shells it was achieved at 250 °C and 15 min (93.66 mg TCH/g pistachio shells). In general, the lowest content of total carbohydrates in the extract and the lowest extraction efficiency were determined in both cases at 300 °C and 60 min (151 mg TCH/g extract (12.01 mg/g pistachio shells) for pistachio shells and 169 mg TCH/g extract (24.85 mg TCH/g walnut shells) for walnut shells). It can be concluded that the decrease in carbohydrate content at temperatures above 200 °C and longer reaction times (>15 min) is due to the hydrolysis of poly- or oligosaccharides and the higher decomposition rate of monosaccharides, which is due to the high ionic product of water at these temperatures [5].

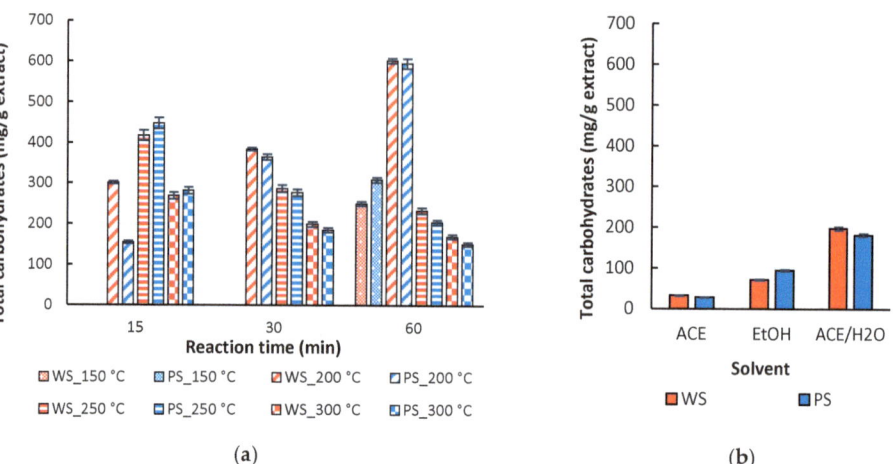

Figure 7. Total carbohydrate content (TCH) in the dry extract (PS—pistachio shells; WS—walnut shells) obtained via (**a**) subcritical water at different reaction conditions and via (**b**) conventional extraction (ACE-acetone, EtOH-ethanol, ACE/H$_2$O-50% acetone).

The total carbohydrate content in the extracts obtained by conventional extraction (Figure 7b) was lower than in the extracts obtained with subcritical water. The conventional extraction of walnut shells with 50% acetone gave the highest amount of total carbohydrates (198.11 mg TCH/g extract) in the dry extract. Under these conditions, the extraction yield was quite low and amounted to only 2.53%. The lowest total carbohydrate content in the extract was 27.33 mg TCH/g extract and was obtained with the acetone extraction.

3.8. Sugars and Derivatives

Sugars and sugar derivatives were detected with HPLC. Cellobiose, glucose, fructose and lactose were the main sugars in the extract solutions (Table 2). Cellobiose was detected after hydrothermal degradation of pistachio and walnut shells at 150 °C, 200 °C and 250 °C for all reaction times. The highest amount of cellobiose was detected in walnut shell extract at 200 °C and 15 min and amounted to 83.39 mg/g extract. The concentration of cellobiose in walnut shell extract decreased with increasing temperature and reaction time. At 250 °C and 60 min it was still present in the extract solution, while at 300 °C it could no longer be detected. In pistachio shell extracts, the cellobiose concentration was very low at 200 °C (up to 2 mg/g extract), while at 250 °C it was only present at 15 min. No cellobiose was detected when the extract solutions were prepared from pistachio and walnut shells using conventional extractions. In subcritical water, cellobiose was converted to glucose [63], which reached the maximum concentration in the walnut shell extract at 250 °C and 60 min (51.3 mg/g extract), while in the pistachio shell extract the maximum amount of glucose (17.9 mg/g extract) was detected earlier, namely at 200 °C and 60 min. In conventional extraction, the maximum glucose concentration was detected in the extract from pistachio shells (6.3 mg/g extract), which was obtained with 50% acetone. Glucose is converted to fructose in subcritical water by an isomerization reaction [48]. The highest amount of fructose (117.10 mg/g extract) in the extract from walnut shells was achieved at 250 °C and 15 min. In conventional extraction, similar to glucose, a high concentration of fructose (8.7 mg/g extract) was also detected in the extract from pistachio shells obtained with 50% acetone. Lactose was determined in low concentrations (2.65 mg/g extract) only in the pistachio shell extract, which was obtained at 200 °C and 15 min, and in the ethanol extract

(2.3 mg/g extract). The lactose was probably converted from cellobiose via an isomerization reaction [63].

Table 2. The content of sugars and sugar derivatives in extracts of pistachio and walnut shells obtained via SWE and via conventional extraction (mg component/g extract).

Conditions	Cellobiose	Glucose	Fructose	Lactose	1,6-AG *	5-HMF *	F *	MF *	LA *
			Walnut shells						
150 °C, 60 min	11.21	8.69	12.75	/	/	2.15	9.32	0.74	3.15
200 °C, 15 min	83.39	10.32	92.08	/	/	4.28	36.90	2.49	1.85
200 °C, 30 min	14.34	24.13	86.62	/	4.18	8.69	42.18	5.14	5.40
200 °C, 60 min	2.76	25.76	60.39	/	5.32	12.07	59.02	8.11	15.15
250 °C, 15 min	13.66	29.9	117.10	/	8.1	19.99	30.62	5.28	22.25
250 °C, 30 min	3.69	44.03	94.5	/	37.68	18.7	11.6	7.46	29.15
250 °C, 60 min	3.7	51.3	54.16	/	52.11	16.9	9.5	2.95	37.33
300 °C, 15 min	/	14.94	7.1	/	55.01	5.6	5.4	1.79	53.61
300 °C, 30 min	/	6.09	3.04	/	13.6	2.68	1.25	1.74	40.54
300 °C, 60 min	/	1.18	1.9	/	5.9	1.15	0.99	1.96	56.39
ACE	/	/	1.52	/	/	/	/	/	/
ACE/H$_2$O	/	5.6	11.84	1.61	/	/	/	/	/
EtOH	/	2.8	3.6	/	/	/	/	/	/
			Pistachio shells						
150 °C, 60 min	/	0.39	49.30	0.18	/	1.17	6.13	0.08	/
200 °C, 15 min	0.49	/	21.28	2.65	/	3.55	71.8	4.44	3.15
200 °C, 30 min	1.06	1.72	42.12	/	/	10.25	167.6	3.85	9.31
200 °C, 60 min	1.71	17.9	61.26	/	3.24	60.6	430.2	13.59	25.83
250 °C, 15 min	0.48	10.21	4.45	/	4.24	101.4	167.8	6.03	48.17
250 °C, 30 min	/	7.70	4.31	/	16.36	124.7	126.8	9.74	53.19
250 °C, 60 min	/	5.71	2.13	/	66.07	47.7	67.7	8.89	56.1
300 °C, 15 min	/	/	/	/	39.2	28.3	63.5	12.13	25.39
300 °C, 30 min	/	/	/	/	12.9	6.7	57.6	6.92	48.63
300 °C, 60 min	/	/	/	/	4.2	0.06	37.68	5.10	65.26
ACE	/	1.68	4.11	/	/	/	/	/	/
ACE/H$_2$O	/	6.3	8.7	/	/	/	/	/	/
EtOH	/	2.37	3.22	2.3	/	/	/	/	/

* 1,6 AG—1,6-anhydroglucose, 5-HMF—5-hydrohxmethylfufrural, F—furfural, MF—methylfurfural, LA—levulinic acid.

Sugar derivatives, namely 1,6-anhydroglucose, levulinic acid, 5-hydroxymethylfurfural (5-HMF), furfural (F) and methylfurfural (MF) were also formed in the aqueous phase during the hydrolysis of pistachio and walnut shells in subcritical water (Table 2), whereas these components were not formed during conventional extraction with organic solvents. 1,6-Anhydroglucose was first detected at 200 °C and 30 min in the case of walnut shells. 1,6-Anhydroglucose is formed via the dehydration of glucose. As shown in Table 2, the concentration of 1,6-anhydroglucose increased, while the glucose content decreased with increasing temperature and reaction time. The maximum concentration of 1,6-anhydroglucose in the extract is reached at 250 °C and 60 min in the case of pistachio shells (66.07 mg/g extract) and at 300 °C and 15 min in the case of walnut shells (55.01 mg/g extract). Furfurals (5-HMF, furfural and 5-MF) are the main degradation products of sugars. 5-HMF can be produced from glucose or fructose via glucose isomerization, while furfural is formed when 5-HMF loses the formyl group [65]. The content of furfurals (5-HMF, furfural and 5-MF) increased with increasing temperature and reaction time, reaching the highest value at 250 °C and 30 min for 5-HMF (124.7 mg/g extract) and at 200 °C and 60 min for furfural (430.2 mg/g extract) and for 5-MF (13.59 mg/g extract) in the case of pistachio shells. The high content of furfurals in the extract is a consequence of the higher content of total carbohydrates. In addition, the pistachio shells consist of a low lignin content and a high content of hemicellulose and cellulose, so more carbohydrates and furfural are formed during hydrolysis than in the walnut shells. In comparison to the literature, the highest yield of furfurals was also determined in the chestnut shell at 200–250 °C for up to 30 min [38]. Another sugar derivative detected in the dry extracts of pistachio and walnut shells is levulinic acid, the main product of the hydrolysis of 5-HMF. The concentration of levulinic acid increased with increasing temperature up to 300 °C, with the maximum concentration in the dry extract being reached after 60 min (walnut shells—56.39 mg/g extract, pistachio shells—65.26 mg/g extract). Levulinic acid and furfurals (5-HMF and furfural) were also determined in the study in which the walnut shells were hydrolyzed via microwave-assisted autohydrolysis. At 210 °C and a reaction time of 10–55 min, the concentrations of the compounds were between 0.46 g/L and 0.85 g/L for levulinic acid, between 0.6 g/L and 2.24 g/L for 5-HMF and between 2.14 and 0.40 g/L for furfural [22].

3.9. The Electricity Costs of the Chemical Conversion of Waste Biomass into Valuable Products in Subcritical Water

It has been estimated that the electricity consumption for the chemical conversion of pistachio and walnut shells with subcritical water on a laboratory scale at 200 °C and a reaction time of 15 min and 60 min is about 9 kWh and 28 kWh per kg of shells, respectively, while the electricity costs would increase accordingly at 300 °C and amount to 22 kWh and 57 kWh per kg of walnut and pistachio shells, respectively. Increasing the reactor capacity (200–10,000 L) would reduce electricity costs. In a 200 L pilot reactor at 200 °C and at a reaction time of 15 min and 60 min, the electricity costs would be 1.2 kWh and 3.8 kWh per kg of shells, respectively, while at 300 °C the electricity costs would be 3.2 kWh and 8.3 kWh per kg of shells, respectively.

By using an industrial reactor (10,000 L), the electricity costs would decrease further and would be 0.95 kWh per kg of shells after 15 min and 2.9 kWh per kg of shells after 60 min at 200 °C, while at 300 °C they would amount to 2.4 kWh per kg of shells after 15 min and 6.3 kWh per kg of shells after 60 min of reaction time.

4. Conclusions

Bioactive and valuable components from pistachio and walnut shell waste were obtained via SWE at different temperatures (150–300 °C), three different reaction times (15 min, 30 min, 60 min) and a material:solvent ratio of 1:10 (g/mL). The conventional extraction was carried out for 2 h at 40 °C with three different solvents (acetone, ethanol and a 50% aqueous solution of acetone) and a material:solvent ratio of 1:20 (g/mL).

It was found that the extraction yield of pistachio and walnut shells with subcritical water was significantly higher (from 8% to 41%) than extraction with conventional solvents (0.23 to 2.85%), which is due to the decomposition of the material in subcritical water during processing. The extracts obtained with subcritical water at 300 °C have excellent antioxidant properties, reaching an antioxidant activity of up to 91% for pistachio shells, while a slightly lower value of 72% is obtained for walnut shells. When the waste material was extracted with 50% acetone, high (80%) antioxidant activity was also observed in the extract from pistachio shells. The extract of walnut shells obtained with subcritical water contains significantly higher amounts of total phenols (127.08 mg GA/g extract) than the extract of pistachio shells (53.52 mg GA/g extract), while the ethanol extract of pistachio shells achieves a slightly higher content of total phenols (86.17 mg GA/g extract). The extracts also contain low concentrations of total flavonoids (up to 10.18 mg QU/g extract).

The content of total carbohydrates and sugars (glucose, fructose and lactose) in the extracts obtained with SWE was significantly higher than in the extracts obtained by conventional extraction with organic solvents, while cellobiose and sugar derivatives, namely 1,6-anhydroglucose, levulinic acid, 5-hydroxymethylfurfural, furfural and methylfurfural were detected only in the extracts obtained with subcritical water. Namely, in conventional extractions, the decomposition reactions of the material that lead to the formation of these components do not take place. The highest carbohydrate content, which can be a good source for the production of bioethanol, was obtained from the waste shells (595 mg TOH/g extract in the case of pistachio shells and 602 mg TOH/g extract in the case of walnut shells) at the lowest temperature (200 °C). In general, glucose and fructose were the most represented sugars in all extracts, while furfurals dominated among the derivatives, which are a valuable component as they are widely used in various industries (plastics, paints, pharmaceuticals, agriculture and chemicals).

In any case, it can be confirmed that subcritical water is an excellent and environmentally friendly medium that can efficiently hydrolyze lignocellulosic biomass and, by modifying and optimizing the process parameters to obtain the desired products, can extract valuable components such as phenolic compounds and sugars in higher yields compared to organic solvents and also valuable degradation products such as furfurals and levulinic acid. In further research, it would be necessary to investigate possible methods for separating the individual compounds.

Author Contributions: M.Č.: Formal analysis, Investigation, Conceptualization, Visualization, Writing—original draft and Writing—review & editing. M.I.: Formal analysis. A.P.: Formal analysis. M.Š.: Investigation, Conceptualization, Writing—review & editing and Supervision. All authors have read and agreed to the published version of the manuscript.

Funding: This research was funded by the Slovenian Research Agency (research core funding No. P2-0421).

Data Availability Statement: The original contributions presented in the study are included in the article, further inquiries can be directed to the corresponding author.

Conflicts of Interest: The authors declare no conflicts of interest.

References

1. Herrera, R.; Hemming, J.; Smeds, A.; Gordobil, O.; Willför, S.; Labidi, J. Recovery of Bioactive Compounds from Hazelnuts and Walnuts Shells: Quantitative-Qualitative Analysis and Chromatographic Purification. *Biomolecules* **2020**, *10*, 1363. [CrossRef] [PubMed]
2. Pistachios: Global Production 2022/23. Available online: https://www.statista.com/statistics/933073/pistachio-global-production/ (accessed on 18 August 2023).
3. Walnut Production Worldwide 2022/23. Available online: https://www.statista.com/statistics/675967/walnut-production-worldwide/ (accessed on 18 August 2023).
4. Han, H.; Wang, S.; Rakita, M.; Wang, Y.; Han, Q.; Xu, Q. Effect of Ultrasound-Assisted Extraction of Phenolic Compounds on the Characteristics of Walnut Shells. *Food Nutr. Sci.* **2018**, *9*, 1034–1045. [CrossRef]
5. Yang, W.; Shimizu, I.; Ono, T.; Kimura, Y. Preparation of Biodegradable Foam from Walnut Shells Treated by Subcritical Water. *J. Chem. Technol. Biotechnol.* **2015**, *90*, 44–49. [CrossRef]
6. Robles, E.; Izaguirre, N.; Martin, A.; Moschou, D.; Labidi, J. Assessment of Bleached and Unbleached Nanofibers from Pistachio Shells for Nanopaper Making. *Molecules* **2021**, *26*, 1371. [CrossRef]
7. Marett, J.; Aning, A.; Foster, E.J. The Isolation of Cellulose Nanocrystals from Pistachio Shells via Acid Hydrolysis. *Ind. Crops Prod.* **2017**, *109*, 869–874. [CrossRef]
8. Wartelle, L.H.; Marshall, W.E.; Toles, C.A.; Johns, M.M. Comparison of Nutshell Granular Activated Carbons to Commercial Adsorbents for the Purge-and-Trap Gas Chromatographic Analysis of Volatile Organic Compounds. *J. Chromatogr. A* **2000**, *879*, 169–175. [CrossRef]
9. Khoshraftar, Z.; Ghaemi, A. Evaluation of Pistachio Shells as Solid Wastes to Produce Activated Carbon for CO_2 Capture: Isotherm, Response Surface Methodology (RSM) and Artificial Neural Network (ANN) Modeling. *Curr. Res. Green Sustain. Chem.* **2022**, *5*, 100342. [CrossRef]
10. Harini, K.; Chandra Mohan, C. Isolation and Characterization of Micro and Nanocrystalline Cellulose Fibers from the Walnut Shell, Corncob and Sugarcane Bagasse. *Int. J. Biol. Macromol.* **2020**, *163*, 1375–1383. [CrossRef]
11. Barczewski, M.; Sałasińska, K.; Szulc, J. Application of Sunflower Husk, Hazelnut Shell and Walnut Shell as Waste Agricultural Fillers for Epoxy-Based Composites: A Study into Mechanical Behavior Related to Structural and Rheological Properties. *Polym. Test.* **2019**, *75*, 1–11. [CrossRef]
12. Thiagarajan, A.; Velmurugan, K.; Sangeeth, P.P. Synthesis and Mechanical Properties of Pistachio Shell Filler on Glass Fiber Polymer Composites by VARIM Process. *Mater. Today Proc.* **2021**, *39*, 610–614. [CrossRef]
13. Aydin, H.; Baysal, G.; Bulut, Y. Utilization of Walnut Shells (*Juglans regia*) as an Adsorbent for the Removal of Acid Dyes. *Desalination Water Treat.* **2009**, *2*, 141–150. [CrossRef]
14. Şentürk, İ.; Alzein, M. Adsorptive Removal of Basic Blue 41 Using Pistachio Shell Adsorbent—Performance in Batch and Column System. *Sustain. Chem. Pharm.* **2020**, *16*, 100254. [CrossRef]

15. Kali, A.; Amar, A.; Loulidi, I.; Jabri, M.; Hadey, C.; Lgaz, H.; Alrashdi, A.A.; Boukhlifi, F. Characterization and Adsorption Capacity of Four Low-Cost Adsorbents Based on Coconut, Almond, Walnut, and Peanut Shells for Copper Removal. In *Biomass Conversion and Biorefinery*; Springer: Berlin/Heidelberg, Germany, 2022. [CrossRef]
16. Siddiqui, S.H.; Ahmad, R. Pistachio Shell Carbon (PSC)—An Agricultural Adsorbent for the Removal of Pb(II) from Aqueous Solution. *Groundw. Sustain. Dev.* 2017, *4*, 42–48. [CrossRef]
17. Pavlovič, I.; Knez, Ž.; Škerget, M. Hydrothermal Reactions of Agricultural and Food Processing Wastes in Sub- and Supercritical Water: A Review of Fundamentals, Mechanisms, and State of Research. *J. Agric. Food Chem.* 2013, *61*, 8003–8025. [CrossRef] [PubMed]
18. Knez, Ž.; Hrnčič, M.K.; Čolnik, M.; Škerget, M. Chemicals and Value Added Compounds from Biomass Using Sub- and Supercritical Water. *J. Supercrit. Fluids* 2018, *133*, 591–602. [CrossRef]
19. Jalili, A.; Heydari, R.; Sadeghzade, A.; Alipour, S. Reducing Power and Radical Scavenging Activities of Phenolic Extracts from *Juglans regia* Hulls and Shells. *Afr. J. Biotechnol.* 2012, *11*, 9040–9047. [CrossRef]
20. Erşan, S.; Güçlü Üstündağ, Ö.; Carle, R.; Schweiggert, R.M. Subcritical Water Extraction of Phenolic and Antioxidant Constituents from Pistachio (*Pistacia vera* L.) Hulls. *Food Chem.* 2018, *253*, 46–54. [CrossRef]
21. Ganesapillai, M.; Mathew, M.; Singh, A.; Simha, P. Influence of Microwave and Ultrasound Pretreatment on Solvent Extraction of Bio-Components from Walnut (*Julgans regia* L.) Shells. *Period. Polytech. Chem. Eng.* 2016, *60*, 40–48. [CrossRef]
22. Ahorsu, R.; Cintorrino, G.; Medina, F.; Constantí, M. Microwave Processes: A Viable Technology for Obtaining Xylose from Walnut Shell to Produce Lactic Acid by Bacillus Coagulans. *J. Clean. Prod.* 2019, *231*, 1171–1181. [CrossRef]
23. Cardullo, N.; Leanza, M.; Muccilli, V.; Tringali, C. Valorization of Agri-Food Waste from Pistachio Hard Shells: Extraction of Polyphenols as Natural Antioxidants. *Resources* 2021, *10*, 45. [CrossRef]
24. Capaldi, G.; Binello, A.; Aimone, C.; Mantegna, S.; Grillo, G.; Cravotto, G. New Trends in Extraction-Process Intensification: Hybrid and Sequential Green Technologies. *Ind. Crops Prod.* 2024, *209*, 117906. [CrossRef]
25. Zhang, J.; Wen, C.; Zhang, H.; Duan, Y.; Ma, H. Recent Advances in the Extraction of Bioactive Compounds with Subcritical Water: A Review. *Trends Food Sci. Technol.* 2020, *95*, 183–195. [CrossRef]
26. Zakaria, S.; Mustapa Kamal, S. Subcritical Water Extraction of Bioactive Compounds from Plants and Algae: Applications in Pharmaceutical and Food Ingredients. *Food Eng. Rev.* 2015, *8*, 23–34. [CrossRef]
27. Cheng, Y.; Xue, F.; Yu, S.; Du, S.; Yang, Y. Subcritical Water Extraction of Natural Products. *Molecules* 2021, *26*, 4004. [CrossRef] [PubMed]
28. Akiya, N.; Savage, P.E. Roles of Water for Chemical Reactions in High-Temperature Water. *Chem. Rev.* 2002, *102*, 2725–2750. [CrossRef] [PubMed]
29. Gbashi, S.; Adebo, O.A.; Piater, L.; Madala, N.E.; Njobeh, P.B. Subcritical Water Extraction of Biological Materials. *Sep. Purif. Rev.* 2017, *46*, 21–34. [CrossRef]
30. Ravber, M.; Knez, Ž.; Škerget, M. Hydrothermal Degradation of Fats, Carbohydrates and Proteins in Sunflower Seeds after Treatment with Subcritical Water. *Chem. Biochem. Eng. Q.* 2015, *29*, 351–355. [CrossRef]
31. Toor, S.S.; Rosendahl, L.; Rudolf, A. Hydrothermal Liquefaction of Biomass: A Review of Subcritical Water Technologies. *Energy* 2011, *36*, 2328–2342. [CrossRef]
32. Chemat, F.; Vian, M. *Alternative Solvents for Natural Products Extraction*; Springer: Berlin/Heidelberg, Germany, 2014; ISBN 978-3-662-43627-1.
33. Cravotto, C.; Grillo, G.; Binello, A.; Gallina, L.; Olivares-Vicente, M.; Herranz-López, M.; Micol, V.; Barrajón-Catalán, E.; Cravotto, G. Bioactive Antioxidant Compounds from Chestnut Peels through Semi-Industrial Subcritical Water Extraction. *Antioxidants* 2022, *11*, 988. [CrossRef]
34. Shitu, A.; Izhar, S.; Tahir, T.M. Sub-Critical Water as a Green Solvent for Production of Valuable Materials from Agricultural Waste Biomass: A Review of Recent Work. *Glob. J. Environ. Sci. Manag.* 2015, *1*, 255–264. [CrossRef]
35. Kapoor, S.; Sachdev, P. Drying Method Affects Bioactive Compounds and Antioxidant Activity of Carrot. *Int. J. Veg. Sci.* 2014, *21*, 141217142840007. [CrossRef]
36. Jokić, S.; Gagić, T.; Knez, Ž.; Šubarić, D.; Škerget, M. Separation of Active Compounds from Food By-Product (Cocoa Shell) Using Subcritical Water Extraction. *Molecules* 2018, *23*, 1408. [CrossRef] [PubMed]
37. Pinto, D.; Vieira, E.F.; Peixoto, A.F.; Freire, C.; Freitas, V.; Costa, P.; Delerue-Matos, C.; Rodrigues, F. Optimizing the Extraction of Phenolic Antioxidants from Chestnut Shells by Subcritical Water Extraction Using Response Surface Methodology. *Food Chem.* 2021, *334*, 127521. [CrossRef] [PubMed]
38. Gagić, T.; Knez, Ž.; Škerget, M. Subcritical Water Extraction of Horse Chestnut (*Aesculus hippocastanum*) Tree Parts: Scientific Paper. *J. Serbian Chem. Soc.* 2021, *86*, 603–613. [CrossRef]
39. Zhu, G.; Zhu, X.; Xiao, Z.; Zhou, R.; Zhu, Y.; Wan, X. Kinetics of Peanut Shell Pyrolysis and Hydrolysis in Subcritical Water. *J. Mater. Cycles Waste Manag.* 2013, *16*, 546–556. [CrossRef]
40. Gur, C.S.; Dunford, N.T.; Gumus, Z.P. Cytotoxicity of Subcritical Water Extracts Obtained from Byproducts Generated at Commercial Pecan Shelling Operations on Cancer Cells. *Bioresour. Bioprocess.* 2023, *10*, 47. [CrossRef]
41. Liu, A.; Park, Y.; Huang, Z.; Wang, B.; Ankumah, R.O.; Biswas, P.K. Product Identification and Distribution from Hydrothermal Conversion of Walnut Shells. *Energy Fuels* 2006, *20*, 446–454. [CrossRef]

42. Safari, F.; Salimi, M.; Tavasoli, A.; Ataei, A. Non-Catalytic Conversion of Wheat Straw, Walnut Shell and Almond Shell into Hydrogen Rich Gas in Supercritical Water Media. *Chin. J. Chem. Eng.* **2016**, *24*, 1097–1103. [CrossRef]
43. Safari, F.; Tavasoli, A.; Ataei, A. Gasification of Iranian Walnut Shell as a Bio-Renewable Resource for Hydrogen-Rich Gas Production Using Supercritical Water Technology. *Int. J. Ind. Chem.* **2017**, *8*, 29–36. [CrossRef]
44. Demirbas, A. Hydrogen-Rich Gas from Fruit Shells via Supercritical Water Extraction. *Int. J. Hydrogen Energy* **2004**, *29*, 1237–1243. [CrossRef]
45. Čolnik, M.; Knez, Ž.; Škerget, M. Sub- and Supercritical Water for Chemical Recycling of Polyethylene Terephthalate Waste. *Chem. Eng. Sci.* **2021**, *233*, 116389. [CrossRef]
46. Čolnik, M.; Kotnik, P.; Knez, Ž.; Škerget, M. Hydrothermal Decomposition of Polyethylene Waste to Hydrocarbons Rich Oil. *J. Supercrit. Fluids* **2021**, *169*, 105136. [CrossRef]
47. Talmaciu, A.I.; Ravber, M.; Volf, I.; Knez, Ž.; Popa, V.I. Isolation of Bioactive Compounds from Spruce Bark Waste Using Sub- and Supercritical Fluids. *J. Supercrit. Fluids* **2016**, *117*, 243–251. [CrossRef]
48. Gagić, T.; Perva-Uzunalić, A.; Knez, Ž.; Škerget, M. Hydrothermal Treatment of Sugars to Obtain High-Value Products. *J. Serbian Chem. Soc.* **2020**, *85*, 97–109. [CrossRef]
49. El Hamdouni, Y.; El Hajjaji, S.; Szabó, T.; Trif, L.; Felhősi, I.; Ab, K.; Labjar, N.; Hermouche, L.; Shaban, A. Biomass Valorization of Walnut Shell into Biochar as a Resource for Electrochemical Simultaneous Detection of Heavy Metal Ions in Water and Soil Samples: Preparation, Characterization, and Applications. *Arab. J. Chem.* **2022**, *15*, 104252. [CrossRef]
50. Yang, H.; Yan, R.; Chen, H.; Lee, D.H.; Zheng, C. Characteristics of Hemicellulose, Cellulose and Lignin Pyrolysis. *Fuel* **2007**, *86*, 1781–1788. [CrossRef]
51. Kaya, M.; Şahin, Ö.; Saka, C. Preparation and TG/DTG, FT-IR, SEM, BET Surface Area, Iodine Number and Methylene Blue Number Analysis of Activated Carbon from Pistachio Shells by Chemical Activation. *Int. J. Chem. React. Eng.* **2018**, *16*, 20170060. [CrossRef]
52. Açıkalın, K. Thermogravimetric Analysis of Walnut Shell as Pyrolysis Feedstock. *J. Therm. Anal. Calorim.* **2011**, *105*, 145–150. [CrossRef]
53. Okonkwo, C.E.; Hussain, S.Z.; Onyeaka, H.; Adeyanju, A.A.; Nwonuma, C.O.; Bashir, A.A.; Farooq, A.; Zhou, C.; Shittu, T.D. Lignin Polyphenol: From Biomass to Innovative Food Applications, and Influence on Gut Microflora. *Ind. Crops Prod.* **2023**, *206*, 117696. [CrossRef]
54. Gagić, T.; Knez, Ž.; Škerget, M. Hydrothermal Hydrolysis of Sweet Chestnut (*Castanea sativa*) Tannins. *J. Serbian Chem. Soc.* **2019**, *85*, 108. [CrossRef]
55. Dizhbite, T.; Telysheva, G.; Jurkjane, V.; Viesturs, U. Characterization of the Radical Scavenging Activity of Lignins—Natural Antioxidants. *Bioresour. Technol.* **2004**, *95*, 309–317. [CrossRef] [PubMed]
56. You, S.; Xie, Y.; Zhuang, X.; Chen, H.; Qin, Y.; Cao, J.; Lan, T. Effect of High Antioxidant Activity on Bacteriostasis of Lignin from Sugarcane Bagasse. *Biochem. Eng. J.* **2022**, *180*, 108335. [CrossRef]
57. Meng, W.; Shi, J.; Zhang, X.; Lian, H.; Wang, Q.; Peng, Y. Effects of Peanut Shell and Skin Extracts on the Antioxidant Ability, Physical and Structure Properties of Starch-Chitosan Active Packaging Films. *Int. J. Biol. Macromol.* **2020**, *152*, 137–146. [CrossRef] [PubMed]
58. Anjum, S.; Gani, A.; Ahmad, M.; Shah, A.; Masoodi, F.A.; Shah, Y.; Gani, A. Antioxidant and Antiproliferative Activity of Walnut Extract (*Juglans regia* L.) Processed by Different Methods and Identification of Compounds Using GC/MS and LC/MS Technique. *J. Food Process. Preserv.* **2017**, *41*, e12756. [CrossRef]
59. Paysepar, H.; Venkateswara Rao, K.T.; Yuan, Z.; Shui, H.; Xu, C. Production of Phenolic Chemicals from Hydrolysis Lignin via Catalytic Fast Pyrolysis. *J. Anal. Appl. Pyrolysis* **2020**, *149*, 104842. [CrossRef]
60. Balasundram, N.; Sundram, K.; Samman, S. Phenolic Compounds in Plants and Agri-Industrial by-Products: Antioxidant Activity, Occurrence, and Potential Uses. *Food Chem.* **2006**, *99*, 191–203. [CrossRef]
61. Yang, J.; Chen, C.; Zhao, S.; Ge, F.; Liu, D. Effect of Solvents on the Antioxidant Activity of Walnut (*Juglans regia* L.) Shell Extracts. *J. Food Nutr. Res.* **2014**, *2*, 621–626. [CrossRef]
62. Sultanova, M.; Dalabayev, A.; Saduakas, A.; Nurysh, A.; Akzhanov, N.; Yakiyayeva, M. The Potential of Non-Traditional Walnut Shells Waste for the Production of Antioxidant Reach Extracts Intended for the Food Industry. *Potravinarstvo Slovak J. Food Sci.* **2023**, *17*, 391–404. [CrossRef]
63. Gagić, T.; Perva-Uzunalić, A.; Knez, Ž.; Škerget, M. Hydrothermal Degradation of Cellulose at Temperature from 200 to 300 °C. *Ind. Eng. Chem. Res.* **2018**, *57*, 6576–6584. [CrossRef]
64. Mok, W.S.L.; Antal, M.J., Jr. Uncatalyzed Solvolysis of Whole Biomass Hemicellulose by Hot Compressed Liquid Water. *Ind. Eng. Chem. Res.* **1992**, *31*, 1157–1161. [CrossRef]
65. Rasmussen, H.; Sørensen, H.R.; Meyer, A.S. Formation of Degradation Compounds from Lignocellulosic Biomass in the Biorefinery: Sugar Reaction Mechanisms. *Carbohydr. Res.* **2014**, *385*, 45–57. [CrossRef] [PubMed]

Disclaimer/Publisher's Note: The statements, opinions and data contained in all publications are solely those of the individual author(s) and contributor(s) and not of MDPI and/or the editor(s). MDPI and/or the editor(s) disclaim responsibility for any injury to people or property resulting from any ideas, methods, instructions or products referred to in the content.

Article

Graphene Oxide from Graphite of Spent Batteries as Support of Nanocatalysts for Fuel Hydrogen Production

Gabriel Sperandio, Iterlandes Machado Junior, Esteefany Bernardo and Renata Moreira *

Departament of Chemistry, Campus Universitário, Universidade Federal de Viçosa, Av. Peter Henry Holfs, s/n, Viçosa 36570-900, Brazil; gabriel.sperandio@ufv.br (G.S.); iterlandes.junior@ufv.br (I.M.J.); esteffany.bernardo@ufv.br (E.B.)
* Correspondence: renata.plopes@ufv.br; Tel.: +55-31-3612-6676

Abstract: The increasing production of electronic waste and the rising demand for renewable energy are currently subjects of debate. Sustainable processes based on a circular economy are required. Then, electronic devices could be the main source for the synthesis of new materials. Thus, this work aimed to synthesize graphene oxide (GO) from graphite rod of spent Zn-C batteries. This was used as support for Ni/Co bimetallic nanocatalysts in the evolution of hydrogen from $NaBH_4$ for the first time. The graphene oxide (GO) exhibited a diffraction peak at 2θ = 9.1°, as observed using X-ray diffraction (XRD), along with the presence of oxygenated groups as identified using FTIR. Characteristic bands at 1345 and 1574 cm^{-1} were observed using Raman spectroscopy. A leaf-shaped morphology was observed using SEM. GO sheets was observed using TEM, with an interplanar distance of 0.680 nm. Ni/Co nanoparticles, with an approximate size of 2 nm, were observed after deposition on GO. The material was used in the evolution of hydrogen from $NaBH_4$, obtaining an efficiency close to 90%, with a kinetic constant of 0.0230 s^{-1} at 296.15 K and activation energy of 46.7 kJ mol^{-1}. The material showed an efficiency in seven reuse cycles. Therefore, a route of a new material with added value from electronic waste was obtained from an eco-friendly process, which can be used in $NaBH_4$ hydrolysis.

Keywords: e-waste; metallic nanoparticles; catalysis; eco-friendly process; sustainability

Citation: Sperandio, G.; Junior, I.M.; Bernardo, E.; Moreira, R. Graphene Oxide from Graphite of Spent Batteries as Support of Nanocatalysts for Fuel Hydrogen Production. *Processes* **2023**, *11*, 3250. https://doi.org/10.3390/pr11113250

Academic Editors: Dimitris Zagklis and Georgios Bampos

Received: 24 October 2023
Revised: 8 November 2023
Accepted: 16 November 2023
Published: 19 November 2023

Copyright: © 2023 by the authors. Licensee MDPI, Basel, Switzerland. This article is an open access article distributed under the terms and conditions of the Creative Commons Attribution (CC BY) license (https://creativecommons.org/licenses/by/4.0/).

1. Introduction

Demand for portable electrical energy storage devices has increased in recent years due to rapid technological advances and the lifestyle adopted by society. This phenomenon has led to an increase in the disposal of obsolete equipment, which is denominated e-waste [1]. According to the report of the International Renewable Energy Agency, in 2023, batteries will be responsible for the storage of 14,000 MW of charge, with an annual revenue of USD 18 billion [2].

Among the different types of batteries, Zn-C cells have a cathode made of graphite carbon, which can be used as a precursor for graphene oxide (GO). Among various types of batteries, Zn-C cells feature a cathode constructed from graphite carbon, which can serve as a precursor for graphene oxide (GO). Moreover, within this type of battery, zinc cups are still available for metal recycling [3], and the electrolytic paste contains zinc manganite dispersed in graphite powder, which has demonstrated utility as a photocatalytic to various catalytic reactions [4].

Graphene oxide is a material that precedes graphene or reduced graphene oxide (GO-r) in graphite chemical exfoliation processes. This material is obtained from graphite through an oxidation reaction, leading to the formation of surface oxygenated groups, including carbonyls, carboxyls, and epoxy groups. This creates a carbon-rich structure with sp^3 hybridization. Despite the structural differences, which lead to specific chemical behavior, GO has thermal, optical and mechanical properties similar to graphene [5]. Graphene oxide has been obtained using different raw materials, from graphite to pomelo peels [6]. This combination of characteristics makes this material highly appealing for a wide range of applications, paving the way for exploring new methods of synthesis [7].

There are different chemical exfoliation processes for graphite to obtain GO such as the Staudenmaier method [8], the Hoffman method [9] and the Hummers method [10]. In general, such processes differ from each other according to the type of oxidizing agent used, as well as different concentrations of reagents [11]. The Staudenmaier method uses fuming nitric acid, concentrated sulfuric acid and potassium chlorate to promote the oxidation of graphite. For the method proposed by Hoffman, the fuming nitric acid is replaced by concentrated nitric acid [9]. For the Hummers method, concentrated sulfuric acid, sodium nitrate and potassium permanganate are used [10]. In all three cases, the product obtained is always the same, with subtle structural differences that do not affect its properties. The Hummers method has variations in the literature that make it more environmentally friendly. Among these modifications, Loudiki et al. performed the ultrasound-assisted oxidation of graphite [12]. According to the authors, the amount of reagent used is smaller compared to the original method, reducing production costs, generating less waste, and making the method eco-friendly. Furthermore, the material presented better characteristics, as its performance was evaluated using voltametric techniques.

Graphene oxide can be used for different purposes [13]. An interesting application consists in its use as a support for metallic nanoparticles [14]. The advantage of the support is to minimize the agglomeration of these materials at a nanometer scale, improving the efficiency of the nanocatalysts [15]. In addition, they configure a heterogeneous system, allowing their reuse in other catalytic cycles, in addition to preventing their leaching. Grad et al. used GO as a nanoparticle support for formic acid dehydrogenation [16]. Singla et al. used carbon-based nanomaterials, including GO, as photosensitizers in photocatalytic water separation reactions [17]. Another application that has shown to be very promising is its use in sodium borohydride decomposition reactions for the production of hydrogen [18].

Hydrogen gas is a strong candidate to replace fossil fuels due to its high specific heat of 28.851 J/(mol × K), in addition to generating water vapor as a combustion product [19]. However, its storage and transport cause serious risks because it is a flammable gas. Therefore, generating hydrogen in the place where it will be consumed is a highly promising alternative. This technology may be possible through the evolution of hydrogen from metal hydrides. These substances are solid at room temperature and have large amounts of hydrogen in their composition. Sodium borohydride, for example, contains 10.5% (w/w) of hydrogen, whose decomposition produces hydrogen gas (Equation (1)). Several catalysts can be used in the process, such as Co [18], Ni [20], Au [21] and Pt [16], among others.

$$NaBH_4 + 2H_2O \rightarrow NaBO_2 + 4H_2 \tag{1}$$

The bimetallic composition, which involves more than one metal, has been highlighted due to the synergistic effect between the two metals. Among the bimetallic compositions, those of nickel and cobalt, which are anchored in different support materials, stand out. Sun et al. synthesized a Co-Ni bimetallic inlaid carbon sphere catalyst that showed promise in the evolution of hydrogen from $NaBH_4$ [22]. According to the authors, a hydrogen generation rate (HGR) of 6364 mL $min^{-1} g_{cat.}^{-1}$ was obtained, with an efficiency of 83.4% after five cycles of use. Chou et al. produced a bimetallic catalyst of Ni and Co anchored in reduced graphene oxide that presented a hydrogen generation rate of 1280 mL $min^{-1} g_{cat.}^{-1}$, with an activation energy of 55.12 kJ mol^{-1} [23]. A three-dimensional graphene network-supported nickel–cobalt bimetallic alloy nanocatalyst was prepared by Karaman [24]. This catalyst showed a hydrogen production rate of 82.65 mL $min^{-1} g_{cat.}^{-1}$, with an efficiency of 95.96% after five cycles of use [25]. Didehban et al. anchored nickel and cobalt bimetallic nanoparticles on magnetic zeolite and bentonite to produce a catalyst for the borohydride hydrolysis reaction [25]. The catalyst anchored in magnetic bentonite showed a hydrogen evolution rate of 186 mL $min^{-1} g_{cat.}^{-1}$. According to the authors, activation energies of 37.62 and 44.98 kJ mol^{-1} were obtained for nanoparticles anchored in magnetic zeolite and bentonite, respectively. Yue et al. produced nickel and cobalt microfibers decorated with

Pd nanocatalysts for the evolution of hydrogen from $NaBH_4$ [26]. According to the authors, a hydrogen evolution rate of 680 mL $min^{-1}g_{cat.}^{-1}$ was obtained, maintaining 90% of its catalytic activity after 10 cycles.

In view of the above, this work aims to synthesize GO from spent Zn-C batteries as a support of metallic nanoparticles (Co and Ni) for the first time for use in borohydride hydrolysis catalysis to produce hydrogen gas. Although other components of the Zn-C cell can be recovered for diverse applications, the aim of this study was solely to enhance the value of the graphite component.

2. Materials and Methods

2.1. Standards and Reagents

Analytical-grade reagents were used in this work. Sodium nitrate 99% (CAS 7631-99-4) and sulfuric acid 97% (CAS 7664-93-9) were purchased from NEON (Suzano/São Paulo–Brazil). Potassium permanganate 99% (CAS 7722-64-7), hydrogen peroxide 30% (CAS 7722-84-1), sodium borohydride 98% (CAS 16940-66-2), nickel sulfate heptahydrate 98% (CAS 10101-97-0) and cobalt nitrate hexahydrate 98% (CAS 10026-22-9) were purchased from VETEC (Duque de Caxias/Rio de Janeiro–Brazil). Hydrochloric acid 37% (CAS7647-01-0) was obtained from ALPHATEC (São Bernardo do Campo/São Paulo–Brazil). Graphite (CAS 7782-42-5) was purchased from ACS Cientifica (Sumaré/São Paulo–Brazil). All solutions were prepared using type 1 water, obtained with the Milli-Q system (Millipore Corporation, São Paulo/São Paulo–Brazil), and were always freshly prepared.

2.2. Obtaining and Processing of Raw Material

Zn-C batteries were purchased at a used battery collection center in the city of Viçosa, Minas Gerais, Brazil. Seven Zn-C batteries were opened with pliers to break the external zinc cup. The rod-shaped carbon cathode was removed with pliers and crushed to obtain a fine powder. Then, the material was sieved through an 80-mesh screen.

2.3. Synthesis of Graphene Oxide

The graphene oxide was synthesized according to the adapted Hummers method [10]. Then, 1000 g of processed graphite from spent Zn-C batteries, 1000 g of sodium nitrate and 50.00 mL of concentrated sulfuric acid were added to a round-bottomed flask. The system was affixed on an ultrasound device (frequency 40 kHz) containing an ice bath in its vat, for temperature control at 0 °C. The system was kept in an exhaust hood for 15 min. A dark green color was observed. Subsequently, 6000 g of potassium permanganate was added slowly to the system at 0 °C under sonication. A violet coloration was observed due to the presence of manganese (+7). The system was maintained under sonication at 0 °C for another hour. Then, the color of the system changed from violet to brown, due to the change in the oxidation state of manganese. After this time, 100 mL of type 1 water was slowly added to the system, and the color changed to a dark brown. The system was sonicated for another two hours, and its temperature was controlled to not exceed 80 °C. Then, another 400 mL of type 1 water was added, followed by the addition of 12 mL of hydrogen peroxide (30%). This step was necessary to eliminate the permanganate residues. Then, the system was centrifuged at 6000 rpm for 7 min, followed by three wash steps with hydrochloric acid 3% v/v solution. The solid GO was dried in an oven at 35 °C for 12 h and stored at room temperature (25 °C). For the sake of comparison, an identical synthesis was performed using analytical-grade graphite.

2.4. Synthesis of Metallic Nanoparticles Decorated on GO (NPs-M/GO)

For the NPs-M/GO synthesis, where M is the metal decorated on GO, 100 mg of GO was dispersed in 10 mL of type 1 water in a beaker. Subsequently, a certain amount of the metal precursor salt, $NiSO_4 \cdot 7H_2O$ and/or $Co(NO_3)_2 \cdot 7H_2O$, according to Table 1, were added to the system, which remained under stirring for 15 min at room temperature (25 °C). Then, 1.00 mL of a solution of $NaBH_4$ (1.00 mol L^{-1}) was added to the system, which remained under stirring for another 15 min. The system was centrifuged at 6000 rpm for 7 min and washed three times with type 1 water. The freshly prepared material was used in the hydrogen evolution. Six different compositions of GO-decorated nanoparticles were prepared, as described in Table 1.

Table 1. Composition of nanoparticles decorated in graphene oxide.

System	Composition
NiNPs-GO	NiNPs
Co/Ni-NPs-GO (20:80 w/w)	Co/Ni ratio 20:80 w/w
Co/Ni-NPs-GO (40:60 w/w)	Co/Ni ratio 40:60 w/w
Co/Ni-NPs-GO (60:40 w/w)	Co/Ni ratio 60:40 w/w
Co/Ni-NPs-GO (80:20 w/w)	Co/Ni ratio 80:20 w/w
CoNPs-GO	CoNPs

2.5. Characterization of Materials

The materials were characterized using different techniques. X-Ray diffraction was performed with a Bruker D8-Discovery diffractor (Billerica, MA, USA), using copper metal as a target, working with a wavelength of 1.54 Å and horny of 45 kV. The sweep speed was 0.05° 2.5 s^{-1} in a range of 5° to 40°. The materials were also characterized using Raman spectroscopy, using a MicroRaman—InVia Renishaw equipment (Kansai, Japan). A laser with a wavelength of 633 nm and power of 3 mW was used, with a number of co-additions equal to 5 and an integration time of 30 s. Thermogravimetric analysis was carried out using a NETZSCH (Selb, Germany), STA 449, with a reading range of 25 to 900 °C, with a variation of 10 °C min^{-1}, in a synthetic air atmosphere. The size of the metallic nanoparticles was evaluated and characterized using Transmission Electron Microscopy (TEM) with the equipment Tecnai, G2-20 Supertwin FEI–200 kV (Hillsboro, OR, USA). The particle size and interplanar distance were determined using ImageJ software (Version: 1.8.0). The morphology was evaluated using Scanning Electron Microscopy (SEM) in a FEI Quanta and model 200 FEG device coupled with an X-ray energy dispersive detector. The functional groups present in the material were evaluated with Fourier Transform Infrared Spectroscopy. A VARIAN 660-IR instrument (Palo Alto, CA, USA) with a PIKE GladiATR attenuated total reflectance accessory with diamond crystal was used. The measure was evaluated in the wave number range from 200 to 4000 cm^{-1}. An analysis of the surface area of the material as well as its element was performed using Scanning Electron Microscopy (SEM) and an Energy-Dispersive X-ray Spectrometer (EDS). The equipment used was a JEOL Scanning Electron Microscope (Kyoto, Japan), model JSM-6010LA, with a resolution of 4 nm and 20 kV, with application from 8 times to 300,000 times, accelerated voltage from 500 V to 20 kV, and an electron gun with formed tungsten filament pre-centered. An Everhart–Thornley detector for secondary electron imaging and a solid state detector for backscattered electrons with topography contrast, composition and variable shading were used. A silicon drift detector was used for EDS analysis with 133 eV resolution. The samples were also subjected to nitrogen adsorption measurement at −196 °C using a Nova Station A surface area analyzer from Quantachrome Instruments (Boynton Beach, FL, USA). Before conducting the measurements, the sample underwent a vacuum drying process at 100 °C for 4 h to eliminate any remaining water and gases. The specific surface area of the sample was then calculated using the BET method.

2.6. Hydrogen Evolution from Borohydride

An image of the reactor used in the catalysis of hydrogen evolution from borohydride catalysis is shown in Figure S1. The conditions used in this work were made according to (Su et al., 2023 [27]). The freshly prepared NPs-M/GO were dispersed in 10.00 mL of type 1 water in a kitassate, which was sealed with a rubber septum. The system was stirred on a magnetic stirrer at controlled temperature. The system was connected through the kitassato side outlet to the hydrogen gas collector by a rubber hose. Subsequently, 1.00 mL of sodium borohydride solution (0.500 mol L^{-1}) was introduced into the system with the aid of a syringe and the reaction time was timed.

2.7. Reaction Parameters Evaluation

Under the conditions mentioned above, assays were carried out to evaluate the influence of (1) different concentrations of $NaBH_4$, (2) different dose of the catalyst, (3) different concentrations of NaOH, (4) different temperatures, and (5) reuse of the material.

2.7.1. Evaluation of the Influence of $NaBH_4$ Concentration

The hydrogen evolution was carried out using different $NaBH_4$ concentrations, i.e., 0.200, 0.300, 0.400 and 0.500 mol L^{-1}. The amount of catalyst Ni/Co NPs (60:40 w/w) was fixed in 0.700 mmol anchored in 100 mg of GO support; volume of 1.00 mL $NaBH_4$ solution (at the target concentration); temperature at 296.15 K.

2.7.2. Evaluation of the Influence of Catalyst Dose

Hydrogen evolution was carried out using different Ni/Co NPs (60:40 w/w) doses, i.e., 0.175, 0.350, 0.525, 0.700 mmol. In these assays, other parameters were fixed, such as GO support mass (100 mg) and volume of 1.00 mL $NaBH_4$ solution (0.500 mol L^{-1}).

2.7.3. Temperature

Hydrogen evolution was carried out at different temperatures: 296.15; 304.15; 313.15 and 321.15 K. In these assays, the other parameters were fixed, such as 0.700 mmol of Ni/Co NPs (60:40 w/w), GO support mass (100 mg); volume of 1.00 mL $NaBH_4$ solution (0.500 mol L^{-1}).

2.7.4. NaOH Influence

Four sodium hydroxide solutions were prepared: 0.010, 0.050, 0.100, 0.200 mol L^{-1} in type 1 water. The nanoparticles were dispersed in 10.00 mL of each alkaline solution. In these assays, the other parameters were fixed, such as GO support mass (100 mg); 0.700 mmol of Ni/Co NPs (60:40 w/w); volume of 1.00 mL $NaBH_4$ solution (0.500 mol L^{-1}); temperature at 296.15 K.

2.7.5. Reuse of the Material

The reuse of Ni/Co-GO NPs was evaluated. For this, the above-mentioned initial conditions were used, setting the parameters as follows: mass of catalyst (100 mg); 0.700 mmol of Ni/Co NPs (60:40 w/w); 1.00 mL of $NaBH_4$ solution (0.500 mol L^{-1}); temperature at 296.15 K. Following every cycle, the resulting suspension was washed with 30 mL of type 1 water, followed by centrifugation at 5000 rpm for 7 min to recover the solid material. The recovered solid was dispersed again in 10.00 mL of type 1 water and reintroduced into the kitassate for another cycle. This operation was carried out until the deactivation of the catalyst was observed.

2.7.6. Activation Energy

Firstly, the kinetic constant of the reaction was determined according to Equation (2) for each temperature; the procedure is described in Section 2.7.3. The temperatures evaluated were 296.15; 304.15; 313.15 and 321.15 K.

$$k = -4d[NaBH_4]/t = d[H_2]/dt \quad (2)$$

The activation energy was calculated using the Arrhenius equation (Equation (3)).

$$\ln(k) = \ln(A) - \frac{Ea}{RT} \quad (3)$$

where k is the kinetic constant of the reaction, A is the pre-exponential factor, E_a is the apparent activation energy in kJ/mol, R is the universal gas constant and T is the absolute temperature.

3. Results and Discussion

3.1. Material Characterization

The obtained graphene oxide from the graphite of spent batteries showed a 95% yield. The small loss of material can be attributed to stages of purification, i.e., washing and centrifugation steps. The GO presented a black color (Figure S2). Its appearance in powder form showed good separation between its grains, which provides good dispersion in water. Similar results were obtained by Loudiki et al. [12]. The SEM image of GO is shown in Figure 1. It can be seen that GO has a leaf-like morphology with different sizes and a highly porous structure. The material had a specific surface area of 31.048 m² g^{-1}. Jia et al. [18] reached a value of 89 m² g^{-1} for the formation of a GO-supported phosphorus/cobalt boride catalyst via in situ reduction. This catalyst was employed in the hydrolysis of NaBH$_4$ to generate hydrogen gas. Liu et al. [20] found a specific surface area of 1.98 m² g^{-1} and 1.15 m² g^{-1} for Ni powder and Co powder, respectively. These materials were utilized in the hydrolysis reaction of borohydride for hydrogen production.

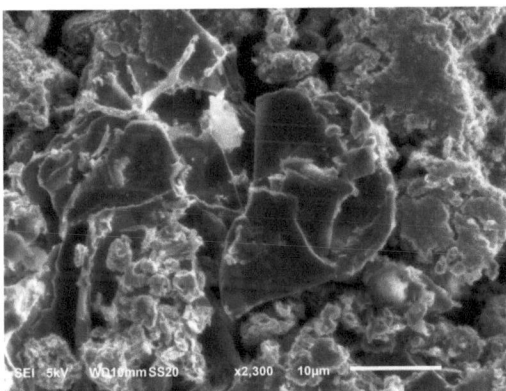

Figure 1. Scanning Electron Microscopy of graphene oxide obtained from spent Zn-C batteries synthesized using the adapted Hummers method.

XRD analysis was used to investigate the conversion of graphite from Zn-C batteries to GO. Figure 2a shows the graphite diffractogram from spent batteries. A sharp diffraction peak can be observed at 2θ = 26.4°, which can be attributed to the basal plane (002) of the graphite, with a lamellar distance of 3.37 Å [28]. Such results indicate a hexagonal crystal structure for the carbon atoms, characteristic of graphite. Additionally, wide diffraction peaks are also observed at 42.5 and 55°, which can be attributed to the (100) and (004) planes, respectively. On the other hand, GO presented a broad peak between 15 and 30°. More detailed information can be observed in Figure 2b, which indicates the formation of an amorphous structure. This occurs due to the oxidation of graphite and detachment of the carbon planes [12]. The peak at 2θ = 9.2° is related to the emergence of interactions between the functional groups that are formed in the GO [19]. Based on the results, it can be concluded that GO was successfully synthesized. However, the presence of peaks attributed to graphite, at 2θ = 26.4° and 42.4°, indicate a residual amount of graphite in the GO obtained. For Ni/Co-GO NPs, a more amorphous character after the deposition of the NPs was observed. According to Zhang et al., the diffraction peak at 2θ = 34° can be attributed to the metal hydroxides formed during the deposition of nanoparticles [29]. The peaks of Ni and Co were not observed due to the low concentration of these metals in the material.

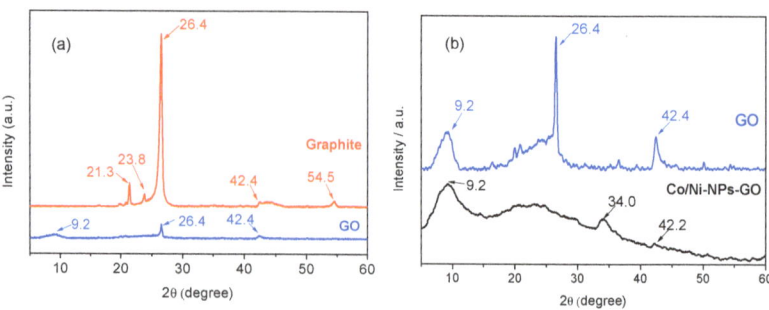

Figure 2. (a) Diffractogram of graphite and graphene oxide (GO) obtained from spent Zn-C batteries synthesized using the adapted Hummers method; (b) diffractogram of GO and Ni/Co-GO NPs (60:40 w/w).

The materials were also characterized using Transmission Electron Microscopy and the GO results can be seen in Figure 3. GO leaf-like morphology with different transparencies can be observed, corroborating the results obtained using SEM. Dark areas indicate stacking of several layers of GO, while areas of greater transparency indicate a thinner film of a few layers of GO. Similar results were observed by Stobinski et al. [30]. The electron diffraction rings obtained from Selected-Area Electron Diffraction (SAED) measurements (Figure S3) exhibited spacings of approximately 0.98 Å, 1.19 Å, 2.10 Å, and 3.00 Å. These findings are indicative of "d" spacings of graphene, signifying the existence of graphitic regions. Similar results were documented by Saxena et al. [31]. After the Ni/Co NPs deposition on GO, a modification of the diffraction pattern was observed, with "d" spacing of about 1.22 Å; 1.65 Å; 2.06 Å; 3.19 Å; and 3.80 Å (Figure S4). Therefore, it can be concluded that Ni/Co NPs deposition was successfully performed. The material presented an interplanar distance of 0.680 nm, as shown in Figure 3a. Similar results were found by Aliyev et al. [32], who found an interplanar distance of 0.65 nm between the GO layers. The Ni/Co NPs were evenly distributed over the material surface, with a size of 1.55 nm ± 0.05 (Figure 3b). Similar results were observed by Dong et al. [15], who obtained nanoparticles with sizes between 2.9 nm and 4.2 nm. The determined interplanar distance was 0.269 nm, which can be attributed to the presence of Ni/Co nanoparticles [33,34].

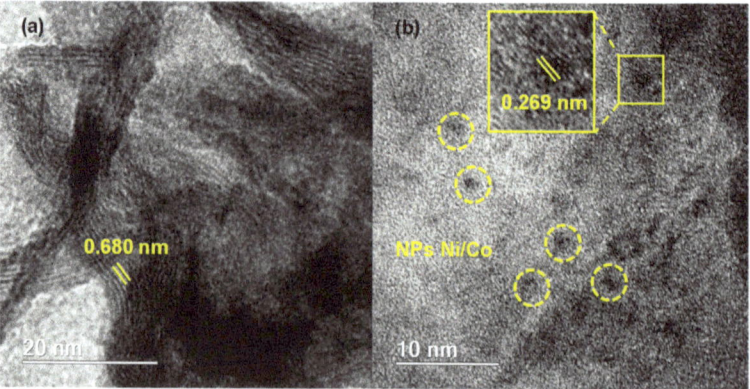

Figure 3. Transmission Electron Microscopy images of graphene oxide obtained from spent Zn-C batteries synthesized using the adapted Hummers method. (a) Interplanar distance between the GO planes (b) Ni/Co nanoparticles decorated on the GO.

The X-ray Energy Dispersive Spectroscopy results, extracted from the images displayed in Figures S3 and S4, are presented in Figure S5. The GO is composed of carbon (40.7%) and oxygen (12.7%). Other elements are also observed in smaller amounts, such as sodium, aluminum, silicon, sulfur, potassium, and manganese, which can be attributed to impurities arising from graphite or the reagents used in the synthesis. The presence of copper is due to the grid used in the analysis. After the deposition of the nanoparticles, the presence of Ni (9.8%) and Co (6%) elements can be observed, in addition to carbon (25.1%) and oxygen (12.5%).

The FTIR spectra of the materials obtained are shown in Figure S6. The results of graphite and GO are shown in Figure S6a. A main band at 3435 cm^{-1} can be observed, which can be attributed to the stretching of hydroxyl groups (νOH) bonds [35], due to the presence of water in the materials. After the graphite oxidation process to obtain GO, two bands are observed at 1730 cm^{-1} and 1630 cm^{-1}, which can be attributed to the stretching of carbonyl (νC=O) of carboxylic acids, esters, and ketones [36]. The bands at 1226 cm^{-1} and 1051 cm^{-1}, also present in GO, can be attributed to the C–O stretching vibrations [28]. The presence of the carbonyl group formed in GO facilitates the fixation of metallic nanoparticles on the surface of the composite [36]. According to Naveen et al. [37], the band at 1081 cm^{-1} can be attributed to stretching vibrations of epoxy (CO). The Ni/Co-GO NPs spectrum is shown in Figure S6b. Bands at 520 cm^{-1} and 611 cm^{-1} are observed, and can be attributed to the Co-O and Ni-O bond, respectively [37].

Raman spectroscopy is a sensitive and non-destructive technique, widely used to detect structural defects in systems containing C sp^2. The results obtained using this technique are shown in Figure S7. For both materials, peaks are observed at 1574 cm^{-1} (G band) and another at 1345 cm^{-1} (D band). The G band corresponds to the first-order scattering of the E$_{2g}$ phonon, in the center of the Brillouin zone, and is typically associated with graphitic carbon structures [36,38]. The D band is attributed to the collective respiration modes of the rings within the graphene lattice, which may indicate a reduction in the size of the C sp^2 domains via chemical oxidation of graphite [36,39]. The D band refers to amorphous carbon. The band at 2699 cm^{-1} can also be observed, historically denominated the G' or 2D band. This band has nothing to do with the G peak, but is the second order of the zone boundary phonons [40]. According to López-Díaz et al. [41], the apparent band at 2936 cm^{-1} corresponds to the D + D' band. This band corresponds to phonons with different moments, which for their activation, require structural defects caused by the change in the chemical structure of the material, caused by the oxidation of graphite.

According to the data obtained, it can be concluded that the synthesis of Ni/Co-GO NPs from spent Zn-C batteries was successful. This material was used in the catalysis of NaBH$_4$ hydrolysis to produce hydrogen.

3.2. Hydrogen Evolution from NaBH$_4$

It is known that the production of hydrogen via hydrolysis of NaBH$_4$ can be accelerated with the addition of inorganic or organic acids, but the rate of hydrolysis is better controlled by transition metals and their salts [42]. In general, doping the active components or supporting them on a porous substrate is also a viable way to increase the surface area of catalysts and reaction efficiency [43]. Nickel and cobalt metals were selected as catalysts for the hydrogen evolution reaction because they are low cost and do not present a risk of extinction. For this, different compositions involving an m(Ni)/m(Co) ratio were evaluated, and the results are shown in Figure 4.

It can be observed that the monometallic composition, i.e., Ni-GO NPs and Co-GO NPs, presented higher reaction speed, but with low efficiency, close to 50% for both materials. Probably, the hydrogen gas produced an agglomerate around the nanoparticle, preventing the decomposition of more borohydride in this saturated site. This phenomenon reduces the efficiency of reaction. On the other hand, bimetallic compositions showed better efficiency when compared to monometallic NPs, except for the composition of Ni/Co-GO NPs (50:50 w/w). These compositions also presented longer induction time, close to 35 s.

The induction time occurs as a moment of pre-catalysis of the reaction, in which a reactive species is formed to catalyze the reaction. Among the bimetallic compositions, the Ni/Co-GO NPs (60:40 w/w) showed better efficiency and speed, with a Hydrogen Generation Rate (HGR) of 212.1 mL min^{-1} g^{-1} from borohydride consumed. This value is similar to the value reported by Liu et al. [20], who found a rate of 228.5 mL min^{-1} g^{-1} using nickel–cobalt boride as a catalyst for the same reaction. Other works that used Ni- and Co-based catalysts for hydrogen evolution from NaBH$_4$ hydrolysis are showed in Table 2, along with the material used in this work for comparison.

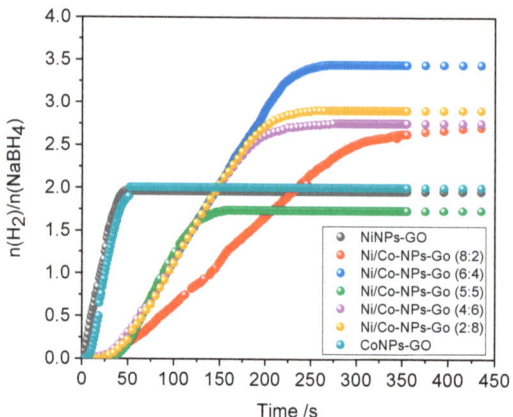

Figure 4. Hydrogen evolution from NaBH$_4$ for different compositions of m(Ni)/m(Co) decorated in GO obtained from spent Zn-C batteries. Reaction conditions: GO support mass: 100 mg; 0.700 mmol of the catalyst; 1.00 mL of NaBH$_4$ (0.500 mol L^{-1}); temperature: 296.15 K.

Table 2. Different Ni- and Co-based catalysts applied in the evolution of hydrogen from NaBH$_4$.

Catalyst	Hydrolysis Conditions	Ea *	HGR **	Reference
Raney Ni–Co	0.5 g catalyst; 1 g NaBH$_4$; 10% wt NaOH; 293 K	52.3	228.5	[20]
Co-Ni@C	50 mg catalyst; 0.1 g NaBH$_4$; 0.1 g NaOH; 298 K	30.3	6364	[22]
Ni-Co/r-GO	5 g of 10 wt% NaBH$_4$; 5 wt% NaOH; 0.05 g catalysts; 25 °C	55.12	1280	[23]
Ni-Co@3DG	0.02 g catalyst; 25 °C; 1 mol L^{-1} NaBH$_4$; 20.0 mL NaOH; (pH = 10.0)	Not informed.	82.65	[24]
Co@C-650	10 mg of catalyst/5 mL H$_2$O 2% m/m NaOH; 2% m/m NaBH$_4$, 30 °C	41.5	330	[27]
Ni/Dolomita	5 mL de 0.25 mol L^{-1} of NaOH; 60 °C; 100 mg NaBH$_4$; catalyst: 100 mg.	38.33	88.16	[44]
CoB-Ni$_4$B$_3$	25 °C; 20 mg of catalyst; 10 mmol NaOH; 5 mL NaBH$_4$ 0.2 mol L^{-1}	32.7	404.6	[45]
Ni/Co-GO NPs	0.500 mol L^{-1} NaBH$_4$; catalyst: 100 mg; 296.15 K; Without of NaOH	51.6	212.1	This work

* Ea = Activation energy; ** HGR = Hydrogen Generation Rate.

Control assays were performed using GO without Ni and Co nanoparticles in the hydrogen evolution from borohydride. The material did not show considerable hydrogen formation. It can be concluded that the GO as a support for the nanoparticles favors the reaction kinetics.

NaBH$_4$ hydrolysis involves the dissociative chemisorption of BH$_4^-$ on the catalyst surface as the first kinetic step. According to Guo et al. [46], BH$_4^-$ ions are adsorbed on electron-enriched Co active sites, forming the Co-BH$_3^-$ and Co-H intermediates, according to Equation (4). Co-BH$_3^-$ reacts with water to form the intermediates Co-H and BH$_3$(OH)$^-$. Two Co-H sites combine to form H$_2$, regenerating part of the active sites (Equation (5)).

$$2\text{Co} + \text{BH}_4^- \rightleftharpoons \text{Co-BH}_3^- + \text{Co-H} \tag{4}$$

$$\text{Co-H} + \text{Co-H} \rightleftharpoons \text{Co-H}_2 + \text{Co} \tag{5}$$

$$\text{Co-H}_2 + \text{Ni} \rightleftharpoons \text{Ni-H}_2 + \text{Co} \tag{6}$$

$$\text{Ni-H}_2 \rightarrow \text{Ni} + \text{H}_2 \tag{7}$$

The adsorption of H$_2$ can block the active sites, decreasing the catalytic efficiency of the material. Thus, the bimetallic composition may allow the transport of H$_2$ to Ni sites (Equations (6) and (7)), preventing the agglomeration and gas saturation on the surface of active Co sites, improving catalyst efficiency. Similar results were observed by Paksoy et al. [45], who used Bo-Ni-Co nanospheres in NaBH$_4$ catalysis, and whose speed obtained was 404.6 mL min^{-1} g^{-1}, for a composition 35/36% w/w Co-Ni.

3.3. Evaluation of the Influence of NaBH$_4$ Concentration

The evaluation of NaBH$_4$ concentration in the evolution of hydrogen mediated by Ni/Co NPs-GO is shown in Figure 5a. It should be noted that the H$_2$/NaBH$_4$ ratio is practically the same, regardless of the concentration of NaBH$_4$ used. The kinetic constants were equal to 4.2 × 10^{-3} s^{-1}, 3.1 × 10^{-3} s^{-1}, 3.2 × 10^{-3} s^{-1}, and 3.6 × 10^{-3} s^{-1} for 0.2, 0.3, 0.4, and 0.5 mol L^{-1}, respectively. The plot of the kinetic constant vs. the ln of NaBH$_4$ concentration is shown in Figure 5b, showing an almost horizontal line with a slope of −0.18. This suggests that the hydrolysis of NaBH$_4$ catalyzed by Ni/Co-GO follows a zero-order reaction with respect to NaBH$_4$ concentration. Consequently, this rules out NaBH$_4$ activation as the sole rate-determining step. Similar results are discussed by Fu et al. [47].

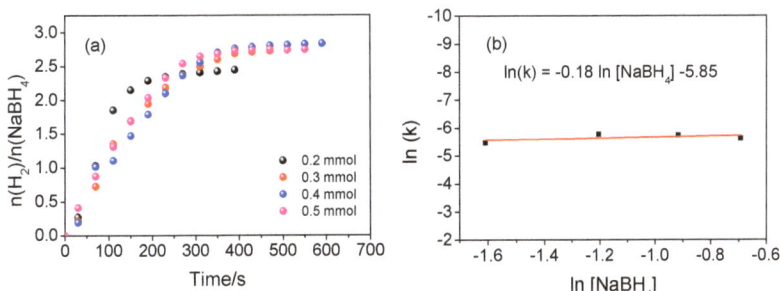

Figure 5. (a) Hydrogen evolution from different NaBH$_4$ concentration. (b) ln of kinetic constant vs. the ln of NaBH$_4$ concentration. Reaction conditions: 0.700 mmol of Ni/Co NPs (60:40 w/w); GO support: 100 mg; temperature: 296.15 K.

3.4. Evaluation of the Influence of Catalyst Dose

The evaluation of catalyst dose in the evolution of hydrogen mediated by Ni/Co NPs-GO is shown in Figure 6a. The catalyst dose increase from 0.175 mmol to 0.700 mmol increased the HGR from 71.7 mL g$_{cat}^{-1}$ min^{-1} to 212.1 mL g$_{cat}^{-1}$ min^{-1}. This result can be attributed to an increase in active sites, favoring the reaction kinetics.

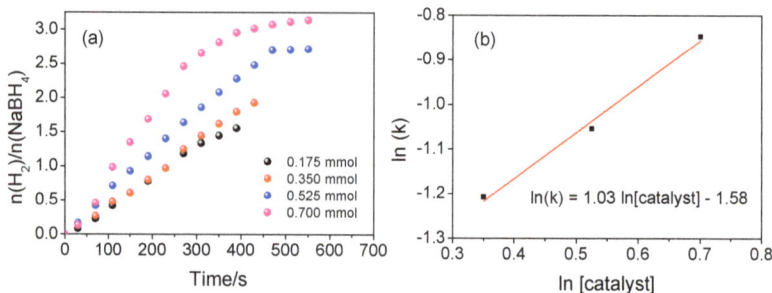

Figure 6. (**a**) Hydrogen evolution from NaBH$_4$ for different doses of catalyst Ni/Co-GO NPs. (**b**) ln of kinetic constant vs. the ln of catalyst dose. Reaction conditions: 0.700 mmol of Ni/Co NPs (60:40 w/w); GO support: 100 mg; 1.00 mL of NaBH$_4$ (0.500 mol L^{-1}); temperature: 296.15 K.

It is evident that the data for doses of 0.175 mmol and 0.350 mmol largely coincide. As a result, the data for 0.175 mmol were disregarded to create the plot of the kinetic constant versus the natural logarithm of catalyst dose (Figure 6b). The slope was 1.18, indicating a first-order kinetics with respect to the catalyst. Similar findings have been discussed by Fu et al. [47].

3.5. Evaluation of NaOH Presence in the Hydrogen Evolution

NaBH$_4$ is considered a very promising hydrogen storage. However, it presents low stability and a slow reaction rate in water in the absence of a catalyst. According to Schlesinger and coworkers [48], borohydride tends to stabilize in alkaline liquid solution, and therefore, this parameter is widely studied. The results of hydrogen evolution using Ni/Co-GO NPs (60:40 w/w) at different concentrations of NaOH are shown in Figure 7. As can be seen, the addition of NaOH decreases the yield. The increase in NaOH concentration from 0.010 to 0.05 mol L^{-1} reduces the reaction yield from 71.4 to 8%, respectively. According to Guo et al. [46], the increase in sodium hydroxide concentration increases the concentration of Na$^+$ ions. This is also due to the borohydride counterion being present in the solution. These ions can be deposited on the active sites of the catalyst, reducing the reaction rate and reaction yield. Thus, the other assays were performed without the addition of NaOH.

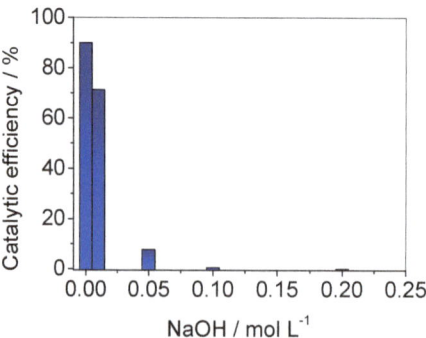

Figure 7. Catalytic efficiency of hydrogen evolution from NaBH$_4$ in the presence of different concentrations of NaOH. Reaction conditions: 0.700 mmol of Ni/Co NPs (60:40 w/w), GO support: 100 mg; 1.00 mL of NaBH$_4$ (0.500 mol L^{-1}); temperature: 296.15 K.

3.6. Evaluation of Temperature in the Hydrogen Evolution

The results of hydrogen evolution using the Ni/Co-GO NPs (60:40 w/w) at different temperatures are shown in Figure 8. The reaction rate is dependent of the temperature, reaching higher kinetics at higher temperature values. The pseudo first-order kinetic models were fitted to the experimental data. The kinetic constants values (k_{obs}) for each temperature are shown in the Table 3.

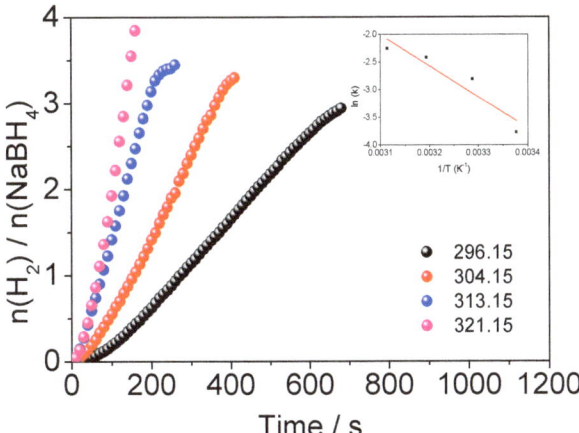

Figure 8. Hydrogen evolution from $NaBH_4$ catalyzed with Ni/Co-GO NPs (60:40 w/w) in different temperatures. Reaction parameters: 0.700 mmol of Ni/Co-GO NPs (60:40 w/w), GO support: 100 mg; 1.00 mL of $NaBH_4$ (0.500 mol L^{-1}). Inset. Arrhenius plot (lnK versus absolute temperature ratio). Data using 0.500 mol L^{-1} $NaBH_4$ solution and using NP-Ni/Co-GO (60:40 w/w) as flexible at different solution temperatures.

Table 3. Kinetic constants (k_{obs}) of hydrogen evolution reaction from $NaBH_4$ with Ni/Co-GO NPs (60:40 w/w) at different temperatures. Reaction parameters: 0.700 mmol of Ni/Co-GO NPs (60:40 w/w), GO support: 100 mg; 1.00 mL of $NaBH_4$ (0.500 mol L^{-1}); temperature: 296.15 K.

Temperature (Kelvin)	Reaction Kinetic Constant (s^{-1})
296.15	0.0230
304.15	0.0606
313.15	0.0893
321.15	0.1047

From the kinetic constants, the Arrhenius graph was constructed (inset of Figure 6). The linear model was fitted to the experimental data, obtaining a coefficient of determination of 0.833. The activation energy of the system was determined according to Equation (2), which presented a value of 46.7 kJ mol^{-1}. This result is consistent with the findings of Amendola et al. [49], who obtained a value of 47 kJ mol^{-1}. The authors used a ruthenium-based catalyst for borohydride decomposition reactions to produce hydrogen gas. Paksoy et al. used the same metals, Co and Ni, supported with metal-boron crystals, which found an activation energy of 32.7 kJ mol^{-1} [45]. Akbayrak et al. found an activation energy of 65 kJ mol^{-1} using cobalt ferrite as a support for platinum nanoparticles [50]. The results indicate that it was possible to obtain a suitable material from spent Zn-C batteries for the efficient evolution of H_2 from $NaBH_4$. From the obtained results, it was possible to determine the rate equation, according to Equation (8).

$$\text{Rate} = k\,[NaBH_4]^0[\text{catalyst}]^1 \tag{8}$$

3.7. Reuse of the Material

The reuse of Ni/Co-GO NPs (60:40 w/w), which presented the better performance in hydrogen evolution from borohydride, was reused until it lost its efficiency. The results are shown in Figure 9. There was a loss of efficiency (17%) between the first and second cycles, but it remained constant until the seventh cycle (70% yield). From the eight cycle onwards, the efficiency decreases again, reaching an efficiency of 50% in the tenth cycle. Probably, the decline in efficiency from the eighth cycle onwards may be linked to catalyst leaching [51]. Comparable findings were noted by Khan et al., who detected catalyst leaching starting from the third cycle [52]. Efficiency in the reaction exhibited a decline over the course of three cycles when employing a Cu-based catalyst for hydrogen evolution in the methanolysis of $NaBH_4$ [53]. Therefore, it can be concluded that the material is stable, as its performance remains satisfactory even after seven cycles of use.

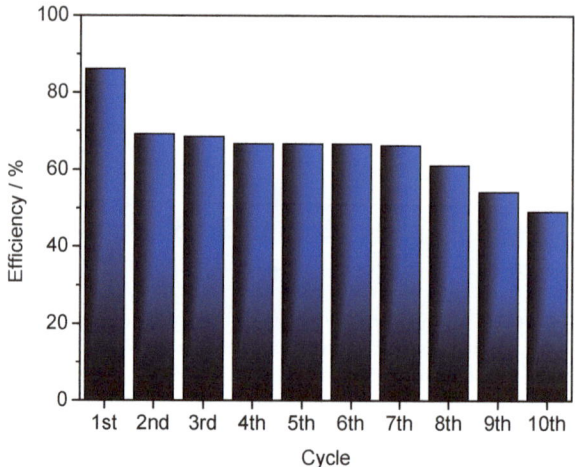

Figure 9. Reuse of Ni/Co-GO NPs (60:40 w/w) in hydrogen evolution from $NaBH_4$. Reaction parameters: 0.700 mmol of Ni/Co-GO NPs (60:40 w/w), GO support: 100 mg; 1.00 mL of $NaBH_4$ (0.500 mol L^{-1}); temperature: 296.15 K.

3.8. Performance of Ni/Co Supported on GO Derived from Graphite in Zn-C Batteries and Analytical Grade

For comparative analysis, Ni/Co nanoparticles were deposited on analytical-grade Zn-C stack graphite-supported graphene oxide (GO). The results are shown in Figure S8. It is noticeable that the performance of both materials was quite similar, with a slightly higher yield for the material obtained from spent Zn-C batteries, while the kinetics were more favorable for the material derived from analytical-grade graphite. The commercial GO value is USD 0.045/g. Considering the inputs for producing GO from spent Zn-C batteries, the value reaches half. Considering the price and environmental appeal, the material obtained in this work appears to be competitive.

4. Conclusions

Based on the results achieved in this study, it can be asserted that a novel, value-added material was successfully obtained from graphite extracted from spent Zn-C batteries using an eco-friendly process. This approach offers a new method for treating and addressing waste that poses numerous environmental challenges, particularly in the context of urban mining. The synthesis of graphene oxide using the adapted Hummers method demonstrated characteristics comparable to those reported in the literature. Commercial graphene oxide is valued at USD 0.045/g, but when considering the inputs for producing graphene oxide from batteries, the cost is reduced by half. From both a cost and environmental perspective, the material obtained in this study appears to be competitive. When used as a support for metallic nanoparticles, this material exhibited promise in hydrogen evolution from sodium borohydride. It displayed kinetic constants in line with the literature, and the rate of hydrogen generation was considered satisfactory. Notably, this study represents the first instance in the literature where graphene oxide obtained from e-waste is utilized as a support for metallic nanoparticles in hydrogen evolution. This aligns with the ongoing discourse surrounding alternative energy sources, opening new possibilities for hydrogen production from various sources. Furthermore, the material can be reused in multiple catalytic cycles, showcasing significant potential for applications in hydrogen evolution. Further studies are required to elucidate the reaction mechanism and explore the reasons behind the performance decline observed after the eighth cycle, as well as to explore other potential applications for graphene oxide support.

Supplementary Materials: The following supporting information can be downloaded at: https://www.mdpi.com/article/10.3390/pr11113250/s1, Figure S1: Hydrogen production reactor. Highlights: (a) Kitassato-type reactor; (b) rubber septum for sealing the system and injecting the $NaBH_4$ solution; (c) bath for temperature control; (d) magnetic stirrer with heating; (e) plastic hose connection between the reactor and the volume measurement system; (f) burette-type volume meter attached to the system to measure the volume of hydrogen gas produced; (g) water reservoir for water leveling in the volume measurement system; (h) digital thermometer; Figure S2: Graphene oxide produced from the rods of used Zn-C batteries; Figure S3: Transmission Electron Microscopy (TEM) image of graphene oxide (GO) obtained from spent Zn-C batteries. Inset: Selected-Area Electron Diffraction (SAED). Polycrystalline structure characterized by the main interplanar distances: 0.98 Å; 1.19 Å; 2.10 Å; 3.00 Å; Figure S4: Transmission Electron Microscopy image of Ni/Co-NPs-GO. Inset: Selected-Area Electron Diffraction (SAED). Polycrystalline structure characterized by the main interplanar distances: 1.22 Å; 1.65 Å; 2.06 Å; 3.19 Å; 3.80 Å; Figure S5: Energy Dispersive Spectroscopy (EDS). (A) Graphene oxide (GO) obtained from spent Zn-C batteries. (B) Ni/Co-NPs-GO (60:40 w/w); Figure S6: FTIR of (a) graphite obtained from spent Zn-C batteries (red) and graphene oxide (GO) obtained from spent Zn-C batteries (black) (b) Ni/Co-NPs-GO (60:40 w/w); Figure S7: Raman spectroscopy. (a) Graphite obtained from spent Zn-C batteries (b) graphene oxide (GO) obtained from spent Zn-C batteries; Figure S8: Hydrogen evolution from $NaBH_4$ mediated by Ni/Co-GO NPs. Reaction conditions: 0.700 mmol of Ni/Co NPs (60:40 w/w); GO support: 100 mg; 1.00 mL of $NaBH_4$ (0.500 mol L^{-1}); temperature: 296.15 K.

Author Contributions: G.S.: conceptualization, methodology, investigation, formal analysis, writing—original draft, writing—review and editing; I.M.J.: conceptualization, methodology, investigation, formal analysis; E.B.: conceptualization, methodology, investigation; R.M.: conceptualization, methodology, resources, funding acquisition, investigation, formal analysis, writing—original draft, writing—review and editing, supervision. All authors have read and agreed to the published version of the manuscript.

Funding: This research received no external funding.

Data Availability Statement: Data sharing not applicable. No new data were created or analyzed in this study. Data sharing is not applicable to this article.

Acknowledgments: The authors thank the Coordenação de Aperfeiçoamento de Pessoal de Nível Superior—Brazil (CAPES), Conselho Nacional de Desenvolvimento Científico e Tecnológico (CNPq-Process: 405828/2022-5 and 312400/2021-7), Fundação de Amparo à Pesquisa do Estado de Minas Gerais (FAPEMIG, RED-00144-22), Department of Chemistry of Universidade Federal de Viçosa, Department of Physics of Universidade Federal de Viçosa, and the Center of Microscopy at the Universidade Federal de Minas Gerais (http://www.microscopia.ufmg.br, accessed on 10 September 2023, for providing the equipment and technical support for experiments involving electron microscopy.

Conflicts of Interest: The authors declare that they have no known competing financial interest or personal relationships that could have appeared to influence the work reported in this paper.

References

1. Karthik, P.E.; Rajan, H.; Jothi, V.R.; Sang, B.I.; Yi, S.C. Electronic Wastes: A near Inexhaustible and an Unimaginably Wealthy Resource for Water Splitting Electrocatalysts. *J. Hazard. Mater.* **2022**, *421*, 126687. [PubMed]
2. Albright, G.; Edie AllCell Technologies, J.; Crossley, P.; Vassallo, A. *Battery Storage for Renewables: Market Status and Technology Outlook*; International Renewable Energy Agency: Masdar City, United Arab Emirates, 2015.

3. Bernardes, A.M.; Espinosa, D.C.R.; Tenório, J.A.S. Recycling of Batteries: A Review of Current Processes and Technologies. *J. Power Sources* **2004**, *130*, 291–298. [CrossRef]
4. Alcaraz, L.; García-Díaz, I.; González, L.; Rabanal, M.E.; Urbieta, A.; Fernández, P.; López, F.A. New Photocatalytic Materials Obtained from the Recycling of Alkaline and Zn/C Spent Batteries. *J. Mater. Res. Technol.* **2019**, *8*, 2809–2818. [CrossRef]
5. Vieira Segundo, J.E.D.; Vilar, E.O. Grafeno: Uma Revisão Sobre Propriedades, Mecanismos de Produção e Potenciais Aplicações Em Sistemas Energéticos. *Rev. Eletrônica De Mater. E Process.* **2016**, *11*, 54–57.
6. Yang, Q.; Cao, L.; Li, S.; Zeng, X.; Zhou, W.; Zhang, C. Upgrading Pomelo Peels into Laser-Induced Graphene for Multifunctional Sensors. *J. Anal. Appl. Pyrolysis* **2023**, *173*, 106074. [CrossRef]
7. Liu, Z.; Yang, Q.; Cao, L.; Li, S.; Zeng, X.; Zhou, W.; Zhang, C. Synthesis and Application of Porous Carbon Nanomaterials from Pomelo Peels: A Review. *Molecules* **2023**, *28*, 4429. [CrossRef] [PubMed]
8. Staudenmaier, L. Verfahren Zur Darstellung Der Graphitsäure. *Eur. J. Inorg. Chem.* **1898**, *31*, 1481–1487. [CrossRef]
9. Hofmann, U.; Rudorff, W. The Formation of Salts from Graphite by Strong Acids. *Trans. Faraday Soc.* **1938**, *45*, 1017–1021. [CrossRef]
10. Hummers, W.S.; Offeman, R.E. Preparation of Graphitic Oxide. *J. Am. Chem. Soc.* **1958**, *80*, 1339. [CrossRef]
11. Camargos, J.S.F.; Semmer, A.D.O.; Da Silva, S.N. Características e Aplicações do Grafeno e do Óxido de Grafeno e as Principais Rotas Para Síntese. *J. Eng. Exact Sci.* **2017**, *3*, 1118–1130. [CrossRef]
12. Loudiki, A.; Matrouf, M.; Azriouil, M.; Laghrib, F.; Farahi, A.; Bakasse, M.; Lahrich, S.; El Mhammedi, M.A. Graphene Oxide Synthesized from Zinc-Carbon Battery Waste Using a New Oxidation Process Assisted Sonication: Electrochemical Properties. *Mater. Chem. Phys.* **2022**, *275*, 125308. [CrossRef]
13. Joshi, D.J.; Koduru, J.R.; Malek, N.I.; Hussain, C.M.; Kailasa, S.K. Surface Modifications and Analytical Applications of Graphene Oxide: A Review. *TrAC-Trends Anal. Chem.* **2021**, *144*, 116448. [CrossRef]
14. Li, W.; Liu, Y.; Guo, F.; Du, Y.; Chen, Y. Self-Assembly Sandwich-like Fe, Co, or Ni Nanoparticles/Reduced Graphene Oxide Composites with Excellent Microwave Absorption Performance. *Appl. Surf. Sci.* **2021**, *562*, 150212. [CrossRef]
15. Dong, J.; Sun, T.; Zhang, Y.; Zhang, H.; Lu, S.; Hu, D.; Chen, J.; Xu, L. Mesoporous NiCo Alloy/Reduced Graphene Oxide Nanocomposites as Efficient Hydrogen Evolution Catalysts. *J. Colloid Interface Sci.* **2021**, *599*, 603–610. [CrossRef] [PubMed]
16. Grad, O.; Mihet, M.; Coros, M.; Dan, M.; Lazar, M.D.; Blanita, G. Reduced Graphene Oxide Modified with Noble Metal Nanoparticles for Formic Acid Dehydrogenation. *Catal. Today* **2021**, *366*, 41–47. [CrossRef]
17. Singla, S.; Sharma, S.; Basu, S.; Shetti, N.P.; Aminabhavi, T.M. Photocatalytic Water Splitting Hydrogen Production via Environmental Benign Carbon Based Nanomaterials. *Int. J. Hydrogen Energy* **2021**, *46*, 33696–33717. [CrossRef]
18. Jia, X.; Sang, Z.; Sun, L.; Xu, F.; Pan, H.; Zhang, C.; Cheng, R. Graphene-Modified Co-B-P Catalysts for Hydrogen Generation from Sodium Borohydride Hydrolysis. *Nanomaterials* **2022**, *12*, 2732. [CrossRef] [PubMed]
19. Rabia, M.; Hadia, N.M.A.; Farid, O.M.; Abdelazeez, A.A.A.; Mohamed, S.H.; Shaban, M. Poly(M-toluidine)/Rolled Graphene Oxide Nanocomposite Photocathode for Hydrogen Generation from Wastewater. *Int. J. Energy Res.* **2022**, *46*, 11943–11956. [CrossRef]
20. Liu, B.H.; Li, Z.P.; Suda, S. Nickel- and Cobalt-Based Catalysts for Hydrogen Generation by Hydrolysis of Borohydride. *J. Alloys Compd.* **2006**, *415*, 288–293. [CrossRef]
21. Darabdhara, G.; Amin, M.A.; Mersal, G.A.M.; Ahmed, E.M.; Das, M.R.; Zakaria, M.B.; Malgras, V.; Alshehri, S.M.; Yamauchi, Y.; Szunerits, S.; et al. Reduced Graphene Oxide Nanosheets Decorated with Au, Pd and Au-Pd Bimetallic Nanoparticles as Highly Efficient Catalysts for Electrochemical Hydrogen Generation. *J. Mater. Chem. A* **2015**, *3*, 20254–20266. [CrossRef]
22. Sun, L.; Gao, X.; Ning, X.; Qiu, Z.; Xing, L.; Yang, H.; Li, D.; Dou, J.; Meng, Y. Cobalt-Nickel Bimetal Carbon Sphere Catalysts for Efficient Hydrolysis of Sodium Borohydride: The Role of Synergy and Confine Effect. *Int. J. Hydrogen Energy* **2023**, *48*, 3413–3428. [CrossRef]
23. Chou, C.C.; Hsieh, C.H.; Chen, B.H. Hydrogen Generation from Catalytic Hydrolysis of Sodium Borohydride Using Bimetallic NiCo Nanoparticles on Reduced Graphene Oxide as Catalysts. *Energy* **2015**, *90*, 1973–1982. [CrossRef]
24. Karaman, O. Three-Dimensional Graphene Network Supported Nickel-Cobalt Bimetallic Alloy Nanocatalyst for Hydrogen Production by Hydrolysis of Sodium Borohydride and Developing of an Artificial Neural Network Modeling to Forecast Hydrogen Production Rate. *Chem. Eng. Res. Des.* **2022**, *181*, 321–330. [CrossRef]
25. Didehban, A.; Zabihi, M.; Babajani, N. Preparation of the Efficient Nano-Bimetallic Cobalt-Nickel Catalysts Supported on the Various Magnetic Substrates for Hydrogen Generation from Hydrolysis of Sodium Borohydride in Alkaline Solutions. *Polyhedron* **2020**, *180*, 114405. [CrossRef]
26. Yue, C.; Yang, P.; Wang, J.; Zhao, X.; Wang, Y.; Yang, L. Facile Synthesis and Characterization of Nano-Pd Loaded NiCo Microfibers as Stable Catalysts for Hydrogen Generation from Sodium Borohydride. *Chem. Phys. Lett.* **2020**, *743*, 137170. [CrossRef]
27. Su, S.; Chen, K.; Yang, X.; Dang, D. Coronavirus-like Core—Shell-Structured Co@C for Hydrogen Evolution via Hydrolysis of Sodium Borohydride. *Molecules* **2023**, *28*, 2–9. [CrossRef]
28. Zhao, W.; Kido, G.; Hara, K.; Noguchi, H. Characterization of Neutralized Graphite Oxide and Its Use in Electric Double Layer Capacitors. *J. Electroanal. Chem.* **2014**, *712*, 185–193. [CrossRef]
29. Zhang, D.; Cui, X.; Jin, G.; Jiao, Y.; Li, D. Preparation, Deposited Behavior and Hydrophobic Property of Modified Graphene Oxide Reinforced Ni Composite Coatings by Magnetic Field Assisted Electro-Brush Plating. *Surf. Coat. Technol.* **2020**, *403*, 126363. [CrossRef]

30. Stobinski, L.; Lesiak, B.; Malolepszy, A.; Mazurkiewicz, M.; Mierzwa, B.; Zemek, J.; Jiricek, P.; Bieloshapka, I. Graphene Oxide and Reduced Graphene Oxide Studied by the XRD, TEM and Electron Spectroscopy Methods. *J. Electron Spectrosc. Relat. Phenom.* **2014**, *195*, 145–154. [CrossRef]
31. Saxena, S.; Tyson, T.A.; Shukla, S.; Negusse, E.; Chen, H.; Bai, J. Investigation of Structural and Electronic Properties of Graphene Oxide. *Appl. Phys. Lett.* **2011**, *99*, 5–8. [CrossRef]
32. Aliyev, E.; Filiz, V.; Khan, M.M.; Lee, Y.J.; Abetz, C.; Abetz, V. Structural Characterization of Graphene Oxide: Surface Functional Groups and Fractionated Oxidative Debris. *Nanomaterials* **2019**, *9*, 1180. [CrossRef] [PubMed]
33. Jacob, B.; Mohan, M.; Dhanyaprabha, K.C.; Thomas, H. NiCo2O4 Nanoparticles Anchored on Reduced Graphene Oxide with Enhanced Catalytic Activity towards the Reduction of P-Nitrophenol in Water. *Colloids Surf. A Physicochem. Eng. Asp.* **2022**, *643*, 128717. [CrossRef]
34. Xu, H.; Shi, Z.X.; Tong, Y.X.; Li, G.R. Porous Microrod Arrays Constructed by Carbon-Confined NiCo@NiCoO2 Core@Shell Nanoparticles as Efficient Electrocatalysts for Oxygen Evolution. *Adv. Mater.* **2018**, *30*, e1705442. [CrossRef] [PubMed]
35. Shi, C.; Cao, H.; Li, S.; Guo, L.; Wang, Y.; Yang, J. Flexible Nickel Cobalt Metal-Organic Frameworks/Reduced Graphene Oxide Hybrid Film for High-Performance Supercapacitors. *J. Energy Storage* **2022**, *54*, 105270. [CrossRef]
36. Rattana, T.; Chaiyakun, S.; Witit-Anun, N.; Nuntawong, N.; Chindaudom, P.; Oaew, S.; Kedkeaw, C.; Limsuwan, P. Preparation and Characterization of Graphene Oxide Nanosheets. *Procedia Eng.* **2012**, *32*, 759–764. [CrossRef]
37. Naveen, A.N.; Selladurai, S. Novel Low Temperature Synthesis and Electrochemical Characterization of Mesoporous Nickel Cobaltite-Reduced Graphene Oxide (RGO) Composite for Supercapacitor Application. *Electrochim. Acta* **2015**, *173*, 290–301. [CrossRef]
38. Caridad, J.M.; Rossella, F.; Bellani, V.; Grandi, M.S.; Diez, E. Automated Detection and Characterization of Graphene and Few-Layer Graphite via Raman Spectroscopy. *J. Raman Spectrosc.* **2011**, *42*, 286–293. [CrossRef]
39. Gao, J.; Liu, F.; Liu, Y.; Ma, N.; Wang, Z.; Zhang, X. Environment-Friendly Method to Produce Graphene That Employs Vitamin C and Amino Acid. *Chem. Mater.* **2010**, *22*, 2213–2218. [CrossRef]
40. Ferrari, A.C.; Meyer, J.C.; Scardaci, V.; Casiraghi, C.; Lazzeri, M.; Mauri, F.; Piscanec, S.; Jiang, D.; Novoselov, K.S.; Roth, S.; et al. Raman Spectrum of Graphene and Graphene Layers. *Phys. Rev. Lett.* **2006**, *97*, 187401. [CrossRef]
41. López-Díaz, D.; López Holgado, M.; García-Fierro, J.L.; Velázquez, M.M. Evolution of the Raman Spectrum with the Chemical Composition of Graphene Oxide. *J. Phys. Chem. C* **2017**, *121*, 20489–20497. [CrossRef]
42. Liu, Y.; Yang, Y.; Gao, M.; Pan, H. Tailoring Thermodynamics and Kinetics for Hydrogen Storage in Complex Hydrides towards Applications. *Chem. Rec.* **2016**, *16*, 189–204. [CrossRef]
43. Zou, Y.; Yin, Y.; Gao, Y.; Xiang, C.; Chu, H.; Qiu, S.; Yan, E.; Xu, F.; Sun, L. Chitosan-Mediated Co–Ce–B Nanoparticles for Catalyzing the Hydrolysis of Sodium Borohydride. *Int. J. Hydrogen Energy* **2018**, *43*, 4912–4921. [CrossRef]
44. Kiren, B.; Ayas, N. Nickel Modified Dolomite in the Hydrogen Generation from Sodium Borohydride Hydrolysis. *Int. J. Hydrogen Energy* **2021**, *47*, 19702–19717. [CrossRef]
45. Paksoy, A.; Kurtoğlu, S.F.; Dizaji, A.K.; Altıntaş, Z.; Khoshsima, S.; Uzun, A.; Balcı, Ö. Nanocrystalline Cobalt–Nickel–Boron (Metal Boride) Catalysts for Efficient Hydrogen Production from the Hydrolysis of Sodium Borohydride. *Int. J. Hydrogen Energy* **2021**, *46*, 7974–7988. [CrossRef]
46. Guo, J.; Hou, Y.; Li, B.; Liu, Y. Novel Ni–Co–B Hollow Nanospheres Promote Hydrogen Generation from the Hydrolysis of Sodium Borohydride. *Int. J. Hydrogen Energy* **2018**, *43*, 15245–15254. [CrossRef]
47. Fu, F.; Wang, C.; Wang, Q.; Martinez-Villacorta, A.M.; Escobar, A.; Chong, H.; Wang, X.; Moya, S.; Salmon, L.; Fouquet, E.; et al. Highly Selective and Sharp Volcano-Type Synergistic Ni2Pt@ZIF-8-Catalyzed Hydrogen Evolution from Ammonia Borane Hydrolysis. *J. Am. Chem. Soc.* **2018**, *140*, 10034–10042. [CrossRef] [PubMed]
48. Schlesinger, H.I.; Brown, H.C.; Finholt, A.E.; Gilbreath, J.R.; Hoekstra, H.R.; Hyde, E.K. Sodium Borohydride, Its Hydrolysis and Its Use as a Reducing Agent and in the Generation of Hydrogen. *J. Am. Chem. Soc.* **1953**, *75*, 215–219. [CrossRef]
49. Amendola, S.C.; Sharp-Goldman, S.L.; Saleem Janjua, M.; Kelly, M.T.; Petillo, P.J.; Binder, M. An Ultrasafe Hydrogen Generator: Aqueous, Alkaline Borohydride Solutions and Ru Catalyst. *J. Power Sources* **2000**, *85*, 186–189. [CrossRef]
50. Akbayrak, S.; Özkar, S. Cobalt Ferrite Supported Platinum Nanoparticles: Superb Catalytic Activity and Outstanding Reusability in Hydrogen Generation from the Hydrolysis of Ammonia Borane. *J. Colloid Interface Sci.* **2021**, *596*, 100–107. [CrossRef]
51. Xu, D.; Zhang, Y.; Guo, Q. Research Progress on Catalysts for Hydrogen Generation through Sodium Borohydride Alcoholysis. *Int. J. Hydrogen Energy* **2022**, *47*, 5929–5946. [CrossRef]
52. Khan, S.B.; Ali, F.; Asiri, A.M. Metal Nanoparticles Supported on Polyacrylamide Water Beads as Catalyst for Efficient Generation of H2 from NaBH4 Methanolysis. *Int. J. Hydrogen Energy* **2020**, *45*, 1532–1540. [CrossRef]
53. Khan, S.B. Metal Nanoparticles Containing Chitosan Wrapped Cellulose Nanocomposites for Catalytic Hydrogen Production and Reduction of Environmental Pollutants. *Carbohydr. Polym.* **2020**, *242*, 116286. [CrossRef] [PubMed]

Disclaimer/Publisher's Note: The statements, opinions and data contained in all publications are solely those of the individual author(s) and contributor(s) and not of MDPI and/or the editor(s). MDPI and/or the editor(s) disclaim responsibility for any injury to people or property resulting from any ideas, methods, instructions or products referred to in the content.

Article

Techno-Economic Assessment of PEM Electrolysis for O$_2$ Supply in Activated Sludge Systems—A Simulation Study Based on the BSM2 Wastewater Treatment Plant

Mario Alejandro Parra Ramirez [1], Stefan Fogel [1], Sebastian Felix Reinecke [1,*] and Uwe Hampel [1,2]

[1] Institute of Fluid Dynamics, Helmholtz-Zentrum Dresden-Rossendorf, 01328 Dresden, Germany; m.parra-ramirez@hzdr.de (M.A.P.R.); s.fogel@hzdr.de (S.F.); u.hampel@hzdr.de (U.H.)
[2] Chair of Imaging Techniques in Energy and Process Engineering, Technical University of Dresden, 01062 Dresden, Germany
* Correspondence: s.reinecke@hzdr.de

Citation: Parra Ramirez, M.A.; Fogel, S.; Reinecke, S.F.; Hampel, U. Techno-Economic Assessment of PEM Electrolysis for O$_2$ Supply in Activated Sludge Systems—A Simulation Study Based on the BSM2 Wastewater Treatment Plant. *Processes* **2023**, *11*, 1639. https://doi.org/10.3390/pr11061639

Academic Editors: Dimitris Zagklis and Georgios Bampos

Received: 22 March 2023
Revised: 22 May 2023
Accepted: 24 May 2023
Published: 26 May 2023

Copyright: © 2023 by the authors. Licensee MDPI, Basel, Switzerland. This article is an open access article distributed under the terms and conditions of the Creative Commons Attribution (CC BY) license (https://creativecommons.org/licenses/by/4.0/).

Abstract: The conversion of renewable energy into hydrogen (H$_2$) by power-to-gas technologies involving electrolysis is seen today as a key element in the transition to a sustainable energy sector. Wastewater treatment plants (WWTP) could be integrated into future green H$_2$ networks as users of oxygen (O$_2$) produced alongside H$_2$ in water electrolysis. In WWTPs, O$_2$ is required for biological treatment steps, e.g., in activated sludge (AS) systems. However, the production costs of electrolysis O$_2$ should be competitive with those of conventional O$_2$ production processes. In this study, mathematical models of a polymer electrolyte membrane electrolyser (PEME) plant and the WWTP of the Benchmark Simulation Model No. 2 (BSM2) were used to simulate electrolysis O$_2$ supply to an AS system and estimate net costs of production (NCP) for produced O$_2$ via a techno-economic assessment (TEA). Assuming that produced H$_2$ is sold to a nearby industry, NCPs for O$_2$ were calculated for two different PEME plant dimensions, four alternatives regarding electricity supply and costs, and three sets of assumptions regarding system performance and market conditions. The analyses were performed for 2020 as a reference year and 2030 based on forecasts of relevant data. Results of the dimensioning of the PEME show the O$_2$ demand of a municipal WWTP with an installed capacity of 80,000 population equivalents (PE), such as the one of the BSM2, can be covered for more than 99% of the simulated period by either a 6.4 MW PEME operated for 4073 full load hours or a 4.8 MW PEME operated for 6259 full load hours. Investment costs for the PEME stacks and the operational costs for electricity make up most of the NCP of electrolysis O$_2$. The projected decrease in PEME stack costs and renewable energy prices in favourable market conditions can result in a competitive NCP for electrolysis O$_2$ in 2030. The approach described in this study can be applied to analyse O$_2$ supply to biological wastewater treatment in WWTPs with different characteristics, in processes different from AS, and under different assumptions regarding economic conditions.

Keywords: wastewater treatment; activated sludge; PEM electrolysis; techno-economic assessment

1. Introduction

The installed capacity of renewable energy sources has continued to increase at an ever-faster pace over the last few decades, promoted by growing concerns regarding the effects of climate change and technological improvements in wind and photovoltaic (PV) power generation systems. However, as the share of weather-dependent, variable renewable energy sources in the energy mix continues to increase, new approaches for grid management become necessary to cope with fluctuating energy availability and ensure a stable and safe supply [1]. Power-to-gas technologies in which electrical renewable energy is converted into green hydrogen (H$_2$) via electrolysis are considered a key process in the energy grid of the future with applications in transport, chemical, and industrial processes, as well as for long-term energy storage and management [2–4]. Until recently, one of the main barriers to the industrial-scale production of green H_2 was the high cost of the electrolyser stacks. Nevertheless, if the current trends of decreasing renewable energy costs and improvements in electrolyser technologies continue in the future, green H_2 will have the potential to become a competitive and sustainable alternative to fossil H_2 in large-scale applications [3,5,6].

Wastewater treatment plants (WWTPs) stand out among other industrial facilities for potential synergies with renewable based energy networks [7]. Their widespread location, the open areas usually available at their sites, and the expertise of personnel in the use of technical gases are among the advantages that WWTP offers for the installation of electrolyser systems [8]. From the WWTP site, produced H_2 can then be valorised internally as fuel, injected into the natural gas network, or supplied to industrial consumers nearby. H_2 can also be converted to methane by taking advantage of the carbon dioxide (CO_2) produced in the anaerobic digestion of sludge as a carbon source. This allows for the use of the biogas infrastructure available at WWTPs and existing natural gas networks [9,10]. Michailos et al. [10] have performed a techno-economic assessment (TEA) of five scenarios for biological methanation of electrolysis H_2 together with biogas coming from an anaerobic digester in a WWTP. The analysed scenarios differed in type of electrolyser, biological methanation process, and source of electricity. They concluded that, given a continuous trend of reduced costs for electrolysers and renewable power in the coming years, the produced methane could achieve lower levelized costs of energy (LCOE) than conventional natural gas.

Apart from the potential for H_2 use and storage, WWTP offers the possibility of exploiting produced oxygen (O_2) instead of discarding it into the atmosphere as a by-product. O_2 is required in WWTPs by microorganisms in biological treatment steps and can also be transformed into ozone (O_3) to be used for disinfection, micropollutant removal, and/or sludge conditioning through ozonation [7,8]. Gretzschel et al. [11] have carried out a feasibility study on the use of O_3 produced from electrolysis O_2 for micropollutant removal at a WWTP in Mainz, Germany. There, surplus energy coming from an on-site PV plant is used to operate a 1.25 MW alkaline water electrolyser to supply the 465,206 kg·a^{-1} of O_2 needed for the ozonation process. The authors concluded that savings of 47,000 €·a^{-1} could be achieved by using electrolysis O_2 instead of buying liquid O_2 from an external provider. Regarding the use of pure O_2 for biological wastewater treatment, Skouteris et al. [12] have carried out a literature review on the effects of the use of pure O_2 on microorganism metabolism and pollutant removal. A higher treatment rate, reduced excess sludge, and better control of filamentous bacteria are presented as advantages reported for pure O_2, while lower pH in the mixed liquor and more refractory effluents are mentioned as possible disadvantages. With the aim of comparing the O_2 transfer process with air and pure O_2 in AS, Mohammadpour et al. [13] presented a mathematical model for bubble rising velocity and volumetric O_2 transfer coefficient ($k_L a$) depending on bubble size. The model is used to calculate the O_2 transfer rate (OTR) and transfer efficiency (OTE) for single bubbles of air and pure O_2 in clean water. Their results show an increase in OTE of approx. 10% for pure O_2 fine bubbles with respect to air injected at a 4 m water depth for conventional AS tanks, which leads to energy savings given by a lower required gas flowrate.

Industrial O_2 production costs have been sufficiently high so far to limit the number of WWTPs using pure O_2 for biological treatment, mainly those in locations with access to cheap O_2 from nearby producers or those requiring a higher OTR to treat heavily polluted and/or saline wastewater [12,14]. However, cost reductions associated with electrolysers and the respective increase in the installed capacity for green H_2 and O_2 production may lead to more favourable conditions for the use of electrolysis O_2 at WWTPs.

In the present study, mathematical models have been used to estimate the dimensions and costs of an electrolyser plant capable of covering the O_2 demand of a conventional AS system in a municipal WWTP and carry out an analysis of the economics of such a project under varying design, operational, and boundary conditions. The results obtained with the models are used together with reference values for economic parameters, namely prices of pieces of equipment, supplies, electricity from conventional and renewable energy sources, H_2, and O_2, as the basis for a TEA on different scenarios.

2. Materials and Methods

2.1. Modelled System and Simulation Process

The modelled system consists of two sub-systems, namely a WWTP with a conventional AS system and a polymer electrolyte membrane electrolyser (PEME) plant installed at the WWTP site. PEME electrolysis was chosen for this study because, although the investment costs of PEMEs are currently higher than those for alkaline electrolysers, the first have shorter response times [15,16] and are therefore better qualified for green H_2 production with volatile a renewable energy supply. The PEME plant consists of sub-models for the PEME stack itself and its associated components, namely an AC/DC converter, a compressor, an intermediate gaseous O_2 storage tank, and a contingency liquid O_2 storage tank. Figure 1 shows a graphical representation of the modelled system. Further components, i.e., the PEME cooling system and water recirculation, are outside the scope of this study.

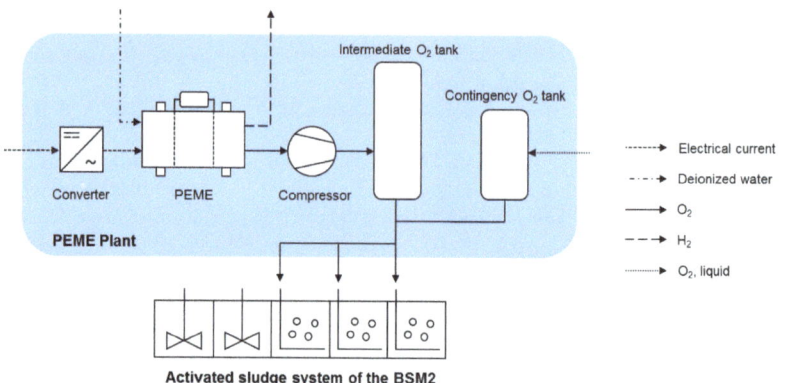

Figure 1. Graphical representation of the modelled system.

The electrolysis O_2 produced by the PEME is pressurized by the compressor and supplied to the intermediate storage tank before being injected into the AS tanks of the WWTP. The O_2 in the contingency storage tank is to be used when the intermediate storage is empty and the flowrate coming from the PEME is insufficient to cover the demand of the AS system. Produced H_2 is assumed to be directly supplied to an industrial site located near the PEME plant; therefore, H_2 storage tanks are not included in the system. The models were implemented into the SIMBA3 software tool developed by the Institute for Automation and Communication in Magdeburg, Germany [17]. All simulations were performed for one year of operation using a 15-min time step. The following sections describe the individual mathematical models for each of the subsystems.

2.2. WWTP Model Implementation and Estimation of O_2 Demand

The conceptual WWTP of the Benchmark Simulation Model No. 2 (BSM2) developed by the International Water Association (IWA) is used as a reference in this investigation. The BSM plant has an installed capacity of 80,000 population equivalents (PE) and includes primary settling, the AS system, secondary settling, and sludge treatment steps. The biological removal of nitrogen and carbon from wastewater is modelled using the Activated Sludge Model No. 1 (ASM1), a widely used mathematical model for the biochemical processes in AS systems, including oxygen demand, nitrification, and denitrification. The AS system of the BSM2 consists of five perfectly mixed tanks connected in series: two tanks for anaerobic denitrification and three tanks for aerobic nitrification. A complete description of the BSM2 plant and simulation procedure, as well as an overview of the ASM1, can be found in [18]. The operation of the WWTP is simulated by using the dynamic influent file described in [19] as an input. This influent file is based on models for household and industrial wastewater production regimes and integrates the impact of weather conditions, i.e., dry, rain, and stormy weather, and temporal variations such as changes in wastewater production during workdays vs. weekends or population dynamics during holiday periods. Water temperature variations are also included in the influent file, affecting O_2 solubility and model parameters for biological activity in the ASM1 [18].

The oxygenation process is modelled in the BSM2 as variations in $k_L a$ values in nitrification tanks. The IWA has defined a default control scheme for the oxygenation system of the BSM2, consisting of a closed-loop configuration with a proportional integral controller (PI) that regulates the dissolved O_2 (DO) in the second nitrification tank by manipulating the values of $k_L a$ in all three nitrification tanks. In this study, the O_2 demand is calculated for the BSM2 operating with the default control strategy, for which the DO set-point is 2 gr·m^{-3}. A full description of the default control strategy can be found in [18]. Starting from the $k_L a$ time series resulting from BSM2 simulations, the OTR at a given time step is calculated for each nitrification tank i as follows:

$$OTR_i = \frac{1}{\alpha} \cdot k_L a_i \cdot (DO_{sat} - DO_i) \cdot V_{AS,i} \qquad (1)$$

where α is the alpha factor for the AS (here, taken as 0.6 based on values reported in literature for pure O_2 AS systems [20]), DO_i and DO_{sat} are the measured and saturation O_2 concentrations, respectively, and $V_{AS,i}$ is the volume of the nitrification tank. In the BSMs, DO_{sat} at 15 °C is defined as 8 gr·m^{-3}; its dependency on temperature is described by the van't Hoff equation [21]. Since this study assumes the use of a 100% O_2 gas stream rather than air, the BSM2 has been modified in a way that DO_{sat} at 15 °C is equal to around 38.1 gr·m^{-3}, which corresponds to the original 8 gr·m^{-3} divided by 21% O_2 content in air. Temperature dependence is assumed to be described in the same way as in the original BSM2.

The corresponding nominal molar flow into the liquid phase ($\dot{n}_{O_2,nom}^{AS}$) is then calculated as the sum of the OTR_i values for all three nitrification tanks:

$$\dot{n}_{O_2,nom}^{AS} = \frac{1}{M_{O_2}} \cdot \sum_{i=1}^{3} OTR_i \qquad (2)$$

where M_{O_2} is the molar mass of O_2. In conventional AS systems, a large share of the O_2 injected through diffusers is not transferred into the liquid phase but rather flows through into the atmosphere as bubbles. These losses can be represented by including a factor for the OTE of the diffuser system. The actual or effective O_2 flowrate that needs to be injected into the AS tanks ($\dot{n}_{O_2,eff}^{AS}$) can be expressed as:

$$\dot{n}_{O_2,eff}^{AS} = \frac{1}{OTE} \cdot \dot{n}_{O_2,nom}^{AS} \qquad (3)$$

The OTE is taken here as a constant with a value of 60% for a conventional AS system [13,22]. Temporal variations in the OTE due to the effects of fouling or temperature changes have not been considered in this study.

2.3. PEME Plant Model Implementation

The PEME plant model includes mathematical expressions for power consumption and mass balances of O_2, H_2, and deionized water. The PEME follows an operation cycle with a one-day period, alternating between full and minimal load. The number of hours at full load operation depends on the availability of electricity, which is location-dependent in the case of renewable sources. Two scenarios for the PEME plant operation and corresponding dimensions are analysed, where scenario 2 has a longer time in full load operation than scenario 1 (see Table 1). The values selected for the duration of full load operation are within the range of the scenarios reviewed in [23] and are meant to represent average and optimal electricity availability. An interlock is implemented in both scenarios to avoid breaching defined maximum (p_{max} of 15 bar) and minimum (p_{min} of 1.5 bar) overpressures in the intermediate O_2 tank. If the pressure in the intermediate tank approaches the defined limits (values above 14 bar or below 2.5 bar), the PEME switches to minimal or full load operation regardless of the predefined cycle.

Table 1. Time at full load operation of the PEME plant for the analysed scenarios.

Scenario	Nominal % of Day at Full Load	Nominal Full Load Hours $t_{FLH,nom}$ (h·a^{-1})
1	40	3504
2	75	6750

The PEME stack is assumed to operate in a low-pressure range, and the produced gases are extracted at atmospheric pressure. At full load, the input current density J is assumed to be 2.0 A·cm^{-2}, at a minimum of 0.4 A·cm^{-2}. The PEME cells have a total active area a_c of 1250 cm^2. The power of the PEME (P_{PEME}) can then be calculated as:

$$P_{PEME} = J \cdot a_c \cdot \varphi_{EZ} \qquad (4)$$

where φ_{EZ} is the voltage of the electrolyser cells, which in turn depends on the input current density. Values for φ_{EZ} of 1.9 V at full load and 1.6 V at minimum load have been selected based on the compilation of PEME polarization curves presented in [24].

Since the starting times of PEMEs are usually below 15 min [16,25], changes in stack temperature and their effect on polarization curves during the start-up are neglected in the simulations. The gas and water flowrates have been calculated following the approach proposed in [15]. The molar flowrates of O_2, H_2, and deionized water in the electrolysis process are modelled using Faraday's law:

$$\dot{n}^{EZ}_{O_2,nom} = \frac{n_c \cdot J \cdot a_c}{4 \cdot F} \cdot \eta_f \qquad (5)$$

$$\dot{n}^{EZ}_{H_2,nom} = \frac{n_c \cdot J \cdot a_c}{2 \cdot F} \cdot \eta_f \qquad (6)$$

$$\dot{n}^{EZ}_{H_2O} = 1.25 \cdot \frac{n_c \cdot J \cdot a_c}{2 \cdot F} \cdot \eta_f \qquad (7)$$

where $\dot{n}^{EZ}_{O_2,nom}$, $\dot{n}^{EZ}_{H_2,nom}$, and $\dot{n}^{EZ}_{H_2O}$ are nominal produced O_2, nominal produced H_2, and consumed deionized water, respectively. Furthermore, n_c is the number of electrolytic cells connected in the series, F is Faradays constant, and η_f is the faradaic efficiency (above 99% for water electrolysis). The effective H_2 and O_2 molar flowrates supplied by the PEME are then calculated by introducing the efficiency factor η_p, taken here as a constant equal to 75%, to account for losses during drying and purification steps after the cells:

$$\dot{n}^{EZ}_{O_2,eff} = \dot{n}^{EZ}_{O_2,nom} \cdot \eta_p \qquad (8)$$

$$\dot{n}^{EZ}_{H_2,eff} = \dot{n}^{EZ}_{H_2,nom} \cdot \eta_p \qquad (9)$$

The intermediate storage tank and the compressor are modelled following the approach described in [26]. The change in pressure in the intermediate storage tank, assuming ideal gas behaviour, can be expressed as:

$$\frac{dp_{sto}}{dt} = \frac{T_{sto} \cdot R}{V_{sto}} \cdot \left(\dot{n}^{EZ}_{O_2,eff} - \dot{n}^{AS}_{O_2,eff} \right) \qquad (10)$$

where p_{sto}, T_{sto}, and V_{sto} are the pressure, temperature, and volume of the tank. T_{sto} is ideally controlled at 25 °C. The flow of O_2 gas from the intermediate storage tank in the PEME plant to the AS system is assumed to show ideal behaviour, and no further components (e.g., operation of valves) have been considered. The power consumption of the compressor P_{comp}, assumed here to be a centrifugal compressor, can be expressed as Equation (11):

$$P_{comp} = \frac{\dot{n}_{O_2,eff}^{EZ}}{\eta_{comp}} \cdot \frac{\kappa \cdot R \cdot T_{PEME}}{\kappa - 1} \cdot \frac{p_{sto}}{p_{PEME}}^{\frac{\kappa-1}{\kappa}} \quad (11)$$

where η_{comp} is the compressor efficiency (63%), κ is the polytropic exponent (1.62), T_{PEME} is the temperature of the PEME (ideally controlled at 80 °C), and p_{PEME} is the pressure of the PEME, taken here as atmospheric pressure.

The behaviour of the contingency O_2 storage tank is not modelled. The required flowrate of external O_2 ($\dot{n}_{O_2,ext}$) is equal to the demand of the AS system during the periods where the pressure in the intermediate tank is below the defined limit p_{min}:

$$\dot{n}_{O_2,ext} = \begin{cases} p_{sto} > p_{min}, & 0 \\ p_{sto} \leq p_{min}, & \dot{n}_{O_2,eff}^{AS} \end{cases} \quad (12)$$

The required contingency storage volume (V_{cont}) is then calculated based on the integral of $\dot{n}_{O_2,ext}$ over the simulation period. In a similar way, the behaviour of the AC/DC converter (transients and efficiency) is not modelled, and its capacity is assumed to be equal to the full load power of the PEME stack.

2.4. Techno-Economic Assessment

The TEA performed in this study considers the installation and operation of the PEME plant at the site of the conceptual BSM2 WWTP. The goal of the TEA is to gain insights on the development of the economics for the use of electrolysis O_2 in AS systems. For this, estimates of the net cost of production (from here on, C_{NCP}) of electrolysis O_2 are retrieved for PEME plants dimensioned according to the scenarios described in Table 1 and operating under different economic conditions. The obtained C_{NCP} values are then compared with those corresponding to O_2 produced in conventional industrial processes (e.g., in cryogenic air separation units). The presented TEA focuses on the implementation of the PEME plant, which means that the costs related to modifications in the design and operation of the WWTP (e.g., modifications to gas injection systems in AS tanks) are outside the scope of this investigation.

2.4.1. Cost Estimation Framework

The cost estimation framework for chemical industries described in [27] has been used as a reference for the calculation of C_{NCP} in the present study. C_{NCP} are derived based on the apparent capital (C_{CAPEX}) and operational expenditures (C_{OPEX}) attributed to the system components and operation. Capital expenditures are calculated using the factorial method. As a first step, the investment costs of the main pieces of equipment or purchased equipment costs (C_{PEC}) are estimated. The C_{PEC} include the costs of all components of the PEME plant model. The costs for the PEME stack, AC/DC converter, and compressor (C_i) are calculated using the capacity method as described in Equation (13) [27]:

$$C_i = C_{i,base} \cdot \left(\frac{S_i}{S_{i,base}}\right)^{\delta_i} \cdot \left(\frac{CEPCI}{CEPCI_{base}}\right) \quad (13)$$

where $C_{i,base}$ is the reference cost for an equipment unit i with a size or capacity $S_{i,base}$, S_i is the actual size or capacity of the equipment to be purchased, and δ_i is a reference empirical scaling exponent. The second term in Equation (13) accounts for historical changes in component costs. The Chemical Engineering Plant Cost Index (CEPCI) [28] is used here for historical cost scaling. The $CEPCI_{base}$ is the value of the index for the year of publication of $C_{i,base}$ and $CEPCI$ is the value for the year of estimation. The reference values used for $C_{i,base}$, $S_{i,base}$, and δ_i can be found in Table 2, together with the year of publication of $C_{i,base}$. The corresponding values for $CEPCI_{base}$ and $CEPCI$ can be consulted under [29].

Table 2. Data used for the cost estimation for PEME stacks, the AC/DC converters, and compressors following the capacity method.

Equipment Item	$C_{i,base}$ (€)	$S_{i,base}$ (kW)	δ_i (-)	Reference	Year of Publication
PEME stack	1000 [a]	1	1	[3,30]	2020
AC/DC converter	160	1	1	[31,32]	2012
Compressor	267,000	445	0.67	[32,33]	2012

[a] Varies according to the value of PEME stack costs C_{PEME} in cost inventory (see Section 2.4.2).

The costs for the intermediate and contingency O_2 storage tanks for the AS ($C_{T,i}$) are calculated using a component-specific capacity method expression as:

$$C_{T,i} = n_{T,i} \cdot \left(a_{T,i} + b_{T,i} \cdot S_{T,i}^{\delta_{T,i}}\right) \cdot \left(\frac{CEPCI}{CEPCI_{base}}\right) \quad (14)$$

where $n_{T,i}$ is the number of tanks required to cover the designed volume. The corresponding values for the factors $a_{T,i}$, $b_{T,i}$, $\delta_{T,i}$, and the tank capacity $S_{T,i}$ can be found in Table 3.

Table 3. Data used for the cost estimation of the O_2 tanks following the capacity method.

Equipment Item	$a_{T,i}$ ($)	$b_{T,i}$ ($·kg^{-1})	$S_{T,i}$ (kg)	$\delta_{T,i}$ (-)	Reference	Year of Publication
Intermediate O_2 tank	12,800	73	7800	0.85	[27,34]	2010
Contingency O_2 tank	17,400	79	900	0.85	[27,34]	2010

The total purchased equipment costs (C_{PEC}) are determined as follows:

$$C_{PEC} = \sum C_i + \sum C_{T,i} \quad (15)$$

The obtained C_{PEC} are used to estimate the remaining cost items of C_{CAPEX}. All involved C_{CAPEX} cost items are estimated using the factorial approach based on the so-called Lang factors ($f_{CAPEX,i}$), which can be represented as an example of the case of ISBL costs (C_{ISBL}) as follows:

$$C_{ISBL} = \underbrace{C_{PEC}}_{\text{Cost basis} \atop (C_{CAPEX,i})} \sum_{i=1}^{n} f_{CAPEX,i} \quad (16)$$

Table 4 summarizes the employed Lang factors $f_{CAPEX,i}$ for all superordinate cost items (C_{ISBL}, C_{OSBL}, C_{CC}, C_{DE}, C_{WC} and C_{SE}) that have been used in this study. Depending on the respective superordinate cost item, the different cost basis $C_{CAPEX,i}$ may be employed. Taking into account that the PEME plant is supposed to be installed at the site of an existing WWTP, cost items related to civil engineering and yard improvement required when a project is to be developed at a completely new site (so-called green field site) are not considered here.

Table 4. Capital expenditure C_{CAPEX} estimation methodology via the factorial method and chosen cost items and Lang factors based on literature data taken from [27,34,35].

Superordinate Cost Item $\sum_i C_{CAPEX,i} \cdot f_{CAPEX,i}$	CAPEX Cost Item Description $C_{CAPEX,i} \cdot f_{CAPEX,i}$	Cost Basis (€) $C_{CAPEX,i}$	Index i	Lang Factor $f_{CAPEX,i}$
Inside battery limits (C_{ISBL})	Equipment purchase	C_{PEC}	1	1
	Equipment installation		2	0.3
	Piping (installed) (valves, fittings, pipes, supports, and labour)		3	0.3
	Instrumentation and controls (installation labour, auxiliary equipment)		4	0.3
	Electrical systems (installed) (wiring, lighting, transformation, and services)		5	0.1
Outside battery limits (C_{OSBL})	Additions to site infrastructure Water, air and electricity supply nodes Piping, storage, and distribution	C_{ISBL}	6	0.1
Contingency charges (C_{CC})	Compensation of cost estimates Price/currency fluctuations Contractor/labour disputes	$C_{ISBL} + C_{OSBL}$	7	0.2
Design and engineering (C_{DE})	Engineering and supervision	$C_{ISBL} + C_{OSBL}$	8	0.3
	Construction expenses		9	0.3
	Contractor fee		10	0.1
Working capital (C_{WC})	Feed/product/spare parts inventory Cash on hand	$C_{ISBL} + C_{OSBL}$	11	0.1
Start–up expenses (C_{SE})	General start-up expenses	$C_{ISBL} + C_{OSBL}$	12	0.05

After calculating all relevant cost items, the total capital expenditures C_{CAPEX} can be determined based on the so-called fixed capital investments C_{FCI}, which represent the entirety of investment costs attributed to the planning/designing, construction, and erection of the plant, and the working capital C_{WC} and start-up expenses C_{SE}, which account for the capital used to maintain the plant's operation over its lifetime.

$$C_{CAPEX} = \underbrace{C_{ISBL} + C_{OSBL} + C_{CC} + C_{DE}}_{=C_{FCI}} + C_{WC} + C_{SE} \qquad (17)$$

The operational costs C_{OPEX} can be subdivided into variable costs of production C_{VCP}, fixed costs of production C_{FCP}, and by-product revenues R_{H_2} from the sale of H_2:

$$C_{OPEX} = C_{VCP} + C_{FCP} - R_{H_2} \qquad (18)$$

C_{VCP} are operational costs directly related to the plant's output and therefore change with the operation mode, e.g., full or minimal load. For the estimation of C_{VCP}, the expression in Equation (19) is used:

$$C_{VCP} = C_{H_2O} + C_{O_2,ext} + C_E + C_{R,PEME} \qquad (19)$$

where C_{H_2O} are the costs of the consumed deionized water, $C_{O_2,ext}$ are the costs of consumed liquid O_2 from the contingency tank, C_E are the costs of electricity, and $C_{R,PEME}$ are the costs for the replacement of PEME stacks until the plants end of lifetime (EOL). The yearly consumption of deionized water, liquid O_2, and electricity is obtained from the simulation results and is assumed to be constant until plants reach EOL. The respective specific costs of deionized water c_{H_2O}, external liquid O_2 $c_{O_2,ext}$, and electricity c_E are described in detail in Section 2.4.2.

The cost of PEME stack replacement $C_{R,PEME}$ is calculated based on the stack lifetime, plant lifetime, and cumulative full load operating hours. It is assumed that stack costs for each replacement are comprised of 50% of the initial specific PEME stack capital costs, as only the cells are replaced and the periphery and housing remain intact and are still usable.

Contrary to C_{VCP}, fixed costs of production C_{FCP} are independent of the actual operation or output of the plant. For the calculation of C_{FCP}, a factorial estimation methodology has also been applied (see Table 5 and Equation (20)).

$$C_{FCP} = \underbrace{c_{OL} \cdot y_{PL}}_{=C_{OL}} + \underbrace{(C_{WC} + C_{SE}) \cdot i_d \cdot y_{PL}}_{\substack{\text{Capital charges} \\ \text{on WC/SE loan}}} + \sum_{i=1}^{6} C_{OPEX,i} \cdot f_{OPEX,i} \quad (20)$$

Table 5. Fixed costs of production C_{FCP} estimation methodology based on the factorial method and retrieved Lang factors from the literature according to [27].

Superordinate OPEX/FCP Cost Item $C_{OPEX,i} \cdot f_{OPEX,i}$	Cost Basis (€) $C_{OPEX,i}$	Index i	Lang Factor $f_{OPEX,i}$
Supervision (C_{SV})	C_{OL}	1	0.25
Direct salary overhead (C_{DSO}) (Non-salary costs: Health insurance and benefits)	$C_{OL} + C_{SV}$	2	0.4
Maintenance (C_{MT})	C_{ISBL}	3	0.03
Property taxes and insurance (C_{PTI})	C_{ISBL}	4	0.01
Rent of land (C_{ROL})	$C_{ISBL} + C_{OSBL}$	5	0.01
Environmental charges (C_{EV})	$C_{ISBL} + C_{OSBL}$	6	0.01

The total operating labour costs C_{OL} represent the costs for the personnel in charge of the plant and are calculated based on the specific operating labour costs c_{OL}, taken here as 60,000 €·a^{-1}, and the plant's lifetime y_{PL}. Capital charges included within C_{FCP} are attributed to the interest payments on the loan of working capital and start-up expenses, which are supposed to be entirely funded by debt. These capital charges are included within C_{FCP}, since the total working capital and total start-up expenses are recovered at the EOL of the plant, and hence the incurring interest payments must not be included in the estimation of C_{CAPEX} via Equations (15) and (16) and Table 4 [27]. In Equation (20), i_d is the interest rate of the capital charges on working capital and total start-up expenses loan, taken here as 0.05. As in the case of the cost items of C_{CAPEX}, the remaining items of C_{FCP} are estimated based on the superordinate OPEX cost items $C_{OPEX,i}$ and their respective Lang factors $f_{OPEX,i}$, as indicated in Table 5.

By-product revenues (R_{H_2}) considered in this study correspond to the income generated by the sale of the produced H$_2$ during the PEME plant lifetime. In the same way as with the costs for deionized water, liquid O$_2$, and electricity, R_{H_2} is calculated based on the simulation results for yearly H$_2$ production ($\sum \dot{m}_{H_2,eff}^{EZ}$) and the specific selling or market price c_{H_2} (also see Section 2.4.2). The yearly amount of produced H$_2$ is also assumed to remain constant until the plants reach EOL.

In order to calculate the C_{NCP} of electrolysis O$_2$, the annuity method based on the total spent fixed capital investment costs C_{FCI} is applied. The total C_{FCI} is annualized by determining the annual capital charge (C_{ACC}) required to fully reimburse the initial capital investment until the plants reach EOL. As a result, the fixed capital investments after interest ($C_{FCI,ai}$), also known as depreciation costs, are determined:

$$C_{FCI,ai} = y_{PL} \cdot C_{FCI} \cdot \underbrace{\frac{i_c(i_c+1)^{y_{PL}}}{(i_c+1)^{y_{PL}} - 1}}_{\substack{\text{Annual capital} \\ \text{charge } (C_{ACC})}} \quad (21)$$

The FCI are financed by debt and equity represented by a compound interest rate i_c (also weighted average cost of capital; see Equation (22)) with respective interest rates for debt i_d and equity i_e, as well as a specific debt ratio r_d for both capital sources. In the present studies, i_e is taken as 0.1 and r_d as 0.5, resulting in an i_c value of 0.075.

$$i_c = r_d \cdot i_d + (1 - r_d) \cdot i_e \tag{22}$$

Based on the retrieved values of $C_{FCI,ai}$ and C_{OPEX}, as well as potential revenues (R_S) from plant salvage (PEME stacks) at plant EOL and the cumulative annual O_2 production ($\sum \dot{m}_{O_2,eff}^{EZ}$), the net costs of O_2 production (C_{NCP}) are determined (Equation (23)).

$$C_{NCP} = \frac{C_{FCI,ai} + C_{OPEX} - R_S}{y_{PL} \cdot \sum \dot{m}_{O_2,eff}^{EZ}} \tag{23}$$

The chosen annuity approach assumes that investments and cash flows start immediately and, due to the integral nature of this approach, no specific timing of investments and revenues has been considered. Moreover, taxes and depreciation charges have been neglected in the annuity approach and hence the determination of C_{NCP}. Revenues from PEME stack salvage are only considered if the remaining lifetime of the installed PEME stack at EOL is larger than 8000 h. The salvage value is derived from the initial stack investment costs, the ratio of the remaining and initial stack lifetime (y_{PEME}), as well as an additional salvage factor of 0.5.

In addition to the annuity method, the potential specific minimum selling price of O_2 through the PEME plant (c_{MSP,O_2}) is calculated via a cash flow analysis, i.e., determination of the net present value (NPV) at the plant EOL. With the annual gross profit (P_n), the depreciation tax allowances (D_n), and the corporate tax rate (t_{cp}), the annual cash flow (CF_n) in each year n can be assessed (Equations (24) and (25)). Subsequently, the NPV is calculated based on Equation (26). To comply with the initial assumption of an NPV of zero at the plant's EOL, c_{MSP,O_2} is varied via a simple search algorithm until the condition formulated in Equation (26) is reached.

$$P_n = c_{MSP,O_2} \cdot \sum \dot{m}_{O_2,eff}^{EZ} + c_{H_2} \cdot \sum \dot{m}_{H_2,eff}^{EZ} + \frac{R_S - C_{VCP} - C_{FCP}}{y_{PL}} \tag{24}$$

$$CF_n = P_n \cdot (1 - t_{cp}) + D_n \cdot t_{cp} \tag{25}$$

$$NPV = \sum_{n=1}^{y_{PL}} \frac{CF_n}{(1 + i_c)^n} = 0 \tag{26}$$

A straight-line depreciation over 10 years and a corporate tax rate (t_{cp}) of 0.3 are assumed. All capital expenses are spent in year zero. The TEA studies are carried out within the software framework of MATLAB R2017b.

2.4.2. Cost Inventory and Market Analysis

To provide economic data for the calculations described in Section 2.4.1 and allow for the realization of the TEA under various conditions, a cost inventory for the items with significant impact on the economic performance of the PEME plant has been defined. The items selected for the cost inventory include the following:
- Electricity price (LCOE) depending on the source of origin.
- Selling price of produced H_2 depending on market conditions.
- Price of O_2 from conventional sources.
- The investment and replacement costs attributed to the PEME.

The presented TEA is performed for the reference year 2020 based on current data and also for 2030 based on forecasts presented in literature to reflect the development of the process's economics. Three different sets of economic parameters have been defined for each of the selected years in order to represent optimistic, neutral, and pessimistic economic conditions for the project's implementation. Four different electricity sources have been considered in the present study, namely conventional, PV, and wind (off-shore and on-shore) energy plants. The costs defined for the different items in the cost inventory, as well as the PEME stack lifetime y_{PEME}, are presented in Table 6. For 2020, the plant's lifetime y_{PL} is assumed to be 20 years, while for 2030, it is assumed to be 30 years.

Table 6. Cost inventory for the estimation of net costs of production (NCP) for electrolysis O_2 based on reference values taken from literature [36–42].

		2020			2030		
		Optimistic	Neutral	Pessimistic	Optimistic	Neutral	Pessimistic
LCOE c_E (€·MWh^{-1})	Conventional	31	43	55	47	71	94
	PV	31	57	140	21	51	81
	Wind on shore	39	61	83	25	53	81
	Wind off shore	72	105	138	56	78	101
H_2 price c_{H_2} (€·kg^{-1})		6	5	4	4	3	2
PEME stack lifetime y_{PEME} (h)		67,500	59,000	50,500	85,000	75,500	66,125
PEME stack cost c_{PEME} (€·kW^{-1})		867	1000	1225	453	600	780
O_2 price $c_{O_2,ext}$ (€·t^{-1})		100	100	100	134 [a]	122 [b]	110 [c]

[a] annual price increase of 3%, [b] annual price increase of 2%, [c] annual price increase of 1%.

The projections of the cost inventory reflect the trends reported in the literature [36–42]. While electricity prices for all renewable sources are expected to decrease, the price for conventional sources is expected to increase due to higher costs for CO_2 emission certificates. Improvements in electrolyser performance and the corresponding decrease in investments are expected to result in decreasing H_2 selling prices in 2030. It is important to point out that, although a stronger reduction in H_2 production costs would be a positive trend regarding the transition to a sustainable energy system, this would increase the calculated NCP for O_2, and therefore the pessimistic scenario considers lower H_2 selling prices. Conventional O_2 prices are assumed to increase at a different rate for each economic condition. The cost of deionized water c_{H_2O} is also assumed to increase with time, taking a value of 2 €·m^{-3} and 3 €·m^{-3} in 2020 and 2030, respectively.

3. Results and Discussion

3.1. O_2 Demand of the BSM2 WWTP

The behaviour of the O_2 demand of the AS system in the BSM2 can be seen in Figure 2 after converting $\dot{n}_{O_2,eff}^{AS}$ to kg·d^{-1} ($\dot{m}_{O_2,eff}^{AS}$). The average daily O_2 demand for the BSM2 was calculated at 10,388 kg·d^{-1}. The use of larger DO_{sat} values to account for the use of pure O_2 (see Section 2.2.) results in higher transfer rates OTR for a given k_La and measured DO concentration when compared with air (see Equation (1)). The k_La values calculated by the PI controller are therefore lower in this study than in the original BSM2, i.e., less gas volume and therefore less energy for gas injection is required when using pure O_2. When k_La values are too low, the additional mixing energy for maintaining the sludge in suspension in the nitrification tanks is to be calculated as part of the operational costs in the BSM2 [18]. However, since the TEA scope includes only the PEME plant, these effects of pure O_2 use on the operational costs of WWTP are not further assessed.

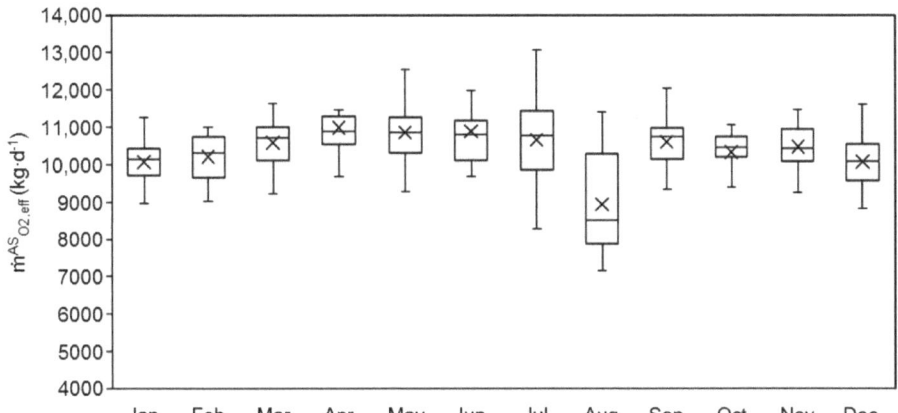

Figure 2. Daily O_2 demand from the AS system of the BSM2 plant. Average values are represented by an ×, median values by a line, the limits of the boxes are the first and third quartile, and outliers are excluded.

The effect of seasonal changes can be seen in higher O_2 demand during warmer months, which can be explained by the decrease in DO_{sat} at higher temperatures and the corresponding decrease in the amount of O_2 that can be maintained in the water phase. A further seasonal effect that can be seen in Figure 2 is the decrease in O_2 demand caused by less household wastewater production during the summer holiday season [19]. Intraday variations in O_2 demand follow the profile of wastewater inflow into the WWTP, i.e., are higher during daytime with peaks around midday and in the evening (see Figure 3).

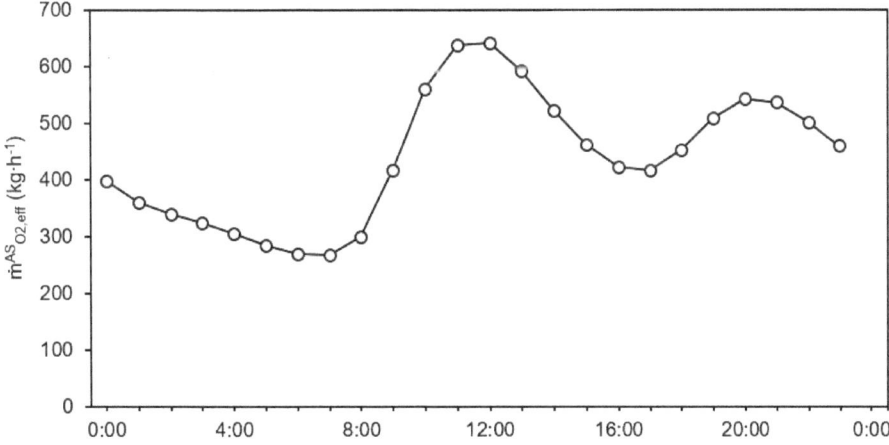

Figure 3. Intraday O_2 demand from the AS system of the BSM2 plant.

The cumulative histogram for $\dot{m}^{AS}_{O_2,eff}$ can be seen in Figure 4, showing that during 80% of the simulation time, the O_2 demand is between approx. 9200 and 11,300 kg·d^{-1}.

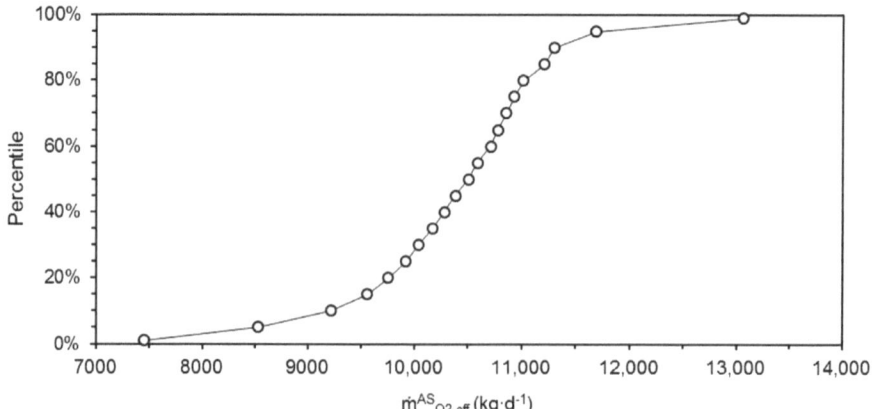

Figure 4. Histogram of daily O_2 demand from the AS system of the BSM2 plant.

3.2. Dimensioning of PEME Plant

The selected capacities of the PEME plant components for each scenario and the corresponding simulation results are shown in Table 7. The operation cycles defined in Section 2.3 are subject to changes due to the activation of the interlock, resulting in an effective amount of hours at full load $t_{FLH,eff}$ that differs from the $t_{FLH,nom}$ presented in Table 1. When analysing gas production, it can be seen that the difference in PEME capacity between both scenarios is compensated by the difference in $t_{FLH,real}$, resulting in a very similar production of H_2 and O_2. In both scenarios, there are periods where, despite the activation of the interlock, the O_2 flowrate produced by the PEME at full load capacity is under the O_2 demand, resulting in p_{sto} values below p_{min} and the need to supply O_2 from the contingency tank. The higher PEME capacity and storage tank volume in scenario 1 results in a significantly shorter period with p_{sto} below p_{min} when compared with scenario 2, leading to a larger volume of the contingency tank in scenario 2. These critical periods are, however, relatively short; in both scenarios, the PEME plant is capable of supplying enough O_2 to the BSM2 WWTP during more than 99% of the simulated time without recurring to the contingency tank. For neither of the scenarios is there a period where p_{sto} is above p_{max}.

Table 7. Result of the dimensioning of the PEME plant for both scenarios.

Parameter	Scenario 1	Scenario 2
n_c (-)	1350	1000
P_{PEME} (kW)	6400	4750
P_{comp} (kW)	37	27
V_{sto} (m^3)	250	200
V_{cont} (m^3)	5	28
Effective % of time at full load	47	72
$t_{FLH,eff}$ (h·a^{-1})	4073	6259
$\Sigma \dot{m}_{O_2,eff}$ (t·a^{-1})	3782	3780
$\Sigma \dot{m}_{H_2,eff}$ (t·a^{-1})	476	476
Time with $p_{sto} < p_{min}$ (d·a^{-1})	0.4	2.5
Time with $p_{sto} > p_{max}$ (d·a^{-1})	0	0

3.3. Economic Assessment

The cost breakdown of all relevant cost categories of purchased equipment costs C_{PEC}, total capital expenses C_{CAPEX}, operational costs C_{OPEX}, as well as the net O_2 production costs C_{NCP} are presented in Figure 5 for an exemplary case (scenario 1 in 2020, under neutral economic conditions and supplied with PV electricity). The breakdowns shown in Figure 5a to 5e are representative for all other assessed cases, i.e., the proportion of cost items is similar. In all cases, C_{PEC} is dominated by the initial PEME investment cost (between 53.2% and 73.4% of C_{PEC} for scenario 1 and between 50.7% and 71.5% for scenario 2), followed by the investments for O_2 tanks, the converter, and the compressor. The share of C_{PEC} made up by PEME investment costs is between 13.2% and 7.5% lower in 2030 than in 2020 due to the assumed decrease in the PEME stack price. C_{FCI}, which make up 92.7% of C_{CAPEX}, are dominated by investments inside battery limits C_{ISBL} (47.8%) and the costs of design and engineering C_{DE} (36.8%).

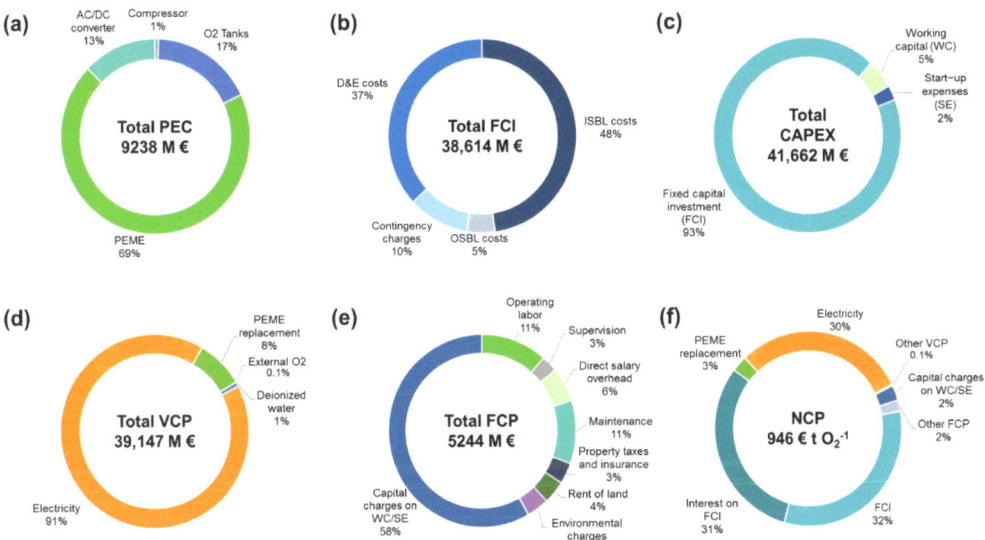

Figure 5. Breakdown of (**a**) purchased equipment costs C_{PEC}; (**b**) fixed costs of investment C_{FCI}; (**c**) capital expenditures C_{CAPEX}; (**d**) variable costs of production C_{VCP}; (**e**) fixed costs of production C_{FCP} and; (**f**) net costs of production C_{NCP} for scenario 1 in 2020, neutral economic conditions, and PV electricity supply.

The costs of electricity consistently make up more than 85% of C_{VCP}. The cost share of PEME stack replacement in C_{VCP} is always below 10%, while the sum of the shares of deionized water and external O_2 for the contingency tank is always below 3%. Capital charges on working capital and total start-up expenses make up the majority of the fixed costs of production C_{FCP} (between 50 and 59.8%).

An overview of all calculated C_{NCP} after revenues are presented in Table 8. Lower investment costs for the PEME stacks result in overall lower C_{NCP} for scenario 2. In 2020, all calculated C_{NCP} are higher than the price of O_2 from conventional sources (100 €·t^{-1}).

In 2030 and under positive economic conditions, competitive production costs below or near the conventional O_2 price (134 €·t^{-1}) are achieved for the PEME plant designed according to scenario 2 and supplied by PV (128 €·t^{-1}) and wind on-shore electricity (161 €·t^{-1}). Such relatively low C_{NCP} are the result of optimistic trends regarding costs of PEME stacks and renewable electricity supply.

Table 8. Calculated net costs of production C_{NCP} in €·t^{-1}.

Year	Scenario	Electricity Source	Optimistic	Neutral	Pessimistic
2020	Scenario 1	Conventional	500	830	1232
		PV	500	945	1935
		Wind on shore	566	978	1464
		Wind off shore	839	1342	1919
	Scenario 2	Conventional	286	609	977
		PV	286	727	1693
		Wind on shore	353	761	1212
		Wind off shore	631	1131	1676
2030	Scenario 1	Conventional	452	874	1311
		PV	237	709	1203
		Wind on shore	270	725	1203
		Wind off shore	526	932	1369
	Scenario 2	Conventional	347	751	1165
		PV	128	582	1055
		Wind on shore	161	599	1055
		Wind off shore	423	810	1224

As can be seen in Figure 5f, C_{NCP} are dominated by fixed costs of investments, the interest on these investments, and electricity costs. However, the share of electricity costs in C_{NCP} varies greatly among the analysed cases (between 20.2 and 51.5% in scenario 1 and between 25 and 57.6% in scenario 2). In 2020, the difference between optimistic and pessimistic PV electricity costs is largest among all energy sources considered (see Table 6). For this reason, both the highest and lowest C_{NCP} values in 2020 correspond to the PV electricity supply. In 2030, the costs of PV and wind on-shore electricity are very similar, with PV resulting in slightly lower C_{NCP}, while more expensive conventional and wind off-shore electricity supply results in higher production costs. The sum of all cost items aside from electricity, C_{FCI}, and interests on C_{FCI} consistently make up less than 10% of C_{NCP}.

It is important to consider that items in the cost inventory were all assigned either optimistic, neutral, or pessimistic values in each case (see Table 6); thus, the results presented in Table 8 do not include combinations of economic conditions. For example, if optimistic values are selected for the cost of PV electricity and the selling price of H$_2$ in 2030 while pessimistic values are kept for all other items in the cost inventory, the resulting C_{NCP} for scenario 2 would be 296 €·t^{-1} rather than 1055 €·t^{-1}.

The maximum and minimum calculated potential O$_2$ selling prices c_{MSP,O_2} are shown in Table 9. Values for c_{MSP,O_2} are always higher than C_{NCP} since plant depreciation and tax on income are included in their calculation (see Equation (24)). The obtained selling prices are therefore not competitive with conventional O$_2$ sources with prices of 100 €·t^{-1} (2020) and 134 €·t^{-1} (2030) in any of the studied cases.

Table 9. Range of calculated minimum selling prices c_{MSP,O_2} in €·t^{-1}.

	Scenario 1		Scenario 2	
	2020	2030	2020	2030
c_{MSP,O_2} max.	2184	1525	1882	1343
c_{MSP,O_2} min.	695	350	436	215

3.4. Further Research

The present study offers a methodology for the analysis of the economics of O$_2$ valorisation in biological treatment steps of WWTPs based on a recognized benchmark such as the BSM2 and simple models for the components of a PEME plant. Regarding possible subjects for further investigations, in this study both the efficiency factor used to represent O_2 losses in gas separation steps η_p and the OTE of the oxygenation system installed at the WWTP are taken as constant. New developments in gas separation units and oxygenation systems are expected to lead to higher efficiencies [43,44], which in turn would help to reduce C_{NCP}. Furthermore, many of the AS systems using pure O_2 are designed with a closed headspace to enable the collection and reuse of injected O_2 [12], which would result in lower electrolyser capacities being required. Future TEAs could address a closed AS system, however additional effects of closed headspace design such as the inhibition of nitrification processes due to CO_2 accumulation and pH decrease should also be considered [12,45,46]. The costs for the adaption of the WWTP infrastructure to the use of pure O_2 should also be analysed.

Further effects of pure O_2 in biological and chemical processes in AS systems are outside the scope of this study. These include benefits such as reduction in sludge production, reduction in fouling foaming and improvements in treatment efficiency [12,13]. Such effects of the use of pure O_2 from electrolysers in AS systems should therefore also be investigated experimentally. Possible synergies between electrolyser plants and other processes in WWTPs can be considered in future simulation studies. These may include the use of heat recovered from the electrolysers cells or the methanation of biogas produced in sludge treatment with the H_2 from the electrolyser [10].

The dimensioning of the PEME plant was done to cover the whole O_2 demand from the BSM2 WWTP with a capacity of 80,000 PE. In Germany this correspond to the second largest category for WWTP capacity defined by the national environment agency. More than 60% of wastewater in Germany is treated at WWTPs with installed capacities above 10,000 PE, although these larger plants make less than 10% of the total number of WWTPs [47]. The proposed methodology can be applied to analyse the economics of similar projects to fully supply smaller WWTPs or partially cover the O_2 demand in larger ones (e.g., pre-treatment step with pure O_2 before conventional AS system supplied with air). A rough estimation of the required PEME capacity for a smaller WWTP of 10,000 PE treating wastewater with a typical O_2 demand of 1200 kg $O_2 \cdot d^{-1}$ [48] can be done by a lineal extrapolation of the PEME capacities presented in Section 3.2. This results in a required capacity of around 740 kW for scenario 1 and 550 kW for scenario 2. The use of pure O_2 is recommended for the treatment of highly-strength wastewater [12], thus future analyses should be done by using models of industrial WWTPs. The same is true for membrane bioreactors (MBR), for which the use of pure O_2 has been shown to increase treatment efficiency and reduce membrane fouling [49].

Regarding the analysed economic conditions, further investigations could integrate changes in electricity prices during the simulated period. In future renewable-based electricity networks, the operation of electrolysers can be adjusted through demand side management according to prices and availability of energy [16]. Within a flexible electricity pricing scheme, plants operators could benefit from reduced electricity costs by adjusting the operation scheme of the PEME accordingly while at the same time providing network regulation services. Moreover, analyses in this study do not consider variations in the cost inventory during the plants lifetime; the prices and performance of the PEME plant are assumed constant until EOL for simplification. More detailed consideration of the H_2 valorisation processes should also be included in future studies (e.g., variations in sold amount and price or the implementation of internal valorisation measures).

4. Conclusions

Power-to-gas technologies based on water electrolysis are expected to play a central role in future renewable energy networks, where green H_2 and derived synthetic fuels are used as alternatives to fossil fuels. In the electrolysis process, large amounts of O_2 are produced alongside H_2, however O_2 is usually seen as a by-product and discarded into the atmosphere. In the present study the economics of the valorisation of electrolysis O_2 in biological treatment steps of municipal WWTPs has been analysed based on the results of mathematical simulation models.

The operation WWTP of the BSM2 has been modelled alongside a PEME system and used to simulate O_2 supply for an operation period of one year. Two scenarios regarding full load hours per year and corresponding PEME plant dimensions have been considered. Simulation data on the amount of consumables required and the produced gas flowrates was used as an input for a TEA on the net costs of O_2 production NCP, assuming that the produced H_2 is sold to a nearby industry. The TEA was performed for the years 2020 and 2030 under sets of optimistic, neutral and pessimistic conditions regarding costs and revenue streams.

Simulation results show that for 80% of the simulation period the O_2 demand of the AS of the BSM2 plant is between approx. 9200 and 11,300 $kg \cdot d^{-1}$. The dimensions of the PEME stack and amount of full load hours were 6.4 MW and 4073 $h \cdot a^{-1}$ for scenario 1, whereas 4.8 MW and 6259 $h \cdot a^{-1}$ for scenario 2. The PEME plants in both scenarios were able to cover the O_2 demand for more than 99% of the simulated time without having to rely on contingency O_2 storage. The results of the TEA show that NCP are dominated by the investment and respective interests on the PEME stacks, as well as the electricity costs. The sum of other cost components makes less than 10% of the NCP. Although for the year 2020 NCP for O_2 produced by the PEME plant are higher than references for the costs of industrial O_2, in 2030 the combination of lower investment costs for PEME stacks and lower renewable electricity prices (PV and wind on shore) resulted in competitive electrolysis O_2 costs when assuming optimistic economic conditions.

Further studies can follow the approach described here to analyse the economics of electrolysis O_2 supply to conventional WWTPs of different size or different systems such as MBRs. The simple models for the PEME plant and the O_2 supply process described here should also be expanded to include the effects of using pure O_2 in AS system, more detailed considerations regarding H_2 valorisation, as well as changes in electricity prices and system performance during the plants lifetime. The use of electrolysers at WWTPs for demand side management by adjusting the operation according to the energy networks behaviour should also complement the presented results.

Author Contributions: Conceptualization, M.A.P.R., S.F.R., S.F. and U.H.; methodology, M.A.P.R. and S.F.; software, M.A.P.R. and S.F.; formal analysis, M.A.P.R. and S.F.; investigation, M.A.P.R. and S.F.; writing—original draft preparation, M.A.P.R. and S.F.; writing—review and editing, S.F.R. and U.H.; visualization, M.A.P.R. and S.F.; supervision, S.F.R. and U.H.; project administration, S.F.R. and U.H.; funding acquisition, S.F.R. and U.H. All authors have read and agreed to the published version of the manuscript.

Funding: This work is partly funded by the Initiative and Networking Fund of the Helmholtz Association in the frame of the Clean Water Technology Lab CLEWATEC—a Helmholtz Innovation Lab under the reference number HIL-A02. The authors are responsible for the content of this publication.

Data Availability Statement: The data presented in this study are openly available in RODARE–Rossendorf Data Repository at http://doi.org/10.14278/rodare.2274.

Acknowledgments: The authors would like to thank Michael Ogurek and Gloria Robleto for the support in the implementation of the models into the SIMBA software. Additionally, the authors would like to thank Anjan Goswami for the contributions made to the implementation of the models as part of his internship at HZDR.

Conflicts of Interest: The authors declare no conflict of interest. In addition, the funders had no role in the design of the study; in the collection, analyses, or interpretation of data; in the writing of the manuscript, or in the decision to publish the results.

Abbreviations and Acronyms

AC/DC	Alternating Current/Direct Current
ACC	Annual Capital Charge
AS	Activated Sludge
ASM1	Activated Sludge Model No. 1
BSM2	Benchmark Simulation Model No. 2
CC	Contingency Charges
CAPEX	Capital Expenditures
CEPCI	Chemical Engineering Plant Cost Index
DE	Design and Engineering
DSO	Direct Salary Overhead
EOL	End of Lifetime
EV	Environmental Charges
FCI	Fixed Capital Investment
FCP	Fixed Costs of Production
HZDR	Helmholtz-Zentrum Dresden-Rossendorf
ISBL	Inside Battery Limits
IWA	International Water Association
LCOE	Levelized Cost of Energy
MBR	Membrane Bioreactor
MT	Maintenance
NCP	Net Costs of Production
NPV	Net Present Value
OL	Operating Labour
OPEX	Operational Expenditures
OSBL	Outside Battery Limits
OTE	Oxygen Transfer Efficiency
OTR	Oxygen Transfer Rate
PE	Population Equivalent
PEC	Purchased Equipment Costs
PEM	Proton Exchange Membrane
PEME	Proton Exchange Membrane Electrolyser
PI	Proportional Integer Controller
PTI	Property Taxes and Insurance
PV	Photovoltaic
ROL	Rent of Land
SE	Start-Up Expenses
SV	Supervision
TEA	Techno-Economic Assessment
VCP	Variable Costs of Production
WC	Working Capital
WWTP	Wastewater Resource Recovery Facility

Symbols

a_c	Active cell area of the electrolyser
$a_{T,i}$	Scaling parameter of storage tank i
$b_{T,i}$	Scaling parameter of storage tank i
c_E	Specific electricity costs
c_{H_2}	Specific hydrogen selling price
c_{H_2O}	Specific feed water costs electrolyser
c_{MSP,O_2}	Minimum selling price of oxygen
$c_{O_2,ext}$	Specific costs of oxygen from external sourcing
c_{PEME}	Specific electrolyser cost
C_E	Total electricity costs

$C_{FCI,ai}$	Fixed capital investments after interest payments
C_{H_2O}	Total feed water costs electrolyser
C_i	Total costs of component i
$C_{i,base}$	Total costs (base year) of component i
$C_{O_2,ext}$	Total costs of oxygen from external sourcing
$C_{R,PEME}$	Total replacement costs electrolyser stacks
$C_{T,i}$	Total costs of storage tank i
$CEPCI$	CEPCI of the estimation year
$CEPCI_{base}$	CEPCI of the base year
CF_n	Annual cash flow
D_n	Annual depreciation tax allowances
DO	Dissolved oxygen
DO_{sat}	Saturation oxygen concentrations
$f_{CAPEX,i}$	Lang factor of CAPEX cost item i
$f_{OPEX,i}$	Lang factor of OPEX cost item i
F	Faraday constant
i_c	Compound interest rate
i_d	Interest rate debt
i_e	Interest rate equity
J	Average current density
$k_L a$	Volumetric oxygen transfer coefficient
M_{O_2}	Molar mass oxygen
$\dot{m}_{O_2,eff}^{AS}$	Effective mass flow into the liquid phase (activated sludge)
$\dot{m}_{H_2,eff}^{EZ}$	Effective mass production rate hydrogen (electrolyser)
n	Year (for NPV analysis)
n_c	Number of electrolyser cells
$n_{T,i}$	Number of subordinate single tanks of storage tank i
$\dot{n}_{O_2,ext}$	Required external molar oxygen intake (contingency tank)
$\dot{n}_{O_2,nom}^{AS}$	Nominal molar flow into the liquid phase (activated sludge)
$\dot{n}_{O_2,eff}^{AS}$	Effective molar flow into the liquid phase (activated sludge)
$\dot{n}_{H_2,nom}^{EZ}$	Nominal molar production rate hydrogen (electrolyser)
$\dot{n}_{H_2,eff}^{EZ}$	Effective molar production rate hydrogen (electrolyser)
$\dot{n}_{H_2O}^{EZ}$	Molar consumption of deionized water (electrolyser)
$\dot{n}_{O_2,nom}^{EZ}$	Nominal molar production rate oxygen (electrolyser)
$\dot{n}_{O_2,eff}^{EZ}$	Actual molar production rate oxygen (electrolyser)
OTE	Oxygen transfer efficiency
OTR	Oxygen transfer rate
p_{PEME}	Electrolyser pressure
p_{max}	Maximum pressure intermediate oxygen tank
p_{min}	Minimum pressure intermediate oxygen tank
p_{sto}	Pressure intermediate oxygen storage tank
P_{comp}	Compressor power
P_n	Annual gross profit
P_{PEME}	Electrolyser power
r_d	Debt ratio
R	Universal gas constant
R_{H_2}	By-product revenue H_2
R_S	Revenue of plant salvage
S_i	Actual scale of component i
$S_{i,base}$	Reference scale of component i in the base year
$S_{T,i}$	Scale of storage tank i
t_{cp}	Corporate tax rate
$t_{FLH,nom}$	Nominal full load hours
$t_{FLH,eff}$	Effective full load hours
T_{PEME}	Electrolyser temperature
T_{sto}	Temperature intermediate oxygen storage tank

$V_{AS,i}$	Volume of nitrification tank i
V_{cont}	Volume contingency oxygen storage tank
V_{sto}	Volume intermediate oxygen storage tank
y_{PEME}	PEM electrolyser stack lifetime
y_{PL}	Plant lifetime
α	Alpha factor
δ_i	Scaling exponent of component i
$\delta_{T,i}$	Scaling exponent of tank i
η_f	Faradaic efficiency
η_{comp}	Compressor efficiency
η_p	Efficiency factor electrolysis
κ	Polytropic exponent
φ_{EZ}	Cell voltage
$\sum \dot{m}_{H_2,eff}^{EZ}$	Cumulative annual H_2 production
$\sum \dot{m}_{O_2,eff}^{EZ}$	Cumulative annual O_2 production

References

1. Staffell, I.; Pfenninger, S. The increasing impact of weather on electricity supply and demand. *Energy* **2018**, *145*, 65–78. [CrossRef]
2. Kanellopoulos, K.; Blanco, H. The potential role of H2 production in a sustainable future power system—An analysis with METIS of a decarbonised system powered by renewables in 2050. *Eur. Comm. JRC Tech. Rep.* **2019**, *10*, 540707. [CrossRef]
3. Glenk, G.; Reichelstein, S. Economics of converting renewable power to hydrogen. *Nat. Energy* **2019**, *4*, 216–222. [CrossRef]
4. BMU Nationale Wasserstrategie—Entwurf des Bundesumweltministeriums. Bonn, 2021. Available online: www.bmu.de (accessed on 28 October 2021).
5. IRENA. Green Hydrogen Cost Reduction—Scaling Up Electrolysers to Meet the 1.5 °C Climate Goal. Abu Dhabi, 2020. Available online: https://www.irena.org/-/media/Files/IRENA/Agency/Publication/2020/Dec/IRENA_Green_hydrogen_cost_2020.pdf (accessed on 25 February 2022).
6. Holst, M.; Aschbrenner, S.; Smolinka, T.; Voglstätter, C.; Grimm, G. Cost forecast for low temperature electrolysis—Technology driven bottom-up prognosis for PEM and alkaline water electrolysis systems. Freiburg, 2021. Available online: https://www.ise.fraunhofer.de/content/dam/ise/de/documents/publications/studies/cost-forecast-for-low-temperature-electrolysis.pdf (accessed on 17 October 2022).
7. Schäfer, M.; Gretzschel, O.; Steinmetz, H. The possible roles of wastewater treatment plants in sector coupling. *Energies* **2020**, *13*, 2088. [CrossRef]
8. DWA. DWA Wasserstoff trifft Abwasser—Arbeitsbericht der DWA-Arbeitsgruppe KEK-7.1 "Wasserstoffbasierte Energiekonzepte". *KA Korrespondenz Abwasser* **2022**, *7*, 597–605.
9. Calbry-Muzyka, A.S.; Schildhauer, T.J. Direct Methanation of Biogas—Technical Challenges and Recent Progress. *Front. Energy Res.* **2020**, *8*, 570887. [CrossRef]
10. Michailos, S.; Walker, M.; Moody, A.; Poggio, D.; Pourkashanian, M. A techno-economic assessment of implementing power-to-gas systems based on biomethanation in an operating waste water treatment plant. *J. Environ. Chem. Eng.* **2021**, *9*, 104735. [CrossRef]
11. Gretzschel, O.; Schfer, M.; Steinmetz, H.; Pick, E.; Kanitz, K.; Krieger, S. Advanced wastewater treatment to eliminate organic micropollutants in wastewater treatment plants in combination with energy-efficient electrolysis at WWTP Mainz. *Energies* **2020**, *13*, 3599. [CrossRef]
12. Skouteris, G.; Rodriguez-Garcia, G.; Reinecke, S.F.; Hampel, U. The use of pure oxygen for aeration in aerobic wastewater treatment: A review of its potential and limitations. *Bioresour. Technol.* **2020**, *312*, 123595. [CrossRef]
13. Mohammadpour, H.; Cord-Ruwisch, R.; Pivrikas, A.; Ho, G. Utilisation of oxygen from water electrolysis—Assessment for wastewater treatment and aquaculture. *Chem. Eng. Sci.* **2021**, *246*, 117008. [CrossRef]
14. Hu, Y.-Q.; Wei, W.; Gao, M.; Zhou, Y.; Wang, G.-X.; Zhang, Y. Effect of pure oxygen aeration on extracellular polymeric substances (EPS) of activated sludge treating saline wastewater. *Process Saf. Environ. Prot.* **2019**, *123*, 344–350. [CrossRef]
15. García-Valverde, R.; Espinosa, N.; Urbina, A. Simple PEM water electrolyser model and experimental validation. *Energy* **2012**, *37*, 1927–1938. [CrossRef]
16. Allidières, L.; Brisse, A.; Millet, P.; Valentin, S.; Zeller, M. On the ability of PEM water electrolysers to provide power grid services. *Int. J. Hydrogen Energy* **2019**, *44*, 9690–9700. [CrossRef]
17. SIMBA# | ifak Magdeburg. Available online: https://www.ifak.eu/de/produkte/simba (accessed on 18 October 2022).
18. Gernaey, K.V.; Jeppsson, U.; Vanrolleghem, P.A.; Copp, J.B. *Benchmarking of Control Strategies for Wastewater Treatment Plants*; IWA Publishing: London, UK, 2015.
19. Gernaey, K.; Flores-Alsina, X.; Rosen, C.; Benedetti, L.; Jeppsson, U. Dynamic influent pollutant disturbance scenario generation using a phenomenological modelling approach. *Environ. Model. Softw.* **2011**, *26*, 1255–1267. [CrossRef]

20. Stenstrom, M.K.; Kido, W.; Shanks, R.F.; Mulkerin, M. Estimating oxygen transfer capacity of a full-scale pure oxygen activated sludge plant. *J. Water Pollut. Control Fed.* **1989**, *61*, 208–220.
21. Lide, D. *CRC Handbook of Chemistry and Physics*, 84th ed.; CRC Press: Boca Raton, FL, USA, 2004.
22. Wang, L.K.; Shammas, N.K.; Hung, Y.-T. *Advanced Biological Treatment Processes*; Springer Science & Business Media: Totowa, NJ, USA, 2010; Volume 9.
23. Lehner, F.; Hart, D. Chapter 1—The importance of water electrolysis for our future energy system. In *Electrochemical Power Sources: Fundamentals, Systems, and Applications*; Smolinka, T., Garche, J., Eds.; Elsevier: Amsterdam, The Netherlands, 2022; pp. 1–36.
24. Carmo, M.; Fritz, D.L.; Mergel, J.; Stolten, D. A comprehensive review on PEM water electrolysis. *Int. J. Hydrogen Energy* **2013**, *38*, 4901–4934. [CrossRef]
25. Bertuccioli, L.; Chan, A.; Hart, D.; Lehner, F.; Madden, B.; Standen, E. Development of Water Electrolysis in the European Union. Lausanne, 2014. Available online: https://refman.energytransitionmodel.com/publications/2020 (accessed on 9 February 2023).
26. Rizwan, M.; Alstad, V.; Jäschke, J. Design considerations for industrial water electrolyzer plants. *Int. J. Hydrogen Energy* **2021**, *46*, 37120–37136. [CrossRef]
27. Towler, G.; Sinnott, R. *Chemical Engineering Design—Principles, Practice and Economics of Plant and Process Design*, 2nd ed.; Elsevier: Oxford, UK, 2013.
28. The Chemical Engineering Plant Cost Index—Chemical Engineering. Available online: https://www.chemengonline.com/pci-home (accessed on 19 October 2022).
29. Plant Cost Index Archives—Chemical Engineering. Available online: https://www.chemengonline.com/site/plant-cost-index/ (accessed on 19 October 2022).
30. Schmidt, O.; Gambhir, A.; Staffell, I.; Hawkes, A.; Nelson, J.; Few, S. Future cost and performance of water electrolysis: An expert elicitation study. *Int. J. Hydrogen Energy* **2017**, *42*, 30470–30492. [CrossRef]
31. Fu, Q.; Mabilat, C.; Zahid, M.; Brisse, A.; Gautier, L. Syngas production via high-temperature steam/CO_2 co-electrolysis: An economic assessment. *Energy Environ. Sci.* **2010**, *3*, 1382–1397. [CrossRef]
32. De Saint Jean, M.; Baurens, P.; Bouallou, C.; Couturier, K. Economic assessment of a power-to-substitute-natural-gas process including high-temperature steam electrolysis. *Int. J. Hydrogen Energy* **2015**, *40*, 6487–6500. [CrossRef]
33. Park, S.H.; Lee, Y.D.; Ahn, K.Y. Performance analysis of an SOFC/HCCI engine hybrid system: System simulation and thermo-economic comparison. *Int. J. Hydrogen Energy* **2014**, *39*, 1799–1810. [CrossRef]
34. Peters, M.S.; Timmerhaus, K.D.; West, R.E. *Plant Design and Economics for Chemical Engineers*, 5th ed.; McGraw-Hill Professional: New York, NY, USA, 2002.
35. Michailos, S.; McCord, S.; Sick, V.; Stokes, G.; Styring, P. Dimethyl ether synthesis via captured CO_2 hydrogenation within the power to liquids concept: A techno-economic assessment. *Energy Convers. Manag.* **2019**, *184*, 262–276. [CrossRef]
36. Wietschel, M. *Integration erneuerbarer Energien durch Sektorkopplung: Analyse zu technischen Sektorkopplungsoptionen*; Umweltbundesamt: Dessau-Roßlau, Germany, 2019.
37. Frontier Economics Strompreiseffekte eines Kohleausstiegs. 2018. Available online: https://www.frontier-economics.com/de/de/news-und-veroeffentlichungen/news/news-article-i4367-analysing-the-economic-impact-of-german-carbon-reduction-targets/ (accessed on 14 February 2023).
38. Winkler, J.; Sensfuß, F.; Pudlik, M. Leitstudie Strommarkt—Analyse ausgewählter Einflussfaktoren auf den Marktwert Erneuerbarer Energien. Karlsruhe, 2015. Available online: https://www.bmwk.de/Redaktion/DE/Publikationen/Studien/leitstudie-strommarkt_analyse-ausgewaehlter-einflussfaktoren-auf-den-martkwert-erneuerbarer-energien.html (accessed on 14 February 2023).
39. Kost, C.; Shammugam, S.; Fluri, V.; Peper, D.; Memar, A.D.; Schlegel, T. Levelized Cost of Electricity-Renewable Energy Technologies. Freiburg, 2021. Available online: https://www.ise.fraunhofer.de/en/publications/studies/cost-of-electricity.html (accessed on 14 February 2023).
40. Adnan, M.A.; Kibria, M.G. Comparative techno-economic and life-cycle assessment of power-to-methanol synthesis pathways. *Appl. Energy* **2020**, *278*, 115614. [CrossRef]
41. Battaglia, P.; Buffo, G.; Ferrero, D.; Santarelli, M.; Lanzini, A. Methanol synthesis through CO_2 capture and hydrogenation: Thermal integration, energy performance and techno-economic assessment. *J. CO_2 Util.* **2021**, *44*, 101407. [CrossRef]
42. Bellotti, D.; Rivarolo, M.; Magistri, L. Economic feasibility of methanol synthesis as a method for CO_2 reduction and energy storage. *Energy Procedia* **2019**, *158*, 4721–4728. [CrossRef]
43. Mohseni, E.; Herrmann-Heber, R.; Reinecke, S.F.; Hampel, U. Bubble generation by micro-orifices with application on activated sludge wastewater treatment. *Chem. Eng. Process. Process Intensif.* **2019**, *143*, 107511. [CrossRef]
44. Herrmann-Heber, R.; Reinecke, S.F.; Hampel, U. Dynamic aeration for improved oxygen mass transfer in the wastewater treatment process. *Chem. Eng. J.* **2020**, *386*, 122068. [CrossRef]
45. Gieseke, A.; Tarre, S.; Green, M.; de Beer, D. Nitrification in a biofilm at low pH values: Role of in situ microenvironments and acid tolerance. *Appl. Environ. Microbiol.* **2006**, *72*, 4283–4292. [CrossRef]
46. Fabiyi, M.; Connery, K.; Marx, R.; Burke, M.; Goel, R.; Snowling, S.; Schraa, O. Extending the Modeling of High Purity Oxygen Wastewater Treatment Processes: Transition from Closed to Open Basin Operations—A Full Scale Case Study. *Proc. Water Environ. Fed.* **2012**, *2012*, 4250–4262. [CrossRef]
47. DWA 31. *Leistungsnachweis Kommunaler Kläranlagen—Verfahren der Stickstoffelimination im Vergleich*; DWA: Hennef, Germany, 2018.

48. Institut für Wasserwirtschaft Halbach. Der biologische Sauerstoffbedarf im Ablauf von Kläranlagen. 7 August 2019. Available online: https://www.institut-halbach.de/2019/08/biologischer-sauerstoffbedarf-im-ablauf-von-klaeranlagen/ (accessed on 7 May 2023).
49. Larrea, A.; Rambor, A.; Fabiyi, M. Ten years of industrial and municipal membrane bioreactor (MBR) systems—Lessons from the field. *Water Sci. Technol.* **2014**, *70*, 279–288. [CrossRef]

Disclaimer/Publisher's Note: The statements, opinions and data contained in all publications are solely those of the individual author(s) and contributor(s) and not of MDPI and/or the editor(s). MDPI and/or the editor(s) disclaim responsibility for any injury to people or property resulting from any ideas, methods, instructions or products referred to in the content.

Article

Techno-Economic Evaluation of the Thermochemical Energy Valorization of Construction Waste and Algae Biomass: A Case Study for a Biomass Treatment Plant in Northern Greece

Georgios Manthos [1], Dimitris Zagklis [1], Sameh S. Ali [2,3], Constantina Zafiri [4] and Michael Kornaros [1,*]

1. Laboratory of Biochemical Engineering & Environmental Technology (LBEET), Department of Chemical Engineering, University of Patras, 1 Karatheodori Str., 26504 Patras, Greece
2. Biofuels Institute, School of the Environment and Safety Engineering, Jiangsu University, Zhenjiang 212013, China
3. Botany Department, Faculty of Science, Tanta University, Tanta 31527, Egypt
4. Green Technologies Ltd., 5 Ellinos Stratiotou Str., 26223 Patras, Greece
* Correspondence: kornaros@chemeng.upatras.gr

Abstract: Biomass treatment for energy production is a promising way for achieving fossil fuel replacement and environmental relief. Thermochemical processes are a common way of processing biomass, but their potential economic benefits are not always clear to investors. In this work, three basic thermochemical processes (combustion, gasification, and pyrolysis) are examined in terms of their theoretical yields and their products, as well as their economic viability. The goal of this analysis was to look into the total amount of available biomass streams and compare business plans in terms of sustainability from a technical and economic perspective. The estimation of the fixed capital investment was based on ready−made solutions that are already available on the market. The analysis showed that the gasification unit has the optimum sustainability results since the total amount of gross income was EUR 0.13/kg of biomass while the treatment cost was estimated at EUR 0.09/kg of biomass. The internal rate of return of the investment was calculated at 9%, establishing a promising alternative solution to sustainable "green" energy production.

Keywords: techno−economic analysis; combustion; gasification; pyrolysis; biomass treatment; thermochemical treatment

1. Introduction

The linear economy model can be described as a series of steps that include extracting resources from the environment, producing goods and services, consuming them, and finally disposing of the residues in a landfill. In recent years, it has become more and more obvious that this is not a sustainable economic concept. An alternative economy model described by a circle that utilizes the produced waste for the recovery of energy and materials has been promoted by the European Union (EU) during the last two decades. This has been advocated in a number of documents issued by the European Commission, such as the Roadmap to Resource Efficient Europe, the Ecodesign Directive, the circular economy package, and the EU directive on waste [1,2].

Waste biomass can play an important role in the circular economy model, as it contains valuable resources that can be recovered, including energy and other by−products. A number of resource recovery methods from biomass have been examined in the literature, leading to the production of energy and the recovery of by−products, as illustrated in Figure 1. Landfilling of biomass leads to the production of biogas, which is in some cases used for the production of electricity, while in other cases it is burnt to prevent its release into the atmosphere (methane is approximately 30 times more potent as a greenhouse gas than carbon dioxide). Moreover, a significant amount of methane escapes as onsite emissions, making landfilling a subpar resource recovery method [3]. Composting can be a very useful resource recovery method, mainly for biomass that has a relatively high moisture content and is not suitable for other forms of resource recovery [4]. Its use leads mostly to the recovery of nutrients in the form of compost, while some applications have been proposed for the recovery of the produced heat [5], though this is not a widespread application. Anaerobic digestion is typically used in the case of high moisture (liquid) biomass, leading to the recovery of biogas and by−products (in the form of anaerobic digestate) [6]. When dealing with low−moisture biomass, combustion, gasification, and pyrolysis are typically more suitable.

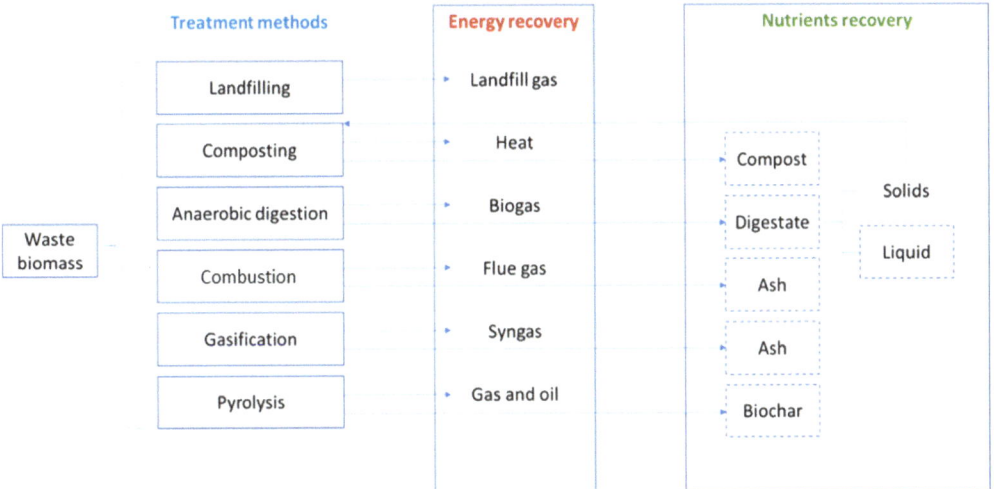

Figure 1. Most prominent resource recovery methods from waste biomass.

Combustion units have widespread use and applicability since this technique is a very common waste treatment method in countries of Northern Europe, such as Finland and Denmark [7]. The electric efficiency of these units is close to or above 80% (of lower heating value), with the highest capital cost typically occurring from the combined heat and power production unit (CHP) [8].

In order to initiate the combustion of biomass, its temperature must exceed a certain point (ignition temperature), which is different for each type of combustible biomass. Biomass during combustion goes through three different stages, which are overlapping and occur simultaneously. These stages are the drying, devolatilization, and burning of solid carbon [9]. Several challenges can occur using this biomass treatment method related to the biomass characteristics (moisture, minor constituents, etc.) [10]. The biomass chamber parameters need to be designed according to the biomass characteristics as well as the ash and gas emissions composition [11,12].

The gasification process converts a solid/liquid organic residue into a gas phase ("syngas") and, in some cases, a solid fraction ("char"). In this process, the biomass is heated in the presence of limited amounts of oxygen in order to release maximum amounts of gases such as CO and H_2. The oxygen requirements can be provided to the system either in the form of pure O_2 or as air [13]. The most widely used medium is air due to its low cost; however, using pure oxygen instead of air can increase the calorific value of the produced gas up to four times due to the absence of nitrogen in the gas phase [14]. Worldwide, several gasification plants are operating or are under construction with most of them dedicated to electricity production [15].

Pyrolysis is a thermochemical process for biomass degradation in the absence of oxygen which provides three different products (biochar, bio−oil, and fuel gas products) [16]. During this process, a large number of reactions take place, but it is mainly accepted that pyrolysis consists of three main stages (biomass drying, primary decomposition, and secondary decomposition reactions) [17,18]. This process can be sustainable and economically feasible only with the upgrading of the bio-–oil to a pure and stable product [19]. Depending on the rate of thermochemical treatment and the residence time, the process is characterized as fast or slow. Slow pyrolysis can increase the yield of biochar produced whereas fast pyrolysis leads to an increase in bio—oil production [20].

This work provides a case study of a potential biomass thermochemical treatment unit constructed in Greece, implementing combustion, gasification, or pyrolysis. The study took into account the mass and energy balances of the different processes considering the biomass characteristics. Equipment cost (Cp) and bioenergy efficiency were estimated for each process in order to assess the business plans during the lifetime of the investment. This analysis could be a guide for decision—making for biomass treatment in coastal regions of Europe since the subsidy percentage used is common throughout the EU [21]. Moreover, the present study investigates the energy production from a waste stream (algal biomass) that is not commonly used for energy recovery and constitutes a typical biomass solid effluent in coastal regions. The aim of this paper is to offer readers a general perspective of thermochemical processes and to evaluate the energy potential of construction and algal biomass (AB), considering their economic feasibility.

2. Materials and Methods

2.1. Feed Material and Pretreatment

The analysis was carried out with the implementation of three different substrates to evaluate the sustainability of the proposed processes. The quantitative characteristics of the final substrate mixture were based on full—scale data of an enterprise that manages construction waste in the region of Northern Greece. The feed material mixture consisted of woody biomass (WB) (branches, wood, tree trunks, and wooden pallets), construction materials (CM) (plastic, pipes, wires, and nylon), and AB (coastal seaweed). According to the data provided by the enterprise, the amounts of WB, CM, and AB to be managed were 30,000, 10,000, and 20,000 t/y, respectively. According to these quantities, the feed material consisted of the aforementioned substrates with a ratio of WB/CM/AB equal to 3/1/2. Several samples of the three different types of substrates were pretreated in order to evaluate the feed's main characteristics. The scope of this process was to calculate the specific elements (C, N, O, and H) and the moisture and ash content in order to estimate the substrate's biomass empirical formula and calorific value from each process reaction. The pretreatment included the initial shredding by a pilot scale shredder (CRUSHERS Monorotor, M4230-700, BLik, Milly-la-Forêt, France) and the subsequent pulping into 1×1 mm pieces by a hand-held crusher (IKA A11 Basic Griding mill—Gemini BV, IKA, Staufen, Germany). After the pretreatment steps, the samples were analyzed. Apart from the aforementioned substrates, the enterprise also manages excavation and demolition waste which are both used as inert materials and were out of the scope of this analysis.

2.2. Analytical Techniques

The measurement of total organic carbon (TOC) was carried out using the TOC—VWS and Solid Module SSM-5000A apparatus (Shimadzu, Kyoto, Japan). Total nitrogen was measured through a Micro—Kjeldahl apparatus (VELP SCIENTIFICA, UDK 129, Usmate, Italy) by the conversion of the organic nitrogen to ammonium salt in the presence of K_2SO_4 and HgO/H_2SO_4 [22]. Moisture was determined by weighing an amount of fresh sample before and after drying at 105 °C overnight, while ash was determined by measuring the weight difference of the dried samples after burning at 550 °C for 45 min [22].

2.3. Description of the Proposed Processes

Regarding the biomass combustion unit, it was assumed that the plant equipment includes a biomass crusher and a main biomass combustion chamber, as well as a combined heat and power system for energy production. The thermal energy produced could potentially be used to cover the thermal requirements of the unit, which has not been included in this analysis. The cogeneration unit includes an electricity and heat production unit and facilities for receiving, storing, and preparing fuel.

Biomass combustion as well as electricity production were carried out in the main unit of the plant. The unit was considered to be installed next to the existing biomass storage structures, and the composition of the feed was assumed to remain constant during the whole operation period. Small changes in the feed lead to different system productivity; nevertheless, the annual biomass amount was assumed to be constant as well as the total annual energy production.

A prototype unit from an American supplier was selected for the evaluation of the gasification process, which included a biomass drying system, a gasification unit, and a CHP unit. A biomass crusher was considered in the analysis for biomass shredding. A solid organic residue fraction (biochar) is obtained from the gasification chamber, which can be further exploited for soil amendment [23] or as material in building constructions [24]. This type of biochar tends to have a higher surface area and a more porous structure compared to biochar produced by other processes (such as pyrolysis). This fact may occur due to the high process temperatures with a limited supply of oxygen. This type of biochar can also be used in animal feed to reduce the occurrence of digestive problems [25]. This analysis describes the construction of a 6.05 MW$_e$ unit. The characteristics of the plant construction site remain the same as those mentioned in the assessment of the biomass combustion plant. Furthermore, this supplier markets a prefabricated treatment system with a maximum productivity of 200 kW. Thus, the 'two—-thirds' rule was used to calculate the C_p for the process.

For the design and analysis of the pyrolysis unit, a unit installed in the Pieria region, Greece, was chosen as a model. This unit includes a mechanical separation unit, a crusher, a thermal converter in the absence of oxygen (main pyrolysis unit) with simultaneous production of gas fuel, heat, and biochar, a thermal oxidizer for pyrolysis gas burning, heat recovery, and a superheated steam production boiler, a waste gas cleaning unit, and a CHP unit with a steam turbine electric generator. This unit has been built for a capacity of 125 tonnes per day of municipal solid waste.

The steps of the processes examined in this work are summarized in Figure 2.

The equipment size for each unit was estimated through the coefficient yields of each piece of equipment and the mass and energy balances of the processes. A figure of 9% equipment downtime for maintenance and repairs was considered. The total Cp was then estimated through the two—thirds rule [26,27]. The fixed capital investment (FCI) for each process was calculated through the total Cp according to Table 1. The individual costs for each FCI element were calculated through the equations in Table 1 according to the methodology by Peters et al. [26]. This method is capable of a preliminary estimation with a confidence of ±30%.

The operational costs, such as waste treatment (C_{wt}) and energy requirements, were estimated for each process, and different treatment costs were implemented for the analysis depending on the waste characteristics. The total treatment cost (TTC) was calculated through Equation (1):

$$TTC = 1.481\ C_{ol} + 1.235\ C_{wt} + 0.143\ FCI + 0.082\ C_p \tag{1}$$

where C_{ol} refers to the labor cost.

A lifetime of 15 years was assumed for the equipment, and 30 years was assumed for the erected buildings. The total operational cost can be divided again into direct costs connected with the production process and other costs such as the depreciation of the equipment and buildings, taxes and insurance, direct work, etc.

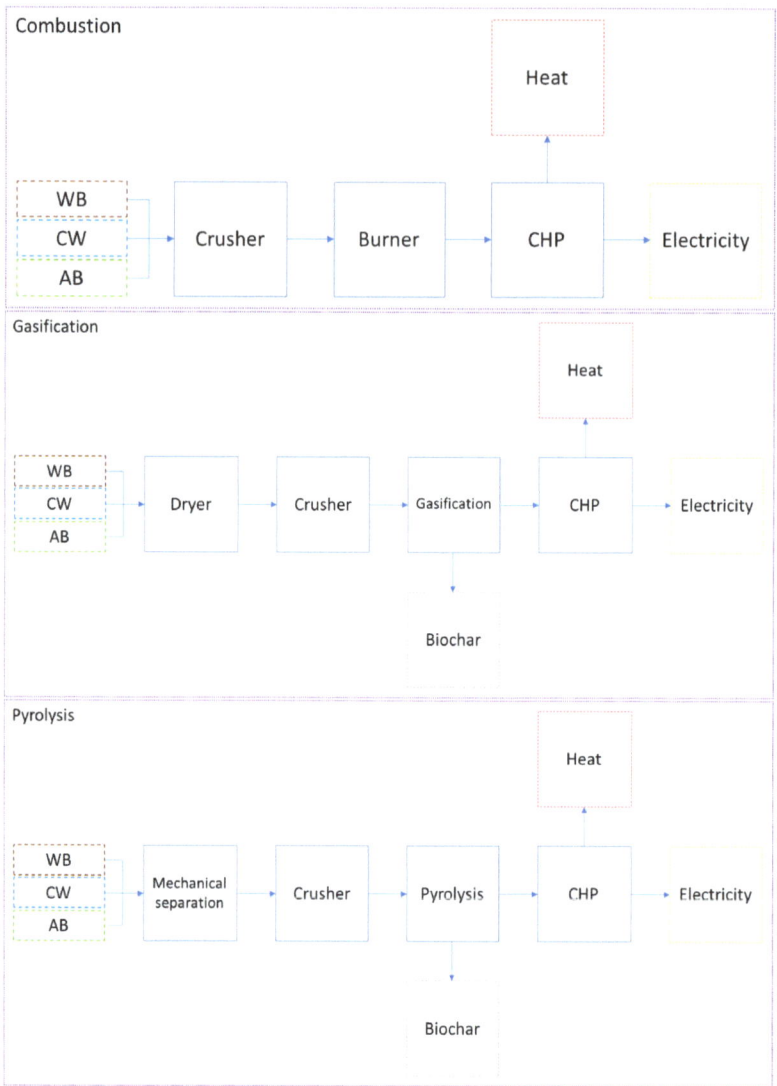

Figure 2. Main steps of the three thermochemical processes examined in this work.

For the investment plan estimation for the installation and operation of the proposed units, it was considered that 25% of the FCI could be covered by the investor's own funds, while 40% could be covered by subsidies according to the development law of Greece 3299/2004. The remaining percentage could be covered by a loan with an interest rate of 8% that must be repaid in the first three years of unit operation. Subsequently, working capital (14% × FCI) must be calculated in the total cash flows, which will be returned to the investor at the end of the life of the unit. Income tax was assumed to be 20% on business profits.

Table 1. Equations used for the economic evaluation of the processes.

Fixed Capital Investment (EUR)	Direct Cost (EUR)	Onsite	
		Purchased equipment	C_p
		Equipment installation	0.06 FCI
		Automatic control and instruments	0.02 FCI
		Piping	0.04 FCI
		Electrical equipment	0.02 FCI
		Offsite	
		Buildings	0.02 FCI
		Yard improvements	0.02 FCI
		Service facilities	0.08 FCI
		Land	0.01 FCI
	Indirect Cost (EUR)	Engineering and supervision	0.04 FCI
		Construction expenses	0.04 FCI
		Contractor's fee	0.02 FCI
		Contingency	0.05 FCI
	FCI (EUR)		$1.724\, C_p$
Total Product Cost (EUR)	Direct Cost (EUR/y)	Energy requirements	0.1 TTC
		Waste treatment	C_{wt}
		Direct work	C_{ol}
		Operating supervision	$0.1\, C_{ol}$
		Maintenance and repairs	0.02 FCI
		Operating supplies	0.005 FCI
		Laboratory charges	$0.1\, C_{ol}$
		Royalties and patents	0.01 FCI
		Depreciation	$0.082\, C_p + 0.06\, FCI$
		Taxes and insurances	0.03 FCI
		Fixed charges	0.05 FCI
	General expenses (EUR/y)	Administrative expenses	0.02 TTC
		Distribution and marketing expenses	0.02 TTC
		Research and development	0.05 TTC

3. Results and Discussion

3.1. Biomass Characterization

The basic physicochemical characteristics of the substrates as well as their elemental analysis are presented in Table 2.

Table 2. Physicochemical characteristics of the substrates.

Characteristic	WB	CW	AB	MIXTURE	Reference
C (% DM *)	50.20 ± 0.9	14.93 ± 3.1	37.14 ± 1.1	51.53 ± 0.6	This work
O (% DM *)	41.57 ± 1.2	3.20 ± 4.0	50.38 ± 8.9	38.11 ± 9.7	[28–32]
H (% DM *)	5.49 ± 0.2	12.59 ± 1.2	5.28 ± 0.2	6.60 ± 0.1	[28–32]
N (% DM *)	0.30 ± 0.1	0.49 ± 0.7	3.04 ± 1.9	1.24 ± 3.0	This work
Moisture (%)	11.95 ± 6.2	2.25 ± 0.3	81.58 ± 0.1	33.53 ± 9.5	This work
Ash (%)	6.78 ± 4.7	65.52 ± 3.3	1.10 ± 0.1	14.67 ± 5.8	This work
Calorific value (MJ/kg$_{DM}$)	18.31 ± 0.6	43.53 ± 2.7	12.33 ± 3.0	20.11 ± 1.8	Calculated

* DM: Dry matter.

WB is characterized by a high carbon content in terms of dry weight as well as a high oxygen content. The percentages of moisture and ash are relatively low (12% and 7%, respectively), making it an ideal waste for thermochemical treatment. CW showed less favorable characteristics for this type of treatment than WB as its carbon content reaches 15%. This fact was mainly due to the high content of wire inside the cables and other materials. The percentage of oxygen in this substrate is reduced by 3%, forming an O/C ratio of 0.21. AB has a high content of ash and moisture, which reduces the thermal value of the mixture material since they increase the latent heat (LH) of the feedstock. The specific substrates appeared to have high complementarity in their individual components, which demonstrates that the final mixture will have a typical biomass composition. The calorific value (CV) for each waste stream was calculated from the elemental analysis considering the percentage of C, H and O in dry biomass according to the equation:

$$CV\left(\frac{MJ}{kg_{DM}}\right) = 0.339\,(\%C) + 0.114\,(\%H) - 0.018\,(\%O) \qquad (2)$$

The highest CV was exhibited in the WB waste stream mainly due to the high organic content of this type of biomass. The CV of the current waste streams was considered as a crucial parameter for the analysis. Nevertheless, only an estimation of this value was carried out without direct measurement. Slightly different values in CV may lead to different system performance, but the comparison results would be the same according to the analysis presented herein. Based on the above, the final characteristics of the biomass after the mixing of different substrates can be found in Table 2. The final characteristics of the biomass are quite similar to those of the WB, which is expected since it was mixed in a higher amount. The moisture after mixing increased by over 30%, which indicates that for this particular substrate, there may be a need for pre−treatment and drying before entering the main process.

3.2. Techno−Economic Evaluation of Alternative Treatment Methods of Biomass

3.2.1. Biomass Combustion Unit

An energy analysis was conducted regarding the specific feed material in order to evaluate the performance of the combustion unit. In the analysis, the high calorific value (HCV) of the specific biomass was calculated based on its characteristics as well as the energy losses that would result from the moisture contained in it through LH. The excess air of the system was 25% more than the stoichiometrically required amount in order to achieve maximum performance and the absence of intermediate combustion products. Based on this excess air, it was assumed that the percentage of monoxide in the gases leaving the system was 1%. The temperature of the main combustion unit was set at 800 °C. The composition of the gas stream leaving the combustion chamber was estimated as $CO_2/CO/O_2/H_2O/N_2$ equal to 12.6/1/2.5/19.5/64.4.

Based on the composition of the gases, the temperature of the chamber, and the excess air in the process, the efficiency of the burner for the specific type of biomass is estimated through Equations (3)–(5).

$$EP\left(\frac{MJ}{d}\right) = \dot{n}_{CO2}\Delta H_{f,CO2} + \dot{n}_{CO}\Delta H_{f,CO} + \dot{n}_{H,in}\frac{\Delta H_{f,H2}}{2} - \dot{m}_{DM}\Delta H_{DM} \quad (3)$$

$$LH\left(\frac{MJ}{d}\right) = \left(\frac{\dot{n}_{H,in}}{2} + \dot{n}_{H2O}\right)\Delta H_{f,H2O} \quad (4)$$

$$UH\left(\frac{MJ}{d}\right) = EP - LH \quad (5)$$

where EP denotes the energy produced, $\dot{n}$ refers to the molar flow of the elements in mol/d, ΔH_f refers to the formation enthalpy in MJ/mol, $\dot{m}_{DM}$ refers to the mass flow of dry biomass in kg/d, and ΔH_{DM} refers to the enthalpy of dry biomass in MJ/kg_{DM}. The molar flows were calculated stoichiometrically from the biomass combustion reaction.

It can be observed that an efficiency of 96% of the calorific value of the biomass was achieved, which makes the process particularly efficient for this specific feed stream. The process's LH, useful heat (UH), and HCV were estimated to be 343, 2674, and 2776 GJ/d, respectively.

Due to the high ash content of the biomass mixture, ash amounts of 20 tonnes per day are produced simultaneously from the treatment. This constitutes a waste stream of the process and needs special management, as it mainly consists of inorganic elements, metals, and wire scraps. For its processing, a cost of EUR 0.42/kg of ash is foreseen [33].

After treatment, the gas produced is used at a CHP plant. The yields of such plants vary depending on their specific type. For this study, the overall efficiency of the cogeneration plant was considered to be 87%, with individual efficiencies of 63% in thermal energy and 24% in electricity [34]. The produced thermal energy from the treatment was not an exploited stream. Some authors propose the exploitation of this stream for heating nearby residential areas after appropriate modification of the network (district heating) [35,36].

This specific project is a challenge as the cost of building substations for the transfer of thermal energy is quite high, considering that there is no previous installation in the area. Furthermore, a specific fraction of energy can be used to heat greenhouses in the winter months [37,38]. These practices potentially increase the viability of the plant. However, they were excluded from this study as they would further increase the total fixed costs as well as the size of the overall processing plant. The total energy production capacity of the biomass combustion unit was assumed at 6.41 MW of electric energy according to the analysis.

The C_p was estimated based on the description of a combustion unit of a specific capacity from the work of [34], by increasing the cost of the unit in relation to the capacity using the two-thirds rule. The total C_p for the combustion unit was estimated at EUR 6,461,358. The FCI of the combustion unit was estimated through Table 1 as EUR 9,621,144. In the work of Sagani et al. [39], the specific capital cost (SCC) was estimated at EUR 3000/kWel for a plant designed for the region of Argolis, Greece, with a capacity of 4.5 MWel. In the present work, the SCC was calculated at EUR 1636/kWel for a capacity of 6.41 MWel, which is in good agreement with the work of Sagani et al. and the economy of scale. For the calculation of the immediate labor, it was assumed that three workers were required per MW of electricity [34]. Moreover, annual staff remuneration was set at EUR 24,000 gross revenue per employee. Based on this analysis, the treatment cost per kg of feed material was estimated at EUR 0.09. The unit's total annual revenue (TAR) was the profit from electricity production, as the development of a district heating network has not been included in the analysis. The sale price for electricity derived from biomass, based on Greek legislation, is set at EUR 140/MWhel for units larger than 5 MW and EUR 162/MWhel for units larger than 1 MW [40]. The gross income per kg of feed material was calculated at EUR 0.12.

The loan for the investment was estimated at EUR 4,714,361. The cash flows for the fifteen years of unit operation are presented in Figure 3a. It becomes clear that the specific investment plan shows great sustainability as all economic parameters have acceptable values. The profitability index (PI) was estimated to be greater than 1 (PI = 1.72). When this investment index estimated greater than 1, the investment could be made, and it is a measure of the investment's attractiveness [41]. At the same time, the net present value (NPV) after the end of the investment is positive (EUR 4,826,477) at the given rate of return (5%). The economic parameter values are presented in Table 3. The internal rate of return (IRR) of the business plan was calculated at 10%, comparable with the same economic parameter for the combustion units described in the works of Candia et al. and Morato et al. [42,43], with a value of 12%.

Table 3. Economic parameters of the analysis carried out for the proposed treatment methods.

Characteristic	Combustion	Gasification	Pyrolysis
IRR	10%	9%	0%
PI	1.72	1.9	0.73
NPV (M EUR)	4.8	5.3	−21.1
Payback Time	8.9	9.3	-

3.2.2. Biomass Gasification Unit

A theoretical analysis was conducted regarding the specific mixture of biomass streams, corresponding to the analysis examined in the combustion unit, in order to estimate the outputs and inputs of the gasification unit. The percentages of gas compounds in the output of the main gasification unit were estimated for $CO_2/CO/CH_4/H_2/N_2$ to be equal to 24/3/3/39/32. The oxygen entering the gasifier was set at 20% of the amount required for complete oxidation of the biomass. At the same time, the extent of the reaction was set at 94% based on the technical characteristics disclosed by the supplier. The temperature of the produced gas (syngas) was set at 600 °C. Regarding the solid stream outflow, the daily mass flow was calculated at 24 t/d with an organic/ash ratio equal to 0.36 with 90%

of carbon, 9% of oxygen, and 1% hydrogen. The volume of the outflow gas from the main gasification unit was calculated at 992,000 m^3 (STP) with a ratio of $N_2/H_2/CO/CO_2/CH_4$ equal to 0.35/0.34/0.06/0.22/0.03.

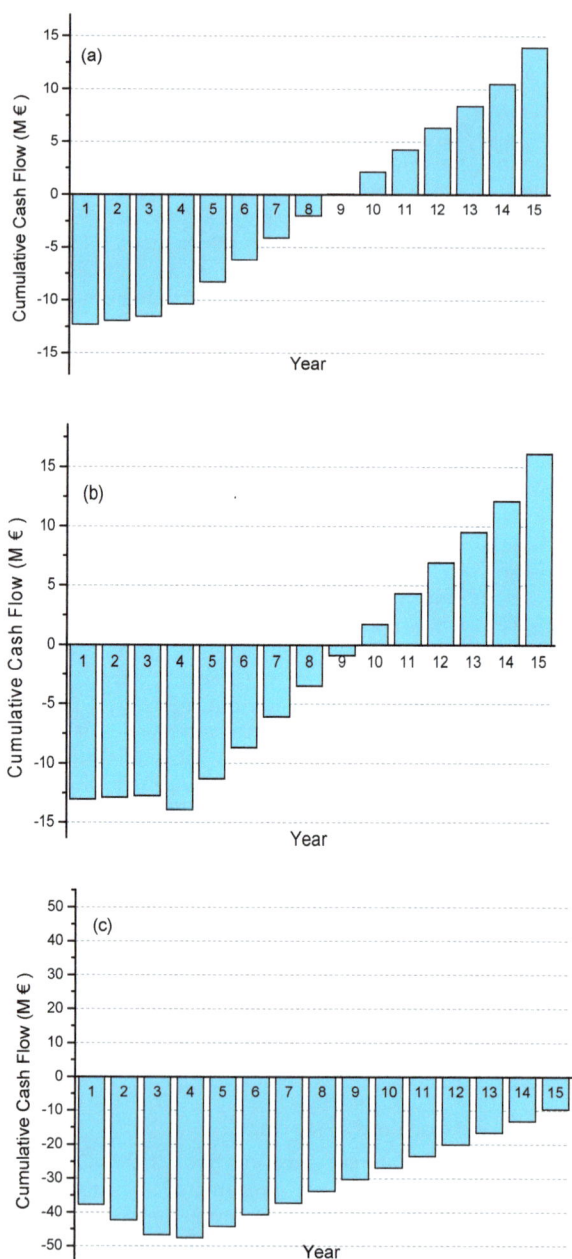

Figure 3. Annual discounted cash flow representation for the combustion (**a**), gasification (**b**), and pyrolysis (**c**) business plan.

The main gasification unit was estimated to recover 84% of the HCV of the biomass in the gas stream. Certain amounts of ash were identified in the solid effluent stream, which can potentially be removed by sieving. The amount of ash that is left over can be handled in the same way as in the combustion unit. The system has an electricity and heat cogeneration unit with efficiencies of 26% in electricity and 37% in thermal energy. Part of the thermal energy is utilized in the biomass dryer of the plant.

The C_p was estimated through the two–thirds rule from data provided by a supplier for a 200 kW unit. Based on this, the total Cp was estimated at EUR 5,730,869 and the FCI was estimated at EUR 9,880,808. Regarding the treatment cost of the process, it was calculated through Equation (1) to be EUR 5,203,955/year. The total number of employees was estimated to be 18. Finally, the treatment cost per kg of feed material was calculated to be EUR 0.09. This value indicates that the processes of combustion and gasification lead to similar treatment costs even though the combustion plant produces a higher amount of electric energy (6% higher).

The total annual revenue (TAR) of the plant came from electricity production, as well as the sale of the total amount of the organic fraction of the solid residue (biochar). The price for electricity derived from biomass was established at EUR 140/MWhel [40], based on Greek legislation, while for the organic solid fraction, this was estimated at EUR 540/t based on the market price. The gross income of electric energy production and biochar was calculated at EUR 6,811,945 and EUR 1,157,506, respectively. The income per kg of biomass was estimated at EUR 0.13. The total revenues are 25% higher than those of the combustion unit, which is mainly due to the sale of biochar. On the other hand, the total revenues from the sale of electricity are reduced by 6%, which is mainly due to the different yields of the two processes, both in the main processing unit and the CHP unit.

For the assessment of the investment cash flows over a 15-year period, it was also assumed that 25% of the investment was covered by equity capital. The amount of the loan, after receiving a subsidy of 40% of the initial investment, was estimated at EUR 4,714,361. Based on the development law 3299/2004 and the characteristics of the investment mentioned in the combustion unit, the investment plan for the construction of a gasification unit is presented in Figure 3b. At the same time, the financial parameters showed a profitable investment compared to the other studied treatment units that could potentially be financed with an IRR of 9% (Table 3). This IRR value is in line with the work of Luz et al. [44] where the IRR for a gasification unit plant for municipal solid waste was estimated at 7.5–15% depending on the plant's capacity. The payback period of the investment was estimated at 9.34 years, the PI was estimated at 1.9, while the NPV was calculated at EUR 5,348,112 after the 15–year period of unit operation. The results for the gasification unit were considered similar to the results of the work of Rentizelas et al. [45] where the gasification process has about a 50% increased NPV compared to the combustion plant unit.

3.2.3. Biomass Pyrolysis Unit

The case study of pyrolysis of biomass fractions considered in the present work can be analyzed according to the mass and energy balances of the process. In the pre–treatment step of the unit, glass and metal can be removed. Since most of the remaining ash after the thermochemical treatment comes from the wire inside the construction waste cables, a first screening of the copper part of the wire can be carried out at this point. This amount is estimated to be 75% of the total ash and therefore 10% of the total biomass. The fuel for the operation of the burner is natural gas, which is considered in the analysis. The resulting inert solid can be used as a soil fertilizer in further processes. The biochar produced was calculated at 19 t/day (11% of the feed material) and the cost for the energy demands of the unit were estimated at EUR 805/d. The estimated energy produced from this type of feed stream was estimated at 11.7 MJ/kg_{DM} which is in the same order of magnitude with the values of other studies with microalgae biomass as feedstock (18.4 MJ/kg_{DM}) [46].

In addition to the financial part, the manufacturing company of the unit also provides detailed information on the waste gases that come out of it after cleaning. Their values are extremely low and certified by the strict specifications of the state of California. Moreover, a cogeneration unit of electricity and thermal energy with an efficiency of 67% in thermal energy and 22% in electricity was derived from the analysis of the energy balances of the unit.

Several products could be produced from the pyrolysis process (bio–-oil and biochar) which could be used as the final product and channeled into the market. Nevertheless, in this study electricity was considered as the main product of the process considering that energy is a stable product that can be fed directly into the power grid. Moreover, this type of unit can be easily compared with the units of combustion and gasification for power generation.

The total C_p was estimated from the FCI of the unit from Table 1 and the two–thirds rule. The FCI of the proposed unit was calculated at EUR 31,949,131. This value is two times higher than the processes of combustion and gasification. This observation was established in the work of Solarte-Toro [47], where the capital cost of the pyrolysis unit was 2.24 times higher than the gasification plant. This fact has a very strong effect on the selection of the optimal investment scenario, as the first parameter for comparison is the FCI value. The cost of natural gas, according to the current provider charges in Greece, was set at EUR 0.83/kg. Most of the processing costs are depreciation due to the high price of equipment compared to the aforementioned biomass processing methods. The final treatment cost per kg of feed material was estimated at EUR 0.1.

The revenues of the plant come from the production of electricity and the organic solid residue (biochar) in the proportions of 61% and 39%, respectively. This type of biochar tends to have a lower surface area and denser structure compared to biochar produced by gasification. This is because pyrolysis is typically performed at lower temperatures and without oxygen, resulting in a higher yield of biochar. Biochar produced by pyrolysis units, with its denser structure, is often used as a carbon sequestration method and for long–term soil improvement [48]. Pyrolysis biochar can also be used as a feedstock for the production of activated carbon, which is used for water and air purification applications [49]. The TAR was estimated at EUR 8,990,000/y or EUR 0.15/kg of feed material. The revenues from the pyrolysis unit are considered approximately the same as those from the gasification unit.

The loan for the pyrolysis unit investment was calculated at EUR 22,045,000. The business plan was considered unsustainable, mainly because of the high equipment costs (Figure 3c). The economic parameters support this claim since the PI is estimated at 0.73 while the NPV was negative at the end of the equipment operation period (Table 3). In the work of Pighinelli et al. [50], it was also reported that a fast pyrolysis unit of biomass (eucalyptus as the substrate) for electricity production presents negative NPV values and cannot be financially competitive. For this reason, a break–even cost for the electricity produced was set (USD 0.62/kWh). In addition, in the work of He et al., it was denoted that other processes such as hydrothermal liquefaction could be more sustainable than pyrolysis or gasification for biomass with high moisture content, but further research must be carried out in order to optimize the process conditions [51].

3.3. Comparison of the Sustainability of the Business Plans

A strategy based on total investment or incremental investment should be followed in order to compare alternative and mutually exclusive business plans [52]. Based on the above criteria, an analysis was conducted for the definition of the optimum investment plan for biomass processing.

The minimum allowable rate of return (MARR) is set at 5%. The first step of the analysis was to reject investment plans where the investment exceeded the available funds. An initial assumption was made that the available funds are sufficient for the implementation of any of the alternative scenarios since this fact lies with each investor. The business plan for pyrolysis was rejected because of IRRpyrolysis< MARR. Comparing the case studies on the combustion and gasification of biomass, the combustion unit was considered as the baseline scenario due to the smaller FCI value. The incremental investment is characterized by Equations (6) and (7):

$$FCI_{Incremental} = FCI_{Gasification} - FCI_{Combustion} = EUR\ 9\ 880\ 808 - EUR\ 9\ 621\ 144 = EUR\ 259\ 664 \quad (6)$$

$$TAR_{Incremental} = TAR_{Gasification} - TAR_{Combustion} = EUR\ 7\ 969\ 451 - EUR\ 7\ 216\ 496 = EUR\ 753 \quad (7)$$

The incremental investment was characterized by a $\delta IRR = 1\% < MARR$. For this reason, the alternative solution of the combustion treatment plant is rejected. The gasification plant is regarded as the optimal investment plan, with it having a higher capital return rate. This scenario was estimated as optimal with the assumption that the entire quantity of the final organic residue would be channeled to the market by the end of each year. For this reason, a promotion strategy for the product would potentially increase the cost of biomass processing.

The proposed technical solutions for the processing of these types of biomass have been extensively studied in the literature [45,53–55]. In the work of Ramos et al. [53], a comparison of environmental and techno−economic analyses was conducted to evaluate different thermochemical techniques, resulting in slightly improved results for the combustion unit compared to gasification, with a plant capacity of 1 t of feed per hour (8 times less than in this work). On the other hand, in the work of Rentizelas et al. [45], the gasification of olive tree, almond tree, and peach tree prunings showed better results for the combustion unit, with a calculated IRR of 18.1%.

4. Conclusions

Thermochemical processes are environmentally friendly and efficient methods for waste treatment and energy production. In the present study, a comparison of different biomass processing methods was completed in order to assess the economic sustainability of the alternative management solutions. The comparison included three thermochemical treatment methods (combustion, gasification, and pyrolysis), indicating encouraging results for the processes of combustion and gasification, while the pyrolysis process was unsuitable because of the high Cp. Regarding the gasification process, the analysis showed that the investment in such a unit provides great economic sustainability, with higher revenues than combustion, even though a smaller amount of energy is produced. This fact is due to the production of biochar. The analysis predicted the TAR of approximately EUR 7.9 million for an initial investment of EUR 9.8 million with an IRR of 9% for a subsidized processing plant in the region of Greece.

Author Contributions: Conceptualization, G.M.; methodology, G.M.; software, G.M.; validation, G.M. and D.Z.; formal analysis, G.M.; investigation, G.M.; resources, C.Z.; data curation, G.M.; writing—original draft preparation, G.M.; writing—review and editing, D.Z. and S.S.A.; visualization, G.M. and D.Z.; supervision, M.K.; project administration, M.K.; funding acquisition, C.Z. All authors have read and agreed to the published version of the manuscript.

Funding: This research received no external funding.

Institutional Review Board Statement: Not applicable.

Informed Consent Statement: Not applicable.

Data Availability Statement: Not applicable.

Conflicts of Interest: The authors declare no conflict of interest.

Abbreviations

$\dot{m}_{DM}$	Mass flow of dry biomass [kg/d]
$\dot{n}$	Molar flow [mol/d]
ΔH_{DM}	Enthalpy of dry biomass [MJ/kg$_{DM}$]
ΔH_f	Enthalpy of formation [MJ/mol]
AB	Algal biomass
CHP	Combined heat and power unit
CM	Construction materials
CV	Calorific Value [MJ/kg$_{DM}$]
C_{ol}	Labor cost
C_p	Equipment cost
C_{wt}	Waste treatment cost
EP	Energy produced
EU	European Union
FCI	Fixed capital investment
HCV	High calorific value
IRR	Internal rate of return
LH	Latent heat
MARR	Minimum allowable rate of return
NPV	Net present value
O/C	Oxygen/carbon ratio
PI	Profitability index
TAR	Total annual revenue
TOC	Total organic carbon
TTC	Total treatment cost
UH	Useful heat
WB	Woody biomass

References

1. European Commission Roadmap to a Resource Efficient Europe. *COM.* 2011, 571. Available online: https://www.eea.europa.eu/policy-documents/com-2011-571-roadmap-to (accessed on 1 February 2023).
2. European Parliament and Council Directive 2000/76/EC of the European Parliament and of the Council of 4 December 2000 on the Incineration of Waste. *Off. J. Eur. Communities L* **2000**, *332*, 91–111.
3. Mønster, J.; Kjeldsen, P.; Scheutz, C. Methodologies for Measuring Fugitive Methane Emissions from Landfills—A Review. *Waste Manag.* **2019**, *87*, 835–859. [CrossRef] [PubMed]
4. Awasthi, M.K.; Sarsaiya, S.; Patel, A.; Juneja, A.; Singh, R.P.; Yan, B.; Awasthi, S.K.; Jain, A.; Liu, T.; Duan, Y.; et al. Refining Biomass Residues for Sustainable Energy and Bio-Products: An Assessment of Technology, Its Importance, and Strategic Applications in Circular Bio-Economy. *Renew. Sustain. Energy Rev.* **2020**, *127*, 109876. [CrossRef]
5. Fan, S.; Li, A.; ter Heijne, A.; Buisman, C.J.N.; Chen, W.-S. Heat Potential, Generation, Recovery and Utilization from Composting: A Review. *Resour. Conserv. Recycl.* **2021**, *175*, 105850. [CrossRef]
6. Zagklis, D.; Tsigkou, K.; Tsafrakidou, P.; Zafiri, C.; Kornaros, M. Life Cycle Assessment of the Anaerobic Co-Digestion of Used Disposable Nappies and Expired Food Products. *J. Clean. Prod.* **2021**, *304*, 127118. [CrossRef]
7. Smith, M.; Smit, T.; Gardiner, A. *Financial Support for Electricity Generation & CHP from Solid Biomass*; Natural Resources Defense Council: Rotterdam, The Netherlands, 2019.
8. Jenkins, B.M.; Baxter, L.L.; Koppejan, J. Biomass Combustion. In *Thermochem Process Biomass Convers into Fuels, Chemicals and Power*; Willey Online Library: Hoboken, NJ, USA, 2019; pp. 49–83. [CrossRef]
9. Vainio, E. *Fate of Fuel-Bound Nitrogen and Sulfur in Biomass-Fired Industrial Boilers*; 2014.
10. Hupa, M.; Karlström, O.; Vainio, E. Biomass Combustion Technology Development–It Is All about Chemical Details. *Proc. Combust. Inst.* **2017**, *36*, 113–134. [CrossRef]
11. Nunes, L.J.R.; Matias, J.C.O.; Catalão, J.P.S. Biomass Combustion Systems: A Review on the Physical and Chemical Properties of the Ashes. *Renew. Sustain. Energy Rev.* **2016**, *53*, 235–242. [CrossRef]
12. Obaidullah, M.; Bram, S.; Verma, V.K.; De Ruyck, J. A Review on Particle Emissions from Small Scale Biomass Combustion. *Int. J. Renew. Energy Res.* **2012**, *2*, 147–159.
13. Arena, U. Process and Technological Aspects of Municipal Solid Waste Gasification. A Review. *Waste Manag.* **2012**, *32*, 625–639. [CrossRef]
14. AlNouss, A.; McKay, G.; Al-Ansari, T. A Comparison of Steam and Oxygen Fed Biomass Gasification through a Techno-Economic-Environmental Study. *Energy Convers. Manag.* **2020**, *208*, 112612. [CrossRef]

15. Shahabuddin, M.; Alam, M.T.; Krishna, B.B.; Bhaskar, T.; Perkins, G. A Review on the Production of Renewable Aviation Fuels from the Gasification of Biomass and Residual Wastes. *Bioresour. Technol.* **2020**, *312*, 123596. [CrossRef]
16. Wang, G.; Dai, Y.; Yang, H.; Xiong, Q.; Wang, K.; Zhou, J.; Li, Y.; Wang, S. A Review of Recent Advances in Biomass Pyrolysis. *Energy Fuels* **2020**, *34*, 15557–15578. [CrossRef]
17. White, J.E.; Catallo, W.J.; Legendre, B.L. Biomass Pyrolysis Kinetics: A Comparative Critical Review with Relevant Agricultural Residue Case Studies. *J. Anal. Appl. Pyrolysis* **2011**, *91*, 1–33. [CrossRef]
18. Kan, T.; Strezov, V.; Evans, T.J. Lignocellulosic Biomass Pyrolysis: A Review of Product Properties and Effects of Pyrolysis Parameters. *Renew. Sustain. Energy Rev.* **2016**, *57*, 1126–1140. [CrossRef]
19. Hu, X.; Gholizadeh, M. Biomass Pyrolysis: A Review of the Process Development and Challenges from Initial Researches up to the Commercialisation Stage. *J. Energy Chem.* **2019**, *39*, 109–143. [CrossRef]
20. Ascher, S.; Watson, I.; You, S. Machine Learning Methods for Modelling the Gasification and Pyrolysis of Biomass and Waste. *Renew. Sustain. Energy Rev.* **2022**, *155*, 111902. [CrossRef]
21. European Environment Agency. *EN34 Energy Subsidies*; European Environment Agency: Copenhagen, Denmark, 2005; pp. 1–9.
22. Eaton, A.D.; Clesceri, L.S.; Greenberg, A.E.; Franson, M.A.H. *Standard Methods for the Examination of Water and Wastewater*, 22nd ed.; APHA: American Water Works Association: Washington, DC, USA, 2012.
23. Sohi, S.P.; Krull, E.; Lopez-Capel, E.; Bol, R. A Review of Biochar and Its Use and Function in Soil. *Adv. Agron.* **2010**, *105*, 47–82.
24. Legan, M.; Gotvajn, A.Ž.; Zupan, K. Potential of Biochar Use in Building Materials. *J. Environ. Manage.* **2022**, *309*, 114704. [CrossRef]
25. Schmidt, H.-P.; Hagemann, N.; Draper, K.; Kammann, C. The Use of Biochar in Animal Feeding. *PeerJ* **2019**, *7*, e7373. [CrossRef]
26. Peters, M.S.; Timmerhaus, K.D.; West, R.E. *Plant Design and Economics for Chemical Engineers*; McGraw-Hill: New York, NY, USA, 2003; Volume 4.
27. Tsigkou, K.; Zagklis, D.; Tsafrakidou, P.; Zapanti, P.; Manthos, G.; Karamitou, K.; Zafiri, C.; Kornaros, M. Expired Food Products and Used Disposable Adult Nappies Mesophilic Anaerobic Co-Digestion: Biochemical Methane Potential, Feedstock Pretreatment and Two-Stage System Performance. *Renew. Energy* **2021**, *168*, 309–318. [CrossRef]
28. Olanders, B.; Steenari, B.-M. Characterization of Ashes from Wood and Straw. *Biomass Bioenergy* **1995**, *8*, 105–115. [CrossRef]
29. Bourgois, J.; Guyonnet, R. Characterization and Analysis of Torrefied Wood. *Wood Sci. Technol.* **1988**, *22*, 143–155. [CrossRef]
30. Rispoli, A.L.; Verdone, N.; Vilardi, G. Green Fuel Production by Coupling Plastic Waste Oxy-Combustion and PtG Technologies: Economic, Energy, Exergy and CO_2-Cycle Analysis. *Fuel Process. Technol.* **2021**, *221*, 106922. [CrossRef]
31. Gala, A.; Guerrero, M.; Serra, J.M. Characterization of Post-Consumer Plastic Film Waste from Mixed MSW in Spain: A Key Point for the Successful Implementation of Sustainable Plastic Waste Management Strategies. *Waste Manag.* **2020**, *111*, 22–33. [CrossRef]
32. Bae, Y.J.; Ryu, C.; Jeon, J.-K.; Park, J.; Suh, D.J.; Suh, Y.-W.; Chang, D.; Park, Y.-K. The Characteristics of Bio-Oil Produced from the Pyrolysis of Three Marine Macroalgae. *Bioresour. Technol.* **2011**, *102*, 3512–3520. [CrossRef]
33. Zagklis, D.; Konstantinidou, E.; Zafiri, C.; Kornaros, M. Assessing the Economic Viability of an Animal Byproduct Rendering Plant: Case Study of a Slaughterhouse in Greece. *Sustainability* **2020**, *12*, 5870. [CrossRef]
34. Manelis, G.C. *Techno-Economic Evaluation of Energy Crops for the Production and Exploitation of Biomass*; 2012.
35. Chau, J.; Sowlati, T.; Sokhansanj, S.; Preto, F.; Melin, S.; Bi, X. Techno-Economic Analysis of Wood Biomass Boilers for the Greenhouse Industry. *Appl. Energy* **2009**, *86*, 364–371. [CrossRef]
36. Ghafghazi, S.; Sowlati, T.; Sokhansanj, S.; Melin, S. Techno-economic Analysis of Renewable Energy Source Options for a District Heating Project. *Int. J. Energy Res.* **2010**, *34*, 1109–1120. [CrossRef]
37. Semple, L.; Carriveau, R.; Ting, D.S.-K. A Techno-Economic Analysis of Seasonal Thermal Energy Storage for Greenhouse Applications. *Energy Build.* **2017**, *154*, 175–187. [CrossRef]
38. Chau, J.; Sowlati, T.; Sokhansanj, S.; Preto, F.; Melin, S.; Bi, X. Economic Sensitivity of Wood Biomass Utilization for Greenhouse Heating Application. *Appl. Energy* **2009**, *86*, 616–621. [CrossRef]
39. Sagani, A.; Hagidimitriou, M.; Dedoussis, V. Techno-Economic Evaluation of Tree Pruning Biomass Fired Power Plants for Electricity Generation: The Case of Three Prefectures in Greece. In Proceedings of the 22nd European Biomass Conference and Exhibition, Hamburg, Germany, 23–26 June 2014; pp. 2282–5819.
40. Goverment, G. 4414/2016- New Support Regime for Power Plants from Renewable Energy Sources and High-Efficiency Cogeneration of Electricity and Heat—Provisions for the Legal and Operational Separation of Supply Sectors 2016. Available online: https://www.rae.gr/7089-2/?lang=en (accessed on 2 January 2023).
41. Al-Rikabi, N.S. Profitability Index and Its Impact on Short And Long–Term Decisions. *J. Leg. Ethical Regul. Issues* **2021**, *24*, 1–14.
42. Candia, R.A.R.; Subieta, S.L.B.; Ramos, J.A.A.; Miquélez, V.S.; Balderrama, J.G.P.; Florero, H.J.; Quoilin, S. Techno-Economic Assessment of High Variable Renewable Energy Penetration in the Bolivian Interconnected Electric System. *Int. J. Sustain. Energy Plan. Manag.* **2019**, *22*.
43. Morató, T.; Vaezi, M.; Kumar, A. Techno-Economic Assessment of Biomass Combustion Technologies to Generate Electricity in South America: A Case Study for Bolivia. *Renew. Sustain. Energy Rev.* **2020**, *134*, 110154. [CrossRef]
44. Luz, F.C.; Rocha, M.H.; Lora, E.E.S.; Venturini, O.J.; Andrade, R.V.; Leme, M.M.V.; del Olmo, O.A. Techno-Economic Analysis of Municipal Solid Waste Gasification for Electricity Generation in Brazil. *Energy Convers. Manag.* **2015**, *103*, 321–337. [CrossRef]
45. Rentizelas, A.; Karellas, S.; Kakaras, E.; Tatsiopoulos, I. Comparative Techno-Economic Analysis of ORC and Gasification for Bioenergy Applications. *Energy Convers. Manag.* **2009**, *50*, 674–681. [CrossRef]

46. Wang, S.; Mukhambet, Y.; Esakkimuthu, S. Integrated Microalgal Biorefinery–Routes, Energy, Economic and Environmental Perspectives. *J. Clean. Prod.* **2022**, 131245. [CrossRef]
47. Solarte-Toro, J.C.; González-Aguirre, J.A.; Giraldo, J.A.P.; Alzate, C.A.C. Thermochemical Processing of Woody Biomass: A Review Focused on Energy-Driven Applications and Catalytic Upgrading. *Renew. Sustain. Energy Rev.* **2021**, *136*, 110376. [CrossRef]
48. Burrell, L.D.; Zehetner, F.; Rampazzo, N.; Wimmer, B.; Soja, G. Long-Term Effects of Biochar on Soil Physical Properties. *Geoderma* **2016**, *282*, 96–102. [CrossRef]
49. Tan, X.; Liu, S.; Liu, Y.; Gu, Y.; Zeng, G.; Hu, X.; Wang, X.; Liu, S.; Jiang, L. Biochar as Potential Sustainable Precursors for Activated Carbon Production: Multiple Applications in Environmental Protection and Energy Storage. *Bioresour. Technol.* **2017**, *227*, 359–372. [CrossRef]
50. Pighinelli, A.L.M.T.; Schaffer, M.A.; Boateng, A.A. Utilization of Eucalyptus for Electricity Production in Brazil via Fast Pyrolysis: A Techno-Economic Analysis. *Renew. Energy* **2018**, *119*, 590–597. [CrossRef]
51. He, S.; Barati, B.; Hu, X.; Wang, S. Carbon Migration of Microalgae from Cultivation towards Biofuel Production by Hydrothermal Technology: A Review. *Fuel Process. Technol.* **2023**, *240*, 107563. [CrossRef]
52. Kookos, I. *Introduction to Chemical Plant Design*; Tziolas: Thessaloniki, Greece, 2009; ISBN 978-960-418-173-5.
53. Ramos, J.S.; Ferreira, A.F. Techno-Economic Analysis and Life Cycle Assessment of Olive and Wine Industry Co-Products Valorisation. *Renew. Sustain. Energy Rev.* **2022**, *155*, 111929. [CrossRef]
54. Yang, Y.; Wang, J.; Chong, K.; Bridgwater, A. V A Techno-Economic Analysis of Energy Recovery from Organic Fraction of Municipal Solid Waste (MSW) by an Integrated Intermediate Pyrolysis and Combined Heat and Power (CHP) Plant. *Energy Convers. Manag.* **2018**, *174*, 406–416. [CrossRef]
55. Ramirez, J.A.; Rainey, T.J. Comparative Techno-Economic Analysis of Biofuel Production through Gasification, Thermal Liquefaction and Pyrolysis of Sugarcane Bagasse. *J. Clean. Prod.* **2019**, *229*, 513–527. [CrossRef]

Disclaimer/Publisher's Note: The statements, opinions and data contained in all publications are solely those of the individual author(s) and contributor(s) and not of MDPI and/or the editor(s). MDPI and/or the editor(s) disclaim responsibility for any injury to people or property resulting from any ideas, methods, instructions or products referred to in the content.

Article

Candidatus Scalindua, a Biological Solution to Treat Saline Recirculating Aquaculture System Wastewater

Federico Micolucci [1,2,†], Jonathan A. C. Roques [1,2,*,†], Geoffrey S. Ziccardi [1,2,3], Naoki Fujii [4], Kristina Sundell [1,2] and Tomonori Kindaichi [4,*]

1. Department of Biological and Environmental Sciences, University of Gothenburg, P.O. Box 463, SE-405 30 Gothenburg, Sweden
2. Swedish Mariculture Research Center (SWEMARC), University of Gothenburg, P.O. Box 463, SE-405 30 Gothenburg, Sweden
3. Department of Marine Sciences, University of Gothenburg, P.O. Box 100, SE-405 30 Gothenburg, Sweden
4. Department of Civil and Environmental Engineering, Graduate School of Advanced Science and Engineering, Hiroshima University, 1-4-1 Kagamiyama, Higashihiroshima JP-739-8527, Japan
* Correspondence: jonathan.roques@bioenv.gu.se (J.A.C.R.); tomokin@hiroshima-u.ac.jp (T.K.); Tel.: +46-72-566-4951 (J.A.C.R.); +81-82-424-5718 (T.K.)
† These authors contributed equally to this work.

Highlights:

- The anammox process is a promising technique to treat nitrogen-rich marine RAS WW.
- The anammox strain *Ca.* Scalindua was successfully acclimated to high salinity marine RAS wastewater.
- Despite a slight decrease in population over the time, *Ca.* Scalindua remained the major species within the granules and was able to maintain a high nitrogen removal rate while exposed to RAS WW in the absence of TE supplementation.

Abstract: Recirculating aquaculture systems (RAS) are promising candidates for the sustainable development of the aquaculture industry. A current limitation of RAS is the production and potential accumulation of nitrogenous wastes, ammonium (NH_4^+), nitrite (NO_2^-) and nitrate (NO_3^-), which could affect fish health and welfare. In a previous experiment, we have demonstrated that the marine anammox bacteria *Candidatus* Scalindua was a promising candidate to treat the wastewater (WW) of marine, cold-water RAS. However, the activity of the bacteria was negatively impacted after a direct exposure to RAS WW. In the current study, we have further investigated the potential of *Ca.* Scalindua to treat marine RAS WW in a three-phase experiment. In the first phase (control, 83 days), *Ca.* Scalindua was fed a synthetic feed, enriched in NH_4^+, NO_2^- and trace element (TE) mix. Removal rates of 98.9% and 99.6% for NH_4^+ and NO_2^-, respectively, were achieved. In the second phase (116 days), we gradually increased the exposure of *Ca.* Scalindua to nitrogen-enriched RAS WW over a period of about 80 days. In the last phase (79 days), we investigated the needs of TE supplementation for the *Ca.* Scalindua after they were fully acclimated to 100% RAS WW. Our results show that the gradual exposure of *Ca.* Scalindua resulted in a successful acclimation to 100% RAS WW, with maintained high removal rates of both NH_4^+ and NO_2^- throughout the experiment. Despite a slight decrease in relative abundance (from 21.4% to 16.7%), *Ca.* Scalindua remained the dominant species in the granules throughout the whole experiment. We conclude that *Ca.* Scalindua can be successfully used to treat marine RAS WW, without the addition of TE, once given enough time to acclimate to its new substrate. Future studies need to determine the specific needs for optimal RAS WW treatment by *Ca.* Scalindua at pilot scale.

Keywords: "*Candidatus* Scalindua"; anaerobic ammonium oxidation (anammox); recirculating aquaculture system (RAS); wastewater treatment; trace elements

Citation: Micolucci, F.; Roques, J.A.C.; Ziccardi, G.S.; Fujii, N.; Sundell, K.; Kindaichi, T. *Candidatus* Scalindua, a Biological Solution to Treat Saline Recirculating Aquaculture System Wastewater. *Processes* **2023**, *11*, 690. https://doi.org/10.3390/pr11030690

Academic Editors: Dimitris Zagklis and Georgios Bampos

Received: 7 February 2023
Revised: 20 February 2023
Accepted: 22 February 2023
Published: 24 February 2023

Copyright: © 2023 by the authors. Licensee MDPI, Basel, Switzerland. This article is an open access article distributed under the terms and conditions of the Creative Commons Attribution (CC BY) license (https://creativecommons.org/licenses/by/4.0/).

1. Introduction

The world population has reached 8 billion at the end of 2022, and is predicted to reach 9.7 billion by 2050 [1]. There is an urgent need to increase healthy, nutritious and sustainable food production to feed this growing world population [2]. Fish products are rich in high quality protein and are generally considered to be healthy (i.e., rich in long-chain omega-3 fatty acids, vitamins and trace elements) [3]. With the stagnation of capture fisheries, there is a global consensus about the importance of the aquaculture sector as an essential source of food [2,3]. The intensification of this sector is, however, accompanied by the raising of environmental concerns, especially regarding the leakage of nutrients to the environment [4]. It is, therefore, important to develop novel techniques for treatment of wastewater (WW) from fish farms, including chemical, mechanical and biological filtrations, in order to further develop this sector in a sustainable way [5–8].

Land-based closed and semi-closed fish farming systems, such as recirculating aquaculture systems (RAS) have been proposed as potential candidates to improve the sustainability of the aquaculture sector. These systems allow for a high degree of water reuse and provide a more stable farming environment and reduced environmental impact compared to traditional open-cage systems [9–12].

In RAS, nitrifying bacteria convert the ammonium (NH_4^+) produced by the fish into nitrate (NO_3^-) via nitrite (NO_2^-) in the presence of oxygen (O_2) (Figure 1A). As a result, NO_3^- can slowly accumulate over time and reach concentrations which could affect fish health and welfare [10,13,14]. High NO_3^- can be managed through biological conversion of NO_3^- to nitrogen gas (N_2) in anaerobic denitrifying biofilters, or by regular water exchanges [15,16]. However, denitrification compartments are not always present in RAS, as this process can lead to the formation and accumulation of intermediate, extremely toxic substances (i.e., NO_2^-, NO and N_2O) [17,18]. As a result, part of the water has to be exchanged regularly in systems without a denitrification compartment, which constitute the vast majority of RAS today.

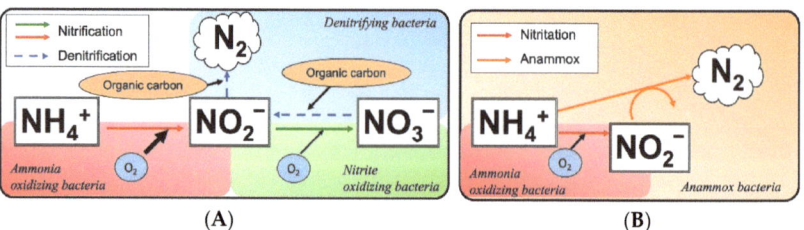

Figure 1. The conventional nitrogen removal process in RAS, with nitrification and denitrification compartments (**A**); the nitritation (partial nitrification)/anammox process (**B**).

The anammox (anaerobic ammonia oxidation) process is a cost-effective and environmentally-friendly way to remove nitrogen compounds from WW [19]. It is a chemoautotrophic biological process, where 1 mol of NH_4^+ is transformed into 1.02 mol of N_2 gas using NO_2^- (1.32 mol) as the electron acceptor and, therefore, needing a partial nitrification (nitritation, Figure 1B) [20–22]. The additional advantages of this process are its low requirements for both O_2 and organic carbon sources, as well as a low production of global warming gases [23–26]. Therefore, the anammox process has attracted more and more attention throughout the world. The anammox-related nitrogen removal process presented here provides a new perspective for future RAS WW treatment.

In 2013, Borin and colleagues [27] detected the presence of the marine strain of anammox, "*Candidatus* Scalindua" (hereafter *Ca.* Scalindua) in deep marine hypersaline gradient systems in the Eastern Mediterranean Sea. The anammox granules were found at 204‰ salinity (204 g L^{-1}). Furthermore, a high nitrogen removal rate (10.7 kg N m^{-3} day^{-1}) was obtained in an anaerobic sludge blanket reactor [28]. Moreover, these marine anammox strains could maintain stable nitrogen removal at a salinity of 50 ‰ [29]. These results suggest that the anammox process has good potential to treat saline (>30‰) WW from marine aquaculture systems [30–32]. Despite these promising results, few studies have focused on the use of anammox bacteria for treatment of marine WW in aquaculture to date.

In our previous study, we have demonstrated that *Ca.* Scalindua remained the dominant species found in the granules of our anaerobic anammox rector throughout the different experimental phases, including after exposure to RAS WW [33]. In this experiment, the anammox was either fed a standard synthetic anammox feed enriched with NH_4^+ and NO_2^- and supplemented with a mix of trace elements (TE) or they were abruptly exposed to 100% RAS WW enriched with NH_4^+ and NO_2^- for short periods, in the absence or presence of TE. This TE mix, composed of 9 TE (Table 1)) was developed when the first freshwater anammox species was isolated and is currently used as a standard in anammox cultures worldwide [34]. The nitrogen removal capacity of the anammox was negatively affected by the abrupt changes to 100% RAS WW without TE, while a subsequent addition of TE led to a slight recovery [33]. We concluded that the reduction in activity could be caused by the abrupt change of medium (from synthetic feed to RAS WW), either because of high levels of unknown compounds (i.e., NO_3^-) present in the RAS WW, and/or the lack/or inappropriate concentration of certain key TE in this new medium.

Table 1. Composition of the TE mix (as reported by van de Graaf and colleagues [34]).

TE	B	Co	Cu	Fe	Mn	Mo	Ni	Se	Zn
Concentration ($\mu g\ L^{-1}$)	2.4	28.3	63.6	1840	274.8	96.4	46.9	47.9	97.8

In the current study, we aim to investigate in greater detail, the growth mechanisms and medium requirements of the marine anammox bacteria *Ca.* Scalindua for use in marine RAS. The specific objectives were to investigate: (1) if a slow adaptation to RAS WW could lead to a better functioning of the *Ca.* Scalindua, and (2) if the TE supplementation is necessary for the normal functioning of this marine strain of anammox bacteria. As all the 9 TE elements used in the standard feed [34] are already present in seawater [33], there might not be a need for a supplementation.

2. Materials and Methods

2.1. RAS WW Collection and Characteristics

RAS WW (Table 2) was collected from the aquarium facilities of the University of Gothenburg (Gothenburg, Sweden), hosting a pilot-scale research and development facility for development of land-based marine RAS at low temperatures (ca. 10 °C). The fish species in the marine RAS were rainbow trout (*Oncorhynchus mykiss*) and Atlantic wolffish (*Anarhichas lupus*). The water samples were collected 3–8 h after the feeding of the animals to capture a peak in NH_4^+ [35–37] and immediately used to prepare the feed for the anammox reactors.

Table 2. Physicochemical characteristics of the RAS WW. Values show the average and standard deviation during the period.

Parameter	Salinity (‰)	NH_4^+ (mg-N L^{-1})	NO_2^- (mg-N L^{-1})	NO_3^- (mg-N L^{-1})	pH	TSS [1] (mg L^{-1})	COD [2] (mg-C L^{-1})	Total P [3] (mg-P L^{-1})
Value	29 ± 1	6.22 ± 2.34	2.24 ± 0.69	1.81 ± 0.88	7.3 ± 0.3	58.8 ± 5.6	39.5 ± 5.3	2.6 ± 0.7

[1] TSS, Total dissolved solids; [2] COD, Chemical oxygen demand; [3] Total P, Total phosphorous.

2.2. Reactors Operation

Ca. Scalindua granules were harvested from an up-flow column anammox stock culture that has been operating with a continuous supply of inorganic nutrient media containing NH_4^+ (28 mg-N L^{-1}) and NO_2^- (34 mg-N L^{-1}) [34] at the University of Hiroshima (Higashihiroshima, Japan) for more than 10 years [38–40]. A biomass (ca. 5 g wet weight) was brought to the University in Gothenburg in August 2019 and was used as inoculum into a glass column reactor (Ø 50 mm; volume, 325 cm^3, KF-50, AS ONE, Tokyo, Japan, Figure 2) with a nonwoven fabric sheet (Japan Vilene, Tokyo, Japan) as biofilm carrier material. The reactor was fed with synthetic marine WW (Aquaforest, Brzesko, Poland) supplemented with nitrogen (NH_4^+ and NO_2^-) and TE, as described earlier [33,34] (Table 1). The reactor temperature was maintained at 28 °C throughout the experimental period, and the initial hydraulic retention time (HRT) was 4.6 h (Table 3). The reactor reached a steady state (removal rates of NH_4^+ and NO_2^- over 95% and it was kept under the same conditions until the start of the experiment (ca. 700 days after the initial inoculation). The reactor used in this study was operated for 280 days in 3 experimental phases.

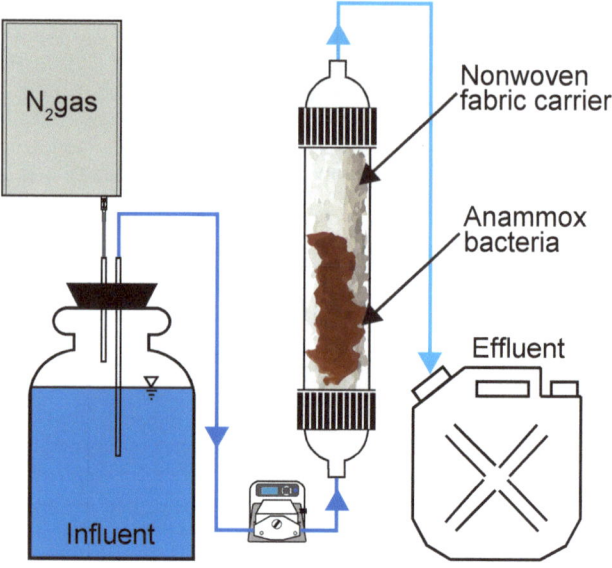

Figure 2. Schematic drawing of the up-flow column reactor.

Table 3. Operational conditions of the column rector.

Phase	Period (d)	AS/RAS [1]	TE [2]	HRT (h)	Nitrogen Loading Rate (g-TN L^{-1} day^{-1}) [3]
1	0–83	AS	+	4.6	0.38 ± 0.03
2	84–200	RAS	+	4.4	0.32 ± 0.06
3	201–280	RAS	−	4.8	0.35 ± 0.04

[1] AS, Artificial seawater; RAS, recirculating aquaculture system WW; [2] TE: Trace element mix (+, presence; −, absence), reported by van de Graaf and colleagues [34]; [3] Values show the average and standard deviation during the period.

During Phase 1 (days 0–83), the reactor was fed with the same synthetic marine WW supplemented with nitrogen (NH_4^+ and NO_2^-) and TE as was arranged earlier [33,34]. During Phase 2 (days 84–200), the reactor was exposed to gradually increasing concentrations of RAS WW. The substitution of the synthetic feed to 100% RAS WW was gradual; 10–30% of RAS WW was substituted every 10–20 days. The RAS WW characteristics were adjusted to approximately match the standard medium for *Ca.* Scalindua regarding salinity (29‰), NH_4^+ (28 mg-N L^{-1}), NO_2^- (30 mg-N L^{-1}) and inorganic carbon ($KHCO_3$, 1000 mg L^{-1}) [38,39]. During Phases 1 and 2, the feed was supplemented with a mix of TE. In the final phase, Phase 3 (days 201–280), the reactor was fed with 100% RAS WW, still supplemented with nitrogen, but in the absence of TE. During Phases 2 and 3, the reactor was slowly adapted to RAS WW with fluctuating concentrations of NH_4^+, NO_2^- and NO_3^- (6.22 ± 2.34 mg-N L^{-1}, 2.24 ± 0.69 mg-N L^{-1} and 1.81 ± 0.88 mg-N L^{-1} on average, respectively, Table 2). The NH_4^+ and NO_2^- supplementation was adapted accordingly to ensure concentrations of these compounds, similar to Phase 1 (Figure 3). However, there was some slight fluctuation in terms of concentration regarding these nitrogen compounds, mimicking what can occur in a full-scale RAS. Although the inlet concentrations varied, the system maintained a high removal efficiency of the compounds (Figure 4).

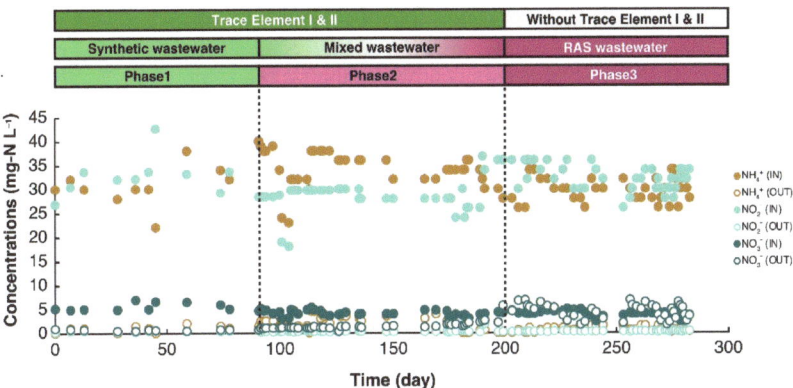

Figure 3. Concentration of NH_4^+, NO_2^- and NO_3^- in the influent (filled circles) and effluent (open circles) throughout the experiment.

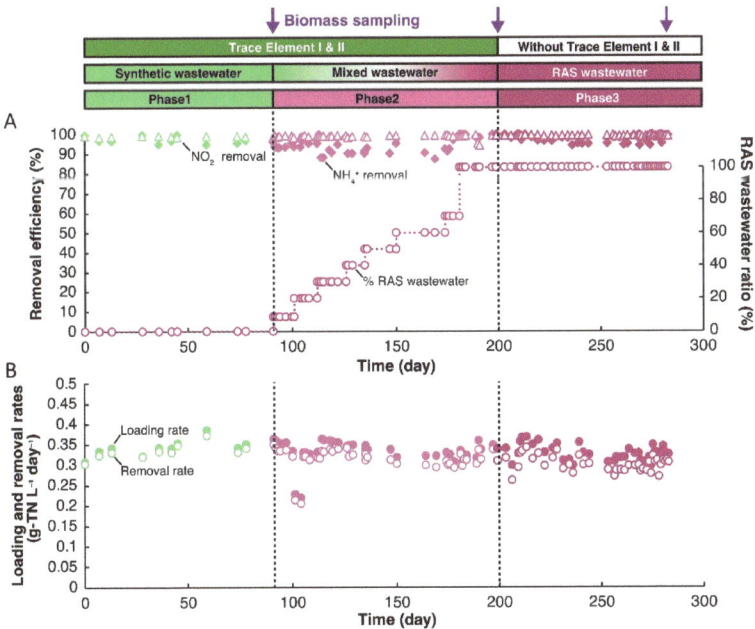

Figure 4. Anammox performance in the reactor. (**A**) NH_4^+ (closed diamonds) and NO_2^- (open triangles) removal efficiencies. (**B**) Nitrogen loading and removal rates (filled and open circles, respectively). Dotted lines and open circle indicate changes in operational phase (artificial seawater or RAS WW, the presence of TE). RAS, recirculating aquaculture system WW; TE, trace element solutions. Purple arrows indicate biomass sampling on days 83, 200, and 280.

Each WW feed was flushed with N_2 gas for at least 30 min before adding the different chemicals to achieve a concentration of dissolved O_2 below 0.5 mg L^{-1}, and the pH was adjusted to ca. 7.0 with a solution of 1 mol L^{-1} H_2SO_4 [34]. The influents were continuously introduced into the reactor using a peristaltic pump (Masterflex L/S Economy Drive, Cole-Parmer Instruments, Vernon Hills, IL, USA).

2.3. Analytical Methods

The total nitrogen (TN) loading and removal rates were calculated based on the concentrations of the nitrogenous compounds (NX; NH_4^+, NO_2^-, and NO_3^-) as well as the HRT (Figures 3 and 4, Table 3), according to the following:

Removal efficiency (%) = [[Influent NX-N (mg-N L^{-1})] − [Effluent NX-N (mg-N L^{-1})]]/ [Effluent NX-N (mg-NL^{-1})] × 100

Removal rate (g-TN L^{-1} day^{-1}) = [[Influent NX-N (mg-N L^{-1})] − [Effluent NX-N (mg-N L^{-1})]] × [Influent volumetric flow rate (L day^{-1})]/[Volume of the tank (L)]

HRT (h) = Volume of the reactor (L)/Influent volumetric flow rate (L h^{-1})

Salinity, O_2 and temperature was determined using a conductivity meter portable Multimeter pHenomenal MU 6100 H (VWR international, Radnor, PA, USA). Analyses of total suspended solids (TSS) were carried out in accordance with the Standard Methods [41]. COD and Total P were measured with a DR-2800 UV-visible spectrophotometer (Hach-Lange, Dusseldorf, Germany) using the LCK1814 and the powder pillow PhosVer 3 (ascorbic acid method, 8048) methods, respectively (Hach-Lange, Dusseldorf, Germany).

The NH_4^+ and NO_2^- concentrations were determined using the powder pillow methods (salicylate method, 8155, and diazotization method, 8507, respectively, Hach-Lange, Dusseldorf, Germany) and the DR-2800. The concentrations of NO_3^- were determined using ion-exchange chromatography (HPLC 20A; Shimadzu, Kyoto, Japan) with a Shodex Asahipak NH2P-50 4D anion column (Showa Denko, Tokyo, Japan) and UV–Vis detector (SPD-20AV, Shimadzu) after filtration of samples through 0.2-μm pore-size PTFE membranes (Advantec, Tokyo, Japan) [42].

2.4. Microbial Community Analysis

To determine the potential changes in the microbial community composition during the different phases, biomass samples for the amplicon sequencing were collected from the reactor at the end of each experimental phase (days 83, 200 and 280). DNA was extracted using a FastDNA SPIN kit for soil (MP Biomedicals, Santa Ana, SC, USA). PCR amplification of the bacterial 16S rRNA gene was performed with a primer set for amplification of the V3-V4 region as follows: 341F (5′-CCTACGGGNGGCWGCAG-3′) and 805R (5′-GGACTACHVGGGTATCTAATCC-3′). The details of PCR amplification were as described previously [43]. PCR products were purified using the Agencourt AMPure XP system (Beckman Coulter, Brea, CA, USA) according to manufacturer instructions. Purified DNA was sequenced using a MiSeq platform with a MiSeq reagent kit (v.3; Illumina, San Diego, CA, USA).

Obtained sequences were trimmed and assembled as described previously [44]. Sequence data were analyzed using QIIME 2 Core 2020.2 distribution [45]. Operational taxonomic units (OTUs) were assigned with the SILVA 132 database [46]. OTUs that accounted for >0.5% of the total reads were used for bar-plots representation. The sequence data in the present study was deposited in the DNA Data Bank of Japan (DDBJ) database under the DDBJ/EMBL/GenBank accession number DRA015143.

2.5. Fluorescence In Situ Hybridization (FISH)

Biomass samples were collected from the up-flow column reactor at the end of each experimental phase (days 83, 200, and 280). Sample fixation and the following FISH procedure were described previously [47]. The probes used in this study were as follows: a mixture of EUB338, II, III, and IV probes labelled with Alexa Fluor 647 specific for all bacteria [48,49] and Sca1129b probes labelled with Alexa Fluor 555 specific for Ca. Scalindua [39]. Hybridized samples were observed with an Axiomager M1 epifluorescence microscope with a 100 W HBO lamp. Images were obtained using an AxioCam MRm version 3 FireWiremonocrome camera and AxioVision software, version 4.5 (Carl Zeiss, Oberkochen, Germany).

3. Results

3.1. Reactor Performance

During Phase 1 (synthetic WW and TE), the TN removal rate showed high efficiency while maintaining constant TN loading rates (Figure 4). Once the reactor continued to maintain a stable state (from day 0 to 83), the average TN loading and removal rates were 0.32 ± 0.05 and 0.30 ± 0.03 g-TN L^{-1} day^{-1}, respectively (HRT 4.6 h). At the end of Phase 1 (day 83), the removal efficiency had reached 94% for NH_4^+ and 99% for NO_2^-, showing a successful establishment of the anammox process in the reactor [38].

During Phase 2 (days 84–200), the use of RAS WW instead of artificial seawater was implemented with a gradual substitution within about a 3-month period (10–30% every 10–20 days, Figure 4). The average TN loading rate during this phase was kept constant at 0.32 ± 0.06 g-TN L^{-1} day^{-1}. During this phase, the removal efficiencies of NH_4^+ and NO_2^- were 94,3% and 98,8%, respectively (HRT 4.4 h) and the TN removal rate was 0.31 g-TN L^{-1} day^{-1}. These results clearly indicated that the method of acclimation lead to the removal of nitrogenous compounds by the anammox microorganisms at a high level of efficiency.

During Phase 3, RAS WW was used without the addition of TE and the HRT was slightly increased to 4.8 h (i.e., a slight decrease of TN loading rate). The NH_4^+ and NO_2^- removal efficiencies showed high efficiency in removal even during this phase.

3.2. Microbial Community Analysis and FISH

A total of 25 603, 30 130 and 28 109 non-chimeric reads and 139, 172 and 206 operational taxonomic units (OTUs) were obtained from days 83, 200 and 280, respectively. In this study, OTUs that accounted for >0.5% of the total reads were used for the analysis, and OTUs accounting for <0.5% of the reads were grouped as "Others" (Figure 5). Ca. Scalindua was identified as the most abundant species in the reactor throughout the experiment. Interestingly, the relative abundances of Ca. Scalindua did not drastically change over time. Despite a slight decrease (from 21.4% at the end of Phase 1 and 16.7% at the end of the experiment), it remained the most dominant species in the anammox granule, even during the phases with 100% RAS WW. The stability of the population of Ca. Scalindua, throughout all the different experimental phases, was also supported by FISH observations (Figure 6).

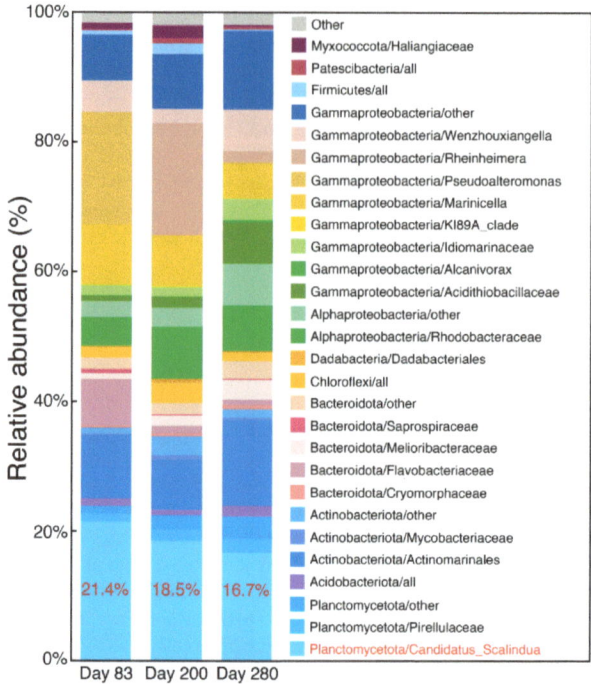

Figure 5. Microbial community composition at the end of each experimental phase (days 83, 200 and 280), based on 16S rRNA gene amplicon sequencing. Red percentages correspond to the relative abundance of the marine anammox *Ca.* Scalindua.

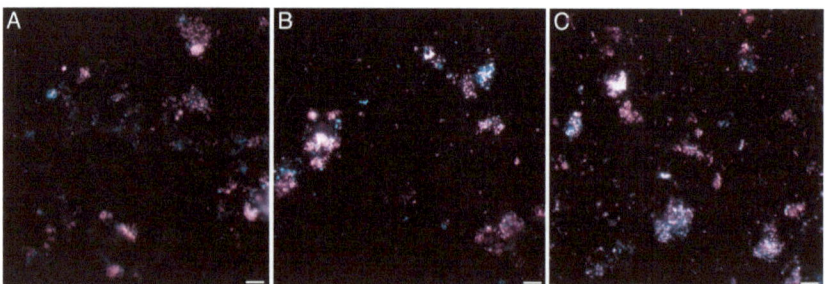

Figure 6. FISH micrographs of biomass collected from the column reactor at days 83 (**A**), 200 (**B**) and 280 (**C**). FISH was performed with Alexa Fluor 647-labelled EUB338mix probe (cyan) for all bacteria, and an Alexa Fluor 555-labelled Sca1129b probes (red) for *Ca.* Scalindua. *Ca.* Scalindua appears magenta and other bacteria appear blue. Scale bars represent 10 μm.

4. Discussion

4.1. Reactor Performance

The marine anammox species *Ca.* Scalindua has been isolated from coastal sediments from Hiroshima bay in 2007 [38]. Since then, inocula from the original samples have been successfully cultivated in Japan and Sweden, using the standard protocol developed by van de Graaf and colleagues [34]. During the first 83 days of our experiment, we continued to feed the anammox reactor with standard feed in order to maintain a steady state of high removal efficiencies with the utilization of synthetic WW as feed for the microorganisms. The efficiencies in terms of removal rate were extremely high and stable, with 98.3%

and 99.5% on average for NH_4^+ and NO_2^-, respectively. These removal rates remained stable when the synthetic feed was gradually replaced by RAS WW during the second phase (days 84–200), with average removal rates of 95.9% and 99.2% for NH_4^+ and NO_2^-, respectively. These removal rates were comparable to the removal rates obtained with the original sediment from Hiroshima bay (95% and 99%, respectively) [38]. These results confirm both the successful establishment and upkeep of the anammox process and the successful acclimation to RAS WW. The gradual increase of RAS WW, slowly replacing the standard feed, in the anammox feed method helped the microorganism to acclimate to this new substrate, as seen with the high and stable removal rates observed during this phase. Unlike what we observed in our previous experiment, the nitrogen removal efficiency was not compromised when allowed to slowly acclimate to RAS WW [33].

In this experiment, we further hypothesized that the reduction in removal rate observed could be due to the absence of certain key TE missing from the RAS WW [33]. Therefore, the last phase of our experiment was designed to verify this hypothesis, if once adapted to 100% marine RAS WW, supplemented with TE, the biomass would be able to maintain the removal capacity over time using pure marine RAS WW without TE supplementation. During this last phase, we continued to observe relatively high and stable removal rates for both NH_4^+ and NO_2^- (92.1% and 98.7%, respectively). Therefore, we can conclude that the required TE must have been present in appropriate quantities in the marine RAS WW to allow for the normal functioning of the anammox granules.

Today, the vast majority of anammox reactors are cultivated using a feed supplemented in 9 TE, which was originally designed for the first freshwater anammox bacteria isolated [34]. TE are essential for the normal functioning, growth and proliferation of the anammox bacteria [50–52]. It is essential to identify the specific TE requirements for each anammox species, as insufficient concentrations can limit normal cell functioning, division and proliferation within the granule, while too high concentrations can negatively impact the anammox process and potentially be lethal for the bacteria [51–54]. It is reasonable to hypothesize that different species of anammox bacteria may have different TE requirements. Marine strains of anammox bacteria, such as *Ca.* Scalindua, may have requirements that differ to those of the freshwater anammox most frequently studied [33,51,55]. To date, knowledge of the specific requirements regarding each individual TE is still scarce [51]. We have previously shown that all those 9 TE were present in the sea salt (Sealife, Marinetech, Tokyo, Japan) used to make the artificial marine water for the RAS from which RAS WW was used [33]. Finally, we have maintained the optimal culture condition for *Ca.* Scalindua throughout the different experimental phases. We have maintained strict anaerobic conditions through the degassing of the feed with N_2 gas prior connection to the reactor. *Ca.* Scalindua was further fed with RAS WW containing low NO_3^- levels and supplemented with NH_4^+ and NO_2^- [34]. As those optimal culture conditions might not be met in commercial-scale RAS, future studies need to investigate the performance of *Ca.* Scalindua under these real-life conditions.

4.2. Microbial Community

FISH and microbiological analysis have reflected a relatively stable population of *Ca.* Scalindua during all the phases of the experiment. Despite a slight decrease over time, *Ca.* Scalindua remained the main bacterial phylum present in the granule across the three experimental phases.

Overall, the relative abundance of bacterial phyla in the biomass samples also remained relatively stable throughout the different phases of the experiment. The small changes observed in the bacterial communities could be attributed to the high protein concentrations and/or the presence of other organic and inorganic residues (including NO_3^-) from waste, fish feces and uneaten feed in the RAS WW during Phases 2 and 3. Indeed, we observed an increase in non-chimeric reads and number of OTUs after the addition of RAS WW to the anammox feed. This additional load of bacteria from the RAS WW could have led to an artefact resulting in a slight reduction of *Ca.* Scalindua in the granule. This is supported by the fact that most of the changes observed concerning bacterial groups belonged to the *Gammaproteobacteria* class. These bacteria, mostly aerobic, are found in freshwater and marine environments including RAS, where they are often the predominant species [56–59]. Slight changes in the bacterial communities over time in the RAS, from which we obtain the WW, could therefore be the reason for the transient, differential colonization of anammox granules over the course of the experiment. Further studies specifically designed to follow the evolution and quantification of the biomass could help detail this.

At the taxonomic level, the main differences observed concern some changes in relative abundance within the class of *Gammaproteobacteria*. Here, we witnessed the total disappearance of *Pseudoalteromonas* after Phase 1 that were replaced by *Rheinheimera* in Phase 2, which are then almost totally replaced by *Wenzhouxiangella* and *Acidithiobacillaceae* during Phase 3 (Figure 5).

Pseudoalteromonas is a genus of gram-negative rods belonging to the family *Pseudoalteromonadaceae* [60]. Members of this family have very versatile metabolic capacities and are thought to play important ecological roles in marine environments [60]. These organisms accounted for a third of the species found in the denitrifying compartment of the denitrification bioreactor of an experimental, warm-water marine RAS [61]. This disappearance could be caused by the change of environment and less favorable conditions for these organisms driven by the addition of RAS WW.

Rheinheimera is a genus of gram-negative bacteria from the family of *Chromatiaceae*. These chemoheterotrophic organisms are widely found in freshwater and seawater environments, including fishponds, but prefer aerobic or microaerobic environments to grow [62–66]. These organisms may have originated from the RAS WW, being aerobic and probably bringing microorganisms from the system, during the slow introduction period during Phase 2. However, after the next phase, these bacteria were exposed to more than 200 days of anaerobic conditions, which most probably have impacted their growth and their relative abundance within the granules [62].

The *Wenzhouxiangella* genus belongs to the gram-negative *Wenzhouxiangellacea* family, they are found in marine, hypersaline, and soda lake environments [67]. Although some species are obligately aerobic and chemoheterotrophic [68], some species have shown a successful adaptation and steady growth under anaerobic conditions in the presence of NO_3^-, which corresponds well to the environment in the anammox reactor [67].

5. Conclusions and Perspectives

This study demonstrates that *Ca.* Scalindua can be used as an alternative denitrifying component in RAS. We have shown that a slow and gradual exposure of *Ca.* Scalindua resulted in a successful acclimation to full marine RAS WW, with maintained high removal rates (over 92%) of both NH_4^+ and NO_2^- throughout the different experimental phases.

The activity of *Ca.* Scalindua was not negatively affected by the organic compounds present in the marine RAS WW nor by the absence/imbalance of certain TE, as hypothesized earlier. The current study, thus, suggests that anammox reactors containing marine strains such as *Ca.* Scalindua could be directly applied to treat RAS WW, without TE supplementation. This represents a clear advantage of using marine anammox strains in marine RAS, as seawater already contains all the essential TE for the normal growth and functioning of these bacteria.

In this study, we maintained optimal culture condition for *Ca.* scalindua throughout the experimental phases. We maintained strict anaerobic conditions and *Ca.* Scalindua was fed with RAS WW containing high concentrations of NH_4^+ and NO_2^- and low concentration NO_3^-. Future studies need to investigate the performance of *Ca.* Scalindua under typical up-scaled RAS conditions regarding nitrogen compounds and O_2, in order to validate the use of marine anammox bacteria as nitrogen treatment technology in commercial scale RAS.

Author Contributions: Conceptualization, J.A.C.R., F.M. and T.K.; methodology, J.A.C.R., F.M., G.S.Z., N.F. and T.K.; software, N.F. and T.K.; validation, T.K.; formal analysis, J.A.C.R., F.M. and T.K.; investigation, J.A.C.R., F.M., G.S.Z., N.F. and T.K.; resources, J.A.C.R., F.M., K.S. and T.K.; data curation, J.A.C.R., F.M. and T.K., writing—original draft preparation, J.A.C.R., F.M. and T.K.; writing—review and editing, J.A.C.R., F.M., K.S. and T.K.; visualization, J.A.C.R., F.M. and T.K.; supervision, J.A.C.R., K.S. and T.K.; project administration, J.A.C.R.; funding acquisition, F.M., J.A.C.R., K.S. and T.K. All authors have read and agreed to the published version of the manuscript.

Funding: This research was conducted within the frame of the MIRAI project and was supported by FORMAS (2020-00867), the Carl Tryggers foundation, Stockholm, Sweden (20:418) the Helge Axelsson Johnsons foundation, Stockholm, Sweden (F19-0425 and F20-0272), the Wilhelm & Martina Lundgrens foundation, Gothenburg, Sweden (2020-3431 and 2021-3828), the Royal Society of Arts and Sciences in Gothenburg (KVVS), Gothenburg, Sweden, the Royal Swedish Academy of Agriculture and Forestry (KSLA), Stockholm, Sweden (VAT2020-0007), The Birgit och Birger Wåhlströms Minnesfond för den bohuslänska havs-och insjömiljön, Stockholm, Sweden, STINT, Stockholm, Sweden (mobility grant for internationalization, MG2019-8483), SWEMARC, the Swedish mariculture research center, strategic funding university of Gothenburg, Gothenburg, Sweden, JSPS KAKENHI Grant Numbers JP20KK0244, JP21K19866, Japan, and JSPS Bilateral Program, Grant number JPJSBP120219926, Japan.

Data Availability Statement: The sequence data in the present study was deposited in the DNA Data Bank of Japan (DDBJ) database under the DDBJ/EMBL/GenBank accession number DRA015143.

Acknowledgments: The authors are grateful to Hiromi Kambara, Darragh Doyle, James Hinchcliffe, Niklas Warwas, Miyuki Roques, Md Ashraful Alam and Linda Frank Hasselberg for their technical assistance.

Conflicts of Interest: The authors declare no conflict of interest.

References

1. United Nations, Department of Economic and Social Affairs, Population Division. *World Population Prospects, Online Edition*; Rev. 1; United Nations, Department of Economic and Social Affairs: New York, NY, USA, 2019.
2. Béné, C.; Barange, M.; Subasinghe, R.; Pinstrup-Andersen, P.; Merino, G.; Hemre, G.-I.; Williams, M. Feeding 9 billion by 2050–Putting fish back on the menu. *Food Secur.* **2015**, *7*, 261–274. [CrossRef]
3. FAO. *The State of World Fisheries and Aquaculture (SOFIA) 2022*; Food and Agriculture Organization of the United Nations: Rome, Italy, 2020.
4. Pahri, S.D.R.; Mohamed, A.F.; Samat, A. LCA for open systems: A review of the influence of natural and anthropogenic factors on aquaculture systems. *Int. J. Life Cycle Assess* **2015**, *20*, 1324–1337. [CrossRef]
5. Martins, C.; Eding, E.H.; Verdegem, M.C.; Heinsbroek, L.T.; Schneider, O.; Blancheton, J.-P.; d'Orbcastel, E.R.; Verreth, J. New developments in recirculating aquaculture systems in Europe: A perspective on environmental sustainability. *Aquac. Eng.* **2010**, *43*, 83–93. [CrossRef]
6. Kolarevic, J.; Baeverfjord, G.; Takle, H.; Ytteborg, E.; Reiten, B.K.M.; Nergård, S.; Terjesen, B.F. Performance and welfare of Atlantic salmon smolt reared in recirculating or flow through aquaculture systems. *Aquaculture* **2014**, *432*, 15–25. [CrossRef]
7. Padervand, M.; Gholami, M.R. Removal of toxic heavy metal ions from waste water by functionalized magnetic core–zeolitic shell nanocomposites as adsorbents. *Environ. Sci. Pollut. Res.* **2013**, *20*, 3900–3909. [CrossRef]
8. Abdelfatah, A.G.; Ali, M.A.; Abdelbary, K.M. Mechanical filtration pretreatment effect on ammonia biofiltration performance indicators in fish aquaculture wastewater. *Misr J. Agric. Eng.* **2022**, *39*, 555–570. [CrossRef]
9. Øvrebø, T.K.; Balseiro, P.; Imsland, A.K.D.; Stefansson, S.O.; Tveterås, R.; Sveier, H.; Handeland, S. Investigation of growth performance of post-smolt Atlantic salmon (*Salmo salar* L.) in semi closed containment system: A big-scale benchmark study. *Aquac. Res.* **2022**, *53*, 4178–4189.
10. Van Rijn, J. Waste treatment in recirculating aquaculture systems. *Aquac. Eng.* **2013**, *53*, 49–56. [CrossRef]
11. Ahmed, N.; Turchini, G.M. Recirculating aquaculture systems (RAS): Environmental solution and climate change adaptation. *J. Clean. Prod.* **2021**, *297*, 126604. [CrossRef]
12. Ahmad, A.; Abdullah, S.R.S.; Hasan, H.A.; Othman, A.R.; Ismail, N.I. Aquaculture industry: Supply and demand, best practices, effluent and its current issues and treatment technology. *J. Environ. Manag.* **2021**, *287*, 112271. [CrossRef]
13. Camargo, J.A.; Alonso, A.; Salamanca, A. Nitrate toxicity to aquatic animals: A review with new data for freshwater invertebrates. *Chemosphere* **2005**, *58*, 1255–1267. [CrossRef] [PubMed]
14. Roques, J.A.C. *Apects of Fish Welfare in Aquaculture Practices*; Radboud University Nijmegen: The Netherlands, 2013; p. 200.
15. Preena, P.G.; Rejish Kumar, V.J.; Singh, I.S.B. Nitrification and denitrification in recirculating aquaculture systems: The processes and players. *Rev. Aquac.* **2021**, *13*, 2053–2075. [CrossRef]

16. Chen, S. *Recirculating Systems Effluents and Treatments*; Aquaculture and the Environment in the United States, World Aquaculture Society: Baton Rouge, LA, USA, 2002; pp. 119–140.
17. Stavrakidis-Zachou, O.; Ernst, A.; Steinbach, C.; Wagner, K.; Waller, U. Development of denitrification in semi-automated moving bed biofilm reactors operated in a marine recirculating aquaculture system. *Aquac. Int.* **2019**, *27*, 1485–1501. [CrossRef]
18. Hu, Z.; Lee, J.W.; Chandran, K.; Kim, S.; Khanal, S.K. Nitrous oxide (N_2O) emission from aquaculture: A review. *Environ. Sci. Technol.* **2012**, *46*, 6470–6480. [CrossRef]
19. Kartal, B.; van Niftrik, L.; Keltjens, J.T.; den Camp, H.J.O.; Jetten, M.S. Anammox—Growth physiology, cell biology, and metabolism. *Adv. Microb. Physiol.* **2012**, *60*, 211–262.
20. Dapena-Mora, A.; Campos, J.; Mosquera-Corral, A.; Jetten, M.; Méndez, R. Stability of the ANAMMOX process in a gas-lift reactor and a SBR. *J. Biotechnol.* **2004**, *110*, 159–170. [CrossRef]
21. Strous, M.; Kuenen, J.G.; Jetten, M.S. Key physiology of anaerobic ammonium oxidation. *Appl. Environ. Microbiol.* **1999**, *65*, 3248–3250. [CrossRef]
22. Strous, M.; Heijnen, J.; Kuenen, J.G.; Jetten, M. The sequencing batch reactor as a powerful tool for the study of slowly growing anaerobic ammonium-oxidizing microorganisms. *Appl. Microbiol. Biotechnol.* **1998**, *50*, 589–596. [CrossRef]
23. Kartal, B.; Van Niftrik, L.; Rattray, J.; Van De Vossenberg, J.L.; Schmid, M.C.; Sinninghe Damsté, J.; Jetten, M.S.; Strous, M. Candidatu s 'Brocadia fulgida': An autofluorescent anaerobic ammonium oxidizing bacterium. *FEMS Microbiol. Ecol.* **2008**, *63*, 46–55. [CrossRef]
24. Okabe, S.; Oshiki, M.; Takahashi, Y.; Satoh, H. N_2O emission from a partial nitrification-anammox process and identification of a key biological process of N_2O emission from anammox granules. *Water Res.* **2011**, *45*, 6461–6470. [CrossRef]
25. Kuenen, J.G. Anammox bacteria: From discovery to application. *Nat. Rev. Microbiol.* **2008**, *6*, 320–326. [CrossRef]
26. Van Dongen, U.; Jetten, M.S.; van Loosdrecht, M. The SHARON®-Anammox® process for treatment of ammonium rich wastewater. *Water Sci. Technol.* **2001**, *44*, 153–160. [CrossRef]
27. Borin, S.; Mapelli, F.; Rolli, E.; Song, B.; Tobias, C.; Schmid, M.C.; De Lange, G.J.; Reichart, G.J.; Schouten, S.; Jetten, M. Anammox bacterial populations in deep marine hypersaline gradient systems. *Extremophiles* **2013**, *17*, 289–299. [CrossRef]
28. Yokota, N.; Watanabe, Y.; Tokutomi, T.; Kiyokawa, T.; Hori, T.; Ikeda, D.; Song, K.; Hosomi, M.; Terada, A. High-rate nitrogen removal from waste brine by marine anammox bacteria in a pilot-scale UASB reactor. *Appl. Microbiol. Biotechnol.* **2018**, *102*, 1501–1512. [CrossRef] [PubMed]
29. Wei, Q.; Kawagoshi, Y.; Huang, X.; Hong, N.; Van Duc, L.; Yamashita, Y.; Hama, T. Nitrogen removal properties in a continuous marine anammox bacteria reactor under rapid and extensive salinity changes. *Chemosphere* **2016**, *148*, 444–451. [CrossRef]
30. Dapena-Mora, A.; Fernandez, I.; Campos, J.; Mosquera-Corral, A.; Mendez, R.; Jetten, M. Evaluation of activity and inhibition effects on Anammox process by batch tests based on the nitrogen gas production. *Enzym. Microb. Technol.* **2007**, *40*, 859–865. [CrossRef]
31. Liu, C.; Yamamoto, T.; Nishiyama, T.; Fujii, T.; Furukawa, K. Effect of salt concentration in anammox treatment using non woven biomass carrier. *J. Biosci. Bioeng.* **2009**, *107*, 519–523. [CrossRef] [PubMed]
32. Malovanyy, A.; Plaza, E.; Trela, J.; Malovanyy, M. Ammonium removal by partial nitration and Anammox processes from wastewater with increased salinity. *Environ. Technol.* **2015**, *36*, 595–604. [CrossRef] [PubMed]
33. Roques, J.A.C.; Micolucci, F.; Hosokawa, S.; Sundell, K.; Kindaichi, T. Effects of recirculating aquaculture system wastewater on anammox performance and community structure. *Processes* **2021**, *9*, 1183. [CrossRef]
34. Van de Graaf, A.A.; de Bruijn, P.; Robertson, L.A.; Jetten, M.S.; Kuenen, J.G. Autotrophic growth of anaerobic ammonium-oxidizing micro-organisms in a fluidized bed reactor. *Microbiology* **1996**, *142*, 2187–2196. [CrossRef]
35. Sikora, M.; Nowosad, J.; Kucharczyk, D. Nitrogen compound oxidation rate in recirculation systems using three biological filter medias in rearing common carp (*Cyprinus carpio* L.) juveniles. *Aquaculture* **2022**, *547*, 737532. [CrossRef]
36. Brazil, B.L.; Summerfelt, S.T.; Libey, G.S. Application of Ozone to Recirculating Aquaculture Systems. In *Successes and Failures in Commercial Recirculating Aquaculture (Conference Proceedings)*; Libey, G.S., Timmons, M.B., Eds.; Northeast Regional Agricultural Engineering Service: Ithaca, NY, USA, 1996; pp. 373–389.
37. Krumins, V.; Ebeling, J.; Wheaton, F. Part-day ozonation for nitrogen and organic carbon control in recirculating aquaculture systems. *Aquac. Eng.* **2001**, *24*, 231–241. [CrossRef]
38. Kindaichi, T.; Awata, T.; Tanabe, K.; Ozaki, N.; Ohashi, A. Enrichment of marine anammox bacteria in Hiroshima Bay sediments. *Water Sci. Technol.* **2011**, *63*, 964–969. [CrossRef] [PubMed]
39. Kindaichi, T.; Awata, T.; Suzuki, Y.; Tanabe, K.; Hatamoto, M.; Ozaki, N.; Ohashi, A. Enrichment using an up-flow column reactor and community structure of marine anammox bacteria from coastal sediment. *Microbes Environ.* **2011**, *26*, 67–73. [CrossRef] [PubMed]
40. Mojiri, A.; Nishimoto, K.; Awata, T.; Aoi, Y.; Ozaki, N.; Ohashi, A.; Kindaichi, T. Effects of salts on the activity and growth of "*Candidatus Scalindua* sp.", a marine Anammox bacterium. *Microbes Environ.* **2018**, *33*, 336–339. [CrossRef]
41. American Public Health Association. *Standard Methods for the Examination of Water and Wastewater: Selected Analytical Methods Approved and Cited by the United States Environmental Protection Agency*; APHA-AWWA-WEF: Washington, DC, USA, 2012.

42. Mojiri, A.; Ohashi, A.; Ozaki, N.; Aoi, Y.; Kindaichi, T. Integrated anammox-biochar in synthetic wastewater treatment: Performance and optimization by artificial neural network. *J. Clean. Prod.* **2020**, *243*, 118638. [CrossRef]
43. Shoiful, A.; Kambara, H.; Cao, L.T.T.; Matsushita, S.; Kindaichi, T.; Aoi, Y.; Ozaki, N.; Ohashi, A. Mn (II) oxidation and manganese-oxide reduction on the decolorization of an azo dye. *Int. Biodeterior. Biodegrad.* **2020**, *146*, 104820. [CrossRef]
44. Awata, T.; Goto, Y.; Kuratsuka, H.; Aoi, Y.; Ozaki, N.; Ohashi, A.; Kindaichi, T. Reactor performance and microbial community structure of single-stage partial nitration anammox membrane bioreactors inoculated with Brocadia and Scalindua enrichment cultures. *Biochem. Eng. J.* **2021**, *170*, 107991. [CrossRef]
45. Bolyen, E.; Rideout, J.R.; Dillon, M.R.; Bokulich, N.A.; Abnet, C.C.; Al-Ghalith, G.A.; Alexander, H.; Alm, E.J.; Arumugam, M.; Asnicar, F. Reproducible, interactive, scalable and extensible microbiome data science using QIIME 2. *Nat. Biotechnol.* **2019**, *37*, 852–857. [CrossRef]
46. Quast, C.; Pruesse, E.; Yilmaz, P.; Gerken, J.; Schweer, T.; Yarza, P.; Peplies, J.; Glöckner, F.O. The SILVA ribosomal RNA gene database project: Improved data processing and web-based tools. *Nucleic Acids Res.* **2012**, *41*, D590–D596. [CrossRef]
47. Awata, T.; Oshiki, M.; Kindaichi, T.; Ozaki, N.; Ohashi, A.; Okabe, S. Physiological characterization of an anaerobic ammonium-oxidizing bacterium belonging to the "*Candidatus Scalindua*" group. *Appl. Environ. Microbiol.* **2013**, *79*, 4145–4148. [CrossRef]
48. Daims, H.; Brühl, A.; Amann, R.; Schleifer, K.-H.; Wagner, M. The domain-specific probe EUB338 is insufficient for the detection of all Bacteria: Development and evaluation of a more comprehensive probe set. *Syst. Appl. Microbiol.* **1999**, *22*, 434–444. [CrossRef] [PubMed]
49. Schmid, M.C.; Maas, B.; Dapena, A.; van de Pas-Schoonen, K.; van de Vossenberg, J.; Kartal, B.; van Niftrik, L.; Schmidt, I.; Cirpus, I.; Kuenen, J.G. Biomarkers for in situ detection of anaerobic ammonium-oxidizing (anammox) bacteria. *Appl. Environ. Microbiol.* **2005**, *71*, 1677–1684. [CrossRef] [PubMed]
50. Aklujkar, M.; Coppi, M.V.; Leang, C.; Kim, B.C.; Chavan, M.; Perpetua, L.; Giloteaux, L.; Liu, A.; Holmes, D. Proteins involved in electron transfer to Fe (III) and Mn (IV) oxides by *Geobacter sulfurreducens* and *Geobacter uraniireducens*. *Microbiology* **2013**, *159*, 515–535. [CrossRef] [PubMed]
51. Li, H.; Yao, H.; Zhang, D.; Zuo, L.; Ren, J.; Ma, J.; Pei, J.; Xu, Y.; Yang, C. Short-and long-term effects of manganese, zinc and copper ions on nitrogen removal in nitritation-anammox process. *Chemosphere* **2018**, *193*, 479–488. [CrossRef]
52. Huang, X.; Gao, D.; Peng, S.; Tao, Y. Effects of ferrous and manganese ions on anammox process in sequencing batch biofilm reactors. *J. Environ. Sci.* **2014**, *26*, 1034–1039. [CrossRef]
53. Lotti, T.; Cordola, M.; Kleerebezem, R.; Caffaz, S.; Lubello, C.; Van Loosdrecht, M. Inhibition effect of swine wastewater heavy metals and antibiotics on anammox activity. *Water Sci. Technol.* **2012**, *66*, 1519–1526. [CrossRef]
54. Yang, G.-F.; Ni, W.-M.; Wu, K.; Wang, H.; Yang, B.-E.; Jia, X.-Y.; Jin, R.-C. The effect of Cu (II) stress on the activity, performance and recovery on the anaerobic ammonium-oxidizing (Anammox) process. *Chem. Eng. J.* **2013**, *226*, 39–45. [CrossRef]
55. Kimura, Y.; Isaka, K. Evaluation of inhibitory effects of heavy metals on anaerobic ammonium oxidation (anammox) by continuous feeding tests. *Appl. Microbiol. Biotechnol.* **2014**, *98*, 6965–6972. [CrossRef]
56. von Ahnen, M.; Aalto, S.L.; Suurnäkki, S.; Tiirola, M.; Pedersen, P.B. Salinity affects nitrate removal and microbial composition of denitrifying woodchip bioreactors treating recirculating aquaculture system effluents. *Aquaculture* **2019**, *504*, 182–189. [CrossRef]
57. Chen, Z.; Liu, Y.; Liu, L.Z.; Wang, X.J.; Liu, Z.P. Heterotrophic bacterial community structure of multistage biofilters in a commercial pufferfish *Takifugu rubripes* RAS. In *Advanced Materials Research*; Trans Tech Publications: Zurich, Switzerland, 2013.
58. Interdonato, F. *Recirculating Aquaculture System (RAS) Biofilters: Focusing on Bacterial Communities Complexity and Activity*; Università Degli Studi di Messina: Messina, Italy, 2012; p. 128.
59. Sanchez, F.A.; Vivian-Rogers, V.R.; Urakawa, H. Tilapia recirculating aquaculture systems as a source of plant growth promoting bacteria. *Aquac. Res.* **2019**, *50*, 2054–2065. [CrossRef]
60. Ivanova, E.P.; Ng, H.J.; Webb, H.K. The Family *Pseudoalteromonadaceae*. In *The Prokaryotes: Gammaproteobacteria*; Rosenberg, E., DeLong, E.F., Lory, S., Stackebrandt, E., Thompson, F., Eds.; Springer: Berlin/Heidelberg, Germany, 2014; pp. 575–582.
61. Brailo, M.; Schreier, H.J.; McDonald, R.; Maršić-Lučić, J.; Gavrilović, A.; Pećarević, M.; Jug-Dujaković, J. Bacterial community analysis of marine recirculating aquaculture system bioreactors for complete nitrogen removal established from a commercial inoculum. *Aquaculture* **2019**, *503*, 198–206. [CrossRef]
62. Brettar, I.; Christen, R.; Höfle, M.G. *Rheinheimera baltica* gen. nov., sp. nov., a blue-coloured bacterium isolated from the central Baltic Sea. *Int. J. Syst. Evol. Microbiol.* **2002**, *52*, 1851–1857.
63. Zhong, Z.-P.; Liu, Y.; Liu, L.-Z.; Wang, F.; Zhou, Y.-G.; Liu, Z.-P. *Rheinheimera tuosuensis* sp. nov., isolated from a saline lake. *Int. J. Syst. Evol. Microbiol.* **2014**, *64*, 1142–1148. [CrossRef] [PubMed]
64. Baek, K.; Jeon, C.O. *Rheinheimera aestuari* sp. nov., a marine bacterium isolated from coastal sediment. *Int. J. Syst. Evol. Microbiol.* **2015**, *65*, 2640–2645. [CrossRef]
65. Chen, W.-M.; Chen, W.-T.; Young, C.-C.; Sheu, S.-Y. *Rheinheimera riviphila* sp. nov., isolated from a freshwater stream. *Arch. Microbiol.* **2019**, *201*, 919–926. [CrossRef] [PubMed]
66. Liu, Y.; Jiang, J.-T.; Xu, C.-J.; Liu, Y.-H.; Song, X.-F.; Li, H.; Liu, Z.-P. *Rheinheimera longhuensis* sp. nov., isolated from a slightly alkaline lake, and emended description of genus *Rheinheimera* Brettar et al. 2002. *Int. J. Syst. Evol. Microbiol.* **2012**, *62*, 2927–2933. [CrossRef]

67. Sorokin, D.Y.; Mosier, D.; Zorz, J.K.; Dong, X.; Strous, M. *Wenzhouxiangella* strain AB-CW3, a proteolytic bacterium from hypersaline soda lakes that preys on cells of gram-positive bacteria. *Front. Microbiol.* **2020**, *11*, 597686. [CrossRef]
68. Wang, G.; Tang, M.; Li, T.; Dai, S.; Wu, H.; Chen, C.; He, H.; Fan, J.; Xiang, W.; Li, X. *Wenzhouxiangella marina* gen. nov, sp. nov, a marine bacterium from the culture broth of *Picochlorum* sp. 122, and proposal of *Wenzhouxiangellaceae fam.* nov. in the order Chromatiales. *Antonie Van Leeuwenhoek* **2015**, *107*, 1625–1632. [CrossRef]

Disclaimer/Publisher's Note: The statements, opinions and data contained in all publications are solely those of the individual author(s) and contributor(s) and not of MDPI and/or the editor(s). MDPI and/or the editor(s) disclaim responsibility for any injury to people or property resulting from any ideas, methods, instructions or products referred to in the content.

Review

Crude Oil Bioremediation: From Bacteria to Microalgae

Rosa Paola Radice [1,2,*], Vincenzo De Fabrizio [1], Antonietta Donadoni [1], Antonio Scopa [3,*] and Giuseppe Martelli [1]

1. Department of Science, University of Basilicata, Viale dell'Ateneo Lucano, 10, 85100 Potenza, Italy
2. Bioinnova srls, Via Ponte Nove Luci, 9, 85100 Potenza, Italy
3. School of Agricultural, Forestry, Food and Environmental Sciences, University of Basilicata, Viale dell'Ateneo Lucano, 10, 85100 Potenza, Italy
* Correspondence: rosapaolaradice@gmail.com (R.P.R.); antonio.scopa@unibas.it (A.S.)

Abstract: Crude oil is one of the major pollutants present. Its extraction and processing generate processing waters contaminated by hydrocarbons which are harmful to both human health and the flora and fauna that come into contact with it. Hydrocarbon contamination can involve soil and water, and several technologies are used for recovery. The most used techniques for the recovery of spilt oil involve chemical-physical methods that can remove most of the pollutants. Among these, must consider the bioremediation by microorganisms, mostly bacterial capable of degrading many of the toxic compounds contained within the petroleum. Microalgae participate in bioremediation indirectly, supporting the growth of degrading bacteria, and directly acting on contaminants. Their direct contribution is based on the activation of various mechanisms ranging from the production of enzymes capable of degrading hydrocarbons, such as lipoxygenases, to the attack through the liberation of free radicals. The following review analyzed all the works published in the last ten years concerning the ability of microalgae to remove hydrocarbons, intending to identify in these microorganisms an alternative technology to the use of bacteria. The advantages of using microalgae concern not only their ability to remove toxic compounds and release oxygen into the atmosphere but their biomass could then be used in a circular economy process to produce biofuels.

Keywords: microalgae; petroleum; hydrocarbons; bioremediation; environmental pollution; crude oil

1. Introduction

Today, the world economy is based on fossil fuels to obtain energy and, specifically, coal and petroleum. Petroleum consumption in 2020 increased by 0.9 million barrels per day while the demand for liquid fuels reached historic highs reaching 100 million barrels per day. The use of oil governs stock exchanges and world markets. For this reason, the extraction and refining of crude oil remain an extremely intense activity. This massive extraction causes numerous problems critical for the environmental pollution of soil and water. Furthermore, there are many accidents recorded over the years related to the transport of petroleum that have caused environmental problems. By focusing primarily on spills in aquatic environments, oil has a major impact on flora and fauna healthy. For this reason, in recent years, a solution has been sought that allows the removal and degradation of oil in a green way, limiting the use of chemical dispersants, which are themselves toxic. Microalgae are unicellular, photosynthetic microorganisms that constitute phytoplankton in the aquatic environment. In the last decade, microalgae have been studied for their nutraceutical, pharmaceutical and industrial applications, being producers of many metabolites such as carotenoids, antioxidants and lipids; these useful for biofuel production [1]. In this review, we analyzed the literature about the ability of microalgae, with particular attention to green microalgae, to remove contaminants deriving from pure crude oil. Microalgae can represent an excellent solution given their ability to metabolize various pollutants, using them as carbon sources, in a green process, releasing oxygen

Citation: Radice, R.P.; De Fabrizio, V.; Donadoni, A.; Scopa, A.; Martelli, G. Crude Oil Bioremediation: From Bacteria to Microalgae. *Processes* **2023**, *11*, 442. https://doi.org/10.3390/pr11020442

Academic Editor: Zongbi Bao

Received: 22 December 2022
Revised: 26 January 2023
Accepted: 31 January 2023
Published: 1 February 2023

Copyright: © 2023 by the authors. Licensee MDPI, Basel, Switzerland. This article is an open access article distributed under the terms and conditions of the Creative Commons Attribution (CC BY) license (https://creativecommons.org/licenses/by/4.0/).

into the atmosphere and subtracting CO_2. To do that, we search all the manuscripts about microalgae and crude oil treatment published from 2010 to 2022. Papers concerning the bioremediation of other contaminants (i.e., municipal wastewaters or heavy metal) have not been included in this manuscript. The search, carried out on the main search databases (PubMed, Scopus, and Web of Science), using as keywords "microalgae and petroleum", "microalgae and crude oil", "microalgae and petroleum and bioremediation", "microalgae and crude oil and bioremediation". A comparison between the different microorganism involved in the process has made to highlight the benefits of using microalgae.

Petroleum Composition

Usually, methane, ethane and propane, which represent the lightest hydrocarbons in natural conditions, are present in the gaseous state; the heavier ones are present in the solid or liquid. However, this can vary by oil field [2]. Petroleum is mainly composed of aliphatic and non-aliphatic compounds, but sulfur, nitrogen and oxygen atoms are also present. Linear hydrocarbons vary their state based on the number of carbon atoms that constitute them [3]. Alkanes with a number of carbon atoms greater than five are present in a liquid state, such as heptadecane ($C_{17}H_{36}$), while compounds with less than five carbon atoms, in a gaseous state [4]. Cycloalkanes, on the other hand, are formed starting from compounds, such as cyclopentane and cyclohexane, from which, in rare cases, cyclopropane and cyclobutane originated [5]. It is not difficult to find compounds such as polycyclic naphthenes within the crude oil, including pregnane and dinosterane [6]. There are aromatic compounds among the hydrocarbons present in the liquid state. The most famous, also for their toxicity, are the BTEX compounds (benzene, toluene, ethylbenzene and xylene) and makeup up to 60% of the light fraction of petroleum, where they do not have substituents in their chemical composition, both in the heavier fraction in which have one or more alkyl substituents or other connected cycloalkane rings [7]. PAHs are formed by multiple aromatic rings fused together and are divided into soluble resins such as anthracene, phenanthrene and pyrene, or as non-soluble asphaltenes [8]. The heteroatoms in the crude oil, present for less than 1% of the total composition, are mainly oxygen and sulfur. Phenols, carboxylic acids, alcohols, esters and ketones contain oxygen [9]. Carboxylic acids also contain fatty acids and naphthalenic acid, which come to a weight of around 1000 Da [10]. The amount of sulfur present affects the properties of the crude oil. It can be more or less acidic, depending on the amount of sulfur present. It is not uncommon to also find ionic compounds such as sodium chlorite or metal porphyrins such as nickel or vanadium in petroleum [11].

2. Current Bioremediation Techniques

Currently, there are several technologies for oil recovery that differ according to the matrix to be purified. Usually, multi-step protocols involve the use of chemical agents and the action of bacterial microorganisms (Table 1) [12].

Table 1. Principal enzyme involved in bacteria crude oil bioremediation.

Bacteria	Pollutants Degraded	Enzyme
Alcanivorax spp.	n-alkanes	Hydrolase (AlkB1 and AlkB2)
	cycloalkanes	Cytochrome P-450 dependent alkane monooxygenase
Gammaproteobacteria	Long C_{22} and C_{36} n-alkanes	Monooxygenase binding flavin (AlmA)
Cyclocasticus	PAHs	Peptidase
Colweillia		Hydrolase
Pseudoalteromonas		
Halomonas	PAHs	Exopolysaccharides
Methylomirabilis oxyfera	Methane	Methane monooxygenase

2.1. Bacteria Biodegradation

The bacteria are also used in the recovery of the crude oil lost during the extraction process, exploiting the ability of various species of bacteria and archaea to metabolise organic carbon and to produce biosurfactant solvents which improve the chemical-physical characteristics of the oil to recover [13,14]. The most used bacterial strains are *Clostridium*, *Zymomonas*, *Klebsiella*, *Enterobacter* and the archaeon *Methanobacterium* [15]. Oil and its constituents have existed in nature for millions of years, and consequently, there are organisms capable of using them as a source of nourishment and energy. Among the microorganisms that can grow in the presence of hydrocarbons, there are about 175 bacterial genera, many archaea and some eukaryotic microorganisms [16]. However, the bioremediation implemented by microorganisms is a complex mechanism that requires numerous steps and cooperation between different species capable of acting on hydrocarbons synergistically. Furthermore, it must be considered that there are numerous factors such as temperature and nutrient concentration that play a fundamental role in the remediation process [17]. Bioremediation generally begins with some bacterial genera capable of attacking straight-chain and branched alkanes present in high quantities. Between these *Oceanispirillales* order (class gammaproteobacteria; phylum proteobacteria), and specifically the genre *Alcanivorax* spp. intervene on n-alkanes and cycloalkanes [18]. To generate energy from alkanes, *Alcanivorax* spp. uses different hydrolases (a non-haem diiron monooxygenase AlkB1 and AlkB2) and three cytochrome P450-dependent alkane monooxygenases [19]. Given the different conditions in which these bacteria operate, some gammaproteobacteria activate special monooxygenases to survive in the presence of ultraviolet light. For example, they use the monooxygenase capable of binding flavin (AlmA) to metabolize the long-chain C_{22} and C_{36} n-alkanes as an energy source [20], instead *Cycloclasticus* spp., *Colwellia* and *Pseudoalteromonas* (class gammaproteobacteria; phylum proteobacteria), degrade aromatic hydrocarbons when, in a second phase, they are found in larger quantities [21,22]. Heterotrophic bacteria degrade exopolymer by-products thanks to peptidase and hydrolase. These enzymes are more expressed in contaminated environments. *Halomonas* bacteria fall into this category by producing exopolysaccharides. They reduce the solubilization of PAHs in an aqueous environment, making them more vulnerable to biodegradation and the formation of aggregates. [14,23]. However, the bioremediation processes mediated by microorganisms are in the balance between the increase of bacteria due to the degradation of toxic compounds and the lack of nutrients which decrease indirectly in proportion to the growth of bacterial biomass [24]. For this reason, it is sometimes necessary to add nutrients, and in particular, nitrogen, to improve performance. In a protected environment, this aspect is easy to solve, but in nature, the consumption of hydrocarbons by microorganisms causes a high degradation of the oxygen necessary for the sustenance of the other species present in the environment [25]. The bioremediation processes can also take place in the absence of oxygen in anaerobic conditions, where specialized bacteria use an alternative metabolism [26]. For example, some species of archaea can decompose methane through a process of reverse methanogenesis under anaerobic conditions. This process involves the use of different terminal electron acceptors [27]. Although the metabolic pathway is not entirely clear, the anaerobic methanotrophic archaea may use methyl-coenzyme M reductase as a key enzyme, exploiting its reverse reaction. In addition to the domain of the archaea, also the bacterium *Methylomirabilis oxyfera* can attack methane. It can convert nitrogen oxides (NO) from reduced nitrite into N_2 and O_2, thus activating methane monooxygenases [28].

2.2. Different Bacteria Consortium

It is evident that there is a collaboration between the different domains for the bioremediation process. In fact, in contaminated waters, phytoplankton and zooplankton collaborate synergistically due to the degradation of hydrocarbons, very often forming agglomerates that settle on the seabed. These agglomerates are rich in crude oil and are formed thanks to the coagulation of phytoplankton, which incorporates oil droplets and precipitates on the seabed. [29]. In the vicinity of oil spills, the indigenous microbial community increases the expression of genes, which are involved in the biodegradation process. It improves bacterial motility, chemotaxis and enzymes involved in aliphatic degradation. Even the very action of the currents favors bacterial blooms and accelerate the degradation [30]. Furthermore, the degradation of the various oil components involves different plasmid genes, depending on the hydrocarbons involved. For the metabolism of alkanes, aerobic microorganisms mainly use various monooxygenases, rubredoxin and rubredoxin reductase to convert alkanes into alcohol by increasing the expression of several *alk* genes. The PAHs metabolism, on the other hand, is more complex given the size of the hydrocarbons. The genes involved are mainly naphthalene dioxygenase (*nah*) genes [31], naphthalene dioxygenase (*ndo*) [32], doxycycline-inducible system (*dox*) [33].

3. Microalgae and Petroleum Bioremediation

Microalgae constitute a fundamental element in the treatment of water contaminated by crude oil and hydrocarbons. Ugya et al. evaluated the ability of some microalgae grown on a biofilm to remove contaminants of petroleum origin, including PAHs and total petroleum hydrocarbon (TPH). The results showed a significant reduction of phytochemical parameters such as sulphate −17.5%, chloride −14.65%, nitrates −33% total suspended solids (TSS) −26%, total dissolved solids (TDS) −7.9%, and chemical oxygen demand (COD) and biochemical oxygen demand (BODs) reduced by 8% and 16.7% respectively. Although not in high percentages, the removal of TPH was equal to 15% after 14 days of exposure [34]. Kuttiyathil et al., on the other hand, analysed not only the removal of crude oil by the microalga *Chlorella* spp. but also how, in nature, the mechanical action of sea waves contributes to creating an emulsion of water and crude oil that could favour the removal of pollutants making them more available. Their results show that following an initial period of adaptation, the Total Organic Carbon (TOC) of the solution was drastically reduced and that, after 5 days, *Chlorella* removed 80% of the emulsified oil [35]. Water mixing and how it can alter bioremediation was also studied in 2014 by Özhan et al., which demonstrated how the bioavailability of crude oil is altered by physical mixing applied in the laboratory. The mixing of the water column containing crude oil does not significantly affect the concentration of total petroleum hydrocarbons (TPH) but increases the concentration of some alkanes and PAHs and causes the formation of colloidal micro-particles (1–70 μm), which improve the degradation of hydrocarbons. [36]. *Chlorella* spp. has been the subject of several studies precisely because of its ability to survive in contaminated media. Znad et al., reported that the treatment of petroleum effluent (PE) with *Chlorella* spp. completely removed phosphorus after 13 days, reduced nitrogen by 78% and reduced COD from 504 mg/L to 144 mg/L. However, treatment of petroleum effluent with *Chlorella* spp. initially increased the biomass, but in the long term, start to be toxic and inhibits cell growth [37]. The nature and concentration of the crude oil, and its constituents, greatly influence the growth and removal of *Chlorella*. For example, the use of Water-Accommodated Fraction (WAF) deriving from diesel is more toxic for *Chlorella* than diesel as it is containing many low molecular weight hydrocarbons (LMW-HC), which can cause damage to cell membranes and affect the production of protective pigments, as reported by Ramadass et al. in its 2017 study [38]. Further studies carried out on *Chlorella* have confirmed its ability to remove various compounds contained in crude oil. For example, Xaaldi Kalhor et al., in both of their studies [39,40] tested different concentrations of crude oil (10 and 20 g/L) on *Chlorella vulgaris* for two intervals (7 and 14 days). The results were encouraging, and the best removal of low molecular weight hydrocarbons (LW), equal to 100%, was achieved with 10 g/L for 14 days, while at higher concentrations (20 g/L), after 14 days, the LW were reduced by 82%. The removal of heavy molecular weight hydrocarbons (HW) followed the same trend as the light ones, reaching higher values for the 14-day intervals and at a concentration of 10 g/L (reduction of HW equal to approximately 78%) [39]. Hamouda et al. (2016) and El-Sheekh et al. (2013) evaluated how the addition of crude oil to the *Chlorella* culture affected its metabolism and, specifically, whether the microalgae preferred a mixotrophic and heterotrophic mechanism rather than the classic autotrophic one. Hamouda et al. tested the growth of *Chlorella* in mixotrophic conditions using 1% crude oil, and the results on the hydrocarbons concentrations, present after 30 days of incubation, showed that the following aliphatic compounds: 3-methyl decane, heptadecane, octadecane, nonadecane, docosane, and tetracosane were removed, while decane, undecane, tridecane, hexadecane, tricosane were significantly reduced compared to the control [41]. El-Sheekh et al. instead, tested *Chlorella's* bioremediation capacity using up to 2% crude oil. The results obtained by gas chromatography-mass spectrometry (GC-MS) showed that, after 15 days of incubation, Indole-3-acetic acid was removed at all tested concentrations, while decane, Indole-3-acetic acid, p-Phenyltoluene, Naphthalene, 3-ethyl, Tridecane, phenanthracene, 1-methyl, Benzene, decyl, phenanthracene, 2-methyl, cyclohexane undecyl, b-pregnane and Octacosane were removed at a concentration of 2% crude oil [42]. One of the most interesting aspects concerning the El-Sheekh study is that PAHs were reduced more efficiently in heterotrophic conditions. This supports the hypothesis that eukaryotic microalgae, such as *Chlorella*, use organic carbon, present in solution, improving their growth range and biomass using a heterotrophic metabolism that allows them to use, split and/or convert hydrocarbons into intermediate metabolites. Confirming this hypothesis is also the study conducted by Das et al. in 2019, which demonstrated how *Chlorella* reached the highest biomass yield (1.72 g/L) in mixotrophic conditions with the addition of pre-treated produced water (PPW) of petroleum origin and removed 92% of the total nitrogen (TN) and 73% of the TOC [43].

4. Mechanism of Action

From the studies analysed, it is evident that green microalgae, in particular *Chlorophyceae*, are excellent candidates to remove crude oil pollutants (Table 2). The mechanism of action with which this happens is not yet completely known, but the principal hypotheses are two: either they use organic carbon deriving from hydrocarbons, or they accumulate them inside by carrying out a defence mechanism and treating them as real contaminants. Ugya et al. analysed both hypotheses, and their results show that, in the microalgae, there was a net increase of saponins after the treatment of petroleum contaminants [34]. Saponins usually play a protective role thanks to their glycosidic-terpenic nature, lowering the surface tension and forming colloidal and foamy solutions [44]. Their amphipathic and surfactant nature increases the bioavailability of petroleum contaminants which are easier to "attack". Ugya et al., demonstrated that the production of ROS increased, highlighting cellular stress induced by crude oil after the treatment. This is related also to the increase of alkaloids, flavonoids and carotenoids within the algae after treatment, suggesting that the ROS produced by the microalgae have degraded the hydrocarbons, protecting them from their toxic action. Furthermore, analyzes carried out by scanning electron microscopic show how the oil has affected the morphology and the surface of the microalgae [34]. If the cell surface was rough before the treatment, it was smooth and polished afterwards; moreover, an analysis of some elements such as silicones, aluminium and iron, showed how these have accumulated on the biofilm thanks to the production of extracellular polymeric substances (EPS) by the microalgae and that have accumulated thanks to the presence of groups functional such as OH, C = O, CO, as also confirmed by the study of the composition of the polysaccharide produced by *Chlorella* spp. conducted by El-Naggar et al. [45]. Ghodrati et al., instead, focused on the genetic nature underlying the bioremediation mechanism. At the basis of their study, there is the idea that PAHs could be a source of ROS, alkoxyl (RO °) and hydroxyls (OH °) inside of cells. Starting from the knowledge on degrading bacteria [46], Ghodrati et al., hypothesized that green algae, being aerobic, could also use dioxygenases to remove and degrade PAHs, focusing specifically on lipoxygenases (LOXs) which oxidize PAHs through the insertion of two oxygen atoms which lead to the rupture of the aromatic ring through ortho-cleavages or meta-cleavages. The addition of oxygen in the hydrocarbon skeleton generates the formation of hydroperoxydes activated by becoming oxylipins. The molecular mechanism in microalgae has not yet been studied, but it would seem that lipoxygenases have both lipoxygenase and hydroperoxidase activity. Consequently, the results of Ghodrati et al. show that exposure to 1% crude oil for 21 days induced the expression of the LOX genes, ultimately leading to the decomposition of hydrocarbons and the production of hydroperoxy acids, fats and oxylipins which are useful to the algae for growth and sustenance, as well as for the resistance to stress-induced by crude oil [47]. SureshKumar et al. hypothesized that the degradation mechanism of PAHs in microalgae could be similar to that implemented by prokaryotes, turning an eye to the bacterial world. Starting from the idea that higher plants and animals share enzymatic and genetic pathways in the removal of exogenous substances, the group of researchers carried out a non-laboratory predictive analysis, considering as a metabolizing mechanism the oxidative system of cytochrome P450 (CYP450), which intervenes in the degradation of those molecules resistant to dioxygenases. Several parameters were analysed to create a model that could simulate the link between PAHs and CYP450 of *Haematococcus pluvialis*. Thirty-eight PAHs formed from 1 to 6 benzene rings were involved in the analysis, and the results showed that hydrogen, hydrophobic, electrostatic, π-π, and Van der Waals interaction occurred in the active site of CYP450. Specifically, 18 PAHs interacted with Threonine282 (Thr282), Alanine337 (Ala337), Serine404 (Ser404) and Lisyne407 (Lys407) via hydrogen bonds. However, in this study, it is evident that only LMW-PAHs were able to bind CYP450, while HMW-PAHs did not [48]. Therefore, there is an antioxidant mechanism for the degradation of petroleum pollutions, in particular, hydrocarbons. It acts in a double capacity, removing the toxic agent and producing nutrients useful for cell growth. Low doses of toxins could activate mechanisms to repair not only the damage induced by the toxin but also other damages previously accumulated by the cell, according to hormesis hypothesis [49]. The hormesis hypothesis claims that an organism responds to small doses of stress adaptively to survive [50]. However, some studies show that the ability of microalgae to remove contaminants continues even after the cell is dead as the microalgae can adsorb micro-drops of crude oil on their surface and, consequently, TOC, removing it from the solution as demonstrated by Kuttiyathil et al. [35].

Table 2. Principal enzymes and molecules involved in bioremediation process.

Microalgae	Pollutants Degraded	Enzyme
Chlorophyceae	Total Crude oil	Saponine
	PAHs	Lypoxygenase
		Hydroperoxidase
	THC	ROS production
Chlorella spp.	THC	Extracellular polymeric substances
Haematococcus pluvialis	PAHs	Cytochrome P450

5. Consortium Microalgae and Bacteria

Nowadays, bacteria are widely studied as bioremediators, and several species suitable for this process are known. On the other hand, microalgae could be valid substitutes. For this reason, many studies have focused on bacteria and microalgae collaboration to degrade crude oil and its pollutants. This collaboration can be of various types, but the basic principle sees the microorganisms work synergistically to obtain a better result (Figure 1). For example, Ashwaniy et al. found that the microalga grown in petroleum refinery effluent (PRE) can reduce the concentration of COD, 81% of BOD, 61% of sulphide, 61% of TSS by 70%. 67% phosphorous and TDS and can act as a substrate for bacterial growth in a microbial desalination cell (MDC) to produce clean energy [51]. Chernikova et al. described how microalgae and bacteria collaborate continuously in nature. The microalgae provide oxygen, exopolymers and organic-material useful for bacterial growth. In turn, bacteria support microalgae growth, producing vitamins, micronutrients, iron and carbon dioxide. Furthermore, Chernikova et al., in their work, demonstrated that in two petroleum-enriched microalgae cultures, *P. lutheri* and *N. oculata*, there was a selection of hydrocarbonoclastic alpha and gammaproteobacteria, especially *Alcanivorax* and *Marinobacter* spp., identifying in total 48 non-redundant bacterial strains also belonging to the genera *Thalassospira*, *Hyphomonas*, *Halomonas*, *Marinovum* and *Roseovarius*. These results are interesting as they candidate microalgae as possible host organisms for these bacteria whose housing niches are ignored [52]. Das et al. found that the ability of *Chlorella* spp. to remove various contaminants supported the growth of aerobic bacteria present in the unsterilized pretreated waters deriving from petroleum processing (PPW). In addition, the bacteria made nitrogen more available by promoting the microalgae biomass [38]. These results confirm the studies conducted by Mahdavi et al. in 2015 where algae produce oxygen through photosynthesis, which is necessary for aerobic bacteria for toxic compounds biodegradation. But the results support the ability of some algal strains to degrade directly and completely, some compounds such as naphthenic acids. In their study, a sample of freshwater taken directly from a pond in northern Alberta was tested for removal. Various conditions were tested, such as the absence of oxygen, presence of a Navicula pelliculosa diatom, and light variations. Only bacteria were tested, and bacteria with algae. The results showed how the algae-bacteria consortium led to an increase in the removal of toxic compounds given by the increase in microbial biomass in the algae-bacteria consortium. The higher rate of detoxification, obtained with bacteria alone, was improved by microalgae, which improved bacterial growth [53]. The coexistence of bacteria and microalgae was also observed by Hodges et al. where filamentous cyanobacteria dominated the reactor used for the decontamination and bio-removal of nutrients and suspended solids petrochemical wastewater [54]. So far, it has been analyzed how algae have been supporting bacterial growth in bioremediation, but Abid et al. have conducted a study in which the opposite occurs. A double-chamber bioreactor was built in which in one the bacteria biodegraded petroleum wastewater and the CO_2 produced was channelled into the chamber containing the microalga Spongiochloris sp, which used it to increase its growth, sequestering the CO_2 produced by the bacteria from the atmosphere [55]. However, these two paths of mutual exchange are accompanied by a third possibility. Tang demonstrated how a microalgae-bacteria consortium, artificially created, can optimize the removal of different petroleum constituents. In his study conducted in 2010, he separately tested four bacterial strains known for their ability to degrade PAHs (*Shingomonas* GY2B, *Burkholderia capacia* GS3C, *Pseudomonas* GP3A and *Pandoraea pnomenusa* GP3B) and the microalga *Scenedesmus obliquus* GH2, both as unialgal and axenic algae. Unialgal GH2 alone was able to remove various contaminants even with high percentages, such as 46% of alkanes and 51% of alkylcycloalkanes, or by reducing PAHs and alkylated naphtalenes by 81%, while axenic GH2 did not show potential for removal. However, these results were disproved by the union of microalgae with bacterial strains. Unialgal GH2, added with the various strains, has not increased its degradative properties, indeed in some cases, it has reduced its efficiency; axenic GH2 in conjunction with the different bacteria, on the other hand, has shown an increase in all degradation rates, completely removing toxic compounds such as PAHs, naphthalene, fluorene and phenanthrene [56]. Although there are not many studies in this regard, Ozhan et al., have shown how the oil spill in southern Louisiana has created dysfunctions in the phytoplankton, which is a valid indicator of toxicity for the health of the compromised marine ecosystem [36]. Jung et al. confirm this and argues that the dose of oil with which the phytoplankton comes into contact is responsible for the imbalance between bacteria and microalgae, reporting that concentrations greater than 1000 ppm inhibit the growth of microalgae by stimulating the bacterial one instead [57].

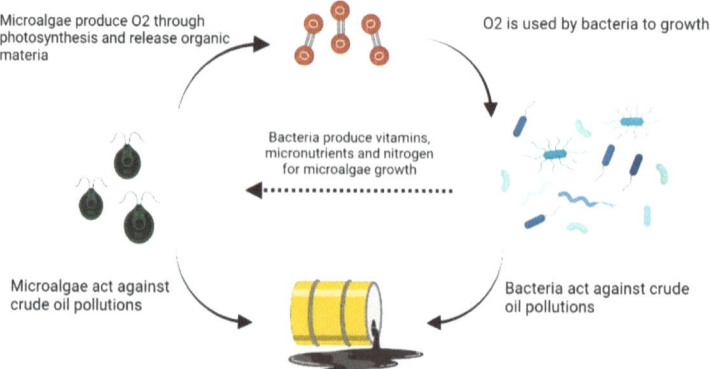

Figure 1. Microalgae and bacteria consortium: mechanisms of action.

6. Conclusions

The bibliography shows how microalgae are a valid alternative for the bioremediation of hydrocarbons and contaminants from crude oil. However, the current techniques used, through the action of specific bacteria, create waste material that must be disposed of, represent an additional cost, and release carbon dioxide into the atmosphere, resulting from their metabolism. Microalgae release oxygen into the atmosphere, sequestering carbon dioxide, being great bioremediators and carrying out a double purification action. Furthermore, in recent years microalgae have been a source of study for their application in the production of biofuels thanks to the quality of their fatty acids; it is possible to enrich the lipids used for conversion using alternative organic carbon-containing media, such as contaminated water [58]. This chain begins with the recovery and degradation of fossil fuel by a microorganism, which in itself constitutes the basis for the production of alternative biofuel [59]. The biofuel deriving from microalgae is extremely interesting as it is part of a circular economy mechanism that allows the reuse of a polluting matrix such as oil to form a new efficient and economical fuel. [60]. Furthermore, microalgal biomass can also be used in various fields, in addition to energy, as microalgae are excellent natural sources of nutrients such as vitamins, proteins, fatty acids and antioxidants. Some microalgae mentioned in this work (such as Chlorella and *Haematococcus pluvialis*), after bioremediation, are used in the nutraceutical field, thanks to important elements such as lipids and astaxanthin, respectively [61,62]. The results of this review demonstrate how microalgae could be used in the direct removal of petroleum hydrocarbons and lay the foundations for further specific studies to investigate the pathways involved in bioremediation to carry out any work of selecting the most performing strains. In conclusion, we believe that green microalgae, such as those described in this review, which already find application in various fields, can become a new biotechnological tool to solve a problem of global interest.

Author Contributions: Conceptualization, G.M. and R.P.R.; methodology, A.S.; investigation, R.P.R.; writing—original draft preparation, R.P.R.; writing—review and editing, V.D.F. and A.D.; visualization, R.P.R., V.D.F. and A.D.; supervision, G.M.; project administration, G.M. and A.S. All authors have read and agreed to the published version of the manuscript.

Funding: This research received no external funding.

Data Availability Statement: No applicable.

Conflicts of Interest: The authors declare no conflict of interest.

References

1. Ferreira Mota, G.; Germano de Sousa, I.; Luiz Barros de Oliveira, A.; Luthierre Gama Cavalcante, A.; da Silva Moreira, K.; Thálysson Tavares Cavalcante, F.; Erick da Silva Souza, J.; Rafael de Aguiar Falcão, Í.; Guimarães Rocha, T.; Bussons Rodrigues Valério, R.; et al. Biodiesel Production from Microalgae Using Lipase-Based Catalysts: Current Challenges and Prospects. *Algal. Res.* **2022**, *62*, 102616. [CrossRef]
2. Hsu, C.S.; Robinson, P.R. *Springer Handbook of Petroleum Technology*; Springer: Berlin/Heidelberg, Germany, 2017.
3. Walters, C. Petroleum. In *Kirk-Othmer Encyclopedia of Chemical Technology*; John Wiley & Sons: Hoboken, NJ, USA, 2020; pp. 1–44. [CrossRef]
4. Kissin, Y. Catagenesis and Composition of Petroleum: Origin of n-Alkanes and Isoalkanes in Petroleum Crudes. *Geochim. Cosmochim. Acta* **1987**, *51*, 2445–2457. [CrossRef]
5. Dooley, S.; Heyne, J.; Won, S.H.; Dievart, P.; Ju, Y.; Dryer, F.L. Importance of a Cycloalkane Functionality in the Oxidation of a Real Fuel. *Energy Fuels* **2014**, *28*, 7649–7661. [CrossRef]
6. Cheng, Q.; Huang, G.; Zhang, M. Distribution Difference and Significance of Short-Chain Steranes in Humic Coal and Coal-Measure Mudstone of Triassic Xujiahe Formation in Sichuan Basin, SW China. *Arab. J. Geosci.* **2021**, *14*, 1–14. [CrossRef]
7. Heibati, B.; Pollitt, K.J.G.; Karimi, A.; Yazdani Charati, J.; Ducatman, A.; Shokrzadeh, M.; Mohammadyan, M. BTEX Exposure Assessment and Quantitative Risk Assessment among Petroleum Product Distributors. *Ecotoxicol. Environ. Saf.* **2017**, *144*, 445–449. [CrossRef]
8. Ossai, I.C.; Ahmed, A.; Hassan, A.; Hamid, F.S. Remediation of Soil and Water Contaminated with Petroleum Hydrocarbon: A Review. *Environ. Technol. Innov.* **2020**, *17*, 100526. [CrossRef]
9. Palacio Lozano, D.C.; Ramírez, C.X.; Sarmiento Chaparro, J.A.; Thomas, M.J.; Gavard, R.; Jones, H.E.; Cabanzo Hernández, R.; Mejia-Ospino, E.; Barrow, M.P. Characterization of Bio-Crude Components Derived from Pyrolysis of Soft Wood and Its Esterified Product by Ultrahigh Resolution Mass Spectrometry and Spectroscopic Techniques. *Fuel* **2020**, *259*, 116085. [CrossRef]
10. Ni, W.; Zhu, G.; Liu, F.; Li, Z.; Xie, C.; Han, Y. Carboxylic Acids in Petroleum: Separation, Analysis, and Geochemical Significance. *Energy Fuels* **2021**, *35*, 12828–12844. [CrossRef]
11. Gab-Allah, M.A.; Goda, E.S.; Shehata, A.B.; Gamal, H. Critical Review on the Analytical Methods for the Determination of Sulfur and Trace Elements in Crude Oil. *Crit. Rev. Anal. Chem.* **2019**, *50*, 161–178. [CrossRef]
12. Nikolova, C.; Gutierrez, T. Use of Microorganisms in the Recovery of Oil from Recalcitrant Oil Reservoirs: Current State of Knowledge, Technological Advances and Future Perspectives. *Front Microbiol.* **2020**, *10*, 2996. [CrossRef]
13. Tourova, T.P.; Sokolova, D.S.; Semenova, E.M.; Ershov, A.P.; Grouzdev, D.S.; Nazina, T.N. Genomic and Physiological Characterization of Halophilic Bacteria of the Genera Halomonas and Marinobacter from Petroleum Reservoirs. *Microbiology* **2022**, *91*, 235–248. [CrossRef]
14. Gutierrez, T.; Berry, D.; Yang, T.; Mishamandani, S.; McKay, L.; Teske, A.; Aitken, M.D. Role of Bacterial Exopolysaccharides (EPS) in the Fate of the Oil Released during the Deepwater Horizon Oil Spill. *PLoS ONE* **2013**, *8*, e67717. [CrossRef] [PubMed]
15. Nwidee, L.N.; Theophilus, S.; Barifcani, A.; Sarmadivaleh, M.; Iglauer, S.; Nwidee, L.N.; Theophilus, S.; Barifcani, A.; Sarmadivaleh, M.; Iglauer, S. EOR Processes, Opportunities and Technological Advancements. In *Chemical Enhanced Oil Recovery (cEOR)—A Practical Overview*; InTechOpen: London, UK, 2016. [CrossRef]
16. Prince, R.C.; Gramain, A.; McGenity, T.J. Prokaryotic Hydrocarbon Degraders. In *Handbook of Hydrocarbon and Lipid Microbiology*; Springer: Berlin/Heidelberg, Germany, 2010; pp. 1669–1692.
17. Kebede, G.; Tafese, T.; Abda, E.M.; Kamaraj, M.; Assefa, F. Factors Influencing the Bacterial Bioremediation of Hydrocarbon Contaminants in the Soil: Mechanisms and Impacts. *J. Chem.* **2021**, *2021*, 9823362. [CrossRef]
18. Dong, C.; Bai, X.; Sheng, H.; Jiao, L.; Zhou, H.; Shao, Z. Distribution of PAHs and the PAH-Degrading Bacteria in the Deep-Sea Sediments of the High-Latitude Arctic Ocean. *Biogeosciences Discuss* **2014**, *11*, 13985–14021. [CrossRef]
19. Mcgenity, T.J.; Folwell, B.D.; Mckew, B.A.; Sanni, G.O. Marine Crude-Oil Biodegradation: A Central Role for Interspecies Interactions. *Saline Syst.* **2012**, *8*, 10. [CrossRef] [PubMed]
20. Liu, C.; Wang, W.; Wu, Y.; Zhou, Z.; Lai, Q.; Shao, Z. Multiple Alkane Hydroxylase Systems in a Marine Alkane Degrader, Alcanivorax Dieselolei B-5. *Env. Microbiol.* **2011**, *13*, 1168–1178. [CrossRef] [PubMed]
21. Niepceron, M.; Portet-Koltalo, F.; Merlin, C.; Motelay-Massei, A.; Barray, S.; Bodilis, J. Both *Cycloclasticus* Spp. and *Pseudomonas* Spp. as PAH-Degrading Bacteria in the Seine Estuary (France). *FEMS Microbiol. Ecol.* **2010**, *71*, 137–147. [CrossRef]
22. Dubinsky, E.A.; Conrad, M.E.; Chakraborty, R.; Bill, M.; Borglin, S.E.; Hollibaugh, J.T.; Mason, O.U.; Piceno, Y.M.; Reid, F.C.; Stringfellow, W.T.; et al. Succession of Hydrocarbon-Degrading Bacteria in the Aftermath of the Deepwater Horizon Oil Spill in the Gulf of Mexico. *Environ. Sci. Technol.* **2013**, *47*, 10860–10867. [CrossRef] [PubMed]
23. Valentine, D.L.; Kessler, J.D.; Redmond, M.C.; Mendes, S.D.; Heintz, M.B.; Farwell, C.; Hu, L.; Kinnaman, F.S.; Yvon-Lewis, S.; Du, M.; et al. Propane Respiration Jump-Starts Microbial Response to a Deep Oil Spill. *Science* **2010**, *330*, 208–211. [CrossRef] [PubMed]
24. Ławniczak, Ł.; Woźniak-Karczewska, M.; Loibner, A.P.; Heipieper, H.J.; Chrzanowski, Ł. Microbial Degradation of Hydrocarbons—Basic Principles for Bioremediation: A Review. *Molecules* **2020**, *25*, 856. [CrossRef]
25. Ron, E.Z.; Rosenberg, E. Enhanced Bioremediation of Oil Spills in the Sea. *Curr. Opin. Biotechnol.* **2014**, *27*, 191–194. [CrossRef] [PubMed]

26. Nagarajan, D.; Dong, C.D.; Chen, C.Y.; Lee, D.J.; Chang, J.S. Biohydrogen Production from Microalgae—Major Bottlenecks and Future Research Perspectives. *Biotechnol. J.* **2021**, *16*, 2000124. [CrossRef]
27. Truskewycz, A.; Gundry, T.D.; Khudur, L.S.; Kolobaric, A.; Taha, M.; Aburto-Medina, A.; Ball, A.S.; Shahsavari, E. Petroleum Hydrocarbon Contamination in Terrestrial Ecosystems—Fate and Microbial Responses. *Molecules* **2019**, *24*, 3400. [CrossRef] [PubMed]
28. Fan, L.; Reynolds, D.; Liu, M.; Stark, M.; Kjelleberg, S.; Webster, N.S.; Thomas, T. Functional Equivalence and Evolutionary Convergence in Complex Communities of Microbial Sponge Symbionts. *Proc. Natl. Acad. Sci. USA* **2012**, *109*, E1878–E1887. [CrossRef] [PubMed]
29. Beyer, J.; Trannum, H.C.; Bakke, T.; Hodson, P.V.; Collier, T.K. Environmental Effects of the Deepwater Horizon Oil Spill: A Review. *Mar. Pollut. Bull.* **2016**, *110*, 28–51. [CrossRef]
30. Mason, O.U.; Hazen, T.C.; Borglin, S.; Chain, P.S.G.; Dubinsky, E.A.; Fortney, J.L.; Han, J.; Holman, H.Y.N.; Hultman, J.; Lamendella, R.; et al. Metagenome, Metatranscriptome and Single-Cell Sequencing Reveal Microbial Response to Deepwater Horizon Oil Spill. *ISME J.* **2012**, *6*, 1715–1727. [CrossRef] [PubMed]
31. Singh, S.K.; Haritash, A.K. Bacterial Degradation of Mixed-PAHs and Expression of PAH-Catabolic Genes. *World J. Microbiol. Biotechnol.* **2022**, *39*, 1–13. [CrossRef]
32. Lee, D.W.; Lee, H.; Lee, A.H.; Kwon, B.O.; Khim, J.S.; Yim, U.H.; Kim, B.S.; Kim, J.J. Microbial Community Composition and PAHs Removal Potential of Indigenous Bacteria in Oil Contaminated Sediment of Taean Coast, Korea. *Environ. Pollut.* **2018**, *234*, 503–512. [CrossRef] [PubMed]
33. Lu, C.; Hong, Y.; Odinga, E.S.; Liu, J.; Tsang, D.C.W.; Gao, Y. Bacterial Community and PAH-Degrading Genes in Paddy Soil and Rice Grain from PAH-Contaminated Area. *Appl. Soil Ecol.* **2021**, *158*, 103789. [CrossRef]
34. Ugya, Y.A.; Hasan, D.B.; Tahir, S.M.; Imam, T.S.; Ari, H.A.; Hua, X. Microalgae Biofilm Cultured in Nutrient-Rich Water as a Tool for the Phycoremediation of Petroleum-Contaminated Water. *Int. J. Phytoremediation* **2021**, *23*, 1175–1183. [CrossRef]
35. Kuttiyathil, M.S.; Mohamed, M.M.; Al-Zuhair, S. Using Microalgae for Remediation of Crude Petroleum Oil-Water Emulsion. *Biotechnol. Prog.* **2020**, *37*, e309. [CrossRef] [PubMed]
36. Özhan, K.; Miles, S.M.; Gao, H.; Bargu, S. Relative Phytoplankton Growth Responses to Physically and Chemically Dispersed South Louisiana Sweet Crude Oil. *Environ. Monit. Assess* **2014**, *186*, 3941–3956. [CrossRef] [PubMed]
37. Znad, H.; Al Ketife, A.M.D.; Judd, S.; AlMomani, F.; Vuthaluru, H.B. Bioremediation and Nutrient Removal from Wastewater by Chlorella Vulgaris. *Ecol. Eng.* **2018**, *110*, 1–7. [CrossRef]
38. Ramadass, K.; Megharaj, M.; Venkateswarlu, K.; Naidu, R. Toxicity of Diesel Water Accommodated Fraction toward Microalgae, Pseudokirchneriella Subcapitata and Chlorella Sp. MM3. *Ecotoxicol. Environ. Saf.* **2017**, *142*, 538–543. [CrossRef] [PubMed]
39. Xaaldi Kalhor, A.; Movafeghi, A.; Mohammadi-Nassab, A.D.; Abedi, E.; Bahrami, A. Potential of the Green Alga Chlorella Vulgaris for Biodegradation of Crude Oil Hydrocarbons. *Mar. Pollut. Bull.* **2017**, *123*, 286–290. [CrossRef]
40. Xaaldi Kalhor, A.; Mohammadi Nassab, A.D.; Abedi, E.; Bahrami, A.; Movafeghi, A. Biodiesel Production in Crude Oil Contaminated Environment Using Chlorella Vulgaris. *Bioresour. Technol.* **2016**, *222*, 190–194. [CrossRef]
41. Hamouda, R.A.E.F.; Sorour, N.M.; Yeheia, D.S. Biodegradation of Crude Oil by Anabaena Oryzae, Chlorella Kessleri and Its Consortium under Mixotrophic Conditions. *Int. Biodeterior. Biodegrad.* **2016**, *112*, 128–134. [CrossRef]
42. El-Sheekh, M.M.; Hamouda, R.A.; Nizam, A.A. Biodegradation of Crude Oil by Scenedesmus Obliquus and Chlorella Vulgaris Growing under Heterotrophic Conditions. *Int. Biodeterior. Biodegrad.* **2013**, *82*, 67–72. [CrossRef]
43. Das, P.; AbdulQuadir, M.; Thaher, M.; Khan, S.; Chaudhary, A.K.; Alghasal, G.; Al-Jabri, H.M.S.J. Microalgal Bioremediation of Petroleum-Derived Low Salinity and Low PH Produced Water. *J. Appl. Phycol.* **2019**, *31*, 435–444. [CrossRef]
44. Kregiel, D.; Berlowska, J.; Witonska, I.; Antolak, H.; Proestos, C.; Babic, M.; Babic, L.; Zhang, B. Saponin-Based, Biological-Active Surfactants from Plants. In *Application and Characterization of Surfactants*; InTechOpen: London, UK, 2017.
45. El-Naggar, N.E.A.; Hussein, M.H.; Shaaban-Dessuuki, S.A.; Dalal, S.R. Production, Extraction and Characterization of Chlorella Vulgaris Soluble Polysaccharides and Their Applications in AgNPs Biosynthesis and Biostimulation of Plant Growth. *Sci. Rep.* **2020**, *10*, 1–19. [CrossRef]
46. Haritash, A.K. A Comprehensive Review of Metabolic and Genomic Aspects of PAH-Degradation. *Arch. Microbiol.* **2020**, *202*, 2033–2058. [CrossRef]
47. Ghodrati, M.; Kosari-Nasab, M.; Zarrini, G.; Movafeghi, A. Crude Oil Contamination Enhances the Lipoxygenase Gene Expression in the Green Microalga Scenedesmus Dimorphus. *Biointerface Res. Appl. Chem.* **2021**, *11*, 11431–11439. [CrossRef]
48. SureshKumar, P.; Thomas, J.; Poornima, V. Structural Insights on Bioremediation of Polycyclic Aromatic Hydrocarbons Using Microalgae: A Modelling-Based Computational Study. *Environ. Monit. Assess* **2018**, *190*, 92. [CrossRef]
49. Stebbing, A.R.D. Hormesis—The Stimulation of Growth by Low Levels of Inhibitors. *Sci. Total Environ.* **1982**, *22*, 213–234. [CrossRef] [PubMed]
50. Burbano, M.S.J.; Gilson, E. The Power of Stress: The Telo-Hormesis Hypothesis. *Cells* **2021**, *10*, 1156. [CrossRef]
51. Ashwaniy, V.R.V.; Perumalsamy, M.; Pandian, S. Enhancing the Synergistic Interaction of Microalgae and Bacteria for the Reduction of Organic Compounds in Petroleum Refinery Effluent. *Environ. Technol. Innov.* **2020**, *19*, 100926. [CrossRef]
52. Chernikova, T.N.; Bargiela, R.; Toshchakov, S.V.; Shivaraman, V.; Lunev, E.A.; Yakimov, M.M.; Thomas, D.N.; Golyshin, P.N. Hydrocarbon-Degrading Bacteria Alcanivorax and Marinobacter Associated with Microalgae Pavlova Lutheri and Nannochloropsis Oculata. *Front. Microbiol.* **2020**, *11*, 572931. [CrossRef] [PubMed]

53. Mahdavi, H.; Prasad, V.; Liu, Y.; Ulrich, A.C. In Situ Biodegradation of Naphthenic Acids in Oil Sands Tailings Pond Water Using Indigenous Algae-Bacteria Consortium. *Bioresour. Technol.* **2015**, *187*, 97–105. [CrossRef]
54. Hodges, A.; Fica, Z.; Wanlass, J.; VanDarlin, J.; Sims, R. Nutrient and Suspended Solids Removal from Petrochemical Wastewater via Microalgal Biofilm Cultivation. *Chemosphere* **2017**, *174*, 46–48. [CrossRef]
55. Abid, A.; Saidane, F.; Hamdi, M. Feasibility of Carbon Dioxide Sequestration by Spongiochloris Sp Microalgae during Petroleum Wastewater Treatment in Airlift Bioreactor. *Bioresour. Technol.* **2017**, *234*, 297–302. [CrossRef]
56. Tang, X.; He, L.Y.; Tao, X.Q.; Dang, Z.; Guo, C.L.; Lu, G.N.; Yi, X.Y. Construction of an Artificial Microalgal-Bacterial Consortium That Efficiently Degrades Crude Oil. *J. Hazard Mater.* **2010**, *181*, 1158–1162. [CrossRef]
57. Jung, S.W.; Park, J.S.; Kown, O.Y.; Kang, J.H.; Shim, W.J.; Kim, Y.O. Effects of Crude Oil on Marine Microbial Communities in Short Term Outdoor Microcosms. *J. Microbiol.* **2010**, *48*, 594–600. [CrossRef] [PubMed]
58. Chen, Z.; Wang, L.; Qiu, S.; Ge, S. Determination of Microalgal Lipid Content and Fatty Acid for Biofuel Production. *Biomed Res. Int.* **2018**, *2018*, 1–17. [CrossRef] [PubMed]
59. Ma, X.; Mi, Y.; Zhao, C.; Wei, Q. A Comprehensive Review on Carbon Source Effect of Microalgae Lipid Accumulation for Biofuel Production. *Sci. Total Environ.* **2022**, *806*, 151387. [CrossRef] [PubMed]
60. Rahman, A.; Agrawal, S.; Nawaz, T.; Pan, S.; Selvaratnam, T. A Review of Algae-Based Produced Water Treatment for Biomass and Biofuel Production. *Water* **2020**, *12*, 2351. [CrossRef]
61. Feng, Y.; Li, C.; Zhang, D. Lipid Production of Chlorella Vulgaris Cultured in Artificial Wastewater Medium. *Bioresour. Technol.* **2011**, *102*, 101–105. [CrossRef]
62. Nishshanka, G.K.S.H.; Liyanaarachchi, V.C.; Nimarshana, P.H.V.; Ariyadasa, T.U.; Chang, J.-S. Haematococcus Pluvialis: A Potential Feedstock for Multiple-Product Biorefining. *J. Clean. Prod.* **2022**, *344*, 131103. [CrossRef]

Disclaimer/Publisher's Note: The statements, opinions and data contained in all publications are solely those of the individual author(s) and contributor(s) and not of MDPI and/or the editor(s). MDPI and/or the editor(s) disclaim responsibility for any injury to people or property resulting from any ideas, methods, instructions or products referred to in the content.

Review

Life Cycle Assessment and Its Application in Wastewater Treatment: A Brief Overview

Siti Safirah Rashid [1,*], Siti Norliyana Harun [2,*], Marlia M. Hanafiah [2,3], Khalisah K. Razman [3], Yong-Qiang Liu [4] and Duratul Ain Tholibon [1]

1. School of Civil Engineering, College of Engineering, Universiti Teknologi MARA (Pahang), Bandar Tun Abdul Razak 26400, Pahang, Malaysia
2. Centre for Tropical Climate Change System, Institute of Climate Change, Universiti Kebangsaan Malaysia, Bangi 43600, Selangor, Malaysia
3. Department of Earth Sciences and Environment, Faculty of Science and Technology, Universiti Kebangsaan Malaysia, Bangi 43600, Selangor, Malaysia
4. Faculty of Engineering and Physical Sciences, University of Southampton, Southampton SO17 1BJ, UK
* Correspondence: sitisafirah@uitm.edu.my (S.S.R.); sitinorliyana@ukm.edu.my (S.N.H.)

Abstract: This paper provides a brief review on wastewater treatment system and the application of life cycle assessment (LCA) for assessing its environmental performance. An extensive review regarding the geographical relevance of LCA for WWTPs, and the evaluation of sustainable wastewater treatment by LCA in both developed and developing countries are also discussed. The objective of the review is to identify knowledge gap, for the improvement of the LCA application and methodology to WWTPs. A total of 35 published articles related to wastewater treatment (WWT) and LCA from international scientific journals were studied thoroughly and summarised from 2006 to 2022. This review found that there is lack of studies concerning LCA of WWTPs that consider specific local criteria especially in the developing countries. Thus, it is important to: (1) assess the influence of seasonality (i.e., dry and wet seasons) on the environmental impact of WWT, (2) investigate environmental impacts from WWTPs in developing countries focusing on the site-specific inventory data, and (3) evaluate environmental sustainability of different processes for upgrading the wastewater treatment system. The environmental impact and cost assessment aspects are crucial for the sustainable development of WWTP. Therefore, environmental impacts must be thoroughly assessed to provide recommendation for future policy and for the water industry in determining environmental trade-offs toward sustainable development.

Keywords: life cycle assessment; wastewater treatment plant; sustainability; environmental impact

Citation: Rashid, S.S.; Harun, S.N.; Hanafiah, M.M.; Razman, K.K.; Liu, Y.-Q.; Tholibon, D.A. Life Cycle Assessment and Its Application in Wastewater Treatment: A Brief Overview. *Processes* **2023**, *11*, 208. https://doi.org/10.3390/pr11010208

Academic Editors: Dimitris Zagklis and Georgios Bampos

Received: 8 November 2022
Revised: 29 November 2022
Accepted: 9 December 2022
Published: 9 January 2023

Copyright: © 2023 by the authors. Licensee MDPI, Basel, Switzerland. This article is an open access article distributed under the terms and conditions of the Creative Commons Attribution (CC BY) license (https://creativecommons.org/licenses/by/4.0/).

1. Municipal Wastewater Treatment System

A municipal wastewater treatment system is encompassed of a sewer system and wastewater treatment plant (WWTP) and characterized by Sikosana et al. [1] as the most common sort of wastewater belonging to the low-strength waste stream category. There are two types of sewer system connected to WWTP: (i) separate sewer system with different flow/network for rainwater runoff and domestic/industrial wastewater, and (ii) combined sewer system of the same sewer pipe for both rainwater runoff and domestic/industrial wastewater. A WWTP consists of different processes or operating units (e.g., pre-treatment, primary treatment, secondary treatment, sludge treatment and tertiary treatment) as shown in Figure 1. Pre-treatment and primary treatment are mainly focused on removal of particulate pollutants such as solids, grit, and greases. Secondary treatment treats organic matter, nitrogen, and phosphorus contained in the sewage through biological and chemical processes [2–4]. Tertiary treatment is applied to remove remaining small particles and pathogens in some WWTPs.

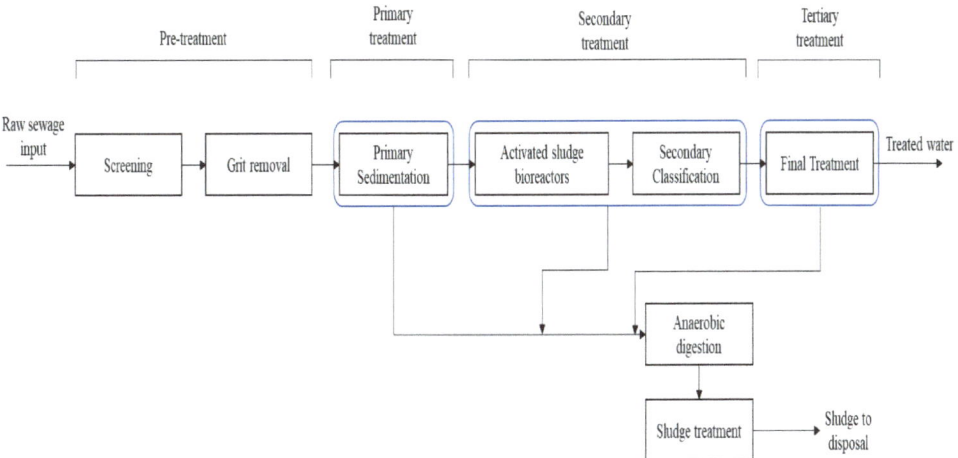

Figure 1. Flow diagram of the WWTP process.

Finally, sludge treatment treats the excess sludge for stabilisation and volume reduction through sludge thickening and dewatering. The sludge is sent to landfill, used in agriculture, incinerated, or transported to composting plant. Meanwhile, constructing a WWTP is a challenging process that implicates various types of materials such as concrete, timber, steel, and plastics, and involves detail operational design and equipment. The operation of WWTP requires: (i) a large amount of electricity for pumping or aeration, (ii) chemicals for sludge treatment and phosphorus removal, and (iii) transportation of waste, sludge, and chemicals [5]. Consequently, WWTP has substantial environmental impacts during its life cycle (i.e., construction, operation, and demolition) due to the energy consumption, chemical usage, sludge generation, effluent discharge, and gas emissions [6].

2. The State-of-the-Art Methods for Applying LCA in Wastewater Treatment Plants

Over the last 50 years, an increased awareness has developed in global society about protecting the environment particularly water resources. In relation to that, the European Commission Council Directive (1991/271/EEC) concerning urban wastewater treatment stated that the objective of wastewater treatment is to protect the environment from adverse effects of discharging urban and industrial wastewater. A large number of wastewater treatment plants (WWTPs) are designed and operated to prevent pollution to the environment by removing a variety of contaminants from wastewater before discharge, restoring desirable quality to water that has been contaminated by humans or nature [7].

However, to some extent, the pollutants in wastewater could be transferred to air such as greenhouse gases (GHGs) emissions [8,9] and soil such as disposal of sludge due to wastewater treatment, which could lead to negative effects on human health and the environment in other forms. This holistic environmental impact from WWTPs is very challenging to evaluate, and thus, a cradle-to-grave approach is needed to analyse the consequences of these plants to the environment. Some environmental impacts from the operation of WWTPs include climate change from the emission of GHGs, eutrophication from the emission of nutrients to the water body, and ecosystem damage from the emission of heavy metals, with the United Nation's sustainable development goals addressing climate change, eutrophication, and acidification of water bodies as the most pressing impacts. Therefore, conducting an environmental impact assessment for particular technologies, products or processes is very important to identify their environmental impacts and potential mitigation strategies.

The application of environmental assessment tools provides reliable environmental impact information that assists in decision-making toward sustainable operation of a system or process [10]. At present, the impact of a wastewater treatment system can be assessed through different evaluation tools such as the LCA method, economic and exergy analysis, the environmental impact assessment (EIA) method, and net environmental benefit analysis (NEBA) [8]. LCA is an approach in assessing the environmental impact associated with all stages in the life cycle of commercial products, processes, or services, and according to Nizam et al. [3] should be assessed in order to create environmentally acceptable technology for future development. In LCA, environmental impacts are assessed from raw material extraction of the product or process to the final disposal of the materials, i.e., cradle to grave [3,8].

The use of LCA has started to draw great attention of many researchers and industrial practice in identifying environmental impacts and evaluating the sustainability of wastewater treatment/technology selection [6,11,12]. This is because LCA provides a complete framework of assessment starting from the goal and scope (objective), life cycle inventory, life cycle impact assessment, and interpretation. Meanwhile, an economic analysis could be assessed using cost-benefit analysis (CBA), life cycle costing (LCC), and techno-economic analysis (TEA) [13–15]. Usually, this economic evaluation can be combined with LCA to produce a robust evaluation for a system-level analysis towards the sustainable operation of WWTPs.

Compared with LCA analysis for the manufacturing sector, an LCA of wastewater treatment is fairly established with about 20 years of practice. Since 1995, more than 70 international peer-reviewed articles dealing with WWT and LCA have been published with different inventories, boundary conditions, functional units (FU), and impact assessment methods. The various research papers have shown that LCA has evolved in the past two decades to include more improvement and systematic assessment. An extensive review of existing LCA studies was conducted for this research to assess the state-of-the-art knowledge on the environmental impact and benefit of LCA to identify the knowledge gap. Based on the selection of related journals, 60 published articles were found to be related to WWT and LCA from the international scientific journals reviewed, but only 58% of the papers published from 2006 to 2022 (Figure 2) were selected and summarised. The criteria of searched for the published articles was based on the topic of 'Life Cycle Assessment' and 'Wastewater Management and Treatment' for various countries to analyse various studies conducted on this topic.

A LCA is an approach that considers environmental, economic, and social impacts that a product or service will produce throughout its life cycle. A life cycle sustainability assessment (LCSA) considers the environmental, economic, and social ramifications of a product's whole life cycle, i.e., from "cradle to grave," as well as its use and waste disposal [16]. It can be used as a technical tool to identify opportunities to reduce the environmental effects associated with a specific product, system, material or activity through consideration of the burdens during manufacturing and as a finished product [17]. LCA has been applied in various research settings to analyse the environmental impacts of different WWTPs as they have a significant environmental impact on receiving water bodies and cost municipalities or industrial facilities a lot of money [18]. However, the scope of assessment is rather challenging due to the variation in defining the system boundaries and the difficulty in considering wastewater composition and the type of pollutants. Different options of wastewater treatment technology have different performances and impacts on the environment, which may take place during different phases in a WWTP's life cycle. In the following overview, relevant studies within this field of research are briefly described mainly to provide a benchmark of LCA methodology application in the wastewater treatment.

Figure 2. Number of LCA studies from 2006–2022.

Based on the detailed review discussed in Section 7, published research on the LCA of wastewater treatment can be classified into two types. One type focuses on using LCA to facilitate technology comparison and selection from the environmental impact point of view. The other type focuses on working on different steps of the LCA method itself (i.e., goal and scope, inventory, impact assessment, and interpretation) to improve the reliability of the LCA results. Some researchers have even developed new models for the calculation of new characterisation factors or new impact categories, such as a new characterisation factor for pollutants or substances to provide more representative and reliable analysis. For instance, one study conducted an environmental evaluation of common technical options for urban wastewater treatment [19], whereas another identified the overall environmental impact of WWTPs (for both water and sludge treatment) using LCA methodology [20]. Some studies have also conducted specific evaluations of GHG emissions from WWTPs [21–23], including one environmental–economic evaluation of the sludge treatment process in Korea that used life cycle analysis [6].

In more detail, LCA methodology was also used by Ontiveros and Campanella [24] to evaluate the environmental performance of three different advanced biological nutrient removal processes in Argentina: modified UCT, five stages Bardenpho, and modified Bardenpho from WWTPs. This evaluation can guide the selection of the biological nutrient removal process in the Argentina context from both technological and environmental points of views. In a different aspect, Yoshida et al. [25] conducted a study on the improvement of life cycle inventory and methodology involving the consideration of onsite GHG emissions and long-term emission data in the land application of sewage sludge. In addition, Morera et al. [5] worked on the improvement of LCA methodology in the urban wastewater treatment system and emphasized the improvement of construction detailed inventory including sewer system and inventory improvement with scale assessment. Recent research identified that most studies using LCA for WWTPs aim to evaluate the environmental impact of different technologies including identifying advanced and conventional emission parameters [26,27], analysing control strategies of WWTP performance [12] and identifying the environmental trade-off of different process alternatives. These findings showed that LCA can assess various aspects of identifying environmental impact from wastewater treatment but the methodology from the framework provided by the International Standard Organisation (ISO) could be further improved. The social factor is more complicated and is not included in this review.

A review of 35 published LCA studies of WWTPs (from 2006 to 2022) identified that most of the published studies have been concentrated in the European continent, followed by the Asian continent, mainly contributed by China with little application from other developing countries such as Thailand and Malaysia (Figure 3). In terms of technology coverage, only a few studies have applied LCA to resource recovery, especially in developing countries. The analysis in these 35 papers also revealed that there is variability in the definition of the functional unit (FU) and the system boundaries, the selection of the life cycle inventory and impact assessment methodology, and the procedure results interpretation. As supported by Hauschild et al. [28], the LCA standard of ISO 14040 is still general and unspecific in its requirement. Besides that, there is a scarcity of secondary data which is commonly obtained from published data of LCA studies, and the data may be incomplete [29,30]. Therefore, there is a need to investigate the standardized guidelines for the wastewater treatment operation by evaluating the key steps in the LCA methodology to improve the quality of LCA–WWTP.

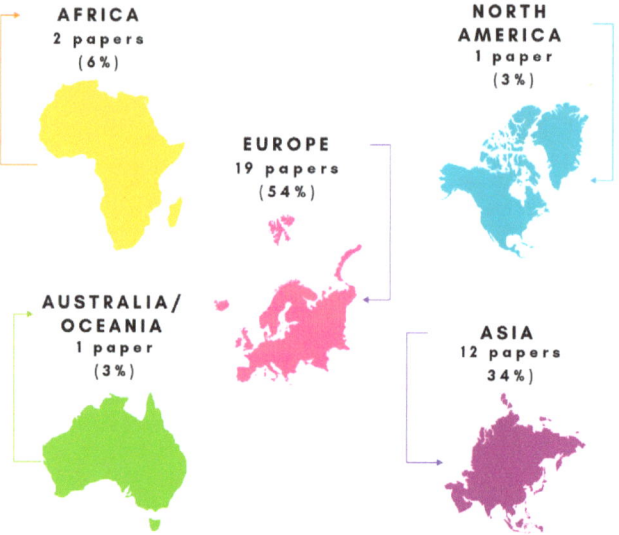

Figure 3. LCA studies based on their continents.

3. Key Steps for LCA Assessment

LCA is a standardised methodology to evaluate the environmental impacts associated with a product or process during its complete life cycle as described in two ISO norms, ISO 14040 and 14044 [31]. The concept of LCA first emerged in the late 1960s. In the 1970s, LCA only focused on energy and raw materials, but later the analysis system expanded to emissions, water, air, and soil. Starting in the 1990s, LCA was applied in wastewater treatment after being identified as suitable for related environmental assessments. In 1994, the ISO began developing standards for the LCA method as part of its 14,000 series on environmental management; however, the method was not yet designed in detail for all fields of assessment [32]. Nevertheless, since then more studies on LCA have been undertaken and published in various disciplines, including a variety of boundary conditions, databases, impact assessment methods, and interpretations.

Several software programs have been developed including free and commercial software to assist in the analysis of LCA. At present, various types of commercial LCA software are available such as SimaPro, Gabi, Umberto and, openLCA [33,34]. SimaPro was developed by Pre-Sustainability Consultants in the Netherlands and has been used for more than 20 years in various studies and projects. It is a user-friendly tool that helps to model and analyse complex products or systems such as water and wastewater treatment. It can also calculate environmental impacts and detect environmental hotspots in a systematic way [5].

In addition, OpenLCA, developed in Germany, is another free software for LCA user [24]. All of these programs are professional life cycle modelling tools and available with various embedded databases such as Ecoinvent, European Life Cycle Database (ELCD), and U.S. Life Cycle Inventory (USLCI). However, one of the challenges of LCA is that it requires detailed inventory information for each system assessed [35].

A detailed review on LCA methodology steps was conducted to understand more about the application of LCA. The structured methodology in LCA as stated in ISO starts with defining the goal and scope followed by life cycle inventory (LCI), and life cycle impact assessment (LCIA), and ends with a results interpretation as shown in Figure 4. This methodology highlights the general steps or flow of LCA with general characteristics that have been identified within each step.

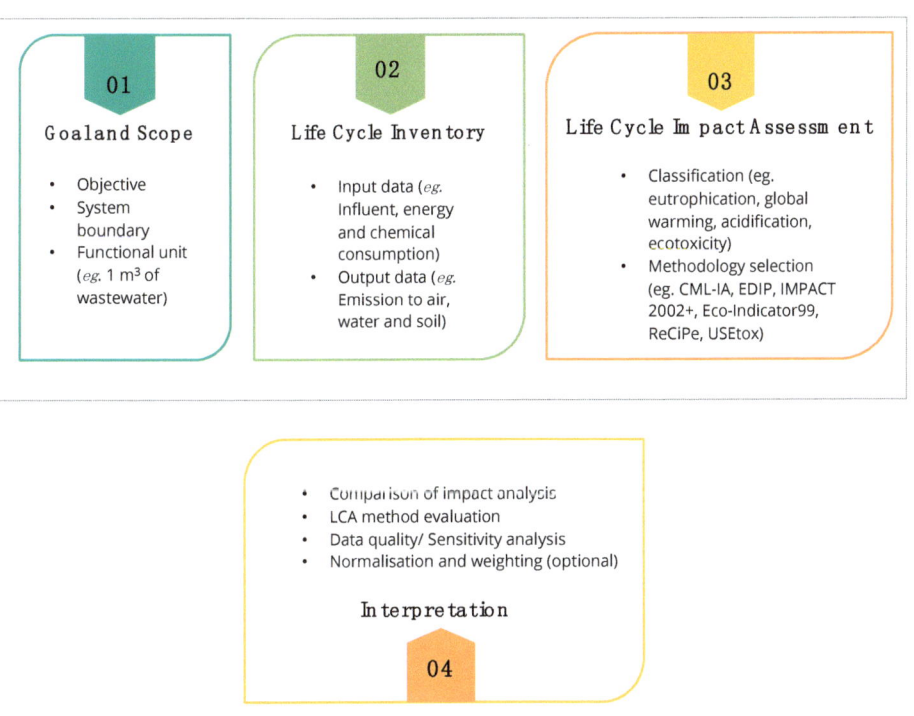

Figure 4. LCA methodology steps for environmental impact assessment from WWTPs.

3.1. Goal and Scope

In detail, the goal and scope of LCA consist of the objectives, system boundary, and functional unit. The objectives consist of the environmental analysis, the technology comparison, and their effect on the environment or the analysis of life cycle inventory and methodology to various impact categories. The system boundary determines which unit process shall be included in LCA analysis [31] such as construction stage, operation, sludge treatment and disposal, and demolition phase. As shown in Figure 5, all of the studies covered operation since it contributes to the highest to the total environmental impact [12,33,36] with merely 7% of the studies analysing the phases of construction up to its disposal/demolition. Lorenzo-Toja et al. [37] reported that the environmental impact from the construction phase is almost negligible for many impact categories compared with the operational phase.

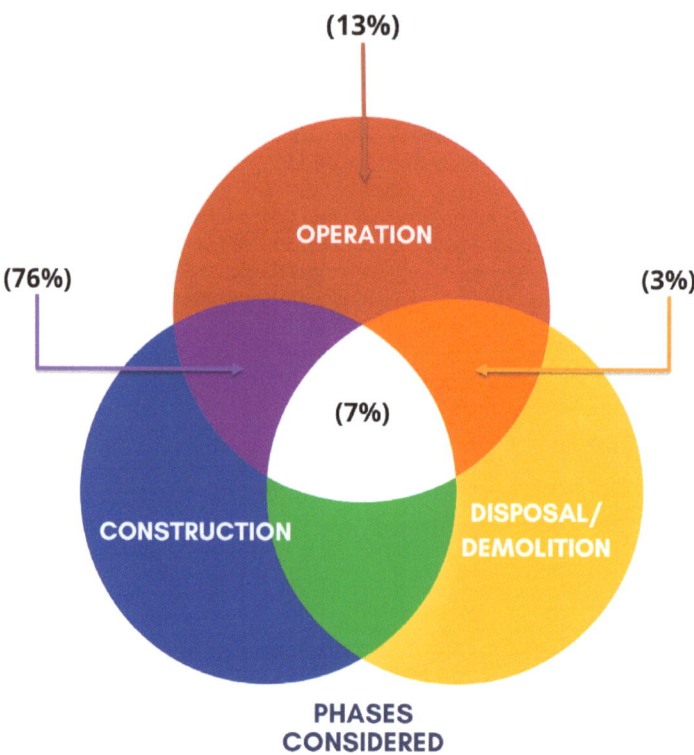

Figure 5. Phases of processes considered for the LCA.

Similarly, Pasqualino et al. [20] stated that the environmental impact from the construction and demolition phases also could be considered negligible. In the operational phase, approximately 80% of the studies included sludge treatment and disposal in the system boundary due to the importance of this stage to the overall impact [32]. Finally, the functional unit is usually defined as the treatment of a volume of wastewater in 1 m³; however, some studies have used population equivalents (PE/year). In addition, several other options are available for the functional unit in LCA–WWTP such as the quantity of sludge produced and the quantity of removed pollutants [38]. However, no strong justification appears to exist between its selection and technologies used in a specific system of WWT. To analyse this issue, Rodriguez-Garcia et al. [39] studied the effect of a functional unit based on wastewater volume (m³) to identify the different effluent quality of six typologies of WWTPs. They found that global warming and economic cost decrease following better eutrophication.

By contrast, studies with similar FU found that a trade-off exists between lower eutrophication, higher environmental, and economic impact when involving more demanding/upgrading treatment such as water reuse. These conflicting results show that discrepancies still exist when using single FU to identify the effect of different treatment technologies. Therefore, Rodriguez-Garcia et al. [39] have suggested that a second FU should be introduced in specific studies such as those on eutrophication reduction (kg PO_4^{3-}) to overcome this limitation and strengthen the system under study. This suggestion was supported by Corominas et al. [32] who determined that a FU of a system could influence the final result, especially when comparing WWTPs with different influent qualities or different removal rates.

3.2. Life Cycle Inventory

After the goal and scope are determined, the second step in a LCA is data collection and inventory build-up, a crucial stage when performing an LCA study. In general, life cycle inventory (LCI) aims to identify the inputs (resources), the outputs (effluent and waste), and the respective amounts of emissions over the entire life cycle of the specific process. Generally, it is given in physical units such as kilogram (kg), cubic metre (m^3), and kilowatt–hour (kWh). Wastewater treatment data inventory includes the foreground as the primary data (operation), which is usually compiled from the operational record, detailed design document, sampling works, and vendor-supplied information. By contrast, background data (secondary input) such as energy production and chemical production are normally provided by the LCI database (e.g., the Ecoinvent and the ELCD). Ecoinvent, which was developed by the Ecoinvent Centre in Switzerland, is one of the major data inventory providers used in various sectors. In the LCI phase, identified inventories are collected for all processes of the boundary and calculated to the same functional unit.

3.3. Life Cycle Impact Assessment

Prior to the calculation of the environmental impacts, the assessment methodology must be selected to give direction to the category of impact required, such as the midpoint level or the endpoint level. Several different methodologies are available to identify related impact categories in the LCA such as Eco-Indicator99 [33], Recipe [36], EDIP 2003, USEtox, IMPACT2002+, and CML2001 [40]. CML2001 is found to be the highest number in the methodology used by researchers due to its extensive impact categories, high relevance to wastewater treatment at the midpoint level, and accurate results as shown from a previous study [20]. For the life cycle impact assessment (LCIA) phase in every method, the inventory data (LCI) emitted to air, water, and soil compartments are multiplied with their characterisation factor (CF) to convert to environmental impacts in various categories, as shown in Equation (1) [41].

$$\text{LCIA} = \text{LCI} \times \text{CF}$$
$$\text{E.g. Freshwater Ecotoxicity Potential (FEP)} = \qquad (1)$$
$$(\text{LCI}_{air} \times \text{CF}_{air}) + (\text{LCI}_{water} \times \text{CF}_{water}) + (\text{LCI}_{soil} \times \text{CF}_{soil}) \text{ (unit: kg1,4-dBeq.)}$$

Characterisation factors (CFs) of inventory data or pollutants are provided to practitioners either in the literature or by the software used [42]. CF models are built based on the mechanism of the cause–effect chain starting from the emission of pollutants until the receiving compartments. CF values are the total results of environmental fate, exposure, and the resulting effect on the exposed section such as human [43]. CFs were calculated by multiplying fate factor (FF) to exposure factor (XF) and effect factor (EF). Fate factor (FF) denotes the residence time of the substances/pollutants in the receiving compartments. Exposure factor (XF) relates to the actual concentration of substances taken by the receiving compartment, e.g., human. Effect factor (EF) is correlated to the route of exposure, e.g., ingestion and inhalation effect to human toxicity. Exposure factor and fate factor are combined to form the intake factor (IF) of a substance [44].

Nevertheless, various discrepancies still exist between methods provided in LCA. To address this issue, Pizzol et al. [45] compared nine different methodologies focusing on the impact of metals on human health. The results showed a poor agreement between the methods. For example, the contribution of metal to total human health changed greatly between the methods. This poor agreement is due to the different types of metal considered and the different techniques used to calculate the characterisation factor. This indicates that there is no unified LCIA method, especially for the human health impact category. Table 1 lists the origin or provider of each methodology provided in LCA.

Table 1. List of environmental impact assessment methods.

Method	Developer
CML 1992/CML-IA	Centre for Environmental Studies, University of Leiden
Eco-indicator 95/99	Pre Consultant B.V
Eco-points 97	Swiss ministry of the environment
EDIP 2003	Institute for product development (IPU) at the Technical University of Denmark
IMPACT 2002+	Swiss Federal Institute of Technology Lausanne (EPFL), Switzerland

Midpoint environmental impact categories are provided in each method. For example, in CML-IA, the midpoint categories involving wastewater treatment normally include abiotic depletion (fossil fuel), eutrophication, global warming, acidification, ozone depletion, and human toxicity potentials. However, water, land, and energy use have been increasingly gaining attention in this research area as new impact categories, depending on the objective of the study. In contrast to midpoint categories, the endpoint damage category is always considered in the LCA assessment as an endpoint area of protection. The categories include damages to human health, ecosystems, and resource availability.

3.4. Interpretation

The final stage of LCA methodology is interpretation. This final stage can identify and evaluate information from the result of the life cycle impact assessment because it can determine the level of confidence in the final results. It starts with an understanding of the accuracy of the result and how it meets the goal of the study. According to Corominas et al. [32] and based on the ISO 14040:2006, the interpretation part in the LCA includes: (a) identification of important issues based on the results of the LCI and LCIA; (b) evaluation of the study considering completeness, sensitivity, and consistency checks; and (c) conclusions, limitations, and recommendations.

4. Geographical Relevance of LCA for WWTPs

Before the 2000s, the majority of the traditional LCA approach was based on site-independence where no consideration was given to geographical and temporal factors. The reviewed study showed that some published papers used secondary data (e.g., from literature) or simulated data to conduct LCA analysis due to the lack of the available primary data, leading to much less reliable results. However, the results still could provide some guidance to a certain degree. For the inventory practice, approximately 55% of studies for LCA–WWTP were based on site operation while others still depended on the estimations, existing simulation data, previous reports, and literature due to the limited availability of reliable databases. The other reason was that performing onsite measurements that obviously can reduce the data uncertainty is often not feasible as the process is expensive and time-consuming.

The analysis of the geographical distribution in LCA found that only a few studies were conducted in developing countries such as India, Egypt, Thailand, and Malaysia. As a consequence, the distributions of studies with regard to the assessed wastewater management systems by LCA on environmental concerns are specific to a few regions only. The drawback of this analysis system is that another country in a different region with a different temperature or economic value cannot meaningfully refer to the existing available data and impact results. This situation shows that the fairly distributed databases around the world are still lacking in LCA analysis studies for WWTPs, especially in developing countries. This idea was supported by Renou et al. [46] who reported that location-specific factors are critical especially for eutrophication and terrestrial ecotoxicity impact category due to the transportation effect by pollutants. Therefore, the selection of inventory data is critical to LCA analysis especially when local factors such as dry and wet season are accounted in the analysis to provide reliable results.

To overcome this limitation, there was a trend after 2000 towards making LCA more site-dependent, considering more site-specific characterization factors such as eutrophication, toxicity impact, and acidification potentials. This is because the point of emission may have a strong impact on these regional and local impact categories. For global warming and ozone layer depletion, characterization factors are justifiable because the emission location has no influence on the transportation effect [47]. Therefore, it is important to identify specific characterisation factors that impact the different countries that have different geographical, climatic, and economic factors, which are significantly lacking in developing countries. This brings into question how the importance of regionalisation criteria and the database influence the LCA results.

Therefore, there is still some possibility that the LCA method for wastewater treatment impact assessments can be improved, especially outside of Europe with consideration for the variability of treatment technology. For example, Yoshida et al. [25] studied the effects of three different inventory databases to the LCA results that are from the European Pollution Release and Transfer Registry (EPRTR), the Denmark national discharge limit data and data collection scheme conducted at the WWTP in Copenhagen, Denmark. They found that the LCA results depended heavily on the onsite data input. For instance, the EPRTR did not capture impact for particulate matter and terrestrial eutrophication. They found that primary data (i.e., site data collection scheme) from WWTPs gave the most reliable LCA results but still needed some improvements, such as the expansion of substance coverage and additional detail collection of energy and chemical usage. On the other hand, for the temporal effect, even though Lorenzo-Toja et al. [37] and Alfonsín et al. [27] identified no clear difference in environmental performance between WWTPs from the Atlantic and Mediterranean regions of Spain, the effectiveness of using the existing secondary databases in a different region, especially in a different climate of a developing country, is uncertain. Therefore, it is well proved that site-specific inventory data is the key to obtaining reliable LCA results.

The review in this chapter shows that research focused on specific local conditions and inventory effects to the LCA results have been rarely assessed in LCA–WWTP related studies. Most of the studies also did not stress the importance of geographically different impacts in terms of data inventory and local factors (e.g., temperature and rainfall). In fact, some of the research outside of Europe uses European datasets for its region without adjusting for uncertain information such as the local impact factors of electricity. One of these factors is the availability of a generic database, which decreases the need for the importance of local primary data. Furthermore, most of the characterisation and normalisation factors are also based on European conditions, where these factors are currently used globally only due to their availability.

However, very few studies have been conducted using LCA in developing countries. The lack of primary data and underrepresentation of the life cycle thinking concepts in developing countries are possibly the main causes for the restricted number of studies published. In the wastewater sector, besides energy and chemical production data, the most important aspects are the effects of temperature, rainfall intensity, local pollutants, and design criteria (e.g., combined or separate sewer systems), all of which could be included and analysed. Moreover, the impact of treatment technology is greatly dependent on the local situation/factors such as geographic location, wastewater characteristic, energy type and source, choices of sludge and waste disposal options, and size of markets for products derived from WWT system such as fertiliser.

The review in this chapter suggests that it is important to have inputs based on a localised primary and secondary database with regard to local characteristic representing specific region such as tropical developing regions or Europe. In other words, the new localised database can keep the commercial data inventory as a benchmark. For example, Europe has a temperate climate (i.e., warm in summer and cold in winter) while tropical zones having warm weather year-round. Indeed, regionalisation is recognised as an important step towards improving the accuracy, precision, and confidence in LCA results.

5. Benefits of LCA for Environmental Impact Evaluation of WWTPs

The current LCA is well described in terms of the framework and can be applied to a wide range of products including waste and water cycles. Therefore, in this situation, LCA could be a tool to identify environmental factors and assess impacts from the wastewater treatment operation [12,24]. Furthermore, Foley et al. [48] pointed out that while their research had provided new inventory data needed about WWTPs, without life cycle impact assessment modelling they could only identify a limited comparison for the impacts by the newly provided data.

Besides identifying the environmental impacts from WWTPs, LCA can assess the trade-off of the new integration of existing technologies in terms of cost and environmental impact [49]. For example, Meneses et al. [12] concluded that the technologies adopted for more stringent effluent standards from WWTPs (i.e., 10–15 mgN/L and 1–2 mgP/L by EU Urban Waste Water Directive) could improve effluent quality but, at the same time, may require additional energy consumption, use chemical reagents, and produce more sludge. Hauck et al. [50] found the trade-off between different environmental impacts by conducting an LCA. They reported a 16% reduction in marine eutrophication, but the climate change impacts increased with 9% from the traditional operation of the Dokhaven Wastewater Treatment Plant in the Netherlands. This increase was due to the increasing use of electricity and shows that the trade-off between effluent quality and other environmental impacts should not be neglected when applying advanced technology. In nutrient recovery, a similar phenomenon was observed. For example, struvite precipitation for phosphorus recovery improved the effluent quality from WWT while recovering nutrient resources. However, the chemical addition for pH control accounted for up to 97% of total struvite cost [51]. Thus, by applying an established methodology, LCA can identify the trade-off of different technologies adopted in WWTPs.

Besides its benefits, LCA still has a series of shortcomings and limitations, especially related to the data quality and methodology choice. Therefore, research is needed to provide recommendations to future LCA practitioners on the suitable data requirement and impact assessment methodology for WWT. To evaluate these limitations, rigorous assessments should be considered especially from various aspects of the LCA to wastewater treatment to identify the most significant environmental issues, including the economic effects.

6. Evaluation of Sustainable Wastewater Treatment by LCA

The world is moving towards sustainable development and a circular economy. In 2015, the United Nations set 17 sustainability-developing goals. This global strategic platform included developing countries, even though developed countries generally have more resources for sustainable development. One of these 17 goals focuses on water and sanitation. The goal includes supporting developing countries in water and sanitation programmes including water efficiency, wastewater treatment, and recycling and reuse technologies. Some developing countries such as China have planned to build concept WWTPs to reconceptualise water, carbon, and energy systems from the systems level, which can help build a 'circular economy' that closes resource loops to achieve sustainable development. Thus, further studies on the sustainable application in WWTPs combined with LCA, especially in developing countries, are crucial for continuous guidance towards reaching a circular economy in the wastewater industry. Hence, it was observed that the top journals publishing on LCA studies were from the Journal of Cleaner Production, Water Research, and Science of the Total Environment throughout 2006–2022 (Figure 6) in line with their respective goals surrounding efficient water management and usage.

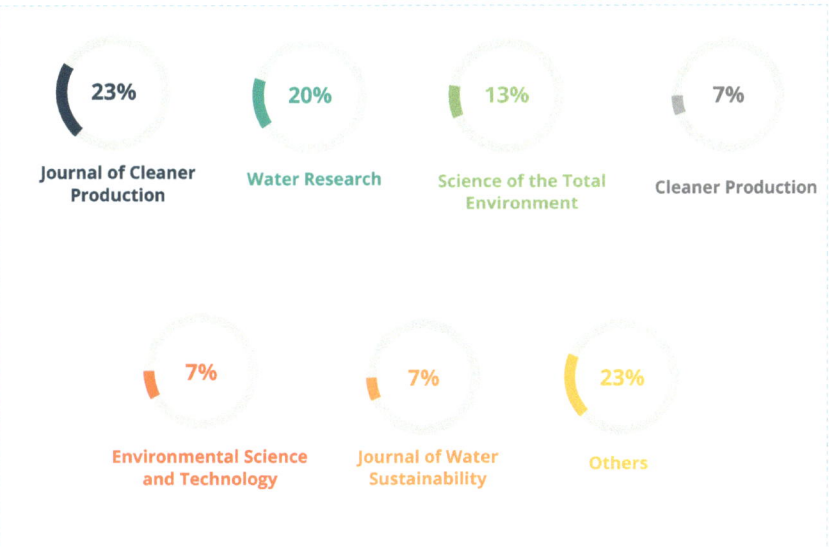

Figure 6. Published LCA studies on WWTP from various journals.

6.1. Sustainable Application in Wastewater Treatment

A WWTP consists of various processes that are typically in series (e.g., pre-treatment, primary treatment, secondary treatment, and sludge treatment) [51]. Each unit has a specific function designed to remove pollutants in wastewater. Pre-treatment largely removes large solids, grit, and oil, whereas primary treatment is designed to remove suspended solids. Secondary treatment is usually based on a biological process that treats organic matter, nitrogen, and phosphorus. Finally, sludge treatment treats the excess sludge by a thickening and dewatering process, and the dewatered sludge is sent to landfills, agriculture land, or incineration plants. An operating WWTP normally uses a large amount of electricity (e.g., for pumping and aeration), as well as chemicals that enhance nutrients removal and improve sludge dewatering process. The operation of a conventional WWTP is not sustainable and generates various environmental impacts such as eutrophication, acidification, and global warming potentials. This chapter reviews and discusses in detail the environmental issues derived from a WWTP and its potential sustainable treatment by using the LCA application.

6.1.1. GHG Emissions

Wastewater treatment operation generates a significant amount of GHGs including carbon dioxide (CO_2), methane (CH_4), and nitrous oxide (N_2O) [52,53]. CO_2 is mainly produced from the process of fossil fuels to energy as indirect emissions, which involves with 14–36% of total emissions from a WWTP. Methane is formed in the sewer system and under anaerobic conditions, whereas N_2O contributes to 23–43% of emissions during the biological nitrogen removal process [21,23]. Reducing these direct and indirect emissions from WWTPs could assist in tackling global warming wherein energy reduction and recovery through AD, nitritation–anammox, and A–B process (A stage for carbon capture to improve energy recovery by digestion, and B stage for biological treatment to improve effluent quality) in WWTPs could further reduce GHG emissions. For example, the combination of the anaerobic digestion with combined heat and power, and energy-optimising activated sludge could save over 102,000 tonnes CO_2/year, which equals 50% of energy optimization [54].

However, to quantify the correct emission, an established environmental tool is required because a complex calculation must be completed, including the range of electricity and chemical consumption, as well as site-specific factors. Currently, the quantification of direct GHG emissions is implemented by observing CH_4 and N_2O emission, which present global warming potentials (GWP) of 21 kg CO_2 eq. and 310 kg CO_2 eq. per kg of compound emitted, respectively [55]. The GHGs are produced within the WWTP in various locations and treatments. The main sources of CH_4 emission are in anaerobic conditions such as sludge thickeners and sludge storage tanks [22]. Nonetheless, another important source of CH_4 is the sewer system [56]. Thus, CH_4 is not only emitted from the anaerobic tanks but also in aerated areas via stripping. Meanwhile, N_2O is mainly reported to be released from anoxic zones of activated sludge configurations where nitrification and denitrification reactions lead to the production of N_2O [57]. Additionally, some studies have also pointed out that N_2O emissions occur in de-gritter units, sedimentation tanks, secondary clarifiers, and sludge treatment tanks [58]. Overall, a suitable methodology needs to be identified to calculate GHG emissions from WWTP and find suitable technologies to reduce these emissions.

6.1.2. More Stringent Discharge Standards

The discharging of nitrogenous components of wastewater effluent to a water body can cause the deterioration of water quality and eutrophication to aquatic life [59]. Therefore, the higher limit of effluent discharge from WWT has been introduced especially in urban areas and developed countries such as the USA, Europe, and Japan. For example, the EU Urban Waste Water Directive has set requirements at 10–15 mg N/L and 1–2 mg P/L, which require the improvement and upgrading of wastewater treatment technology such as applying enhanced biological phosphorus removal (EBPR), anaerobic ammonium oxidation (anammox), and aerobic granular sludge (AGS).

Meanwhile, in most developing countries, the discharge requirement is lower because most of the technology is still at a lower efficiency for treatments than that used in developed countries. For example, most of the WWTPs in developing countries only consider nutrient and organic matter removal, whereas most treatment plants in Europe have already applied resource recovery technology such as anaerobic digestion and water reuse technology. Therefore, the scale of environmental impact varies depending on the local factor, as well as regulation and technology adopted mainly for eutrophication impact, which is regularly monitored. The monitoring of effluent data is normally compulsory for all WWTPs to identify the level of nutrients discharged into the water body where it could affect the quality of river or ocean. Thus, the assessment of site-specific discharge standards from a WWTP is crucial, especially in urban areas. These assessments can potentially be used by decision-makers to assess effluent quality regulation and consider upgrading requirements in the future.

6.1.3. Sludge Treatment and Disposal

For the sewage sludge generated from WWT, approximately 10 million and 8 million tonnes of dry sludge were generated in the European Union and United States, respectively, in 2010 [60]. This problem affects the environment where energy is consumed for the treatment and disposal process, polluting underground water and soil by heavy metals and GHG emissions; an estimated 32–39% of CH_4 is emitted from the sludge [53]. Apart from a 90% reduction of sludge volume after incineration [61], integrating technologies of anaerobic digestion and struvite recovery could help to reduce the amount of sludge from WWTPs. For instance, Amersfoort WWTP in the Netherlands, which has commissioned three advanced technologies including struvite recovery by Ostara, could reduce 17% sludge volume while recovering 45% of phosphate and producing 60% more biogas to energy.

6.1.4. Nutrient Removal and Material Recovery

Nutrient removal from WWTPs consists of treatments to remove nitrogen and phosphorus before being discharged to water body and requires different processes. In nitrogen removal, nitrogen is oxidised from ammonia to nitrate through nitrification process, which takes place in aeration tanks/secondary treatment tanks. This process is followed by denitrification where nitrate is converted to nitrogen gas, which is released into the atmosphere and consequently removed from the wastewater. The denitrification process needs anoxic conditions to encourage proper biological reaction. Various technologies are increasingly available for nitrogen removal from wastewater that leads to a cleaner discharge to a water body and sustainable application. For instance, nitrification–denitrification is increasingly applied worldwide due to its technical maturity.

Other nitrogen removal technologies such as aerobic granular sludge (AGS) and anammox are increasingly applied because they have the potential to reduce energy and chemical consumption. Apart from this, the A-stage from the A–B process removes about 55–65% of the organic load, and approximately 80% of nitrogen elimination is achieved in the B-stage [62]. Phosphorus removal can be achieved by chemical phosphorus precipitation such as using iron chloride. Phosphorus can also be biologically removed using polyphosphate-accumulating organisms (PAOs) in EBPR. PAO could accumulate great quantities of phosphorus within their cells, and separate the phosphorus from the treated water. Other phosphorus removal technologies include ion exchange chemical removal and the emerging aerobic granular sludge (AGS) process.

The regular application of nutrient reuse from WWTPs is applying sludge to agricultural lands such as composting due to the nitrogen and phosphorus content in the sludge, both of which can be nutrient sources for plants. However, not all the sludge can be directly applied to agricultural lands due to the pollutant contents such as heavy metals, which can harm the environment. This is the reason why more nutrient recovery research and application is increasingly conducted worldwide for better, more sustainable consumption. Recently, the focus has been on chemical phosphorus product due to its scarcity. For instance, various technologies have been developed to recover phosphorus from WWTPs such as Ostara from Canada and Gifhorn, Airprex, and Unitika from Japan where the struvite can be sold as fertiliser. For example, struvite crystallisation by Airprex was used to retrieve phosphorus following the anaerobic digestion process and EBPR. Struvite was produced by air stripping the reactor, while adding chemical product such as magnesium.

In addition, P recovery process could improve the effluent quality and minimize sludge production while meeting the stringent P discharge limit (<2 mg/L). In terms of efficiency, the recovery of phosphorus from the side stream can achieve up to 50% of P recovery potential, whereas 90% can be recovered from sewage sludge ashes by incineration. However, the combination of EBPR systems for P removal with P recovery technology has received wide interest because EBPR could increase the potential for P recovery by more than 90% [63]. Meanwhile, floatation is another process that recovers heavy metals from wastewater, including copper, zinc, chromium, nickel, lead, and iron, through mechanisms of either precipitate, ion flotation, or sorptive flotation [64].

6.1.5. Energy Recovery to Achieve Energy Neutral or Positive Wastewater Treatment

Basically, energy can be recovered from WWTPs by the process of anaerobic digestion of sludge. However, according to Stillwell et al. [65], this type of technology can only recover approximately 30–40% of the total energy requirements in WWTPs. Therefore, single technology such as the AD of sludge is not enough to achieve energy-neutral or -positive WWTPs, requiring appropriate optimization and technology improvements. For example, technologies such as anammox or the A–B process have to be integrated into the traditional operation of a WWTP to achieve energy-neutral status. As a reference, the Strass WWTP in Austria, which was designed and operated with two-stage activated sludge plant (A–B process) integrated with side-stream anammox and sludge digestion has significantly achieved an 8% energy surplus [66].

This is possible due to achieving an average energy consumption of 0.3–0.5 kWh/m^3 while the source of carbonaceous materials in wastewater reached a recovery of 1.7 kWh/m^3 energy. Therefore, by combining the emerging technologies such as side stream anammox with the adsorption-biological (A–B) stage process followed by anaerobic digestion (AD), energy self-sufficient wastewater treatment could be achieved. An environmental assessment tool such as LCA can be used to evaluate this technology integration and identify the environmental benefits from the energy recovery. However, an intensive assessment methodology should be identified for a convincing result due to the complex technology integration, which requires every detailed aspect of the design and assessment.

6.1.6. Integrated Technology to Upgrade Wastewater Treatment Plant

Conventional WWTPs remove organic matter for the protection of the aquatic environment. However, with an increasing population, municipal WWTPs are faced with the challenge of ensuring sustainable treatment, which includes nutrient removal and resource recovery. Sustainable wastewater treatment greatly relies on treatment technologies. Several new technologies have been developed to treat wastewater more efficiently with low energy and chemical consumption, great potential for resource recovery, higher effluent quality, reduced sludge production, and reduced GHG emission. However, the vast majority of these novel technologies are still in the early stages of research without foreseeable commercialisation. For the pressing task of achieving or moving towards sustainability, plants must rely on existing and mature technologies. In fact, it has been widely accepted that applying the existing technologies and integrating them effectively can achieve more sustainable wastewater treatment instead of waiting for the maturity of novel technologies [60].

Furthermore, it has been found that some technologies can reduce energy consumption and GHG emissions, whereas others achieve resource recovery. Besides the environmental impact, the integration of various technologies also deals with technical and economic impact assessments to identify those technologies that are technically applicable and economical [67]. However, research on the holistic analysis of integrated technologies in the wastewater treatment area is still a fairly new approach. The lack of a comprehensive analysis about the comparison of the environmental impacts and benefits from integration treatment technology to existing plants hinders the practical application of the proposed technologies [68]. In addition, most of this type of research so far has not considered local factors, which may cause great discrepancies.

Thus, there is a possibility to introduce a new configuration of WWT involving nutrient removal and resource recovery (e.g., water, energy, and nutrients) from suitable existing technologies that may retrofit current technology treatment for the future. WWTPs could generate electricity and heat from the methane produced by sewage sludge in anaerobic digestion, in addition to the energy efficiency, nitrogen and phosphorus removal that has been adopted in many WWTPs mainly to reduce eutrophication impact in the water body. The elimination of phosphorus by chemical precipitation could achieve low phosphate concentration in the effluent, making this technology widely used [69].

A few technologies have been developed towards more sustainable treatment, and among the technologies that have been practised on full-scale systems are EBPR and struvite recovery. EBPR is able to decrease the number of chemicals used for the phosphorus removal [69], and P recovery technology produces a high grade of P minerals in the form of magnesium ammonium phosphate (e.g., struvite—$NH_4MgPO_4 \cdot 6H_2O$) for use as fertiliser [70]. EBPR can be a less expensive process to construct and operate; it also generates less sludge and does not use a chemical substance [71]. Solids generated in EBPR can significantly offset the demand for synthetic fertilisers through integration with P struvite recovery technology [48]. However, this nutrient removal and resource recovery treatment has some limitations, such as increases in energy consumption, chemical consumption, and cost [72], so holistic assessments are needed for the sustainable upgrading of wastewater treatment. Sena and Hicks [73] highlighted that environmental impacts associated with

P recovery that involve infrastructure construction, energy, and chemicals required could outweigh the benefits. Furthermore, hotspot analysis to upgrade WWTPs for nutrient removal and resource recovery is important for the identification and selection of efficient technology.

6.2. Application of LCA to Select Sustainable WWTPs

This review clearly shows that different technologies have been developed, integrated, and applied to achieve energy and phosphorus recovery, improve effluent quality, and reduce GHG emissions. In addition, the successful demonstration of STRASS is an aspiring example to show that utilising a combination of existing technologies can lead to energy-neutral wastewater treatment and gain environmental benefits. As seen, the achievements of this plant are a promising demonstration of the sustainable wastewater treatment system. However, the question on how to apply this to a wider context still needs systematic level assessment in environmental and economic aspects, with consideration for local factors. As more technologies are being developed or applied to upgrade existing wastewater treatments for resource (e.g., water, energy, and nutrients) recovery and more stringent discharge standards are being implemented, environmental impact analysis from different aspects is imperative to achieve 'real' sustainable wastewater treatment. This situation shows that the selection of a mature and efficient environmental and economic assessment tool is important to achieve convincing results towards more efficient wastewater treatment with low impact to the environment.

In essence, sustainable wastewater treatment should, over a long-term perspective, be able to treat wastewater while protecting human health and environment with minimal use of scarce resources. In addition, it should also produce beneficial recovery products and be socially, technically, and financially viable. This is because wastewater, which was previously considered as a disposal liability, can now become valuable resources. Water reuse, nutrient removal and recovery, and energy self-sufficiency are among the core parts of wastewater treatment operations working towards sustainability. Apart from this, other environmental factors such as eutrophication, GHG emissions, and pollution from residual sludge have to be considered at the same time to evaluate the sustainability of wastewater treatment. This is because the current global concern is to identify the trade-off between environmental issues such as eutrophication, global warming, toxicity, and electricity used, with more stringent effluent limits and the increased utilisation of some resource recovery technologies such as struvite precipitation of phosphorus.

Due to the significant effect of upgrading technology to the environment and economic, a few studies have evaluated the effect of upgrading plants compared with the existing treatment. Nevertheless, research regarding upgrading wastewater treatment using LCA are various and inconsistent in terms of technology integration and assessment methodology, and most studies have not included an economic assessment. Studies have been conducted to identify the environmental effects of upgraded processes in WWTPs [4,74], but the complexity of these studies vary with different system boundaries and selected technologies and impact categories. The impact of phosphorus recovery from WWT is rarely considered where, for example, comprehensive and quantitative LCA studies involving the impact of phosphorus struvite recovery from WWT technology are still limited [36]. In fact, only a few studies of LCA focused on energy recovery and, for these, important methodological issues in LCA still need to be addressed. Therefore, due to the lack of methodology consistency and transparency in the current practice for LCA–WWT, it is important to emphasize the need for a robust, transparent, and standard method for sustainable technology assessment.

A holistic assessment is especially important for the mature technology that is increasingly applied worldwide, including in developing countries. In a study by [75], LCA was applied to evaluate the impact from WWTPs with upgrading technology of phosphorus removal. They concluded that biological P removal as a best practice should only be added with a chemical process if necessary, based on the life cycle environmental analysis of two P removal scenarios (e.g., biological versus chemical P removal). The results by Hao et al. [4]

who studied LCA of resource recovery technology (e.g., water reuse, electricity, thermal, and P recovery) of WWTP in China found that thermal energy recovery from sludge incineration significantly contributed to 40% of total resource recovery score, followed by 30% electricity recovery, and achieved net-zero impact from total environmental value. Meanwhile, P recovery only achieved 6% from the total resource recovery process. This review indicates the need to combine both nutrient removal and resource recovery using local data to further identify their impact and benefit to the environment while improving LCA methodology itself.

6.3. Life Cycle Economic Assessment of Wastewater Treatment

Economic assessment is one of the most important criteria in identifying the feasibility and efficiency of integrated technology in WWTPs [49,76]. Evaluation of the capital, operations and maintenance costs, and product revenue are important criteria for technology integration. Standard LCA practices encompass only environmental impacts, which excludes economic and social impacts. However, some researchers have increasingly conducted economic analysis for WWTPs, such as a life cycle costing assessment for the selection of wastewater treatment [77], an economic valuation of environmental benefits from the wastewater treatment process [76], and an economic assessment for greywater recycling using whole life cost (WLC) [78] developed a novel method integrating environmental and economic criteria for selecting the best process for WWTPs.

On the other hand, Lin et al. [79] suggested exploring a weighting system to monetize the environmental issues and convert all the economic and environmental criteria into a single sustainability score. Lorenzo-Toja et al. [26] proposed a system value assessment using LCA and LCC for WWTPs based on ecoefficiency concepts. A modelling approach is needed to have a holistic environmental and economic performance of a diverse process [79,80]. Less than 10% of the reviewed studies included an economic efficiency analysis. Furthermore, none of the previous studies assessed the consequence of product value from the wastewater industry involving energy recovery and nutrient recovery to agriculture in specific countries that integrated with the nutrient removal process. This issue carries some questions about how LCA and LCC can support the creation of a circular economy concept in WWT and ensure a positive environmental impact. Additional questions include where should the substituted materials and products be accounted for and who can claim the benefit.

To answer the questions above, a complete economic evaluation for the integration of the technologies proposed should be included and thoroughly evaluated towards a circular economy and sustainable development. This is because some technologies have not been applied in the wastewater treatment industry, and the recovered products such as struvite have yet to be fully accepted by agricultural organisations especially in developing countries. Therefore, an in-depth evaluation needs to be conducted on the economic aspects of the proposed integrated technology identify its compatibility mainly for energy and nutrient recovery. For example, the market value of recovered product such as P fertiliser could influence the economic situation where the price can be different across the world, depending on the demand, regulations, and social acceptance. In addition, economic evaluations of the capital, operation and maintenance, and product revenue are other important criteria for the integration technology besides environmental factors.

In summary of the environmental and economic assessments, an increasing number of wastewater evaluation methods only focus on a limitation aspect of sustainability, while the roles and contributions of the whole system are difficult to understand and thus could exacerbate problems when planning for achieving sustainability. Therefore, although some work on environmental and economic assessments has been done as mentioned previously, a lack of systematic analysis exists for the sustainable development of integrated WWTPs with resource removal and recovery. Furthermore, even though LCA application in wastewater treatment has grown significantly in the last few years, LCA was not originally designed for wastewater treatment analysis, and thus, some issues exist that could be improved including refining the data inventory, impact methodology, and economic indicators for more reliable LCA. This is because to achieve true sustainability, an assessment from an integrated perspective is needed wherein the environmental impacts of WWTPs do not exceed its benefits [36]. Further research should consider wider impact categories through system analysis that considers temporal, spatial, and local specific criteria of WWTPs. This is because it is important to acknowledge the barriers that may vary based on geographical and cultural contexts [81], so a study should focus on a tropical region, such as Malaysia.

7. Review for the Sustainable Strategies in Malaysia

Local factors such as government guidance, policy, wastewater characteristics, pollution of water bodies, climate, main fuel, and local practices for wastewater treatment could affect the selection of technologies towards sustainable development and environmental impact of the integrated wastewater treatment. Therefore, a detailed review of Malaysia information and related characteristic is further discussed in this section.

Malaysia is located in Southeast Asia with a current population of 32.8 million people, producing the total volume of wastewater of 7.53 million m^3/day. As a developing country, the wastewater collection and treatment coverage is very low. Until 2013, only 50% of the wastewaters treated by mechanized plants while others still use untreated individual septic tanks and oxidation ponds [82]. For the mechanical WWT, activated sludge (AS), aerated lagoons, rotating biological contactors (RBC), extended aeration (EA) and trickling filters are the current treatment technologies used. Malaysia's current strategy is to reduce individual untreated wastewater by planning towards a proper centralised treatment system. With more WWTP facilities to be built, it is in a good position to directly adopt well-developed technologies for sustainable wastewater treatment. This is because more than 90% of current wastewater treatment technologies in Malaysia only involve conventional treatment (i.e., without energy recovery). This type of treatment cannot achieve sustainable operation for the rapid growth of municipal WWTPs.

Moreover, many resources are required such as energy and money for transportation, treatment, and final disposal of sludge. As mentioned before, due to the chemical energy contained in wastewater, it is seen as valuable fuel to supplement power generation in Malaysia. However, it has not yet been determined how policy and environmental regulation from the government of developing country can best serve in improving sustainability. Upon the UN Climate Conference in Paris 2015, Malaysia has striven to reduce 45% of its carbon emission intensity by 2030. Previously, it has introduced a feed-in tariff (FiT) in 2004 and subsequently established the Sustainable Energy Development Authority (SEDA) Act in 2011 to fulfil the national aspiration towards achieving energy self-sufficiency and mitigating climate change. As of 2014, only 3.3% of consumed energy is renewable and produced in Malaysia, while 96.7% of its consumed energy is generated from fossil fuels [83].

Based on this situation, Malaysia has adopted a target of 11% installed renewable energy capacity by 2020. Since the water sector consumes 3–5% of total energy consumption of the country, it is an important factor in leading Malaysia to sustainable development, in which we could include renewable energy and nutrient recovery in WWTP. Moreover, with possibly strong municipal wastewater due to the implementation of separate sewer collection system, and a hot climate throughout the year with temperatures ranging from 22 °C to 32 °C, this situation is more favourable to adopt anaerobic digestion, anammox treatment, and the A–B process. This is because more energy could be recovered from stronger municipal wastewater, less or no energy is required by anaerobic digestion and anammox, and treatment efficiency is higher due to higher bacteria activity at a higher temperature.

On the other hand, the previous survey in 2005 by National Hydraulic Research Institute of Malaysia (NAHRIM) identified that 62% of lakes and reservoirs in Malaysia were in serious eutrophic condition. In 2013, out of 473 rivers monitored by Department of Environment Malaysia (DOEM), 72% were polluted and 6% were classified as heavily polluted [84,85]. As such, the Department of Irrigation and Drainage of Malaysia is working towards cleaner water bodies, having introduced the River of Life Project in 2012 which requires cleaner effluent, especially from WWTPs, even though there is no concrete decision yet on the improvement of the wastewater effluent standard. Current effluent discharge limit to the river is 20–50 mgN/L, 20–50 mg BOD_5/L, and 120–200 mg COD/L, but the phosphorus limit is only required when discharging into stagnant water bodies with 5–10 mg P/L.

Meanwhile, due to rapid expansion in crop production in Malaysia (e.g., rubber, oil-palm, cocoa etc.), the importation of phosphate fertilisers is significantly increasing from China and Australia, amounting to GBP 28.8 million in 2005 and GBP 58.8 million in 2011. Based on this situation, P recovery to fertiliser from WWTP is a favoured option which should be considered. Finally, most of the sludge from WWTP in Malaysia is disposed of in landfills, which could impose potential risk and pollution of the underground water and soil. Therefore, these situations would require more research and planning towards sustainable technology which could reduce the volume of sludge and other environmental impacts. However, the existing technologies from developed countries should be carefully evaluated by considering the difference in culture, land, climate, and economy. Currently, there are a lack of policies and regulations in Malaysia regarding resource recovery from water and wastewater sector. Therefore, based on the future results of this research, the suggestions of new regulation and policy can further be explored on a country-wide basis. For instance, economic incentives to enhance technologies and markets for nutrient recovery from WWTP can be proposed and brought about through regulation.

Although Malaysia is not as ambitious as China, how to develop sustainable wastewater treatment in Malaysia for the global strategic platform of sustainable development is still pressing. The research on sustainable wastewater treatment from the system level is still very new, and little work has been done in the Malaysian context with the consideration of local factors, specifically on the overall environmental impact of wastewater treatment. Therefore, a detailed review of Malaysian information and the related local wastewater situation is further discussed in this section.

In Malaysia, the Environmental Quality Act 1974 (Act 127) is the primary federal legislative for water quality. As for sewage, the latest regulations are set in the Environmental Quality (Sewage) regulations 2009, which are applicable to any premises discharging sewage into Malaysian waters except for housing development with less than 150PE. Therefore, those treatment system developed after 2009 have a stricter standard in terms of concentration limit and numbers of parameters regulated [85]. For example, a phosphorus limit was introduced for the first time in 2009 with 5 mg/L for standard A and 10 mg/L for standard B. The other standard parameters included BOD, COD, suspended solid, pH, oil and grease, and NH_3-N. Indah Water Konsortium Sdn Bhd (IWK) is currently the biggest wastewater treatment operator in Malaysia, managing more than 70% of wastewater treatment management. The list of all effluent discharge limits is shown in Table 2.

Table 2. Environmental Quality (Sewage) Regulation 2009 for new sewage treatment system (Malaysia).

Parameter	Unit	Standard A	Standard B
Temperature	°C	40	40
pH value	-	6.0–9.0	5.5–9.0
Biochemical oxygen demand (BOD_5) at 20 °C	mg/L	20	50
Chemical oxygen demand (COD)	mg/L	120	200
Total suspended solids (TSS)	mg/L	50	100
Oil and grease (OandG)	mg/L	5	10
Ammoniacal nitrogen, AMN (river)	mg/L	10	20
Ammoniacal nitrogen, AMN (stagnant water body)	mg/L	5	5
Nitrate-nitrogen (river)	mg/L	20	50
Nitrate-nitrogen (enclosed water body)	mg/L	10	10
Phosphorus (stagnant water body)	mg/L	5	10

For sewage sludge production from WWTPs, Malaysia generates approximately 5 million m³ per year. However, the amount has been predicted by Indah Water Konsortium to reach 7 million m³ per year by 2022. Sewage sludge/biosolids is the sludge waste that has been produced after wastewater is treated in a wastewater treatment facility. This sludge is usually in a dilute suspension form, which typically contains 0.25 to 12% of solid matter. Pathogens, heavy metals, and toxic pollutants are present in the untreated wastewater. Sewage sludge also contains high amounts of heavy metals such as lead, cadmium, nickel, chromium, and copper due to its industrial origin [86,87]. This is why most countries strictly regulate the usage of sewage sludge in agriculture or as a soil amendment because of its potential of being harmful to humans, animals, and the environment [87–89]. Sewage sludge is also comprised of organic matter (e.g., COD) and nutrients (e.g., nitrogen and phosphorus) that make it suitable to be used as an organic fertiliser [88,89]. However, sewage application to land for a long period may result to the accumulation of heavy metals in soil. The increased amounts of heavy metals are dangerous because they are usually non-degradable.

The environmental impacts from WWTP such as greenhouse gas emission, toxicity [88,89], and acidification potentials is not properly measured since they are not regulated by the environment agency. To date, these environmental impacts have been ignored in the regulatory framework. Hence, a detailed life cycle inventory and assessment for identifying a correct environmental burden from WWTP is required. For the life cycle development in Malaysia, by the initial review, existing databases providing for local life cycle inventory involving wastewater management are limited. The Malaysian Life Cycle Inventory Database (MY-LCID) was established in 2005 by the Malaysian government under SIRIM Berhad (Scientific and Industrial Research Institute of Malaysia) but it is still at the very beginning stage and seeking to enhance its contents to wider aspects. This research could provide holistic operational databases acquired from variety sources including operational parameters, site sampling database, government websites, technical reports, and local journal articles. The database is up-to-date and reflects the current environmental performance of wastewater treatment. Table 3 shows the overview of existing study of LCA in wastewater management from 2006 to 2022.

The role of environmental impact and cost assessment is important for the sustainable development of WWTP. The technologies that will be adopted towards sustainable WWT could not only be assessed based on the single factor. Thorough environmental impacts must be evaluated to provide guidance for future policy, and for the water industry to find trade-offs for environmental factors and move towards to sustainable development. To enhance the dependability and reproducibility of results, a more consistent implementation of LCA should be proposed, such as allowing deployment on new or current membrane systems [89,90].

8. Summary and Knowledge Gaps

Based on the overall review, LCA has been used as an effective and efficient methodology for the environmental impact of WWTPs. However, LCA applied for WWTPs is still relatively new compared with other manufacturing processes, especially in the developing countries. The question on how WWTPs can implement LCA to achieve reliable results of their environmental impact still needs further research. Additional questions on how to implement LCA in developing countries such as Malaysia to provide guidance to policy makers and WWTPs on operations and upgrading remain and prove to be challenging. This paper identified three main knowledge gaps of LCA for WWTPs and three challenges in the LCA methodology to address for WWTPs in developing countries such as Malaysia: (1) There is a need to critically assess the influence of seasonality (i.e., dry and wet season) on the environmental impact by LCA; (2) there is a need to investigate environmental impacts from WWTPs in developing countries focusing on the site-specific databases; and (3) there is a need to evaluate environmental sustainability of different processes for upgrading wastewater treatment systems.

Therefore, it is important to upgrade existing WWTPs with regards to nutrient removal and resource recovery for more efficient treatment, but identifying the impacts or trade-offs is also important for future reference, an aspect which is rarely discussed. Secondly, there is a lack of comparisons of environmental and economic impacts for the integrated nutrient (i.e., nitrogen and phosphorus) removal and resource recovery. For example, energy and P recovery could further reduce the other environmental impact within the same treatment scheme, but the economic cost is uncertain due to additional chemical and electricity consumption. The real trade-off between these upgrading systems needs to be identified for future implementation strategies towards more efficient and sustainable WWTPs. This is because, to achieve true sustainability, an assessment from an integrated perspective is needed where the environmental impacts of WWTP should not exceed its benefits [36].

Thus, the comprehensive design for upgrading and a method for evaluating both environmental and economic burdens are needed to provide useful information for policy makers and practitioners on the rectification or upgrading of WWTPs. Thirdly, the lack of environmental impact weighting for different phases of operation leads to difficulties in identifying environmental burden hotspots. Most studies remain limited to single-unit operations such as sludge treatment without conducting a comprehensive impact from the whole treatment. Thus, it is crucial to investigate the hotspot impact from upgrading treatment to identify which process has the most burden. Finally, few studies have been conducted in developing countries especially when involving the integration of nutrient removal and resource recovery. Thus, a comprehensive assessment for evaluating both environmental and economic burdens from site-specific data is needed to provide useful information for upgrading wastewater treatments plants in terms of technical, environmental, and economic impacts.

Table 3. Overview of existing study of LCA in wastewater management from 2006 to 2022.

No	Author	Journal	Country/Area	Goal	Functional Unit (FU)	Processes Considered	Sludge Disposal	Data Source/Inventory	LCIA Method and Tool	Impact Category	Scale
1.	[91]	Egyptian Journal of Chemistry	Iraq	Analysis and evaluation of environmental impacts in AL Najaf wastewater treatment plants	1 cubic meter of wastewater for the studied station	Treatment units related to sewage treatment processes, sludge treatment, and other processes such as construction and material transportation	-	Foreground data: WWTP Background data: Ecoinvent	Tool: SimaPro 7 Method: IMPACT2002+	GWP, Respiratory Organics, non-renewal energy	-
2.	[92]	Journal of Cleaner Production	Sweden	Evaluating the sustainable value of municipal WWTPs	Volume of wastewater treated (m^3) by the WWTP in one year.	Construction and operation	-	Foreground data: WWTP Background data: Ecoinvent ver 3.2	SimaPro (PhD v 9.0)	GWP, EP, AP, ADP, HTP,	50,000 m^3 of influent wastewater per day.
3.	[93]	Environmental Science and Pollution Research	China	Analysing environmental performance with respect to life cycle GHG emissions and eutrophication impact	1 m^3 of treated wastewater	Construction, operation, sludge treatment	-	Foreground data: WWTP Background data: Gabi	Tool: Gabi	GHG, EP	30,000 m^3/day
4.	[94]	International Journal of Environmental Science and Technology	Brazil	Evaluating environmental impacts of WWTP based on an upflow anaerobic sludge blanket followed by a high-rate aerobic pond	1 m^3 of pre-treated wastewater	Operation	Agriculture	Foreground data: WWTP Background data: Ecoinvent	Tool: OpenLCA 1.9 Method: ReCiPe v.1.13 2008	GWP, GTP, CED, TEP	Capacity to attend 10,000 people
5.	[95]	Cleaner Production	Iran	Evaluating the sustainability of two actual wastewater treatment plants using the eco-efficiency index based on energy and life cycle analysis	Total of produced dry sludge or effluent from Al-Teymour and Khin Arab WWTPs with 453,000 and 472,000 Population Equivalent (PE) during one year starting from April 2017	Operation	Agriculture	Foreground data: WWTP	Method: ReCiPe	GWP, HH	453,000 and 472,000 Population Equivalent (PE)
6.	[4]	Water Research	China	To evaluate environmental impacts of a WWTP and compare with resource recovery option	PE/year	Construction, operation, demolition	-	Foreground data: WWTP Background data: Chinese life cycle database	Tool: - Method: CML2001	GWP, EP, AP, ADP, HTP,	200,000 m^3/day
7.	[96]	Journal of Environmental Management	China	To provide assessment of environmental impacts involving 126 PPCPs in advanced wastewater treatment by LCA	1 m^3/day	Construction and operation	-	Foreground data: WWTP Background data: Gabi	Tool: Gabi 6.0 Method: Usetox and Traci	AP, EP, HTP, GWP, OLDP, FEP	-
8.	[97]	Science of the Total Environment	Egypt	To study environmental performance of different scenarios in developing country	1 m^3/day	Construction and operation	-	Foreground data: WWTP Background data: Ecoinvent	Tool: - Method: CML2000	AP, GWP, EP, POP, OLDP, DARP, TEP, FEP	40,000 m^3/day

313

Table 3. Cont.

No	Author	Journal	Country/Area	Goal	Functional Unit (FU)	Processes Considered	Sludge Disposal	Data Source/Inventory	LCIA Method and Tool	Impact Category	Scale
9.	[98]	Journal of Cleaner Production	Denmark and Sweden	To investigate the contribution of direct CH_4 and N_2O to annual carbon footprint of seven WWTPs	1 mg of input, 1 kg carbon, N and P removed	Operation	On-site incineration and application to agricultural land	Foreground data: WWTP Background data: Ecoinvent, EASETECH, ELCD	Tool: EASETECH v2.3.6 Method: IPCC 2006	GWP	-
10.	[70]	Science of the Total Environment	France	To assess impact of recovered phosphorus from WWTP	1 kg of struvite recovered	Construction and operation	Use for fertiliser	Foreground data: WWTP Background data: Ecoinvent v2.2	Tool: Gabi v6 Method: CML-IA	ADFFP, AP, EP, FEP, MEP, TEP, HTP, OLDP, POP	300,000 PE
11.	[67]	Resources, conservation and recycling	Austria	To analyse impact of P recovery form WWTP	PE/year	Operation	-	Foreground data: Literature Background data: Ecoinvent v2.2	-	GWP, AP	-
12.	[99]	Journal of Cleaner Production	China	To investigate how, and to what extent, the LCA results could be influenced by the adoption of various LCA methodologies, via a case study of a representative WWTP in China	10,000 m^3 of waste-water	Operation, sludge treatment	-	Foreground data: WWTP Background data: Ecoinvent V2.1, Chinese life cycle database (CLCD)	Tool: - Method: CML and e-balance (China)	EP, FWEP, HTP, OLDP, GWP, ADP, ACP	-
13.	[100]	Journal of Cleaner Production	Mexico and Canada	To compare the environmental performance of two WWTP technologies across all environmental impact categories in Latin America and the Caribbean	1 m^3/day	Construction and operation	-	Foreground data: WWTP Background data: Ecoinvent, national database and literature	Tool: - Method: Impact 2002 and Recipe	MEP, GWP, FWEP, PM	-
14.	[26]	Science of the Total Environment	Spain	To set new benchmark regarding environmental performance of WWTPs (different climatic regions—Atlantic and Mediterranean) for summer/winter	1 m^3/day	Construction, operation, sludge treatment	-	Foreground data: WWTP Background data: Ecoinvent 2.2 and Spanish electricity production	Tool: Simapro Method: CML 2001, USES-LCA (heavy metals and PPCPs)	EP, GWP, OLDP, HTP, MEP, FWEP	25,000 PE (Atlantic), 70,000 PE (Mediterranean)
15.	[101]	Water Research	Denmark	Evaluation to capture necessary infrastructure additions, operational changes, and reuse option for EBPR2 and side stream microalgae cultivation in photobioreactor	1 m^3/day	Construction, operation, sludge treatment	Incinerator and microalgal fertiliser	Foreground data: Operating reports of an existing process, databases, and model result. Background data: Ecoinvent (Swiss and European market)	Tool: EASETECH Method: ILCD 2011, Usetox (human toxicity)	GWP, ACP, TEP, MEP, POF, Etox, Htc, Htnc, PM, RD	-

Table 3. Cont.

No	Author	Journal	Country/Area	Goal	Functional Unit (FU)	Processes Considered	Sludge Disposal	Data Source/Inventory	LCIA Method and Tool	Impact Category	Scale
16.	[102]	Journal of Cleaner Production	Spain	To identify and quantify the main environmental contributors derived from the treatment of urban wastewater and water reclamation opportunities in Tarragona, Spain	1 m^3/day	Operation, sludge treatment	Agriculture	Foreground data: WWTP Background data: Ecoinvent 3.1 and literature	Tool: Monte Carlo simulation Method: CML 2001	TA, CC, FE, ME, POF, MD, FD, OD, TI, WD, CED	132,000 PE
17.	[12]	Journal of Cleaner Production	Spain	To investigate the main environmental contributors derived from the treatment of urban wastewater and water reclamation opportunities in Tarragona, Spain	1 m^3/year	Operation, sludge treatment	Agriculture	Foreground data: Benchmark simulation model 2 Background data: Ecoinvent-sludge transportation and Spanish Energy for electricity production, literature	CML2000	AP, GWP, EP, PHO, DAR, ODP, TAETP	-
18.	[103]	Journal of Cleaner Production	Korea	Evaluating several wastewater treatment plant (WWTP) processes, including an integrated sludge management system and waste sludge disposal methods in a large city based on life cycle analysis (LCA) and economic efficiency analysis (EEA)	1 m^3/day	Operation, sludge treatment	-	Foreground data: Operation of WWTP Background data: LCI database of Korean ministry of environment	Tool: Gabi Method: CML 2001	AP, EP, GWP, HTP	CAS-340,000 m^3/d A2O-680,000 m^3/d MLE-80,000 m^3/d
19.	[104]	Water Research	France	To propose a holistic, life cycle assessment (LCA) of urban wastewater systems (UWS) based on a comprehensive inventory including detailed construction and operation of sewer systems and wastewater treatment plants (WWTPs)	1 day of operation	Construction, operation, sludge treatment	-	Foreground data: operation of WWTP Background data: Ecoinvent	Tool: Simapro Method: Recipe v1.07	TA, CC, FE, ME, POF, MD, FD, OD, TI, WD, CED	5200 PE
20.	[25]	Water Research	Denmark	To investigate how the basis of inventory data affects the outcome of a WWTP LCA by using specific WWTP located in Denmark based on the TRENS system	1 m^3/day	Operation, sludge treatment	-	Foreground data: operation of WWTP Background data: European Pollutant Release EPRTR) and Transfer Registry, Danish emission monitoring, state of the art LCA, Ecoinvent v2.2	Tool: EASETECH Method: ILCD 2011	GWP, AP, EP, PHO, ETP, PM	265,000 PE

Table 3. Cont.

No	Author	Journal	Country/Area	Goal	Functional Unit (FU)	Processes Considered	Sludge Disposal	Data Source/Inventory	LCIA Method and Tool	Impact Category	Scale
21.	[105]	Journal of Cleaner Production	Denmark	To compare four types of wastewater treatment plants	1 m³/day	Operation, sludge treatment	Incinerator, Agriculture	Foreground data: WWTP Background data: Ecoinvent 2.2, ELCD, and Danish Environmental Protection Agency	Tool: Monte-Carlo Method: ILCD 2011, IPCC, Recipe, UseTox, CML2002	AD, AC, EU, GWP, ODP, HT, TE, MET, FET, PO	Between 20,000 PE to 100,000 PE
22.	[106]	Science of the Total Environment	Spain	To compare three side-stream technologies treating anaerobic digestion supernatant at two different levels, as independent processes and as part of a modelled WWTP	1 m³/day	Operation, sludge treatment	Landfill	Foreground data: WWTP Background data: Ecoinvent 2.2, Swiss centre for life cycle inventory 2012	Tool: Biowin Method: CML2002	AD, AC, EU, GWP, ODP, HT, TE, MET, FET, PO	-
23.	[40]	Water and Environment Journal	India	To compare 4 WWT technologies	PE/year	Operation, sludge treatment	Land application, etc.	Foreground data: WWTP Background data: Ecoinvent 2.2 and literature	Tool- Method:CML2 baseline 2000	AP, GWP, EP, FWAT, HT, MAET, ADP, TE	ASP:200k PE, UASB-FAL:300k PE, CW:30k PE, SBR:100 k PE
24.	[22]	Water Research	Netherlands	To determine the contribution of methane to the greenhouse gas footprint of a wastewater treatment plant and to suggest measures to curb methane emissions	-	Operation, sludge treatment	-	Foreground data: One-year measurement campaign	-	GHG	360,000 PE
25.	[21]	Journal of Water Sustainability	India	To evaluate and quantify the greenhouse gas emissions, mainly methane and nitrous oxide, from the wastewater treatment system	-	Operation, sludge treatment	-	Foreground data: WWTP	Tool: - Method: IPCC 2006	GHG emissions	33 MLD
26.	[23]	Biotechnology and Bioengineering	Spain	To demonstrate the importance of using process-based dynamic models to better evaluate GHG emissions	-	Operation, sludge treatment	-	-	Tool: Benchmark Simulation Model Platform No. 2 (BSM2)	GHG emissions	-
27.	[55]	Journal of Water Sustainability	Korea	Development of a comprehensive impact assessment of gaseous emission from urban wastewater infrastructure and treatment facilities	-	Operation, sludge treatment	-	Foreground data: WWTP	Method: Technical Guidelines (DCCEE, 2010)	GHG emissions	-
28.	[48]	Water Research	Australia	To analyse 10 different wastewater treatment scenarios, covering six process configurations and treatment standards ranging from raw sewage to advanced nutrient removal	-	Construction, operation, sludge treatment	Agriculture	Foreground data: WWTP Background data: Ecoinvent 2.2 and literature	Tool: Biowin simulator	GHG	-

Table 3. Cont.

No	Author	Journal	Country/Area	Goal	Functional Unit (FU)	Processes Considered	Sludge Disposal	Data Source/Inventory	LCIA Method and Tool	Impact Category	Scale
29.	[107]	Bioresource Technology	China	Illuminate the environmental benefit of a WWT and reuse project using LCA model	1 m³/day	Construction, operation, and demolition	-	Foreground data: WWTP Background data: Chinese database for construction material	Tool: - Method: Eco-indicator 99	Energy use	-
30.	[33]	Cleaner Production	Egypt	Develop scenarios to improve the total environmental performance and the sustainability of Alexandria's urban water system	1 m³	Operation	-	Foreground data: WTP and WWTP Background data: Literature	Tool: Simapro Method: Eco-indicator	Various	Various scale of water and wastewater treatment
31.	[20]	Environmental Science and Technology	Spain	Identify the environmental impact of a WWTP in order to determine the environmental loads associated with the plant's operation and compare the total environmental impact of the various stages in both water and sludge treatment lines	1 m³/day	Operation, sludge treatment and disposal	Incinerator, Agriculture, landfill, compost plant	Foreground data: WWTP Background data: Ecoinvent 2.2, Spanish energy mix, and the European model for transport and water	Tool: SiSOSTAQUA Method: CML2002	AP, GWP, EP, PHO, DAR, ODP, ETP	144,000 PE
32.	[46]	Cleaner Production	France	Evaluate the environmental performance of a full scale WWTP	1 m³ of ww/year	Operation, sludge treatment	Agriculture	Foreground data: Operation Background data: Estimation (air emission) for chemical and electricity	Tool: Simapro Method: CML2000, Eco-indicator 99, EDIP96, EPS, Eco-points97	GWP, ARD, AP, EP, TP	140,000 PE
33.	[19]	The International Journal of Life Cycle Assessment	Spain	Environmental evaluation of the most common technical options for urban wastewater	PE	Operation, sludge treatment	-	Foreground data: Operation Background data: Ecoinvent	Tool: Simapro Method: CML2000,	EU, OP, GWP, ACP, AC, PO, AD, TOXILOGICAL (HT, FET, MET, TET)	72,000 to 125,000 PE
34.	[108]	Environmental Science and Technology	Germany	To provide a modular gate-to-gate inventory model for industrial wastewater purification in the chemical and related sectors	1 m³	Operation	-	Foreground data: Operation Background data: Ecoinvent	-	-	>500,000 m³
35.	[109]	Proceedings of LCE	Belgium	To assess the environmental impact of WWTP using LCA methodology	1 m³	Construction, operation, sludge treatment	-	Foreground data: Operation	Tool:- Method: eco-indicator 99, CML and Impact 2002+	HT, FWT, MET, TE, EU, AC, GW, FF	170,000 PE

Author Contributions: Conceptualization, S.S.R. and S.N.H.; validation, M.M.H. and Y.-Q.L.; writing—original draft preparation, S.S.R.; writing—review and editing, S.N.H.; visualization, K.K.R. and D.A.T.; funding acquisition, S.N.H. All authors have read and agreed to the published version of the manuscript.

Funding: The APC was funded by [FRGS/1/2022/WAB02/UKM/02/1] and [GGPM-2022-072].

Conflicts of Interest: The authors declare no conflict of interest.

References

1. Sikosana, M.L.; Sikhwivhilu, K.; Moutloali, R.; Madyira, D.M. Municipal wastewater treatment technologies: A review. *Procedia Manuf.* **2019**, *35*, 1018–1024. [CrossRef]
2. Al-Raad, A.A.; Hanafiah, M.M. Removal of inorganic pollutants using electrocoagulation technology: A review of emerging applications and mechanisms. *J. Environ. Manag.* **2021**, *300*, 113696. [CrossRef] [PubMed]
3. Nizam, N.U.M.; Hanafiah, M.M.; Mahmoudi, E.; Halim, A.A.; Mohammad, A.W. The removal of anionic and cationic dyes from an aqueous solution using biomass-based activated carbon. *Sci. Rep.* **2021**, *11*, 8623. [CrossRef]
4. Hao, X.; Wang, X.; Liu, R.; Li, S.; Van Loosdrecht, M.C.; Jiang, H. Environmental impacts of resource recovery from wastewater treatment plants. *Water Res.* **2019**, *160*, 268–277. [CrossRef] [PubMed]
5. Morera, S.; Corominas, L.; Poch, M.; Aldaya, M.; Comas, J. Water footprint assessment in wastewater treatment plants. *J. Clean. Prod.* **2016**, *112*, 4741–4748. [CrossRef]
6. Piao, W.; Kim, Y.; Kim, H.; Kim, M.; Kim, C. Life cycle assessment and economic efficiency analysis of integrated management of wastewater treatment plants. *J. Clean. Prod.* **2016**, *113*, 325–337. [CrossRef]
7. Englande, A.J., Jr.; Krenkel, P.; Shamas, J. Wastewater Treatment & Water Reclamation. *Ref. Modul. Earth Syst. Environ. Sci.* **2015**. [CrossRef]
8. Harun, S.N.; Hanafiah, M.M.; Noor, N.M. Rice Straw Utilisation for Bioenergy Production: A Brief Overview. *Energies* **2022**, *15*, 5542. [CrossRef]
9. Campos, J.L.; Valenzuela-Heredia, D.; Pedrouso, A.; Del Río, A.V.; Belmonte, M.; Mosquera-Corral, A. Greenhouse Gases Emissions from Wastewater Treatment Plants: Minimization, Treatment, and Prevention. *J. Chem.* **2016**, *2016*, 3796352. [CrossRef]
10. Campos-Guzmán, V.; García-Cáscales, M.S.; Espinosa, N.; Urbina, A. Life Cycle Analysis with Multi-Criteria Decision Making: A review of approaches for the sustainability evaluation of renewable energy technologies. *Renew. Sustain. Energy Rev.* **2019**, *104*, 343–366. [CrossRef]
11. Awasthi, M.K.; Sarsaiya, S.; Wainaina, S.; Rajendran, K.; Awasthi, S.K.; Liu, T.; Duan, Y.; Jain, A.; Sindhu, R.; Binod, P.; et al. Techno-economics and life-cycle assessment of biological and thermochemical treatment of bio-waste. *Renew. Sustain. Energy Rev.* **2021**, *144*, 110837. [CrossRef]
12. Meneses, M.; Concepción, H.; Vrecko, D.; Vilanova, R. Life Cycle Assessment as an environmental evaluation tool for control strategies in wastewater treatment plants. *J. Clean. Prod.* **2015**, *107*, 653–661. [CrossRef]
13. Escobar, N.; Laibach, N. Sustainability check for bio-based technologies: A review of process-based and life cycle approaches. *Renew. Sustain. Energy Rev.* **2020**, *135*, 110213. [CrossRef]
14. Aziz, N.I.H.A.; Hanafiah, M.M. Application of life cycle assessment for desalination: Progress, challenges and future directions. *Environ. Pollut.* **2020**, *268*, 115948. [CrossRef] [PubMed]
15. Rashid, S.S.; Liu, Y.Q.; Mokhtar, H.; Zainudin, M.R.; Muda, M.F. The review of toxicity emission from municipal wastewater treatment by life cycle assessment. *Gading J. Sci. Technol.* **2020**, *5*, 10–18.
16. Dahiya, S.; Katakojwala, R.; Ramakrishna, S.; Venkata Mohan, S. Biobased products and life cycle assess-ment in the context of circular economy and sustainability. *Mat. Circ. Econ.* **2020**, *2*, 7. [CrossRef]
17. Hanafiah, M.M.; Leuven, R.S.E.W.; Sommerwerk, N.; Tockner, K.; Huijbregts, M.A.J. Including the introduction of exotic species in life cycle impact assessment: The case of inland shipping. *Environ. Sci. Technol.* **2013**, *47*, 13934–13940. [CrossRef]
18. Teodosiu, C.; Barjoveanu, G.; Sluser, B.R.; Popa, S.A.E.; Trofin, O. Environmental assessment of municipal wastewater discharges: A comparative study of evaluation methods. *Int. J. Life Cycle Assess.* **2016**, *21*, 395–411. [CrossRef]
19. Hospido, A.; Moreira, M.T.; Fernández-Couto, M.; Feijoo, G. Environmental performance of a municipal wastewater treatment plant. *Int. J. Life Cycle Assess.* **2004**, *9*, 261–271. [CrossRef]
20. Pasqualino, J.; Meneses, M.; Abella, M.; Castells, F. LCA as a Decision Support Tool for the Environmental Improvement of the Operation of a Municipal Wastewater Treatment Plant. *Environ. Sci. Technol.* **2009**, *43*, 3300–3307. [CrossRef]
21. Gupta, D.; Singh, S.K. Greenhouse gas emissions from wastewater treatment plants: A case study of Nnoida. *J. Water Sustain.* **2012**, *2*, 131–139.
22. Daelman, M.R.; Van Voorthuizen, E.M.; Van Dongen, U.G.; Volcke, E.I.; Van Loosdrecht, M.C. Methane emission during municipal wastewater treatment. *Water Res.* **2012**, *46*, 3657–3670. [CrossRef] [PubMed]
23. Corominas, L.; Alsina, X.F.; Snip, L.; Vanrolleghem, P. Comparison of different modeling approaches to better evaluate greenhouse gas emissions from whole wastewater treatment plants. *Biotechnol. Bioeng.* **2012**, *109*, 2854–2863. [CrossRef] [PubMed]
24. Ontiveros, G.A.; Campanella, E.A. Environmental performance of biological nutrient removal processes from a life cycle perspective. *Bioresour. Technol.* **2013**, *150*, 506–512. [CrossRef] [PubMed]

25. Yoshida, H.; Clavreul, J.; Scheutz, C.; Christensen, T.H. Influence of data collection schemes on the Life Cycle Assessment of a municipal wastewater treatment plant. *Water Res.* **2014**, *56*, 292–303. [CrossRef]
26. Lorenzo-Toja, Y.; Alfonsín, C.; Amores, M.J.; Aldea, X.; Marin, D.; Moreira, M.T.; Feijoo, G. Beyond the conventional life cycle inventory in wastewater treatment plants. *Sci. Total Environ.* **2016**, *553*, 71–82. [CrossRef]
27. Alfonsín, C.; Hospido, A.; Omil, F.; Moreira, M.; Feijoo, G. PPCPs in wastewater—Update and calculation of characterization factors for their inclusion in LCA studies. *J. Clean. Prod.* **2014**, *83*, 245–255. [CrossRef]
28. Hauschild, M.Z.; Goedkoop, M.; Guinée, J.; Heijungs, R.; Huijbregts, M.; Jolliet, O.; Margni, M.; De Schryver, A.; Humbert, S.; Laurent, A.; et al. Identifying best existing practice for characterization modeling in life cycle impact assessment. *Int. J. Life Cycle Assess.* **2012**, *18*, 683–697. [CrossRef]
29. Razman, K.K.; Hanafiah, M.M.; Mohammad, A.W.; Lun, A.W. Life cycle assessment of an integrated membrane treatment system of anaerobic-treated palm oil mill effluent (POME). *Membranes* **2022**, *12*, 246. [CrossRef]
30. Hanafiah, M.M.; Ghazali, N.F.; Harun, S.N.; Abdulaali, H.S.; AbdulHasan, M.J.; Kamarudin, M.K.A. Assessing water scarcity in Malaysia: A case study of rice production. *Desalination Water Treat.* **2019**, *149*, 274–287. [CrossRef]
31. *ISO 14040*; Environmental Management—Life Cycle Assessment—Principles and Framework. International Organisation for Standardisation (ISO): Geneva, Switzerland, 2006.
32. Corominas, L.; Foley, J.; Guest, J.; Hospido, A.; Larsen, H.; Morera, S.; Shaw, A. Life cycle assessment applied to wastewater treatment: State of the art. *Water Res.* **2013**, *47*, 5480–5492. [CrossRef] [PubMed]
33. El-Sayed Mohamed Mahgoub, M.; Van der Steen, N.P.; Abu-Zeid, K.; Vairavamoorthy, K. Towards sustainability in urban water: A life cycle analysis of the urban water system of Alexandria City, Egypt. *J. Clean. Prod.* **2010**, *18*, 1100–1106. [CrossRef]
34. Tomei, M.C.; Bertanza, G.; Canato, M.; Heimersson, S.; Laera, G.; Svanström, M. Techno-economic and environmental assessment of upgrading alternatives for sludge stabilization in municipal wastewater treatment plants. *J. Clean. Prod.* **2016**, *112*, 3106–3115. [CrossRef]
35. Balkema, A.J.; Preisig, H.A.; Otterpohl, R.; Lambert, F.J. Indicators for the sustainability assessment of wastewater treatment systems. *Urban Water* **2002**, *4*, 153–161. [CrossRef]
36. Zang, Y.; Li, Y.; Wang, C.; Zhang, W.; Xiong, W. Towards more accurate life cycle assessment of biological wastewater treatment plants: A review. *J. Clean. Product.* **2015**, *107*, 676–692. [CrossRef]
37. Lorenzo-Toja, Y.; Vázquez-Rowe, I.; Amores, M.J.; Termes-Rifé, M.; Marín-Navarro, D.; Moreira, M.T.; Feijoo, G. Benchmarking wastewater treatment plants under an eco-efficiency perspective. *Sci. Total Environ.* **2016**, *566*, 468–479. [CrossRef]
38. Gallego, A.; Hospido, A.; Moreira, M.T.; Feijoo, G. Environmental performance of wastewater treatment plants for small populations. *Resour. Conserv. Recycl.* **2008**, *52*, 931–940. [CrossRef]
39. Rodriguez-Garcia, G.; Molinos-Senante, M.; Hospido, A.; Hernández-Sancho, F.; Moreira, M.; Feijoo, G. Environmental and economic profile of six typologies of wastewater treatment plants. *Water Res.* **2011**, *45*, 5997–6010. [CrossRef]
40. Kalbar, P.P.; Karmakar, S.; Asolekar, S.R. Assessment of wastewater treatment technologies: Life cycle approach. *Water Environ. J.* **2012**, *27*, 261–268. [CrossRef]
41. Ortiz-Gutiérrez, R.A.; Giarola, S.; Bezzo, F. Optimal design of ethanol supply chains considering carbon trading effects and multiple technologies for side-product exploitation. *Environ. Tech.* **2013**, *34*, 2189–2199. [CrossRef]
42. Muñoz, I.; Gómez, M.; Molina-Díaz, A.; Huijbregts, M.; Fernández-Alba, A.; García-Calvo, E. Ranking potential impacts of priority and emerging pollutants in urban wastewater through life cycle impact assessment. *Chemosphere* **2008**, *74*, 37–44. [CrossRef] [PubMed]
43. Huijbregts, M.A.; Struijs, J.; Goedkoop, M.; Heijungs, R.; Hendriks, A.J.; Van de Meent, D. Human population intake fractions and environmental fate factors of toxic pollutants in life cycle impact assessment. *Chemosphere* **2005**, *61*, 1495–1504. [CrossRef] [PubMed]
44. Rosenbaum, R.K.; Bachmann, T.M.; Gold, L.S.; Huijbregts, M.A.; Jolliet, O.; Juraske, R.; Koehler, A.; Larsen, H.F.; MacLeod, M.; Margni, M.; et al. USEtox—The UNEP-SETAC toxicity model: Recommended characterisation factors for human toxicity and freshwater ecotoxicity in life cycle impact assessment. *Int. J. Life Cycle Assess.* **2008**, *13*, 532–546. [CrossRef]
45. Pizzol, M.; Christensen, P.; Schmidt, J.; Thomsen, M. Impacts of "metals" on human health: A comparison between nine different methodologies for Life Cycle Impact Assessment (LCIA). *J. Clean. Prod.* **2011**, *19*, 646–656. [CrossRef]
46. Renou, S.; Thomas, J.; Aoustin, E.; Pons, M. Influence of impact assessment methods in wastewater treatment LCA. *J. Clean. Prod.* **2008**, *16*, 1098–1105. [CrossRef]
47. Gallego, A.; Rodríguez-Lado, L.; Hospido, A.; Moreira, M.T.; Feijoo, G. Development of regional characterization factors for aquatic eutrophication. *Int. J. Life Cycle Assess.* **2009**, *15*, 32–43. [CrossRef]
48. Foley, J.; De Haas, D.; Hartley, K.; Lant, P. Comprehensive life cycle inventories of alternative wastewater treatment systems. *Water Res.* **2010**, *44*, 1654–1666. [CrossRef]
49. Mayer, B.K.; Baker, L.A.; Boyer, T.H.; Drechsel, P.; Gifford, M.; Hanjra, M.A.; Parameswaran, P.; Stoltzfus, J.; Westerhoff, P.; Rittmann, B.E. Total Value of Phosphorus Recovery. *Environ. Sci. Technol.* **2016**, *50*, 6606–6620. [CrossRef]
50. Hauck, M.; Maalcke-Luesken, F.A.; Jetten, M.S.; Huijbregts, M.A. Removing nitrogen from wastewater with side stream anammox: What are the trade-offs between environmental impacts? *Resour. Conserv. Recycl.* **2016**, *107*, 212–219. [CrossRef]
51. Doyle, J.D.; Parsons, S.A. Struvite formation, control and recovery. *Water Res.* **2002**, *36*, 3925–3940. [CrossRef]
52. Metcalf and Eddy. *Wastewater Engineering: Treatment and Reuse*, 4th ed.; McGraw-Hill: New York, NY, USA, 2014.

53. Chai, C.; Zhang, D.; Yu, Y.; Feng, Y.; Wong, M.S. Carbon Footprint Analyses of Mainstream Wastewater Treatment Technologies under Different Sludge Treatment Scenarios in China. *Water* **2015**, *7*, 918–938. [CrossRef]
54. Georges, K.; Thornton, A.; Sadler, R. *Evidence: Transforming Wastewater Treatment to Reduce Carbon Emissions*; European Environment Agency: Bristol, UK, 2009. Available online: https://www.gov.uk/government/uploads/system/uploads/attachment_data/file/291633/scho1209brnz-e-e.pdf (accessed on 8 November 2022).
55. Listowski, A.; Ngo, H.H.; Guo, W.S.; Vigneswaran, S.; Shin, H.S.; Moon, H. Greenhouse gas (GHG) emissions from urban wastewater system: Future assessment framework and methodology. *J. Water Sustain.* **2011**, *1*, 113–125.
56. Masuda, S.; Suzuki, S.; Sano, I.; Li, Y.-Y.; Nishimura, O. The seasonal variation of emission of greenhouse gases from a full-scale sewage treatment plant. *Chemosphere* **2015**, *140*, 167–173. [CrossRef]
57. Kampschreur, M.J.; Temmink, H.; Kleerebezem, R.; Jetten, M.S.; Van Loosdrecht, M.C. Nitrous oxide emission during wastewater treatment. *Water Res.* **2009**, *43*, 4093–4103. [CrossRef] [PubMed]
58. Harriss, R.; Systems, C.; Hall, M. Nitrous Oxide Emissions from Municipal Wastewater Treatment. *Environ. Sci. Technol.* **1995**, *29*, 2352–2356.
59. Sun, S.-P.; Pellicer-Nàcher, C.; Merkey, B.; Zhou, Q.; Xia, S.-Q.; Yang, D.-H.; Sun, J.-H.; Smets, B.F. Effective Biological Nitrogen Removal Treatment Processes for Domestic Wastewaters with Low C/N Ratios: A Review. *Environ. Eng. Sci.* **2010**, *27*, 111–126. [CrossRef]
60. Wan, J.; Gu, J.; Zhao, Q.; Liu, Y. COD capture: A feasible option towards energy self-sufficient domestic wastewater treatment. *Sci. Rep.* **2016**, *6*, 25054. [CrossRef] [PubMed]
61. Kasina, M.; Wendorff-Belon, M.; Kowalski, P.R.; Michalik, M. Characterization of incineration residues from wastewater treatment plant in Polish city: A future waste based source of valuable elements? *J. Mater. Cycles Waste Manag.* **2019**, *21*, 885–896. [CrossRef]
62. Nowak, O.; Keil, S.; Fimml, C. Examples of energy self-sufficient municipal nutrient removal plants. *Water Sci. Technol.* **2011**, *64*, 1–6. [CrossRef]
63. Urdalen, I. *Phosphorus Recovery from Municipal Wastewater—Literature Review*; Norwegian University of Science and Technology: Trondheim, Norway, 2013.
64. Kyzas, G.Z.; Matis, K.A. Flotation in Water and Wastewater Treatment. *Processes* **2018**, *6*, 116. [CrossRef]
65. Stillwell, A.S.; Hoppock, D.C.; Webber, M.E. Energy Recovery from Wastewater Treatment Plants in the United States: A Case Study of the Energy-Water Nexus. *Sustainability* **2010**, *2*, 945–962. [CrossRef]
66. Jonasson, M. Energy Benchmark for Wastewater Treatment Processes—A Comparison between Sweden and Austria. Benchmarking. 2007. Available online: https://www.iea.lth.se/publications/ms-theses/full%20document/5247_full_document.pdf (accessed on 8 November 2022).
67. Amann, A.; Zoboli, O.; Krampe, J.; Rechberger, H.; Zessner, M.; Egle, L. Environmental impacts of phosphorus recovery from municipal wastewater. *Resour. Conserv. Recycl.* **2018**, *130*, 127–139. [CrossRef]
68. Mininni, G.; Laera, G.; Bertanza, G.; Canato, M.; Sbrilli, A. Mass and energy balances of sludge processing in reference and upgraded wastewater treatment plants. *Environ. Sci. Pollut. Res.* **2015**, *22*, 7203–7215. [CrossRef] [PubMed]
69. Maurer, M.; Boller, M. Modelling of phosphorus precipitation in wastewater treatment plants with enhanced biological phosphorus removal. *Water Sci. Technol.* **1999**, *39*, 147–163. [CrossRef]
70. Pradel, M.; Aissani, L. Environmental impacts of phosphorus recovery from a "product" Life Cycle Assessment perspective: Allocating burdens of wastewater treatment in the production of sludge-based phosphate fertilizers. *Sci. Total Environ.* **2019**, *656*, 55–69. [CrossRef] [PubMed]
71. Blackall, L.L.; Crocetti, G.; Saunders, A.; Bond, P. A review and update of the microbiology of enhanced biological phosphorus removal in wastewater treatment plants. *Antonie Leeuwenhoek* **2002**, *81*, 681–691. [CrossRef]
72. Bashar, R.; Gungor, K.; Karthikeyan, K.; Barak, P. Cost effectiveness of phosphorus removal processes in municipal wastewater treatment. *Chemosphere* **2018**, *197*, 280–290. [CrossRef]
73. Sena, M.; Hicks, A. Life cycle assessment review of struvite precipitation in wastewater treatment. *Resour. Conserv. Recycl.* **2018**, *139*, 194–204. [CrossRef]
74. Hospido, A.; Moreira, T.; Martin, M. Environmental Evaluation of Different Treatment Processes for Sludge from Urban Wastewater Treatments: Anaerobic Digestion versus Thermal Processes. *Int. J. Life Cycle Assess.* **2005**, *10*, 336–345. [CrossRef]
75. Coats, E.R.; Watkins, D.L.; Kranenburg, D. A Comparative Environmental Life-Cycle Analysis for Removing Phosphorus from Wastewater: Biological versus Physical/Chemical Processes. *Water Environ. Res.* **2011**, *83*, 750–760. [CrossRef]
76. Hernández-Sancho, F.; Molinos-Senante, M.; Sala-Garrido, R. Economic valuation of environmental benefits from wastewater treatment processes: An empirical approach for Spain. *Sci. Total Environ.* **2010**, *408*, 953–957. [CrossRef] [PubMed]
77. Rawal, N.; Duggal, S.K. Life Cycle Costing Assessment-Based Approach for Selection of Wastewater Treatment Units. *Natl. Acad. Sci. Lett.* **2016**, *39*, 103–107. [CrossRef]
78. Memon, F.A.; Butler, D.; Han, W.; Liu, S.; Makropoulos, C.; Avery, L.M.; Pidou, M. Economic assessment tool for greywater recycling systems. *Proc. Inst. Civ. Eng. Eng. Sustain.* **2005**, *158*, 155–161. [CrossRef]
79. Lin, Y.; Guo, M.; Shah, N.; Stuckey, D.C. Economic and environmental evaluation of nitrogen removal and recovery methods from wastewater. *Bioresour. Technol.* **2016**, *215*, 227–238. [CrossRef] [PubMed]
80. Haruna, S.N.; Hanafiah, M.M. Consumptive use of water by selected cash crops in Malaysia. *Malays. J. Sustain. Agric. (MJSA)* **2017**, *1*, 6–8. [CrossRef]

81. Larsen, T.A.; Alder, A.C.; Eggen, R.I.L.; Maurer, M.; Lienert, J. Source Separation: Will We See a Paradigm Shift in Wastewater Handling? *Environ. Sci. Technol.* **2009**, *43*, 6121–6125. [CrossRef]
82. Din, M. Special Interview with Datuk Ir Abdul Kadir Mohammad Din, CEO of Indah Water Konsortium (IWK) Returning Malaysia's Rivers To Life: Kuala Lumpur. *Malaysia* **2013**, 1–44. Available online: https://www.yumpu.com/en/document/read/39288651/returning-malaysias-rivers-to-l-malaysian-water-association (accessed on 8 November 2022).
83. Dudley, B. *BP Statistical Review of World Energy—Full Report*; British Petroleum: London, UK, 2016; pp. 1–48.
84. Huang, Y.F.; Ang, S.Y.; Lee, K.M.L.A.T.S.; Lee, T.S. Quality of Water Resources in Malaysia. *Res. Pract. Water Qual.* **2015**, *3*, 65–94. [CrossRef]
85. Ariffin, M.; Sulaiman, S.N.M. Regulating Sewage Pollution of Malaysian Rivers and its Challenges. *Procedia Environ. Sci.* **2015**, *30*, 168–173. [CrossRef]
86. Rashid, S.S.; Liu, Y. Assessing environmental impacts of large centralized wastewater treatment plants with combined or separate sewer systems in dry/wet seasons by using LCA. *Environ. Sci. Pollut. Res.* **2020**, *27*, 15674–15690. [CrossRef]
87. Harun, S.N.; Hanafiah, M.M.; Aziz, N.I.H.A. An LCA-Based Environmental Performance of Rice Production for Developing a Sustainable Agri-Food System in Malaysia. *Environ. Manag.* **2020**, *67*, 146–161. [CrossRef]
88. Rashid, S.S.; Liu, Y.Q.; Zhang, C. Upgrading a large and centralised municipal wastewater treatment plant with sequencing batch reactor technology for integrated nutrient removal and phosphorus recovery: Environmental and economic life cycle performance. *Sci. Total Environ.* **2020**, *749*, 141465. [CrossRef] [PubMed]
89. Razman, K.K.; Mohammad, A.W.; Hanafiah, M.M. Life cycle design and efficiency strategy for sustainable membrane technology. In *Proceedings of the IOP Conference Series: Earth and Environmental Science*; IOP Publishing: Bristol, UK, 2021; Volume 880, p. 012053.
90. Ghani, L.A.; Ali, N.; Nazaran, I.S.; Hanafiah, M.M. Environmental Performance of Small-Scale Seawater Reverse Osmosis Plant for Rural Area Water Supply. *Membranes* **2021**, *11*, 40. [CrossRef] [PubMed]
91. Al-Anbari, M.A.; Altaee, S.A.; Kareem, S.L. Using Life Cycle Assessment (LCA) in Appraisal Sustainability Indicators of Najaf Wastewater Treatment Plant. *Egypt. J. Chem.* **2022**, *65*, 9. [CrossRef]
92. Shanmugam, K.; Gadhamshetty, V.; Tysklind, M.; Bhattacharyya, D.; Upadhyayula, V.K. A sustainable performance assessment framework for circular management of municipal wastewater treatment plants. *J. Clean. Prod.* **2022**, *339*, 130657. [CrossRef]
93. Shao, S.; Mu, H.; Keller, A.A.; Yang, Y.; Hou, H.; Yang, F.; Zhang, Y. Environmental tradeoffs in municipal wastewater treatment plant upgrade: A life cycle perspective. *Environ. Sci. Pollut. Res.* **2021**, *28*, 34913–34923. [CrossRef]
94. Rebello, T.A.; Gonçalves, R.F.; Calmon, J.L. Mitigation of environmental impacts in warm-weather wastewater treatment plants using the life cycle assessment tool. *Int. J. Environ. Sci. Technol.* **2022**, *19*, 4763–4778. [CrossRef]
95. Alizadeh, S.; Zafari-Koloukhi, H.; Rostami, F.; Rouhbakhsh, M.; Avami, A. The eco-efficiency assessment of wastewater treatment plants in the city of Mashhad using emergy and life cycle analyses. *J. Clean. Prod.* **2019**, *249*, 119327. [CrossRef]
96. Li, Y.; Zhang, S.; Zhang, W.; Xiong, W.; Ye, Q.; Hou, X.; Wang, C.; Wang, P. Life cycle assessment of advanced wastewater treatment processes: Involving 126 pharmaceuticals and personal care products in life cycle inventory. *J. Environ. Manag.* **2019**, *238*, 442–450. [CrossRef]
97. Awad, H.; Alalm, M.G.; El-Etriby, H.K. Environmental and cost life cycle assessment of different alternatives for improvement of wastewater treatment plants in developing countries. *Sci. Total Environ.* **2019**, *660*, 57–68. [CrossRef]
98. Delre, A.; Hoeve, M.T.; Scheutz, C. Site-specific carbon footprints of Scandinavian wastewater treatment plants, using the life cycle assessment approach. *J. Clean. Prod.* **2018**, *211*, 1001–1014. [CrossRef]
99. Bai, S.; Wang, X.; Huppes, G.; Zhao, X.; Ren, N. Using site-specific life cycle assessment methodology to evaluate Chinese wastewater treatment scenarios: A comparative study of site-generic and site-specific methods. *J. Clean. Prod.* **2017**, *144*, 1–7. [CrossRef]
100. Hernández-Padilla, F.; Margni, M.; Noyola, A.; Guereca-Hernandez, L.; Bulle, C. Assessing wastewater treatment in Latin America and the Caribbean: Enhancing life cycle assessment interpretation by regionalization and impact assessment sensibility. *J. Clean. Prod.* **2016**, *142*, 2140–2153. [CrossRef]
101. Fang, L.L.; Valverde-Pérez, B.; Damgaard, A.; Plósz, B.G.; Rygaard, M. Life cycle assessment as development and decision support tool for wastewater resource recovery technology. *Water Res.* **2016**, *88*, 538–549. [CrossRef] [PubMed]
102. Pintilie, L.; Torres, C.M.; Teodosiu, C.; Castells, F. Urban wastewater reclamation for industrial reuse: An LCA case study. *J. Clean. Prod.* **2016**, *139*, 1–14. [CrossRef]
103. Piao, W.; Kim, Y.-J. Evaluation of monthly environmental loads from municipal wastewater treatment plants operation using life cycle assessment. *Environ. Eng. Res.* **2016**, *21*, 284–290. [CrossRef]
104. Risch, E.; Gasperi, J.; Gromaire, M.-C.; Chebbo, G.; Azimi, S.; Rocher, V.; Roux, P.; Rosenbaum, R.K.; Sinfort, C. Impacts from urban water systems on receiving waters—How to account for severe wet-weather events in LCA? *Water Res.* **2018**, *128*, 412–423. [CrossRef]
105. Niero, M.; Pizzol, M.; Bruun, H.G.; Thomsen, M. Comparative life cycle assessment of wastewater treatment in Denmark including sensitivity and uncertainty analysis. *J. Clean. Prod.* **2014**, *68*, 25–35. [CrossRef]
106. Rodriguez-Garcia, G.; Frison, N.; Vázquez-Padín, J.; Hospido, A.; Garrido, J.; Fatone, F.; Bolzonella, D.; Moreira, M.; Feijoo, G. Life cycle assessment of nutrient removal technologies for the treatment of anaerobic digestion supernatant and its integration in a wastewater treatment plant. *Sci. Total Environ.* **2014**, *490*, 871–879. [CrossRef]

107. Zhang, Q.H.; Wang, X.C.; Xiong, J.Q.; Chen, R.; Cao, B. Application of life cycle assessment for an evaluation of wastewater treatment and reuse project–Case study of Xi'an, China. *Bioresour. Technol.* **2010**, *101*, 1421–1425. [CrossRef]
108. Köhler, A.; Hellweg, S.; Recan, E.; Hungerbühler, K. Input-dependent life-cycle inventory model of industrial wastewater-treatment processes in the chemical sector. *Environ. Sci. Technol.* **2007**, *41*, 5515–5522. [CrossRef] [PubMed]
109. Halleux, H.; Lassaux, S.; Germain, A. Comparison of life cycle assessment methods, application to a wastewater treatment plant. In Proceedings of the 13th CIRP International Conference on Life Cycvle Engineering, Leuven, Belgium, 31 May–2 June 2006.

Disclaimer/Publisher's Note: The statements, opinions and data contained in all publications are solely those of the individual author(s) and contributor(s) and not of MDPI and/or the editor(s). MDPI and/or the editor(s) disclaim responsibility for any injury to people or property resulting from any ideas, methods, instructions or products referred to in the content.

MDPI AG
Grosspeteranlage 5
4052 Basel
Switzerland
Tel.: +41 61 683 77 34

Processes Editorial Office
E-mail: processes@mdpi.com
www.mdpi.com/journal/processes

Disclaimer/Publisher's Note: The title and front matter of this reprint are at the discretion of the Guest Editors. The publisher is not responsible for their content or any associated concerns. The statements, opinions and data contained in all individual articles are solely those of the individual Editors and contributors and not of MDPI. MDPI disclaims responsibility for any injury to people or property resulting from any ideas, methods, instructions or products referred to in the content.